A HISTORY OF WINE IN AMERICA

THE PUBLISHER GRATEFULLY ACKNOWLEDGES
THE GENEROUS CONTRIBUTION TO THIS BOOK
PROVIDED BY THE GENERAL ENDOWMENT FUND
OF THE UNIVERSITY OF CALIFORNIA PRESS
ASSOCIATES.

A HISTORY OF WINE IN AMERICA

From Prohibition to the Present

Thomas Pinney

UNIVERSITY OF CALIFORNIA PRESS
Berkeley   Los Angeles   London

Title page vignette: Wrought-iron sign at Boordy Vineyards in Maryland,
commissioned by winegrower Philip Wagner. Though it obviously alludes
to the story of the scouts sent by Moses into the Promised Land (Numbers
13:23), the sign, Wagner said, shows "two vignerons bringing the French
hybrids to Maryland."

University of California Press
Berkeley and Los Angeles, California

University of California Press, Ltd.
London, England

© 2005 by The Regents of the University of California

Library of Congress Cataloging-in-Publication Data

Pinney, Thomas.
    A history of wine in America : from prohibition to the present / Thomas
Pinney.
        p.   cm.
    Includes bibliographical references and index.
    ISBN 0-520-24176-2 (alk. paper)
    1. Wine and wine making—United States—History.   2. Wine industry—
United States—History.   I. Title.
TP557.P57   2005
641.2'2'0973—dc22   2004017999

Manufactured in the United States of America
14   13   12   11   10   09   08   07   06   05
10   9   8   7   6   5   4   3   2   1

Natures Book contains 50% post-consumer waste and meets the minimum
requirements of ANSI/NISO z39.48–1992 (R 1997) (Permanence of Paper).♾

To Charles Sullivan,
il maestro di color che sanno

CONTENTS

ILLUSTRATIONS

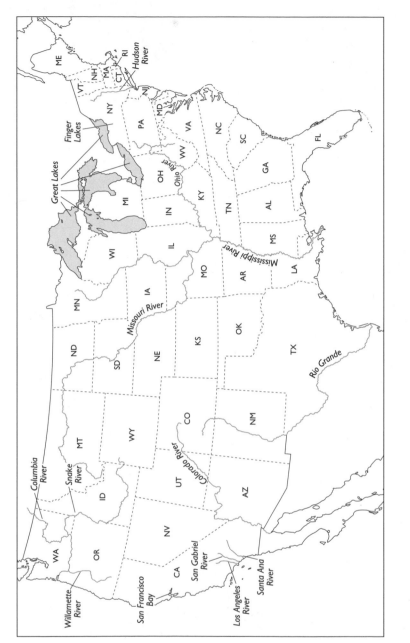

MAP 1

The United States and its major rivers. Historically, winegrowing developed along the rivers and lakes of the United States, beginning with the Ohio River, then moving to the Finger Lakes, the Hudson, the Great Lakes, and the Missouri River valley between Omaha and St. Louis. The Rio Grande is the site of the oldest winegrowing in the country, even before there was a United States. The Columbia, the Willamette, and the Snake run through the Northwest wine country. In arid Southern California, the first winegrowing was established along the banks of the Los Angeles, San Gabriel, and Santa Ana Rivers. San Francisco Bay is the center of California's most highly regarded winegrowing districts. These old patterns still persist.

Del Norte

Siskiyou

Modoc

Humboldt Trinity

Shasta

Lassen

Tehama

Mendocino

Glenn Butte

Plumas

Lake Colusa

Yuba Sierra

Nevada

Sonoma

Sutter

Placer

Napa Yolo

Sacra-
mento

El Dorado

Marin

Solano

Amador Alpine

Contra
Costa

San
Joaquin

Calaveras

San
Francisco

Alameda

Tuolumne

San Mateo

Santa Stanislaus
Clara

Mariposa Mono

Santa Cruz

Merced

San
Benito

Madera

Fresno

Monterey

Kings

Tulare

Inyo

San
Luis
Obispo

Kern

Santa
Barbara

0 20 40 60 80 100 miles

Ventura

Los
Angeles

San Bernardino

Orange

Riverside

San Diego Imperial

MAP 2

The counties of California. Almost every county of California has made some trial
of winegrowing in the more than two hundred years of the state's viticultural history.
Winegrowing today extends from Mendocino County in the north to San Diego County
on the Mexican border, and eastward to the foothills of the Sierra Nevada in El Dorado
and Amador Counties. Only the northern counties and the mountain and desert
counties of Alpine, Mono, and Inyo are today without some reported viticulture.

PREFACE AND ACKNOWLEDGMENTS

This book is a continuation of my *History of Wine in America: From the Beginnings to Prohibition*, published by the University of California Press in 1989. Although the two books are connected, they have had to take very different forms. The task of the first volume was mainly to recover the story of repeated efforts to establish a wine industry that repeatedly failed and then, because they had failed, had been forgotten. In many places the surviving record was vestigial or almost nonexistent. It was possible, then, to think of writing a survey that would cover more than three hundred years of history and yet keep it within the confines of one substantial—though not, I hope, overlong—volume.

For the period covered by this second book, the task has been just the opposite: so much has been done and so much is known that it is impossible to pack it all into the space of a single volume. In the first book I could be reasonably comprehensive; in this volume I have had to be severely selective. No historian can know what questions will interest future generations; but in making my selection of what to include I have tried to choose what seems important from the vantage point of the beginning of the twenty-first century.

Only after I had finished writing the book and was thinking about prefatory statements did it occur to me that there is another, enormous omission: Why have I said nothing to explain why the subject of wine deserves to be written about at such length? To one who knows nothing about wine, the question will no doubt be very real; but for those who take an interest in the subject—and they are my audience—no explanation will be required. They will know already that the subject of wine is, from every point of view, infinitely varied and interesting. I will therefore leave the philosophical defense of wine as a valid subject to others and take for granted here that the enterprise needs no apology.

Having said so much in defense of my omissions, I may now make a modest claim to have provided a good deal of information that is not generally known. The fate of American wine under Prohibition; the conditions of renewal after Repeal; the various measures of the New Deal affecting wine; the early markets and methods; the effects of the war, of varietal labeling, and of postwar adjustments; the breakthrough in the 1960s; and the spread of winegrowing to almost every state: these and a good many other things in the story I tell here have not yet been narrated at length in a connected way. Just for that reason, much that I have written will certainly need to be corrected or adjusted. As I wrote in the preface to my earlier volume, "There is a history of winegrowing to be written for almost every state in the nation. . . . For the most part, the work remains undone. I have therefore had to depend all too frequently on my own resources. I sincerely hope that one effect of this book—perhaps the most important one that it can have—is to stimulate others to take up the historical inquiry" (p. xvi).

The volume of writing about wine in this country has increased mightily in the years since those words were written, but as far as the work of serious historical writing is concerned, they still apply to a large extent. Leon Adams had already published his invaluable book *The Wines of America* (1973; 4th ed. 1990), but that is mostly concerned with the present scene. The Napa Valley has been excellently served by two authoritative works, Charles Sullivan's *Napa Wine* (1994), a historical account from the beginning, and James Lapsley's *Bottled Poetry* (1996), an analysis of the rise of Napa to a position of leadership since Repeal. An older California has been authoritatively documented in Ernest Peninou, *History of the Sonoma Viticultural District* (1998), and Ernest Peninou and Gail Unzelman, *The California Wine Association* (2000). Ronald Irvine's *The Wine Project* (1997) is a thorough survey of its subject, winegrowing in Washington State, as is *Indiana Wine* (2001), by James L. Butler and John J. Butler. Most of the rest of the considerable current literature takes the form of guidebooks that do not derive from any original historical inquiry.

For a very incomplete account of my dependence on the work of others and on library materials, see "Sources and Works Cited" at the end of the volume. I would like to make special acknowledgment to Axel Borg, wine bibliographer at the Shields Library of the University of California, Davis, and to John Skarstad in Special Collections there.

1

FORMS OF LIFE IN A DRY WORLD

THE VOLSTEAD ACT

On 16 January 1919 the senators of the Nebraska state legislature, by a vote of thirty-one to one, ratified the Eighteenth Amendment to the Constitution of the United States, prohibiting the sale of alcoholic drink throughout the nation. With the Nebraska vote, the amendment received the required support of a two-thirds majority of the states for it to pass into law. Now it would become effective a year from the day of the clinching vote—that is, at midnight on 16 January 1920—and it seemed clear that at that time, the drinking of wine (to say nothing of beer and whiskey) must come to an end for the people of the United States. The language of the amendment was curt and uncompromising:

> The manufacture, sale, or transportation of intoxicating liquors within, the importation thereof into, or the exportation thereof from the United States and all territory subject to the jurisdiction thereof for beverage purposes is hereby prohibited.

To convert this sweeping command into practical administration, the U.S. Congress passed the National Prohibition Act on 28 October 1919, over the veto of President Wilson.[1] This piece of legislation was thereafter always called the Volstead Act, in reference to its ostensible author, Andrew Volstead, a veteran Republican congressman from Minnesota. Volstead's congressional career was devoted mostly to defending the interests of the farmers of the upper Midwest, but as a teetaler and chairman of the House Judiciary Committee, he took on the task of drafting the bill that was to enforce Prohibition. Although

Volstead always said otherwise, it was generally understood that the real author of the bill was Wayne B. Wheeler, the animating spirit of the Anti-Saloon League, the main organizing power behind the successful drive for constitutional prohibition.[2] The act thus was an opportunity for the forces that had brought about Prohibition to dictate their terms to the nation.

The key provision of the Volstead Act was its definition of *intoxicating liquor* as anything containing more than 0.5 percent alcohol. The basis of the definition was simply the measure traditionally used for purposes of taxation, but its intent was obviously to cast the net of prohibition as widely as the most ambitious reformer could hope. The definition was devastating to the brewers of beer and the makers of wine. Unlike the distillers of spirits, who had always been the main target of the prohibition campaign, they had at least been able to hope, down to the last moment, that their produce would be spared and their livelihoods continue. The terms of the act extinguished that hope.

Yet the Volstead Act's severe notion of what constituted an intoxicating drink was modified by some important omissions and exceptions. The significance of these irregularities was probably not clearly grasped by the act's framers, but it became increasingly evident during the course of the Prohibition years. The act, like the amendment itself, did not specify "alcoholic" but only "intoxicating" drink; nor, like the amendment, did it prohibit any "use" or "purchase" of such drink—these important details, it has been said, are evidence of a practical recognition on the part of the Drys that they could not successfully achieve a "radical, bone-dry amendment."[3]

Both the act and the amendment were directed not against the consumer, but instead against the producer and dealer (the "traffic," in the language of the Anti-Saloon League). Thus the purchase, possession, and consumption of alcoholic beverages had no penalty attached to them. The bootlegger might be subject to the rigors of the law, but his customer was secure. People prudent enough to supply themselves before the trade shut down could enjoy their cellars with impunity.[4] And if they could manage, illegally, to replenish them, the supplies once in hand were theirs, legally, to drink and to share with friends. Apart from these omissions, the act was further weakened by an exception allowing heads of families to make up to 200 gallons annually of "fruit juices" exclusively for consumption in the home. The language of the provision was obscure and contradictory, but as we shall see, its effect was to license home winemaking.

Another exception allowed the production of alcohol for "non-beverage" purposes. Mostly, this meant the large-scale production of alcohol for industrial uses—in paints, solvents, and chemicals, and in the manufacturing processes for textiles, rubber goods, film, smokeless powder, and many other blameless products. There was also provision for winemaking itself to continue: Wine for sacramental use in Christian and Jewish congregations continued to be produced commercially. And since wine could be prescribed as medicine, or used in foods as a flavoring agent, winemakers who obtained permits could compete for those restricted markets too.

Such anomalies and exceptions point to the important fact that Prohibition, over the fourteen years of its existence, was not one undeviating, uniform condition but a complicated, sometimes contradictory arrangement that passed through several distinct phases and that affected the country in different ways at different times. Since the history of wine in America is bound up with the fortunes of Prohibition, the changing developments in the drama that took place between the passage of the Eighteenth Amendment, which established it, and the Twenty-first, which repealed it, should be briefly sketched.

THE PHASES OF PROHIBITION

At first, Prohibition seemed to work, especially if one took a restricted view of its aims. If, as has been plausibly argued, it was mainly concerned to curb the drinking of the American working class, then its first few years of operation were a decided success.[5] The legal sale of alcoholic drink of course disappeared, and by other measures, too, American drinking appeared to be on the way down: arrests for drunken driving and the number of cases of alcoholism were reported to be greatly reduced.[6] It could also be—and was—asserted that the general condition of the American workingman and his family was better under Prohibition than ever before.

Another sign of the early effectiveness of Prohibition is that to all appearances, drinking did not increase in those communities where it had not been established before—for instance, among women, and at most of America's colleges and universities. Yet another, more dubious result of the early operation of Prohibition was to increase the proportion of spirits in the total of what was actually drunk: if one was seeking merely an alcoholic jolt, and if it took no more trouble to get spirits than to get beer or wine, then beer and wine would lose out. And so they did. But that development could be of no concern to the Drys, who lumped all alcoholic drinks together under the heading of Demon Rum. And in the early going, as reports came in of the newly sobered style of the nation, their cry was a triumphant "long live Prohibition."

The legality of Prohibition was challenged almost at once and from many directions. Since the ratification of the Eighteenth Amendment came on a vote of state legislatures, it was argued that the people had not been properly heard from: there ought to have been popular referendums instead. In Ohio, in 1919, such a referendum was in fact held, and it overturned the earlier vote of the legislature in favor of ratification. But the Supreme Court upheld the legislature against the referendum, and so that hope went glimmering. The constitutionality of the amendment was challenged repeatedly in the courts on various grounds: it was an encroachment on states' rights and on local self-government; it invaded privacy; it was an illicit act of legislation in the guise of a constitutional change. No doubt there were other arguments too.

Nothing worked. The Supreme Court, under Chief Justice William Howard Taft, uniformly repelled all attacks on the amendment, not only in the early years of Prohibition but to the very end.[7] No amendment to the constitution had ever been repealed; and in the early years of Prohibition there seemed little reason to suppose that the Eighteenth would prove to be the exception. The exuberant certainty of the Drys broke out in extravagant imagery. Evangelist Billy Sunday proclaimed that you could no more repeal the amendment "than you could dam Niagara Falls with toothpicks." As late as 1930, when cracks had already appeared throughout the structure of Prohibition, Senator Morris Sheppard, a Dry from Texas, declared that "there is as much chance of repealing the Eighteenth Amendment as there is for a hummingbird to fly to the planet Mars with the Washington Monument tied to its tail."

Despite such boastings, a process of erosion was going on. It showed itself in one way as a problem of enforcement. To patch up leaks in the law, new legislation had to be passed, such as the Wills-Campbell Act (1921), which restricted the quantity of beer and wine that doctors could prescribe for medicinal use. A more serious sign of trouble was the harsh provision of punishment in the Jones Act of 1929. This was a late stage in the evolution of Prohibition, and the extent to which the law was being violated may be guessed at from the desperation of the measure: where the Volstead Act prescribed penalties of up to six months' imprisonment *or* a thousand dollars for a first offense, the Jones Act imposed five years *and* ten thousand dollars.[8]

The difficulties of enforcement were partly caused by a growing sentiment that the law did not deserve to be obeyed. The enemies of Prohibition—despairing at the impossibility, as it seemed, of repealing the Eighteenth Amendment and baffled by the repeated failure of efforts to modify the law in any way—often turned to a simple policy of nullification: if the law could not be changed, then it would be ignored. Quite respectable people argued for this view: a former president of Yale University, for example, and the distinguished journalist Walter Lippmann.[9] And what such respected public figures were prepared to set forth in public must surely have been acted on by great numbers of ordinary and anonymous citizens in private.

Another sign of change was the reluctance of many states to take an active hand in enforcing Prohibition. The second section of the Eighteenth Amendment provided that "the Congress and the several States shall have concurrent power to enforce this article by appropriate legislation." *Concurrent power* was interpreted to mean that the federal law could be paralleled or even strengthened by state law. The intention of this provision was to respect the laws of those states that already had Prohibition, especially if those laws were as tough as or tougher than the Volstead Act. The Drys also hoped that the states would help keep down the cost to the federal government of policing Prohibition by enforcing their own laws. The "concurrent" clause created a legal confusion, since offenders might be prosecuted twice for the same crime, once by the state and again by the federal authorities—a kind of double jeopardy. But in fact, the concurrent system offered a target that the Wets could hit with some effect, even while the Eighteenth Amendment itself seemed secure against all assaults. In New York in 1923, the Democratic governor, Al Smith, in response to popular pressure signed a bill repealing the state's prohibition legislation. This did nothing to alter the conditions of national Prohibition, but it registered, in terms that politicians could understand, popular resentment of the state of things. By 1927, only a few states were spending any money to enforce their own Prohibition laws, and thereafter many states, well in advance of Repeal, did away with their concurrent laws.[10]

The main energy of the developing Wet counterattack went into efforts to secure not repeal but modification. Repeal, in the middle of the Prohibition era, still looked like an impossible task. But perhaps the bone-dry definition enshrined in the Volstead Act— nothing over 0.5 percent alcohol allowed—could be changed.[11] The aim was to modify the act so as to allow, as a first step, the legalization of 2.75 percent beer.[12] Later, the legalization of so-called light wines was added to the objectives of the campaign. Congressional hearings on the proposed modifications were held in 1924 and again in 1926, but the hopeful were disappointed on each occasion.[13] The time was not yet ripe for lawmakers to venture the risk.

Meanwhile, the country seemed to be growing restless under the law. The docile acceptance of Prohibition that marked the first years, at least according to some observers, had now disappeared. Arrests for violations of the Volstead Act went up, not down. More important, the popular impression was growing that Prohibition had proved to be a failure: it didn't prevent drinking, but on the contrary only produced a nation of lawbreakers. Such, at any rate, was the theme of the Wet propagandists, whose main strategy now lay in discrediting the effectiveness of the law. What the truth of the matter was—if there was any clear truth—is probably impossible to know now. While the Wets proclaimed the failure of the experiment, the Drys just as noisily asserted its success. The choice of evidence, and the method of interpreting it, were determined by the purposes of the disputants: neither side had any trouble in making a case for its own view of the question.[14]

Whatever the reality, the *idea*—some have called it a fiction or a myth—that Prohibition was a failure began to win out over the doctrine of its success.[15] With this shift, the third and terminal stage of national Prohibition began. Leading the attack for the Wets was the Association Against the Prohibition Amendment (AAPA), founded in 1919 in the last, futile days of the struggle against the Eighteenth Amendment, but reorganized in 1928 and now operating in the excited hope that repeal was possible. The organization in its new form was a combination of the rich, the well known, and the reactionary. They were at least as much concerned with states' rights and limitations on big government as they were with such issues as the morality of drinking or the social effects of the saloon.[16]

The opposition to federal authority that animated the AAPA leadership is clear in the resolution they adopted early in 1928: they were determined to work for "entire repeal of the Eighteenth Amendment," they said, for the simple and sufficient reason that Prohibition "never should be the business of the Federal Government."[17] They were working in an atmosphere greatly changed since the beginning of Prohibition, nearly a decade earlier. The impetus of evangelical reform that had originally impelled the Drys to triumph had now run down. Resistance—overt or silent—to the enforcement of the law had grown more and more stubborn, and the "failure" of Prohibition had become more and more an article of public faith. The initiative had now passed from the Drys, who had had their chance and lost it, to the Wets, who like all oppositions were rich in promises.

An opportunity arose in the 1928 presidential elections. Both parties attempted, more or less successfully, to avoid making clear commitments on the matter of Prohibition. But the outcry over the failure of the law could not be wholly evaded: Herbert Hoover, the Republican candidate, was prompted to promise an investigation into the question. Following his election, he performed his promise by appointing a national commission on law observance and enforcement, called the Wickersham Commission after its chairman, a former U.S. attorney general, George Wickersham. The commission was charged to review "the entire federal system of jurisprudence and the administration of laws" and did so in a series of fourteen lengthy reports. But its main business was with the enforcement of Prohibition, and its report on that subject, published in five volumes early in 1931, got all the attention.[18] The Wickersham report fully reflects the confusion and contradictions of opinion about what Prohibition actually was and what it actually did.

The commission interviewed representatives of every segment of the community, ordered special research inquiries, collected the opinions of experts, listened to the testimony of Wets and Drys of all stripes, and accumulated the statistics and documents of official agencies. The outcome, perhaps inevitably, was deeply contradictory. President Hoover, in transmitting the report, announced that the commissioners had concluded in favor of Prohibition. And so they had: the official recommendation was against repeal. But it was not much in favor of Prohibition as it had so far been known, and the evidence it had collected seemed, as much as anything, to confirm the charges of the AAPA that Prohibition didn't work. The general sense that the commission's report contradicted itself was put into verse by Franklin P. Adams in his *New York World* "Conning Tower":

> Prohibition is an awful flop.
> > We like it.
> It can't stop what it's meant to stop.
> > We like it.
> It's left a trail of graft and slime,
> It don't prohibit worth a dime,
> It's filled our land with vice and crime.
> Nevertheless, we're for it.[19]

The AAPA, which had had much to say to the Wickersham Commission, was soon joined by other, like-minded groups. The Voluntary Committee of Lawyers, founded early in 1929, brought together a number of distinguished New York City attorneys whose influence was out of all proportion to their numbers, though membership was soon extended outside New York to other cities.[20] Another group, calling itself the Crusaders, was formed in Cleveland in 1929 to recruit young men to the cause of repeal. The religious zeal implicit in the name is a clear expression of the shift of righteousness from Dry to Wet.[21] Most important of the new organizations to appear in the wake of the AAPA was the Women's Organization for National Prohibition Reform, organized in 1929 under Pauline Sabin, the socially prominent wife of a wealthy New York banker. At its first convention, in 1930, the Women's Organization roundly declared for repeal: "We are convinced that National Prohibition is fundamentally wrong," the conference resolved, mainly because Prohibition was opposed to the Constitution—the women agreed with the political position of the AAPA, to which the new organization was closely allied.[22] By 1933 the Women's Organization claimed a membership of nearly 1.5 million women. Even allowing for inflation in the figure, the group was certainly the biggest of the anti-Prohibition associations, though it aimed more at prestige than at mere numbers in its membership.[23]

It was also, symbolically at least, the unkindest cut of all to the embattled Drys. The defection of women from the Dry standard, which, it had been supposed, they would defend to the last, was a blow as serious as it was unexpected. According to Mrs. Sabin's own testimony, she had been inspired to form the Women's Organization when she heard Mrs. Ella Boole, the veteran head of the Woman's Christian Temperance Union (WCTU), assert at a Congressional hearing in 1928 that she, Mrs. Boole, represented "the women of America." Mrs. Sabin thought to herself, *Well, lady, here's one woman you don't represent.*[24] She thereupon founded the Women's Organization. She was, inevitably, vilified as a traitoress, but she proved quite capable of defending herself with energy and aplomb.

The last, and irrecoverable, stroke was the Great Depression. After the moral argument, the economic argument had always been the reliance of the Drys: Prohibition was prosperity. After the crash of 1929, when the nation faced economic disaster, that argument too was taken from their hands. The Wets, for their part, could and did make as many claims for the certain economic benefits of repeal as the Drys had before them for the economic benefits of Prohibition. Repeal, it was said, would generate such revenues as would pay off the federal deficit.[25] It would also generate new jobs, so it was promised; and on this point organized labor eagerly joined in the agitation for repeal. So did the farmers: agricultural surpluses had depressed prices throughout the decade. The promise of a new market for grain to make beer and spirits was impossible to resist.

By the time of the presidential elections of 1932, the question of Prohibition hardly seemed problematic any longer; it had been absorbed into larger economic issues. It had also become identified with party politics. Hoover and the Republicans were, to their considerable discomfort, identified with the Eighteenth Amendment. Roosevelt—who had at best a wavering and cautious record on the question—and the Democrats were now firmly identified with repeal.[26]

After Roosevelt's landslide victory, the lame-duck Congress immediately acted on what was seen as a Wet mandate. A resolution for repeal passed the Senate on 16 February 1933 and the House on 20 February; it was then submitted to the states for ratification—not by the legislatures, as had been the done with the Eighteenth Amendment, but by specially elected conventions, so that "the people" could be heard directly on the question. On 5 December 1933 the necessary two-thirds majority of the states was secured by the vote of the Utah convention—but this was by now merely a pro forma action. The outcome had long been foreseen, since the conventions had been elected earlier, and their votes were foregone conclusions. The ratification of the Twenty-first Amendment, repealing the Eighteenth, had been achieved in well under a year's time from the beginning of the formal process—the first-ever repeal of a constitutional amendment in American history.[27]

The newly elected Congress that met in March 1933 at once enacted alterations to the Volstead Act—alterations that had been repeatedly but vainly sought in the past but that now could hardly be granted fast enough. In early April all restrictions were lifted on medical prescriptions of whiskey.[28] At the same time, the Volstead Act was altered by the so-called Cullen Beer Act (after Representative Thomas Henry Cullen, Democrat of New York) to allow the sale of 3.2 percent beer, at least in those nineteen states whose laws did not still obstruct this federal permission. According to one historian, the return of beer on 7 April 1933, even at 3.2 percent, produced a more excited binge than the actual moment of Repeal, eight months later.[29] Wine was allowed back at the same time, but only on the same terms as beer—that is, at a strength of 3.2 percent alcohol.

THE WINE INDUSTRY UNDER PROHIBITION

It is now time to turn back and inquire into the fate of wine and winemaking during the complex history of the Prohibition era.

After the Volstead Act first passed, all was predictably confusion and gloom; some people might choose to think that it was all a bad dream and would soon go away, but after passage it was hard for even the most stubborn to be hopeful. The giant of the American wine industry, the California Wine Association (CWA), began to take itself apart and dispose of the pieces as soon as Prohibition seemed certain. At the peak of its operations the CWA had distributed more than 80 percent of California's wine, the produce of some fifty-two wineries under such distinguished labels as Brun and Chaix, De Turk, Greystone, and Italian Swiss Colony.[30] Now it concentrated on selling off as much of its stock as it possibly could in a race against the Prohibition deadline, and for a time at least, it made no more wine. Others, large and small, entered the same race against time in selling their wine. Louis Petri recalled that his grandfather sold wine from his San Francisco cellar "right up to the last hour. . . . They started maybe at 25 or 30 cents a gallon. The last of it was sold at a couple of dollars a gallon. . . . They were lined up for blocks, people with jugs, as if there would never be another gallon of wine produced in the world."[31] Philip Wagner tells of a million-dollar shipment of 10,000 cases of sparkling wine and 7,000 barrels of still wine that left San Francisco for the Far East at the last minute, 31 December 1919.[32] One of the few shrewd enough to exploit the coming of Prohibition on a large scale was H. O. Lanza, then living in upstate New York and later a power on the California wine scene. He bought 1.3 million gallons of wine from the CWA and sold it at a high profit in the interval between the passage of the constitutional amendment and the coming into force of the Volstead Act.[33]

Wine, however, did not simply disappear. In order to make this point clear, it will be necessary to load the narrative with a great many statistics, but the point is worth making because it is not generally understood. There were in storage at the outset of Prohibition some 17 million gallons of wine in the United States—down 30 million gallons from the preceding year, the result of the panic selling that went on in the final Wet year.[34] The regular market for the wine left in storage was now, of course, gone, but in fact the Volstead Act allowed wine to be used in a number of ways. Wine could be prescribed as medicine. It could be used in food or in tobacco as flavoring: thus the Colonial Grape Products Company during Prohibition had an extensive trade with Campbell's Soup for sherry as a seasoning, and with the Bayuk Cigar Company for wine to cure tobacco leaves.[35] Wine was permitted to rabbis and priests for the celebration of the sacraments; it could be distilled and the resulting spirits used in a variety of applications (in fortifying sacramental wines, for example); it could be turned to vinegar and sold. All of this was allowed by the language of the amendment, which prohibited manufacture only for "beverage purposes."

These permitted outlets were, however, comparatively small and inelastic. The quantity of wine for sacramental use, for example, never exceeded 3 million gallons in a year, and averaged much less than that.[36] Yet wine for sacramental use appears to have been the largest single legal market open to the industry. Wine tonics were the next largest part of the market, varying from half a million to a million gallons a year. The quantities of wine prescribed as medicine and of wine used as flavoring were too small to mean much, though the flavoring category grew steadily during the Prohibition years.[37] The scale of continued commercial production was by no means inconsiderable; it is, in fact, quite surprising to discover just how considerable it was during the time that the sale of alcoholic beverages was forbidden by the nation's basic law. This anomaly is explained by the fact that established wineries were allowed, if they applied for the appropriate permits, to make wine and store it, in recognition of the fact that crops of wine grapes continued to be produced. Having made the wine, they could sell it only for the approved nonbeverage uses: but they might keep it indefinitely, again under permit. The arrangement made little sense, but so it was. When Repeal came at last, there was a lot of wine waiting to be sold—most of it, despite what one would expect, having been made during the Prohibition years themselves.

Even so, the production of wine was only a fraction of what it once had been, and it continued to decline. In 1921, before other arrangements to dispose of the grape crop were firmly established, more than 20 million gallons of wine were made. The next year the figure was just over 6 million. There was a sudden spurt of production in 1923 and 1924, when rain damage compelled growers to salvage their substandard grapes as wine rather than send them to the fresh market.[38] Another spurt occurred in 1929. The crop in that year was a short one, but there was by that time a deliberate effort to divert grapes away from the unremunerative fresh market into wine. The figures sagged to their lowest point in 1930: under the combined weight of the Depression and national Prohibition, the United States managed to produce a bare 3 million gallons of wine in that difficult year.

The stocks of wine held in American wineries during Prohibition hovered around an average of 25 million gallons: the lowest figure was the 17 million gallons in 1920 already mentioned; the highest was the 31 million gallons of 1924.[39] The point is that, at any time during Prohibition, there was a lot of wine legally made and legally stored by licensed wineries in the United States. Indeed, the records of the Prohibition authorities housed at the University of California, Davis, cover more than five hundred wineries and winemakers who, at one time or another during Prohibition, made or stored wine in California. The reports of the revenue men are sometimes detailed enough to let us see with some particularity what these Prohibition wines were. A little more than half were dry table wines. In 1930, for example, there were 1 million gallons of Angelica in storage in California, 4 million of claret, 2.5 million of port, and 3.75 million of sherry. The leading white wine was "riesling" (by which any dry white wine might be meant) at 1,647,968 gallons. In New York State, Catawba and, again, riesling led the way; more exotic items included 35,000 gallons of Cabernet in California, 27,000 gallons of Ives Seedling in Ohio, and 97,000 gallons of Barbera in New York (presumably the latter was all of California origin).[40]

As annual wine production declined, so inevitably did the number of wineries still holding licenses. In 1922 there were 919 bonded wineries—694 in California, 123 in New York, 28 in Ohio, 15 each in Missouri and New Jersey, the rest scattered over fourteen other states. Each year these numbers diminished, mostly, one supposes, because the owners of wineries increasingly lost hope that the day on which they might sell their wine in the ordinary way would ever come. Relatively few of the hundreds of wineries that were legally bonded at the outset of Prohibition were in fact making wine on a regular basis. They were merely storehouses for a commodity that could not be much used but that could not simply be thrown away. In order to produce wine they must obtain a permit from the Bureau of Prohibition. In the first half of 1920 the bureau issued only 242 permits to manufacture. How many of these permits were issued to wineries is not stated, but the total would include the distillers of industrial alcohol.[41]

By 1933, the last year of Prohibition, the number of bonded wineries had dwindled to 268: California had 177; New York, 50; Ohio, 9; Missouri, 3; New Jersey, 10; a few more were scattered over what were now only eleven other states.[42] Paradoxically, at the lowest ebb in the number of wineries, in 1933, the production of wine shot up to more than 18 million gallons, now that Repeal was confidently expected.[43]

In view of these figures, it is hardly correct to say that Prohibition put an end to the American wine industry. According to the official statistics, nearly 135 million gallons of wine were produced by bonded wineries in the fourteen vintages of the Prohibition years, and nearly 43 million gallons of this wine were legally sold for permitted uses.[44] But, of course, even though the industry was not absolutely finished off, it was seriously diminished, obstructed, and distorted.

The simplest and most common response to Prohibition on the part of American wineries was to go out of business rather than try to stay alive by undertaking new enterprises. The equipment for making wine—crushers, stemmers, presses, tanks, filters—and the ovals, casks, and barrels for storing it were not of much use for anything else. Thus the capital machinery of the winemaker could neither be used nor sold in the United States.[45] The winery building might well be put to some other use, but only after its furnishings had been cleared away and somehow disposed of. The winemakers themselves had to find some other line of work.

A typical case—only one among very many—was the Hammondsport Wine Company, of Hammondsport, New York, the center of sparkling-wine production in the eastern United States.[46] The company, which produced Golden Age Champagne from native hybrid grapes, had never been very prosperous. As Prohibition neared, the directors considered, without enthusiasm, the idea of going into the grape juice business. The prospect was not sufficiently attractive, and in 1920 it was decided to wind up the business and pay off the stockholders if anything should remain after the debts were met.

As its main asset, the company had 3,000 cases of sparkling wine on hand, with an estimated value of $35,000. It also had unofficial—and illegal—offers of $100 a case for the wine. At that price, the company would have been able to pay off its $50,000 indebtedness and have a handsome $250,000 left over to distribute to the shareholders, who would otherwise be left with nothing for their investment. But the wine could not be legally sold at all. Faced with this impasse, the directors went on helplessly waiting and hoping that they might realize something from the sale of a winery that no one wanted and that could not be used.

At the end of 1921, the Hammondsport people were surprised to learn that a majority interest in the company was now in the hands of new stockholders, people from New York City unknown to the old officers of the company. The new stockholders held a meeting to elect new directors, and very shortly thereafter the stock of wine stored in the company's cellars began mysteriously to shrink. By June 1922, when the Internal Revenue Service men moved in, only 300 cases were left at the plant. The winery was then sold at public auction to satisfy the government's claim to back taxes on the vanished wine. But the new owners had paid far less for the property than they had illegally realized on the wine, and they seem to have entirely escaped prosecution. The missing Golden Age Champagne, it was said, had been disposed of under "foreign labels" and had no doubt brought very fancy prices indeed. The original stockholders, however, got next to nothing, the government was defrauded, and Hammondsport had already lost a local industry.

A few miles to the northwest of Hammondsport, in Naples, at the foot of Canandaigua Lake, the firm of Widmer's Wine Cellars illustrated another response to Prohibition. Widmer's was a much larger operation than the Hammondsport Wine Company, and perhaps the relatively large scale of the business made it seem not only more important but more possible to run a winery under Prohibition. It was, indeed, a struggle, but it was done. Widmer's Wine Cellars had been founded by a Swiss immigrant, John Jacob Widmer, in 1888; it now became Widmer Grape Products Industry, since *wine* had been deleted from the official vocabulary of the United States. Widmer was still in control of the winery and would continue to be until 1924, when he sold it to his sons Carl, Frank, and Will; they operated it through Prohibition and afterward.[47]

Running a winery under Prohibition left one between Scylla and Charybdis: since processing grapes to make an alcoholic beverage was illegal under the basic law of the land, anyone handling grapes was closely policed so that the dangerous trade he engaged in was not allowed to pass over into criminality. At the same time, since "intoxicating liquors" *could* be produced for purposes other than drinking, the Department of the Treasury continued its traditional surveillance of the winemakers in order to guard the revenue. These doubled attentions, from police and from revenue officers, generated a welter of permits, regulations, forms, reports, bonds, and other bureaucratic restraints. Only a very determined person would be prepared to cope with them.

The Widmers obtained their basic operating license, permit A, from the federal Prohibition Administration.[48] This permit authorized them to produce up to 90,000 gallons of wine per quarter, a figure presumably based on the winery's past production. To the basic permit A they added permit H, allowing them to withdraw up to 1,500 gallons of wine per quarter for the manufacture of flavoring syrups for soft drinks. Permit H required a bond of $30,000. Permit K allowed the Widmers to produce cider in what had been a winery; and permit L allowed them to receive wines to be dealcoholized for beverage purposes (a trade that never amounted to much). All traffic in wine—whether withdrawing it from one's own stocks to be converted to some legal form, or buying it from some other source—was carried on by means of "permits to purchase intoxicating liquors for other than beverage purposes." These permits were issued by the Prohibition Administration, and the transactions that the agency authorized were closely monitored. The slightest irregularity in the reports was instantly challenged and a strict accounting demanded by both the Internal Revenue Service and the Prohibition Administration. The enforcement of Prohibition upon the nation at large was woefully inadequate, and most people who could pay the prices were able to indulge their tastes without effective restraint from the law. But for a law-abiding winemaker, the case was very different. He was visible, he was on record, and he was thus helplessly vulnerable to regulation and interference.

The Widmers never, during Prohibition, produced wine in the quantity legally allowed to them by their basic permit—360,000 gallons a year. They seem instead to have drawn on the stocks that they had already on hand at the beginning of Prohibition. In 1922, for example, they had about 120,000 gallons of wine; the next year, the figure was about 105,000 gallons. But in 1927 they produced 30,000 gallons, to add to the 98,000 gallons already in storage. And as the prospect of Repeal became more and more certain, they increased production against the coming of the new day, as did all the other winemakers who had survived the drought. Their inventory for 1933, at the end of the last year of Prohibition, shows that they had 362,000 gallons on hand, nearly a third of which had been produced in that year's vintage. So by the end of Prohibition the Widmers had more wine than they had had on hand at the beginning. They were thus rather better prepared than most to meet the demand for decent wine when Repeal came. Even as late as 1936 Widmer's was able to offer "Prohibition" wines: port from 1920 and 1925, sherry from 1924 and 1927.[49]

Grape juice was, so to speak, the Widmers' bread and butter during Prohibition. In this, too, they had an advantage, for they had been making grape juice since 1912 and had a considerable establishment devoted to it by the time Prohibition arrived. They continued to produce it long after Repeal. Selling grape juice was a highly competitive business during Prohibition, however, and it is doubtful that Widmer's share of the market would use up the grapes available. Besides, it was mainly the Concord that was used for grape juice: what was to be done with all the other varieties of native grape in New York State vineyards, the Catawbas, Delawares, Elviras, and Dutchesses from which the region's white wines, and especially its sparkling wines, had traditionally been made?

Everything that ingenuity could suggest and desperation venture seems to have been tried or at least considered. They inquired into the production of grapeseed oil for cooking, of dried grape skins for stock feed, and of argol and lees for industrial use. They made grape jellies and grape sauces, and they invented a wine tonic that seems to have had a good success. The variety of resource displayed is summed up on the company's letterhead in 1933, on which the following list of products appears: "Altar wines, wine tonics, wine sauces, mint sauces, wine jellies, mint jellies, fruit jellies, grape jellies, grape syrups, grape pomace, medicinal wines, grape concentrates, de-alcoholized wines, manufacturing wines, rum and brandy jellies, rum and brandy sauces, cider for vinegar stock, manufacturing wine syrups, sweet cider in glass and bulk, creme de menthe wine cordial de-alcoholized." Widmer's wine tonics were available with a port, sherry, or tokay base and could be bought without prescription, so they helped to soak up some wine. They were sold at "not over 22% alcohol," and they can hardly have provided much sensual gratification: the ingredients, apart from the wine, were dextrose, peptone, and sodium of glycerophosphate crystals. I leave to medical opinion the question whether such a compound had useful tonic principles. It did, however, help the Widmers to struggle on to the day of Repeal.

The experiences illustrated by the Hammondsport Wine Company and by Widmer's were general in the winemaking regions. Outside New York and California there were few wineries large enough to manage the diversification improvised by the Widmers: the old Sandusky, Ohio, firms of Engels and Krudwig, M. Hommel, and Sweet Valley Wine Company were among them. Many held on in more or less the position that they had been in when Prohibition came into force, keeping their wine in storage and perhaps even adding to it on occasion, but unable to do anything with it. So after a few years they were likely to succumb. Most of the small-scale wineries in such states as Virginia, New Jersey, Ohio, and Missouri were extinguished—one reason among others that winemaking has been so slow to recover in those places. It is particularly puzzling that there should have been almost no vestige of life left in the Missouri industry. One suggested explanation is that the winegrowers of the state, who were mostly German and had made a point of preserving their German identity, had suffered badly during World War I from the virulent anti-Germanism of the time. Prohibition had followed hard on the heels of the war, and the Missouri Germans, who had been bullied into an all-American style (they ceased to teach German in the Hermann schools in 1918), were not about to do anything that might make them seem other than law-abiding Americans.

The point that Prohibition did not create a single, uniform condition of things is very fully illustrated by the situation in California.[50] At the beginning of Prohibition, there were nearly seven hundred wineries in California holding licenses from the Bureau of Prohibition to store, to make, or to sell wine. They were of all sizes, from the very smallest to the very largest, and they were scattered through every winemaking region of the state. The winemakers who had the toughest time were the small producers with a merely local traffic. They could be licensed to hold on to the wine already in storage, and even to produce more if they could not otherwise deal with their grapes, but more often than not they had no way to get rid of what they made and could not afford to keep what they had in sound condition. Giosue Agostini of Healdsburg, for example, took out a license to make wine in 1920, and continued to make a little in succeeding years. But by 1929 it had all gone sour: the wine was dry table wine, and there was no demand for that in the legal markets. By 1931 Agostini's winery, described as "quite a large one" before Prohibition, was almost derelict. The once-solid structure was now an "old dilapidated building with a shingle roof. . . . The cooperage is old and some of the tanks are about to collapse, and all of the wine is spoiled." Agostini had to petition to have the wine destroyed (that is, allowed to run down the drain: such an operation had to be closely supervised so that the wine was not "diverted"). Agostini meantime earned his living as a dairyman, but he had at least persisted longer than others.

For another example, Blanche Marie Albertz of Cloverdale took out the necessary permits in 1920, but in 1924 the inspectors found that "no interest has been taken to keep the wine in good condition. The wine has evaporated and the containers remain unfilled. . . . The containers were covered with dust and spider webs. There is no desire to make more wine." Three years later all the wine that remained was run down the drain and the permits surrendered. The Hollis Black winery in Cloverdale, one of the highly regarded wineries of Sonoma County, also saw most of its wine go bad: in 1931 the winery converted 22,000 gallons of wine into vinegar and returned its permits to the authorities. (Black, however, reentered the trade after Repeal.) One of the pioneer names in Sonoma winemaking, Dresel and Company, went through the same dismal process. Carl Dresel, who was born on the property in 1851, made a little wine during Prohibition in order to salvage the grapes from his vineyard that could not be sold as fresh fruit. By 1930 he, too, decided to wind up the business, converted his wine into vinegar, and requested the return of his bond from the authorities. The firm was not revived by Repeal.

In Napa County a typical small producer was Peter Jaeger of Yountville, who made, under the usual permit, a small quantity of wine after 1920. In 1923 the Prohibition director declined to renew Jaeger's permit, on the grounds that there could be no real market for the wine, and "it is not believed advisable to encourage the continued manufacturing of wine where the outlet is so limited, the supply far exceeding the demand." Jaeger soon found the truth of this; in 1925 the wine was dumped and Jaeger's bond canceled. Another longtime Napa winegrower, one with connections going back to the early days of the industry there, was John H. Wheeler, who had become secretary of the State Board of Viticultural Commissioners soon after its founding in 1880. Wheeler, whose winery was at Zinfandel Lane, south of St. Helena, had been replanting his vineyards to walnuts and other crops in anticipation of the coming of Prohibition, but he still had some 60 acres of vines in 1924. He made only a little wine during Prohibition, but he could not manage to get rid of even that little and had to ask the authorities for permission to dump it. In 1930 the operation was wound up, and though Wheeler reopened his winery on Repeal, he was by then an old man, able to continue for only a few years.

One anecdote recorded by a Prohibition Administration inspector suggests how perverse the situation must have seemed to the people who grew grapes, made wine, and then had to stand by while the wine deteriorated in storage. John Cereghino, whose winery was near Concord, discontinued business in 1919 but then made 7,520 gallons of wine in 1922 without filing with the authorities. When the inspectors came to ask why, he answered that he meant only to make grape juice from the unsold grapes in his vineyard, but the stuff turned to wine. He then paid the required taxes. The next year, Cereghino died. When the inspectors called again in 1927, they found that the wine was now down to 1,040 gallons, and they demanded of Mrs. Cereghino by what authority she had removed wine from bonded premises. She replied, "What do you expect me and my children and my help to drink? Water?" The agent who reported this encounter was more amused than angry, and concluded that there were no signs of "wilful intent to break the law." In the next year Mrs. Cereghino, like so many others, reported that the wine was spoiled and requested that it be destroyed under official supervision. It was.

Larger, better-known wineries than those just mentioned did not fare much better. Paul Masson, for example, who had a great reputation for champagne and table wines, found that he could not sell them in the tiny, legal nonbeverage market: that is, as medicinal or sacramental wines (though he produced what he called a medicinal champagne). He had some 500 acres of vineyards, but Masson made little wine through most of the Prohibition years.[51] In 1932, when prospects were clearly changing, he applied for permission to resume winemaking. The inspector sent to analyze the wines that Masson then still had on hand reported that they were all so acidic that he doubted whether they could be "ameliorated and saved," even though the winery was "operated by one of the best known winemakers in California, and believed to have been maintained in the best possible condition, as to cooperage etc."

The famous To-Kalon Vineyard, at Oakville in the Napa Valley, had all sorts of troubles: the manager was fined in 1925 for "illegal possession." In the next year an inspector reported that "this winemaker does not bear a good reputation for honesty," and in 1927 the winery's application for a renewal of its permit was disapproved, even though no evidence of wrongdoing had been provided. The permit was later restored, but an inspector's report in 1932 tells a sad story: the winery was in poor condition; the wine mostly old, kept in a dirt-floored space; the tanks leaking; bungs loosely fitted; some wine still fermenting in storage; vinegar flies abounding; wines not properly racked; tanks not properly cleaned and sulfited. The only winemaking instruments on the premises were "one gauging rod, 1 wantage [deficiency] rod, and 1 Saccarometer [sic] (not serviceable)." And yet this had once been one of the model wineries of the Valley. When the winery was wholly destroyed by fire in 1939, there was no wine on the premises.[52]

There were cases, a few at any rate, in which a winery quietly held on and managed to stay in reasonably good shape. Fountaingrove, in Santa Rosa, made wine regularly, succeeded in selling some of it, and kept what it had in good condition, or so the inspectors reported. Felix Salmina, at St. Helena, managed in the same way: he made a little wine each year, after most of his grapes had been disposed of in the fresh market, and, the inspectors said, kept it in good condition. When Repeal came, he had nearly 300,000 gallons of wine on hand, ready to sell.[53] Andrew Mattei, a Swiss who had developed his Fresno County winery to a capacity of 3 million gallons before Prohibition, also operated in a diminished but uninterrupted way.[54] Samuele Sebastiani, in Sonoma, contrived to hang on to his property by diversifying into any opportunities that arose: he owned rental properties, and he built a theater, a cannery, a bowling alley, and a skating rink. When Repeal came, he still had a winery.[55]

No winery could be said to have flourished under Prohibition, but a few of the very largest did contrive to dominate such markets as existed. Beaulieu is perhaps the best-known instance. It enjoyed most-favored status with the Catholic diocese of San Francisco and was able to continue production uninterruptedly as a supplier of altar wine. Not only that, but demand reached such a point that Beaulieu took over the Wente Brothers property on a lease so that it could add Wente's well-regarded white wines to its range of sacramental wines.[56] Colonial Grape Products, a combination of wineries around the state carpentered together in 1920 from parts of the wreck of the CWA, produced a good deal of wine at one location or another, mostly for distillation into high-proof brandy or for conversion to vinegar—though it also sold quite a lot of wine in the New York market.[57] But it could not keep up all its properties equally. The distinguished La Perla winery in Napa County—perhaps the best of the lot—fell into decay. In 1927, of the 50,000 gallons of wine then on hand at La Perla, only 600 were regarded as "fit for consumption" (were consumption allowed); the rest would have to be distilled. The decline of the property had gone so far by Repeal that the winery could not be revived, and in 1935 it expired. The Italian Vineyard Company, Secundo Guasti's large enterprise at Cucamonga, maintained itself mostly by shipments of grapes to the home winemaking market from its huge vineyards ("the largest in the world," the company boasted), but kept the winery going too: it made concentrates, and when all other outlets were closed, it made wine. An inspection in 1925 reported that the entire plant was in full operation, and by 1930 the inventory at Cucamonga showed more than 2.5 million gallons of wine on hand. Perhaps this was the largest operation in all of California. It included wines under the whole gamut of borrowed names that characterized provincial California: claret, burgundy, riesling, sauterne, marsala, tokay, port, malaga, sherry.

There were, improbably, even new winemaking enterprises founded during the Prohibition years. The Christian Brothers, already operating a winery at Martinez, bought and moved into the much larger Theodore Gier winery in Napa County in 1930. Louis Martini entered the market for grape products in 1923 in a large winery formerly belonging to the CWA at Kingsburg, in the Central Valley, and prospered there sufficiently to be able to build a completely new winery in St. Helena just before Repeal.

These were notable exceptions, however. For the most part, the winemaking that went on during Prohibition was not undertaken with any hope that the wine could be sold but only as a salvage operation when all other means to get rid of a grape crop had failed: one reads such explanations again and again in the records of the federal authorities: "an emergency measure to salvage unsaleable grapes"; "it depended largely upon the market for grapes, as to whether or not wines would be produced"; "we cannot otherwise dispose of our grapes"; "will make wine only in order to salvage the crop"; "the only purpose in maintaining the winery is to use it for . . . salvaging grapes not otherwise marketable."

There were, inevitably, licensed wineries whose wines flowed into the illegal traffic and were put to the purpose outlawed by the Eighteenth Amendment by being consumed as a beverage, but not very many. It is not easy to get distinct information on this head, since one had to be caught selling wine illegally in order to enter into the record. The commissioner of the Internal Revenue Service reported in 1923 that thirty-eight wineries had been seized for violating the law and that convictions had been secured against most of them, but he gave no further details.[58] Wineries obviously operated at some risk, yet Leon Adams recalled that the restaurants of San Francisco were well supplied by small wineries in the Bay Area that continued to work despite Prohibition. A winemaker in the Hecker Pass said that the Prohibition agents knew what the wineries were doing and that the wineries knew that the agents knew, but that "everybody got along as best they could."[59] That story would seem to be confirmed by Everett Crosby's recollection of the practice in Pleasanton, in the Livermore valley; there, he says, the mayor and his aides were regularly to be seen through the unshuttered windows of the speakeasy across the street from city hall as they stood at the bar drinking the local red wine.[60] Over on Monterey Bay, the Bargetto family served Sunday dinners to the public with wine from the barrels stored in the basement; the dinner was $2.50 and included a bottle of wine for every four diners. If a diner wanted more, the young daughter of the house fetched it from the basement for another $2.50.[61] In Boulder Creek, the hotel operated by the Locatelli family was a principal outlet for the wine they produced in their winery and continued to serve that purpose through the Prohibition years.[62] But it is to be noted that all of these operations were hardly to be distinguished from home winemaking and thus only accidentally or intermittently subject to the interference of the law.

For its part, the federal government reported fairly large seizures of illegal wine, though there is no indication of where it might have come from. In 1923, for example, the revenue men seized a reported 490,000 gallons of wine; nearly half of this total was seized in California, and one supposes that it came from the local grapes. New York contributed nearly 100,000 gallons to the total, but much of that was probably smuggled from various sources. It is interesting to note that 44,000 gallons were seized in Louisiana, which had a long-established partiality for French wines.[63]

On the whole, however, it seems clear that licensed American wineries had only a negligible part in the notorious bootleg trade that is supposed to have operated almost at will under Prohibition. Lurid stories abound of bootleggers careening down the midnight roads of the wine country, pursued by revenue men; of wine flowing from the staved-in heads of confiscated barrels and running down the gutters of city streets; of raids on speakeasies whose patrons fled in panic to avoid arrest (presumably they were ignorant of the fact that drinking liquor was not criminal—only the seller was liable). These are the clichés, the popular stereotypes, in the American imagination of Prohibition, and the forbidden booze that was the cause of it all certainly included wine. But such images have little or nothing to do with the wineries that existed before Prohibition and managed to endure through it.

These licensed wineries were under close supervision; it was known precisely how much wine they had on hand and what sort of wine it was. If any discrepancy occurred between what was on the record and what the inspectors actually found on the premises, an explanation was at once demanded. Under such close surveillance, the winemaker had little chance to cheat, whatever his wishes might have been. Inspectors could, of course, be bought off, but presumably not all of them were venal.[64] In the second place, the produce of legitimate wineries was not in (illegal) demand when one could legally make wine at home, or in a rented basement, or in a convenient warehouse. The supply of grapes was unlimited and unpoliced. The law permitted home winemaking and had no means of confining it, once begun, within those limits. Only the eradication of the vineyards could have prevented wholesale unlicensed winemaking, and as will be seen, the nation's vineyards, so far from disappearing, doubled in acreage under Prohibition. There was certainly a large traffic in illegal wine, but practically speaking, it had little to do with the licensed American winemaking establishment.

VITICULTURE AND HOME WINEMAKING

While the winemakers struggled to keep alive some fragments of their business, things were very different among the grape growers. There were prophecies of doom for the growers as the shadow of Prohibition neared: the small farmers who had invested years of work in their vines would, at a stroke, lose their markets and be driven from the land, or so people said. The vineyardists of the Lake Erie islands, their representative declared in Congress, would be pauperized should the Volstead Bill pass into law; as for the growers of California, it would cost them $2 million just to dig up their vines after Prohibition had put an end to their use.[65] The State Board of Viticultural Commissioners in California and the University of California, recognizing the need to assist the grape growers in these desperate circumstances, undertook to develop alternative products from grapes: there were experiments in dehydrating grapes and in condensing grape syrup from fresh grape juice. At the beginning of Prohibition there was even some effort made to promote such processes. But the doctors despaired of their patient. F. T. Bioletti and W. V. Cruess, two most eminent names among the experts, published a discouraged bulletin in May 1919, after the passage of the Eighteenth Amendment but before the passage of the Volstead Act, under the title "Possible Uses for Wine-Grape Vineyards." They concluded that the possible uses were few indeed. One could dry grapes for hog feed, but that would not cover the costs of production; neither would converting grapes to industrial alcohol. Grape syrup could not compete with syrups from cane, sorghum, or sugar beets; it was, Bioletti and Cruess thought, "hopeless" to try to compete against the established taste for grape juice from the eastern Concord grape. In a prediction that proved spectacularly wrong, they saw no prospect for selling fresh grapes. Some of the San Joaquin vineyards, they thought, might be grafted over to table grapes, but that would be impossible in the wine-grape vineyards of the coastal regions: "It seems inevitable . . . that most of the wine grapes of this region will have to be abandoned or removed."[66]

As it happened, there was no need at all to search after alternative uses for the produce of California's vineyards.[67] The California vineyardists had already established a growing trade in fresh grapes for the East Coast to supply home winemakers. Now that trade shot up explosively, and growers were delighted to find that their crop was more eagerly sought after than ever before, largely by buyers from the East who came with money in their pockets.[68] These buyers were, as Carl Wente recalled, "an odd group," working without offices: "Trading began *after* grapes had been packaged, a car loaded and a bill of lading issued to the buyer. In the hotel lobby or on the street corner, bidding for this car went on, and the car could be sold by the original buyer only to be re-sold once or several times thereafter. A car which had been originally destined for Pittsburgh might eventually be re-routed to New York City."[69] Grapes that had been selling for $25 a ton were now bid for at prices two and three times that figure. In the first vintage of the Prohibition era, 1920, more than 26,000 railroad cars of fresh grapes rolled out of California.[70] The railroads scrambled to grab a share of this huge market—it exceeded 72,000 carloads in 1927—and developed facilities for distributing the crop in terminal cities such as Chicago, Newark, and Boston.[71]

In conditions like this, a booming growth in vineyards began at once.[72] Bearing vineyard acreage in California in 1920 was about 300,000 acres; by 1927, the peak year, it touched 577,000. The figures of grape production doubled in six years, from 1.25 million tons in 1920 to 2.5 million in 1927.[73] The situation for growers in other states, though not as heatedly expansive as in California, was prosperous enough. By 1926 there were, for example, 4,000 new acres planted to grapes in Missouri and 7,300 in Arkansas.[74] In Ohio, production reached a record 29,000 tons in 1926, and the figures for other grape-growing states such as Michigan, New York, and Pennsylvania all show large rises in average production in the first half of the 1920s. Even Nebraska, hardly thought of as a land suited to the grape, joined in the rush. Its vineyards produced nearly 1,250 tons of grapes in 1919, and "the crops in recent years have been even larger."[75] In 1925 the grape crop outside California totaled half a million tons, precisely double the level of 1920.[76]

SECTION 29:
"NONINTOXICATING IN FACT"

The reason for this startling result of Prohibition was simple: the nation had turned to home winemaking. No one had imagined that the demand would be remotely like what it proved to be. Andrew Volstead, someone said, should be enshrined as the patron saint of the San Joaquin Valley.[77] It is curious to reflect on the possibility that Prohibition, if it had only continued long enough, might at last have done what no other agency has yet succeeded in doing, and made the United States a nation of wine drinkers.[78] Since the wine made at home—or in illegal small-scale wineries in basements and garages across the country—did not enter into the official record, one can only guess at how much was actually made. The members of the Wickersham Commission made such a guess in their report; using a conservative set of possibilities as a basis, they came up with the conclusion that an average 111 million gallons of wine were produced in each year from 1922 to 1929 in American homes.[79] That figure compares with the 55 million gallons of commercial production in 1919, just before Prohibition descended; thus, just as grape production had done, so wine production doubled in the first five years of Prohibition.

The salvation of viticulture in the country came about through an obscurely expressed and much-disputed proviso in the text of the Volstead Act. Section 29, Title II, of the act reads thus:

> The penalties provided in this chapter against the manufacture of liquor without a permit shall not apply to a person manufacturing nonintoxicating cider and fruit juice exclusively for use in his home, but such cider and fruit juices shall not be sold or delivered except to persons having permits to manufacture vinegar.[80]

The section is on the face of it somewhat awkward, since it merely lifts a penalty instead of creating some distinct privilege. It presented many difficulties in interpretation and application, but most of them were resolved in favor of what was presumably its original intent—to authorize home winemaking without interference from the officers of the law. A history of this text (so far as it can be known) and an elucidation (so far as it can be given) should be of interest, considering the importance it had for the fate of grapes and wine in America.

FIGURE 1
How grapes were sold
to home winemakers.
The grapes were packed
in so-called California
lugs holding about 24
pounds and shipped in
a cattle car for the sake
of the ventilation pro-
vided by the open slats.
(From *California Grape
Grower* 13 [October
1932]; reprinted with
permission from *Wines
and Vines*.)

The section was not introduced into the Volstead Act until after it had passed the House of Representatives and gone on to the Senate for debate.[81] There, Section 29 was inserted and agreed to, even though it was recognized as a remarkable and confusing exception: What *were* "fruit juices," and how were they "manufactured"? Why, if they were "nonintoxicating," should they have to be exempted from the prohibition against intoxicating liquors? What did *nonintoxicating* mean?[82] On these points the question of home winemaking depended, for in subsequent rulings made by the Bureau of Prohibition and in a succession of judgments in a number of trials, it appeared that *fruit juices* must include wine, and that *nonintoxicating* meant "nonintoxicating in fact" rather than the Volstead Act's statutory 0.5 percent alcohol.[83] Whether the intention of Section 29 had been to produce this result is not entirely clear, but it seems most likely. One version of its history holds that the section was introduced because some senators were anxious about the farm vote and feared the anger of the apple growers if their cider market should be taken from them. Much more circumstantial and persuasive is an account given by the veteran winemaker and tireless promoter of wine Paul Garrett.[84]

According to Garrett, Section 29 came about in the following manner. During the course of the debates on the Volstead Bill, Garrett attended a hearing in Washington at which the grape growers pleaded their case against the bill. The meeting, as Garrett recalled, was dominated not by the senator presiding but by the Reverend E. C. Dinwiddie, veteran legislative superintendent of the Anti-Saloon League, who repeatedly assured the growers that he had no wish to injure any agricultural interests. He was prepared even to allow the continued production of wine, since he was confident that it could be dealcoholized before being sold and that it would find a ready market. Taking this hint, Garrett called on Dinwiddie and his even more potent associate, Wayne B. Wheeler, at the offices of the Anti-Saloon League: they assured him that they did not wish to cause the loss of any crops. After further discussions, the text of Section 29 was inserted by Wheeler and Dinwiddie into the Volstead Bill, originally with the word *wine* in it; when that word was objected to in Congress, the term *fruit juices* was substituted, and the proviso that such fruit juices be nonintoxicating was added. Garrett then represented to Dinwiddie and Wheeler that these changes made the exception pointless: what had "nonintoxicating fruit juices" to do with wine? But he was reassured by them that this curious formula would serve the purpose. Garrett's account is not quite clear on the point, but apparently Dinwiddie and Wheeler were prepared to disregard the Volstead Bill's definition of *intoxicating* and to accept wine made at home as "nonintoxicating in fact." None of them had any idea that the scale of home winemaking would be what it turned out to be. But, as Garrett concluded, the key point was that home winemaking was "specifically provided for" and was "intended by the framers of the bill."[85]

This account seems to be essentially confirmed by the testimony of both Wheeler and Volstead himself. Wheeler said that the framers of the Volstead Act left the term *nonintoxicating* undefined in Section 29 because they knew that home producers would not have the means of making exact measurements of the alcoholic content in their "fruit juices." If they were held to a strict standard, the courts would not be able to handle the burden of cases; anyone might be charged for the most trivial of infractions by a hostile neighbor or a disgruntled associate. It was enough that everyone knew what the legal limit was and that anything beyond that limit was illegal.[86] Volstead remembered the situation thus:

> In the conference between the two Houses we wrote into the [Volstead] act a proviso to the effect that a person might make nonintoxicating cider and fruit juices. The question as to what construction will be put upon that is still open, except to this extent, former Attorney General Palmer positively held that a person could make his cider or his fruit juices and leave them in his home, no matter how strong they might become, which practically means that a man can make cider and wine in the house. . . . it might contain quite a little more than one-half of one per cent without being intoxicating, and that was the object of keeping that provision in. Otherwise the expression "nonintoxicating" would mean nothing.[87]

The Bureau of Prohibition, the agency of the Treasury Department created to administer the Volstead Act, evidently took the Garrett-Volstead view of the question. The bureau ruled on it as early as June 1920, affirming then that the word *nonintoxicating* in Section 29 did not mean what the Volstead Act said but rather meant "nonintoxicating in fact," and therefore not necessarily subject to the provisions of the act.[88] Things were quietly left in this agreeably indeterminate state until 1923, when a congressman from Maryland, John Philip Hill, determined to compel the Bureau of Prohibition to clarify Section 29.

Hill—a Baltimore lawyer who had been decorated for his services in the war, had taught government at Harvard and Johns Hopkins, had been U.S. Attorney for Maryland, and now sat in the House of Representatives as a Republican congressman—was no ordinary moonshiner. He was in a good position to stir up trouble, he enjoyed publicity, and he had a cause—indeed, he already had a reputation as one of the noisiest opponents of

Prohibition in the House. He wanted to modify the Volstead Act in order to allow the production of 2.75 percent beer, and he thought that he could do so by forcing the government to admit that *nonintoxicating* would in fact permit a good deal more alcohol than the limit set by the Volstead Act.[89] Accordingly, he made some wine in the fall of 1923 at his house in Baltimore, and then loudly advertised the fact that he had done so. He invited the analysts of the Bureau of Prohibition to his house and presented them with samples of his wine (made from New York juice); they duly certified that it was in fact wine, and that the samples offered to them ran from 3 percent to almost 12 percent alcohol. The wary authorities responded only by securing a temporary injunction against Hill and padlocking his wine room.

The next fall, Hill tried again. This time he made cider from the apples growing in the orchard behind his house, and then publicly invited all those who agreed with the aims of his campaign to come to his house on Saturday, 20 September 1924, to "inspect and try a glass of . . . home-made cider."[90] A crowd responded—estimates varied from five hundred to two thousand "guests"—though Wheeler, the power of the Anti-Saloon League, and Roy Haynes, head of the Bureau of Prohibition, were not among them, despite the fact that Hill had made a point of inviting them especially.

To his great satisfaction, Hill was now indicted, though not arrested, for the illegal manufacture of wine and cider. The case was referred to district court in Baltimore, and there the judge held that the defendant was entitled to show evidence that his cider was not intoxicating "in fact"—in other words, that the definition of *intoxicating* in the Volstead Act did not apply to home production of alcoholic drink. The question was then put to the jury, which decided that Hill's cider did not, in fact, intoxicate.[91]

The *New York Times*, in editorializing on the case, agreed that it had revealed a gross contradiction in the act, but doubted that it would do anything to modify the rules "in the direction of common sense."[92] And the *Times* was right. Hill pressed his bill in favor of 2.75 beer to no avail, and then dropped out of national politics. The case was, however, of great value to the grape growers and home winemakers of the country, for the precedent that it set stood up in the courts thereafter. Until Hill began agitating for a ruling, home winemaking had gone on largely undisturbed, indeed, but in uncertainty regarding its status under the law. Now it was certainly legal, as long as the result was "nonintoxicating in fact"; and since no one knew what "intoxicating in fact" was, the Prohibition men took the prudent course and usually left the home winemakers alone.

Not all of the nation's home winemakers began with fresh grapes.[93] Many of them worked instead either with grape juices purchased from a commercial source or with grape concentrate, available at any time of the year. In this way, by producing either juice or concentrate, a few wineries could stay alive and share some crumbs from the grape growers' more prosperous table. Grape concentrate was made by a number of wineries now converted to "grape products": Italian Swiss Colony, for example, offered both fresh juices and its Moonmist concentrate in zinfandel, sherry, riesling, and muscatel styles throughout the Prohibition era.[94] Colonial Grape Products supplied juices and concentrates from

FIGURE 2
Congressman John
Philip Hill making "fruit
juices" at his home in
Baltimore. (From
California Grape Grower 6
[October 1925]; reprinted
with permission from
Wines and Vines.)

its plants in Elk Grove, Napa, and St. Helena, as did L. M. Martini from Kingsburg, to name only a few.

The Prohibition-era records of the George Lonz Winery, on Middle Bass Island, Lake Erie, show us in clear detail a section of the many Americans who took up winemaking at home.[95] The Lonz Winery had been in business since 1884, established by George Lonz's father. Now it carried on by selling fresh juice—Delaware, Concord, and Catawba from the Lake Erie islands—to a growing list of customers throughout the Midwest, but especially to the Germans of Ohio. Hein, Winkler, Kalman, Steinbrecher, Eichorn—such were the names of Lonz's customers. After them, the main traffic was with the residents of Detroit. The juice was shipped off the island in white oak kegs varying from 10 to 50 gallons in capacity. The top price, reached in 1924, was $1.75 a gallon for Delaware grape juice; by the Depression year of 1932 this had slipped to $1.20 a gallon, but even at that Lonz was certainly making far more from a ton of grapes in this form than he ever did as a pre-Prohibition winemaker. Printed instructions on how to convert the juice to wine were sent with the kegs: the recipe for Catawba, for example, was 20 gallons of Catawba juice to 15 pounds of sugar and 6 gallons of water, stored at a temperature of 70 degrees Fahrenheit. The instructions allowed that the juice could be kept from fermentation by pasteurizing it, and that it could be converted to vinegar after fermentation by exposing it to the air. But it was quite clear that the intent of the "directions on the care and preservation of Lonz's Grape Juice right from the press" was to make wine. Sometimes there were anxieties about the law. One customer in Flint, Michigan, wrote to cancel his order in 1923 because, he said, the local revenue officers were keeping track of juice shipments so that they could call later "for the purpose of testing the alcoholic content" of the result. This proved to be a false alarm, however, and neither Lonz nor his customers seem to have been much troubled by the Prohibition officers.

Lonz's customers included doctors, engineers, newspapermen, bankers, lawyers—the whole range of professions—as well as ordinary working people and some very rich men too: the president of the Continental Bank in Detroit, the president of Columbia Motors, and the president of the Ohio Bell Telephone Company, for instance. There were advertising men, accountants, city officials, and at least one artist of distinction: Eliel Saarinen, the architect, then resident at Cranbrook Academy, was a Lonz customer.[96] So too, most improbably, was the president of the Ohio WCTU, who wrote Lonz to thank him for his grape juice: "Instead of doing anything that curses the race," she said, "you are its benefactor." Can she have read his advertisements? Perhaps not. Most of Lonz's advertising appears to have been carried on by word of mouth, and some customers later acted as his agents for the sale of juice.

Not all of them, of course, were entirely happy customers: amateur winemaking is too chancy a business for that. Lonz's correspondence is full of plaintive letters from people whose juice ran into trouble: it went sour, or it wouldn't ferment, or it turned to vinegar; it might blow the bung from the keg, or it might burst the bottles it went into; and after all had been done according to rule it still might turn cloudy and turbid. If needed, Lonz would send a man to superintend things, but the service does not seem to have been much sought after. People took their chances, and though the failures must have been many, the successes—they could never have been very good—were enough to keep things going. In 1928 Lonz bought a new Cadillac and made a two-month trip to France and Germany.

The early instructions sent out by Lonz were careful at least to cite the federal regulations that disallowed any use of homemade wine outside the home. The word *wine* was never used, and the text appealed to customers to help prevent abuses of the privileges they had been given. But by 1932, when repeal was beginning to seem possible, the word *wine* was freely used in Lonz's literature, and his product had become Lonz Wine Juices.

AFTER THE BOOM

The flourishing condition of viticulture under Prohibition did not last. The high-pressure development of vineyards had, by 1926, produced a supply greater than demand, and in an entirely unregulated market, prices crashed.[97] The problem was greatly complicated by the fact that growers had only a few weeks in the year in which to sell fresh grapes, mostly in cities far distant from the source. The means for disposing of the fresh crop were sometimes of the most primitive. Often the grower or an agent (or sometimes the grower's son) would accompany the loaded cars to the distant railroad yards and sell them directly to buyers at the door of the car. More often the load would be offered at auction, subject to every accident of the local market. Young John Parducci, at the age of fourteen, was sent to board in New Jersey so that he could superintend the sale of grapes shipped by his father from Mendocino County:

> We'd open the cars up and people walked down this ramp, which was about a quarter of a
> mile long with cars on both sides. They would look at these grapes and take down the num-

ber of the car and go to the auction market, and when the car came up they would bid on it. If it brought a profit to us, we sold it; if it didn't bring a profit, we'd hold it over for a day or two.[98]

But, he added, "grapes deteriorated very fast after the long trip, and we did not dare to keep them too long."[99] The market thus operated under panic conditions every year.

Another serious problem had developed in the vineyards; it was not recognized at the time, but it proved to be among the most damaging and enduring results of Prohibition. The great explosion of grape planting that took place under Prohibition was not of grapes suited to making good wine but of grapes fit to be transported long distances and capable of attracting an uninstructed buyer—"shipping grapes" rather than true wine grapes. Home winemakers a continent away from the major source of grapes naturally wanted fruit that stood up well to the rigors of a long transport over deserts and mountains and broiling prairies. No wine grape of high quality could withstand such an ordeal. The result, very soon established, was that California vineyards were more and more planted or grafted over to tough, good-looking grapes capable of holding up under shipment but of decidedly inferior merit for winemaking. No matter: they looked better, and so they sold better. In 1931, for example, of the 15,000 cars of black juice grapes shipped from California, almost 6,000 cars were of Alicante Bouschet, a dark, coarse grape of splendid color and form but of marginal value for wine. The other leading varieties were Carignane (3,000 cars), a good but undistinguished grape, and Zinfandel (3,000 cars), an excellent type but very susceptible to rot and far from its best when grown in the Central Valley vineyards, as many of the grapes shipped out were. The situation for white grapes was, if anything, even worse. The leading white varieties were Malaga (1,765 cars), a table grape, and Muscat (2,700 cars), presumably the Muscat of Alexandria, primarily a raisin grape.[100] The varieties nowadays associated with fine wine in California—Zinfandel excepted—did not effectively enter into the shipment of grapes during Prohibition. It is true that there never *had* been a large acreage of such grapes in the state, but Prohibition diminished what had been there.

Prohibition thus encouraged a double-barreled mistake: too many grapes, and when Repeal came, too many grapes of the wrong kind. From the point of view of the winemaker, the vineyards had been deeply degraded. Except for Zinfandel (more often than not planted in the wrong region), superior red varieties were hardly to be found. The case with white wine grapes was even worse. There had not been many before Prohibition, and the demand for them among home winemakers was very restricted. By the time Repeal arrived, they had virtually disappeared. So at the end of Prohibition the vineyards abounded in raisin and table grapes and were almost destitute of wine grapes of any quality. This gross imbalance in the composition of California's vineyards entailed problems that plagued the industry for the next generation: raisin and table grapes were in perennial surplus, wine grapes of quality in perennial shortage. The extent to which California wine—not just in the first years of Repeal but to this day—comes from table and raisin varieties is depressing to contemplate. In the average figures for 1933–35, California wineries crushed 317,000 tons of wine grapes and 302,000 tons of raisin and table grapes. Even in 1937, the figures were 466,000 to 455,000.[101] Such proportions had to mean a severe debasement of the average level of quality, especially when it is considered that mostly the poorer grades of table and raisin varieties—those that could not be sold in the market to which they properly belonged—were diverted to the wineries. A comparable shift in the character of eastern wines seems also to have occurred as the plebeian Concord took over more and more from such varieties as the Catawba and the Delaware. This development had perhaps more to do with the expansive market for grape juice than with the demands of home winemakers. But the result was the same: wine grapes lost out.

After the collapse of 1926 it was clear that something had to be done. The California Vineyardists Association (CVA) was created at the end of that year to act as an industry-wide agency: marketing, advertising, inspection, research, lobbying, and the production of grape products all fell within its scope, but devising methods of orderly marketing was its main object.[102] It was to be voluntary but would charge fees for its services, and it hoped to secure the cooperation of the entire trade. But the CVA's plan for orderly marketing depended heavily on the simple, desperate expedient of leaving much of the grape crop unharvested. On that basis it did not get very far: it came too late to the vintage of 1927 to affect the dreary results of that year, and things were little better in 1928. By that time the directors saw that only if the members entered into firm contractual obligations could the CVA do much to affect the depressed market for fresh grapes, but by then the depression was too deep. The CVA claimed to have twelve thousand grower-members at the beginning of its existence and to have increased its membership thereafter.[103] But it ceased operations around 1932 and officially disappeared in 1936. Before it expired, however, it had generated a powerful child.

This was an organization called Fruit Industries, created in 1929 by a combination of the largest producers of "grape products" in California—that is, by the remnants of the old winemaking industry, as distinguished from the grape growers. Fruit Industries emerged from one of the elements of the CVA, its Grape Products Division, a loose affiliation formed in 1927 to develop products from and markets for the troublesome annual surplus of the California grape crop.[104] The possibilities for such a body suddenly altered in 1929 when, as a part of President Hoover's scheme to rescue American agriculture from its years of economic depression, the Agricultural Marketing Act was passed. This act created the Federal Farm Board, which presided over a large fund to be used for "stabilizing" the production of major agricultural commodities. Growers, according to the plan, would organize cooperatives; the Farm Board would lend them money; and with that money the co-ops would buy up surpluses, control production, and supervise marketing. Thus all would be rationalized. The fledgling Grape Products Division of the CVA

FIGURE 3

A California vineyard in the San Joaquin Valley pulled up, not at the beginning but near the end of Prohibition, after the collapse of prices in the late 1920s. (Courtesy of the Wine Institute.)

fitted quite nicely into this scheme, for its members already controlled most of the grape products business in California.

They now reorganized themselves as a marketing co-op under the name of Fruit Industries, which took over all the plants, stock, and businesses of the participating firms.[105] Paul Garrett, though identified with eastern grapes and wines, was the owner of large California properties and became the chairman of the board and the public personality of Fruit Industries; its executive director was Donald Conn, the man behind the formation of the CWA.[106] By October 1929 they had secured a million-dollar loan from the Federal Farm Board.

But what were they to do with it? Their task was to absorb as much of the California surplus grape crop as they could, but the sale of wine was just as illegal now as it had been before the Farm Board was invented, and the market for grape tonics, grape jellies, and grape sauces was not going to offer much hope. The plan, then, was to promote grape concentrate as it had never yet been promoted.[107] And that plan depended on the Bureau of Prohibition. Would it cooperate? Conn and other officers of Fruit Industries went to

Washington looking for assurances and promptly received them. Mabel Walker Willebrandt, the assistant attorney general in charge of prosecutions under the Volstead Act, declared that the sale of concentrates and their use under the provisions of Section 29 of the act were perfectly legal. The director of the Bureau of Prohibition, Dr. Doran, issued a circular to his agents reaffirming that they were not to interfere with the shipment or sale of "juice grapes, grape juice and concentrates" and that the home winemaker was to be left undisturbed.[108] For its part, Fruit Industries promised, as the announcement of its formation put it, "rigid adherence to the requirements of the National Prohibition Act."[109]

Secure behind the authority of the Bureau of Prohibition and furnished with public money from the Farm Board, Fruit Industries could now go to work on the promotion of its grape concentrate, called Vine-Glo. Here the irrepressible Garrett at once showed his bold inventiveness. He proposed a committee of three referees who would publicly guide the sales policy of Fruit Industries: Dr. Dinwiddie, of the Anti-Saloon League; Mrs. Lenna Yost, legislative superintendent of the WCTU; and Willebrandt, the assistant attorney general. The Farm Board refused to approve the scheme, but its audacity is pleasant to contemplate. And Dr. Dinwiddie actually agreed to serve![110] There were other promotional high jinks too. When, as a part of its opening sales campaign, Vine-Glo entered the Chicago market late in 1930, the papers reported that Al Capone was preparing to treat it with a strong arm. On the heels of this story, Conn of Fruit Industries issued a press release asserting that Fruit Industries would not be intimidated but would "take its chances with the racketeers. It will protect the law, itself, its agencies, and its customers." After a few days of furor in the press, most people concluded that the whole thing was a promotional stunt, as no doubt it was.[111]

Meantime, Vine-Glo did reasonably well in the market. It came in eight varieties and so had something to offer to everyone: port, Virginia Dare (Garrett's famous brand of Scuppernong wine), muscatel, tokay, sauterne, riesling, claret, and burgundy. Conn reported that a million gallons were sold in fiscal 1929–30 and that sales of more than 2 million gallons were expected in the next year. That would account for some 80,000 tons of California grapes, a significant contribution to the stabilization at which the Farm Board aimed. The gratified board continued its support of Fruit Industries, lending it another million in 1930.[112]

The special appeal of Vine-Glo, as opposed to the many other concentrates on the market, was its quasi-official character: backed by the Farm Board and carrying the assurance of its advertisements that the stuff was "legal in your own home," Vine-Glo could be bought without apology or explanation by the most timid householder. This note of public rectitude was reinforced by the device of selling it (at first) exclusively through drugstores. Another selling point was the comprehensiveness of the service offered. The Vine-Glo people would not only sell the concentrate but deliver it to the purchaser's home, supervise its fermentation, and then bottle the result—the householder had only to pay for it and then to drink it.[113] And all was legal—or at least it was, briefly.

The promotion of Vine-Glo immediately produced an outburst of protest from the Dry forces, an outburst that was intensified when it was learned that Willebrandt, who had left government service in mid 1929, was now the attorney representing Fruit Industries and Vine-Glo in Washington, D.C. The woman who, in her capacity as assistant attorney general in charge of prosecuting crimes against the Volstead Act, had pronounced Vine-Glo legal was now its paid defender. Thus she was both judge and advocate in this case, and though her behavior was, in every technical sense, perfectly proper, poor Willebrandt came in for much abuse. At the same time the public authorities, embarrassed by the outcry over Vine-Glo, began to think again about the legality of such frank promotion of winemaking. The Farm Board continued its support of Fruit Industries, making another million-dollar loan in October 1931. But at almost the same time, a federal court ruled that Section 29 of the Volstead Act permitted the householder to make his "fruit juices" only from fresh grapes, not from concentrate.[114] Frightened by this sudden turn, Conn of Fruit Industries announced in November 1931 that the company would give up its Vine-Glo program. This "voluntary" decision was soon made compulsory by a ruling of the Prohibition director excluding grape concentrate from the protection offered by Section 29 of the Volstead Act. The adventure of Vine-Glo was over.[115]

In the meantime, other signs of activity in the winegrowing world were starting to appear as the long-desired repeal began to seem possible. The overconfident promises of the Vine-Glo promotion had backfired, but it is observable from about 1930 that the word *wine* was returning to the national vocabulary, or at least to the vocabulary of those who worked with grapes. The persistence of winemaking throughout Prohibition has already been stressed. The collapse of the fresh-grape trade in 1926 was a reason for more winemakers to take a chance on converting into wine the grapes that no one wanted; they could have little assurance that they could ever sell what they made, but it seemed better to do so than to let the crop rot on the vines. As one veteran grower and winemaker from the Santa Clara Valley, Norbert Mirassou, recalled, if some of the larger wineries had not made wine and stored it for the growers before Repeal, "there would have been a lot more grape growers that would have gone broke than what did go broke."[116] Cribari and Bisceglia Brothers were among those wineries that made an early return to production, but there were many others. The chance that Al Smith, an avowed Wet, might win the presidential election in 1928 caused a hopeful burst of winemaking in that year, though the hopeful were disappointed.

As the coming of Repeal passed from hope to near certainty, the business began to warm up quickly. At vintage time in 1932—when, apparently, the prospect of Roosevelt's election seemed so clear that everyone knew what was going to happen—the *California Grower* reported that the Department of Prohibition was granting winemaking permits to "responsible growers" and that "a number of owners of unused wineries . . . plan this year to crush their surplus grapes and make wine."[117] And so they did—a total of more than 13 million gallons in 1932.[118] The number of licensed wineries in California at the beginning of 1933, 177, had leaped to 380 by the end of the year, the moment of Repeal, and they managed to produce nearly 20 million gallons of wine in that year, while the country still lay under the law of Prohibition.[119] Notable in retrospect among these new wineries licensed in anticipation of Repeal was that of the brothers Gallo, whose business would grow in a generation to be the largest winemaking enterprise in the world. They received a permit to make up to 50,000 gallons of wine in September 1933. On 8 December 1933, three days after Repeal, they requested an amended permit for an "additional 130,000 gallons of wine which we have already manufactured." Such irregularity would have put the brothers in hot water with the Prohibition authorities, but in the first dawn of Repeal no trouble was made.[120]

At the end of 1932 another step toward the reemergence of wine was made with the formation of the Grape Growers League of California. The league was organized with the help of Leon Adams, a San Francisco journalist who was inspired by a mission to "civilize American drinking."[121] In the pursuit of that vision he later assisted in the foundation of the Wine Institute and in its activities aimed at making wine an important and unquestioned part of American life. Adams remained active in the cause for more than sixty years, and through the publication of his *Wines of America* he became the standard authority on the subject.[122]

Despite its name, the Grape Growers League was clearly an organization of interests having to do with wine—its aim was to "protect the interests of every phase of the grape and wine industry."[123] There was no longer any mealymouthed talk of grape products. The league, which was a direct ancestor of the Wine Institute, announced that it would work toward the immediate legalization of light wines and to that end would cooperate with "the grape growers and winemakers in New York, Ohio, New Jersey, Michigan, Missouri, Pennsylvania and other grape states."[124] The representatives of the league managed to get a hearing before the House Committee on Ways and Means, arguing for the legalization of wine.[125] The manufacturers of equipment that might have a use in winemaking also scented the change in the air: an advertisement for irrigation pumps early in 1933 touted the combination of "light wines and pumps." It was as though Prohibition no longer existed, though it certainly still did in every legal sense.[126] Even the federal government acted as though Prohibition had already expired: the appropriation for enforcement was cut, and the attorney general dismissed half of the Bureau of Prohibition's agents in June 1933.[127]

But the effort to get light wines (that is, unfortified dry table wines) legalized proved surprisingly difficult, for no very good or apparent reason. The difficulty suggests that the grape growers and winemakers were not very powerful politically: California, where most of the grapes and wine came from, was still a remote and underpopulated place. The effective agitation for repeal was largely an eastern affair, and beer and spirits were far more prominent objectives than wine ever was. Thus the Volstead Act was successfully amended to allow the sale of 3.2 percent beer, but all efforts to get light wine—something around 10 percent is what the winemakers proposed—attached to the beer bill failed. Instead, the measure for wine was determined by the measure for beer: 3.2 in either case, even though the winemakers protested, quite rightly, that there was "no such thing" as a 3.2 wine.[128] This permission—which went into operation on 7 April 1933, the day that beer "came back"—was of very doubtful promise to the winemakers. Wine drinkers wanted no such watery compromise, and people merely curious about wine would form very wrong notions if their experience began with such ersatz fluids.

Leon Adams says that the campaign for light wines was scuttled in the Senate when a senator from California, William Gibbs McAdoo, himself only a reluctant Wet, agreed to a single formula for both beer and wine as a means of speeding the bill's passage.[129] The winemakers tried again with a bill for the legalization of wine sponsored by Congressman Clarence Lea, but it died in the Ways and Means committee in June 1933. Lea argued that since the Volstead Act already permitted homemade wine, which certainly reached about 10 degrees of "nonintoxicating" alcohol, the legalization of such wine would only recognize what was already permitted.[130] A flood of petitions from California poured in supporting this proposition. But the idea that the Volstead Act could be modified to include wine evidently had little support in high places. A memo from President Roosevelt in response to pleas from the California delegation in the House of Representatives put it clearly: "I am convinced," Roosevelt wrote, "that 10% is unconstitutional."[131]

Nevertheless, since no one knew exactly how long it might be before repeal actually came to pass and since 3.2 was the formula offered in the meantime, some wineries decided that they might as well give it a try. The first to hit the market were a 3.2 claret and "sparkling burgundy" (both Concord-based) put out by the old New Jersey winery of H. T. Dewey and Sons at its New York retail store. The store, according to report, was mobbed by eager customers, who were limited to two bottles each.[132] Other winemakers soon followed Dewey's lead, though perhaps somewhat shamefacedly. Shewan-Jones of Lodi put out a sparkling white called La Conquesta; Scatena Brothers of Healdsburg offered a sparkling Clarette; and Italian Swiss Colony had a burgundy and sauterne. The editor of *California Grape Grower,* who had once worked for Italian Swiss Colony in its great days under Andrea Sbarboro and Pietro Rossi, loyally affirmed that "the new products are excellent," but he could not repress an outburst of regret: "Oh, for a glass of the old Tipo, red or white."[133]

Mercifully, the day of 3.2 wine was brief. When Repeal arrived on 5 December 1933, low-alcohol wines at once disappeared as real wine flowed into the channels of distribution.[134]

WHAT DID PROHIBITION DO?

In one view, it did very little. From what has been said to this point, it must be obvious that Prohibition did not put an end either to the growing of wine grapes or to the production of wine in this country. It may even, as has been suggested, have done something toward familiarizing Americans with wine (and the names of some wine grapes) through the opportunity of home winemaking—the largest of the loopholes in the clumsy structure of Prohibition. The acreage of American vineyards at the end of the Prohibition era was substantially greater than it had been at the beginning.[135] American wineries, at the moment of Repeal, held about 48 million gallons of wine. Thus wine and winemaking seem to have survived the long drought in remarkably vigorous condition.

Incidentally, Prohibition put an end to the CWA, the near-monopoly power that had controlled California wine since the 1890s. The demise of the CWA cleared the way for a renewal of competition after Repeal, and even though the Drys certainly did not intend it that way, this development was probably one of the constructive results of Prohibition.

But in another sense Prohibition did a great deal, all of it bad from the point of view of winegrowing. For nearly fourteen years, Prohibition had associated wine with illegality, and though there is no way to measure the effects of such association, it cannot have been without disturbing consequences. The still-persistent American tendency to think of wine—in common with other alcoholic drinks—only in either-or terms must also have been powerfully reinforced by Prohibition: either one drinks (with the unexpressed qualifier "too much") or one does not drink at all. The moderate, regular consumption of wine as an indispensable adjunct to food simply does not seem to have entered into the American imagination of desirable practices. Prohibition may well have been a symptom rather than a cause of this condition, but it made official the disappearance of a true temperance into the artificial and fantastic opposition between excess and abstinence.[136]

For nearly fourteen years most Americans had no access to anything resembling good wine. Home winemaking is all very well, but without good materials (almost impossible to find at any distance from the vineyards), good methods (unlikely in improvised conditions), and intelligent guidance (hardly to be expected), the results at best cannot have been better than mediocre and at worst were certainly appalling. The idea of wine must have been soon degraded: *basement rotgut, red ink, dago red,* and like terms express the popular notion that inevitably formed under such conditions.

Even had the conditions for winemaking at home been better, good wine would not have resulted, for as we have seen, good wine grapes had been driven from American vineyards in favor of less suitable varieties or of table and raisin types—and for many years to come, these dominated the supply of grapes destined for American wine.

The material damage wrought by Prohibition was of course most obvious in the number of American wineries that had gone out of business, fallen into decay, or been put to other purposes. The 917 licensed wineries of 1922 had shrunk to 268 by 1933, a net loss of 649 establishments, large and small.[137] A good many of them returned to life under the revivifying power of Repeal, but nothing could undo the disruptions that the long suspension had created. When the Rip van Winkle of American wine woke up again, it was to find that its cooperage had dried out and fallen to pieces, its machines had rusted and become obsolete, its channels of distribution had clogged, its markets had dissolved, and its name had been forgotten. No research had been carried out. No instruction had been given to a younger generation. A tradition had been broken, and an orderly growth cut off. In this condition the American wine industry returned to free life—in the midst of the deepest economic depression that the country had ever known. Whatever "normal" conditions might be, they were certainly not to be expected now.

2

THE RULES CHANGE

WHAT MIGHT HAVE BEEN

When the New Deal was yet young and Repeal still so recent that no one knew how things would develop, at least one man in Washington had a vision of what the future of wine in this country might be. This was Rexford Guy Tugwell, a member of President Roosevelt's Brain Trust, that small group of bright, mostly young academics with ideas about what could be done with a well-planned, well-managed economy.[1] Tugwell was now assistant secretary of the Department of Agriculture; before migrating to Washington, he had been a professor of economics at Columbia University with a particular interest in agricultural history. He had, among many other things, edited Jared Eliot's *Essays upon Field Husbandry,* a pre-Revolutionary eighteenth-century work, and through his acquaintance with such material he knew something about the repeated experiments with grape growing and winemaking that ran throughout American colonial history and that had enjoyed constant official support and encouragement.[2] Tugwell, though he had been still a young man when Prohibition closed down on the country, also knew something of the civilized tradition of wine in Europe, where he had lived for intervals after the war.

Now, in the earliest morn of Repeal, it seemed clear to Tugwell that Americans, if they could be led to make wine an integral part of their culture, might move from adolescence to maturity in the matter of drink. Wine, he declared in a speech to the Women's Democratic Club of Washington, D.C., was the drink of moderation and civility; it was a food, an agricultural product, and as such it should be plentiful and it should be cheap. Tugwell thought that wine production should be both small-scale and local, and he was moved to prophesy thus:

> I foresee a plethora of small local vintages, some good, some mediocre, some perfectly dreadful, out of which will arise in future some great names and great traditions of American wine. I foresee the day when the average American home will be able to enjoy good beer and good wine produced in the neighborhood at moderate prices. . . . And better still, I foresee that, with this change in the drinking habits of our people, may come a change of temper and of temperament, a less furious striving for happiness at the bottom of the whisky barrel. I foresee fewer deaths from heart failure, fewer nervous breakdowns, far fewer of the myriad ailments brought about by overwork and overworry. In their place, I anticipate a calmer and more leisurely type of civilization, in which there will be time for friendly conversation, philosophical speculation, gaiety and substantial happiness.[3]

Tugwell went on to say that American wines should have American regional names, so that Keuka, Roanoke, San Joaquin, and Sacramento might some day mean as much on the world's wine lists as Burgundy, Chianti, and Rhine.

Tugwell's vision almost exactly mirrors that of Thomas Jefferson at the beginning of the nineteenth century, when Jefferson saw a nation of temperate wine-drinking farmers enjoying the vintages of their own or local vineyards.[4] And like Jefferson's, Tugwell's vision remained just that: a vision. But Tugwell, like Jefferson, was determined to do what he could toward the realization of the dream. When Repeal was clearly about to come and Roosevelt's government was debating how to respond to the new conditions, Tugwell proposed a plan. Distilled spirits would be closely controlled by being made available only through licensed stores. But wine and beer would be made "easily available in retail stores just about as any other commodity would be." In Tugwell's recollection, this arrangement almost came to pass:

> For some time I thought Roosevelt persuaded. He recalled well enough all the old abuses. We prepared several memoranda and drafted a law we thought adequate. Then he changed. He told me privately that there were those who were so influential that they could almost certainly defeat the necessary legislation. He outlined the arguments they would use. Anyway, he said, the legislative leaders had warned him not to try it. In their warning was an implied threat to much else he was asking for; so temporary codes for the industry were set up instead, and a federal agency was organized on the old plan.[5]

Thus an opportunity was lost through political timidity to put wine into the mainstream of American life. Whether the American wine industry could have responded effectively to the opportunity is another question. Certainly it could not have done so at once. It needed better grapes, better methods of production, and better standards, all of which would take time to provide. But with the prospects of a wholly open market before it, in which it would no longer carry the stigma associated with Demon Rum, and with a friendly public pol-

FIGURE 4

Rexford Tugwell *(right),* undersecretary of Agriculture, and a Colorado farmer in 1935. Tugwell hoped to put wine in the mainstream of American life. (Library of Congress.)

icy encouraging its development by all forms of commercial support, by freedom from taxation, and by agricultural and technical research, who can doubt that wine would have gained a place for itself in American life that can now hardly be imagined? It would be grown in places that have never yet dreamed of doing so, and in styles not yet thought of; there would be regional specialties with strong regional loyalties; wine not only would be familiar in all the range of public eating places, from three-star restaurants to small-town cafés and highway fast-food franchises, but it would also be in college dining halls and company cafeterias and at all outdoor events. It would, in short, be taken for granted, assumed to be a natural and proper part of meals, understood and appreciated without snobbery, affectation, suspicion, or abuse. So, at any rate, Tugwell must have imagined.

We can never know what might have been, but unquestionably, a magnificent opportunity was lost.

If he could not finally persuade the chief executive to create an enlightened national policy for wine, Tugwell, as assistant secretary of Agriculture, might still do something useful. Accordingly, in 1933, he requested that the scientists of the department draw up a plan for a program of research in viticulture and enology.[6] In November the department submitted a memo outlining an impressive plan for research. Noting by way of preamble that "winemaking in the United States has remained up to the present in the group of arts or crafts and has never become a science," the memo warned that such a condition could not continue: "If the resumption of wine manufacture in the United States is to result in anything other than a repetition of past history, with a resultant flooding of our markets with an inferior product which is discriminated against by purchasers in favor of foreign wines, the initiation and continuance of a strong program of research for the guidance of the industry into scientific methods of production is absolutely necessary."[7]

The plan called, first, for the construction of a model winery at the Beltsville, Maryland, station, which was to be the headquarters of the work; other smaller wineries were to be built in one of the northern states, yet undetermined, and at Meridian, Mississippi. In California the Oakville experiment station in the Napa Valley was to be revived, and work there carried out in close cooperation with the University of California.[8] In viticulture, the immediate questions to be studied included rootstock development, the breeding of new varieties (assisted by plant exploration in China and Japan), cultural practices, diseases, and varietal testing for adaptation and wine quality. In winemaking, the program stressed the biochemistry of fermentation, the development of yeasts, and the study of blending. In addition, the department planned "a careful survey of the country to be made with the view to determining whether other regions than those now growing grapes may not be adapted to the development of fine wines."[9]

Early in 1934 one of the Beltsville researchers, C. A. Magoon, a senior bacteriologist, went to California to inquire into the wants of the winegrowers there and to plan for an experimental winery to be built in cooperation with the university. Magoon then went for three months to Europe, where he visited Italy, France, and Switzerland and established contacts with the schools of enology at Conegliano, Montpellier, Bordeaux, Geneva, and Lausanne, as well as with the Institut Pasteur in Paris. Magoon formed a very clear and intelligent idea of what was wanted and what might be done. He saw that the American winemaker must first be able to achieve consistency, to "make it possible for the consumer to know what he is getting when he buys a bottle of wine." He thought that the future lay with table wines, even though the market was currently dominated by sweet fortified wines. And he saw that Americans must be educated in wine, but in the right way:

> The right kind of an educational campaign would be helpful, but the "O, be joyful," "wine, women and song" and the pseudo-poetic and highly lurid treatments of the subject must be eliminated. Decent people don't want to get drunk and they don't want their use of wine

to be considered in the same category with licentiousness. Straightforward and respectable use of light wines in *moderation* but *by many people* will need to be the foundation of a stable wine industry and any educational campaign will need work towards this.[10]

Meanwhile, the department expanded the vineyards at Beltsville, and construction began on the model winery there. When it was completed in the spring of 1936 the new winery displayed the state of the art as it then stood: tiled laboratories, temperature-controlled fermentation rooms, a modern distillery, presses and tanks of the most up-to-date design.[11] Then disaster struck. The still-potent prohibitionist element in Congress got wind of the work and was roused to action. In 1935 the enemies of Demon Rum succeeded in attaching a rider to the agricultural appropriations bill: no funds appropriated for agricultural research could be used for work on "intoxicating beverages."[12] According to Leon Adams, the villain in all this was Clarence Cannon, a representative from Missouri and a "lifelong Prohibitionist." Cannon, as chairman of the House Appropriations Committee, threatened to cut off the entire USDA appropriation unless the wicked work on wine were given up. The USDA could only submit.[13] Adams had excellent means of knowing about such matters, but this story is perhaps somewhat exaggerated. Cannon was on the House Appropriations Committee, but he was not its chairman in 1935; he was a lifelong abstainer himself but not, as far as I can find, an active prohibitionist. There is evidence that he inquired early in 1935 as to the utility of USDA research into winegrowing, but then Cannon was a notorious penny-pincher: he seems to have been interested only in having it demonstrated that the work was necessary rather than in putting a stop to it on prohibitionist grounds.[14]

But there is no question that the work was stopped before it ever got properly under way. The winery never crushed a grape. Its equipment was sold (the still went to a winery in Boulder Creek, California, and the crusher-stemmer to the Hallcrest Winery in Felton, California). The building intended to house the model winery was disguised under the innocuous name of the West Building and given over to such things as the seed production laboratory and the nut investigations section.[15] Worse, the department had been so shaken by the storm over its plans to carry on research in winemaking that for the next generation and more, it hardly dared whisper the word *wine,* much less take a hand in guiding and supporting American winemaking, as it had long done in the days before Prohibition.[16]

The fate of the USDA research program showed, as clearly as anything could, that even after Repeal wine might be legal but it was certainly not legitimate—the shadow of moral reprehension lay over it still, as it continues to do in many parts of the country and for large sections of the population.[17] In this atmosphere such ideas as Tugwell's would always have to struggle merely to survive, let alone flourish.

There was, however, at least one further, though abortive, effort by the New Deal to develop winemaking. This was an undertaking of the Federal Emergency Relief Adminis-

FIGURE 5
Paul Garrett, with his
wife, daughters, and a
governess, at some time
before Prohibition. "The
wine industry," he said,
"ought to be—*it can be*—
bigger than the auto-
mobile industry, bigger
than the steel industry."
(North Carolina Collec-
tion, University of North
Carolina at Chapel Hill.)

tration (FERA), in 1934 and later, to plant muscadine grapes on a large scale throughout the southern United States, from Virginia to Texas. The idea came from Paul Garrett, the energetic promoter whose Scuppernong-based Virginia Dare wine had been one of the nation's favorites before Prohibition. Garrett thought that grapes could redeem the exhausted soils of the South and that winemaking could provide a living for the region's impoverished farmers, who would be allowed to sell their wines directly at the winery door. If the scheme should succeed, Garrett saw no reason why it should not extend to the entire country: in his excited vision he saw 10 million acres planted to vines over the course of a quarter century, acres from which 5 billion gallons of sound cheap wine would flow to put the United States' per capita consumption on a level with that of France and Italy.[18]

Garrett's enthusiasm had some effect on the official planners. In June 1934 they approached him to ask whether he would buy muscadine grapes if the government undertook to plant them in many of the southern states. He would, of course: he said that he needed 20,000 tons and could get only about 2,000 for his current needs. He would also set up a processing plant to handle the grapes whenever a crop should be ready.[19] The officials cautiously consulted the USDA on the matter: would it be practical to grow muscadine grapes (the Scuppernong included) in North Carolina, Alabama, Mississippi, and Louisiana?[20] The answer was yes, and the Rural Rehabilitation Agency, an arm of FERA, was soon at work searching for vines. By October it had rounded up some 600,000; the agency also had a horticulturist named J. G. Woodroof at the agricultural experiment station in Tifton, Georgia, at work propagating a million vines of muscadine grapes for the South. His collection included "five strains of Scuppernongs" and the muscadine varieties Hunt, Thomas, and James.[21]

The plan that emerged was to distribute the grapes to already settled communities in North Carolina, South Carolina, Georgia, and Louisiana or to new communities formed under the Rural Rehabilitation Agency's authority. The farmers would receive vines, planted at 220 per acre in small plots ranging in size from 3 to 5 acres. Some 5,000 acres would be planted in the first phase of the work. It was calculated that a muscadine vineyard would yield 3 tons of grapes an acre, and that a ton would fetch $35 for wine. This would not be enough to support a farm family, but it would provide a crucial source of cash to farmers otherwise doomed to subsistence. Moreover, the Scuppernong had many uses. As Dr. Woodroof wrote, almost lyrically,

> The Scuppernong grape is native to the southern states, and is one of the most reliable fruits to grow around a farmstead. The vines produce a crop of delicious fruit each year at a time when little other fresh fruit or vegetables are to be had. The vines when trained on an arbor furnish shade for chickens and members of the family during the summer. If given a little care Scuppernong vines will live for more than forty years. They are as free of destructive insects and diseases as any fruit grown in the South, and require no especial cultural or fertilizer treatments. Besides furnishing shade and fresh fruit, Scuppernongs may be made into delicious jelly, jam, pies, marmalades, and unfermented grape juice for the home.[22]

The remark about shade for "chickens and members of the family" shows that Woodroof had a decent care for animal comfort. But we may also note his failure to mention wine. He must have been informed about the purposes of his work, yet he could not bring himself to put it into writing. The omission is eloquent.

Garrett, who had no such inhibitions, undertook to buy the produce of 5,000 acres of muscadine grapes for ten years, and he at once set about preparing for the tide of grapes to come, building a new plant in Atlanta and expanding his facilities in North Carolina and Virginia.[23] Some planting was actually carried out. In early 1935 some 200 acres had been planted in Georgia, Florida, and Louisiana, including vineyards in such new "organized" rural communities as Pine Mountain Valley, Georgia (near President Roosevelt's favored Warm Springs), and Cherry Lake Farms, Florida; there were also plantings at Penderton, North Carolina, and McBee, South Carolina, and doubtless other places in the South. But by the end of 1935 expectations for the project, after only a year's trial—long before any of the newly planted vines could have produced anything—were fading. Garrett's eloquence, whatever its effect on bureaucrats in Washington, was not enough to persuade the bewildered farmers of the South that grape growing was a way out of the wilderness for them. Or perhaps the project succumbed to Dry disapproval.[24] In any event, the vines propagated by FERA were put up for public sale at the end of 1937, a move that clearly put an end to the plan for small, subsidized vineyards throughout the South.[25]

WHAT HAPPENED INSTEAD

Tugwell and Garrett represent what may be called the messianic idea of wine generated by the excitement of Repeal. Theirs was the lofty vision of what might be. What actually emerged, more coldly and unattractively, was very different. What the country got in fact was a contradictory combination of purposes that united the prohibitionist's wish to hinder and obstruct the wine trade with the Depression-generated eagerness to tap a new source of revenue. This inauspicious combination—obstructive regulation and heavy taxation—has operated ever since Repeal as the federal government's policy toward American winemaking.

A number of rival plans were eagerly put forward in the vacuum between Prohibition and Repeal to regulate the revived traffic in alcohol. One official of the Department of Agriculture proposed to Secretary Wallace that the entire trade in liquor, imported and domestic, be made a monopoly of the department, under the powers of the Agricultural Adjustment Act.[26] A survey of liquor administrations around the world, paid for by John D. Rockefeller Jr., concluded that the sale of all alcoholic drink should be in the hands of the state.[27] No agreement was reached on the question then, nor has it been since, except in one respect: revenue came first. Table wine had not been taxed in the United States, except in times of war.[28] But now that happy exemption was no longer thinkable. These were times of deep economic depression, when unemployment ran at nearly a quarter of the workforce—about 10 million people at a conservative estimate—and the federal budget was falling into ever deeper deficit as revenues sagged and expenditures soared. In the last phases of the drive for Repeal, the economic argument had been irresistibly attractive, just as it had been for Prohibition fifteen years earlier. Repeal, by legitimizing liquor again, would at once take the trade out of the hands of criminals and enrich the government instead. The time had now come to collect on this promise.

The Liquor Taxing Act of 1934 was passed barely a month after Repeal.[29] It was guided through Congress by Congressman Frank H. Buck, a California Democrat who was himself a fruit grower in Vacaville and a friend of the wine industry (his district included the Napa Valley). Hearings on the question of liquor taxes had been held in anticipation of Repeal in June and December 1933, but the measure as it was passed in January 1934 was inevitably a work of hopeful ignorance.[30] No one had a clue about what the tax should be, or about what revenues might be reasonably expected. Proposals were made to set the tax on table wines as low as 4 cents a gallon and as high as 16 cents; the act compromised on a very modest 10 cents a gallon for table wines and 20 cents for fortified wines. The California Wine Producers Association declared itself satisfied with the arrangement.[31] At the same time, a heavy tariff of $1.25 a gallon was laid on imported wines to protect the domestic producers. Legislators and tax collectors then sat back to await the revenues that would pour in.

They were disappointed; indeed, all concerned, federal authorities and winemakers alike, were disappointed. In 1934, the first year of Repeal, the production of wine reached 42 million gallons, a very respectable figure for an industry that had just been restored to civil life after fourteen years of disability under Prohibition. There were, as well, some 48 million gallons of wine from earlier years in storage. But the sale of tax-paid wine in 1934 reached only about 32 million gallons, including imports.[32] The reasons for this dismal result were no doubt various. Much of the wine offered for sale was substandard and damaged the market. People had lost the habit of drinking wine, or if they had not, they might very well continue to make their own, as they had during Prohibition. But the wine men at once made loud outcry over the heavy burden of taxation laid on them. The tax, they said, kept the bootlegger in business, and this complaint became accepted as an official explanation. It was calculated that the country had in fact drunk nearly 50 million gallons of wine in the first year of Repeal, but most of that quantity, it was said, had been made at home.[33] And it was said too that much of this wine, supposedly for home consumption, was illicitly sold. Maybe so. But the tax of 10 cents a gallon would have added only 2 cents to the price of a bottle of wine, and even in depression times that hardly seems enough to have driven the wine drinker into the arms of the bootlegger.

The perfectly legal practice of home winemaking certainly continued on a large scale. The people who learned to make their own wine under Prohibition preferred, according to Philip Wagner, to make their own wine after Repeal.[34] Robert Rossi, of Italian Swiss Colony, suspected that "as much, and very probably more, wine is being made in basements since repeal than is being sold commercially for consumption."[35] Such suspicions appear to be confirmed by the quantity of grapes shipped fresh from California. It was assumed that half of the quantity shipped would be used for home winemaking; on that assumption the estimated production of such wine in 1934 was 34 million gallons.[36] Even as late as 1937 the Tariff Commission estimated that 29 million gallons of home wine were produced, 30 percent of national consumption.[37] How much of this wine might have been illegally sold instead of being consumed at home can only be guessed.

Whatever the truth of the matter may have been, Congress repented of its first act of Repeal taxation. A delegation of California wine men called on President Roosevelt in February 1935 to ask for lower taxes and continued tariff protection; they found "a friend in the President."[38] After extensive hearings, in which some witnesses argued that there should be no federal taxes at all on wine,[39] a bill was introduced cutting the federal tax to 5 cents a gallon for table wine and 10 cents for fortified wine. The bill was again in charge of Congressman Buck, who explained to Congress that the act of 1934 had been only "a guess in the dark"[40] and that it had clearly failed in its intent to stimulate the sale of wine. The government, he said, had always encouraged the consumption of the "milder alcoholic beverages," and so cutting taxes was the way to go: "It will be an encouragement to the cause of temperance to make the cost of wine with a relatively light alcoholic content as cheap as possible."[41] The bill passed, and the sale of wine did in fact increase, but whether owing to the new tax laws or to other causes no one can now say.[42] The revenue suffered from the change, at least in the short term, for there was a falling off of almost $3 million in the first year of the new tax.[43]

The important effect created by these first post-Repeal measures was not to discourage or encourage the consumption of wine, but to separate wine from the untaxed products of agriculture. The prohibitionists had made wine merely one item under the general category of Demon Rum, and therefore a thing to be prohibited. Now, to the government, it was merely one item in the general class of liquor, and therefore a thing to be taxed. This notion of wine as a productive source of tax revenue was not lost on the states, as we shall see. The history of wine since Repeal in this country has been one of steadily increasing taxation (barring that one anomalous reduction in 1936), and of taxes laid on by a steadily increasing number of authorities. The modern American official idea of wine, unlike the older one, is either as a commodity whose use is to be restrained by taxation, or as a luxury open to sumptuary taxation—never as a desirable item of diet.

Still, the interests of the tax gatherer in the Depression years were obviously in favor of an increasing use of wine. The other post-Repeal development—the creation of a regulatory authority over the liquor trade—had the opposite purpose: restriction and obstruction in the name of control. In the very act of proclaiming the repeal of the Eighteenth Amendment, President Roosevelt had affirmed that "the policy of the Government will be to see to it that the social and political evils that have existed in the pre-prohibition era shall not be revived nor permitted again to exist."[44] What this meant is clarified by the note appended to Roosevelt's proclamation by the editor of his papers, Samuel I. Rosenman, who had been counsel to Roosevelt and presumably knew something of his intention. The federal government, Rosenman wrote, had determined to alter its traditional laissez-faire policy and to take "a large part in controlling the liquor traffic." *Control,* as it turned out, meant not only licensing and regulating, but also restraining and limiting. The object was not just to see that criminals were kept out, but also to offer every discouragement to the growth of the trade—or as Rosenman put it, "to eliminate the pressure for increased sales."[45]

The first step toward this end was the creation, by executive order, of the Federal Alcohol Control Administration (FACA) on 4 December 1933, the day before Repeal.[46] The director of FACA was Joseph H. Choate Jr., a New York lawyer who had been a leader in the fight for Repeal as a founder of the Voluntary Committee, one of the important players in the struggle against Prohibition. The agency worked under the provisions of the National Industrial Recovery Act of 1933, which created the National Recovery Administration (NRA), remembered now for its blue eagle emblem and the slogan "We do our part," displayed in shops and offices all over the country. The NRA's mission was to stimulate production and employment and at the same time to regulate competition and reduce labor abuses. With its related agencies, it operated through the device of industry "codes of fair competition." In this scheme, the economic life of the country was divided into a long list of industries, and each of these, through its own representatives working with federal authorities, drew up a plan of regulatory practices covering such things as wages, hours of work, prices, collective bargaining, manufacturing methods, and advertising. There had never been anything like this measure of government "interference" in American business life before, and the intrusions of the NRA and its creatures were bitterly and fiercely resented. But the codifying went on despite all protest. The whole of the liquor trade was covered by codes for brewers, distillers, rectifiers, importers, wholesalers, and most important for our purposes, winemakers.[47]

The wine industry was divided into two sections, east and west, in recognition of the fact that the conditions and products were so very different in the two regions. In general, that difference arose from the fact that winegrowing in the East was then wholly dependent on the use of native hybrid grapes, whose juice, deficient in sugar and excessively high in acid, typically had to be both diluted with water and ameliorated with sugar. Eastern practice also depended heavily on the addition of neutral California wine to the wines of the native grapes. The juice from California's vinifera grapes rarely needed added sugar (though it might be corrected for a too-low acid content) and was not blended with juice from any other source. These differences made it very difficult for the East (which, after Repeal, mostly meant New York, New Jersey, and Ohio) and the West (California almost entirely) to agree on standards and methods.[48]

The western group—in fact all of its members were from California—formed under the direction of FACA called itself the Association of Western Wine Producers; it appointed a committee to draw up an NRA code, which received formal approval in November 1934. A comparable scheme was followed in the eastern states, and delegates from each group, western and eastern, made up a National Wine Code Authority. The code banned various unfair trade practices (e.g., secret rebates), required winemakers to secure permits before they could operate, and created regulations for labeling and advertising.[49] The federal agency was to be the final authority in all disputes and actions arising out of the code.

When the Supreme Court in May 1935 declared the National Industrial Recovery Act unconstitutional, the codes that it had created ceased to operate, but Congress at once restored federal supervision of the liquor industry by creating the Federal Alcohol Administration (FAA) within the Department of the Treasury.[50] The act creating the new agency effectively continued all the provisions of the FACA codes regulating licensing, labeling, trade practices, and advertising. The wine industry, in common with the rest of the liquor industry, continued to operate under strict regulation. The mood behind such legislation was still powerfully affected by the experience of Prohibition and its excesses. A federal alcohol administration was needed because, as Congressman Thomas Henry Cullen put it, "the legalized liquor traffic cannot be effectively regulated, if the door is left open for highly financed groups of criminals and racketeers to enter into the business of liquor production and distribution."[51] More bluntly, the general assumption was that anyone in the liquor trade, until proved otherwise, was a bootlegger at heart and must be dealt with accordingly.[52]

The regulations for labeling and advertising specified in the FAA act were especially broad. No label could, "irrespective of falsity" (a bureaucratic phrase that I take to mean "it doesn't matter whether it is true or false"), make statements relating to "age, manufacturing processes, analyses, guarantees, and scientific or irrelevant matters as the Administrator finds to be likely to mislead the consumer." The same conditions applied to all advertising in any form.[53] Such terms allowed a large and indefinite scope for the interpretive rulings of the federal administrator: Who is the "consumer"? What is or is not "likely" to "mislead" him or her? Such questions might be argued endlessly; and the administrative decisions made on them over the years since the act was passed have inevitably seemed to be often arbitrary and restrictive.[54] The Widmer winery, for example, was not allowed to use the word *casks* on a label in 1945 on the grounds that the term implied a statement about age; nor could the company state, in a promotional booklet of 1938, that it had made wines during Prohibition for "altar and medicinal purposes." It had in fact done so, according to the letter of the law, but the term *medicinal* was not allowed. In 1950 the statement on a Widmer's point-of-sale leaflet about "the deep relaxing satisfaction in a glass of good wine" was declared unacceptable as creating the impression that wine is "conducive to physical well-being."[55] Such rulings must have been made by the tens of thousands. One cannot but admire the intensity of the bureaucratic scrutiny; at the same time, one might adduce any number of permitted weasel words, distortions, and concealments routinely allowed by the federal authorities for reasons not apparent.

The rule-making authority created by the Federal Alcohol Act, as one writer put it, is "more extensive than in any other field of government authority"; and the industry that is thus supervised "is the most thoroughly regulated and carefully supervised of all industries."[56] It is also a thoroughly anomalous situation in which a fiscal authority, the Department of the Treasury, makes the rules governing the production and the standards of identity of a food product—wine. Some efforts have been made since the creation of this situation to change it by restricting the authority of Treasury to the collection of revenue and by putting all other matters concerning wine under the authority of the Department of Agriculture. So far such efforts have had no effect.

At the same time, the act extended what many consider an unfortunate liberty to the winemakers by permitting the bad old pre-Prohibition practice of appropriating foreign names for American wines. Many European nations had agreed at the Convention of Madrid in 1891 not to use the names of wine regions belonging to others, but the United States had never signed the treaty (nor has it today).[57] The American practice had then been officially permitted by the Food and Drug Act of 1906, Regulation 19: "The use of a geographical name in connection with a food or drug product will not be deemed a misbranding when by reason of long usage it has come to represent a generic term and is used to indicate a style, type or brand; but in all such cases the State or Territory where any such article is manufactured or produced shall be stated upon the principal label."

The winegrowers were not yet prepared to accept Tugwell's faith in native appellations but clung to the idea that their wines must be called sherry, burgundy, chianti, or chablis if they were to sell. Under the conditions of confusion and ignorance about wine prevailing in 1935, they were probably right; but one may still regret so backward-looking a decision. It was Senator Johnson of California who introduced the amendment to the FAA bill that allowed the use of "any trade name or brand of foreign origin not presently effectively registered in the United States Patent Office."[58] This provision was spelled out in detail in the next year. American winemakers had the right "to use wholly or in part the wine names or brands Port, Sherry, Burgundy, Sauterne, Haut Sauterne, Rhine (Hock), Moselle, Chianti, Chablis, Tokay, Malaga, Madeira, Marsala, Claret, Vermouth, Barbera, Cabernet, Saint Julien, Riesling, Zinfandel, Medoc, or Cognac, or any other geographic name of foreign origin (except Champagne)."[59] *Barbera, Cabernet, Riesling,* and *Zinfandel,* which are to us unintelligible except as varietal names, were then held by the California people to be "geographic" or "type" names because of their established usage within the pre-Prohibition wine trade. It was not until 1939 that a new ruling held that such varietal names were not, after all, generic, and could be used only on wines made from the grapes in question. Equally curious was the fact that Burgundy was allowed but not Bordeaux; Moselle but not Mosel. But, as one study of this scheme of things concludes, "the regulations in this area are a result of political and economic compromise, rather than of internally coherent philosophy or public policy."[60]

What to call sparkling wine proved to be an especially tough question. Approval of the use of the name *champagne* was at first withheld pending the decision of the FAA on the question.[61] The FAA concluded that the word *champagne* could be used only by those producers that followed the *méthode champenoise:* that is, the method of carrying out a secondary fermentation in the bottle.[62] Sparkling wines produced by bulk processes could use the word *champagne* but had to add the phrase *bulk process*. This regulation was frequently disputed but was not altered until 1993, when the stigma of *bulk process* was allowed to disappear from labels and other descriptions permitted in its place, such as "fermented outside this bottle."

The federal government was now directly engaged in controlling the wine industry, though largely in a nay-saying way. It had the power of life and death through the system of licenses and regulations; but beyond that it had no interest in the health of its charge, except as it might be made to pay taxes. That the federal government did not go even further in its control was owed to a large extent to the fact that the movement that had brought about Repeal had been a states' rights movement.

THE STATES' RIGHTS MAZE

Prohibition had of course been opposed on many different grounds, but one of the most important was the argument that the national government had no right to interfere in matters that should be left to the states. Drinking, if it were to be regulated at all, was emphatically one of those matters. As the manager of the American Association against the Prohibition Amendment, the most important organization in the overthrow of Prohibition, put the point, "the whole basis upon which the repeal fight has been waged is the theory that each state should handle the matter of liquor control in such a way as seems best to its citizens."[63] If, then, states' rights were one of the central justifications of Repeal, the federal government had been told, in effect, to keep its hands off. It did not do so, as we have seen, but certainly it did nothing to check or guide the confused outpouring of state legislation affecting wine that followed Repeal. And there is a powerful irony in the way that the Repeal argument of states' rights has been used to create formidable barriers to the liquor trade.

The language of the Repeal amendment itself was quite definite in this matter. The Twenty-first Amendment, while declaring the end of national Prohibition in its first section, provided a second section reaffirming the power of the states to enforce prohibition— or any conditions whatever—within their borders. The section reads, "The transportation or importation into any State, Territory, or possession of the United States for delivery or use therein of intoxicating liquors, in violation of the laws thereof, is hereby prohibited." Though formally a recognition of states' rights, this provision was practically a recognition that even though Prohibition might be dead, prohibitionism was certainly not. Indeed, one must emphasize that just as Prohibition was not a single, unvarying condition throughout the country and throughout the years of its existence, neither did Repeal create a single, unvarying condition. At the moment the Twenty-first Amendment was passed, it applied to only twenty of the forty-eight states; and though others soon joined the original Wet states, prohibition continued—and continues—to apply in many places and in many unexpected ways through state and local regulation.[64] Indeed, it may be said that the Twenty-first Amendment is a deeply contradictory instrument: in its first part it enables the return of alcoholic drink, while in its second part it allows for the growth of an unprecedented tangle of restrictive and obstructive regulation. As one winemaker has put it, "Prohibition was never repealed, it was just amended."

The more than byzantine complexity of the regulations that succeeded Prohibition across the states of the union is so tangled and dense that no mere illustrations can give an adequate idea. One can only hope to convey a dim suggestion. Essentially, there were three schemes that the states might follow: a state might grant licenses to wholesale and retail dealers; it might reserve to itself the sale of all liquor through a monopoly system; or it might choose to remain Dry.[65] By 1936, when the dust had begun to settle, twenty-six states followed one or another system of licensing; there were fifteen monopoly states; and seven states called themselves Dry. But what mad variations flourished within each group![66] Both Arkansas and California, for example, were license states, but in Arkansas you could not get wine or spirits in a hotel, restaurant, or club, though you could in California. In California you could buy a drink at a bar, but in Colorado, another license state, you couldn't. In Kentucky, you could have a drink on licensed premises only if the container held two ounces or less. In Massachusetts, women were not allowed in taverns, and in those places where women *could* drink they had to be seated while they did so. In South Carolina, the state constitution forbade the sale of alcoholic beverages by the drink, but the legislature

declared beer of 5 percent alcoholic content and wine of 14 percent to be nonalcoholic! The combinations and permutations of such permissions and restrictions went on endlessly as the rules changed, through all of the license states, seemingly without plan or purpose.

In the monopoly states there was equivalent confusion. In Maine, the state sold wine and spirits, but hotels could sell any liquor by the bottle to guests; restaurants could sell beer and wine only. In Michigan, another monopoly state, restaurants could sell beer, wine, and spirits, but "taverns" only beer. In the cheerless Montana monopoly, anything more than 3.2 percent alcohol could be sold only by the package—no drinking at the bar—and only in state stores—no wine with your restaurant meal. Moreover, the wretched patron of the Montana state store would not be served until he had presented his individual permit to buy, a permit issued by the state Liquor Control Board. The Ohio monopoly laid a lighter hand on its customers: hotels, restaurants, and clubs could all sell all types of liquor, but spirits could not be sold by any more than one place for every two thousand persons.

Nor was Dryness uniform in the Dry states. Kansas reaffirmed its constitutional Dryness "forever."[67] The Dry state of Mississippi, however, determined that beer and wine of 4 percent alcohol were nonintoxicating and might be freely sold. North Carolina declared for prohibition but allowed eighteen counties to operate retail liquor stores under the supervision of county alcoholic beverage control boards. And so on.

This fantastic balkanization of liquor regulation is beyond question the most powerful and enduring effect of Prohibition in America. The process had begun long before the passage of the Eighteenth Amendment, for the country had seen many towns, counties, and states go Dry or impose restrictive legislation on liquor well before 1919. When national Prohibition was imperfectly cleared away, the old, long-planted seeds, now favored by the climate of states' rights, sprang into growth and flourished like weeds. And they could not be eradicated. In the seventy years since Repeal there has been some rationalization of state laws, but not much: the situation now is not essentially different from that which formed so rapidly and bewilderingly immediately following the death of Prohibition.

Since the states were now free to do as they liked with the liquor trade within their borders, and since the states were all desperate for income in the Depression years, it was perhaps inevitable that they should begin to lay taxes on liquor, including wine. At any rate, that is what they did, and enthusiastically. In anticipation of Repeal, an interdepartmental government committee, studying the question of how to tax a revived liquor industry, had recommended to Congress that the federal government should levy a uniform rate and return a part of the revenue thus created to the states on a proportional basis. This proposal was intended to stave off the situation that in fact developed—a chaos of uncoordinated and arbitrary practices—but it did not seem practical and so was disregarded.[68] The states were evidently in no mood to give up their right to do as they pleased with the liquor trade within their own borders—or to share any revenues from it.

What happened was a new thing. Before Prohibition, the states had been content with the revenue from liquor licenses, for they regarded the right to levy an excise tax as belonging to the federal government. Now the liquor trade was regarded as fair game by the states, and even by some municipalities. Like the regulations for the sale and service of liquor, the taxes varied wildly from state to state. To describe, again, the situation as it stood in 1936: California, predictably, levied only 2 cents a gallon on table wines, and some states—Idaho, Georgia, and Maine, for example—had no tax at all. But in other states one can chart a steady rise, from the 5 cents of Louisiana through the 10 cents of Arkansas, the 20 cents of Maryland, to the 40 cents of Delaware. Although the wine industry might effectively lobby against federal taxes, as it managed to do in 1936, there was no quick way for it to do so against the manifold state taxes.

Thus the taxation practices that immediately developed in the early days of Repeal are still with us. They have become long-established traditions, difficult to dislodge or even to challenge. Nowadays the state collects $2.25 on every gallon of table wine sold in Florida but only 11 cents in Louisiana; $1.70 in Alabama but only 19 cents in New York. Louisiana and New York, one might argue, have long had a tradition of wine drinking (by comparison with most other states, at any rate), so they might be expected to tax wine lightly; and Alabama has a long history of prohibition, and might be supposed to wish to obstruct the sale of wine. But Florida? Its urban, mixed population, its large retirement communities, and its vast international tourist traffic give it one of the highest per-capita rates of wine consumption in the country, and seemingly no interest in a high tax on wine. And yet it has the highest in the nation. The tradition of the arbitrary exercise of states' rights seems the simplest way to account for the crazy quilt of taxes, as well as of regulations.

The continuing power of the prohibitionist spirit was also a reason: officially defeated and discredited as constitutional Prohibition now was, the public force that had created it in the first place was still formidable then, as it is now. States' rights made for fragmentation, and that fragmentation created an opportunity for the Dry forces. In the absence of uniform regulations, they could secure obstructive and even punitive regulations in the different states in the interest of control or revenue, or both. Not all regulation was Dry-inspired, of course, but there can be no doubt that a good deal of it was. Even President Roosevelt, in proclaiming the end of Prohibition, solemnly expressed the pious hope that the country would never see "the return of the saloon."[69] This formula, an echo of the rhetoric of the Anti-Saloon League, had become ritual by 1933, but the fact that Roosevelt thought it necessary to use the phrase says much about the habits of thought that still persisted. The result of the conflicting and inconsistent state regulations was that wine had no chance to become an untroubled commodity in general commerce, moving freely with the trade in bread and cheese and fruit. A writer in the *California Grape Grower*, contemplating the growing thicket of regulations, taxes, and fees, sadly concluded that "a well-defined policy among the prohibitionists could not have done a better job in curtailing the wine business, which was presumed to be one which teaches temperance and the use of wines with meals as a part of the article of diet."[70]

Another new impediment, unknown before Prohibition, was the decision by most states to outlaw the retail sale of wine in bulk, so that a man with a cellar could not bottle a barrel for himself or a winemaker fill customers' jugs on demand. Before Prohibition, more than half of all the wine sold in this country was sold to the retail buyer from bulk containers—typically from a barrel. After Repeal, very little of it was. This restriction was laid down partly in order to defend the revenue: the contents of large containers were more difficult to control than what went out in countable bottles, each bearing a tax stamp. It also had the advantage of allowing a much tighter control over what went into the bottle. The winemaker (or, more often, the regional bottler) knew what he was giving his customers in bottles bearing his name; what came from an unmarked barrel might have who knows what source. But bottling greatly raised the cost of wine. In 1936 it was estimated that the costs of bottling amounted to almost half the wholesale price of a gallon of California wine in the New York market, even when the wine was bottled in New York.[71] Moreover, the disappearance of wine direct from the barrel—unpretentious, accessible, familiar, and cheap—made wine seem more strange than ever to a population already unused to it.

Immediately after Repeal, only six states permitted the sale of wine from bulk containers at retail, California among them. But even in California—where, in the early days of Repeal, much wine was sold directly from the barrel as it had been before Prohibition—

the practice was finally ended by legislative action, albeit not until 1945.[72] According to Leon Adams, it was the large wineries that got sales from the barrel outlawed in California in order to deny this valuable outlet to the small fry.[73] The disappearance of retail wine from the barrel in California was long preceded by the disappearance of imported wine in bulk, brought about by importing regulations under the NRA and by most state laws. Before Prohibition, three-quarters of the wine imported into the United States was in bulk for a popular market; by 1936 some 95 percent of all imported wine was in bottles.[74] Since the costs associated with bottling were just as high for inexpensive wines as they were for more costly ones, there was no inducement to deal in inexpensive wines. Even worse, after a large reduction in the tariffs on most imported wines had been negotiated in 1936, the tariff on bulk wines was left at the old high rate. Thus the more expensive bottled wines came in at a rate substantially below that of inexpensive *ordinaire*.[75] These perverse rules, by which the supply of inexpensive wine by simple and direct methods was prevented, have doubtless contributed to the creation of the strange marketing conditions that still obtain in this country.

In view of all the regulations affecting wine and other liquors that sprang up following Repeal, it is impossible not to agree with the conclusion of a writer in the *American Mercury* that "the only effect of Repeal has been to place an article formerly contraband in the bastard category of things legally allowed but morally reprehensible."[76] As if to seal this judgment, Congress in May 1936 voted $10,000 to defray the expenses of the Sixteenth Triennial Convention of the World's Woman's Christian Temperance Union—an extraordinary official act by a body that only three years earlier had submitted the Repeal amendment to the voters of the United States.[77]

Congress also did what it could to enforce the second section of the Twenty-first Amendment, the section guaranteeing to the states the right to enact prohibitory laws. The Liquor Law Repeal and Enforcement Act was passed in 1935 to protect Dry states "against transgressions from the outside" by making it not only a state but a federal offense to bring liquor into any state whose laws prohibited it.[78]

Finally, the right of the states to enjoy an absolute authority over all liquor traffic within their borders was sustained by a series of Supreme Court decisions particularly associated with Justice Louis Brandeis.[79] Brandeis delivered the court's opinion in a series of cases from 1936 to 1939 upholding state liquor laws of widely varying character in California, Michigan, Minnesota, Missouri, and Pennsylvania.[80] Brandeis was opposed to bigness in both government and commerce, which may be a reason for his defense of states' rights on this particular issue. But I do not know that anyone has satisfactorily explained his part in sustaining the second section of the Twenty-first Amendment in its conflict with the commerce clause of the Constitution. The major obstacles to the commerce of wine in the United States came about through the Twenty-first Amendment; but they have been sustained by the Brandeis decisions.[81]

When, at the end of the 1930s, the confused swirl of legislation that Repeal created had taken effect, the situation looked like this.

There was no positive federal policy toward wine. It was not a favored industry; no measures were taken to develop or encourage it; and it was officially regarded for purposes of taxation and regulation as a minor branch of the liquor trade.

New powers of federal regulation had been created by FACA and its successors with decisive authority over all matters of licensing, labeling, and advertising. This regulatory system had been established not in any positive spirit but out of a fear of the criminal element that had flourished during Prohibition and out of an unacknowledged deference to the continuing power of the prohibitionist element in American politics.[82]

Some vestige of the long-honored notion that wine is the drink of temperance lingered, perhaps, in the federal government's willingness to keep the excise tax on wine (itself a new thing) rather lower than higher.

Meanwhile, through the unholy mingling of states' rights and prohibitionist forces, a crazy, ramshackle structure of state and local regulations, taxes, and fees had been built up without design or direction.[83] In the innocent days before Prohibition, as one veteran sadly recalled, there had been a free movement of wine from state to state (except, of course, for those that were already Dry). There were no state or city taxes, nor any state licenses. Anyone might ship a case of wine to a friend or relative from any Wet state to another without question.[84] Now, however, the flow of wine across the country that might have been imagined to follow Repeal was impeded, obstructed, and diverted in a thousand unpredictable and arbitrary ways—and still is.

3

THE DISMAL '30S

A TROUBLED PROSPECT

At the beginning of 1934, when a winemaker, returning to his newly legalized business, looked around him to see what his prospects were, he would have found little enough to cheer him. The economic depression, surpassing in length and intensity anything ever known in this country, showed no signs of lifting. The legislatures of state after state were busy laying new and unpredictable taxes on wine and inventing new laws to confuse commerce in wine. The federal government had taken on a new activity in the licensing and regulation of winemaking while at the same time refusing to resume its role in assisting and encouraging viticulture and winemaking. Yet while hampering regulations proliferated, there was no organization within the wine trade itself, no concerted means whereby it might promote itself, defend itself against attack and injury, or present itself effectively to an uninformed public. It was not merely unorganized: it did not know its own business. Whatever standards and traditions had operated before Prohibition had been effectively lost. Nothing but the barest minimum in the way of legal wine standards existed, and it would be the work of years to discover what desirable standards might be, let alone what they ought to be.[1]

As for the market—that is, the people who would buy and drink whatever wine was made for them by the winemakers—they could hardly know what they wanted. Nor, it soon appeared, were there many who were interested in wine at all. The culture of wine, frustrated and defeated as it had been through more than two hundred years of trial in the history of American settlement, had never managed to grow as more than a sickly, exotic plant in this country. And Prohibition seemed to have killed that growth to the root.

Some recollection of wine still lingered, however, and there were some Americans who were curious about it. One of the very minor, and short-lived, boom industries created by Repeal was the publishing of books about wine to educate the American consumer. These offered to instruct and guide the curious, uncertain American in the nomenclature, etiquette, and ritual of wine.[2] Much of their effect was, unfortunately, to produce wine snobbery—that child of ignorance wedded to anxiety—and just as much was to perpetuate misconceptions and misinformation. In a devastating review article devoted to the books published for the guidance of the innocent American public immediately after Repeal, Frank Schoonmaker concluded that he could not decide which one was the worst.[3] One authority counseled that a bottle of Champagne should be opened with a corkscrew and offered a list of "good recent years in Cognac." Another advised that one should prefer the "French brands" of Sherry and that no Champagne under twenty years old was fit to drink. And yet another revealed that both rum and Spanish brandy are known as *aguardiente,* which, being translated, means "water for the teeth."[4] The authors of *Household Guide to Wines and Liquors* (an instance that Schoonmaker missed) informed their readers that Catawba was "produced from Muscat grapes."

There were some sane voices in the midst of this foolish hubbub: Schoonmaker himself, with Tom Marvel, published the *Complete Wine Book;* Julian Street's *Wines* was reliable; and Philip Wagner's *American Wines and How to Make Them*—published just as Repeal dawned—at last gave Americans experienced and informed directions on how to make wine for themselves.[5] The rest of the instructional literature of the time was laughably bad, but revealed a sad-enough situation of ignorance and confusion.

Neither Schoonmaker nor Street had much to say about American wine. How could they? A few wineries that had resumed production in the years just before Repeal would have had some sound wine to sell: for example, Paul Masson, Beaulieu, and Concannon. But by far the larger part of the available wine was either what had just been made in the vintage of 1933, when the government had averted its gaze so that winemakers could make wine in anticipation of Repeal, or what had been in storage during the Prohibition years. Some of that might have been quite good to start with and might have benefited from long storage.[6] Most of it would not. Good American wine was, therefore, strictly a promise and not a present reality in 1934.

Of course, not all California wine was bad. Leo Berti recalled that some wineries, at least, made wine by sound modern methods and that some good grapes were available: "In fact, Zinfandel, Carignane, Petite Sirah were probably of higher quality than some today, as they were grown on non-irrigated, low-yielding vineyards and had small berries."[7] But, Berti added, "large quantities of poor wine were produced." Under the circumstances, it is not surprising that opinion quickly hardened into prejudice. The popular estimate of California wine may be judged from the ostensibly knowing summary of *Fortune* magazine early in 1934: "Most California Riesling, best of the white wines, is watery and just

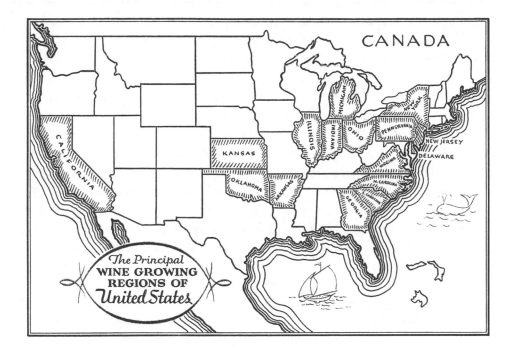

FIGURE 7

One of the early post-Repeal experts instructs the novice that Kansas and Oklahoma are among "the principal wine growing regions of [the] United States"! Both states were legally Dry, and neither had any winegrowing at all. (From S. Dewey, *Wines: For Those Who Have Forgotten and Those Who Want to Know* [1934].)

something to drink with your fish. . . . The red wines, the clarets and the Burgundies and the Chiantis, have neither the authentic flavors of the original nor the strong honest quality of the [bootleg] wines we bought last year. Most California wine, in short, is belly wash."[8]

To add to the problem of not-very-good wine, there was downright bad wine. Street, who wrote as a friend of the wine industry, was forced to admit that when Repeal arrived, the wineries "muddled along as they could" with combinations of raisin grapes, table grapes, fruit concentrates, and "heaven knows what else," and used various desperate processes to "age" the results.[9] Burke Critchfield, who represented the Bank of America in its relations with the California wine industry, agreed with Street: "Concoctions made of raisins, dried grapes, concentrate, extracts, water and sugar," he said, "were put out as 'wine' in elaborate packages, with intriguing vintage statements, sometimes 'guaranteed.'" Another critic found "wines in which the residuary taste was glycerine, others in which a compound of syrup, grape juice (probably synthetic) and a base of old wine which had turned to vinegar were quite apparent."[10]

In 1935 the California Board of Public Health, operating under the authority of the California Pure Foods Act, seized some 115,000 gallons of misbranded and adulterated wines, including "spiked claret."[11] Some of these adulterations and mislabelings no doubt occurred after the wines had left the winery and were at the mercy of unscrupulous bottlers, but some must have been the work of the winemakers themselves. There being no regulations about such matters, it was, for example, perfectly legal to sell wines labeled *port, sherry,* and *muscatel* at 14 degrees of alcohol instead of the usual 20 degrees, and so to avoid paying the higher tax on wine above 14 degrees. The practice appears to have been common.[12] And no doubt there were other abuses.

Simple incompetence in winemaking, rather than deliberate fraud or misrepresentation, might also account for a good deal of bad wine. Uncontrolled high temperatures during fermentation were common, resulting in stuck fermentations and wines susceptible to vinegar bacteria.[13] Or they might turn cloudy and mousy-flavored with the disease called *tourne,* produced by lactic acid bacteria. Wines from overripe grapes of very low acid could develop mold, as happened to large volumes of California muscatel in 1936.[14] Wines might also be spoiled by unclean cooperage or by careless storage—the care of cooperage, one expert observed after the end of the first Repeal vintage, "has caused newcomers no end of grief."[15]

And then there was the need to sell wine at once, before it was properly matured, in order to pay expenses and satisfy the banks. According to an editorial in the *Wine Review* in 1934, many producers shipped immature wines because "the financial institution that held their mortgages told them to unload, and unload at once."[16] Wines might also be shipped in contaminated barrels. According to the editor of the *Wine Review,* in the days before Prohibition new cooperage exclusively was used for shipping wine to market, but in the post-Repeal scramble, barrels "formerly used for vinegar, pickles, glue, molasses, lard, oil and practically every other product shipped in this form of package" might be and were used for wine.[17] Even supposing that a sound wine had been shipped properly, it might be spoiled in the hands of the bottler. Most California wine left the state in tank cars, consigned to local and regional bottlers east of the Rockies; not many of these, especially in the years just after Repeal, had the means to handle their wines in a way that would guarantee to keep them sound.

The disappointing sale of American wine in the first year following Repeal has already been mentioned.[18] Things got better, but production continued to outpace consumption. Most of the wine sold in the country was bought in relatively few states. California came first, with a per capita consumption that averaged a modest three gallons or so in the first years following Repeal. After California there was a long drop in the averages, from three quarters of a gallon per capita consumption in New York, to a quarter of a gallon in Missouri, and down to the two one-hundredths of a gallon that was all that Iowa managed to drink in 1935. The imbalance of the market is strikingly shown by the fact that, of the modest quantity of 32 million gallons of wine sold in 1934, three-fourths was drunk in only five states—California, Louisiana, New Jersey, New York, and Michigan.[19] A large part of the reason for this distortion is that "repeal" was far from complete: so many states or localities were still Dry, and so many states had hampering regulations affecting the sale of wine, that less than half of the nation's population lived where wine was freely available.[20]

This inequality of distribution and consumption continues to the present day. By and large, wine is drunk in the cities rather than in the country; on the coasts rather than in the heartland; and in the North rather than in the South. The result is that large parts of the country continue to be vinous wastelands—as every traveler through those parts of the United States not much frequented by tourists can confirm.

Not only were the sales of wine disappointing, it quickly appeared that there had been a transformation in the national taste. The figures of production and consumption in the first years after Repeal show that fortified wines were far more in demand than table wines. This was a surprise to the winemakers—an "amazing reversal," as one observer wrote.[21] Before Prohibition, dry table wines always dominated the market, usually by a ratio of approximately three to two. That was now changed, and the change endured for many years. The production of wine in California in 1933, when wineries were operating without the index of sales to tell them what to make, was divided between 16 million gallons of sweet (that is, fortified) wine and 19.6 million of table wine, something like the proportion that had obtained in the last years before Prohibition. The proportions of the next year's vintage show that the winemakers had quickly learned what their market wanted: almost 26 million gallons were fortified, to 11 million of dry table wine. In 1937 the proportion zoomed to nearly five to one: 54 million to 11 million. Not until 1967 did the production of table wine once again overtake and pass that of fortified wine. Since then, there has been a dramatic collapse in the fortunes of fortified wines in this country; as of 2003 they represented only about 6.5 percent of annual production, a defect quite as extravagant as the excess of the earlier years. There is no doubt that California can make excellent fortified wines in many styles. One may hope that they will sooner or later regain some of the appreciation that they deserve. But at the time of Repeal, their dominance of the market certainly worked to delay and impede the development of good table wines.

The shift in preference from table wine to fortified wine at the time of Repeal has never been satisfactorily explained. The usual comment is that Prohibition had taught Americans to look only for a "kick" in whatever they might drink, and perhaps that reasoning is right as far as it goes. On this view, fortified wines were a cheap substitute for spirits. It has also been suggested that the taste for dry wines requires some experience, and that the inexperienced American at once preferred sweet wines and stuck to them.[22] That taste for sweetness was also confirmed by the American liking for soft drinks, which had continued to grow in popularity all through the Dry years.

Another argument is that people who wanted dry wine continued to make it in their basements in preference to buying more expensive commercial wine; fortified wines were not made at home, so one had to buy them.[23] It would also have been much easier to have a fortified wine on hand in a household that did not regularly drink wine with meals—

that is to say, almost every American household. A bottle of port, or sherry, or muscatel could be kept in the cupboard for use if a guest might want "wine," or it might be used to mark a celebration of one kind or another. Probably not many other occasions for drinking wine were even imagined by most Americans. Yet another reason for the dominance of fortified wines, especially plausible in the early days, was that unlike dry table wines, they would not spoil—or at least they would not spoil so quickly, or so perceptibly, since the added alcohol and sweetness masked defects in wine quality.[24]

In any case, the so-called sweet wines, under the names *port, sherry,* and *muscatel,* at once became the staple of the reborn American wine trade.[25] Such wines could do nothing toward establishing an identity for American wines; they did nothing to stimulate experiment with new or different grape varieties, and they continued to conceal from an unsuspecting American public that wine might be an agreeable adjunct to meals. "The whole picture is cockeyed," as one wine man wrote: but there it was.[26]

OLD AND NEW

We have seen how many wineries managed, in one form or another, to survive the long siege of Prohibition. Some of them now began energetic new lives. A few, but only a very few, had histories that went back into the nineteenth century. In California, these included Cresta Blanca (founded in 1882) and Wente (1883) in the Livermore Valley; Italian Swiss Colony (1881) and Fountaingrove (circa 1883) in Sonoma County; Inglenook (1884) and Beringer (1876) in the Napa Valley; Almadén (1852) and the Novitiate of Los Gatos (1888) in the Santa Clara Valley; and, among the large producers in the Central Valley, the St. George Winery (1879) and A. Mattei (1892) in Fresno.

In California the ancestral names—the survivors from the era before Prohibition who now became the patriarchs of the reestablished industry—included Sophus Federspiel, Lee Jones, Almond R. Morrow, and the twins Edmund and Robert Rossi. Federspiel (1871–1936), of a Danish family, had entered the wine business through Italian Swiss Colony in 1889 and had become general manager of the company. During Prohibition, with H. O. Lanza, he took over the Elk Grove Winery, the Cordova Vineyard, and other properties and operated under the name of Colonial Grape Products, a name he continued to use after Repeal.

Jones (1879–1961), crippled and, reportedly, a very sharp operator, had been a government gauger before becoming a winemaker for the California Wine Association (CWA) in the Lodi district; he now presided over the National Fruit Products Company of Lodi.[27] Like all such enterprises with the word *products* in their names, it was a creature of the Prohibition years, formed in 1920 by a group of growers to find a market for their produce. The National Fruit Products plant was remodeled and reequipped as Repeal approached and, as the Shewan-Jones Winery, enjoyed the reputation of "the finest winery in the United States" for the splendor of its machinery and technical arrangements. The secretary and treasurer of Jones's firm was F. O. Smith, a veteran who began his career

Lee Jones, of the Shewan-Jones Winery, a link to the pre-Prohibition past. (Courtesy of the Wine Institute.)

with the CWA in 1909; and the winemaker was another veteran, named Elbert M. Brown—a "great" winemaker, according to Leon Adams and many others.[28] The winery could thus boast that it was managed by members of the "three greatest families in America: Smith, Jones, and Brown."[29]

Morrow (1862–1951) went back to the days of Kohler and Frohling and Henry Lachman, pioneer winegrowers and wine merchants in San Francisco.[30] In 1894 Lachman's firm formed part of the original CWA and Morrow went with it; he remained with the CWA, in its various transformations, until his death in 1951. Morrow was tutored by Lachman, a wine taster of legendary powers, and became himself the acknowledged master of his generation of wine tasters in California.[31] When the Wine Institute was formed in 1934, Morrow, in recognition of his standing within the reborn trade, was made its first president.

The Rossis—sons of the manager who helped to create Italian Swiss Colony—had saved the Italian Swiss Colony property and its label from the general wreck of the CWA during Prohibition. They had kept it going by serving the sacramental and medicinal wine

trades and by the manufacture of concentrates, as well as by the sale of fresh grapes. In anticipation of Repeal, they had resumed the production of wine and were poised and ready when the moment arrived: in December 1933, the *California Grape Grower* reported that Italian Swiss Colony had just "staged a gala festival when the first 'California Wine Special' left Asti carrying some 45,000 gallons of choice Riesling, Sauterne, Chianti and Burgundy wines to the Eastern markets."[32] Edmund Rossi, more public than his twin brother, Robert, was now an officer of the California Grape Growers League and frequently acted as the spokesman for the reemergent industry in the months of transition from Dryness to Wetness.

The best-known American winemaker was probably Paul Garrett, who had a genius for promotion and who had, before Prohibition, made his Virginia Dare the most popular wine in America—or so Garrett himself claimed. His headquarters were now in New York, for he still had winemaking properties in the East, where he lived in baronial splendor in a house on Bluff Point, commanding a prospect of the vineyards of Lake Keuka in the Finger Lakes region of New York. He remained, however, a part of the Fruit Industries cooperative that he had organized earlier and so was an important player in California too. Also in the Finger Lakes, the Widmers in Naples and the Taylors in Hammonds-port were among the survivors who helped connect old with new. At this time, when many men in the industry neither knew nor cared much about wine, as Leon Adams recalled, men like Morrow, Federspiel, Jones, and the Rossis, who did know and did care, were particularly valuable.[33]

There were also some new names. Many of them did not long endure, but a few have since achieved prominence. Louis M. Martini, who had managed to make and sell fortified wines from the Central Valley during Prohibition, now struck out in a new direction by building a million-gallon winery in the Napa Valley for the production of table wines.[34] The Cella family, based in Lodi, began the development of the Roma Wine Company, soon to be, for a time, the largest in the state. The brothers Gallo, Ernest and Julio, who had begun winemaking in Modesto only in 1933, had a winery with a 450,000-gallon capac-ity by 1934, a modest step on the path toward becoming the largest winemakers that the world has ever known, anywhere. The big fruit growers in the Central Valley also entered the winemaking business in order to have a home for those grapes from their vast vine-yards that could not be made into raisins or sold fresh: Di Giorgio, California Growers Winery, California Grape Products, and others.[35]

These large interests, which considered winemaking merely a means to salvage a crop otherwise unusable, were a big part of the reason that the California wine trade was so unstable through the '30s and long after World War II. The so-called surpluses that plagued growers and winemakers then were to an important degree not owing to the small grow-ers but to the large ones, not to the winegrowers but to the "three-way" growers, who imagined that one type of grape might be equally suitable for eating as table fruit, for making raisins, and as the source of wine. These were the people whose wines might fairly be called industrial wines, and whom Leon Adams must have had in mind when he said that many of the so-called wine men in California after Repeal cared nothing for wine; they thought of it as "a drink for skid row."[36] They quickly became among the lead-ers of the wine trade in California, dominated as it was by the production of fortified wines from the vineyards of the Central Valley, and were to remain in that position for the next generation. As James Lapsley has said, the history and politics of wine in the Central Val-ley during these years is a story "still waiting to be written."[37] It would do much to ex-plain the way that things went.

The big new wineries quickly dominated the trade, and they were largely in the hands of men who did not go back to a time before Prohibition but who had seized the oppor-tunity presented by grape growing in the Dry years: Joseph Di Giorgio of the Di Giorgio Fruit Company, Arpaxat Setrakian of the California Growers Winery, J. B. Cella of the Roma Wine Company, Krikor Arakelian of the Mission Bell Winery. But though there were a number of important newcomers in the wine trade, the influx of gangsters and get-rich-quick speculators that had been feared seems simply not to have happened. Many of the names in American winemaking immediately after Repeal, both in California and the East, were those not of newcomers but of companies that went back to a time before

Prohibition. Frei Brothers, F. Salmina, Frasinetti, Greystone, Inglenook, Beaulieu, Las Palmas—the list would be a fairly long one. Sometimes, it is true, there were new men behind the old names. More often, though, even when the winery name was new the men behind it were likely to be old-timers. There was much talk about speculators, but the federal licensing regulations, the depressed economy, and the considerable existing establishment did not allow for many such. Such speculators as there were must have been mostly concerned with buying and distributing wine rather than with the slow process of growing it.

A number of new wineries were set up after Repeal; these were likely to be small enterprises opened by people who had been growing grapes through the Prohibition years and were now hoping to make some money with wine. After a few years of undercapitalized and inexperienced existence, they tended to give up the struggle, though the proprietor might well keep his vineyards. The precariousness of the business may be suggested by figures from the Wine Institute: in the nine years 1934–42, some 554 California wineries went out of business, frequently on account of financial difficulties.[38]

THE VINEYARDS

Among the freakish results of Prohibition had been the sudden great expansion in American vineyards to supply the home winemaking market. That boom had peaked in 1926, and since then the total acreage had been shrinking. If Prohibition had, paradoxically, increased the planting of vines, Repeal, paradoxically, did nothing to arrest the decline. Between 1928 and 1936 there was a reduction of more than 150,000 acres in the total of the country's vineyards.[39] The yields from these vines, however, did not decline proportionately, and after 1936, both vineyard acreage and grape production began to go up.[40] The vineyards of California overwhelmingly dominated the national scene, producing an annual average of 2 million tons of grapes over the four years 1934–37. New York was next, with an average of 67,000 tons, followed by Michigan at 55,000 tons. Ohio (30,000), Pennsylvania (21,000), and Arkansas (11,000) were the other leading states.[41]

The damaging effect of Prohibition on the character and quality of vineyards, especially in California, has already been discussed. The relatively small quantity of good wine varieties was greatly diluted by large plantings of undistinguished wine grapes and raisin grapes. White wine varieties virtually disappeared. The condition of things is shown clearly by the figures for California's vineyards in 1930, after ten years of the operation of Prohibition.[42] The state had, in 1930, some 526,844 acres of vineyard, divided thus: raisin grapes, 248,459 acres; table grapes, 98,408; wine grapes, 179,977. It is important to understand that most of these grapes grew in the Central Valley: 380,592 acres out of the total. Fresno County, the queen of the valley, alone had some 192,000 acres of grapes, dominated as always by raisin grapes but including nearly 20,000 acres of wine grapes. Indeed, more than 40 percent of the state's wine grapes—some 75,500 acres—grew in Fresno or other counties of the Central Valley. Even if these had been good varieties (as they mostly were not), they could not have developed in that climate the balance required of grapes from which good dry wine can be made, given the viticultural and winemaking practices of the time. The only object during Prohibition had been to secure volume, since there were no quality distinctions. Varieties were chosen for their productivity, and vines were pruned to yield as much as possible. In the counties around San Francisco Bay, traditionally the source of the state's best wines, only 55,300 acres of grapes, including raisin and table grapes, were reported. Few of those 55,300 acres were planted to superior varieties.[43]

But pity the poor grape grower. What could he do when his labor barely paid him enough to live on, if it even did that? According to a survey made by the University of California in 1934, it would cost a vineyard in Sonoma County yielding three tons to the acre about $19 to produce a ton of grapes.[44] Since the average price for a ton of grapes during the 1930s ran from $20 for choice white varieties down to $15 for Alicantes, the vineyardist was playing a losing game unless he could raise his production substantially. But poverty meant that, more likely, one got poor yields from poor varieties, since growers often could not afford the expenses of proper cultivation. Limited spraying, sloppy pruning, no fertilizing, heavy virus infestation—all this meant reduced yields. In the 1930s, even in the more favored regions, the vineyards of California did not, as James Lapsley says, "provide fertile ground for the gospel of variety improvement."[45]

What were the main varieties of wine grapes? Zinfandel was the leader, being planted on 51,000 acres over the state. More than half of these acres were to be found in the Central Valley. Next came Alicante Bouschet at 38,500 acres; this grape had been the great favorite among home winemakers during Prohibition because its tough skin enabled it to endure rough handling and still remain attractive, and because of the intense color of its juice (it is a *teinturier*, a blue grape with colored rather than clear juice). It yields a wine satisfactorily dark to the eye but never more than common to the palate. And since the greater part of the plantings of Alicante Bouschet were in Fresno and other hot Central Valley counties, the deficiencies of its wine would have been intensified by the low acid level of its juice. This objection did not count for much during Prohibition. Indeed, one of the attractions of the Alicante Bouschet was that its intense color made it possible to add sugar and water to the pressed skins to produce a second wine. The third favored variety was the Carignane with 26,500 acres, again mostly in the Central Valley. Carignane (pronounced by most California growers as "Kerrigan") can produce a respectable wine, and the variety still holds a place in California winemaking as a source of wine for blending. The plantings of these three grapes alone added up to 116,000 acres of the state's total of 180,000 acres of wine grapes.

In that total, white wine varieties, for which there was little demand during Prohibition, had virtually disappeared. In 1930, there were a mere 7,000 acres of white wine grapes in all of California, mostly growing in the Central Valley and without any varietal identity in the reports.[46]

There were even some plantings of eastern varieties in California, including Concord, Delaware, Norton, Lenoir, and, most curious of all, Scuppernong.[47] That California in the

1930s should still grow Catawba and yet know almost nothing of Cabernet or Chardonnay is, to our view from the twenty-first century, an almost incredible fact; but nothing could better illustrate how troubled and confused grape growers and winemakers were in those times.[48]

Since the state's vineyards were dominated by raisin and table grape varieties, much of the state's wine was inevitably made from those same grapes. In the first three years of Repeal, 1933–35, almost half of the table grapes—and on average 14 percent of all the raisin grapes—grown in the state were crushed for wine, which meant, in effect, that half of the California crush was composed of raisin and table grapes.[49] Worse, the table and raisin grapes that went to the wineries were almost always the poorer sorts, culls or rain-damaged or otherwise substandard fruit that could not be sold for the table or converted to raisins and so were "salvaged" by being made into wine, either to be drunk in that form or, more often, to be distilled into high-proof brandy for fortifying the sweet wines that were the staple of the industry.[50] The sad fact was that many growers thought of the wineries merely as their third option, after the fresh and raisin markets had been satisfied. As one California winemaker innocently observed, "The wineries are practically a dumping ground for any variety of grape produced in the state"; this, however, did not trouble him, for he went on to say that "any grape is a wine grape."[51]

The state of the vineyards could not be immediately improved, nor did conditions of economic depression at all encourage replanting to better and more appropriate varieties. The figures make dismal reading. In the six years 1933–38, some 11,000 acres of red-wine grapes were newly planted in California vineyards. Of these, 4,000 were Zinfandel, nearly 2,000 Carignane, and 1,000 Mission. Grenache, Petite Sirah, Alicante Bouschet, and Mataro (Mourvèdre) made up another 2,000. If any varieties superior to these were planted, they are submerged in the figure for 2,000 acres of "others." Nearly 5,000 new acres of white wine varieties were planted in the same years, but the choices were equally retrograde: 1,780 acres of Palomino, 600 acres of Burger, 392 acres of French Colombard, and 1,955 of "others."[52] Meantime, the planting of the already too abundant and, for wine purposes, highly undesirable Thompson Seedless went on unabated. In the years 1933–38 more than half of all new plantings in California were in raisin grapes, nine-tenths of them Thompson Seedless: and this at a time when the market for raisins was declining.[53] The result was that, as late as 1940, Frank Schoonmaker and Tom Marvel could estimate ("decidedly on the high side") that there were then only 50 to 100 acres of Chardonnay, 300 to 400 of Sauvignon Blanc, 800 to 1,000 of Cabernet, and 300 to 500 of Pinot noir growing in the entire state of California.[54]

The fountain cannot rise higher than its source, and as long as the source of California wine—its grapes—remained undistinguished and even unsuited for wine, and as long as grape varieties were grown in regions unsuited to them, the quality of the wine had to suffer.[55] The same thing could be said about eastern winegrowing, which was too much at the mercy of the baleful Concord and hardly had a glimmer of other possibilities.[56] The presence of such large volumes of "alternative" grapes, especially in California, had the effect of depressing prices for wine grapes, so that there was little inducement to plant good wine varieties. The situation was thus a perfect vicious circle: without good wines to offer, the industry could not arouse the interest of the market; and without a growing market, the industry could not pay for the quality that would make it grow. So the situation perpetuated itself.

THE WINERIES

The rebuilding of the wineries was much more obvious and much more dramatic than the slow and misguided changes that took place in the vineyards. The pages of *Wines and Vines* in the early days of the revival are filled with excited accounts of new building and renewed activity. "At the Beringer Bros. Winery at St. Helena," ran one report as early as August 1933, "Fred Abruzzini is superintending the installation of a second crusher, the re-coopering of 60 casks and the construction of a bottling building." At Roma, in Lodi, "modern buildings have been constructed and additions made that provide every up-to-date improvement"; California Grape Products at Delano installs 700,000 gallons of new cooperage, and B. Cribari, of Fresno, adds a million gallons' capacity.[57] The catalog runs euphorically on through a list of new crushers, presses, refrigeration units, storage cellars, distilleries, evaporators, labeling machines, and all the other capital items of modern winemaking. The number of wineries operating in California leaped, in the single month of July 1933, from 167 to 240; by November it had reached 313, and it continued to grow. It was estimated that by the end of 1936, a short three years after Repeal, there were 140 million gallons of storage capacity in California, twice the capacity that was still intact at the time of Repeal, and it was feared, with some reason, that the production capacity of the state had already outgrown the market.[58]

How was all this paid for? The subject is one that has not yet been studied, though it would presumably offer an instructive history. The chief financial power in the state was the Bank of America under its founder, A. P. Giannini, and though Giannini had no high opinion of the wine men of California, his bank was their main resource. J. B. Cella, of the Roma Wine Company, recalled that all they had to do was ask and the loan was theirs; the Petris, Louis Martini, and the Rossis of Italian Swiss Colony were also the beneficiaries of such informal banking.[59] All of these favored clients, it may be noted, were owners of big enterprises. Federal agencies were also important sources of credit for both vineyards and wineries: the Commodity Credit Corporation, the Federal Land Bank, the Production Credit Agency, and the Berkeley Bank for Cooperatives.[60] Other commercial banks had a part too: Antonio Perelli-Minetti said that he owed his success to the "liberal way" he had been financed by the Security Pacific Bank.[61] Ernest Gallo—who, in the days of his small beginnings, had been turned down by the Bank of America—found a friendly backer in the Capital National Bank of Sacramento.[62]

The tendency in the reconstruction of the California wineries was clearly toward bigness—toward larger wineries at the expense of the smaller. The California Growers Winery plant at Cutler, entirely devoted to the production of fortified wines and brandy, was a wholly new establishment, with a storage capacity of 2.5 million gallons. California Grape Products, with several wineries around the state, grew from 2 million to 5 million gallons. Krikor Arakelian, at Madera, had 6,000 acres of vineyards and 2.5 million gallons of storage capacity; Roma, in Lodi, had 5 million gallons of storage ready at the moment of Repeal, and two years later that figure had grown to nearly 8 million. By the end of 1936 there were thirty-nine wineries in California with a storage capacity of more than a million gallons apiece; together, these wineries accounted for more than 60 percent of the state's entire wine storage capacity. It was estimated that another 30 percent of that capacity belonged to 126 wineries with storage of more than 100,000 gallons each. The remaining small wineries, to the number of 423, divided the remaining 10 percent of the state's wine capacity among them.[63] This tendency continued unbroken for the next thirty years and more: as W. V. Cruess wrote in 1947, the small wineries existed to make wine for sale to the large wineries, and really operated in order to provide a local market for the grape crop.[64] There were, of course, some small and medium-size producers that went their own independent way—Korbel, Larkmead, Beringer, Concannon, and the like. The bulk wine trade, however, is what most people were engaged in. In this trade, in which large volumes of standard wine were sold at a low profit in a toughly competitive market, size was an advantage.

The trend toward big wineries was continued by the formation of cooperative wineries. The depressed economic conditions of the 1930s favored the cooperative idea, which was a way for the grape growers, who stood at the bottom of the structure that led from the grapes in the vineyard to the bottle on the table, to get a decent return on their produce.[65] By combining forces in a cooperative venture, they could convert their own grapes into wine and, in some instances, carry out the marketing of the finished product as well: in either case, the growers stood to make a bit more on their grapes by processing them themselves than if they sold them to the commercial wineries. The New Deal encouraged the method, and supported it through the Farm Credit Administration.

The cooperative idea was not new: there had been co-ops in the California wine trade at least since 1904, when the Woodbridge Vineyard Association near Lodi was founded. They now began to proliferate, and since they were joint rather than individual enterprises, they were almost always built on a very large scale. The growers of the Lodi district, with the example of the Woodbridge co-op before them, took the lead in the development.[66] The Bear Creek Vineyard Association of Lodi was formed in 1934 by 102 growers, who put up a reinforced-concrete winery of 1.1 million gallons' capacity in that year. To serve as winemaker, the association lured out of retirement Adolph Bauer, a German-trained technician who had come to California in the 1880s.[67] The East-Side Winery, a co-op of sixty growers, also in Lodi and also established in 1934, was built with an original capacity of 1.5 million gallons. In the next year, six more cooperatives were formed, adding another 4.5 million gallons of capacity.[68]

The cooperatives, like the other large wineries, were essentially bulk wine producers, not interested in developing anything more than a large-scale market for standard wines:

FIGURE 10

Sign outside the Roma winery in Fresno, circa 1937. The renewed California industry lost no time in employing superlatives. (J. B. Cella II, *The Cella Family in the California Wine Industry* [1986].)

indeed, it was said that because their first object was to compensate the growers, they were inclined to unload their wines as quickly as possible, to the unsettling of the market.[69] Some of them did their own marketing—East-Side, for example. But most of them followed the standard pattern and sold their wines in bulk to bottlers around the country. Others came together through the device of a "marketing co-op"—a nonprofit sales agency that advertised and distributed the produce of a number of separate cooperative wineries. In 1937 three large cooperative wineries formed California Wine Sales to market their wines in bulk, and in 1943 this group became the Wine Growers Guild, an important presence in California wine until it was sold in 1991.[70]

The winegrowing map of California very soon after Repeal looked pretty much as it had before Prohibition, since one could hardly expect that new sites would be explored before the old ones had been reestablished. In the first generation after Repeal, the main winegrowing regions were the northern bay counties (Napa, Sonoma, Mendocino, Lake), the eastern and southern bay counties (Contra Costa, Alameda, Santa Clara, San Mateo, Santa Cruz), the Sacramento Valley, the San Joaquin Valley, Southern California, and the foothills of the Sierra Nevada.

The northern bay counties were the best-known sources of table wine before Prohibition, and they at once resumed that position following Repeal. In 1934, Sonoma County led in actual grape acreage (19,000 acres) and in number of wineries (104). Napa County at the time had only fifty-three wineries, but among them were a few better-known than any of the survivors in Sonoma—notably Inglenook, Beaulieu, and Beringer; in the course of the next decade, Napa gradually took over primacy from Sonoma.[71] The scale of operations in Mendocino and Lake Counties was very small and showed no signs of growing: both were in effect satellites of Sonoma and Napa, supplying grapes and bulk wines to the better-known wineries in those counties. Generally, the northern bay counties were in an unhappy position: the huge shift in the market from table wines to fortified wines meant that they were fighting against the tide; and the virtual disappearance in the United States of an informed body of wine drinkers, the people who might be interested in superior table wines, meant that the growers had little incentive to rise above the level at which they had resumed in 1934. For many years following Repeal, the winemakers of the northern bay counties fought what seemed to be a losing struggle. Much of their wine went out in bulk as anonymously as any industrial wine from the Central Valley: it may have helped to improve the reputation of California wine generally, but it did little economically or promotionally for the district.

Essentially the same story was repeated for the eastern and southern bay counties. There are those who hold that the best red wines ever made in California came from Santa Clara and San Mateo Counties; Livermore, in Alameda County, had long held a high reputation for white wines in a state in which white wines were distinctly second fiddle. Contra Costa was known for a number of small wineries producing good sound provincial wines. As in the northern counties, the new energy released by Repeal did not carry things very far; with the exception of Wente and Concannon in Livermore (and briefly Los Amigos), no winery in the eastern and southern bay counties acquired any reputation or prosperity. Diminishing vineyards, unimproved practices in vineyard and winery, and a dependence on anonymous sales in bulk were the norm.[72]

In the Sacramento Valley, the northern part of the Central Valley, the old vineyard regions north and east of Sacramento had shrunk to about 7,000 acres by the time of Repeal. But to the south, around Lodi in San Joaquin County, things were very different. It was here that some of the biggest of the post-Repeal wineries developed: by 1936 there were fifteen large wineries in and around Lodi, including several co-ops and such giant private producers as Shewan-Jones and Roma (before its move to Fresno). They had a combined storage capacity of 25 million gallons, nearly a fifth of the state's total.[73] Lodi was then and for years afterward the winemaking capital of California, producing a mix of table and fortified wines. Indeed, it may be said that Lodi is still the capital of California winemaking, taking volume, variety, and quality together.

The San Joaquin Valley—the southern half of the Central Valley, extending roughly from Merced south through Fresno to Bakersfield—was overwhelmingly the largest region of California viticulture. In 1936 it accounted for 346,000 of the state's total of 468,000 acres of grapes. Most of these, it is true, were raisin grapes (about 215,000 acres);

sol.

but the San Joaquin also led the state's wine grape acreage, with 68,000 out of the total of 162,000. The fortified wines produced from the grapes of the San Joaquin were the dominant element in the market.

The old Los Angeles (Southern California) district, which at this time mostly meant the Cucamonga region, straddling the border of Los Angeles and San Bernardino Counties, had 27,000 acres in 1934, and it held steady in acreage for the next generation. There were some small wineries, mostly owned by Italian Americans, operating in and around Cucamonga, but the pattern of winemaking in the district resembled that in the Central Valley. Big privately owned wineries such as the old Italian Vineyard Company at Guasti, the Paul Garrett Winery, and the Padre Vineyard Winery were joined by several large co-ops such as the Cucamonga Pioneer Winery to dominate both the grape growing and the winemaking. As one would expect in a district classified as regions IV and V, Cucamonga made a lot of fortified wine; but it continued to produce a great deal of table wine as well, which was traditionally in demand in the Italian American communities of Philadelphia and New York. To the west, in Los Angeles County, viticulture had been in gradual decline ever since the late nineteenth century, when Pierce's disease had exterminated the vineyards of Anaheim and seriously damaged the outlook for winegrowing in and around Los Angeles, the cradle of California wine. The great growth of the city and the consequent rise in land values were even more potent causes of disappearing vines. There were, however, still some 4,400 acres of vineyard in Los Angeles County in 1936.

The vineyards in the foothills of the Sierra Nevada, mostly in Placer County, amounted to only about 4,000 acres in 1936, and there was little or no sign of a significant renewal there. For the rest, there was a scattering of vines in the far south of the state—San Diego County—and in the Central Coast counties—around Templeton in San Luis Obispo County, for example, or in San Benito County, where the Valliant Winery near Hollister counted as one of the best in the state.

The seemingly irresistible tendency toward the large scale, combined with the lack of a demanding or critical market, made it almost inevitable that California winemaking in the first years after Repeal knew much about quantity and very little about quality. These industrial conditions also led to the practice of the big wineries each making a complete "line" of wines: dry and sweet, red and white, still and sparkling, fortified and unfortified, through the whole range of recognized names—port, sherry, claret, burgundy, rhine, sauterne, and the rest.[74] The varieties from which such wines were made, the regions in which they may have been grown, were never identified; such information simply did not count. What did count was that a winery should be able to supply the entire spectrum of standard wines, as these were then recognized, to its customers.[75]

THE EASTERN SCENE

Eastern is a very approximate term in the context of American winemaking. Practically speaking, in the era under discussion it meant "not California." Before the 1970s, when winegrowing began to spread into new territories, the term indicated the winegrowing states of New York, New Jersey, Ohio, Michigan, and Arkansas. Climatically and botanically, it meant "everything east of the Rocky Mountains" as well as the Pacific Northwest. The main winemaking difference between *East* and *West* (that is, California) was that vinifera grew in California and not elsewhere in the United States, except for small plantings in eastern Washington and a handful of Mission grapes in New Mexico.

In the "East," then, the same sorts of processes were going on, though much less visibly. It is not generally recognized how widespread winemaking activity was in the United States, since so much of it was small-scale, local, and often short-lived. But the figures are interesting. The number of American wineries in the first years after Repeal peaked at 1,245 in 1936 and then began a slight decline, owing no doubt to the tough times and to the new regulations that made running a winery something more than a simple farm enterprise (though it had never really been that in American practice). The total number was 1,206 in 1937 and 1,175 in 1938.[76] To take 1937 for analysis, the 1,206 wineries then licensed were scattered over thirty-three states, including such unlikely places as Colorado (two wineries) and Hawaii (two).[77] California had 630 wineries, only a little more than half the total, but producing 115 million gallons of that year's total of 122 million. New York was next in production, with 3 million gallons from 123 wineries, but the state with the largest number of establishments after California was Ohio, with 130 licensed wineries. The precariously small scale of operations in Ohio is clear from the fact that the production from these 130 wineries amounted to only 755,000 gallons—an average of a bit under 6,000 gallons per winery, supposing that all 130 actually produced wine in that year. That level might have been enough for survival if the simple and direct method of sales from bulk at the winery door had still been allowed, but the new requirements for bottling and labeling made things difficult, as did the burden of complying with new federal and state regulations and taxes. After Ohio, one may note that in 1937 there were some 73 wineries in Arkansas, 51 in New Jersey, and 35 in Washington State (where the state's other fruits and berries contributed more to winemaking than grapes did). Only Missouri, among the states prominent in pre-Prohibition winemaking, did not see a mushroom crop of small wineries in the morn of Repeal: the state had just 12 wineries in 1937.[78] As has been noted in the first chapter, the Missouri Germans seem to have been devastated by the combined effects of World War I and Prohibition, so thoroughly indeed that there was now almost nothing left to revive.

Despite all the many small wineries in the East, the tendency there, as in California, was toward fewer and larger establishments. By the 1940s, the Finger Lakes industry in New York was dominated by four wineries: Taylor, Great Western, Gold Seal, and Widmer's. These, like their large-scale counterparts in California, had as their stock-in-trade a line of standard imitations—port, sherry, burgundy, and the rest.[79] The same pattern held, on a smaller scale, in Michigan: by 1943, ten years after Repeal, four wineries in Michigan represented more than 80 percent of the state's entire volume of production. Even more than California, the eastern industry just after Repeal seems to have seen mostly a return of the old names rather than any notable new presences: Taylor (1880), Pleasant Valley (1860), Widmer's (1887), and Gold Seal (1865) in the Finger Lakes; Renault (1870), Hiram Dewey (1857), and Kluxen (1865) in New Jersey; Engels and Krudwig (1863), M. Hommel (1878), and Lonz (1884) in Ohio, to name only a few of the better known.

In other respects, the eastern industry was very different from California's.[80] Three centuries of disappointment seemed to have shown conclusively that the vinifera vine—the "wine-bearer," the species from which all European wines derive—would not grow in most of the United States. Climate, indigenous diseases, and indigenous pests unknown in Europe were uniformly fatal to the European vine. Yet all over North America native grapes flourished in variety and profusion—*Vitis labrusca, Vitis aestivalis, Vitis rupestris,* and *Vitis riparia* among the more familiar species. All were unfit for wine; the grapes were mostly small, with little juice, and that little high in acid, low in sugar, and filled with strange and unwelcome flavors. So the situation remained for nearly two centuries. Grapes unfit for wine were found everywhere, and the one grape good for wine would not grow. This stubborn fact, more than any other single condition, explains the failure of a wine-drinking tradition to establish itself in American culture.

The solution was discovered by accident. Somehow, a few of the many European vines repeatedly imported in vain all up and down the early colonies managed to survive long enough to flower and so to enter into hybrid combinations with the vines of the native species. The first of these accidental hybrids was discovered in the mid-eighteenth century; from the first half of the nineteenth century, work in deliberate hybridization between vinifera and native vines was carried on by a growing number of enthusiasts, both commercial and amateur. By the end of the century, some thousands of the resulting grapes had been named and described. From the yield of all this labor, a few sorts have been selected as best suited, in one way or another, for wine: Catawba, Delaware, Dutchess, and a handful of others. Such grapes combine, in varying proportions and intensities, the qualities of their parents, the aim being to secure the resistance to disease of the natives with the winemaking qualities of the European grape. Almost all of them betray their native parentage to some degree, particularly in the quality called foxiness—an unmistakable aroma and flavor said to be largely owing to methyl anthranilate (the Norton, a *Vitis aestivalis* variety, is an exception). They have other peculiarities as well. They are higher in acid and lower in sugar than vinifera grapes, and many of them are "slip-skin," making them difficult to press, so that special presses and techniques for their handling have had to be developed.[81]

The taste for such grapes and their wines can be acquired. The Concord grape—which is not even a hybrid but a pure *Vitis labrusca*—is, indeed, now so widespread in this country that its aroma and flavor define for many what "grapiness" is, and it is preferred over all other grape types. Given some experience, however, and given a choice, few if any prefer the wines of the American hybrids to the wines from European grapes. The American hybrids, however, were all that the eastern winemakers had to work with, and in the course of time they established a market for their wines, which they learned to blend and ameliorate. Their particular successes were almost all with white wines, including sparkling wines, for the peculiar native flavor is stronger in red wines (again, the Norton is an exception).

Two special practices followed from the fact that eastern wines were based on native grapes. Since these grapes are typically high in acid and low in sugar, the musts were routinely "ameliorated" by adding water to dilute the acid and by adding sugar to raise the potential alcohol. And because the juice of these grapes is so strongly flavored, the winemakers routinely blended it with neutral wines from California (which could, as well, be bought for less than it cost to produce wine in the East).

Both of these practices—ameliorating and blending with imported wine—were outlawed in California. There, with grapes that are typically high in sugar and low in acid, the winemaker was allowed to add acid, but no addition of sugar was permitted.[82] And to be called California wine, it had to be exclusively Californian—no addition of out-of-state wine was allowed. These basic differences in the conditions of wine production made it impossible for uniform standards to be devised for American winemaking and were a serious obstacle to cooperation between the eastern and western wings of the American wine trade. Throughout the '30s and beyond, there were conflicts between the Easterners, dependent on amelioration and blending in order to function competitively, and the Californians, eager to establish the "purity" of their wines.

Much of the winemaking in the East was not calculated to raise hopes for the future. In Michigan, for example, it is reported that most of the wine was fermented dry, at 8 or 9 degrees of alcohol by volume: this was all that could be expected from the native American grapes (particularly the Concord) grown almost exclusively in Michigan vineyards. Little of it saw the market in this condition, for most of the wine made in Michigan was then sweetened by the addition of sugar and fortified by the addition either of already fortified wine or of brandy. Such wine was usually sold at 16 percent alcohol; it could contain up to 25 percent wine not made in Michigan, but if it had more than that it would lose its tax advantage (4 cents a gallon versus 50 cents a gallon for wines from other states). This was the "light, sweet wine" evidently widely popular in the first years after Repeal.[83] It was one of the objects of the California wine people that such wine should not be called port or sherry, as it well might have been. Whatever it might be called, the only idea of Michigan wine that a Michigan customer could form in that protected market would be of a foxy, sweet, high-alcohol compound utterly unfit for use with food. For better or worse, production grew from about 350,000 gallons in 1935 to nearly 2 million gallons in 1942.[84]

Another practice allowed in the eastern trade was for wines of any origin—in reality almost always from California—to be bottled under the eastern winemaker's label as "American" wine: thus one could buy "American Zinfandel" under the label of an Ohio or a Finger Lakes winery, even though no Zinfandel vine grew within two thousand miles of the winery.

The one turf on which eastern winemakers felt confident competing against California, even with all its advantages, was that of sparkling wine. The high acids and low sugars of the native American grapes were an asset rather than a handicap in the making of sparkling wine, and "champagne" from the East, particularly from the Finger Lakes of upstate New York, had dominated the domestic market in the years before Prohibition. The cuvée of New York champagne, the outcome of long experiment, was based on blends of Catawba, Delaware, and Elvira grapes, with additions of Dutchess, Isabella, Iona, and Eumelan.[85] New York's domination was restored after Repeal and was to continue for another generation. The champagne-making empire of the eastern states had a westerly province in St. Louis, where the American Wine Company returned to its production of Cook's Imperial, first made in 1859 by the Chicago politician Isaac Cook. In the old days the company had brought in Catawba wine from its vineyards in Ohio and elaborated it after the *méthode champenoise* in caves dug under the streets of St. Louis. Now it blended Ohio and California wine as the basis of its champagne.

California had never been backward in the production of sparkling wine, which had been attempted by the Sainsevain brothers in San Francisco as early as 1857. The Eclipse champagne of Arpad Haraszthy had been one of California's celebrated wines in the nineteenth century, as had the sparkling wines of Paul Masson and others in later years. New York had always had the lead, however. In the first four years after Repeal, the country as a whole produced about 1.7 million gallons of champagne, nearly half of which (772,200 gallons) came from New York, as compared to the 350,000 gallons of such wine produced in California. The rest was made up mostly of wines from New Jersey, Ohio, and Michigan.[86] New York sparkling wine was traditionally made by the *méthode champenoise* of secondary fermentation in the bottle, but the Charmat process of secondary fermentation in large closed containers gained ground there (and in California too) after Repeal.[87]

Winemaking in the eastern United States after Repeal was not an expansive activity but, rather, a holding operation. There was a brief spurt of apparent growth when Repeal came and the number of wineries increased. But there was no equivalent increase in the vineyards, and the vineyards themselves continued to be based almost exclusively on the old native hybrids or, increasingly, on the Concord.[88] Other, better grapes—notably the hybrids developed in France—were now available to eastern growers, but there was no more incentive for the eastern wine industry to improve its viticultural basis than there was for California's.[89] The story of winemaking in the East over the next three decades and more is an undramatic history of erosion and attrition. There were no striking new developments, no new territories conquered. Instead, gaps opened up in the old structure as the inevitable losses brought about by business failure, retirement, and death were not repaired. Some wineries prospered: those in the Finger Lakes region, with their secure hold on the trade in sparkling wine, are the best example. The historical prominence of the Finger Lakes region was institutionalized in the Finger Lakes Wine Growers Association, founded in 1932, the major trade group in eastern winemaking. A few wineries in other regions did well in local or specialty markets: the old Sandusky wineries of John G. Dorn

FIGURE 11

The Grape Festival at Sandusky, Ohio, October 1939. (From *Cleveland Plain Dealer.*)

and Engels and Krudwig with Catawba wines, Paul Garrett with his muscadine-based Virginia Dare wines, H. T. Dewey in New Jersey with a Norton wine.[90]

The general tendency in the East, despite temporary fluctuations, was downward, as may be shown by the outline of winemaking in Ohio through the '30s and after. Historically, Ohio was the navel of American winemaking: it was there, in Cincinnati in the 1830s, that the first successful commercial winemaking in this country was at last achieved through the work of Nicholas Longworth, whose still and sparkling wines from the Catawba grape had been widely hailed. Before the Civil War, winemaking had spread north from Cincinnati to the shores of Lake Erie, where the Catawba found an especially agreeable climate and where a largely German-derived community of winemakers prospered through the production of still and sparkling white wines until Prohibition. Indeed, for a brief time before the rise of California to national dominance of wine production, Ohio was the nation's leading producer of wine.[91]

Upon Repeal, a great many of the old wineries reopened. "Workmen are busy enlarging the plant of the Engels and Krudwig Wine Company, Sandusky, Ohio," the *Wine Review* reported in July 1934. The plant capacity was to be doubled, to a million gallons, and "hundreds of new acres are planned." It is doubtful that the new vineyards were in fact planted. There were some exotic new additions to the Ohio scene as well: in 1935 the Mon Ami Company, managed by Colonel S. Zagonyi, late of the Hungarian army, opened near Sandusky to "make Champagne by a secret patented process which comes all the way from romantic Budapest."[92] Most of Ohio's wineries were still to be found on the shores of Lake Erie, particularly to the west around Sandusky; they were still mostly in the hands of families, most of German descent; and they still depended on the Catawba grape. This was not a combination well adapted to compete with large quantities of neutral wine produced in California by industrial-scale wineries. Indeed, the Ohio wineries themselves depended on just such wine to stretch out their own product, so that they were collaborators with their own competition.[93] The results were not very good: Schoonmaker and Marvel complained that in Ohio the musts were often too heavily dosed with sugar, so that the alcoholic content of the resulting wines was too high. And stretching those wines with neutral California wine deprived them of any regional character. The practice favored in Ohio of long aging in wood meant that the wines—particularly the whites, which would have been the really distinctive wines—lost their fruit and freshness.[94]

The vineyards of Ohio, like those of other regions in the East, did not materially increase during the 1930s. They were typically small, usually a part of a truck-farming or general fruit-growing operation; only one, in 1936, was as large as 50 acres.[95] To the west, around Sandusky and on the Lake Erie islands, the Catawba was the leading variety and the source of Ohio's best wines; to the east, from Cleveland to the Pennsylvania border, the Concord dominated. There were altogether about 15,000 acres of vineyard in the state, less than half of what had grown there in the late nineteenth century. The average crop in the years 1930–39 was 30,000 tons, a very modest yield of 2 tons an acre, as compared with the 10 tons or more an acre of which California's Central Valley vineyards were capable.[96] About three-quarters of this yield was crushed for wine. The average production of wine—most of it table wine—in Ohio from 1935 to 1940 was about 1.3 million gallons. In 1935 there were 112 licensed wineries in the state, only a very few of which made wine in large quantities.[97]

Curiously enough, although the average production of wine in Ohio did not much grow in these years, the number of licensed wineries did, to a high of 149 in 1940. After that, owing no doubt in part to the war but also surely to the continued pressure of competition from California, the decline was rapid. The quality of Ohio wines was not high: there was a market for Catawba wines, but by 1940 some 80 percent of the vineyards of Ohio were given over to the near-worthless Concord.[98] Since the market for Ohio wines could not be improved on that basis, prices for grapes declined, removing all incentive for the planting of better varieties. The 149 wineries of 1940 sank rapidly thereafter—to 93 in 1950, to 47 in 1960. By the latter year, given the rate of decline, there was little reason to think that winemaking would persist much longer: production in that year was just under half a million gallons.[99]

By and large, what was true in Ohio was true in all the other eastern states that had any tradition of winemaking. There was a spasm of new activity at the beginning of Repeal, but it did not advance the industry much beyond the point that it had already reached before Prohibition. In New Jersey, for example, such old enterprises as H. T. Dewey and Company and Herman A. Kluxen reopened, but there was a gradual dwindling there through the '30s. Michigan made an exception; there, a few wineries grew large under the conditions of the protected market. New York, where a few wineries were large enough and well enough established to have a loyal market, made the other exception.

4

MAKING AND SELLING WINE IN THE '30S

HOW WINE WAS MADE

In 1933, before Repeal had come to pass but when its coming was already certain, Lou Stralla, having heard that the wine business might be a good thing, decided that he would give it a try, even though he knew nothing about wine or winemaking.[1] Stralla took a simple and direct path: he approached the wealthy J. K. Moffitt, who owned the historic Charles Krug winery, then lying idle outside St. Helena in the Napa Valley, and asked Moffitt to lease it to him. To Stralla's surprise, Moffitt agreed to do so. Stralla now found himself, as the result of his audacity, with a winery but without any idea of what to do with it; he had to find help, for he was in a position rather like that of the girl in the fairy tale who must somehow learn to spin gold out of straw, and learn quickly.

As in the fairy tale, help was forthcoming: first, the winemaker at Beaulieu Vineyards, on the other side of St. Helena, told Stralla that one Rufus J. Buttimer, who had been the winemaker at the Ewer and Atkinson Winery in Rutherford before Prohibition, might be coaxed out of retirement. Buttimer agreed to do what he could, and he, in turn, recruited Jack Heitz, whose family used to be in the wine business. Then old Joe Cheli, who used to work at Krug and still lived across the road, got interested in what was going on at the old place and gave them a hand. And so it went. Together they cleaned things up, and after the grapes had come in they found that they had made 400,000 gallons of red and white table wine, Cheli making the white and Buttimer the red. "I'll tell you," Stralla said to an interviewer years afterward, "it was an amazing thing to me. . . . I knew nothing about wine at all, and here we had 400,000 gallons of good wine. I couldn't quite understand what happened."[2]

Such improvisations, mixing the ignorance of complete newcomers with the remembered experience of the old-timers, must have been common enough in the revived scene of winemaking in America. Stralla had the advantage of setting up in a region where the memory of winemaking was still strong. Others would not have had the same luck. So how, we may ask, was wine made in and around 1934? And how and in what forms did it reach its market? The answers to these questions will obviously vary according to the winemaker and all the details of his situation, but some reliable general answers can be given. In view of the methods and materials generally in use, California wine just after Repeal and for perhaps too many years afterward was typically either peasant wine, made in a rough-and-ready way by a small proprietor, or industrial wine, made without any concern beyond cheapness and volume. There were exceptions to these rules, but they were very exceptional. As W. V. Cruess put it in 1934, the most common method of winemaking in California then was the "'let alone method'" in which "nature takes its course, often with disastrous results to the quality of the wine."[3]

As the figures for the annual crush show, wine might be made of any sort of grape— table grape, raisin grape, or wine grape—and was not likely to originate in any very distinguished variety, there being hardly any distinguished varieties available. The tendency was to go for high sugars, so that the grapes were picked when they were very ripe. The wines were, as a result, often deficient in acid and high in pH and therefore "flat." One of the first objects of the people at the University of California, Davis, was to persuade California winegrowers to pick at an earlier stage of ripeness, and to help in this aim they managed to secure a slight increase in the minimum total acid allowed by California wine standards. The matter of picking at a proper stage of ripeness, which seems in retrospect so simple a question, was in fact one of the main points of contention in post-Repeal California. In a letter written in 1940, Maynard Amerine indulged an eloquence on the subject that he could not allow himself in his official publications. He wrote,

> There is an appalling lack of recognition of the critical importance of picking at the proper stage. Not only does the sugar rise too high but the acid decreases too low when the grapes are picked late in the season. The resulting wines are heavy, lacking the essential fruité quality and frequently have an overripe grape or raisin taste. . . . But more important is the influence of late picking on the fermentation. As the grapes pass their time of optimum maturity the number of rotten and diseased berries increases and the chemical composition becomes less favorable to yeast growth and more favorable to the growth of harmful organisms, particularly spoilage bacteria. Aside from [Martin] Ray you would be amazed at how few of our growers or vintners have the least conception of these facts. This is one of the recurring reasons for the lack of quality (or even drinkability) of California wines.[4]

The power to control such things as the time of picking was not often in the hands of the wineries (even supposing that they appreciated the importance of the question), for the estate model of winemaking, in which vineyards, winery, and cellar are all parts of an integrated whole, was quite unusual in California.[5] The grower was on his own to prune, cultivate, and harvest his grapes as he saw fit. He might sell his crop to any one or more of a number of wineries, which for their part would buy their grapes wherever they might find the best terms. The only measure of quality in general use was the sugar content of the grapes: the more "sugar points," the better the price, other things being equal.

Labor, of course, in those Depression days, was cheap. A grower could readily find all the help needed to cultivate and pick grapes, so there was little or no incentive to develop machinery for these purposes. A picker might hope to make about three dollars a day for a ton of grapes—"the usual picking of 1 man in a 9-hour day."[6] They worked, after the traditional fashion, with short, curved knives or short-bladed shears, and loaded the clusters into fifty- to sixty-pound lug boxes. The lug boxes might be stacked up on flatbed trucks or they might be emptied into large gondolas, which were then hauled by truck to the winery. The interval between picking and delivery to the crusher was sometimes long, to the detriment of quality: grapes held for many hours under the hot California sun and hauled for long distances would not arrive in good condition.

Most of the wineries themselves were mixtures of the old and the new. There had been no startling changes in the world's winemaking methods and machines in the years that the American industry had lain dormant. Nor would there have been the means, in the Depression years, for most winemakers to begin with new equipment: they used what they could, and replaced what they had to. There were some wineries newly built from the ground up, notably the big co-ops: Cherokee, East-Side, and Bear Creek wineries at Lodi; the Florin Winery; the Elk Grove Winery; and others—but the Louis Martini winery in the Napa Valley was almost the only such winery in the regions where dry table wine was made. These plants had the advantage of starting out with all the latest equipment and the latest ideas in winery design, but there were not many novelties even in the newest of establishments.

One simple but important advance was the use of concrete floors, which made cleaning easy. In pre-Prohibition California the floors might well have been of wood, gravel, or even plain dirt.[7] Another innovation was the use of large concrete tanks in place of the old wooden tanks for fermentation and storage.[8] The main reason for choosing them was that they were inexpensive to build. They could hold more than the largest wooden tanks; they could be lined with glass, wax, or enamel to assure a clean surface; and they posed little risk of leaking. If they were properly lined, they imparted no character to the wine and did not assist aging, so they were suited only to the production of standard wines; but perhaps they made that standard more reliable than it might otherwise have been.[9]

The importance of controlling the temperature of the must during fermentation had long been understood.[10] Because the time of the vintage in California, the end of summer, is also the hottest season of the year, such control is all the more important. Uncontrolled high temperatures affect the balance and flavor of wine for the worse; they may also result in stuck—that is, incomplete—fermentations, making the wine susceptible to

FIGURE 12
Concrete fermenting
tanks in the Petri Winery
at Escalon in the 1930s,
then regarded as the state
of the art. (From *Wine
Review* 14 [October 1946];
reprinted with permission
from *Wines and Vines*.)

vinegar bacteria, or to the disease called *tourne,* or milk-sourness. The new winery build-ings put up after Repeal were built with insulation against the California heat. Inside the winery in the fermenting tanks, the primitive method of cooling was to throw blocks of ice into the fermenting wine, and this method was apparently still to be met with in Cali-fornia.[11] More often, cold water was circulated through several turns of iron pipe immersed in the fermenting vats; this method was not very efficient, and had also the result of dis-solving iron into the wine, making it turbid.[12] The preferred technique was to circulate the fermenting wine itself through water-cooled copper pipe outside the fermenting tank.[13] What proportion of California's wineries were in fact equipped with reliable means of cool-ing to control fermentation is not easy to say.[14] The desirability of such means was clearly if not generally recognized; but complaints about stuck fermentations, and about the wines resulting from them, were common. Stuck wines may result from other causes, but hot fermentations were a main cause in the '30s. Probably very few wineries had really efficient cooling capacity, though their number steadily grew as time went on.[15]

The fundamental rule of all winemaking practice, the rule of strict cleanliness, was of course well understood, but the conditions created by Prohibition and Depression some-times meant that the rule was broken: old vats and barrels infected with vinegar bacteria or molds might be impossible to clean thoroughly yet might still be used for fermenting and storage, with predictable results.

For the rest, California winemaking followed standard international practices.[16] At least, it did in a well-run and well-equipped winery; but of course there were few such anywhere in the United States, owing to the damage done by Prohibition and prolonged by the Depression. But in a well-run winery, such as we may suppose for this discussion, the grapes for red wines were passed through a crusher-stemmer and pumped into the fermenting tank, where sulfur dioxide was added to sterilize the juice.[17] The tank, as has been said, might be made of concrete if the winery were new; more often, it was of redwood, the readily available California wood and long the standard choice in California wineries. Such tanks might reach capacities of many thousands of gallons; these, with their low surface-to-volume ratio, made the control of temperature difficult. If a dry wine was the object, some water might be added to the must in order to dilute the sugar content, for the ripe grapes in California might often produce a sugar content so high that it could be carried through to a complete fermentation only with difficulty.[18] The naturally occurring wild yeasts on the grapes having been inhibited by the sulfur dioxide treatment, a pure yeast starter was next added.[19] While fermentation proceeded, the cap of skins, seeds, and stems that forms at the top under the rising pressure of carbon dioxide gas was regularly punched down or pumped over; this was done to encourage the yeast by aeration, to extract color, and to keep down the growth of vinegar bacteria that thrive at the surface of the cap. The fermenting must would be cooled if needed, at least to the extent that the winemaker had the means to do so.

When fermentation was complete, the wine would be run off into large storage tanks, almost universally made of redwood in California. Electric pumps would be used to transfer large quantities of wine from one container to another. Such pumps would be made of brass, the transfer lines of copper, and the other equipment—presses, crushers, and so on—of either copper or bronze. The aim was to avoid contact of the wine with iron. Stainless steel, so important in the winemaking developments of recent years, was then available but practically out of reach on account of its cost.[20]

The pomace—that is, the stems, seeds, and skins left in the fermenting vat after the free-run wine has been drawn off—would then be shoveled out and taken to the press to yield a press wine. A power-driven continuous press, on the principle of the auger, was in use in California, but the results were considered unsatisfactory—too many solids created by the press's disintegration of the skins produced a muddy wine.[21] Basket presses, operated by hydraulic pressure, were the standard, and there were no doubt some hand-operated basket presses to be found as well. If the press wine was to be distilled, as it often was, then the continuous press was perfectly acceptable. The disposal of the dry pomace from the press was often a troublesome question. It was a breeding ground for undesirable bacteria and for vinegar flies, and a burden on sewage systems. One common practice was to haul it into the vineyards and there spread it out to be plowed under.

White wine was of course fermented off the skins. The grapes, as in the process for red wines, were passed through a crusher-stemmer, but they were then pressed, so that the juice could be fermented by itself.[22] Since the grapes were being pressed before fermentation, when they were still firm and slippery, the stems removed by the crusher-stemmer were often mixed in with the crushed grapes to facilitate the pressing. The juice from the press was then allowed to settle in order to remove the coarser solids, and fermentation would probably take place in a covered rather than an open tank such as was used for red wine.[23] Like the red grapes, the white grapes most in use were likely to develop very high sugars, so that if a dry wine was the aim water might be added to the must. Since this had the effect of diluting the acid as well, and since the acid was often too low to start with, the winemaker could add tartaric or citric acid to the must at this stage.[24] The inability of most wineries to control fermentation temperatures would have been especially damaging to white wines, the delicate flavors and aromas of which are greatly enhanced by cool fermentation. Because white wines are more subject to protein instability than red wines, tannin was sometimes added to the fermenting must to aid in clearing the resulting wine. White wines might also be stored in wood for some years—though long storage was not usual for any post-Repeal wine in California—further reducing their freshness and fruitiness. Pasteurization, which *was* usual in order to stabilize wines before bottling, had the same effect. The predictable result of these procedures was a wine more yellow or brown than white, flat rather than fresh, and without any desirable aroma or flavor. There is general agreement that whatever improvement in red wines may have been achieved in the years after Repeal, the improvement in white wines is still far greater—the starting point was so very low.

The laboratory control of all these procedures was, except in larger wineries that could afford the labor and equipment, pretty elementary. The law required the winemaker to possess a hydrometer to measure the sugar content of his musts and wines and an ebulliometer to determine the alcohol content of the finished wine; some small wineries may have managed with no more than this minimum.[25] Another possibility was for a number of small wineries to band together to provide a common laboratory, as did a group of Sonoma wineries in 1937; by this means they hoped "to obtain advice before something has gone wrong, rather than too late."[26] There were also independent laboratories that would undertake to do the routine work of analysis and control for wineries.[27]

Many of the larger wineries had distilleries devoted to the production of high-proof spirits used for their fortified wines.[28] The stills—invariably of the high-volume continuous mode of distillation—were fed with the pomace from the presses and with base wine from culls and other salvage from the vineyards, including table and raisin grapes. Wines infected by vinegar or other bacterial spoilage might also be distilled into neutral spirit.

The wine once in storage—almost always in vats, tanks, and ovals of large capacity rather than in small containers—would be racked and fined; that is, periodically drawn off from the accumulated sediments at the bottom of the tank and clarified by the addition of some agent. Bentonite, a volcanic clay, began to be used in place of such traditional fining agents as egg white and isinglass.[29] The wine was rendered perfectly clear by passing it through filters, coarse and fine. There was some use of centrifuges to clarify wine, too, particularly in order to make it fit for market at the earliest possible time.[30]

The question of aging wine in cask and in bottle hardly arose in California. The bulk sweet wines that were the staple of the trade could have benefited, no doubt, from proper aging, but there was little or no incentive to take such an expensive step in the process of winemaking. The handful of winemakers who aimed at producing a superior dry table wine might have had some small cooperage for their wines and probably understood the importance of aging. But how far the trade in general was from accepting this practice is vividly shown by the remarks of W. V. Cruess. In the first edition of his standard text, *The Principles and Practice of Wine Making* (1934), he makes no mention at all of the practice of aging in small cooperage. In the second edition (1947), he notes the practice in Bordeaux of aging wines in small barrels—as small as 50-gallon capacity—and pauses in passing to wonder whether the Bordeaux method might be "worthy of consideration" in California. He hastily adds a disclaimer: "I am not recommending that 220 liter casks (or for California the approximately equivalent 50 gal. barrel) be used for the aging of certain of our wines." But something smaller than the usual very large containers might, he suggested, be suitable for "very fine wines." Of course, he added by way of caution, there was "serious danger of development of an oaky flavor unless the casks used are thoroughly treated; or unless sound, old, previously used casks are employed."[31] More attractive at the time than the idea of long storage in barrels was the idea of rapid "aging"—a perennially seductive notion. Cruess listed, among other things that had been tried in California following Repeal, oxidation, pasteurization, cooking, refrigeration and aeration, and ultraviolet light.[32]

Rather than study the matter of aging their wines, the Californian producers spent much time and energy trying to attain perfect clarity. One good reason for this emphasis was doubtless the high incidence of unstable wines arising from defective methods: protein haze, tartrate deposits, metal pickup. Another reason was that wines were shipped to market so soon that they had had no chance to clear themselves. Cloudy wines, or wines with deposits of tartrate crystals at the bottom of the bottle, were automatically suspected of being spoiled, and so the winemakers had to devise methods to achieve a reassuring clarity. "The present domestic demand," as one writer put it, is for "wine of absolute clarity."[33] Hence the various forms of fining and of filtering, including, as L. K. Marshall wrote in 1937, some "hitherto untried methods," were much studied. Marshall added that "the thing has gone so far that I am afraid we are sacrificing the natural quality to the one standard that is set up today—that of clarity."[34]

When an unfortified wine was ready for shipment, it was likely to be pasteurized in bulk. This made the wine stable and secure against infections but at the cost of flavor and delicacy.[35] Most California wineries would not have bottled much or any of their production; that was the work of the regional bottlers. Only the larger enterprises could have afforded automatic bottling lines. These had already been developed for the soft drink trade, but they were expensive. Such bottling as was done would have been carried out mostly by a hand-operated siphon filler; the corks would be put in by hand. The bottles, which might well be secondhand, would also have been cleaned by hand before being filled. Labeling and packing, too, were likely to be done manually.

THE BASIC WINE TYPES

Since winemaking in California was now largely devoted to the production of three standard fortified wines—port, muscatel, and sherry—it is of some interest to know how such wines were made.

No planting of any grape actually used in authentic Port existed in California; port was therefore made from such grapes as Zinfandel, Mission, Mataro, Carignane, and Grenache. Any of these, when grown in the Central Valley, was likely to be low in both acid and tannin and high in sugar, desirable characteristics for keeping the wine sweet, alcoholic, and smooth.[36] Their color, however, might well be deficient, or unstable, or both. The juice of such grapes was fermented until it reached about 14 degrees Balling, then cooled and taken to the fortifying room where, under the eye of a federal gauger who guarded the revenue by supervising the measurements, high-proof brandy was added to the incompletely fermented must to raise it to 21 degrees of alcohol. This stopped further fermentation by killing the yeasts (most yeasts cannot live in a concentration of 16 or more degrees of alcohol), and since unfermented sugar remained, the wine was sweet.[37] To solve the problem of color, such grapes as Alicante Bouschet or Durif might be added at the crusher or their wines blended in later.

Muscatel was almost always produced from the Muscat of Alexandria, a raisin grape, rather than from any of the more distinctive muscat varieties, and was typically even sweeter than California port.[38] Though technically a white wine, muscatel was fermented on the skins in order to extract the maximum of the distinctive muscat flavor. It might also be fortified with a muscat brandy to intensify the sought-after taste. The popularity of the wine was such that a cooperative winery wholly devoted to its production—the Muscat Co-operative Winery—was founded in Kingsburg in 1935.[39] But the popularity of muscatel also meant that much of it was produced with only a minimum of muscat grapes, filled out with neutral varieties.[40]

California sherry—"the most important of California wines"—might be made from any grape.[41] Before Prohibition a wine so called might actually have come from Palomino or Pedro Ximenes grapes; after Repeal, given the degradation of the California vineyards, it probably came from Thompson Seedless or Flame Tokay grapes, or from any grape of an appropriately low acid, mixed in any proportion that might be convenient.[42] In fact, the only widely available grape for white wine—apart from muscat varieties—was the Thompson Seedless. The juice was typically fermented to dryness and then fortified, after which it was called sherry material, or shermat. It might or might not be given some age before the next step: heating the shermat in large closed redwood tanks—up to 30,000 gallons— at a temperature of approximately 125 degrees Fahrenheit or more for three to six months in order to oxidize the wine. As W. V. Cruess observed, the inventor of this method for the treatment of California sherry is not known to history, but whoever he might have been, he was "mixed up," for the method belongs to Madeira, not to Sherry.[43] In one method, the heating—or "baking"—process was achieved by heated coils in the tank; in another, the storage room itself was heated. The latter was the preferred method, since it avoided the caramelizing effect and the turbidity produced by hot metal in the wine, but it was more expensive and therefore not the standard. If a sweet sherry was desired—and most post-Repeal sherry was sweet—any white sweet wine might be added to it.[44]

These methods, for sherry and for the other sweet wines, were essentially those that

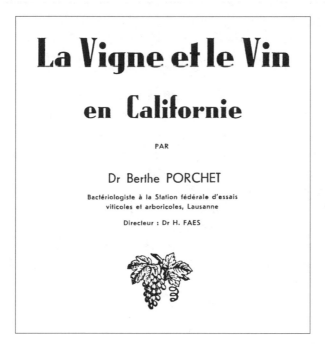

FIGURE 13

Title page of one of the earliest accounts of winemaking in post-Repeal California. Porchet spent the vintage season of 1936 in California and wrote admiringly of the state's fortified wines. (University of California, Davis, Shields Library.)

had been practiced before Prohibition, the only important difference being that before Prohibition there had been a somewhat better supply of appropriate grapes than there was after; there was perhaps a disposition to allow the wine to mature more slowly as well. According to H. H. Marquis, editor of the *Wine Review,* more study and experiment had been given to the production of sherry than to that of any other wine in California following Repeal. At the same time, he added, the results varied widely not only from district to district and from producer to producer, but within the produce of a single winery.[45] There were no agreed standards. Nor was there any resemblance between California's methods and those of Spain: both the *flor* yeast and the solera system were unknown here.[46]

The other familiar sweet wines from California were angelica and tokay. Angelica, which had been produced from the early days of winemaking in California (the name is supposed to derive from Los Angeles), was originally a *mistelle,* that is, a sort of cordial produced by adding brandy to an unfermented grape juice.[47] It was now merely a generic fortified white wine, made from any variety of grape by the usual procedures.

So too was tokay, which had never had any special identity in America, both the grapes and the procedures required for the genuine Hungarian Tokay being quite unknown. According to Maynard Amerine, California tokay was a blend of port, sherry, and a neutral white wine such as angelica, but as Frank Schoonmaker and Tom Marvel observed, in California "'Tokay' and 'Angelica' and 'White Port' come, as often as not, out of the same barrel."[48]

There was also some market for unfortified sweet wines, both red and white, which might be made by any of several methods; the preferred one was to add to a sound dry wine a dose of fresh grape juice or grape concentrate and then to pasteurize the result in order to prevent any further fermentation. Such wine could be sold below the price of a fortified wine because it contained no brandy, and it satisfied the taste for sweetness that seemed to dominate the American market.[49]

The results of California's winemaking methods were, at best, merely standard wines—that is, wines of a reliably consistent quality without distinction.[50] Since they went under names that did not describe them, they were bound to disappoint anyone who knew what those names in fact meant. At the same time, the mislabeling made it difficult to judge them on their own terms.

When winemaking methods were not at their best, the results might be deplorable. W. V. Cruess, who led the revived work in wine research at the University of California, noted after the 1934 vintage that many winemakers had not properly sulfited their wines, so that "tourne has been altogether too prevalent and has taken a very heavy toll this year."[51] It is strongly suggestive that two years later Cruess still felt it necessary to insist on the most elementary considerations. If California were to make better wine, he lectured the winemakers, then they would have to observe certain essentials:

> (1) Grow better and more flavorful grape varieties; (2) pick the grapes at a better degree of ripeness, not too ripe as is too often the case now; (3) transport them carefully and deliver them promptly in clean boxes; (4) conduct clean, sound fermentations at cool temperatures with pure yeast in the presence of SO2; (5) age the wines properly in proper cooperage for a *sufficient time;* and (6) do not market partially spoiled wines; instead, distill them, dump them, or make vinegar of them.[52]

The instruction available to California winemakers was certainly adequate, but the combination of indifference, or ignorance, with inadequate methods and equipment meant that unstable or downright spoiled wines continued to be produced in California throughout the '30s.[53]

In 1938, Maynard A. Amerine and E. H. Twight—both of the University of California, Davis—began a series of articles on California wine types in which, among other things, they compared the wines of each type as currently made in California with the equivalent wines made before Prohibition.[54] Their comparison developed into a sustained litany of lament for good things gone. Before Prohibition, one might buy a so-called claret derived from Cabernet, especially the Cabernet of the Santa Cruz mountains, that "would compare favorably with Bordelais wines"; "today," however, they wrote, "California Claret

FIGURE 14

French-born E. H. Twight, who taught wine to the viticulturists at the University of California, Davis, after Repeal. (From *Wines and Vines* 53 [May 1972]; reprinted with permission from *Wines and Vines*.)

is simply a good standard red wine and the name does not imply that it is made of any special variety."

As for port, there used to be good examples from the Fresno district made from the Trousseau grape. "The authors have tasted some marvelous preprohibition California ports which had been properly made and aged"; now, port in California was made from the wrong varieties, varied unpredictably in color, sugar, and acidity, and was insufficiently aged. The result was "cheap and common."

Angelica, which had been prized as a "smooth, very sweet delicately flavored, fortified wine" when made by the old methods and from Mission grapes, was now likely to have "foreign flavors" imparted by "cooking" it after the manner of California sherry, or to have a "raw alcohol flavor" from insufficient aging.

What, exactly, the wines called burgundy in California were, or ought to be, had never been agreed on. The best were blends. "We need only to turn back to the time prior to prohibition to find a number of blends which were splendid wines of this type. . . . the Refosco (Crabb's Burgundy) wine of the To Kalon Vineyard . . . the dark colored, heavy, but tart Saint Macaire wines; and the robust but superior and flavorsome wines of the

Tannat and Valdepeñas produced by the Stanly Estate." Now, they concluded, whatever the varieties used, they are often "grown under unfavorable conditions or permitted to become overripe so that the wine is too alcoholic, heavy, lifeless, and flat."[55]

HOW WINE WAS MARKETED

The main conditions affecting the marketplace—most of them bad—have already been discussed. Chief among them were the baffling and obstructive laws and regulations that sprang up in the anarchy of states' rights let loose by Repeal. As a result, in many places wine did not appear at all. In places where the demand for wine was weak, the demand remained weak.

Next in order of importance was probably the ignorance of the consumers. They were not likely to know more than the difference between red and white, even supposing that they thought of wine as an available commodity at all. As the inequality of distribution throughout the United States shows, there were many parts of the country in which, effectively, wine simply did not exist.[56]

The main markets after Repeal outside California were, as they had been before Prohibition, the urban centers of the country, particularly New York, Chicago, and New Orleans. Before Prohibition, much domestic wine had been sold from bulk containers: the buyer brought a jug or bottle to the liquor store or grocery and had it filled directly from the barrel. There is no question that this often meant that one got bad wine, kept too long, perhaps in an unclean container, and long gone flat through oxidation. There is no question, either, that wine sold thus was as cheap as it could be.[57] If the dealer knew what he was doing, the buyer might get good value. Otherwise, the chances were not good.

After Repeal this practice greatly diminished and ultimately disappeared. California persisted in allowing sales directly from the barrel at retail: in the first years of Repeal it was estimated that 90 percent of the wine sold in California came directly from the barrel.[58] But the method was generally seen as old-fashioned and, more often than not, as injurious to the trade, since it ran so many risks: substituted wine, spoiled wine, adulterated wine.[59] In most places, wine went out to the public in bottles neatly stamped and sealed to show that the makers had paid their taxes, a practice that greatly assisted the Bureau of Internal Revenue and no doubt helped the consumer to be sure that he was getting what he paid for. The trade, however, was not entirely pleased by this development. Wine in bottles, so it was said, was "a luxury product beyond the means of the average consumer" since the cost of glass had to be added to the costs of bottling machinery, warehousing, and transport.[60] These objections, however, did little to change the fact that bottled wine was now the rule.

The new regulations did not mean that bottling at the winery became the standard practice. Some wineries did take to bottling their own wines, but it meant an expensive investment in equipment, along with further expenses in warehousing and shipping. The

FIGURE 15
A San Francisco liquor store in 1934, the first year after Prohibition; note that the whole of one wall is given over to wine from the barrel. (From *Wine Review* 2 [October 1934]; reprinted with permission from *Wines and Vines*.)

few that took this path were called bottle-wine wineries, to distinguish them as a special class.[61] Few wineries, even those that did bottle some of their production, would have bottled all of it. Wineries that did no bottling at all might sell wine in bulk to wineries that did; such intrastate movement from winery to winery has always been an important part of the trade. As it had been before Prohibition, most California wine continued to be shipped out in bulk—the standard method was by 8,000-gallon rail tank car—to bottlers across the country.[62] The bottlers, who held federal permits to operate bonded wine cellars, then distributed the wine to their local markets, typically under their own brand names.

The pre-Prohibition practice was strengthened by the fact that a winery, if it wanted to sell its own wines outside the state in which they were produced, now faced a maze of regulations, varying from state to state and not only difficult but expensive to comply with. By undertaking to deal with all the licenses, fees, and procedures that might be required by the regulations in their own states and territories, the bottlers performed an essential service. And by promoting their own brands in their own territories, they provided the advertising for wine that the winemakers themselves were not yet ready to pay for.

When the wine at last reached the retail shelf, what the customer saw offered for his choice was an array of bottles labeled Bradshaw's California Sherry, or Old Castle California Claret, or Jovial Monk California Moselle, or something similarly generic and uninformative. A very few of the largest wineries could distribute wine regionally or nationally under their own labels because they could maintain warehouses and bottling establishments in the larger cities. Italian Swiss Colony and Roma did so, as did Fruit Industries, whose constituent wineries represented a large collection of recognized labels from the days before Prohibition, including Virginia Dare, Calwa (the old California Wine Association label), Guasti, and Aristocrat. But more often than not, even the wineries that had nationally distributed labels also sold large volumes in anonymous bulk: it was said that Roma wines, for instance, were sold under four thousand other names.[63]

Under this system there was hardly any way to promote quality or individuality.[64] The few good wines being made were scarcely to be found outside California or a very few metropolitan markets. The rest was standard wine, sold without any indication of the particular region where it was grown, the winery that made it, or the grapes it was made from. The largest of the New York distributors, the Eastern Wine Company, sold thirty different wine "types" from California sources under the brand name Chateau Martin: there were two grades, a red label at 48 cents a quart and a white label at 59 cents.[65] There was no particularization beyond that; nor could there have been, since the bottler would change his sources of supply according to the changes of the market.

At the same time, the association of California's wines with what was taken to be the ritual and the glamour of wine was routinely asserted. As one critic pointed out, there was entirely too much talk about "rare old vintages," "connoisseurs," and "fine wines," when what was wanted was a straightforward campaign in favor of simple, inexpensive wine to be used regularly and without pretense.[66] This failure has only grown worse with the passing years. It did occur to some that selling wine as a popular, uncomplicated drink might make sense. One idea, for example, that attracted some producers was the possibility of selling wine in cans, like soft drinks and beer. There was a brief flurry of interest in canned wine in 1935, but that idea did not catch on then, nor has it since, despite several renewed efforts.[67] Whether it would have helped to popularize wine may be doubted, but at least it assumed that wine could be sold without pretense.

The mislabeling of wine under European names continued after Repeal. How completely this practice dominated, to the exclusion of practically all local and varietal names, may be shown by the names of the wines entered in the first post-Repeal wine judging held at the California State Fair in 1934. The official categories included Haut Sauterne and Chateau Yquem. In the next year, Chianti, White Chianti, and Moselle had been added to the list.[68] Nor was it only the less scrupulous or merely industrial wineries that used such names. Cresta Blanca offered a St. Julien and a Margaux in the '30s; Beaulieu had a Pontet Canet; Concannon and Almadén both had Château Yquem.[69] When the Wine and Food Society of Los Angeles in 1941 drew up a list of fifty "distinguished" California wines, the entries read after this fashion: Fruit Industries Rhine Wine, Italian Vineyard Company Chablis, Wente Brothers Moselle, Concannon Chablis, Bohemian Banquet Claret, Beaulieu Burgundy.[70]

It was not only the use of purloined names that was objectionable. Perhaps even more important was the fact that wines bearing these names had no legal definition. A burgundy was imagined to be red, and a chablis white, but beyond that there was nothing to restrict the winemaker in what he used or guide him in what he aimed at. As one veteran winemaker, Louis Foppiano, remembered, "The red grapes—Zinfandel, Petite Sirah

FIGURE 16

How wine got to market from California; an advertisement from 1936. (From *Wine Review* 4 [June 1936]; reprinted with permission from *Wines and Vines*.)

and Carignane, with a little Alicante—were bottled either as Burgundy or Barberone. The difference was strictly in the color. You'd look at a tank of wine, and if it was heavy and dark it was Barberone."[71] As for white wines, if one was dry it might be called sauterne, but if a little sweetening were added then it could be a riesling—or the names could be reversed.

When Maynard Amerine and his associates at Davis analyzed the wines submitted to the California State Fair and the Los Angeles County Fair—the two established wine judgings in the state—for the years 1937–38, and the wines judged at the Golden Gate Exposition of 1939, they found, in effect, that none of the wine type names meant anything.[72] The entries of a wine called claret, for example, varied so greatly as to be incommensurable. One sample had 16 percent alcohol and 5 percent sugar! As for the general notion that clarets were lighter in color than burgundies, the lightest and the darkest wines that Amerine found were both called burgundy. "A consumer purchasing California burgundy or claret might get a smooth, very light-colored wine, resembling a *rosé,* or a year-old, violet-red Alicante Bouschet."[73]

If there was no discoverable standard uniting the wildly varying samples of a given wine type, there was, conversely, no way to separate the various wines called by different names: riesling, hock, moselle, and chablis might all be effectively indistinguishable. Some white wines were dry, some were slightly sweet, and some were very sweet. But one looked in vain for other reliably distinguishing characteristics. As for the red wines called burgundy, claret, and chianti, it was equally impossible to distinguish among them by any analytical tests. As Amerine temperately observed, in view of such uncontrolled variations and similarities, "the consumer has no way of knowing . . . what kind of wine he is getting except that it is red"—unless it happened to be white.[74]

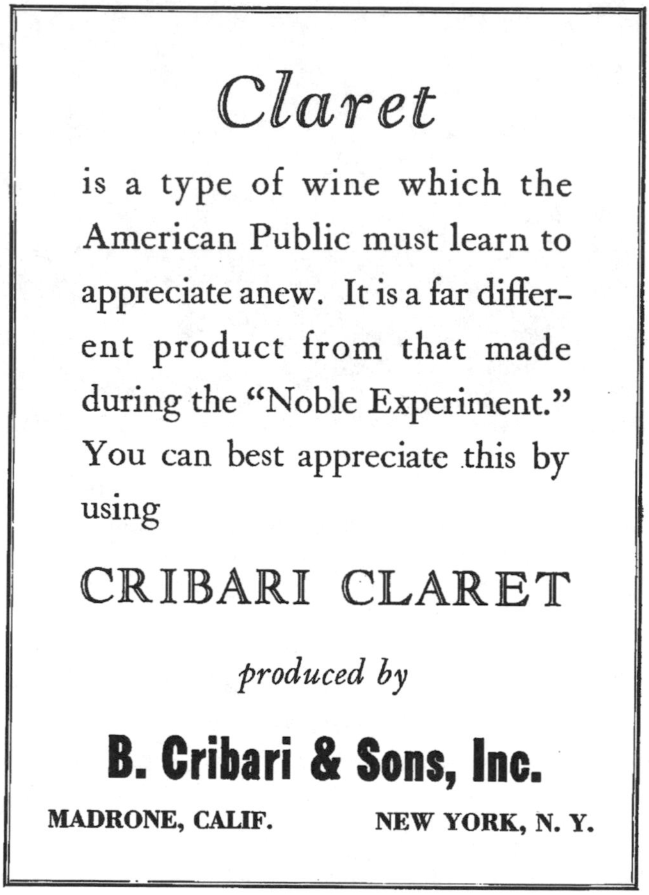

FIGURE 17

This advertisement from 1938 suggests that not much progress had been made yet toward educating the public about table wines. There was no standard for so-called claret, or for any other such mislabeled wines. (From *Wines and Vines* 19 [January 1938]; reprinted with permission from *Wines and Vines*.)

In response to this gaping hole in the regulations for American winemaking, the Wine Institute offered a set of descriptions that, under the circumstances, were as close as anyone could come. Thus, California claret was a "dry, rich red, medium-bodied wine"; Zinfandel was "a Claret-type wine made of the Zinfandel grape"; California burgundy was a "rich, generous, dark ruby-red wine, stronger in flavor, 'body,' and bouquet than California Claret."[75] The futility of such descriptions must be apparent—yet they could perfectly well be used today, since the law in this matter is still just what it was then.[76]

The situation into which the trade had been driven—or had chosen to go—was summed up at the end of the 1930s by Louis Petri, head of the rapidly growing Petri Winery. Good wines were blended into standard wines instead of being identified as special and sold accordingly. Conversely, poor wines were "salvaged" by being blended into sound wines at a rate of 5 percent or 10 percent per batch. No clear categories that allowed the buyer to distinguish between the ordinary and the superior existed; instead, all was confused and mixed in varying and unpredictable qualities.

Port made from Alicante, Angelica from Tokay strippings, Sauterne from Thompson Seedless should not be bottled with expensive labels and wrapped in fancy tissue paper and sold as high price and high quality wines. Such wines should be sold in tank cars and then to markets where only price is the factor. Then again, those who do have truly fancy wines should demand higher prices for these wines and not let such beautiful wines go for almost nothing in tank cars.

Today, the poor consumer cannot tell from the label or from the price whether he is getting the finest wine in California or the poorest bulk wine that ever was lucky enough to get by the minimum standards.[77]

The extent to which American wine failed to reimpose itself in the first years after Repeal is vividly clear from an anecdote in a letter to W. V. Cruess, the leading technical authority on wine in California, from one of his young assistants in the Fruit Products Laboratory at Berkeley, Emil Mrak.[78] Mrak had, for some reason, attended a convention of the American Medical Association in Cleveland, and wrote to Cruess about his observations there. Wine, he said, was practically unavailable in the convention hotels and at the banquets laid on for the doctors: they drank spirits exclusively, scotch if they could get it, bourbon if they couldn't. Mrak himself loyally ordered a glass of sauterne for dinner, though for 35 cents (worth something like $4 or more in 1936) he got only a three-ounce glass. "But that wasn't all—one drink and I almost lost my dinner—the wine was sour and full—just chuck full—of tourne. I can taste it yet. So goes the wine business."

The fact that one might get spoiled wine if one ordered it in restaurants partly accounts for the neglect of wine in American life. But only partly: the main reason would seem to be that many—perhaps most—Americans had very little familiarity with any wine at all, and practically none with American wine. Mrak's report about the indifference to wine even among such well-fed and well-traveled professionals as one would see at a gathering of American doctors is confirmed by other contemporary evidence. A glance at the catalogs of wine merchants and the wine lists of urban hotels shows that the American wine business, wherever it might have been going, had not gone very far: the sixty-four-page catalog of wines from the venerable S. S. Pierce of Boston for November 1935 lists no wine from California; the wine list of the Hotel Stevens in Chicago for 1936 has no American table wine; neither does the list of the Hotel Mayflower in Washington, circa 1937.[79]

The St. Regis Hotel in New York determined in 1935 that it would have the finest wine list in America and hired Julian Street, the author of *Wines: Their Selection, Care, and Service* and a director of the importing firm of Bellows and Company, to draw it up. Their existing wine list, the work of journalist "Baron" G. Selmer Fougner, did in fact contain a few American wines, but the first thing Street did was to get rid of these: they were sold off as carafe wines or otherwise disposed of.[80] The simple truth was that no American wine could possibly appear on a list determined to be of the finest wines exclusively.[81]

Even if a very few American wines might arguably have been good enough to qualify, the fact is that no one thought so then.

After the damage done by the locust years of Prohibition, it would have been unreasonable to expect that the American wine trade would at once be restored to health. And perhaps, in light of the conditions that they had to work under, the winemakers could not have done much otherwise than they did. These concessions, however, need not obscure the fact that much was wrong with the business.

5

COUNTERCURRENTS

THE WINE INSTITUTE

If much was wrong with American winemaking after Repeal, there were at the same time significant efforts under way to make it better—countercurrents that eventually turned the tide. One of these efforts took shape as the Wine Institute.

In 1932, as the prospect of Repeal began to seem not merely possible but probable, the Grape Growers League was created in order to work for the legalization of wine within the Volstead Act, or, more boldly, for Repeal itself.[1] When the passage of Repeal became certain but before it had been passed, the Grape Growers League, in September 1933, transformed itself into the Wine Producers Association. The group, under either name, was made up of the veterans of the trade: the Rossi brothers, A. R. Morrow, Sophus Federspiel, Georges de Latour, F. Cribari, Lee Jones, and others of the same standing. They represented the table wine tradition of California. The producers of fortified wines, largely concentrated in the Central Valley, organized on their own as the California Sweet Wine Producers in 1933, and so underlined a division of interests and a source of conflict that long operated in the state.[2] The first work of both groups was to cooperate in writing the National Recovery Administration code for the western wine industry.[3]

At the beginning of 1934, constitutional Prohibition had been lifted, but in its place stood a host of new problems in the forms already discussed in this history: new federal and state regulations, new taxes, and new requirements for compliance with all the inconsistent rules affecting interstate commerce; besides these burdens, there was an uninstructed public and an absence of clear standards for the production and labeling of wine.

In the face of such problems, the Wine Institute was created. Like all such developments, it could not be credited to a single inventor. The Wine Producers Association and the Sweet Wine Producers were the obvious ancestors. The immediate sponsor was the California Chamber of Commerce, under whose auspices a wine industry conference was convened at Monterey on 7 June 1934—the "industry" being understood to include winemakers, grape growers, glassmakers, label printers, machinery manufacturers, barrel makers, and all others whose services contributed to the making and selling of wine. On the motion of Robert Rossi, the convention voted to establish a committee to work toward the realization of the measures agreed to at the conference for the health of the trade.[4] This Statewide Vintners' Committee then set to work.[5]

After some months of conferences and inquiries, the Vintners' Committee called a meeting of the wine industry in Room D of the Clift Hotel in San Francisco on 20 October 1934.[6] The representatives of some fifty wineries came to the meeting to hear what was proposed.[7] The object was, like that of any trade organization, quite simple: to create the best possible conditions under which to produce and to sell the product—in this case, wine. The means devised to achieve this end was an organization to be called the Wine Institute. Its agenda, as outlined at the 20 October meeting, was as follows: to oppose adverse legislation and support the simplification of regulations; to have wine recognized as "a food product and temperance beverage"; to educate the public about wine; to sponsor research; and to keep its members informed.[8] The degree of emphasis on these different aims has shifted over the years, but the original statement of purpose still pretty closely describes the institute's program.

From this meeting the establishment of the institute was quickly carried through. Some thirty-two wineries signed on at once; a slate of directors was elected; the directors named officers at a meeting on 29 October; and the articles of incorporation were filed on 2 November.[9] The president—an honorary title—was A. R. Morrow.[10] The secretary (in fact the chief executive officer) was Harry Caddow, and the legal officer was Jefferson Peyser; both men were to serve for the rest of their working lives the organization they had helped found.[11] An office was found at 85 Second Street, San Francisco, an address shared at various times by the California Deciduous Fruit Growers Association, the California Vineyardists Association, the California Grape Products Company, Fruit Industries, A. R. Morrow, and the Association of Western Wine Producers. No other address is so rich in the history of American wine.[12]

The first, crucial task was to enlarge the membership. The original members, though they were stated to represent "about half of the wine production of the State," were numerically but a tiny fraction of the 654 bonded wineries then operating statewide.[13] The intended scope of the institute—at least in theory—was not limited to California but took in the whole of the United States: as the articles of incorporation put it, one of the institute's aims was to "promote a more enlarged and friendly intercourse between the business men engaged in the wine and grape growing industry of the United States." In fact, not much effort seems to have been put into pursuing this end; no winery outside California has ever

been a member of the institute, and the institute's publications take for granted that their reference is California. No doubt the officers would have welcomed members from any quarter, but it was hard enough to recruit the Californians. The Wine Institute has never come close to attracting all of California's wineries as members—partly because of the cost of membership, and partly because of the political conflicts of the trade, notably the differences between small and large producers and, especially in the early days, the differences between the sweet wine producers and the table wine producers.

The opening membership drive did, however, make significant progress. According to Ruth Teiser and Catherine Harroun, the work was given a boost first by Congressman Emanuel Celler, who urged banker A. P. Giannini to "be the Moses that will lead the grape and wine industry out of the wilderness" by taking a part in the institute.[14] Since Giannini's Bank of America was the main lender to the California wine industry, Giannini could easily enough have played Moses. He preferred, however, to work indirectly, which he did by urging prominent winemakers to join, with some success.[15] In his first annual report, dated August 1935, Caddow stated that the membership then stood at 188, representing more than 80 percent of American wine production.[16] Since then, membership has not fluctuated much above or below that level. The disproportionate representation of big wineries as opposed to small wineries among the members remained a problem. In 1942, for example, the institute calculated that 62 percent of the large wineries in California were members but only 9 percent of the small ones were.[17] The institute could, as it had from the beginning, proclaim that its members controlled the great bulk of the wine produced in the state, but it could not claim to speak for a wholly united industry: the indifferent, the reluctant, and the dissident always remained outside in significant numbers.

The work of the institute was paid for by a levy on the tonnage of grapes crushed by member wineries and on the wine sold: the original figure was 20 cents per ton of grapes, a fifth of a cent per gallon of table wine, and a quarter cent per gallon of fortified wine.[18] In the first seven months of the institute's operation, this scheme was sufficient to meet the $55,000 of expenses incurred. Caddow's report at the end of that period was, after the fashion of such things, more than a little self-congratulatory, but it did seem to show that the Wine Institute was making a difference. In the mere seven months of its active life, he said, the institute had already secured tax reductions and license fee reductions in a number of states, new permissions for bulk sales, and a reduction in federal regulatory red tape; work had begun toward educating the hotel and restaurant trades in wine sales and toward establishing a statistical service. The institute had also recommended minimum prices for wine grapes averaging some 15 percent higher than growers had received in 1934—this with an eye to recognizing the importance of the grower, "upon whom, as everyone knows, the welfare of the entire viticultural industry depends."[19] The effect of the institute's publicity work, Caddow concluded, was such that "where several months ago everything said publicly about our wine was bad, most of what is said nowadays is good."[20] All this, of course, was only a beginning. And it may be said here at once that, after nearly seventy years of public relations, lobbying, advertising, educating, and informing, the Wine Institute has succeeded only in somewhat mitigating, not in removing, the vexatious and arbitrary restrictions on the commerce of wine in this country. But that has been a highly necessary work: no other organization has had the persistence and the prestige to improve conditions even to the limited extent achieved by the Wine Institute.

One important development in which the Wine Institute took a special interest was that of new regulations for "standards of identity and quality for wine produced in California." This was the first step beyond the minimal standards defined by the Food and Drug Administration, which had so far been the only legal measure available for determining what might be called wine.[21] Since the Federal Alcohol Control Administration had not yet produced its own definitions for identity and quality, it was all the more important for California to come up with some enforceable rules. They were unveiled at the end of 1934 by the California Department of Public Health; the key rules prohibited the addition of sugar to the must (a practice allowed in the eastern United States) and required that wine calling itself *California* must be wholly from California-grown grapes. Maximum limits were set for volatile acidity, and minimum limits for total acidity.[22] There were strict provisions for enforcement too: winemakers could be required to submit samples to the Department of Public Health for analysis, and wine in violation of the rules could be confiscated and disposed of.

When these regulations came into force in April 1935, they produced quick results: within a month, 40,000 gallons of substandard wine had been confiscated, and much more voluntarily withdrawn from the dealers' shelves.[23] At the outset, the Wine Institute provided the money to pay the chemists who ran the necessary tests; the institute was then instrumental in obtaining an appropriation from the state to pay the expenses of inspection both at retail premises and at the wineries themselves. In Caddow's judgment, this was "the outstanding accomplishment of the united wine industry" so far.[24]

When the Federal Alcohol Administration produced its standards at the end of 1935, it allowed, as a concession to the conditions of eastern winemaking, the addition of sugar to the must and the blending of up to 25 percent of wine from other states into wine that would carry a geographical appellation.[25] In other words, a New York State wine, for example, could (and regularly did) contain up to 25 percent of California wine and still be legally identified as New York State wine. The Californians interpreted this to mean that a California wine, once it was shipped out of California, could also be so treated—that is, it might be blended with wine from other sources up to 25 percent of volume, and still be called *California*. The consequence was, as Louis Petri wrote in 1939, that the California wine trade was "suffering from the adulteration, stretching, and misbranding of our wines in other states."[26] To stop such practices, the Wine Institute got the California standards recognized by the federal authorities as covering all California wines in interstate commerce, a measure of which the California industry was particularly proud as a sign of its integrity in trade.[27]

THE RESUMPTION OF RESEARCH

Such standards as those prescribed by California and by federal authorities were highly necessary, but they could, after all, establish only the minimum levels of quality below which commercial wine could not be permitted to sink. To put the nation's renewed winemaking on the path toward producing wines of real quality, more would be required: better grape varieties and better practices in the vineyards, improved technical control in the wineries, a commitment on the part of the winemakers to the highest standards, and—the sine qua non—a public prepared to recognize quality and willing to pay for it. None of these necessary prerequisites existed in 1934, and their achievement would obviously be a work of time. One of the most important forces in making a beginning to that end was certainly the University of California, specifically the Division of Viticulture and Fruit Products in the College of Agriculture at Berkeley and Davis. The division went back to 1880, when work in viticulture and enology, supported by a special legislative grant and directed by the eminent Eugene Hilgard, dean of the School of Agriculture, was begun in order to serve the state's winegrowing industry. The passage of the Eighteenth Amendment put an end to enological work, but the division turned to the study of innocent "fruit products," which might include nonintoxicating uses of the vine. At the moment of Repeal it could at last return to the purpose for which it had been founded, and did. Shortly after this renewal, the division split its work in two, the enological work remaining at Berkeley under the Fruit Products Laboratory (later the Department of Food Technology), and the viticultural work being assigned to the branch of the College of Agriculture at Davis.[28]

The university, in fact, provided a good deal of such continuity in winegrowing knowledge as the state possessed. The senior member of the Division of Viticulture and Fruit Products was Frederic T. Bioletti (1865–1939), who got his start at Stanford's Vina Ranch and who had been hired at the university by Hilgard himself in 1889; he was to serve, with some interruptions, until his retirement in 1935. Bioletti (English-born despite his Italian name) was now an old man who could not provide much more than a symbolic link to a pre-Prohibition California.[29] The active and decisive power in the university department was a food chemist named William Vere Cruess, who had worked with Bioletti in enological research before Prohibition.[30] During the Dry years he studied such products as unfermented fruit juices, dehydrated fruits, and olive oil and produced a textbook on commercial fruit and vegetable products. He also had the doubtful distinction of having invented fruit cocktail. Now he at once picked up where he had left off and published, in 1934, *The Principles and Practice of Wine Making*. This was the first authoritative guide to the subject produced in America since before Prohibition, and it is fair to say that it embodies everything that was then known in this country about winemaking.[31]

Cruess did not confine himself to the laboratory but was an active and visible organizer and participant. The level of winemaking knowledge in California immediately following Repeal was so low, Cruess recalled, that drastic action was needed. To provide it, he led instructional sessions in winemaking up and down the state, sent out his staff to visit wineries, promoted meetings on technical subjects under university sponsorship, attended the trade meetings of wine producers, and wrote about all these things in the trade press as well as publishing technical papers of his own.[32] "Our services during the first four or five years" following Repeal, he thought, "have been our most important and useful."[33] He also gathered a set of young researchers around him who were to contribute importantly to the progress of California winegrowing toward new levels.[34]

Cruess's book marked a beginning. How urgently it was needed may be gathered from a well-known story told by Ernest Gallo. When he and his brother Julio determined to become winemakers, Ernest Gallo said, they knew about winemaking only what they had learned from seeing their father make wine in the basement of their home. There were no trained winemakers to be had for love or money in 1933, but the brothers did find two pamphlets by Professor Bioletti from the pre-Prohibition years, now in storage at the public library in Modesto. "These pamphlets were probably the difference between going out of business the first year because of an unsalable product, and what was to become the Gallo winery."[35] More comprehensive and advanced instructions for winemakers in Cali-

FIGURE 19
William Vere Cruess, head of the Fruit Products Division at the University of California, Berkeley, undertook to teach winemaking to the new California wine industry. (Department of Food Science and Technology, University of California, Davis.)

fornia were later provided in the work of two younger university researchers, Maynard Amerine and Maynard Joslyn.[36] Between 1940 and 1941 they produced three bulletins on the production of table wine, dessert wines, and brandy that became at once the standard texts for California and that rest in part on research carried out by the university after Repeal.[37]

Winemakers who took the trouble to study and to apply the information in these university publications would have moved at once to the front line of enological practice—far in advance of the standards that still characterized the industry and that continued to prevail for years yet. Discouragingly few winemakers appear to have taken any advantage of the help offered them. The Department of Viticulture and Enology at Davis (to give it the name it now has) was not wholly disregarded. It acquired a new building designed expressly for its work in 1939. With its fermentation rooms, aging and bottling rooms, sherry room, distillery, brandy storage, and laboratory, the building was an investment in wine research without precedent in this country.[38] But only the year before, a writer in *Wines and Vines,* after reporting enthusiastically on the research program at Davis, added by way of conclusion, "It is a pity that this work being done at Davis has been so generally ignored by many of the people whom it is benefiting and whom it will ultimately benefit."[39] The inertia to be overcome was heavy, and the apparent failure of the trade to respond was deeply frustrating to the people who could see a better way. Amerine himself said that, after thirty years of apparently unregarded work, he would have left the university for the "right biochemical job" if one had been offered to him, so complete was the apparent indifference toward his work on the part of winemakers in California.[40] Why bother to go on with a labor that had so little effect? No doubt some of the reluctance of the California winemakers to listen to the university men came from the immemorial suspicion of the practical worker for the theorist, a suspicion always especially strong when the work is close to the soil, as winemaking is.[41] The poverty of the Depression years was also a reason: applying good ideas often costs money, and few people had much money. Nevertheless, the instruction and advice of the university researchers was having its effect: the preparation was long and often invisible, but the results in the end were powerful.

One of the renewed activities at the university went back to the very beginnings of viticultural and enological research in California: this was the program of evaluating the different varieties of grapes and their wines on a regional basis, continuing work begun under Hilgard in the 1880s.[42] The state was divided into five viticultural regions on the basis of heat summations. The normal growing temperature for the grape begins at 50 degrees Fahrenheit. The heat summation for a particular region is arrived at by taking the average daily temperature in excess of 50 degrees Fahrenheit during the growing season (1 April to 31 October): the total gives the degree days for that region. Thus a day that ranged from 60 to 90 degrees would yield 25 heat units. At one extreme, the Central Valley around Bakersfield, where the heat summation totals over 4,000, belongs to the hot climate of region V. At the other, Los Carneros in Napa and Sonoma Counties, where the heat summation does not exceed 2,500, belongs to the cool climate of region I. This scheme has since been much criticized, largely on the ground that single-element indicators—in this case temperature—are not adequate to describe the complexity of the problem, which requires such things as length of day, daily temperature ranges, solar radiation, soil moisture, latitude, and any number of others to be taken into consideration. But such objections are not very much to the point: the scheme was meant to provide a beginning, and it did.

Hilgard had analyzed wines from many different varieties of grapes grown in regions all over the state in the 1880s and 1890s, but without exact information about climatic variations. The fact that wines made from grapes grown around Sonoma and wines from the same variety of grape grown around Fresno were very different was of course well known in California. But it was known only in a very general way. On the basis of the newly established classification by heat summation, it was now possible to relate variations in the character and qualities of wines from different grape varieties to the regions in which the grapes were grown. The quality factors analyzed to show the effects of climate included

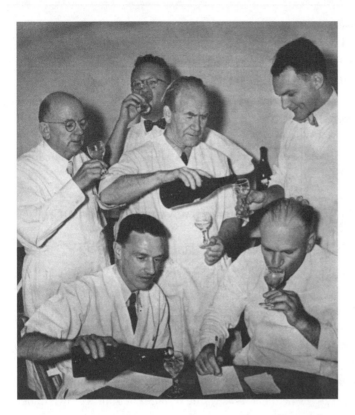

FIGURE 20

The experts who guided the re-created wine industry after Repeal, shown here as judges at the California State Fair in 1938. *Standing, from left:* Louis Wetmore, prominent in the pre-Prohibition wine industry; Maynard Joslyn, chemist in the Fruit Products Division, Berkeley; W. V. Cruess, head of the Fruit Products Division; Maynard Amerine, enologist at Davis. *Seated, from left:* George Marsh, chemist in the Fruit Products Division; A. J. Winkler, viticulturist and head of the department at Davis. Wetmore and Cruess were a link to pre-Prohibition days; Joslyn, Marsh, and Winkler began their work under Prohibition; Amerine was the first new researcher appointed after Repeal. (From *Wines and Vines* 20 [January 1939]; reprinted with permission from *Wines and Vines.*)

the sugar-acid ratio, total acidity, and tannin content. But Maynard Amerine and A. J. Winkler, who carried out this long labor of evaluation, went beyond such conventional analyses by submitting each wine sample to taste testing (or in technical terms, "organoleptic examination").[43] By themselves and with the help of their associates they accumulated thousands of tasting notes to give practical meaning to their analytic data.

In order to obtain uniform samples for analysis, Amerine and Winkler made their own wines, in small lots of five gallons each: the small lots were necessary in order to manage a great many samples, and because a grower would willingly let the Davis men have the required hundred pounds or so free, at a time when they had little money to support their work. In order to get their grapes, they went into the field themselves:

> We would go in the evening to San Jose, pick grapes at five o'clock in the morning and have them here [Davis] at four in the afternoon, crush them, and take care of the other lots that were fermenting, and the next morning at five o'clock go to Napa and pick grapes. This went on for a period of six or eight weeks. Every fall, '35, '36, '37, '38, '39, '40, '41.[44]

By 1939 they had made some 3,000 sample lots of five gallons each.

The first fruits of the project were gathered in the bulletin published in 1944 by Amerine and Winkler, ponderously titled, after the fashion of official publications, "Composition and Quality of Musts and Wines of California Grapes." In this report we learn, for example, that Cabernet Sauvignon wines from regions I, II, and III were "distinctive in aroma, full flavored, soft, well balanced, excellent in quality." But Cabernet wines from regions IV and V were "deficient in acid, and therefore flat, lacking in freshness, and not delicate in aroma."[45] Such general remarks were sustained in detail by analytic reports on many samples of Cabernet wines from all regions of California over a period of five years. Comparable analytic reports were given for the wines from dozens of other grape varieties. Some were recommended for particular regions; some were given limited recommendation; many were not recommended; and others were simply identified as "not fully tested." The comprehensiveness combined with the analytic detail of this bulletin make it one of the important contributions to the history of winegrowing in California—a landmark work.

Although the full report of the work of Amerine and Winkler was not published until 1944, many of their conclusions were available in the interim, supposing that anyone wished to make use of them.[46] Amerine and Winkler revisited growers whose grapes they had used to report on the results; they also issued many individual invitations to try their experimental wines, and on at least two occasions there were general gatherings of winemakers at Davis to sample what was being done. Winkler especially was tireless in proclaiming the need to plant good grapes.[47] When this was done, he wrote, California could produce not merely good table wines but what he called "festive wines," wines that were the "properly made products of the better and really fine varieties of grapes grown under suitable soil and climatic conditions."[48]

Amerine and Winkler's recommendations were not final, nor did they pretend to be. They were unenthusiastic about Zinfandel, for example, because they considered it to be often planted in the wrong places and "too much planted now."[49] They did not recommend such Italian grapes as the Nebbiolo (it was not sufficiently productive to warrant planting in the conditions of California at that time), or such Bordeaux grapes as the Malbec, which they regarded as promising but too problematic to be recommended: "other varieties have equal or greater potentialities."[50] These grapes—and others not particularly recommended by Amerine and Winkler—have their champions in California, who persist in working with them despite the recommendations of the university. And who knows what ultimately might be done with them? Amerine and Winkler did not legislate on such matters but simply offered their evidence, tentative as it might be, along with their opinions. And their work certainly made clear in objective form the mistake of attempting to squeeze good dry wine from Zinfandel grown in a region V vineyard, or interesting white wine from a once-popular variety such as Burger no matter what region it might be grown in. On the other hand, it drew attention to the virtues of a high-acid variety like Barbera for the production of a well-balanced wine in the hot Central Valley. Such observations are now taken for granted; but they had to be established by long and detailed study. Nor is the work in any sense complete. By such painstaking means are we brought a little nearer to that ideal condition, never to be attained, in which the right grape is grown in the right place.

Work on the breeding of new varieties had begun even before Repeal in 1931, when the university established a grape breeding project directed for many years by Professor H. P. Olmo. Over the next fifty years some 300,000 individual experimental vines were produced. From this number only a handful have been selected for commercial propagation.[51] The aim of this project was mainly to develop varieties combining high productivity with superior fruit quality—that is, in California terms, wine grapes suited to the Central Valley. Other programs sought to develop varieties resistant to the many pests and diseases of the vine, including Pierce's disease and phylloxera. Useful results from this sort of genetic lottery are few and unpredictable, however, and it was many years before the work with new crosses contributed anything to winegrowing.[52] Even now, no new grape developed in California has established an important place for itself in American viticulture, with the exceptions of Rubired and Ruby Cabernet.[53] This is not at all surprising, and it reminds us of how long a view the patient people engaged in the production of new varieties must take. The astounding new techniques of genetic manipulation may change all this and rapidly bring in new generations of wonder grapes; but that has not yet happened.

One modest leverage that the university could apply in trying to lift the industry to a higher level of quality was through wine judgings, which were reestablished at the California State Fair in Sacramento beginning in 1934. The work of organizing the judging was in the hands of W. V. Cruess; in the first year of the renewed judging, Professor Bioletti and Frederick Flossfeder, formerly on the Davis faculty, awarded medals to the Beringer, Concannon, Beaulieu, Wente, and Cresta Blanca wineries, among others.[54] For a few years afterward, most of the wineries with any pretension to quality entered their wines; the competition then lost some of its attractive power, but not before it had served to bring to notice some of California's best.

Cruess also had the idea of establishing statutory quality grades for commercial wines, on the analogy of the grades used for such things as canned peaches, or olives, or walnuts. As there were Fancy, Choice, Standard, Second, and Pie grades for canned peaches, why not Fancy, Choice, Standard, Second, and Distilling Material grades for wines? These grades would be applied by a state inspection service and printed on the containers, so consumers would know just what they were getting and would pay accordingly.[55] The idea, though perfectly sound in itself, seems—unsurprisingly—to have met with no success.

In these years the only other institution carrying on research work of interest to the wine industry was the New York Agricultural Experiment Station at Geneva, in the Finger Lakes district. The wine research of the New York station, like that at the University of California, went back to a time long before Prohibition, and was now renewed. Work in New York had concentrated especially on viticulture and on grape breeding, since the quest for improved varieties—cold resistant, disease resistant, more productive, and better-

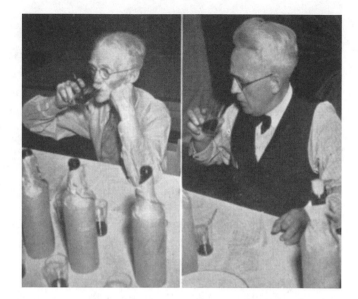

flavored—was the clear priority for the East, made all the more urgent by the great increase in Concord plantings during Prohibition. Unluckily, the emphasis in New York at
that time was mostly on table grapes rather than wine grapes. The Geneva station also
undertook research into the problems of wine production for New York and the East.[56]

THE IDEA OF QUALITY

The immediate task of the scientists at Davis and Geneva was to bring American winemaking to that point of technical competence at which it could produce good, sound, reliable wine. At the time, it seemed to many that they were aiming too high, reaching after a standard of technical control that was neither necessary nor desirable. Later, after
their lessons had been well learned, the scientists came in for the opposite criticism: they
had aimed too low, and were interested only in sound commercial wine rather than in
the lofty goal of a great wine to be achieved by an art beyond technology. That judgment
is of course quite unfair, even foolish: the scientists did the job that it was absolutely necessary for them to do and that would not otherwise have been done. Still, one may wonder about those difficult years following Repeal: Did the ideal of making not just wine,
but really good wine, survive? And if so, how and where?

Before Prohibition, there were more than a few winemakers who were determined,
even fanatical, in their pursuit of the highest quality. One may mention the Gundlach-
Bundschu winery in Sonoma, whose Bacchus brand of Riesling had the highest reputation; Fountaingrove, in Santa Rosa, showed what could be done with Zinfandel; in Napa,
Hiram Crabb at the celebrated To-Kalon vineyard and Tiburcio Parrott on Spring Mountain made Cabernets of distinction; in Livermore, the Mont Rouge Winery excelled in

both red and white wines; and, to complete this circle around the San Francisco Bay, La Questa Vineyard in the hills of San Mateo County and Mira Valle Winery on Monte Bello Ridge enjoyed a high prestige for wines of impeccable style. The wines from such producers as these, though we cannot know them directly now, were certainly excellent things, deservedly admired and sought after.

Not one of the superior producers survived the Prohibition years unscathed. Most did not survive them at all. Fountaingrove persisted, but in a small way; the tradition of fine winegrowing in Sonoma County was all but obliterated. In San Mateo County, La Questa Winery reopened but survived only a few years. In the Napa Valley, only four wineries with any tradition of excellence were still in operation after Repeal: Beaulieu, Inglenook, Beringer Brothers, and Larkmead. Beaulieu, founded in 1900 by Georges de Latour, had stayed busy during Prohibition through its extensive business in altar wines and had managed to maintain its vineyards of fine varieties more or less intact, but its equipment and procedures were old-fashioned and in some respects primitive.[57] Inglenook, the splendid property created after 1879 by the Swedish-German sea captain Gustave Niebaum, had simply vegetated during Prohibition. It now resumed the production of wine from its own vineyards but found so little demand for wine under its own label that some of the production was sold off in bulk.[58] Beringer, established in 1875 by two brothers from the German Rhineland, showed even more clearly the ravages of Prohibition: its vineyards had been largely grafted over to the inferior shipping varieties that home winemakers preferred, so that the winery could now make only standard blends. And Beringer quickly followed the market's turn from dry to sweet wines from 1934 onward. The wines that Beringer bottled under its own name thus had little of the distinction that had marked its pre-Prohibition wines; in any case, most of what Beringer now made was sold anonymously in bulk.[59] The Larkmead Winery—the property of the Swiss family Salmina—like so many other wineries that had produced wine during Prohibition found on Repeal that the wine it had kept so long in storage was now above the legal limit for volatile acidity. Much of the new wine that Larkmead made was blended with the old "pricked" wine and sold off in bulk, and for several years this process did not leave much over for sale under its own name.[60]

Such was the condition of the best-known producers of quality wine in the Napa Valley. There was a tiny market for bottled wines from a few Napa wineries, but the Napa Valley, in common with every other wine-producing region of California, by and large depended on the bulk wine trade.[61] Nor was it any better elsewhere. The number of acres planted to superior varieties in all of California was a minute fraction of the whole. The number of ambitious and experienced winemakers who were in a position to aim at excellence could be counted on the fingers of one hand; and the market for what these few made from the small supply of good grapes available was tiny indeed. André Tchelistcheff estimated that Beaulieu was selling only about three thousand cases of its bottled wines in each of the years 1935 and 1936; the rest went out in bulk.[62] Evidently, the material basis for the production of quality wine had shrunk almost to the vanishing point in California.

The material basis is of course necessary. But what is also necessary is an educated demand. Wine of quality is, after all, not a matter of mere specification: so much acid, so much sugar, a phenolic content of such-and-such compounds, a pH of a certain figure. Nor is the pattern of a fine wine laid up in some unchanging platonic sphere. Fine wine— the idea and the embodiment both—is instead a sort of complex historical institution that is not created at a stroke but grows through a combined effort, often in unpredictable ways. What is "good," in wine or in any other valued thing, is good only because producer and consumer both agree upon what is wanted and, after sufficient experience, agree that the thing wanted has in fact been achieved. Only at that point can the laws of *appellation contrôlée* be written, because only then can we know what varieties, what cultivation practices, what yields, and what winemaking methods are agreed to be desirable. Nor is such an ideal ever fixed: the great Bordeaux, Burgundy, and Rhine wines produced at the end of the twentieth century are still recognizably Bordeaux, Burgundy, and Rhine, but they are not the same as the wines of those names in the eighteenth or nineteenth centuries. That is why we can say that fine wines are an institution, changing and adapting to new conditions, but nonetheless retaining an identity. In the United States in the 1930s, there simply was no effective idea of what the fine wines of the country might be, or ought to be. There were the great European types to refer to; but what relation could or should American wines have to them? And what were the possibilities for a distinctive identity, for an American wine?

All this is to say that American winemakers badly needed an interested group of American wine drinkers who would respond to what was being done and provide a reason to do things better or differently. There were some faint stirrings in that direction, but so small at the outset that one can detect them only in hindsight: they must have been quite unnoticed at the time.

The flurry of books about wine already glanced at in the beginning of chapter 3 might have been a hopeful sign: writing about wine implies that there are people who like to read about it, people who may be (but not necessarily are) interested in drinking it too. But those (mostly bad) books had no successors. After the first year of Repeal, no book on American wine was published in the 1930s.[63] Nor did the magazines take it as a subject. *House and Garden,* alone among American magazines, published an occasional article on wine in the 1930s, but not on American wine. The literature of wine in this country was confined to the promotional ephemera put out by the wineries themselves and to a handful of technical bulletins.[64]

At the end of 1933, the great Anglo-French gourmet and writer André Simon, having lost his job as the English agent for the Champagne house of Pommery, founded with the versatile A. J. A. Symons the Wine and Food Society of London.[65] The repeal of Prohibition shortly thereafter made an opportunity not to be neglected for the new society, and Simon accordingly traveled to New York in November 1934 to promote civilized eating, the familiar use of wine, and, not incidentally, the Wine and Food Society. Interestingly enough, Frank Schoonmaker and Tom Marvel appear to have anticipated Simon by projecting a wine society that should make American wines its particular interest. They must have decided that there was not room for two groups and stepped aside in favor of Simon—who was *not* particularly interested in American wines but who kept an open mind.[66] Simon met an indifferent reception in New York. But how could it have been otherwise? For, as he wrote,

> The men and women in their early thirties to-day have grown up in the foul air of deceit, gangsters and bath-tub gin. The hip-flask was the god of their youth. How can they be expected to turn to the shrine where Bacchus holds his court? They like hard liquor better. They preface what is to be dinner with a few "old-fashioned" cocktails and come to table in a semi-dazed condition, not wanting any food, but craving for cigarettes, which poison the air for their fellow-guests and burn holes in the hostess's best table-cloth. Wine to them, in their state, is nauseating; they want a high-ball or something with a kick in it. They are beyond reform as beyond civilization altogether.[67]

But from Boston on he was well received, and by the time Simon returned to England, chapters of the Wine and Food Society had been founded in Boston, Chicago, San Francisco, Los Angeles, New Orleans, and, after all, New York. These organizations, small but elite and glamourous, made a beginning in the development of connoisseurship in America. Simon himself, on his return to England, published a brief article on "Californian Wines" in the society's journal, *Wine and Food*.[68] At its third meeting, in October 1935, the New York branch of the society presented a tasting of American wines at the Savoy Plaza hotel—the sort of publicity that American wines can only rarely have had.[69] In the next year, the San Francisco branch of the society, not to be outdone, presented a tasting of California wines to some four thousand guests, "most of them epicures and socialites."[70] So there began to be a small but articulate response to the thin trickle of good wine produced in America. Another group, formed in 1939 by the indefatigable Leon Adams at the suggestion of Maynard Amerine, was called the Society of Medical Friends of Wine and based in San Francisco. The public enhancement that such a group might lend to American wine needs no comment. The society continues to flourish, having achieved its 227th quarterly dinner meeting at the end of 2004. Even more gratefully to be noted was a slight augmentation of the ranks of that small, saving remnant of wineries dedicated to quality. In 1936 Martin Ray bought Paul Masson's old La Cresta estate and began to make wines with the highest ambitions for distinction; and in 1940, seven years after he began construction of the winery near St. Helena, Louis M. Martini released the first of his Napa Valley wines, vintage-dated and varietally labeled.[71]

DRIFTING TOWARD THE ROCKS

All the efforts so far discussed in this chapter were not enough to arrest the drift of the wine trade in California toward shipwreck. The figures tell a clear story: 1934 was a year of bad weather in the California vineyards, so that neither the grape crop nor the volume of wine produced was very large. In the next year, however, the weather was favorable and California's vineyards produced a bumper crop—an act of God, no doubt, but distinctly troublesome to growers and winemakers. Wine production leaped from the 37 million gallons of 1934 to nearly 66 million gallons in 1935; but there was not yet enough storage capacity in the rebuilding wineries to provide a home for all the grapes. The season was late as well, so that growers had to sell in a rush. In such a buyer's market, the growers received what were called "pitiful" or "ruinous" prices, an average of $10 a ton, well below anyone's cost of production.[72] But the winemakers fared no better, since consumption did not keep pace with production, and the prices of wine went down just as did the prices for grapes.

In 1936, spring frosts reduced the crop and took a little pressure off the market. Some 494,000 tons of grapes were crushed in 1936, as contrasted to 887,000 tons in 1935; wine production sank from 66 million gallons to 47 million; and the price of grapes rose from the pitiful $10 a ton to about $17. Then disaster struck in the form of two consecutive bountiful harvests—a familiar paradox in the 1930s, when men struggled to cope with abundance in the midst of destitution. The crop in 1937 was the largest in the history of California—2,454,000 tons—and that was followed by an even larger crop in 1938—2,531,000 tons.[73] At the same time, the export market for raisins, always an important element in the economy of the California grape trade, was shrinking in response to approaching war.[74] That meant even more pressure on the wineries to take care of the crop. But the wineries had neither the room nor the markets to handle this flood of grapes. Wine production in 1937 had set a record at more than 91 million gallons, and the inventories of wine in the state had swollen to 114 million. Prices went down to 20 cents a gallon for fortified wines, to 8 cents for dry red wine. In 1938, some thirty-three California wineries, representing a storage volume of nearly 2.5 million gallons of wine, went out of business.[75] Clearly a crisis was at hand.[76]

It was to be a recurring crisis, arising in the first place from the overplanting of grapes in the Prohibition years and now intensified by the slow markets of the Depression years. The surplus crop was the chief headache of the trade, and much ingenuity and experiment went into trying to find a remedy. The surplus was never in wine grapes but always in raisin grapes—which meant almost exclusively Thompson Seedless. But the big industrial-scale winemakers of the Central Valley were also industrial-scale grape growers who made little or no distinction between one sort of grape and another. This was a new thing. Earlier crises—the collapse of prices in the early 1890s, for example—had affected the wine trade and the growers of wine grapes specifically. Now the problem was an excess of grapes that were not properly wine grapes at all but that had, for better or worse, become the staple of the bulk trade in fortified wines. The growers of wine grapes and the makers of table wines would gladly have turned their backs on the whole untidy scene, but they seemed inextricably entangled with their errant brothers: the price of grapes anywhere in the state was always affected by the large crops of the Central Valley, and the price of grapes in turn affected the price of wines.

In 1938, the California Agricultural Prorate Act provided a stopgap measure. It allowed the growers, if they could secure a two-thirds majority, to create a marketing plan under the supervision of a state-appointed committee. The plan was to convert a large part of the perishable grape crop into long-lived brandy, which could then be stored until a satisfactory market was found for it. After a campaign led by the Wine Institute, the necessary majority was achieved in an election in July 1938 by a landslide vote of five to one in favor of the measure. All earlier efforts to get stabilization schemes accepted had failed, but the need for action was now felt to be urgent. About seven thousand growers and 250 wineries were included.[77]

There had been conflict, however. From the point of view of the coastal growers and the table wine producers, the problems of the industry were largely created by the Central Valley growers and by the winemakers who served them or who were a part of the growers' operations. In salvaging their table-grape culls and excess raisin grapes they had created the surplus and, worse, created a surplus of indifferent wine.[78] Since the makers of table wine had a market for their product and saw no surplus of the grapes they used, the measure seemed most unjust to them: "Prorate plan," the lawyer for one group of growers wired President Roosevelt, "contemplates almost confiscation of forty five percent of dry wine grapes to be converted into brandy on false premise that there is dry wine grape surplus. No such surplus exists."[79] There were attempts to kill the loan from the Reconstruction Finance Corporation that would make the plan work, and there were unavailing suits against the prorate scheme itself.[80]

Despite the sometimes bitter opposition, the plan went into operation. Each grower, if he wished to sell his crop, had to deliver 45 percent of it to the Control Commission for distillation into beverage brandy or high-proof spirits, which would be kept off the market until such time as it might be sold at acceptable prices. The rest of the harvest could be sold to wineries at a guaranteed minimum price—the real object of the plan. More than 350,000 tons of that year's grape crop were converted into brandy by this so-called set-aside scheme, producing a pool of 9.25 million gallons of brandy and 4.5 million gallons of high-proof spirits. The work was administered by a corporation invented for the purpose, called the Grape Growers Products Association, and was financed by loans from the federal Reconstruction Finance Corporation and the Bank of America.[81]

The scheme worked: the diversion reduced that year's wine production to about 57 million gallons, some 35 million gallons less than that of the year before. The brandy that went into storage was ultimately sold, and though payment was deferred, the people who had grown the grapes and distilled the wine at last received an acceptable price for it. Such smooth statements, however, often conceal a great deal of irregularity and injustice. The final payments on the brandy pool were not made until 1948, and by that time many growers, especially Japanese American growers who had been interned during the war, could not be found.[82]

Opinions vary on whether the brandy in this vast pool was any good. According to Peter Valaer, a chemist with the Internal Revenue Service, the brandy was made "under certain definite requirements such as lower proof distillation, better distilling material, and the exclusive use of new plain barrels, all tending to produce a better grape brandy than ever before."[83] Maynard Amerine, however, who was on the official committee charged with approving the different batches of prorate brandy, had a different recollection: many were defective, he recalled, having been distilled by people "who had never distilled before."[84] James Riddell agrees with Amerine's recollection: "the general quality of the brandy was rather poor. . . . Large quantities of brandy were redistilled and again put away for aging because the original quality was not satisfactory."[85] Much of the prorate pool of brandy was bought by whiskey distillers, who converted it to neutral spirit and used it in blended whiskies.[86] But Otto Meyer, who spent "four or five months" tasting each lot in the pool, found enough decent brandy there to start The Christian Brothers in the brandy business.[87]

The prorate scheme had been a desperate scramble to avert disaster, not a permanent solution; indeed, it operated only for a year, so strong was the opposition to it.[88] Another measure was the invention of a Vintners' Trade Council in 1938, on the initiative of the Wine Institute under the authority of the California Unfair Practices Act. The act made it unlawful to sell wine below cost, and the Vintners' Trade Council was formed in order to enforce the law.[89] In order to determine what costs actually were, a survey was made, with interesting results. The survey determined that the production cost (exclusive of federal and state taxes) of California wine made in the vintage of 1937 ranged from 36.09 cents to 47.54 cents per gallon for fortified wines; from 18.36 cents to 24.67 cents for dry red wine; and from 20.98 cents to 36.93 cents for dry white wine—to put this in the simplest terms, it cost only 5 cents to make a bottle of California red wine at the top of the price scale.[90]

Before the harvest of 1939 came about—it, too, threatened to be a big one—new measures to stabilize the wine industry were initiated by certain winegrowers acting on their own—or under direction of their banks—rather than through state or federal legislation.[91] There were dark prophecies that grapes would fetch only $3.50 to $5 a ton, which would mean ruin for everyone. In the face of this emergency, the bankers and a group of Central Valley producers formed a co-op called Central California Wineries, Inc., to act as an agent for its members in buying grapes and in holding as inventory the wine made from them; the wine could then be sold in "orderly" fashion.[92] The model was evidently the old California Wine Association (CWA), formed in the economic crisis of the early 1890s to control the California wine market by near-monopolistic domination. There would be no undercutting of prices if buyers had only one source to go to. The money power behind the new corporation was the Bank of America, which preferred working with a big strong group in command of the trade instead of attempting to shore up many small producers or foreclosing a great number of depreciated properties.[93] The role of the Bank of America in all this was made plain by the appointment of Burke Critchfield, a vice president of the bank, as general manager of Central California Wineries: he had not left the bank but had, rather, been loaned to see that the bank's interest was well managed.[94]

Throughout the **WINELAND** of **AMERICA**

Scattered throughout the great wine producing sections of the state—each famous for its own individual types of grapes and each distinguished by its own character of wines—are the producing and aging plants of CCW's member wineries. Of course, you will readily recognize their names:

Acampo Wineries and
    Distilleries, Inc.
Acampo
Alta Winery and
    Distillery
Dinuba
Bisceglia Brothers
    Wine Co.
Wahtoke
*Central Winery
    Greystone Cellars
    St. Helena
*Central Winery, Inc.,
    Kingsburg Plant
    Kingsburg

Colonial Grape
    Products Co. of
    Calif.
Elk Grove
Crest View Winery,
    Inc.
Clotho
DaRoza Winery
Lodi
Earl Fruit Co.
Delano
Franzia Bros. Winery
Ripon
Frasinetti Winery
Florin
Fresno Winery, Inc.
Clovis
Eugenio Morello
Kerman
Italian Vineyard
    Company
Guasti
Mount Tivy Winery,
    Inc.
LacJac
St. George Winery
Fresno
San Joaquin Winery
    & Distillery, Inc.
Fresno
Tulare Winery Co.
Tulare
Village Winery
Escalon

* storing, aging and finishing
plants

Central California Wineries Inc.

BANK OF AMERICA BUILDING   FRESNO, CALIFORNIA

FIGURE 22
Central California Wineries was created in 1939 to stabilize the market by controlling production and prices. It succeeded so well that it was charged by the authorities with restraint of trade. (From *Wine Review* 8 [August 1940]; reprinted with permission from *Wines and Vines*.)

The example of the Central California Wineries arrangement goaded California's cooperative wineries into something similar; most of them joined in forming an organization called California Cooperative Wineries, Inc., to manage inventories and to collaborate with Central California Wineries toward the goal of controlling prices.[95] The *Wine Review* hailed these developments as the dawn of a new day. "We've turned the corner," it declared:

Through the formation of the Central California Wineries and the California Co-operative Wineries, and the co-operation between these groups and non-members, wine production is again placed on a profitable basis. Adequate finances are available, for the first time in years, to cover all production and ageing costs. Wines may no longer be sold below cost, and in fact cannot now be sold at prices which do not guarantee a fair margin of profit.[96]

It was an effective arrangement. The price per ton for grapes in 1939 was higher than in 1938—a base of $13.20 as opposed to $10.60—and Central California Wineries was able to pay growers in cash, thanks to the loan from the Bank of America.[97] In the year after the vintage of 1939, Central California Wineries held some 16 million gallons of wine, some of it added by large purchases from other wineries that had no distributing arrangements.[98] In the next year the group expanded by buying the Kingsburg winery of Louis M. Martini, formerly a CWA property, where grape products had been produced during Prohibition and fortified wines since: this marked the moment when Martini decisively abandoned the Central Valley to concentrate on his Napa Valley winery, whose wines had not yet been put before the public. Central California Wineries also bought the old Greystone Winery north of St. Helena, the biggest single facility in that part of the state. With these two new acquisitions, which not only greatly expanded capacity but put them in the table wine trade as well, Central California Wineries approached a capacity of 35 million gallons.[99]

Its success was perhaps too great. Complaints were made of price fixing, and the Justice Department began preparing an antitrust case against Central California Wineries. The indictment drawn up charged the Bank of America, Central California Wineries, and other wineries having contracts with them with a "conspiracy to raise, fix, control and stabilize" prices—which, of course, had been the whole idea. The indictment was dropped.[100] But Central California Wineries was glad to sell out not long after, when the big distillers began their move into wartime California.

THE WINE ADVISORY BOARD

The alternative to stabilizing measures, which inevitably looked like restraint of trade in some form and were therefore always met with doubt or protest, was simple enough: get more people to drink wine. The Wine Institute, from the very beginning of its life, had urged on the California wine trade the cardinal importance of a national advertising campaign. But who would pay for it? And how would it be managed? Until those hard questions were answered, there would be no campaign, though everyone agreed that it was among those things most highly to be desired. The anxious days of 1938 compelled an answer.

A new law, the California Marketing Act, had created the legal means by which producers of agricultural crops could combine, under the direction of the state Department of Agriculture, to advertise and promote their produce—that is, the pear growers could combine to promote pears, or the rice growers combine to promote rice, and so on. In their early forms, such plans, which had to be authorized in writing by the people concerned, applied only to those growers who actually signed up as willing to pay assessments to support the promotional campaigns. In 1937, however, the act was modified so that if 65 percent of the growers of a certain crop (measured either by numbers or by volume of production) agreed to ask for a "marketing order," as it was called, then *all* growers of that crop in California would be compelled by law to contribute to the program. This new possibility was seized on by the Wine Institute, which sent people out to all the

California winegrowing regions to sign up supporters. A marketing order for the wine industry was drawn up and approved, a public hearing held, and during the course of the year 1938, some 90 percent of California's wine production was signed up in support of the order.[101] Thus was laid the ground upon which the first cooperative national advertising of California wine could be carried out.

Under the marketing order, the Wine Advisory Board was appointed by the director of the California Department of Agriculture. From this body was appointed a subcommittee on advertising, and since advertising was what the board was all about, that is where the real business went on. The board at once hired the Wine Institute to undertake publicity and education within the trade—wholesalers, retailers, hotels, and restaurants all over the country—and the J. Walter Thompson agency to produce the national advertising.[102] The first advertisements appeared in May 1939 on billboards, car cards, and shelf cards, in newspapers and national publications, and in any other form that ingenuity might suggest. There were other sorts of promotional work as well. In 1939 the first of what proved to be a series of "national wine weeks" was proclaimed, and promoted nationwide through print advertising and point-of-sale displays.[103] It also did lobbying—politely called trade barrier work—an activity that consumed half of its budget.[104]

All of this work was paid for by an assessment on all the wine sent to market by California producers: one and a half cents a gallon on fortified wines, three-quarters of a cent a gallon on table wines. The assessment, collected by the state by the same procedures used to collect the state tax, provided $2 million in 1939: the advertising tax it was sometimes called, quite rightly.

This development was anything but smooth.[105] The coercive power of the marketing act was especially resented by those who had not chosen to support it, and suits were at once filed against it. The point of attack was the claim that wine was an agricultural commodity—a claim that had to be made since the marketing orders were available only for agricultural commodities. Indeed, the first efforts to secure a marketing order had been flatly turned down by the Department of Agriculture, which did not recognize winemaking as a part of its domain. The strategists at the Wine Institute, however, had foreseen everything; their clients were, they said, winegrowers, and they insisted on this term as the only appropriate one.[106] With the help of Earl Warren, then the attorney general of California, this claim was recognized, and so the status of the winemakers—or, rather, wine*growers*—of California as a part of agriculture was established. The courts upheld this position, and the suits were denied.[107]

Meantime, the work of the board went on, and measured by sales, it looked as though it were having an effect. In 1939, the first year of the board's activity, the sale of California wine rose to 64,560,000 gallons from the 55,000,000 gallons of 1938; in 1940, the figure was 75,673,000 gallons, and in 1941, 89,237,000. These were heady figures for a trade that had started at 26,000,000 gallons in 1934, and the Wine Advisory Board did not hesitate to claim a large share of the credit. One must remember that the marketing situation had been altered in 1939 by the outbreak of the war: imported wines were, or were soon to be, in dwindling supply, and domestic wines in consequence attracted a degree of attention that they could never otherwise have hoped for. But the volume of imported wine sold in the United States in the years 1934–38 had averaged less than 3,500,000 gallons annually, only a fraction of the sales gain that had occurred coincidentally with the advertising work of the Wine Advisory Board.[108]

The aim of the board's campaign was not simply to increase the use of wine but specifically to increase the use of table wine as a mealtime beverage—a controversial policy in a wine trade dominated by the large-scale producers of fortified wines. As the prorate program had been opposed by the table wine producers, so now the Wine Advisory Board program was opposed by the fortified wine producers. Their suits against the legality of the board failed, as has been noted, but their continued opposition made the renewal of the marketing order that was the basis of the board a chancy proposition: twice the renewal vote, which came up every three years, was nearly defeated, but the table wine interest was strong enough to pull out the victory.[109] The Wine Advisory Board continued in operation for thirty-seven years, succumbing at last in a political fight that had nothing to do with the internal conflicts of the wine trade.

By 1939, five years after Repeal, the structure of the renewed wine industry in California was clear. Fortified wine from the Central Valley dominated the trade. Much of this wine, and of the high-proof spirits used to fortify it, came from the great volumes of table and raisin grapes grown in the valley that were neither sold fresh nor turned into raisins. The periodic oversupply of such grapes, more than anything else, was what unbalanced the wine trade in California. The industry had shown much technical and managerial skill in creating large-volume wineries after the wreck of Prohibition, but the standard wines of California were not more than that, and the standard wobbled a good deal. Good wine grapes were grown in only a small fraction of the state's vineyards, table wines were not much in demand, and hence the production of good table wines from good wine varieties was distinctly a minority element in the trade. It was to be the work of time and unrelenting effort to convert the vineyards of the state to better varieties, and to develop a market that wanted superior table wines. In the meantime, some order had been created through the establishment of the Wine Institute and the Wine Advisory Board, and the work of instructing winegrowers and winemakers had been energetically carried on by the University of California. As the figures for the production and sale of wine went up, the number of active wineries went sharply down. The 733 bonded wineries of 1936, the peak year, were down to 549 in 1938 and to 474 in 1940, a decline that was to continue for years.[110]

At the end of the decade, in 1939, the Golden Gate International Exposition at San Francisco—the first such extravaganza on the West Coast since the Panama-Pacific Exposition of 1915—provided an opportunity to present a comprehensive display of California wines. Plans were made by the Wine Institute for a Wine Palace where individual exhibitors could mount their displays and where a restaurant would serve meals accompanied by California wines to educate the American public about the relations of food and wine.

The restaurant did not materialize, but a "wine temple" (rather than a "palace") was erected in the Foods and Beverages Palace and displayed the wines of some forty-six wineries.[111] A wine judging, using "international" standards, was held at the exposition, but this, too, failed to draw an enthusiastic response.[112] The exposition did something, no doubt, for California wines, but the exhibits appear to have lacked glamour, and the state's wine played only a minor part at Treasure Island. The confidence of the industry was not yet up to anything very bold or very splendid. This muffled sort of celebration seems an appropriate end to the '30s, in which survival rather than splendid achievement had been the main object.

If one looked backward from the vantage point of 1939, the five years preceding had been all ups and downs, abounding in surprises, disappointments, and hairbreadth escapes from disaster. But if one looked around and ahead, the prospect was different: consumption was up, inventories were not alarmingly high, the competition from imports was greatly reduced, and California producers could even think about taking over the export markets that Europe had lost. Curiously enough, despite all the troubles, it was beginning to be an expansive time.

6

WINE IN THE WAR YEARS

FIRST EFFECTS

The chance that the war that was declared in September 1939 would open up the world to American wines—an exciting thought rather widely shared at one time—was more theoretical than real.[1] Those few parts of Europe that were not caught up in the war were not much interested in American wines, even supposing one could safely transport them there; South America had its own supplies; there was war in Asia. None of the necessary work in establishing markets and the means of supplying them had been done.[2] And soon enough, the United States was in the war too.

This is not to deny that there was a surge in exports at the beginning of World War II: the 86,000 gallons of American wine exported in 1939 jumped to 400,000 gallons in 1940.[3] But after America entered the war it was not possible to continue this export trade. On the other side, the gap created by the disappearance of European wine (mostly French and Italian) was not very large—on average the American market had taken fewer than 4 million gallons annually. Nor did this gap take long to repair: though few imports were made in 1942, by 1943 the volume of imports had already reached the prewar level, and in the next year it surpassed even that. Neutral Portugal and Spain had replaced France and Italy, with the anomalous result that the United States imported more wine over the wartime seas than it ever had in times of peace.[4]

What did come about as a result of the war, however, was of inestimable importance to the American wine industry. At first there was not much apparent concern about supply. As late as May 1940 the *New York Times* reported that there were stocks of French wines in the United States sufficient for the next six months, and that there had so far been no increase in prices. The fall of France in the next month abruptly cut off that source. As the modest flow of European wine began to dry up, the East Coast importers, who supplied almost all of such markets for superior wines as then existed, saw that they would soon have to deal in American wines to help replace their lost supplies. And the more perceptive among the winemakers and the wine merchants saw that they now had a chance such as they had not had before to identify American wines with quality.[5] Frank Schoonmaker, who had been importing wine from Europe since 1935 and who, almost alone among the members of the eastern trade, had taken an earlier interest in the future of American wines, toured the wine regions of the country in 1939 seeking reputable wines to sell. He had been preceded by the New York importing firm of Park and Tilford, which had California wines in its catalog by 1939.[6] Soon thereafter, wines from California, New York, and Ohio were being offered by a number of dealers to customers who had never before heard of such wines and who needed considerable encouragement and persuasion before they could be coaxed to buy them.

A 1941 catalog of the Sherry Wine and Spirits Company in New York provides a characteristic instance. It offers American wine frankly as an unfamiliar thing, and is careful to qualify its recommendations ("we do not wish to exaggerate"), to explain the character of the regions the wine came from (in the Livermore valley, "the vineyard soil appears coarse and gravelly—the temperature is higher than in its neighboring wine valleys"), and to describe the wines (Inglenook 1935 Riesling is "produced from the Franken Riesling grape. Frequently this grape is marketed under the varietal name of Sylvaner. Not unlike a Sylvaner from Alsace"). The catalog offered wines from Wente, Concannon, Cresta Blanca, Martini, Salmina (Larkmead), Inglenook, Beringer, Beaulieu, Mt. St. Helena, Fountaingrove, the Novitiate of Los Gatos, La Questa, Paul Masson, Korbel, Valliant, Widmer's, and Engels and Krudwig—a rich collection.[7] The new curiosity about California wines extended even to California. The San Francisco branch of the Wine and Food Society gave a dinner in March 1940 featuring exclusively the wines made by Martin Ray at the Paul Masson Winery, the first time that a California wine had received such attention in its own state.[8]

It was particularly fitting that Schoonmaker and his firm (of which Alexis Lichine was then sales manager) should have been among the leaders in this development. Schoonmaker, ever since he and Tom Marvel published *The Complete Wine Book* in 1934, had been urging American winemakers to aim for quality, with little enough response. If the country were to produce superior wines, he had sensibly argued, the growers would have to plant better varieties, winemakers would have to follow better production methods, and the wines would have to be sold under properly descriptive labels rather than under borrowed and uninformative European names. This last proposition, one that Schoonmaker had repeatedly made in the trade press, had earned him much ill-will among winemakers, who found Schoonmaker's arguments impossible to answer but did not want to be disturbed in their comfortable bad practices.[9] In vain, Schoonmaker urged self-inter-

FIGURE 23

Frank Schoonmaker, who gave a new identity to American wines. (From Frank Schoonmaker, *Encyclopedia of Wine*, 6th ed. [1964], by permission of Hastings House.)

est on the growers and winemakers: the growers should welcome honest labeling because it would lead to higher prices for better grapes; and the wineries should want it because they could achieve recognition for their superior wines and sell them at superior prices.[10] Despite such arguments, things went on pretty much as they had before. Educating the American public in a new style of labeling was not something that the wine trade was eager to undertake.[11]

The new situation created by the war in Europe gave Schoonmaker his opportunity. His quest for salable American wines in 1939 had yielded some results: in New York he had found Delaware from Widmer's; in Ohio, Catawba from Engels and Krudwig; in California, Semillon, Chardonnay, and Sauvignon blanc from Wente, Cabernet from Inglenook, Zinfandel from Salmina, Pinot noir from Fountaingrove.[12] These wines (and ultimately a good many others) he now offered for sale under labels, often of his own design, after the principles that he had so long argued.[13] The labels were regional first: Finger Lakes, Lake Erie, Livermore valley. But since American winegrowing regions were not (and are not) identified with any particular wine, the labels also gave the name of the variety of grape from which the wine was made: Delaware, Catawba, Semillon, Cabernet Sauvignon. Finally, they clearly identified the producer of the wine: Widmer's, Engels and Krudwig, Wente, Larkmead. The buyer could now tell from an American wine label, as he already could from a European label, who made the wine, where it was made, and what it was made of—precisely those things that did not appear on the private label of a bottler selling wine from bulk under a generic name.[14] On this basis, the so-called varietal labeling method, it now became possible for American winemakers to achieve an identity and to cultivate a market for wines of character.[15] As Schoonmaker himself said, "Nothing we have done since we became wine merchants in 1935 has given us as much satisfaction as the inclusion of these good American wines in our catalogue. We can offer, at long last, American wines which are sound, properly made, honestly labeled, clean, which have a good taste and which are inexpensive. This means to us an end, not of Prohibition, but of the effects of Prohibition."[16]

The effects of Prohibition were to be far more lasting than Schoonmaker allowed, since they are still very much with us, but his modest summary of what had been accomplished certainly showed a new direction. That change continued for some time to be resented and resisted by many winemakers, who felt that the new mode of labeling implicitly condemned their wines bearing the old-style labels: it was all, so some of them concluded, a trick of the importers to alienate their customers from American wines even as they dealt in American wines.[17]

The effect of this change, so simple in form and concept yet so difficult to establish, has been so broad and so profound that it requires to be discussed at some length.[18] Since no scheme is perfect, it is also necessary to take into account some of the defects of what has now become the standard method of American wine labeling.

Despite what seems to be the free-and-easy tradition of labeling wine in America, neither the trade nor the regulatory authorities were ever indifferent to the question, though there was more legislation than enforcement. California, for example, passed the Pure Wine Law in 1887, providing for the use of a stamp or label to certify that the wine had met the official standards. The law was violently opposed, and soon after its passage its key provision, the requirement for a stamp of purity, was overturned on appeal: a few wineries continued to use the stamp, but they were the exception.[19] In 1907 an act of the California legislature officially recognized a new nomenclature for California wines, including such names as Calclaret, Calburgundy, and Calriesling. Again, no one seems to have paid any attention to this act, and it was repealed in 1935.[20] The Federal Alcohol Control Administration (FACA), in the early days of the National Recovery Administration code, was dissatisfied with the rules for labeling and attempted, unsuccessfully, to introduce the terms *dry red* and *dry white,* or *light red* and *light white,* so that a California burgundy might carry on its label the qualification "a dry light red wine."[21] The trade also recognized that the development of brand names or proprietary names might be preferable to using European names: Paul Garrett's Virginia Dare and Italian Swiss Colony's Tipo had been notable examples before Prohibition.

When the Federal Alcohol Administration (FAA) at last established its regulations for wine, it allowed—as we have seen—the continuation, essentially unchanged, of the American practice of using European wine names, on the grounds that these had become "generic."[22] Not everyone agreed with this view. In October 1933, in anticipation of Re-

CONTENTS 4/5 PINT • 12% ALCOHOL BY VOLUME

A SCHOONMAKER SELECTION

LAKE ERIE
ISLAND
CATAWBA

A LIGHT WHITE WINE MADE FROM CATAWBA GRAPES

BOTTLED AT THE WINERY BY
THE ENGELS & KRUDWIG WINE CO.
SANDUSKY, LAKE ERIE ISLANDS DISTRICT, OHIO

SELECTED BY
FRANK SCHOONMAKER & CO., INC.
WINE MERCHANTS
NEW YORK, N. Y.

FIGURE 24
Schoonmaker's varietal labels from 1940. (From *Wines and Vines* 21 [November 1940]; reprinted with permission from *Wines and Vines*.)

peal, a writer in the *Fruit Products Journal* had asked rhetorically, "Why masquerade American wines under foreign names?" and argued that since the slate had been wiped clean by Prohibition, American winegrowers could now build their own identities.[23] About the same time, Rexford Tugwell had prophesied that American wines would acquire regional names: he suggested Keuka, Roanoke, and San Joaquin, among others.[24] But establishing a regional identity takes a long time, and meanwhile wine had to be sold under some sort of label. The varietal method offered an alternative to using European names that did not belong to us, or to using American regional names that did not yet stand for anything known in the world of wine. Varietal names, in conjunction with place-names, would provide honest and informative labeling.

The idea was not, of course, new. Far from it.[25] The first successful commercial wine production of any size in this country was achieved by Nicholas Longworth in Cincinnati, beginning in the 1830s: Longworth's wines always went to market as "Catawba," the name of the grape from which they were produced. One might fairly say, then, that varietal labeling is the *oldest* style of labeling for American wines. Nor did the tradition of varietal naming thus established ever disappear. There were eastern wines called Catawba, Delaware, Iona, Ives, and so on, through a long list of native American grapes, in the years down to Prohibition. In California there had been many wines sold under varietal names before Prohibition, including Beclan, Cabernet Sauvignon, Grignolino, Traminer, and Semillon.[26] Zinfandel and Riesling were perhaps the most familiar names on labels.[27] Schoonmaker's principles of labeling were thus already known and followed in America, but very much as a minority tradition.[28] By taking them up in a polemical way as a challenge to the standard practice, by associating such labeling with the best that the country had to offer, and by showing that there was a market for wine so identified, Schoonmaker began a remarkable change in the way that winemakers saw their own product and in the expectations that wine buyers had for the wines that they sought out and drank. Another generation was to pass before varietal labeling became the standard in America, but a decisive turn in that direction was clearly made when the war compelled Schoonmaker to add American wines to his stock in trade.

Without question, the move toward varietal labeling was a giant step toward achieving a new level of quality in American wines, and it is almost impossible, I think, to overstate its importance. The practice has, however, at least two defects: it gives an exaggerated importance to the grape variety at the expense of geographical origin; and it fails to recognize the basic importance of blending in wines of quality. The first point was clearly brought out, curiously enough, in a meeting of winegrowers in 1860, when the American wine business had just barely begun. The Southern Vinegrowers' Convention, meeting in Aiken, South Carolina, debated the subject of "naming the different wines" then beginning to be produced. In response to the suggestion that wines be named after the grapes they came from, it was pointed out that, though hundreds of wines might be made of the Catawba grape and so labeled, no two of them would be alike: "The same grape will make totally different wines in different places."[29] That proposition is just as true now as it was then. And it is not just the region that makes the difference: so do the cultivation and winemaking practices. Zinfandel grown in Fresno County, on irrigated land and pruned to yield ten tons an acre, is certainly Zinfandel; but in respect of character and quality it has little relation to Zinfandel grown in Amador County on unirrigated land and yielding a bare two tons per acre. *Where* a grape is grown and *how* it is grown appear to be quite as essential as *what* grape is grown.[30] And so do the methods by which wines are made from grapes of the same name. So the modern wine drinker, looking at the hundreds of Cabernets now offered for his choice, can have only the most elemen-

A 1948 wines of vinos

tary guarantee from the fact that all the wines are certainly from Cabernet grapes. The simple uniformity of the name conceals an unpredictable variety of styles, characters, and qualities.[31] In recent years the winemakers of California have increasingly recognized this fact and have turned, inevitably, to promoting the idea of location, usually under the fashionable term *terroir,* as a way of establishing an identity and a claim to inimitable character. There is no doubt that different regions have different characters, but it is slow work discovering just what that character is and then getting the public to recognize and appreciate it.

The other defect, the failure to provide for blending, is also a matter of some seriousness. Many of the world's great wines are not the product of a single variety of grape but are made from the blended contributions of a number of different varieties—from two to as many as thirteen.[32] Bordeaux (both white and red), Rioja, Chianti, Port, Champagne—all are blended wines, all based on the perception that the different qualities of different varieties may be combined to produce a result that for balance and complexity no single variety can match. It is also true that some varieties do not have character enough, or distinction enough, to merit treatment as separate varietals. As one commentator on Schoonmaker's arguments for varietal labeling observed, "I don't think, for example, that one would be justified in selling the vin ordinaire from the Midi as 'Aramon' unless the wine were sufficiently distinct to be recognized as a product of the Aramon and the Aramon variety only."[33] Since some varieties did not have character enough to stand alone, and since several varieties might be combined to make a whole greater than the parts, blending was and is a necessary practice in the general scheme of winemaking.

Varietal labeling, unfortunately, does not merely fail to allow for this practice, it is hostile to it. The 51 percent requirement established by federal regulation in 1936 was raised in 1983 to 75 percent; and that regulation was challenged by a lawsuit in which the plaintiffs argued that labels should show the percentages of *all* grapes used in a wine so that winemakers would not use "cheap garbage grapes" to fill out the unspecified 25 percent.[34] No one would want cheap garbage grapes, of course; but the implication of this protest is that any blending is a way of cheating. Instead, we are given an ideal of "purity"—that is, a wine labeled with the name of a grape ought to be made exclusively from that grape. There are cases in which this is so: a great German Riesling is pure Riesling, Burgundy is all Pinot noir, Chablis all Chardonnay, and so on. But a uniform, rigid rule would be simply nonsense. In some cases, one grape alone does the job; in others, a mixture is wanted. But varietal labeling does not allow for—or at least does not encourage—the practice of blending. And the common sense of the matter is that a wine carrying a varietal name ought to be entirely of that variety—otherwise why call it that? Recognizing this point, and being constrained by the varietal regulations, a group of California winemakers in 1988 agreed to use the proprietary name *Meritage* for their wines that are blended according to the classical formula of Bordeaux. The idea seems to have had at least a limited success, and it suggests the possibility of a system of naming that does not depend on the grape variety.[35]

The basis of naming for all the great wines of Europe is geographical: a village (Barolo); a city (Oporto); a district (Champagne); a river (Mosel). But behind these is a tradition, and that is what is really in question. One knows by long tradition what grapes are used for the wines of the Médoc; one knows by long tradition what methods of fermentation are used for Sherry; one knows by long tradition how the wines of Champagne are cleared after the second fermentation. It is only in comparatively recent years that these traditions have also been given the force of law. The tradition had to come first. If strict and inelastic regulations are adopted before experience has shown us what kinds of wine we can make best, and where, and by what methods, they will simply stultify development in the United States: the country has not yet scratched the surface of its winegrowing possibilities. An ideal system of labeling will have to follow on a historical development that has not yet occurred; legislation that protects the soundness and authenticity of wine is of course highly necessary, but laws that specify what varieties to use, what cultivation practices to follow, what yields to allow, what vinification practices to follow, and so on would be absurdly premature in this country.

NEW PLAYERS IN THE GAME

Another change created by the disturbances of a threatened war was the sudden appearance of European exiles on the American wine scene. They were not many, but they made a difference.[36] Hanns Kornell, from a winemaking family in Germany and trained at the distinguished wine school at Geisenheim, arrived in California in 1940 and went to work for Fountaingrove, in Santa Rosa; he was preceded there by another émigré, his cousin Kurt Opper. The sales manager at Fountaingrove in 1942 was Eugene Schoenberger, formerly the manager of a *Sekt* firm in Mainz, and the winemaker at Fountaingrove was Schoenberger's nephew, Hanns Kornblum. Kornell, after leaving Fountaingrove, did a stint as champagne maker for the American Wine Company in St. Louis (maker of Cook's Imperial). Eventually he took over the old Larkmead Winery in St. Helena and made it, under his own name, a leading producer of sparkling wine. Opper, after restoring Fountaingrove to the prestige it had once enjoyed, went on to the Paul Masson Winery, where he worked with yet another German, Hans Hyba, the champagne master for Masson.

Otto Meyer, who came from a family of winemakers and distillers at Bingen, in the Rheinhesse, fled from Nazi Germany in 1939 and was soon having a major impact on the California trade. Meyer gained experience of California conditions by working for Krikor Arakelian's big Mission Bell winery in Madera. He paid special attention to the subject of brandy, then not much studied in this country, and determined to make use of the great pool of brandy produced by the set-aside program of 1938. He was joined in this plan by his brother-in-law, Alfred Fromm, another refugee from Hitler's Germany, then associated with The Christian Brothers. Fromm, like Kornell, was a graduate of the wine school at Geisenheim. He had entered the American wine business in partnership with another German, Franz Sichel, of the family of winegrowers and merchants still prominent in France and England. Fromm and Sichel had been working since 1937 for the national distributors of The Christian Brothers wines and had made a success of it by building up a distribution system and by bottling at the winery. Now Fromm and Meyer persuaded The Christian Brothers to enter the brandy business, and set to work sampling and selecting from the reservoir of prorate brandy. The result was so successful that demand soon outran supply.[37] In 1945 Fromm and Sichel, with the help of Seagram's, took over the Paul Masson winery and began to develop it into one of the most prominent names in the postwar years. Another Geisenheim graduate, Richard Auerbach, joined Roma as a winemaker in 1940 and remained there until his retirement in 1963.[38]

The French, not being under the same pressures, were less numerous than the Germans, but they included Henri Lanson, of the Champagne firm, who was an official of GoLan Wines in 1941; and Paul Rossigneux, formerly with Geisweiler et Fils in Burgundy, who was president of the Napa and Sonoma Wine Company in San Francisco. Before Prohibition, the wine trade had been thoroughly cosmopolitan; now it began to be so again, a welcome effect though from a bad cause. One should add the names of two notable Europeans who came to the American wine trade before the war: Charles Fournier, trained in the cellars of Veuve Cliquot Ponsardin, who joined Gold Seal Vineyards in Hammondsport, New York, in 1933 and eventually became president of the firm; and André Tchelistcheff, a Russian trained in Czechoslovakia and France, who worked at Beaulieu from 1938 and became, before his death in 1994, the doyen of Napa Valley winemakers.

Another change wrought by the war—a change much more publicized and disputed than the small but significant influx of Europeans—was the entry into California winegrowing of the four major American distillers: Schenley, Seagram's, National Distillers, and Hiram Walker and Sons. In just a few years these firms acquired a dozen or so large winery properties controlling some 25 percent of California's production capacity. Their presence on the scene was only temporary—by the 1950s they had largely withdrawn—but it was noisy while it lasted, and the stage was not quite the same after they had left it.

Even before the war there had been some stirrings of interest in the wine business on the part of the distillers. There had not traditionally been any link between the distilling and wine trades in this country. Whiskey was a big and prosperous business; wine was not. Whiskey manufacture was concentrated in Middle America, wine on the remote West Coast. Whiskey was familiar and straightforward; wine was exotic and problematic. The wine people had always resented having to suffer the prohibitionist attacks that should, they thought, be directed against whiskey, and the distillers had always resented the winemakers' assumption of innocence.

The first link between the two groups was brandy. Schenley wished to add an American brandy to its line, and as a beginning to that end bought a small distillery from the Roma Wine Company in 1938.[39] Early the next year, National Distillers made a comparable move by buying the Shewan-Jones winery at Lodi, not so much for its wine production as for its brandy. The move from brandy to wine was not made until shortly after Pearl Harbor when, early in 1942, Schenley bought the Cresta Blanca Winery in the Livermore valley, apparently as a means of supplying its importing subsidiary, Schenley Imports, whose European sources were disappearing. Otherwise, the distillers were not yet much interested in the wine trade. The whiskey business was quite profitable, and the effects of the war, so far, were all to the advantage of American distillers: sales of hard liquor jumped 50 percent between 1939 and 1941, for the national income was rising and the American supply of spirits was unlimited.[40]

In the first months after the American entry into the war, the distillers devoted their excess capacity to the production of industrial alcohol. Then, at the end of August 1942, the War Production Board announced that all production of whiskey would cease on 1 November—a development that suddenly made wineries attractive on a new basis. The distillers were of course prospering as producers of alcohol for the war effort, but if they were to keep their lines of distribution open against the time that whiskey would again be available, they needed something to sell. So they moved quickly into California wine-making, or, as it was more extravagantly said at the time, they staged "an all out invasion of the wine business."[41]

Schenley remained the leader. It already had the Manteca distillery and Cresta Blanca. In September 1942 Schenley bought the Elk Grove winery from Colonial Grape Products, the firm founded by Sophus Federspiel in 1920, and then added, early in November, the Roma winery at Fresno—"the largest winery in the world"—and two properties from Central California Wineries: the former Martini winery in Kingsburg and the Greystone Winery in St. Helena.[42] This was a breathtaking pace: Schenley now had wineries in Kingsburg, St. Helena, Elk Grove, Fresno, San Francisco, Healdsburg, and Livermore, with inventories of almost 20 million gallons of wine and a storage capacity of more than 30 million gallons.[43] In the space of a few months, Schenley had become the major player in American wine. *Fortune* magazine, in reporting on the new action in California, found that the distillers had stirred up an excited speculative spirit; the corridors of the Fresno hotels, where the dealmaking was concentrated, were filled with the "ghosts of proposed and half-consummated deals," and there seemed to be no property that was not for sale. As though to calm the excitement, the head of Schenley Distillers, Lew Rosenstiel, announced that he had not gone into wine merely as a "wartime proposition" but was "working on the future."[44]

Schenley was followed by National Distillers, which almost simultaneously with Schenley's purchase of Roma announced that it had bought the Italian Swiss Colony wineries at Asti and Clovis—then the third-largest winemaking establishment in California. The Schenley and National Distillers purchases were the blockbuster events of 1942, but they were accompanied by some smaller ones. Seagram's moved into California with the purchase in December 1942 of the Mount Tivy Winery at Reedley, and in 1943 of Paul Masson at Saratoga. Hiram Walker did not enter the fray until 1943, when it bought the Valliant Winery at Hollister and the R. Martini Winery at Santa Rosa, though it had earlier—through its purchase of W. A. Taylor, a New York importer and distributor—

established a connection with California wine. When the dust had settled, the score was as follows: the four major U.S. distillers now owned or leased eighteen, mostly big, California wineries, with a total storage capacity of almost 50 million gallons. They did not control a proportionate quantity of California's vineyards, most of which remained separate from the wineries, so they could not automatically dominate production. But they were now a powerful minority in a system in which, only a short time before, they had had no presence whatever.

The response to this development was of course mixed. Some pointed to the clear advantages that new capital strength would give to the wine trade, perennially plagued as it had been by the inability to pay for new developments, for the proper production and maturation of its wines, or for their orderly marketing. The "ramshackle" California wine industry, it was said, would now be organized on a large scale as a "fast-moving business with big capital, big production and nationwide distribution."[45] Others were suspicious: the whiskey people did not understand the trade, would exploit it without regard to standards, and cared nothing for the traditional relations among growers, winemakers, and distributors. Both responses were correct: the distillers did have the money to do useful things, and they did do some dubious things.

One of the things they did—particularly Schenley—was to advertise wine more aggressively than had been done before. Radio advertising was not wholly new to wine— Roma and Gallo had sponsored programs, as had a few others—but now Schenley's Cresta Blanca sponsored a major network show, the *Cresta Blanca Carnival*.[46] The Petri Wine Company followed by sponsoring Basil Rathbone and Nigel Bruce in a weekly *Sherlock Holmes* broadcast on national radio; Italian Swiss Colony sponsored a news program with Fulton Lewis Jr. Wineries also began to buy space on billboards across the country, and pages of ads in major magazines and newspapers.

The result was contradictory: as the demand for wine grew under the pressures of rising incomes, wartime shortages, and advertising, the supply of wine, under wartime controls, dwindled. Schenley's method of resolving the problem was simple: it put all of its wines from all of its sources into bottles with the Cresta Blanca label. What had once been in effect an estate label for wines from the Livermore valley, with a long-established reputation for quality, now became a mere brand, ornamenting bottles filled with sherries made from the strippings of Central Valley Thompson Seedless grapes, or burgundies made from Alicante Bouschet and Carignane. By selling all of its wine, no matter what its quality might be, under its highest-priced label, Schenley no doubt made a good profit, but it was not a tactic that could outlast the war.[47] Cresta Blanca's competitors, Leon Adams later wrote, never forgot or forgave this episode, nor did Cresta Blanca, after such debasement, ever recover its old prestige.[48]

The distillers did another thing for which they were much abused. Since Americans wanted to drink whiskey, of which the distillers did not have enough, and since the distillers had a good deal of wine, which Americans did not particularly want, the distillers inevitably made sales on a tie-in basis: if you want to buy a bottle of whiskey, they said, which we know you badly do, you must first buy this case of wine, which in the course of time you will perhaps learn to love.[49]

But the distillers, whatever their sins in marketing wine, were probably not quite as wicked as they were widely imagined to be. It was claimed that the distillers controlled the Office of Price Administration and set grape ceilings low so as to squeeze the grower and enrich themselves; that they were "taking control" of the entire wine industry; that they were converting their stocks of wine into high-proof spirits and putting that into their whiskies; and that if they were depressing grape prices with one hand, with the other they were paying inflated prices for grapes in order to control the market. All of these accusations, and more, came out during hearings held at the end of 1943 by a subcommittee of the Senate Committee on the Judiciary that was appointed to inquire into the wartime behavior of the liquor industry, particularly into shortages and high prices. The chairman of the subcommittee, Senator Fred Van Nuys of Indiana, was evidently hostile to the distillers and prepared to listen to the worst that could be said, but very little if any evidence of unfair trade practices, let alone of a conspiracy, was turned up by the hearings.[50]

The conditions of war were sufficient to explain most of the things complained of; and, after all, the distillers, having moved so quickly into the California wine industry, did not go much further than their first steps had taken them. The frenzy of buying wineries lasted only a few months. After the early months of 1943 the distillers acquired no further properties in California. Then they were allowed to resume the production of whiskey for the month of August 1944, and the increasingly successful course of the war gave them less and less reason to take an interest in the wine trade. The exit of the distillers, though not quite as rapid as their entrance, was rapid enough. The vicissitudes of the postwar years gave them much reason to think that the wine business could better be left to others. By the '50s they began to withdraw, and they were effectively out of the trade by the end of the '70s.[51]

MAKING WINE IN WARTIME

Grape growers and winemakers now, at last, had a seller's market; they could sell all that they produced, and at good prices. "The war paid off a lot of mortgages," as one observer put it.[52] But in common with every other business in the country, the wine trade had to operate under the restrictive conditions of a country at war. Taxes, of course, went up at once.[53] In August 1942, the War Food Administration of the War Production Board ordered that the entire crop of Thompson Seedless, Sultana, and muscat grapes be made into raisins. Since such grapes were the basis of the California fortified wine industry—in 1941 they had made up 44 percent of the entire crush in California for fortified and table wines alike—diverting them from the wineries meant a precipitous fall in the production of fortified wines (but did not much affect table wine production). The order also came very late, when the harvest was already under way, so it created great confusion. There were loopholes in the order, large enough that some 95,000 tons of raisin grapes found their way to the wineries.[54] But production did go down, thanks to a short crop and the diversion order. Amid cries of disaster, some other voices might be heard. The editor of *Wines and Vines* reported that some winemakers saw the diversion of raisin grapes as an excellent thing:

> They say that the use of table and raisin varieties of grapes in the production of wine originally was largely a salvage action for grape growers. If a way could be found to plant more wine grapes and use raisin and table varieties for the purposes for which they were first intended, it would improve the quality of all wines produced in California; and furthermore would contribute to raising of standards, to a new increase of wine consumption, and to a bettering of prices. This may be mere theory but it should at least be mentioned as the opinion of some vintners.[55]

The editor had clearly seen the future, though the weak-kneed concluding sentence shows how difficult it was to sustain such a vision.

The three wartime vintage years may be summarized as follows. In 1942 the crop was a small one to begin with—2,160,000 tons—and the supply of grapes for wine was further reduced by the diversion of the raisin crop away from the wineries. California produced only 54 million gallons, the smallest production since Repeal, divided into 36 million gallons of fortified wines and just over 18 million gallons of table wines. At the same time, sales rose to an all-time high of 96 million gallons, so inventories of wine in California at the end of 1942 had dwindled by some 40 million gallons from the levels at the beginning of the year. Thus, as James Lapsley has said, the California wine trade went from "glut to scarcity" in the turn of a year.[56] Incidentally, the brandy produced by the controversial prorate program of 1938 was entirely sold during 1942, so that troubled chapter was closed satisfactorily.[57] The average price of grapes in this year was reported to be $33 per ton, and there were stories of sales at figures that would have seemed quite impossible only a few years before.

In 1943 a large crop was produced—2,789,000 tons—and unlike those of the 1930s, it was gladly welcomed. The order diverting raisin grapes from the wineries was still in force, but total production in California reached 80 million gallons, 45 million gallons of which was fortified wine. In these conditions, the price of nonraisin grapes, which were not subject to price control, inevitably rocketed: "Fantastic prices," *Wines and Vines* editorialized, "have become an actuality, and it might well appear to grape growers that the day of the millenium *[sic]* has come."[58] Sales of wine were lower than in the year before—73 million gallons as opposed to 96 million—mainly, it seems, on account of the difficulties of transport. The movement of bulk wine to the East was much reduced.

Another large crop in 1944—2,514,000 tons—and a slightly higher proportion of it crushed for wine yielded over 90 million gallons, two-thirds of it fortified. Grape prices reached an average of $108 per ton. Only a little more wine was sold than in the year before, and the inventory of California wine at the end of 1944 was some 10 million gallons larger than it had been at the end of 1943. By the time of the 1945 harvest, the war was over, and all the conditions that had operated for the previous three years had changed. We may now take a brief look at what these were.

The labor supply was reduced during the war, of course, but I have found no evidence that the figures for grape and wine production were much affected: the average harvest in the war years was just what it had been in the three years preceding.[59] And the vineyard acreage in California remained stable.[60] What did make a difference was the diversion away from the wineries of the raisin grapes on which the industry had grown so much to depend. In the three years 1942–44, about 285,000 tons of raisin grapes were crushed for wine; in the three years 1939–41, that total had been 1,089,000 tons, a difference more than sufficient to account for the decline in wartime production.[61]

If the labor shortage did not make much difference to the general operation of the winemakers, neither did shortages of packaging materials—glass, cork, paper, wood, and the like—and of machinery for processing. A committee from the wine industry was formed to advise the War Food Administration on the requirements of the industry, and it seems to have had its requests reasonably met.[62] The number of sizes and shapes of bottles was restricted, but bottles were still available: most wines were bottled in Bordeaux-style bottles as the standard container.[63] Cork never ceased to be imported, since the main suppliers, Spain and Portugal, managed to remain neutral throughout the war. The idea of developing a native supply of cork was looked at, though not very seriously.[64] There were, certainly, many nuisances and frustrations to be endured by the wartime winemaker, but nothing that threatened to put an end to his work.

Transportation was more affected than production. The main method of shipping wine to the eastern markets that were the mainstay of California was by a fleet of some 1,250 specially lined railroad tank cars. As early as August 1942, some three hundred of these had been requisitioned for shipment of war materials, and the winemakers had had to work out means of using the remainder on a virtually nonstop basis. By June 1943 half of the tank cars had been requisitioned.[65] In consequence, wine shipments went down and inventory went up, though neither by a very large measure. The shipment of wine in barrel or in bottle increased to take up much of the volume that could no longer move by tank car: boxcars, unlike tank cars, would often otherwise travel empty back east, so they were available for wine shipments. Probably the California winemakers were not sorry to keep some of their wine in reserve, since the market was now stabilized as it had never been since Repeal and their inventories were now valuable assets rather than a burden to be gotten rid of. The eastern winemakers also benefited, since they were conveniently close to the main markets: their wines were eagerly sought after when California wines were in limited supply.

In short, although there was no doubt much making shift and although the industry had to operate under strict controls, the war brought prosperity to almost all of its parts. Only the independent bottlers suffered, as we will see, because they could not control their sources.

The car that carried fine old wines . . .

now carries alcohol for ammunition

GATX
GENERAL AMERICAN

A SYMBOL OF INTEGRITY FOR OVER 40 YEARS

GENERAL AMERICAN TRANSPORTATION
CORPORATION
Chicago

FIGURE 25
A force for change: the
shortage of tank cars for
wine helped to bring
about bottling at the
winery. (From *Wines
and Vines* 24 [March
1943]; reprinted with
permission from
Wines and Vines.)

The wine industry also had its small but useful part to play in the war effort. It was the unique source of tartrates, recovered from pomace or in the form of deposits scraped off the sides of storage tanks. For many years the commercial supply had all been imported; now tartrates from domestic sources were used in the manufacture of rayon, in photographic chemicals, and in medicines.[66] Those wineries that had stills for the production of brandy and high-proof spirits for fortification also contributed. Early in the war the War Production Board dismantled a number of California brandy stills, shipped them to the Midwest, and reerected them at whiskey distilleries to produce industrial alcohol. The stated reasons for this action were that brandy stills could produce a higher-proof distillate than could whiskey stills and that it would be more efficient to have them working close to the nation's grain supply. In California, however, it was rumored that the move was a plot by the whiskey people to deprive California of its distilling capacity and so to eliminate a possible competitor in the spirits trade: brandy versus whiskey.[67] In the event, this episode made little difference to California's production of brandy and fortified wine.

Among the other worries produced by wartime conditions was the predictable outburst of prohibitionist activity or, as an alarmed editorial in *Wines and Vines* put it, the determination of the "followers of Volsteadism . . . to lead the nation into the morass of Prohibition once more."[68] Protecting the soldiers against Demon Rum was the easiest pitch to use for the "followers of Volsteadism"; after all, how could drunken officers and soldiers win a war? This argument had worked during World War I, when the Wartime Prohibition Act had been an important step in the run-up to national Prohibition. Excited by that heady memory, the Drys now took the field again with the object, as one hostile observer said, "first . . . to dry up all military camps and establishments; second, to dry up all war industrial areas; and third, to dry up the entire country."[69] Senator Sheppard, he of the Eighteenth Amendment, introduced a bill in 1941 prohibiting the sale of all alcoholic drinks in and around all military bases, and this became the national focus of the Dry campaign. It failed, being resolutely opposed by the secretaries of the Army and the Navy both. It was resurrected at the end of 1942 in the form of a rider to the Draft Bill, when it was again blocked.[70] A bill for national prohibition "for the duration" was introduced in 1943 and actually reached a hearing before a subcommittee of the House Judiciary Committee.[71] A number of states imposed curfews on the sale of alcoholic beverages, and agitation for local option was greatly increased. But despite some ground lost to local option, the most serious threats were fought off. When the war ended, the prohibitionists did not seem to have made any substantial gains.

The most important effects produced by any of the wartime measures were, by all odds, the changes brought about by price controls, and those changes probably could not have been foreseen. To begin with, in an effort to head off wartime inflation, Congress created the Office of Price Administration (OPA) in January 1942. When it directed its attention to the wine industry, the OPA concluded that it would not be possible to fix the prices of grapes for wine, since they were of so many different sorts from widely different regions selling at greatly varying prices. It would, instead, fix the price of wine, and it did so in a regulation published in May 1942.[72] This set the prices at which wine could be sold on the basis of the highest prices prevailing in March 1942. But there were many complications: Wine shipped in bulk between wineries in the same state, for example, was not subject to price control. Or if a winery had, in March 1942, a line of bottled wines at premium prices, it could sell *all* of its wines at that high price, premium or not: that was how Schenley, for example, made use of its Cresta Blanca label. And that was why Seagram's bought Paul Masson from Martin Ray, who had charged higher prices for his small production of varietal wines than had any other producer in California.[73]

Grape prices, as we have seen, went up at once. But the production of wine could not be much expanded, and the price of wine had been fixed. The obvious question was, How could a winemaker stay in business if the costs for his raw material, grapes, exploded, but he couldn't make any more wine than he had made before and he couldn't charge more than he had charged before? In these conditions, the lower-priced brands disappeared. Shipments of bulk wine to established bottlers outside California shrank, and the bottling of wine by the winery at the highest allowable price became the norm.[74] If a winery had no high-priced bottled wine of its own at the time that the original price ceiling was imposed, it could sell in bulk to a winery that did have such a line at prices higher than it would get if it shipped wine in bulk outside the state. The big firms that had already begun to bottle wines before the war had a distinct edge in this situation: Fruit Industries, Roma, Cribari, Petri, and as we have seen, Cresta Blanca. Those who could afford it soon took up bottling: the Gallos bought a used bottling line in New York and had it shipped to California, accompanied by its mechanic.[75] Guild Wineries, a marketing combination of several cooperatives in California, was formed in 1943 in order to exploit the advantages that went with a company's bottling its own wines. In this way did the practice of bottling at the winery, formerly regarded as the province of the premium table-wine producers, become a standard method.

Although the California wineries before the war had been well started on the road toward doing their own bottling and distributing, it had still been the exceptional practice. A few wineries even bottled all of their production, as The Christian Brothers was doing by 1939; but that came about largely because The Christian Brothers had an inspired salesman, Alfred Fromm, in charge of selling its wines.[76] The novelty of the practice before the war is curiously confirmed by that the fact that in 1939 the Wine, Liquor and Distillery Workers Union picketed retail liquor stores in New York City selling wine bottled in California because such wine would cost them their jobs as bottlers of wine on the East Coast.[77]

After this change had been forced on the wineries as a condition of survival, they soon found that they had no wish to return to the old practices. As one writer put it as early as 1942, the winemakers "will never again want to return after the war to the small-margin, cut-rate, cutthroat competitive condition we have become accustomed to over the years as a result of our mad scramble to maintain volume, even without profit, through tank car sales."[78]

The prophecy proved essentially correct. As *Wines and Vines* put it in 1946, the discovery that wineries could successfully sell wine of their own bottling was "the major development in the industry during the war."[79]

Price controls also had some effect in encouraging the production of superior wines. Under the category of "special pricing" the OPA allowed higher prices to be charged for varietal wines or for wines qualifying as "above average." The winemaker who was now bottling his own wine, rather than shipping it out without a name, was newly conscious of the need for making the best wine he could; the recognition by the OPA that superior wine should be allowed a superior price—a recognition that the American market on its own had seemed incapable of reaching—added yet another reason to the argument for quality.[80]

The failure to control the price of bulk wine moving from winery to winery within California was the biggest loophole in the system of price control. The big wineries, it was said—because they had the money, the bottling machinery, and the distribution systems—were able to corner the supply and shut everyone else out. As one eastern bottler complained early in 1943, "I took a certified check for $100,000 to California last week and I couldn't buy a drop of wine."[81] Recognizing its mistake, the OPA put the intrastate traffic in bulk wine under price control in February 1943.[82] At the same time, the Justice Department opened an inquiry into the charges made by embattled independent bottlers that they were being victimized by the power of the big wineries, especially those newly acquired by the invading distillers, who were taking all the wine for themselves.[83]

By 1943 the system of price controls was itself out of control. The wineries were told by the OPA that the ceiling on wine prices would be based on the assumption that grapes were selling at an average price of $30.30 a ton. But in the competition for grapes, some prices had gone up to five or six times that figure, the wineries hoping that by the time the wine from such costly grapes was ready to sell, the era of price controls would be over.[84] Meanwhile, grapes and bulk wines were more and more kept in California until they left the state in the form of bottled wines, or "case goods," at premium prices. Recognizing that its policy had not worked, the OPA in November removed price controls from grapes in interstate commerce so that buyers outside California might compete for some part of the crop—too late to make much difference.[85]

In preparation for the vintage of 1944, new ceilings were announced in August; they raised the one for bottled wines a bit by assuming that grapes would sell for $66 a ton—more than twice the figure used for 1943 but still well below the actuality. The big change was in the ceiling for bulk wines, which went up by nearly 100 percent. The evident intent was to defend the interests of the eastern bottlers, who had been driven to the wall under the old regulations. If bulk wines could be sold for the same price to the eastern bottlers as to wineries in California, then the eastern bottlers could compete on equal terms.[86] There was some hope that the loophole permitting a winery to sell all of its wine under its highest-priced label might be closed, but that hope was disappointed.[87] As the harvest season approached, the wineries grew more cautious about the price they would pay for grapes. A larger proportion of the raisin grape crop was made available; the good news about the war made it prudent to consider a return to "more normal" conditions, and the crop was again going to be a large one. But if the wineries intended to be more restrained in their bidding for grapes, their resolve soon broke down: the price of grapes was again bid up beyond levels that could be justified in light of the ceilings on wine prices. The average price for a ton of grapes in 1944 soared to $108. The same pressures raised prices for eastern grapes as well: the average price for grapes in the New York–Pennsylvania–Ohio–Michigan region in the period 1936–39 was $36 per ton; this rose to $81 per ton in the years 1942–44. A short crop in 1945 drove the price up to $141.[88]

The independent bottlers and distributors of wine outside California were forced to take extraordinary measures to stay in business. If no one would sell them bulk wine directly, they could contract with a California winery to buy grapes and make wine for the bottler's own account (this was called custom crushing). And it was not just the bottlers who used this method. The eastern winemakers also depended heavily on California wine for blending and on California brandy for fortifying. When they found that their California suppliers would give them nothing, they turned to custom crushing as well. Widmer's, D. W. Putnam, and Pleasant Valley, prominent New York Finger Lakes producers, all had agreements in 1943 with the Arvin Wine Company in the Central Valley under which the New Yorkers would buy California grapes and pay Arvin a fee for converting them into fortified wine to be shipped east. Widmer's had a similar agreement with California Products Company for the high-proof brandy used in fortifying.[89]

An even bolder method was for a bottler or dealer simply to purchase a California winery outright. A number of such purchases were in fact made, though without creating anything like the noise that the big distillers' earlier buying spree had. By July 1944 some dozen or so California wineries had been acquired by bottlers for the sake of guaranteeing supplies: the Elk Grove Winery was bought by a Milwaukee distributor; Garden Vineyards Winery went to a group of New Jersey bottlers, Larkmead to a Chicago merchant, and the Burbank Winery to the Eastern Wine Corporation of New York.[90] In one case, at least, the tail wagged the dog: the Gibson Distributing Company, bottlers and distributors of Covington, Kentucky, bought the big (2.25 million gallons capacity) Acampo Winery in 1943 and thus set out on the course that was to make the company one of the major presences in California winemaking for many years.[91] The old Renault Winery in New Jersey also entered the California field, buying St. George Winery in Fresno and Fountain Winery in St. Helena.[92] Renault was a hybrid enterprise: it was still a producer of eastern sparkling wine, but it was also a major distributor of wines from other sources.

It was not just the eastern distillers and the independent bottlers who shook up the system by their purchases. The California wineries themselves were in the market for new properties, especially in order to make sure of a supply of grapes. California Grape Products, for example, bought the Italian Vineyard Company property in Cucamonga in 1943, acquiring thus at a stroke some five thousand acres of established wine grapes.[93]

By the time the vintage season arrived in 1945, the war was over. Even before then, the conditions that had controlled the wine industry in wartime were beginning to break up. In June 1945 the War Food Administration determined that it no longer needed to set aside any of the raisin-grape crop for raisins. At the same time, the predictions were for a large grape crop—the second largest since Repeal, smaller only than that of 1943. In anticipation of these conditions, the OPA announced in June 1945 that it would lower the ceilings on the price of wine for the next vintage. It was soon clear that abundance had now replaced scarcity and that the main changes brought about by scarcity— diversion of bulk wine away from the independent bottlers, a huge increase in winery bottling, and rising prices—would now be slowed or reversed. The wineries were flooded with grapes, whose prices dropped from the average $108 a ton paid in 1944 to an average $55; some varieties fetched as little as $25 a ton.[94] The resulting vintage in 1945 was a record 116 million gallons. The wineries did not wait for the OPA to act but began lowering their prices substantially, so that a bottle of standard fortified wine that sold for $1.06 in August went for 82 cents in September 1945. To confirm the way that things were going, the OPA announced in November that it was suspending all price ceilings on wine.[95]

All of these developments had an ominous look—would there be a return to the familiar prewar condition of overproduction and ruinous prices? No doubt there was much

If We Could Treble Our Present Wine Stocks—

We would still be unable to supply the many buyers old and new who seek

SEBASTIANI WINES

We say this with sincere regrets, for we are anxious to serve all who through their sales efforts are helping to promote a wider consumption of American wines.

However, with a limited inventory, we are duty bound to serve our regular customers first. And even they are getting only a portion of their requirements.

Orders that we refuse are, therefore, done so out of necessity, and with regrets.

SEBASTIANI WINERIES

Producers of Dry and Sweet Wines

Sonoma and Woodbridge, California

FIGURE 26
A seller's market in war-time. Sebastiani, a major supplier of bulk wines to the eastern trade, attempts to mollify the bottlers it must disappoint. (From *Wine Review* 11 [June 1943]; reprinted with permission from *Wines and Vines*.)

anxiety on this score, yet the tone of the remarks made by industry people was determinedly optimistic.[96] People had gotten to know wine during the war years, it was said; now they would continue to buy it, and the market would continue to grow. The more or less official view was expressed by Harry Caddow, secretary-manager of the Wine Institute: "The grape and wine industry emerges from the war period in the soundest position in its history, with its wines greatly improved in quality to meet European competition and with millions of American consumers who have discovered in recent years that the products of their own country's vineyards are as desirable as any from foreign lands."[97] This was not a statement that could stand up to examination: there had been no structural change during the war years in the sources of California wine (except that not as many raisin grapes were used) or in the methods by which it was made, so how could its wines be greatly improved in quality? Such remarks might be taken as a sign of a new confidence—or just as hopeful noises.

But the fact is that the war had been almost wholly advantageous to American wine. It opened the doors of wine merchants, hotels, and restaurants to American wine; it allowed

Frank Schoonmaker and others to find a market for American varietal wines, varietally labeled, so that American wine—some American wine, at any rate—was now both authentic and identifiable. The war also brought the well-financed, commercially sophisticated distillers into California, who taught new lessons about brand identity, distribution, and advertising. And it brought price controls and shortages, so that wineries learned to bottle their own produce rather than ship it in anonymous bulk to independent bottlers.

All of these things added up to some strong commercial arguments: there was more profit (always supposing that the market held up) in a well-advertised wine bottled by the winery under its own name than there was in wine shipped off in tank cars. The experiences of the war also added up to an argument for quality—the most valuable result of all. If American wines had now found entry into those places where they had not been known before, that was largely because the war had compelled their admission. To hold their place when European wines came back, the level of quality would have to go up. Winemakers now began to admit that they could improve their wines and that there was a reason to do so. They began, in fact, to say exactly what their critics had been saying ever since Repeal: that they should plant superior varieties in place of the heavy producers of inferior wine, that they should seek to combine the best varieties with the appropriate locations, and that they should make their wines by the best methods.[98]

There was a chorus of encouraging and hopeful remarks to be heard about American wine toward the end of the war: "There is gradually emerging, through all the turmoil," M. F. K. Fisher wrote, "a quality of production that cannot be harmed by war or prejudice or even man's dishonesty."[99] Frank Schoonmaker, newly returned from the war at the end of 1945, was even more emphatic. "American wines," he declared, "are now on the best tables of New York and Boston and Philadelphia and Washington and Chicago—*and they are there to stay.*" But, he warned, the new demand for American wines of quality could not be met without large new plantings of superior grapes, and those would not be made until the wineries saw the light and paid the higher prices required for shy-bearing varieties of quality.[100] As though in anticipation of Schoonmaker's observations, the Wine Institute, meeting at the beginning of 1945, announced that it would encourage the planting of superior grape varieties in properly chosen locations.[101]

This was a revolutionary shift in perception. Before the war, most American winemakers were content to defend the way they already did things: they made fortified wines because that was what the market wanted; they mislabeled their wines because that was how it had always been done; they used unsuitable grapes because they were what was available, and no market existed for wine from superior varieties. Anyone who questioned these positions—and, fortunately, there were always a redeeming few who did stubbornly question—was dismissed as ignorant or troublesome. Now, however, a new possibility had been glimpsed, not merely by the "impractical idealists" but by the people who made and sold wine in large quantities. Perhaps this turn of things would have come about without a war, but as it happened, it was the war that made it come about.

7

POSTWAR DISAPPOINTMENTS

A BRIEF EUPHORIA

By the end of the war, late in 1945, the winemakers of the United States were like nervous racehorses at the starting gate, eagerly waiting for the signal to go. The end of wartime regulations and the easing of restrictions on materials and supplies did not happen at a single stroke, but conditions were sufficiently changed by the beginning of 1946 to make that a year of unbounded expansion. The official view was euphoric. "Consumption is expected to exceed all past records," *Wines and Vines* declared, no doubt expressing a general belief.[1] Or as Herman Wente, president of the Wine Institute, put it more elaborately,

> Wine sales in America are picking up speed. Like a passenger train on a siding, waiting for the war express to go by, the wine industry found time in the war years to get rid of the clinkers clogging its fire grate, to get everything oiled and in running order, and to build up such a head of steam that it was ready to set new records when the switch was thrown. Now it's on the main track again and all that is needed is cooperation by the men who make the wine train go.[2]

This is clear testimony to the excited optimism of the day. More important, perhaps, it shows a remarkable self-deception. It is all very well to talk about getting rid of clinkers and building up a head of steam, but what, after all, had really changed in American winegrowing? The big distillers had entered the scene, with their money and their distribution systems. But they had done nothing to change the basis of the industry. The same grapes still grew in the same vineyards, the same methods of winemaking still obtained, and the market was still dominated by sweet fortified wines. It is true that the war years had taught the winemakers that brand promotion paid off and that some wines might be sold for more money than others if they could only be given distinct identities: these were highly valuable lessons. But in the first years after the war, there was far more talk about a new day than any concrete action to bring about real change. It was easier to do more and more of the same things. The scale of the industry grew larger, but despite all the talk, it remained essentially the same.

New building was the top priority. The general persuasion that sales were going to go up sharply meant that more production capacity and more storage would be needed. Then, too, prices would certainly fall below the levels that they had reached under the artificial pressures of wartime; thus more wine would have to be made and sold to keep income up. Wineries must therefore expand, and so they did. The new building and new equipment reported in the months following the end of the war recall the exciting first days of Repeal: "Windsor Adds Equipment," "Cal. Cellars Expands," "Cameo Plans Construction," "Cella Builds Winery," "Cal-O-Ky Plans Additions," and "Sonoma Adds Equipment" is the harvest of headlines from a single page of the *Wine Review* in February 1946. At the end of 1946, *Wines and Vines* reported that new construction had broken all records, and that in the Central Valley alone, some 45 million gallons of fermenting and storage capacity had been added in one year.[3]

Brand-new wineries were built by Bisceglia Brothers at Fresno, the Liberty Winery at Acampo, and the Di Giorgio Wine Company at Di Giorgio in Kern County.[4] But most of the action was in expanding and modernizing existing establishments: the Sunnyside Winery at Fresno added 2 million gallons of storage; Cameo Vineyards of Fresno added a million; the old Sun-Maid raisin plant at Fresno was taken over by a new company called Vie-Del Grape Products Company to produce grape concentrate, high-proof brandy, and neutral wine to be sold to eastern winemakers for blending with their native wines.[5] In Madera, Krikor Arakelian's big Madera Winery was completely renovated, including the addition of a million-gallon sherry cooking plant. Substantial remodelings were reported at Petri, Roma, Gallo, and Italian Swiss Colony, among many others.[6] These new buildings gave wineries an opportunity to apply the latest notions about efficient operation and equipment: perhaps the most notable item was the increasing use of stainless steel in such things as cooling coils (but not yet for storage and fermentation tanks). Stainless steel, which pretty well solved the age-old problem of metal contamination in wine, had been produced in volume during the war and was now available at prices lower than had been possible before.

The Di Giorgio plant, at the far southern extremity of the Central Valley, was regarded as defining the state of the art, at least for the industrial-scale production of fortified wines that dominated the trade. The winery, standing in the midst of the vines that supplied it, was fed by a steady stream of tractor-drawn trailers, each holding five tons of grapes. The

FIGURE 27
The new wineries in post-war California continued the line that had been taken in the '30s: more and more fortified wines from larger and larger wineries. (From *Wines and Vines Yearbook* [1947]; reprinted with permission from *Wines and Vines*.)

grapes passed through a battery of crushers to the fermenting building, where thirty concrete tanks, each with a capacity of 60,000 gallons, received the must. Each tank was equipped with stainless steel cooling coils circulating water from a cooling tower. The pomace left after fermentation was removed by continuous mechanical conveyor; it was first passed through a continuous press and then through a pomace still so that no drop of juice was lost. What did not go into wine was distilled into high-proof brandy for fortifying the wines. Everything was on the largest scale: two blending tanks were rated at 260,000 gallons each; there were eight refrigerated, cork-walled tanks of 60,000 gallons each; and the sherry-cooking building held twenty concrete tanks of 60,000 gallons each, equipped with stainless steel heating coils. The finished wine went through overhead pipelines directly into tank cars on the winery's railway siding. All was mechanized, so that twenty men did the work that before had required seventy; and the design allowed for ready expansion to a projected 20 million gallons of storage capacity.[7]

No one questioned the quality of the wines so produced, which were no doubt as sound as careful production controls could make them (the winery's laboratory was "considered one of the most modern in the industry"); they were certainly inexpensive as well.[8] But the Di Giorgio operation, impressive as it was, at the same time illustrated the major defects of the California industry, considered as a potential source of varied and interesting wines.

Sicilian-born Joseph Di Giorgio (1875–1946) came to America at age fourteen and went into the fresh fruit business, first in New York, then in Baltimore, and then in Washington, D.C. He grew rich as a dealer in bananas, operating a fleet of banana boats. Then he sold the banana business and went into Florida citrus. In 1920, the first year of Prohibition, he bought 24,000 acres in Kern County, California, and began developing vast vineyards, having noted that the grapes from this hot southern end of the great Central Valley ripened earlier than those farther north. "With that kind of advantage," he said, "I can make a fortune." And so he did.[9] He became the king of Kern County, far and away the most visible of its developers: his fellow citizens erected a bronze bust of him in the Kern County town of Arvin, a few miles from the center of his operations.[10]

Obviously, Di Giorgio had little interest in wine. He developed his vineyards under Prohibition, when commercial winemaking was illegal; he planted them in one of the hottest regions of the state, where early maturity and large volume were the main considerations; and he saw his opportunity not in making wine but in supplying table grapes to the early markets. There came a time, however, when he simply had too many grapes, and only then did winemaking enter the picture. His first venture came in 1932 when, as he later recalled, "I was thinking about what I could do with thirty thousand tons of grapes on the vines and no market for them."[11] What he did was to make a deal with the Italian Swiss Colony winery, which was at the time, in the latter days of Prohibition, beginning to prepare for Repeal. Di Giorgio would deliver grapes to Italian Swiss Colony, which would make wine for him on a partnership basis. Ultimately Di Giorgio, through the credits he established as the owner of a large part of its wine inventory, became a major stockholder in Italian Swiss Colony and so profited nicely from its sale in 1942 to National Distillers. By that time he had a large winery of his own at Delano, in the south of the Central Valley. And now he had an even larger one at Di Giorgio. Winemaking, however, was for him never anything but a "salvage" operation, even though the salvage was generated in huge volumes. As one of his nephews explained, the only reason that the Di Giorgio Fruit Company acquired the Delano winery "was to have a place to utilize the excess grapes that we grew other than for table purposes."[12] Nor did Di Giorgio himself take any interest in wine—he himself never drank it—apart from its role as a safety valve in his vast operation.[13] "Why did Mr. Di Giorgio have wineries?" Leon Adams asked rhetorically. "He wasn't interested in wine. He never was really interested in wine, only in grapes."[14] But without a winery to make use of them, what could one do with the grapes left over from those thousands of Kern County acres? So wine was made.[15]

In the general rush to obtain new equipment, wineries were particularly eager to set up new bottling lines. As *Wines and Vines* explained, the turn to winery bottling that the war had compelled had been more or less improvised at the time, the machinery being "squeezed into any available part of the winery buildings."[16] Now they could do it right. The St. George Winery at Fresno set up two new lines; Alta put up a new 36,000-square-foot building to accommodate its bottling operations; Guild Wineries erected a central bottling plant at Lodi.[17] And there was an equivalent traffic in new crushers, presses, fermenting and storage tanks, filters, and refrigeration equipment.[18]

New vineyard planting went on up and down the state. Early in 1945, when expansive stirrings were distinctly felt, Vai Brothers in the Cucamonga district bought 1,300 acres of vineyard in Mira Loma; early in 1946, B. Cribari and Sons bought 330 acres of orchard and farm country near Gilroy to convert to vineyards.[19] New planting had begun even earlier in the Napa Valley, where Martin Stelling, a San Francisco businessman, had been buying up old vineyards since 1943 and planting new ones since 1944. Stelling understood the importance of superior varieties, and he set a valuable example for others by his work before his accidental death in 1950. In André Tchelistcheff's view, Stelling was like "new oxygen" to the Napa Valley.[20]

There was considerable buying and selling of established properties as wineries, bottlers, and speculators jockeyed for position in a high-stakes race. Wineries that changed hands included Cordelia Vineyards (with a capacity of 1 million gallons), sold to a St. Paul investment banker in 1946; the Waterford Winery (2 million gallons) was bought by Eastern Wine Corporation, the biggest of the New York City bottlers, in May 1946, and at the same time the Wente Brothers Winery bought the R. C. Williams Cellars in Livermore.[21] The biggest deal of all was the sale in April 1945 of the Italian Vineyard Company at Guasti—the 5,000-acre "world's largest vineyard" and its accompanying winery—by H. O. Lanza to Garrett and Company.[22]

All of this turnover gave out ambiguous signals: was it a sign of confidence or of nervousness? So too did the burgeoning of new cooperative wineries: was the building of new co-ops a vote of confidence in the future, or a warning of impending trouble? After the 1945 vintage, when prices for some grapes had plummeted as low as $25 a ton, many growers took counsel among themselves and decided that their best protection was to go into the wine business on their own account via the cooperative route. Accordingly, the Del Rey Winery near Fresno, based on a group of 140 growers, went up in 1946; so did the Yosemite Winery at Madera, a cooperative of more than 100 growers and the first co-op in Madera County. The Lockeford Winery in Lockeford and the Mendocino Cooperative Winery in Empire were also built in 1946. Together these new wineries had a storage capacity of almost 10 million gallons, and almost all of that productive capacity was devoted to fortified wines.[23]

As this very sketchy summary of postwar renovation and expansion suggests, the emergent pattern clearly continued the developments that had begun with Repeal—that is, toward the large-scale production of standard, blended wines, most of them fortified. One of the big questions about the wine trade after the war was whether Americans would continue their "unusual preference" for sweet fortified wines over dry table wines.[24] That question now seemed to be quite clearly answered: they would. Before the war, practically the entire output of such wines had been sold to bottlers for distribution under the bottlers' own labels. The war, as we have seen, gave the winemakers a reason to change that practice and to begin to do their own bottling and distributing. There was now some tendency to revert to the prewar practice. Production was again unrestricted, price controls were relaxed if not yet gone, transportation presented no difficulties. In these conditions, the simple plan of letting the bottler handle the market had its undeniable appeal.

But things had already changed too much to allow a complete return to the old ways. For one thing, many wineries now had a large investment in bottling lines; for another, many had invested in the promotion of their own brands. There was no point in abandoning these assets as long as the market held up. And after a slight uneasiness at the end of 1945, when prices began to fall sharply, the expansive market that everyone had hoped for actually materialized.[25] The wineries, for the moment at least, seemed not to need the bottlers, and the unlucky bottlers had to scramble again to find supplies. *Wines and Vines* estimated in April 1946 that only some 10 million to 12 million gallons had been sold in bulk from the 1945 crush, as against the prewar rate of 60 million gallons. And the price of bulk wine went up steeply by as much as 50 percent between the beginning and the middle of 1946. The bottlers loudly complained that they were victims of a conspiracy to freeze them out of business, and there was much bad feeling all around.[26] The bottler would soon have his revenge; the boom of '46 was succeeded by the bust of '47, and those bottlers who had survived the hard times were again eagerly courted and could name their own terms.

As the wine trade had plunged headlong down the path that led toward bigger and bigger volumes of monotonously undistinguished wines, the professors at the University of California resumed their work aimed at improving California grapes and wines. The work had not been wholly interrupted by the war; it now began to grow again.[27] The dominant interests of the enologists, as they had been before the war, were the control of fermentation and the relation of variety and location to the quality of wine. The viticulturists had even more to occupy them in importing and testing new varieties and in grape breeding. Phylloxera remained a constant problem.[28]

Most urgent, however, was the challenge presented by a serious outbreak of Pierce's disease. Once known as the Anaheim disease (after the disastrous episode in the 1880s when the flourishing vineyards of the Santa Ana valley near Los Angeles were nearly wiped out by the mysterious affliction), Pierce's disease had reappeared to a troubling extent, this time in the San Joaquin Valley—where it had been unknown—and by 1941 was a serious concern not only there but across the state. In 1943 it was estimated that some 75,000 acres of vineyard were affected, and the losses from crop damage went up steadily: $3.4 million in 1942; $5.8 million in 1943; $7.45 million in 1944.[29] In 1947 the Fresno district appealed to the state legislature for a large appropriation to fight the "insidious, constantly encroaching malady."[30] By that year, however, the epidemic had greatly diminished, and in the next year had so far declined that people could disregard it. Pierce's disease remains, however, a perennial threat, for which no treatment is yet known.[31]

The struggle to understand and control the disease was not restricted to the scientists at Davis but involved many agencies: the U.S. Department of Agriculture, the state Department of Agriculture, and several departments of the university. There was not much that could be done, apart from pulling diseased plants from the vineyards. That slowed the spread of the disease, but of course it also reduced production and left the causes untouched. The main carriers of the disease were identified—a variety of insects called sharpshooters—as were their host plants. Large plantings of experimental seedlings were made in hopes of finding resistant varieties, but without success. One such planting was made on the UCLA campus in Westwood in 1946, a reminder of how recent the agricultural history of Los Angeles still is.[32] For a long time it was thought that the disease was produced by a virus; not until 1974 was it shown to be not viral but bacterial.[33]

The work of the university scientists after the war found a response within the industry that it had not been able to arouse before. This was in part because there was now, twenty years after the resumption of scientific work in viticulture and enology, a small but significant number of university-trained men employed in the industry itself.[34] The growing prestige of the technological approach to winemaking was recognized in 1944 by the formation of the Technical Advisory Committee (TAC) as a standing committee of the Wine Institute. The committee grew out of an informal group gathered in 1942 on the invitation of the Wine Institute. The original members were not very confident that their aims would inspire much support, but they were agreeably surprised: by the end of the decade the committee was an authoritative presence.[35]

In 1950, in a move to enhance the professional prestige of a group now beginning to achieve some numbers, the American Society of Enologists (ASE) was formed.[36] Such a group would have been quite impossible to organize earlier, when people offering to call themselves enologists might have been counted on the fingers of one hand.[37] Now there were sufficient numbers of technical men in the wine industry to sustain a professional group, and, they thought, the time had come to assert themselves. "The truth of the matter," as Edmund Rossi Jr. recalled, "was that in 1950 the American Society of Enologists was formed with the idea of giving more status to the winemakers."[38] Up to that point, the technical men had been confined to their laboratories; they now wanted to be winemakers, in control of operations. Organization and technical interchange were important steps to that end. There were suspicions in the trade that the enologists were organizing a union, but that was a groundless anxiety. It is true that the membership, because of the structure of the wine industry at that time, was largely composed of men working for big businesses, but the aim was, as their president said at their first meeting, simply to learn how to make "better wine at lower cost."[39] The most paranoid employer could not quarrel with that. Both the TAC and ASE inevitably had a strong University of California flavor about them, and university scientists like Maynard Amerine were among the most determined proponents of the idea that the enologist should be a professional, with all the authority and responsibility attached to that character, rather than a simple technician.[40]

The technical understanding of processes within the winery was now well ahead of the state of California's vineyards.[41] Winemakers—in theory at least—had the methods to make very good wines. But they had very few good grapes to make them out of. The need for better varieties, and for ceasing to use those varieties in plentiful supply that yielded only mediocre or neutral wines at best, was clearly understood by anyone who had attended to the subject at all. The annual resolutions of the Wine Institute, for example, regularly called for the improvement of the varietal stock in California. And the university people pointed out again and again that not all varieties were equal, that "three-way" grapes would not make good wine, and that climate and region mattered too. These things were known and admitted, but change came slowly.

There were at least three major problems to be solved in the vineyards: the elimination of inferior varieties and their replacement by superior varieties; the correction of confused and mistaken identifications (how many different varieties were known as Gamay Beaujolais? which "Pinots" really were Pinots? what was Syrah? or Sirah? or Petite Sirah?); and the securing of desirable clones of the varieties chosen.[42] The last point may be illustrated by this observation from H. P. Olmo, in charge of the grape breeding program at Davis, writing in 1951: "I do not know of a single vineyard of the *Pinot noir* in California where I could recommend that a grower obtain propagating wood, because our plantings are largely poor strains and the number of vines showing degeneration is large indeed."[43]

How stubborn was the resistance to planting better varieties may be shown by analyzing the postwar expansion of California's vineyards. The high prices for grapes and the euphoric view of the prospects for the wine trade had the inevitable effect of stimulating grape planting throughout the state. The acreage of nonbearing grapes, roughly the measure of new planting, leaped from 36,000 in 1944 to almost 52,000 in 1945, the largest such increase since the explosion of planting that marked the first years of Prohibition. Moreover, the bulk of this new planting was in wine grapes: of the 52,000 acres of nonbearing vines in 1945, 15,000 were raisin grapes, 12,000 table grapes, and the remainder—almost 25,000 acres—were wine grapes.[44] The excitement that such figures might arouse is tempered when one analyzes them. Most of this planting was in the Central Valley, not only of raisin and table grapes but of wine grapes too: 16,000 acres as opposed to just over 3,000 acres of wine grapes throughout all the North Coast counties.[45] And the varieties planted were overwhelmingly of the old, undistinguished standbys that the growers and wineries were both accustomed to—Carignane, Grenache, Mission, Palomino.[46] A. J. Winkler, reviewing in 1946 the new grape plantings in California for the preceding two years, found almost nothing to promise any improvement in quality: there were, instead, unwarranted increases in the table and raisin grapes that for years had burdened California with annual surpluses. And when a decent grape was planted, it was more often than not in the wrong place. Palomino would help improve the sherries of the Central Valley, but why, Winkler asked, plant it in the coastal counties? Carignane and Petite Sirah were good grapes, but they would sunburn in the lower San Joaquin Valley.[47]

Five years later Winkler surveyed the scene again and found it even more depressing. The total vineyard acreage in California in 1951 was now almost exactly 500,000 acres, a marked drop from the 555,000 of five years earlier.[48] Some of that loss was in raisin grapes, but proportionately more was in wine grapes: the nearly 30,000 nonbearing acres (newer plantings) of wine grapes in 1946 had shrunk to fewer than 5,000 in 1951. It was true, Winkler conceded, that things had been improved by the removal of a considerable acreage of Alicante Bouschet from the state's vineyards (some 17,500 acres remained, only 97 of which were new plantings), but the vineyards of California were still dominated by raisin and table varieties, just as they had been at the beginning of Repeal. "This condition prevails," Winkler wrote, "even though there has been ample opportunity for improvement since repeal; 145,033 acres of vines have been pulled and 147,221 planted. These changes have cost industry about $750,000; a tremendous expense with practically nothing to show for it."[49]

The reason for the continued dominance of table and raisin grapes was, as Winkler well knew, largely a question of money. If wineries did not pay more for better varieties, then there was no reason to give up growing high-yielding, low-quality grapes. Grapes were bought on "sugar points"; as Philip Wagner recalled the practice in 1949, "The winemaking goal everywhere [in California] was still the highest possible sugar rather than a proper sugar-acid balance."[50] And if Thompson Seedless grapes at ten tons an acre were rated at the same sugar levels as Sauvignon blanc at two tons an acre, who would grow Sauvignon blanc?[51] Maynard Amerine published "An Historical Note on Grape Prices" in *Wines and Vines* in October 1946, showing that in 1887 growers received four times as much for Cabernet as they did for Mission, and twice as much for Riesling as for Malvoisie; the difference in prices was clearly reflected in the ratings assigned to the resulting wines. "The moral," he concluded, "is very simple: to secure fine wines fine grapes are necessary; to secure fine grapes the winery must pay more for the low-yielding varieties."[52] But the moral had yet to be taken in any practical way. A very careful observer of the industry might have seen some hopeful signs in Napa, however, where better varieties were beginning to get better prices. In response, growers began to plant more of the better varieties there, so that Napa was almost alone in having a good supply of good grapes when at last the demand for them came in the 1960s.[53]

Paralleling the continued dependence on high-yielding grapes was the trend toward ever-higher yields from the wine varieties themselves. In the decade of the 1940s the average tonnage per acre for wine grape varieties in California was just under four tons; in the 1960s it had risen over five tons.[54] Some of that increase was perhaps owing to better methods of cultivation, but most of it had to come from overcropping. And overcropping—that is, allowing the vine to carry more fruit than it can properly ripen—entailed a serious loss of fruit quality. All this was known, but not much was done about it.

In a market so dominated by quantity and apparently so indifferent to quality, it was

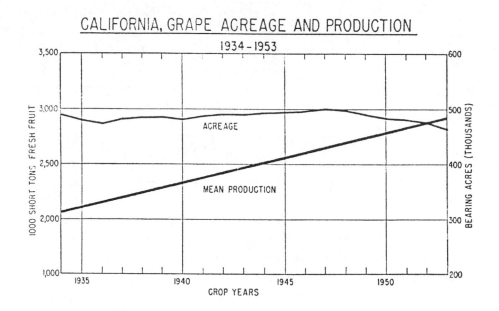

CALIFORNIA, GRAPE ACREAGE AND PRODUCTION
1934–1953

FIGURE 28

Professor Winkler's demonstration of overcropping in California: a 40 percent rise in production from a slightly declining acreage. Most of the defects of California wine, Winkler thought, could be traced to overcropping. (From *Journal of the American Society for Enology and Viticulture* 5:4 [1954]; reprinted by permission of the American Society for Enology and Viticulture.)

even possible to take the gloomy view that growers would give up on fine wine grapes. Writing as late as 1956, Eugene Seghesio, of the Seghesio Winery in Healdsburg (founded in 1902), listed the obstacles that a grower had to surmount: "large overhead, low yield, low return, unsatisfactory help, limited success in replanting, and lack of stability in the industry." In consequence, he warned, "the acreage and tonnage of Sonoma County are slowly declining, so that it may cease to be a grape and wine producing area."[55]

It was not simply that the supply of wine grapes seemed to be going nowhere: it was sinking. In Sonoma County, as Seghesio had gloomily pointed out, the total acreage was decreasing, and so was the proportion of superior varieties in that diminishing total. Olmo, writing in 1950, observed "the disappointing fact that the acreage of the noble varieties is less today than it was fifty years ago."[56] Olmo's solution was to breed new varieties that would combine large production with improved quality, and so allow California to break out of the vicious circle it had been caught in since Repeal: poor grapes making poor wine for an indifferent market that asked only for poor wine from poor grapes.[57] The introduction of Olmo's Ruby Cabernet in 1948 was the main salvo in this campaign, and it had some effect. Ruby Cabernet, a cross of Carignane and Cabernet Sauvignon, was not as productive as Carignane nor its wines as distinguished as those of Cabernet Sauvignon, but it produced more than Cabernet Sauvignon and its wines tasted better than those of Carignane. It was, in short, a compromise, and thus vulnerable to the objections made against all compromises. But growers actually began growing it, which was the main thing. In the first ten years of its commercial life, only about 250 acres of Ruby Cabernet were planted, but by 1971 there were about 5,000 acres, and that total rose to 18,000 acres by 1976. Almost all of this acreage was in the right places, in Central Valley vineyards whose high production was most in need of improved quality. Of that 1976 acreage, almost 90 percent was in Fresno, Kern, Madera, Merced, Stanislaus, and Tulare Counties.[58] After 1976 the planting of Ruby Cabernet began to fade: total acreage was down to 13,000 acres at the beginning of the 1980s, and by the end of the decade the total was only half that. In recent years there has been a rise in the acreage of Ruby Cabernet, but it has not recovered the ground that it once held.[59]

If no substantial improvement had been made in California's vineyards, what about the winemaking? There was, as has been said, a good technical understanding available. And a small but growing movement aimed at making good wine was now under way. A notable step forward was made by André Tchelistcheff in Napa when he set up his Napa Valley Technical Group about 1947. This became a center for people interested in the matter of improving wine quality—in fact, practically a who's who of Napa Valley winemaking: Louis P. Martini, Peter and Robert Mondavi, George Deuer, Lee Stewart, John Daniel, and Al Huntsinger were among the participants. They met "to exchange practical information on the production of high-quality wines."[60] But in general, the available technical understanding had not been widely applied, and the standards of California winemaking left much to be desired. In an important series of articles on wine production from California grapes, Maynard Amerine listed a discouraging set of prevailing practices: overcropping ("a wide-spread evil in California during and since the war"); too-early or too-late harvesting ("perennial problems in California"); uncontrolled fermentation ("the most appalling variations in fermentation procedures"); inadequate aging ("until recently many California wineries were unaware, or acted as if they were unaware, that table wines improved in the bottle"); and "unintelligent blending."[61] Varietal wines were being produced without varietal character, white wines bottled too late, red wines fermented at temperatures too high.[62] And these procedures were based on a grape supply still overwhelmingly dominated by inferior varieties—even where a grower might claim to have a superior variety, examination often showed that the vineyard was in fact planted to some other, inferior, misnamed variety, or was a mixture of varieties.[63] In a later series of articles devoted to the question of aging wines, Amerine added to the list of bad California practices: the winemakers of the state, he said, seemed to regard aging with "extreme suspicion, or even contempt."[64] There were reasons for this view: the winemakers had to turn over their inventories quickly in order to stay in business; California wineries, most of them, were unsuitable for long-term storage, as were the large containers almost exclusively used. The market was not yet prepared to pay for the expense of aging. Vintage-dating was rarely used, so that the fact of aging could not be effectively presented. Other reasons—inexperience and an unwillingness to learn—were less defensible.[65]

In 1949, Philip Wagner—who had established a reputation as one of the very, very few authorities on wine outside the state of California by his work as a vineyardist, winemaker, and author—was invited to be a judge at the wine competition at the California State Fair. He went to California, Wagner recalled, filled with awe at the idea of assisting in the choice of the best wines from the production of such an impressive industry, but soon found that the industry was in fact "touchingly weak and vulnerable." It was, he remembered,

> naïve and irrelevant to the mainstream of American life. Here they were, these men and women, working themselves to the bone for something that the American public couldn't care about less, namely a decent glass of wine. The people at the fair were not even able to provide proper wine glasses; instead, the judges tasted their wines from receptacles that were more appropriate to a small milkshake or a gooey dessert. It turned out that in all of California it was impossible to find a supply of good, serviceable, all-purpose wine glasses of ample size and moderate price.[66]

On his return to Maryland, Wagner began supplying such wineries as Almadén and Martini, as well as the Wine Institute itself, with glasses of appropriate design that he and his wife had arranged to have made some years before. As for the wines to be judged at the fair, these, he found, were made to no standard at all.[67]

The idea of making wine in California was not yet felt to be at all attractive or glamourous. Writing to friends in 1953 at the beginning of a new semester at Davis, Maynard Amerine gloomily observed, "Registration is here—little interest in enology. Perhaps we make it too difficult? But the industry is certainly not prosperous enough to attract the new students. The veterans who came in 1946–47 have nearly all left the wine industry now."[68]

Amid all the discouraging signs, the hopeful one was the scattered appearance of small wineries—and sometimes not so small—devoted to making good wines. These concentrated on making only a few kinds of wine by the best methods from carefully cultivated superior varieties of grapes. Mostly they were created by newcomers—sometimes amateurs—who had not been scarred by the grim struggle for survival during Prohibition and by the Depression following. They could thus see and believe in possibilities that many veterans had long since given up on. They have been called gentleman winemakers, and as such they make a link with California in the late nineteenth century, when the ostensible charm of grape growing and winemaking lured many of the cultivated and the wealthy to vineyard estates in the coastal counties.[69] But if they were gentlemen, they were not dilettantes. The work they set themselves required unlimited energy and dedication; the money that goes typically with being a gentleman was also highly useful.[70]

The first of these invaluable pioneers was Martin Ray (1904–76). He had known Paul Masson and his wines in the days before Prohibition, and his object in becoming a California winegrower was to restore the standards that had once been known. Thus, as is

FIGURE 29

"Receptacles that were more appropriate to a small milkshake or a gooey dessert." Philip Wagner *(left)* with Dr. S. P. Lucia and Professor George Marsh judging red table wines at the California State Fair, 1949. The inability of the fair to provide suitable wineglasses, Wagner thought, said much about the state of the wine industry. (From *Wine Review* 17 [September 1949]; reprinted with permission from *Wines and Vines*.)

true of most reformers, his deepest motive was conservative—to return to the past; the fact that that past might be largely imaginary was a large part of its appeal. The term that invariably occurs in any discussion of Martin Ray is *fanatic*—the more one learns of the man and his work, the more the term seems inevitable—or perhaps *obsessive* might be even better.[71] However one may put it, Ray was certainly a man possessed by his ambition to make great wine. After a career as a stockbroker—the fact that he prospered at this during the Depression says a good deal about him—Ray bought the old Masson winery in the hills above Saratoga from Paul Masson himself in 1936 and proceeded to make it a standing rebuke of the practices prevailing then and long afterward in California.[72] He concentrated on making pure varietal wines from Pinot noir, Cabernet Sauvignon, and Chardonnay from his own unirrigated vineyards, at a time when these vines were so rare in California as to be practically invisible. The grapes were crushed within the hour of their picking; the musts were unsulfited, and barrel fermented: they were pressed in hand presses that Ray had had custom built with stainless steel fittings. Ray aged his wines, unfined and unfiltered, in small oak cooperage, and he kept them back from the market until they were, in his judgment, ready: ten years of bottle age was his preferred measure. And he priced his wines so high as to challenge disbelief.[73] As Ray said, "Quite frankly I would like people to be shocked, shocked first at the type of wines that can be made in California, and second, by the prices which people are willing to pay for them when at

FIGURE 30
Martin Ray in his cellar, where, he maintained, he alone in California made wine in the right way. (Reprinted by permission of the Ray Family Collection, Saratoga, California.)

their best."[74] Incidentally, according to his widow Ray spent $1,000 each month at the end of the '30s on the best French and German wines so that he could educate his palate and know what he aimed at in producing his own.[75] While he was doing these things Ray also was loudly proclaiming that he, and he alone, was following the path of virtue in California winemaking. He was often—not always, but often—right; and he succeeded in offending almost everybody. But as he wrote in 1940, the state of things in California when he began was such that, in his dedication to the pursuit of fine wines, "there is as yet no competition. It is particularly a happy situation because I am doing the thing that I want to do and I cannot do it in any other way."[76]

Ray's winery burned to the ground in 1941, and though he managed through heroic labor to rebuild it, he sold it soon thereafter to Seagram's and moved on to another property nearby. There he continued just as energetically and determinedly to pursue his idea of what California wine should be, but perhaps with not quite the same dramatic impact that he had in those brief years between 1936 and 1941, when he startled the small American wine world by the audacity of his performance.

Martin Ray's example, the restoration (and transformation) of a historic property, was followed by several others in these years, though by none with the same ferocity of single-minded purpose that Ray exhibited. Sometimes such a restoration might originate by purest accident. In 1943 Frank Bartholomew bought at auction the old Buena Vista property just outside the town of Sonoma, the winery estate that Agoston Haraszthy had founded in 1857 and from which he had directed the campaign of publicity that first made the United States aware of California wine. Bartholomew, a newspaperman and later the president of the United Press news service, had no idea at the time of what he had bought: he was looking merely for an agreeable country property. The winery had long been inactive and was in ruinous condition.[77] When he learned what he had acquired, Bartholomew and his wife determined to restore it; Antonia Bartholomew directed the original work while Frank Bartholomew was serving as a war correspondent.[78] Buena Vista was particularly interesting for its old stone building and the tunnels driven into the hill behind it, both from the days of Haraszthy: these too were restored. The first Buena Vista wines from Haraszthy's replanted vineyards appeared in 1949 and were good enough to take prizes in the state judgings. The example of Bartholomew's restoration must have had its imaginative effect in suggesting that the valuable parts of California's winegrowing tradition were still viable. Bartholomew himself gave much credit for the success of his enterprise to the friendly assistance of many of the elite among California's established winemakers, including Herman Wente of Wente Brothers, John Daniel Jr. of Inglenook, and André Tchelistcheff of Beaulieu.[79]

Another restoration was that of Los Amigos winery in Mission San Jose, founded in 1888 and bought in 1936 by Robert Mayock, a Los Angeles lawyer and real estate man. Mayock planted the old vineyards to Pinot noir and Cabernet Sauvignon, and before his death in 1945 had acquired a good reputation for his wines. In Napa County, the old Lombarda winery north of St. Helena was bought by a partnership in 1940 and transformed into the Freemark Abbey winery, which had a short but respectable tenure producing premium wines. To the south, in Santa Clara County, something much more portentous developed when a San Francisco businessman, Louis Benoist, bought the Almadén Winery in Los Gatos in 1941. Almadén could be traced back to the earliest days of winemaking in Northern California, when (as New Almadén) it had been planted by the Frenchman Charles Lefranc in 1857. It continued in a vestigial way through Prohibition and returned to production after Repeal, only to decline into bankruptcy in 1938. Benoist apparently did not begin with serious winegrowing intentions, but that changed when he brought in Frank Schoonmaker as a consultant and a major stockholder: now Schoonmaker could produce his own California wines.[80] Oliver Goulet, who had been Martin Ray's winemaker at the Masson property, was put in charge of production.

The special significance of the Almadén venture was not just that the new owners intended to make good wine but that they meant to do so on a large scale and to advertise widely. The war put most of this plan on hold; nevertheless, Almadén began a program of planting superior varieties in its vineyards in 1942 and introduced its Grenache rosé, one of Schoonmaker's ideas, that same year.[81] When the war ended, Almadén was ready to begin the campaign, under Schoonmaker's promotional guidance; it combined the idea of good wine with *available* wine, a new and effective pairing. It was much easier to promote the idea of buying a good bottle of wine if one could actually find such a bottle to buy, and Almadén had a big part in seeing that this happened. The company developed new vineyards, notably in San Benito County, and introduced a solera system for sherry production, among other innovations. It made large quantities of unpretentious standard wines—chablis and burgundy and so on—but they were made from appropriate wine grapes and made to a decent standard. It made smaller quantities of good varietal wines, but still in a large enough volume to achieve national distribution at prices that ordinary people might afford. It was doing, in short, just what Schoonmaker had long argued should be done: make sound wines from good grapes, and superior wines from superior grapes, authentically labeled.

Another significant restoration began back in Napa County in 1943 when the Mondavi family, producers of bulk wines at Acampo and the Sunny St. Helena winery in St. Helena, bought the Charles Krug winery, which in the nineteenth century had been the flagship operation of the valley. They set to work to improve the vineyard and reestablish the old reputation. Bulk wines paid the bills, but an increasing quantity of good varietals was produced as the vineyards were restored.[82] The Krug label was reserved for these wines.

Restoring an old property and reclaiming a reputation was one way to go; another, just as difficult if not more so, was to establish something quite new. A handful of such wineries appeared in the 1940s, all of them small (they are the models for what later, rather unfortunately, came to be called boutique wineries) and most of them the work of people who did not begin as winemakers. When Englishman J. F. M. Taylor, a chemist with Shell Oil and later an international consultant, and his American wife, Mary, bought property in 1941 on Mount Veeder, in the Mayacamas Mountains that separate the Napa Valley from the Sonoma Valley, they did not quite start from scratch. The region had had a minor part in Napa winemaking before Prohibition, and there was the shell of an old winery building and a neglected vineyard on the site. But in effect they started over from the beginning, planting Chardonnay and Cabernet Sauvignon. Their Mayacamas Winery was bonded in 1947, and by the 1950s they had estate-bottled wines for sale and for distribution to their stockholders as dividends. Another small mountain winery was established in 1941 by Chaffee Hall, a San Francisco lawyer, who had a 14-acre vineyard planted exclusively to Riesling and Cabernet Sauvignon grapes on property near Felton in Santa Cruz County. His Hallcrest Winery operated until Hall's death in 1969, always on a small scale, always dedicated to high quality.

Two other small Napa wineries emerged about the same time and more or less according to the same pattern. Fred McCrea, an advertising man from San Francisco, and his wife, Eleanor (close husband-and-wife partnerships seem to have characterized such enterprises), bought land for a summer home on Spring Mountain, on the west side of the valley, in 1943 and began planting vines, especially Chardonnay, in 1946. They bonded their winery in 1952 and had a little wine to sell in 1953. Their success was immediate, even though McCrea, the advertising man, did no advertising: the only promotion was by word of mouth. By 1990 it took four years on a waiting list before one was eligible to buy any Stony Hill wine.[83] J. Leland Stewart, like the Taylors at Mayacamas, started with an old winery and a neglected vineyard, which he bought in 1943 and renewed under the name of Souverain. This was on Howell Mountain, on the east side of the valley; like the McCreas, Stewart, whose first wines were sold in 1947, made a specialty of white wines but produced distinguished reds as well.

The quest for quality was not entirely confined to those places that—like Napa, Sonoma, and Santa Cruz—had a history of fine wine. In 1948, following the experimental work on *flor* yeasts carried out by W. V. Cruess, Solera Cellars was established in Escalon by a partnership between Parrott and Company, San Francisco wine merchants, and the Village Winery of Escalon. By using Palomino grapes, *flor* yeast, and the solera method of fractional blending, Solera Cellars aimed at a "step-up in the quality of California sherries."[84] In 1950 the enterprise was bought by Almadén and provided the basis for Almadén's very successful line of sherries. And in 1946 Walter Ficklin, a grape grower with some 200 acres of raisin and table varieties south of Madera in the Central Valley, determined to see what could be done for California port by planting the vines from which the real thing was produced—Tinta Madeira, Tinta Cão, Touriga, and others. He and his sons built a winery of adobe to provide cool storage in the valley's heat and had a small quantity of wine to sell by 1953, all of it from the Tinta Cão grape. Since then, their California port has maintained a high reputation; and the winery is still most unusual in California as being devoted to the production of a single wine.[85]

Most of these new wineries had several things in common: They were small (Mayacamas had 50 acres of vines; Stony Hill, 35; Hallcrest, 14). They were the work of amateurs, or at least of people who had no previous connection with the trade (the Ficklins were grape growers, but they knew nothing about making port when they committed themselves to their experiment). And they aimed at the highest quality: their wines came from grapes of good varieties, they were stored in small cooperage, they received bottle aging before being released, and they were the object of close personal supervision at every stage of their production. They were also, of course, expensive.

The total effect of the varied restorations and new beginnings embodied in the wineries just described is impossible to calculate. But it is safe to say that they set an example of the highest importance by showing that people who were determined to do it could produce superior wines; and by staying in business, they showed that this was a practical enterprise as well.[86] They attracted respectful attention from connoisseurs and commercial winemakers both. In general, the trade was inclined to welcome and encourage such newcomers. As Eleanor McCrea recalled, "One of the things that was interesting then was that people like Herman Wente and the senior Louis Martini had seen their businesses get so big that they were almost out of hand, that they cherished the thought of a small jewel of a winery that one could do exactly as one wanted. They were wonderfully helpful."[87]

The trade was beginning to pay attention, but how many obstacles remained to be overcome may be suggested by the fate of a "premium wine program" put forward in 1949. This proposal, drafted by a committee of the Wine Institute, had the admirably simple aim of selling "greater amounts of older and better wine for more money."[88] To do so, wineries would select wines for registration with the state of California, hold them for aging, and then send them to market with a state seal certifying the age. It was evidently the intention that such wines would be largely varietal. The plan was at once vetoed because no one yet wanted to support any official distinction between one sort of wine and another: the prevailing view of the members of the Wine Institute was that wine was wine.[89] Still, there *was* a difference. A few months after the death of the premium wine program proposal, an article in the *Wine Review,* while admitting that there was no agreed definition of what a premium wine was, nevertheless affirmed that perhaps 2 percent of the industry's production qualified as "premium," and that such wines "exercise a tremendous effect on the reputation of California vintages."[90] There, for the moment, we can leave the matter.

A CYCLE OF TRADE

After all these general considerations, it is time to look in some detail at events in the years just after the war: they show quite clearly how feeble a grasp on secure prosperity the wine trade still had.

The grape crop in 1946 was the biggest on record—just under 3 million tons in California. It was, as usual, dominated by raisin grapes, which furnished more than half of the total, and half of those grapes were crushed for wine. This was by far the largest quantity of raisin grapes ever used by the wine industry, an excess that contributed to the marketing disasters of the next year. Equal quantities of wine and table grapes were also used, the result being that more than 1.5 million tons of grapes were used for winemaking in California—by a large margin a record year.[91]

In these conditions of abundance, and given the uncertainties of the market, it would have been reasonable to expect that prices for grapes would go down. They did not. On the contrary, they rose, to the general surprise and pleasure of the growers, to unlikely heights. The average price per ton of grapes in 1945 was $56; now, with a bumper crop, it soared to $90.

What had happened? The received answer is that in the midst of plenty, people feared shortage. Inventories were still at their 1945 level, and in view of the expansive prophecies for the wine market they would not be enough to meet the demand. At vintage time the record-breaking size of the crop had not yet been fully recognized. There were rumors that the raisin processors would compete against the wineries for grapes.[92] And perhaps there was a mild panic reaction as everyone seemed to be jostling to get a good supply of grapes. For these and whatever other reasons, the price of grapes went up and up. Louis Rosenstiel, the head of Schenley, was identified as the villain of the piece. He had concluded that a boom market lay ahead and set out to buy grapes at any cost, not only to meet the projected demand but, it was said, to cut out the competition. Schenley, when it could not buy as many grapes for its wineries as it wanted, turned to buying large quantities of bulk wines at inflated prices, a move that raised the already overheated temperature of the business a few more degrees. National Distillers joined the hunt, even buying in table grapes late in the season.[93] Both firms, as a result, suffered enormous losses in the next year and began to make their exit from the California wine scene.[94] Meanwhile, 1946 was a banner year: as *Wines and Vines* put it, "The grape crop was the largest in history; so was the crush; so was production of dessert wine, red table wine, white table wine; so was apparent consumption in the United States."[95]

The collapse came in 1947, a year still remembered with a shudder by veterans of the wine trade as a time of darkest gloom—it was, as longtime wine industry consultant Louis Gomberg called it, a "super-crash."[96] The huge production from the 1946 vintage did not move through the channels of distribution because these, it was now discovered, were already full. And the promise of a growing demand for wine among the American people was not fulfilled. Wine consumption went up a little in 1947, but in no proportion to the increase in supply: consumption rose from 97 to 107 million gallons in 1947, a respectable increase; but inventory leaped from 86 to 140 million gallons. And that wine newly added to inventory had been made from grapes for which top prices had been paid. It must now be sold, if it could be sold at all, for less than it cost to make.

The explanation the wine industry gave to itself for this situation was that the trade had been overstocked. Distributors, during the war, had been forced to buy large stocks of wine on the tie-in system, and they in turn had forced their customers to buy large stocks of wine on the same terms. The retailers now had more wine than they needed and would buy no more from the distributors. And so the supply backed up on the hands of the producers. Such, at any rate, was the accepted account.[97] It was also said that the excited market of 1946 made the retail dealers think that the price of wine would go up, so they bought largely in anticipation of a rise.[98] A simpler explanation of what happened is that most Americans who wanted something to drink happily bought spirits as soon as they came back in unrestricted supply and stopped buying the wine they had not particularly wanted in the first place. It may be noted here that the collapse of sales was almost entirely felt by the large producers of fortified wines and standard table wines—the so-called jug wines. The producers of quality wine were largely unaffected, a fact that may have had its effect in the long term when people had had a chance to reflect.[99]

Soon all was confusion. Prices were cut, and cut again: bulk wine that had been sought after in 1946 at more than a dollar a gallon now sold for 40 cents.[100] The bottlers, who had been scorned as recently as 1946, were now eagerly wooed again. Any and all means were tried to get things moving. Brother John, winemaker for The Christian Brothers, wrote to Widmer's, the New York State winery and a customer for California wines, offering to make wine for them—"quality dry wines which could be either dry red or dry white." This was, as Brother John admitted, a risk for The Christian Brothers, since they could not afford to have it known that they sold their wines in such a fashion: "bottled at the winery" was their boast.[101] But the times were dire: "Wine sales have taken a sharp decline, and I consider the California situation as being pathetic since every winery has sufficient inventory on hand. I do not know of any winery that needs wine."[102] There were rumors of many financial failures, and it was estimated that for the coming vintage, grapes might fetch only $20 a ton.[103] As we have already seen, there was a postwar revival in cooperative wineries. Now, in anticipation of the projected disaster-level prices for grapes, two more were founded: the Kearney Cooperative Winery Association of Fresno and the Larkmead Cooperative Winery of St. Helena.[104]

As the season of the vintage approached, it was clear that the wineries would greatly reduce their purchases of grapes. The crop was a large one—almost as large as the record-setting one of 1946—but the wineries took only about a third of it, producing 95 million gallons of wine in contrast to the 152 million gallons of the preceding year.[105] Once again there was a grape surplus, as there had been perennially in the '30s; and once again that surplus consisted of raisin grapes, which, though everyone agreed that they had already been much overplanted, continued to be planted. Although the overall grape crop was slightly down in 1947, the raisin-grape crop was up by some 55,000 tons. But where the wineries had taken almost 750,000 tons of raisin grapes in 1946, they now took only 319,000 tons—431,000 tons less of a crop 55,000 tons greater, leaving half a million tons of raisin grapes to be dealt with.[106]

Once again, measures for stabilization dominated industry talk, while the raisin trade was in turmoil. One suggestion was that the raisin men establish a "grape institute" and take care of their own problems by obtaining a state marketing order.[107] Another was to declare the Thompson Seedless a "nonwine" grape and to prohibit making any wine from it.[108] Yet another was that the winemakers voluntarily hold back the wines of 1947 from the market for at least a year to avoid "suicidal price-cutting policies and the flooding of the market with immature wines."[109] The main hope was that the federal government would buy up a large part of the surplus, as in fact it did.[110] That helped to stabilize prices, but it was only a holding measure. It was probably not much comfort for growers to hear the head of the Wine Institute assure them in October that the events of 1947 were only a "postwar readjustment," and that a "permanent" market of 100 million gallons for American wine might easily be doubled and tripled.[111]

By the beginning of 1948, the worst appeared to be over. The drastically reduced production of 1947 had brought inventories more in line with demand, and shipments began to increase. The price for which California wineries sold their bulk wine, however, continued to be lower than what it had cost to produce it in 1946.[112] The 1948 crop was again a large one—at 2,891,000 tons just marginally greater than that of 1947 and marginally less than that of 1946. Production went up considerably: almost 1,400,000 tons of the crop was crushed for wine (in the usual mix overwhelmingly dominated by raisin grapes), yielding nearly 130 million gallons of wine. Fortified wine took an even larger than usual share of the whole. In the past three years it had been produced in a ratio of about four to one over table wine; that figure was now five to one.[113]

Various schemes to deal with the grape surplus were bandied about in 1948: a raisin marketing agreement (essentially a scheme for the government to buy up excess raisins and ship them abroad); a marketing order for California dessert wine; a return to the plan of the Central California Wineries; and a "grape holiday," which would eliminate the chronic surplus by forbidding all new planting for five years.[114] None of these proposals came to pass in 1948, and in the meantime, wine continued to sell at cost or less, sliding below 40 cents a gallon for fortified wine at the end of the year.[115] What this meant for a winery operation was spelled out in detail in a speech by General John Deane, who had moved from superintending the Lend-Lease program to Russia during the war to the presidency of Italian Swiss Colony after the war. In a conservative estimate of expenses, he said, it cost 4 cents a gallon to make the wine; carrying charges (fixed charges and maintenance for operations) were 8 cents a gallon, supposing the winery could turn over its production in eighteen months; selling cost was 2 cents a gallon; so each gallon cost 14 cents exclusive of the price of grapes. If the winemaker were to have any profit on this scale of expenses, he could afford to pay $18 a ton for grapes, but the current price for grapes was more than $20: so those people who sold their wines at 35 cents were paying more than they would receive.[116] The more energetic winemakers groped about to find new markets: Gallo, for one, introduced a "light, sweet, Concord-flavored" wine called Gallo-ette, hoping to exploit the popularity enjoyed by Concord kosher wines such as Manischewitz and Mogen David; the Roma winery quickly followed suit with a similar wine called Jo-Ann. Despite heavy advertising, they soon disappeared: the moment was not propitious.[117]

This state of things persisted into the next year: 1949 began, so *Wines and Vines* observed, "with almost universal pessimism."[118] By midsummer the prospect of a large crop deepened the gloom; it was now impossible to delay action of some kind. The elaborate committee work, the campaigning, the lobbying, and the secretarial and accounting work required to push any proposal to a conclusion were largely provided by the Wine Institute, as it had done in the past and would do in the future. The winemakers first agreed to a state marketing order that would keep the vintage of 1949 off the market until March 1950.[119] California also passed a fair trade law for wine, intended to maintain minimum price levels.[120] And in September the winemakers agreed to the Grape Stabilization Marketing Order, which provided for an assessment on wine actually sold to create a stabilization fund (though no one was quite sure how it should be spent).[121] After these measures were taken, it turned out that the 1949 crop was short, the smallest in six years; the crush that year was also the smallest in six years, producing only 91 million gallons of wine instead of the 130 million of 1948. So there was no surplus to be dealt with after all.

All of these things appeared to have their effect.[122] In 1950 wine shipments went up, bulk wine prices increased, and the assessments on sales to provide a stabilization fund were lifted. In short, confidence had returned, at least until the next vintage season came around. As it happened, 1951 began the cycle anew: a big harvest and a big inventory led to a new slide in prices.

One need not follow these ups and downs in detail, but it should simply be noted here that the outlook in 1950—some five years after the end of the war, when the future of wine in America had been declared to be unboundedly splendid—seemed in truth quite discouraging. It looked, indeed, uncomfortably like the end of the 1930s. Fortified wines continued to dominate the market, and in an ever-growing proportion.[123] The winemakers still accepted vast quantities of grapes from inferior varieties. Desperate measures were resorted to in order to deal with the regular surplus of grapes for which there was no market but which the growers continued to produce. All of this sounds bad enough, and no doubt it was. But the conviction that it was possible to make good wine in California was not lost. The steady advice and encouragement of the university counted for something, and so did the example of those few, small wineries dedicated to quality. The advances were mostly visible in 1950 only to the eye of faith; but they were nevertheless real advances.

8

BACK EAST

TWO SORTS OF WINE

The immediate postwar years are a convenient point from which to take a survey of American winegrowing outside California. In common with their California counterparts, the winegrowers in the rest of the country had had to endure Prohibition, struggle through the Depression years, and hang on during the war. Now, in the first moment of the postwar era, they shared the same euphoria. "Everyone connected with the industry is optimistic," a writer on winegrowing in Arkansas reported in 1946, "and, to the last man, the belief is that the State is but at the threshold of a great development."[1] But what, we may ask, had in fact survived through these years, and in what condition? What expectations could be reasonably held? On what basis? The answers to such sober questions were not particularly encouraging, though few paused to ask them.

Commercial winegrowing had been established in the eastern states in the first half of the nineteenth century after more than two centuries of hopeful experiment and repeated, comprehensive failure.[2] Beginning with small successes in Ohio and New York, winemaking in some form had, by the end of the century, been carried on in almost every state east of the Rocky Mountains, from the Atlantic Coast westward to Kansas, and in the Southwest as well. Almost all of the many wineries in question had only a local trade, and most of them had a very uncertain tenure on life. But a pattern had gradually been established before being obliterated by Prohibition. In the northern parts of the region, exposed to the extremes of continental weather, the tempering effect of water was crucial. Thus the Great Lakes states dominated: New York, Pennsylvania, Ohio, and Michigan. The Missouri River region from Omaha to St. Louis was a district of persistent and varied enterprise in grape growing and winemaking; so was the Ozark region, both in Missouri and in Arkansas. There was a marginal commerce scattered over Texas and along the Rio Grande in New Mexico. On the East Coast a small but distinctive industry existed in New Jersey. Generally, the South lagged behind, though the operations of Paul Garrett in North Carolina and Virginia, based on the rotundifolia grapes native to the region, were an exception. At the opposite corner of the country, in the Northwest, there were significant plantings of grapes in Washington and Oregon from which some wine was made, though the trade was dominated by wines made from the local fruits and berries.

Such, roughly, was the scene up to Prohibition. After Repeal, the recovery of winemaking activity was slower and less complete than in California, where it had been far more extensive and economically important than in any other state. But the old pattern dimly reemerged: the Great Lakes states, the Ozarks, certain spots in the South, and the northwestern corner were still where grapes were grown and where what might emphatically be called American wines were made. For all of the wine made outside California came from pure native varieties (the muscadines in the South, the Concord in the rest of the country) or from the so-called native hybrids, containing more or less vinifera admixture in their blood. More precisely, the wines sold as eastern wines could and did contain up to 25 percent of California wine, and the rest came from native varieties.[3]

There were thus two distinct sorts of American wines offered to Americans, but they were not identified as different. They went to market under the same names: New York made and sold "sauterne," as did California; there were Ohio ports and California ports, Michigan burgundies and California burgundies—to say nothing of the genuine Sauternes, Burgundies, and Ports from France and Portugal—working to the greater confusion of the American wine market. For if California sauterne (the final s was almost invariably omitted in American practice) had little resemblance to what came from the banks of the Ciron, it was equally different from the New York wine of that name. Perhaps it was even more different, because the wines from native grapes and from vinifera are as different as, say, orange juice and grapefruit juice. If you are expecting the one and get the other, you are likely to be unpleasantly surprised; and if you grow up thinking that the one *is* the other, you will certainly be confused. The case either for varietal naming or for clear regional names is particularly strong when we come to the differences between the two kinds of American wine. But it was long before appropriate distinctions in naming were brought about.

Both Easterners and Californians were making what was incontestably wine, but beyond that elementary fact comparisons are difficult to make. The Easterners had a more difficult climate to work with: in some years they might lose half or more of their crop to winter kill or to frosts; they had to protect against black rot and downy mildew, afflictions unknown in California, by a program of regular spraying.[4] Their yields were lower, and their production costs higher; they worked with vines whose habits of growth were different (head pruning, for example, is unknown in the East) and that produced very different kinds of grapes. Many eastern varieties are slip-skin grapes—that is, the skin easily separates from the pulp so that only a very little pressure is needed to slip the skin right off. Thus it is difficult to press the grapes, which slip and slide around instead of lying docilely in place, and require a different pressing technique. After the grapes have been crushed, pectin-splitting enzyme is added to help break them down, and some sort of binder or bulking agent (such as rice hulls or wood pulp) is added to keep them from slipping in the press. The grapes are then wrapped in cloths and built up in layers (called cheeses) in the press, known as a rack-and-cloth press. White grapes especially require this treatment.[5] Since the color of native red grapes is often poor, they are usually heated (to about 140 degrees Fahrenheit) before pressing to extract the maximum of color. The heated grape material is then ameliorated and sent to the press, after which the resulting juice is fermented without the skins, unlike the practice of red wine production in most of the world.[6] Some eastern red grapes may be pressed cold rather than hot and fermented on the skins, but the dominant Concord is typically hot-pressed.

The sugar content of most native varieties is regularly under 20 degrees Balling—the approximate level needed to make a wine of the minimum alcoholic content required to keep it stable—so the eastern winemaker must add sugar.[7] The acid content of the juice, on the other hand, is typically too high, so it is brought down by diluting the juice with water: up to 35 percent per volume of a sugar-water dilution is permitted.[8] And the flavors and aromas of the native hybrids are unlike those of anything else; the word used to describe the most striking of those flavors is *foxy*.[9] The diminution of this flavor in the grapes is one of the main aims in the breeding of new varieties using native grapes, and the amelioration of this flavor in the wines made from native hybrids is one of the main aims of the winemaker.

Such, in quick outline, were the conditions affecting winemaking outside California. And as the character of the wines made differed greatly from that of California wines, so too did the scale of operations. The contrast may be readily shown by some statistics from the decade 1940–49. In that period, the average production of grapes (of all kinds) in California was 2,607,000 tons. In the rest of the United States, average total production was 183,000 tons, so California in the '40s grew on average more than fourteen times as many grapes as all the rest of the country combined. These averages conceal the annual variations, which were significant enough in California (from a high of 2,958,000 tons in 1946 to a low of 2,160,000 in 1942) but could and did vary wildly in the rest of the country, largely for reasons of climate: production was 235,500 tons in 1942 but only 118,400 in 1945—a slide of 50 percent.

Of this production, an average of a million tons of grapes was crushed for wine in California, or about 40 percent of the total crop. In the other states an average of a hundred thousand tons was crushed each year, almost 60 percent of the crop. This difference in the disposition of the crop is readily accounted for by the fact that eastern grapes were either eaten fresh or crushed: there were no raisin grapes.[10] But the term *crush* is misleading, for only a small proportion of the eastern crush went into wine. Reliable figures

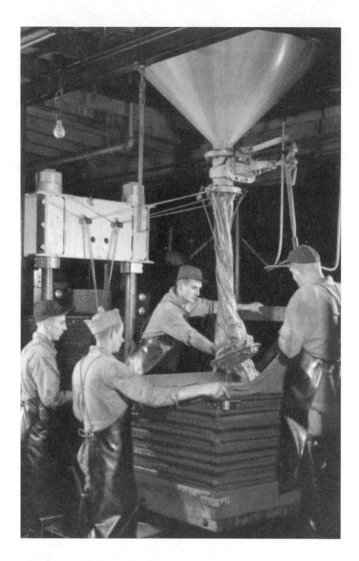

FIGURE 31
Loading a rack-and-
cloth press at Pleasant
Valley Wine Company
of Hammondsport,
New York. (Postcard in
the author's collection.)

do not exist, but on a generous estimate only from a quarter to a third of the crush went to the wineries; the rest was used for grape juice, which was unquestionably the staple market of eastern grape growing.

To get to the central matter in this comparison, California made an average of 109 million gallons of wine annually in the decade; all of the other states combined made an average of 10.5 million gallons.[11] And a substantial part of that eastern total was in fact made up of California wine and California brandy. The wine, usually a neutral blending wine brought in by tank car, was used to dilute the strong flavors of the native product, and the brandy was required for fortifying the large volumes of eastern "port," "sherry," and the like.

The relatively small scale and relatively high costs of eastern winemaking entailed different marketing practices. In the East, there were no vast volumes of bulk wine moving between winery and winery, or winery and bottler, as in California. Instead, the eastern producer was likely to bottle the greater part of its own produce, so that the winery name meant something in the smaller and more local markets for winemakers in New York, Ohio, or Michigan.

NATIVE GRAPE VARIETIES

The distinctive wines of the East were made from what were known as native hybrid grapes, that is, grapes from crosses of different native species with vinifera vines, exhibiting in varying proportions the different qualities of their parents.[12] The important varieties for winemaking were all grapes that had been introduced in the nineteenth century, when eager experimenters, both amateur and commercial, had created a flood of new grapes for trial. It had long been recognized that the varieties inherited from the nineteenth century were far from satisfactory, and that if the eastern wine industry were to make any significant advance toward higher quality, it would have to develop better grapes. Officially, of course, the eastern winemakers took the view that their grapes were not inferior, only different—or even superior. Greyton Taylor, head of the big Finger Lakes winery bearing his name, explained that "New York State wines are more full flavored, with a slight accent towards fruitiness (i.e. 'grapiness')." And, he added, "since wine comes from grapes, wine should taste as though it did."[13] But whatever they might say publicly, privately they knew better.[14]

There was hardly any eastern variety that would yield a decent red wine. The more delicate and attractive white wine varieties were either shy yielders or difficult to grow, and all produced more or less of the wild flavors that anyone accustomed to the wine of vinifera had to learn either to like or to overlook. But no new variety of any commercial importance for winemaking had been introduced for nearly a century. The fact is probably testimony both to the conservative character of grape growing and to the huge odds against success in any grape breeding project. The New York Agricultural Experiment Station at Geneva had produced some 25,000 hybrid seedlings by 1939 and had released some of them for commercial propagation, but without making any real dent on the established choices.[15] Thus the eastern industry continued to be based on varieties it knew to be unsatisfactory, but they were all it had to work with.

As a later chapter will show, the situation has changed dramatically, and the importance of the old native hybrids declined so greatly, that they may be in danger of becoming only a historical memory.[16] That is perhaps all the more reason to say something about them at this point in the narrative, when they were still the mainstay of eastern winemaking, as they had been for more than a century.

The workhorse variety was the Catawba, a chance-found hybrid of an unknown vinifera with a native labrusca; it is also the grape on which the first really successful American winemaking was founded, beginning with John Adlum in Washington, D.C., about 1820.

It was popularized by Nicholas Longworth of Cincinnati from 1830 onward, and by the time of the Civil War it had been planted commercially from New York to Missouri. Longworth had made still Catawba wines both dry and sweet and had also produced a successful sparkling Catawba. This grape's versatility has continued to be exploited: there are dry and sweet, still and sparkling, white and pink Catawba wines. Before Prohibition Catawba was grown all along the Ohio shore of Lake Erie, and after Repeal it continued to be an important variety in that state, especially on the islands at the western end of the lake. It had long been established in the Finger Lakes region of New York. It was even grown to some extent in California, a testimony to the prominence it had obtained among American grape growers. Because it has a very high acid content, it is well adapted to the production of sparkling wine; the high acid also allows it to be heavily diluted before being ameliorated. A part of its attraction is its ability to stand up to such manipulation.

The Delaware—a hybrid of aestivalis, labrusca, and vinifera—came to public notice in 1849; it is named for the town of Delaware, Ohio. Wine from the small, pink grapes of Delaware is among the most delicate and pleasing of all those from eastern grapes. Most of it went into the sparkling-wine cuvées of New York State, though a few bottlings of a still Delaware might be found. As Philip Wagner wrote in 1945, the Delaware is "usually considered the best native white-wine grape."[17] Although it was not widely planted, being mostly a Finger Lakes specialty, it set a standard for quality in eastern wines. For some reason, Delaware is one of the most widely planted grapes in Japanese vineyards.[18]

The Iona, preferred by some even to the Delaware for white wine but difficult to cultivate; the Dutchess, a green grape, insufficiently hardy to be widely grown; the Elvira, a productive grape once much favored in Missouri for winemaking; and a fairly long list of other native hybrids were still grown, mostly in New York State vineyards and mostly for their contribution to the base wines for champagne production. In New York State Widmer's Wine Cellars, at Naples, in the Finger Lakes, was almost alone in offering varietal wines from the traditional native hybrids: it had a long list, including such exotica as Isabella, Moore's Diamond, Salem, Vergennes, and Missouri Riesling. All of these wines were from grapes that were a legacy from the expansive experiments of the nineteenth century, when they had seemed to herald a new day for eastern wine. Their glamour was now much diminished and their future uncertain. A few Ohio wineries offered varietal Catawba and Delaware wines, but one would have had to look very hard indeed to find any such things outside New York and Ohio.

The attention devoted to native hybrids for red wine was much less than to those for white wine. Far and away the most highly regarded of the red varieties was the Norton, a hybrid of aestivalis and labrusca, introduced into cultivation in the 1830s. It does not do well as far north as New York, but before Prohibition it had been established in New Jersey, Virginia, Arkansas, and especially Missouri. Winegrowing in Missouri by the middle of the century had hardly yet revived after the devastation of Prohibition, but the tradition of red wine from Norton was maintained by the Hiram Dewey Winery in Egg Harbor City, New Jersey. In Arkansas some wine was made from a grape called Cynthiana, which is the Norton grape, though the identity of the two was stoutly denied by the Ozark winemakers. Other old-line hybrids for red wine included Ives, Bacchus, and Clinton. Wine has been made from all of these varieties, but never of a kind to inspire enthusiasm. If California winemaking had no consistent standards for the wines that it produced under generic names, the practice was even more chaotic in the East, especially for red wines. Each winemaker would have his own formula for a burgundy or a claret, and any relation between those names and the produce of the native grapes was arbitrary indeed.

In the general confusion that followed the devastation of the European vineyards by phylloxera at the end of the nineteenth century, some of these American hybrids were, in desperation, planted in Europe: since some of them resisted phylloxera, and since they gave a kind of wine, they were better than nothing. Noah (riparia–labrusca) among the white wine varieties and Othello (vinifera–riparia–labrusca) among the red were the most favored. All such American hybrids are now prohibited in European commercial vineyards, but they had a persistent life there; some varieties, in fact, have had a far better reception as émigrés than they ever got at home. The role of American native and hybrid vines in Europe employed as direct producers has never been properly described, and perhaps never will be.

The dread name that has not yet been whispered in this rapid account of native American varieties is that of the Concord grape. The Concord is named for the unoffending town of Concord, Massachusetts, where it was cultivated by Ephraim Bull from seed of a labrusca vine. Introduced in 1853, it was soon planted all over the country outside the South, and it so dominated American grape growing thereafter that it still defines the idea of "grape" for most Americans. Why this should be so is easy to explain. The Concord, a pure labrusca, exhibits all the faults of its kind: it is not particularly resistant to phylloxera; it is aggressively foxy; its sugar content is so low that no wine can be made from it without the addition of sugar; and no matter what methods may be used, its wines are uniformly coarse and undistinguished. But it is tough enough to endure all sorts of growing conditions, especially those of the North American continent; it is fairly good-looking (dark blue); and it is fruitful. When you planted Concord you could be sure of a crop, and it did not cost much to grow it. It thus became the available grape. It is the source of almost all the grape jelly made in America. And perhaps most important, grape juice—that uniquely American child of the union of Temperance with Technology—was from its origin a product of the Concord grape.[19]

The Concord remains by far the most widely planted grape in the United States outside California: it still dominates in the vineyards of Washington and New York, the two biggest wine-producing states after California. It has had an effect analogous to that of the Thompson Seedless in California during and after Prohibition. Since the high-yielding Thompson could be used as a table grape, a raisin grape, or a wine grape, it was the line of least resistance for a grower to plant more and more Thompsons at the expense of other varieties. And so it was with the reliably productive Concord: it had some appeal as a table grape, it was the main source of grape juice, and it could be used for wine. In the conditions created by Prohibition and the Depression years that followed, the Concord swept all before it.

In the American South, especially in the Gulf states, grape culture was even more difficult than in the North, partly on account of the heat and humidity, and partly on account of the devastations of Pierce's disease, which is thought to be native to the region. Many of the different species of American grape do grow in the South, but its preeminent species is the curious grape called rotundifolia, the round-leaf grape. This, the ampelographers agree, is in fact a grape (the question was once disputed), though it is genetically different from other grapes and is in consequence difficult to hybridize. Its habit of growth is rank and vigorous, and it prefers to ramble over a trellis rather than be pruned. Its fruit grows in loose clusters of a few round, tough-skinned berries that fall from the stalk when ripe. Its virtues are that it laughs at phylloxera, ignores Pierce's disease, and resists most other diseases as well; its defects are low sugar, low acid, and a powerful musky aroma. Southerners are loyal to rotundifolia; they usually call it Scuppernong, after only one of its many varieties. That others may be persuaded to like it is illustrated by the success of Paul Garrett's Virginia Dare wine: before Prohibition, this wine—which began as a pure Scuppernong product—was said to be the most popular wine in America. But its popularity meant that it had to be progressively diluted, for there was not enough Scuppernong to meet the demand. When the brand was revived after Prohibition, it depended more and more on California wine as its basis, though Garrett continued to produce Scuppernong wine in the South.

If the winemakers of the East had made a virtue of their necessities and had frankly promoted the wines from native grapes as true regional specialties instead of calling them port, sherry, claret, burgundy, and so on, would they have developed a broader and more solid industry than in fact was achieved? Frank Schoonmaker and Tom Marvel thought so: if only Americans had accepted their native grapes and had honestly exploited them as natives, they argued, we would have had a whole spectrum of distinctive and interesting wines to boast of, unlike any other in the world.[20] That did not happen. Whether it might still happen, who knows?

WINEGROWING IN NEW YORK

In winemaking terms, California was the metropolitan center; all the other places were provinces, which by comparison with the capital did not produce much at all. Still, this provincial production occupied a good many grape growers and winemakers and filled many millions of bottles. There were, in fact, more wineries outside California than within it. In 1940, for example, there were 474 bonded wineries in California and 616 in the rest of the country. Both numbers gradually declined through the decade, but the gap between California and the rest remained pretty much the same: it was 374 to 415 at the end of the decade.[21] Of course, many if not most of these establishments outside California were very small indeed, without much in the way of resources and without any organization to defend and assist them. It is not surprising that they showed no sign of doing anything to advance the state of winemaking.

New York stood at the head of this business, as it had since the nineteenth century. At the end of the war, in 1945, New York had 39,000 acres of vineyards, down only a little from the 41,000 acres of 1940. There were single wineries in California that had the production capacity of all the wineries in New York State combined; but New York typically made more than twice as much wine as any other state except California. Its average production in the decade 1940–49 was almost 7 million gallons, leaving only a little over 3 million gallons of wine to be accounted for by the others outside California. New York also had a more various production than the others; it made a small quantity of distinctive varietal table wines, a large volume of standard table wines, and an even larger volume of fortified wines. Its main identity in the minds of American wine buyers, however, was as a producer of sparkling wines, especially those made in the Finger Lakes region in the middle of the state.

New York also took the lead, outside California, in the scientific and technical support of winegrowing. The Agricultural Experiment Station at Geneva (now administratively a part of Cornell University) had a long and distinguished history of research and applied work in grape growing and winemaking, going back to 1882. The great horticulturist and encyclopedic writer Liberty Hyde Bailey had made Cornell University the outstanding center of agricultural teaching in the United States, and the two institutions contributed together to viticultural research. The great name in the study of vines in New York was Ulysses Prentiss Hedrick, of the Geneva experiment station. His *Grapes of New York* (1908) is a magisterial catalog and description of the native American grapes then cultivated, not just in New York but everywhere that native American varieties were grown. When Prohibition was imminent, Hedrick assisted his fellow Americans to an understanding of how they might grow grapes for themselves with his *Manual of American Grape-Growing* (1919), which includes a section on winemaking. In his old age (he was then seventy-five) he put all his experience into practical form with *Grapes and Wine from Home Vineyards* (1945).

The Geneva station, as has already been mentioned, had a long-standing program for breeding new varieties of grapes. It should be added here that beginning in 1902 it also carried out experiments in the cold-climate culture of vinifera. By that time the major causes of the failure of vinifera in the East were understood: native diseases, including mildew and black rot; insect pests, especially phylloxera; and winter kill. Work could thus begin on breeding and on cultivation practices to discover how vinifera might be protected against its enemies. The publicity given in recent years to Dr. Konstantin Frank and others as the pioneers of vinifera in New York and the East has unfairly obscured the work of the Geneva station. By 1915 it had carried the work far enough to publish a bulletin on the subject.[22] The U.S. Department of Agriculture had also tested vinifera at its Arlington, Virginia, station even during the Dry years. The results were not of a kind to secure the department's recommendation, but it was certainly aware of the possibilities.[23]

At the time of Repeal, the Geneva experiment station resumed work on the problems of practical winemaking for the benefit of the New York industry. The station had a notable success with a new process for the rapid oxidation of New York State sherry, designed by the head of its chemistry division, Donald Tressler.[24] By combining aeration with baking, the process allowed the highly foxy Concord and its close relative, the Niagara, both of which abounded in New York vineyards, to be used in making a fortified wine.[25]

Although New York steadily maintained its position as number two, the winegrowing industry there, in common with that of all the other states apart from California, exhibited the symptoms of a slow decline. As Philip Wagner remembered it, the whole production of the Taylor Wine Company went through "two old-fashioned rack and cloth presses . . . the same was true of Gold Seal and of Great Western." It was, he said, "a small specialty industry—nothing more."[26] Little that was new seemed to be happening. There were 117 bonded wineries in New York in 1940; in 1950 the number had dwindled to 88.[27] The acreage devoted to grapes in New York continued its gradual decline to about 34,000 at the end of the decade.[28] The vineyard practices were very little different from what they had been a century earlier, at the beginning of commercial winemaking in New York, and the declining vineyards of the state averaged a marginal production of one to one and a half tons per acre.[29] Annual wine production fluctuated markedly with the available grape crop, which, as we have seen, might vary by as much as 50 percent from year to year. So New York's production ranged from 9,352,000 gallons in 1944 to a low for the decade of 4,654,000 in 1948.

New York has traditionally been divided into three distinct winegrowing regions. The oldest of these, on the banks of the Hudson River between New York and Albany, was now in almost terminal decline. In the nineteenth century it had been the site of many small winemaking enterprises and a hotbed of grape-breeding activity, led by Dr. C. W. Grant of Iona Island and A. J. Caywood of Newburgh. The old Brotherhood Winery in Washingtonville, some miles back from the river in Rockland County, was still in business but only in a small way. The notable enterprise among the few survivors was the Hudson Valley Wine Company, operated by the children of its founder, Alessandro Bolognesi. They made table and sparkling wines from their own vineyards on the western bank of the Hudson from Catawba, Delaware, Iona, and Bacchus grapes, and they had a good reputation locally. When a writer for the *New Yorker* visited the winery in 1947, the tone of the story he wrote was thoroughly elegiac: Papa had been full of a founder's energy, but the children were now weary and looked forward to getting out of the business. None of the children had married, so there were no heirs. This Chekhovian air no doubt seemed inevitable in 1947 as one surveyed the declining vineyards of the Hudson.[30]

The Finger Lakes region, in the middle of the state, was the largest and most flourishing part of the wine trade in New York, as it had been since its establishment before the Civil War. Vineyards and wineries were mostly to be found around only two of the lakes, both at the western end of the group: Keuka Lake and the town of Hammondsport, and Canandaigua Lake and the town of Naples. Here were the big four companies: Ur-bana (the Gold Seal brand), Pleasant Valley (Great Western), and Taylor were at Ham-mondsport; Widmer lay some miles to the west at Naples. They operated out of build-ings of a Victorian solidity and amplitude that shamed mere utilitarian modern structures. There was a scattering of other wineries—D. W. Putnam at Hammondsport, for exam-ple, or Vineyardists Incorporated (originally a Paul Garrett property) at Penn Yan. The big four had among them a storage capacity of approximately 4 million gallons, dwarfing anything else in the East.[31]

The pride of the Finger Lakes district was its sparkling wine, in which trade Pleasant Valley's Great Western label had long held a leading position. At its best, New York sparkling wine was always a bottle-fermented product. In the decade of 1940–49 the pro-duction of sparkling wine in New York averaged 736,000 gallons, the output of about forty different makers, large and small. By contrast, California in the same years produced an average of 540,000 gallons from about thirty-four makers.[32]

In the scale of operation and economic importance, there was nothing else to com-pete with the Finger Lakes winegrowers outside California. The prominent men of the Finger Lakes were inevitably the prominent men in the eastern industry as a whole: Will Widmer of the Widmer Winery, Greyton Taylor of the Taylor Wine Company, E. S. Under-hill of the Urbana Winery, and Charles Champlin of Pleasant Valley. They were the men who testified at congressional hearings or who consulted with the regulatory authorities; they were the men whose protests or recommendations would be listened to in the state capital. They had formed a Finger Lakes Wine Growers Association in November 1932, more than a year in advance of Repeal. The association was represented by an attorney in Washington, D.C., to defend the interests of its members, who included grape grow-ers as well as winemakers.

The existence of a Finger Lakes Wine Growers Association suggested that the East-erners might organize an equivalent of California's Wine Institute, and no doubt such a thing would have been welcomed. But the balkanization of the United States through the right of each state to determine its own liquor policy made it almost impossible to form an effective industrywide organization outside California. In California, the trade could come together in the Wine Institute because its members were operating under Califor-nia law. But how were New York (no wine sales in grocery stores), Pennsylvania (wine sales only through state liquor stores), and Michigan (preferential tax for Michigan wines) to work together? Or any other combination of states, since in the matter of wine there was no free traffic among any of them? They were thus imprisoned behind whatever bar-riers their home state might have erected—and there were barriers in every case.

Furthermore, the conditions of production and operation were so widely different that there was sometimes almost no common ground. It was hard enough for the Wine In-stitute to hold up under the tensions between the small producers in California who aimed at quality table wines and the huge, industrial-scale producers interested only in the great-est possible quantity of standard fortified wines. But how did one connect Violet Burhard of Leslie, Arkansas, whose winery stored 15,000 gallons of grape, apple, cherry, and black-berry wines under the Lone Wolf label, with the big Monarch Wine Company of Georgia, which dealt only in muscadine wines and fruit wines (storage 1 million gallons)? Or either with the Ehrle Brothers of Homestead, Iowa, whose winery had storage for only 1,000 gallons of dessert and fruit wines? Or with the Val Verde Winery at Del Rio, on the Mexican border of Texas, where Louis Qualia made wines from native hybrids planted by his grandfather in 1883? There were scores of equally out-of-the-way and intensely local operations, whose separateness made any effective combination hard to imagine. It was a provincial, idiosyncratic, and not very prosperous business.

Still, the idea of organizing was a good one in itself. Winemakers from New York, Ohio, Michigan, and Missouri had met in Buffalo as early as July 1936 "to organize an association of Eastern wineries to promulgate legislation favorable to the industry and increase wine consumption."[33] It aimed to include all wineries east of the Rocky Mountains, and would be open to growers as well. The meeting approved the plan, voted to incorporate as the Eastern Wine Growers Association, and then adjourned. An office was duly opened in New York City, and then nothing more seems to have happened. Probably the attractions of membership were not strong enough to overcome the obstacles of expense.

In the early days of the revived wine industry there had been conflict between its eastern and western wings—which meant, substantially, New York and California. When the federal standards for wine were written, the Easterners had had to defend their rights to add sugar and otherwise ameliorate the musts they worked with, and to blend in California wine while still preserving a state appellation. California had taken the holier-than-thou attitude that such things were unnecessary (as they were in California) and that no one, therefore, should be permitted to employ them. This had not endeared the Californians to the Easterners.

The Wine Institute, however, had always thought well of the idea of a national organization that would include all of the wine associations in the country—importers, wholesalers, bottlers, retailers, and not least eastern growers (which meant in effect the members of the Finger Lakes Wine Growers Association and whoever else might be moved to join independently). Accordingly, the Wine Conference of America was founded at a San Francisco meeting in March 1947. The Wine Institute took on the burden of the secretarial work but was careful to see that the offices were distributed: E. S. Underhill of the Urbana Winery in Hammondsport was the first chairman.[34] The conference, which met twice yearly, began with thirteen members and, for a time, managed to stay alive and even to grow: by 1954 there were twenty member associations. Then it seems to have faded away.[35] Since then a number of other efforts to organize the wine interest on a national scale have been made, but the difficulties remain formidable. Some of those difficulties lie in genuine regional differences; but no doubt more of them arise from the confusion of laws and regulations created by the second article of the Twenty-first Amendment.

The third winegrowing district of New York State was the so-called Grape Belt, the flatlands running along the south shore of Lake Erie all the way from Buffalo to the Ohio border, home to the largest concentration of grape culture in the country outside California. New York's part of this territory, from just north of Buffalo to the Pennsylvania border, had been almost entirely given over to the Concord grape and was therefore more concerned with grape juice than with wine. The Welch Grape Juice Company had set up its headquarters at Westfield in 1897 and had steadily expanded its operations in the region over the next half-century. Still, immediately after Repeal some eight wineries were operating between Niagara Falls and the Pennsylvania border. Only three were still operating in 1945: the Fredonia Products Company in Fredonia; the Colonial Winery, also in Fredonia; and Chateau Gay in Lewiston, on the Canadian border. One of those that did not survive the war years was the Niagara University Winery, also in Lewiston, a part of the farm operation belonging to the Vincentians of the university. They made altar wines from the grapes of their own vineyards between 1931 and 1944, in a winery of some 120,000 gallons' capacity.

New York had in effect a fourth "district" that was not so much a place as a certain sort of wine for a special market: the kosher wine trade, centered on New York City with outposts in other urban regions, particularly Chicago. This trade had for its basis the Concord grape, especially the Concord grape from the vineyards of New York. For wine to be kosher, it does not matter what kind of grape it is made from; nor does it matter what style of wine is produced: red or white, dry or sweet, still or sparkling. As long as the wine is produced by approved methods, it is kosher. Those methods essentially aim at guarding purity and cleanliness but include some strict religious requirements as well. All phases of production, beginning with the blessing of the grapes at the moment of crushing all the way through to bottling, must be under rabbinical supervision. The wine may not come into contact with anything unkosher (so isinglass or gelatin or casein, all products derived from prohibited sources, may not be used for fining). No food may be eaten on the winemaking premises. All handling of grapes, juice, and wine must be performed by "a Sabbath-observant Jewish male," called a *mashgiah* ("supervisor").[36] And no work may be done on the high holy days, even if they should (and they usually do) fall at the time of the vintage.[37] Considering these requirements, it is not surprising that much of the wine thought of as kosher in this country is in fact no such thing but only a type. It should be added that as there are various forms of Judaism in this country, so there are varying definitions of what is kosher. Or as one kosher winemaker put it, "What's kosher and what isn't is so complicated that you wouldn't have space in a popular magazine to discuss all the distinctions."[38]

The recognized kosher type in the United States is a highly sweetened wine based on Concord grapes, and it has so dominated the American idea of what kosher wine is that many people are surprised to learn that there is in fact no necessary connection among Concord and sweetness and kosher. The connection came about only by historical accident. The first large Jewish communities in this country were on the East Coast, and the only grapes available in sufficient quantities on a reliable basis were, by the time those communities were formed in the nineteenth century, Concord grapes. In that situation,

American kosher wine became Concord wine. And because the Concord will not make a stable wine without added sugar, and because the defects of Concord wine are to some extent masked by sweetness, American kosher wine became sweet wine. It has been suggested that since most of the Jews in the United States came from European regions without vineyards and without a wine-drinking tradition, they preferred sweet wines.[39] Perhaps so, though it seems doubtful. But there is no reason for the accidental association of kosher with Concord to remain permanent, and there are many signs that it is beginning to break up.

Some kosher wines in the years just after the war were made in the vineyard regions themselves, notably by the Star brothers at the Fredonia Products Company in the Lake Erie Grape Belt. Their enterprise went back to before the days of Prohibition. In the Finger Lakes region, kosher wines were produced by Canandaigua Industries. But even more kosher wines were made not where the grapes grew but in urban wineries. These might be small, like the New York State Fruit Products Company of New York City, where House of David and Belmont Kosher wines were made; or large, like the Monarch Wine Company in Brooklyn, founded in 1934, which owned the Manischewitz brand. This winery processed Concord juice from upstate vineyards at its plant in the Bush Terminal, Brooklyn, far from any vines. In an interesting variation of things, Monarch acquired the Garden Vineyards Winery in Fowler, California (with a capacity of 3 million gallons), in 1944 and converted it exclusively to kosher wines. These wines followed the standards of the Central Valley rather than those of New York State: muscatel, sherry, and port were the staples, produced from "almost every variety . . . including Carignanes, Palominos, Fresno Beauties, Feherzogas [Feher Szagos], and Zinfandels."[40]

Other New York City wineries producing kosher wines were the Crystal Wine Company on lower Broadway, the Monterey Wine Company (Lipschutz kosher wine) in Brooklyn, and the curiously named California Valley Wine Company, then as now on the lower east side of Manhattan on Rivington Street. Founded in 1899, it is now called the Schapiro Winery after its owners. The Kedem Winery, originally founded in Czechoslovakia, migrated to the lower east side of Manhattan in 1948 and then to the Hudson Valley, at Milton, New York. Streit's kosher wine came from Mount Vernon, New York. Another large urban winery was Mogen David, in Chicago. It started in the bottling business as the California Wine Company in 1933; in 1941, as the Wine Corporation of America, it began winemaking; and in 1947 it changed its name to Mogen David, as its most popular wine was called. This wine was produced from Concord grapes purchased from New York, Ohio, and Pennsylvania vineyards and shipped as juice or concentrate to the Chicago winery.[41]

The market for kosher wines was by no means restricted to the Jewish community. Mogen David, for example, was a favorite wine in the Midwest, where the Concord flavor and aggressive sweetness were regarded as desirable qualities: by 1952 Mogen David expected to sell 5 million gallons of its wine.[42] In fact, the sweet Concord wines became, briefly, among the hottest commodities in the trade. This led to an amusing historical irony. The Welch Grape Juice Company had been founded by the teetotalling Methodist dentist Dr. Thomas Welch, who had devised a way of preserving fresh grape juice through pasteurization with the express purpose of delivering the church, and the population at large, from the evils of wine. In 1950, faced by a surplus of Concords from a heavy harvest and tempted by the heady success of kosher wines, the backsliding officers of Welch's announced that the company would produce wine as well as juice. No doubt the shade of Dr. Welch was grimly satisfied by the result: the competition of Manischewitz and Mogen David was too much, and Welch's soon got out of the wine business.[43]

OHIO AND MICHIGAN

The condition of the wine business in Ohio following Repeal was summarized in chapter 3; to that account not much need be added here for the immediate postwar years. Because the grape growers of the state had turned almost exclusively to the Concord grape, the few remaining wineries bought land and planted vineyards of their own to provide a supply of Catawba and a small assortment of other native varieties.[44] As a result, the remaining independent growers virtually ceased to produce any wine grapes at all.

The wineries on the Lake Erie islands depended more and more on tourism for their markets, but the increases in land value and taxes created by tourism made it harder to sustain a grape-growing business. As the island vineyards declined in productivity, they were not renewed. In the northeast, the growth of the city of Cleveland effectively put an end to viticulture in that region.[45] No particular effort seems to have been made to assist winegrowing in Ohio. The wineries complained that the agricultural research station at Wooster did no work on winegrowing, even though the industry was willing to pay for a program of research.[46] The general assumption appears to have been that winegrowing in Ohio was in a fatal decline, not to be arrested.

The vineyards of Michigan were in the southwestern corner of the state, where the effect of Lake Michigan provided a climate for fruit growing: the lake effect delayed budding in the spring and delayed frosts in the fall, and the prevailing westerly breezes helped to keep down fungal diseases. Most of the state's 28,000 acres of vines in 1946 were in but two counties, Berrien and Van Buren, where the Concord was varied only by some small plantings of Delaware and Niagara.[47] The major customer for these grapes was not the few wineries of the state but the Welch Grape Juice Company, which had two plants in the Michigan grape country. In the five years from 1944 through 1948, for example, an average of only 14 percent of Michigan's grape crop was crushed for wine; the rest was sold for the table or went into jams, jellies, and juice.

After the war, in 1946, eleven wineries were operating in Michigan, four of which were a good deal larger than the others. None of them antedated Repeal.[48] Originally they had set up in Detroit, where La Salle Wine and Champagne Company, with a capacity of a million gallons, remained. The Bronte Champagne and Wines Company, with a capacity in 1946 of more than a million gallons, had moved from Detroit to Hartford in 1944. The St. Julian Winery had migrated from Detroit to the vineyards of Paw Paw, where it had as a neighbor the Michigan Wineries (now Warner Vineyards). Both of these ultimately had storage capacities of over a million gallons. Bronte and La Salle made a little sparkling wine by the Charmat process, as well as a little wine from other fruits; La Salle also made carbonated wine. For the rest, Michigan wine was sweet Concord made up in various forms, both red and white.

One appeal—from a certain point of view—of the Concord grape was that it would first yield a white wine from the free-run juice, and then the skins, suitably watered and sugared, could be fermented to yield a red wine as well. The traditional formula holds that a ton of grapes will yield 150 gallons of wine; but the practices in Michigan were such that a ton of Concords yielded 246 gallons of wine![49]

The Michigan wine industry had hardly existed before Prohibition. After Repeal it was the prisoner of two bad conditions: the fact that more than 90 percent of the grapes grown in the state were Concords, and the fact that the local industry, after a few years of struggle, had been protected by a discriminatory tax. Wine produced within the state paid a tax of 4 cents a gallon; all other wine paid a tax of 50 cents. Being thus secured against competition, Michigan wineries were content to follow the line of least resistance by making large quantities of sweetened Concord wines. Michigan wine had another peculiarity: most of it was lightly fortified to bring it up to 16 percent alcohol. As has been described in chapter 3, the Concord wines of Michigan were typically fermented dry at about 9 percent alcohol and then sweetened by the addition of sugar and raised to 16 percent alcohol by the addition of either brandy or already fortified wine. Such wines, because they were officially classified as "natural," could be sold in grocery and drug stores; the more usual fortified wines from California and elsewhere, of from 18 percent to 21 percent alcohol, could be sold only in state liquor stores.[50] The 16 percent measure, which was under the federal minimum for fortified wines, meant that the ports and sherries of Michigan were sold with the word *light* on the label: "light sherry wine" or "light port wine."

This strange state of things was the work of one William Geagley, chief chemist of the Michigan State Department of Agriculture, who served some forty-seven years in the position and managed, during his tenure, to dictate the idea of wine to the people of Michigan. Geagley held that wines of more than 16 degrees of alcohol were not wines but "distilled spirits." To reach 16 percent, the Concord wines of Michigan had to add brandy (from California), but Geagley nevertheless proudly affirmed them to be "natural fermented wines of low alcohol," and he succeeded in embodying his views in the Michigan law of 1937 that created the protected market.[51] Geagley had other curious notions; one was that the Concord grape was of unsurpassed excellence: "A lot of grape growers would give their right arm if they could match it," he said, and added that "in Europe . . . vineyard farmers after years of experimenting have failed to develop the Concord type which readily grows in Michigan."[52] Another notion was that Michigan wine law was not discriminatory, but only a wholesome protection; anyone who might object did so "for selfish reasons" and to deprive the people of its "beneficial effect."[53]

Ironically, the wineries that Geagley sought to protect soon found their protection irk-

FIGURE 32
Dr. W. C. Geagley passing
judgment on a Michigan
wine; he greatly admired
the wine of the Concord
grape. (From *Berrien
County Record*, 16
September 1960.)

some. The only kind of wine that Michigan knew was fortified wine, and California wines, being more strongly fortified than those of Michigan, were preferred.[54] By 1947 the Michigan producers complained that California fortified wines at 20 percent dominated the market, even though they could be sold only through state liquor stores and paid a higher tax while their own 16 percent wines might be sold by private licensees throughout the state: "90 per cent of last year's output," they said, lay "unsold in their warehouses."[55] At least one Michigan winery attempted to exploit the Michigan law that held 16 percent wine to be natural and everything above that to be distilled spirits. It sued the state's Liquor Control Board to stop the sale of all wines fortified above 16 percent unless they were labeled "spirits." Since federal law forbade wine to be so labeled, a favorable ruling would have eliminated the out-of-state competition at a stroke.[56]

When such desperate measures failed, the Michigan wineries petitioned that they, too, should be allowed to make wines fortified to 20 percent. The necessary amendment to the law was passed in 1950, and in the next year Michigan wines of 20 percent—still, no doubt, regarded as natural—entered the market.[57]

That market, protected as it was by an exclusive tax, was wholly within the state, which drank wine from Michigan and very little else, despite the outcries of the winemakers about competition from outside. In 1940, for example, out of 1,665,000 gallons of wine moving to market, only 295,000 came from outside Michigan, and eight years later things had not changed much: more than 70 percent of the wine drunk in Michigan was produced in Michigan.[58] The effects of such provincialism were predictable. When a wine lover from Chicago on vacation in Michigan's Upper Peninsula in 1948 sought out the local liquor store, he found that its entire stock consisted of light, sweet Michigan wines, varied only by a few bottles of Petri wine from California. "What a level of vinous intelligence there must be in Michigan!" he was moved to exclaim in his book of tasting notes.[59] Michigan had been thoroughly geagleyized.

The state's average annual production of wine was about 1.25 million gallons in the decade 1940–49. The small circle of winemakers who enjoyed this closed, apparently stable business formed a Michigan Wine Institute in 1938 to "maintain consistent high standards" and to "co-operate with the liquor control commission, the Michigan department of agriculture, and the grape growers."[60] It was perhaps fitting that Dr. Geagley, after his forty-seven years of service to the state, joined the institute as its director. The reference to "high standards" was presumably without irony, and reminds us how conventional and unexamined such phrases too quickly and easily become. The fact is that Michigan's history after Repeal is one of the most deplorable in the story of American wine.

A SOUTHWESTERN CURVE:
FROM MISSOURI TO NEW MEXICO

In moving south from Michigan to Missouri we may note in passing two sites of local winegrowing at opposite ends of the state of Iowa. One is the small group of settlements called the Amana Colony in southeastern Iowa. Founded by the German Community of True Inspiration in the middle of the nineteenth century, Amana had flourished as a communitarian society in which wine from the community's vineyards had been a part of both daily life and religious ritual. In 1932, under the strains of the Depression, Amana gave up its communal system and allowed its members to fend for themselves. The Ehrle brothers chose to keep up the tradition of winemaking that had been exclusively communal before. Since the war and the development of tourism, other Amana wineries have been opened, and there are now eight scattered about the colony. The Amana vineyards were not maintained, but wine is made from purchased grapes as well as from a variety of other fruits, vegetables, and greens, including wild grapes, dandelions, and red clover.[61] An Amana specialty is a rhubarb wine called Piestengel; it is so heavily sugared that it must be sold as "other than standard" wine, but it appears to have a ready sale at the retail shops in Amana.[62]

In western Iowa, on the banks of the Missouri River, the Council Bluffs Grape Growers Association—a cooperative that went back to 1893—made more conventional wines, mostly from Concords. In 1946 the association's winery had 300,000 gallons of storage capacity. It went out of the wine business in 1977, its vineyards destroyed by the weed killer 2,4-D, which was widely applied to the corn and bean fields of the region. Such are the hazards of midwestern viticulture. The winemaking at Amana and at Council Bluffs has only a local interest, but it is worth noting, perhaps, as a reminder that the possibilities in this country are by no means yet fully explored.

New York pretty much held its own after Repeal; Michigan exploited a protectionist market to create an industry where none had existed; but Missouri, like Ohio, failed to prosper. In the nineteenth century, Missouri had been the scene of highly significant experimentation and a widespread and active interest in grapes and wine. At the middle of the continent, exposed to every extreme of American weather, it had nonetheless shown that good wine could be grown: Missouri made dry wines both white and red (the Norton was particularly at home here), and sparkling wine in the cellars of St. Louis. Its vineyards followed the course of the Missouri River across the state, from Westport near Kansas City to Florissant, outside St. Louis, where Jesuit fathers had made wine since the early nineteenth century. The German settlers at Hermann and other communities had developed a substantial wine industry based on Norton, Elvira, and other native types. In a region farther south, winemaking was carried on at the Italian colonies of Rosati and St. James.

Missouri, and particularly the Missouri Germans, had also contributed importantly to the scientific development of viticulture. Charles V. Riley, not a German but the state entomologist of Missouri, was the first to establish the identity of the vine pest then devastating the vineyards of Europe with the American plant louse phylloxera. George Engelmann, a St. Louis physician, was the leading American ampelographer of his day. George Husmann, of Hermann, was a tireless promoter of winegrowing in America and a leader in supplying American rootstocks to reconstitute the ravaged vineyards of Europe. Jacob Rommel, Nicholas Grein, and Hermann Jaeger did valuable work in grape breeding. Missouri, in short, was one of the active sites of productive work in American winegrowing down to the moment of Prohibition. In that expansive period the Stone Hill Winery of Hermann had grown to be one of the largest American producers. Missouri wine was an important tributary to the mainstream of American wines.

For reasons that are not at all clear, Prohibition seems to have had an especially destructive effect in Missouri.[63] The American Wine Company—producers of Cook's Imperial Champagne, elaborated in tunnels under the streets of downtown St. Louis—made a strong comeback. But hardly any other winery did. And the American Wine Company by that time was largely dependent on California wine for the basis of its popular Cook's Imperial brand of sparkling wine. The flow of wine actually produced from Missouri's own vineyards had dried to a mere rivulet. Vineyard plantings had expanded under the artificial pressures of Prohibition, as they had elsewhere, to take advantage of the opportunities of home winemaking and the increased demand for grape juice. But as elsewhere in the East, the Concord grape had ousted almost everything else. When Repeal came, there were precious few wine grapes left.

Some ten wineries operated in Missouri in the first years after Repeal, but with the exception of the American Wine Company, they were all so small as to be almost invisible. The Ruegsegger Winery, in St. Joseph, had a capacity of 4,000 gallons of wine, divided between "claret" and "sweet concord"; Alfred Nahm, in the old German winemaking town of Augusta on the Missouri River, had a capacity of 3,000 gallons; the Wepprich Winery at St. Charles, a few miles down the river, had a capacity of 4,700 gallons. These were not new enterprises but rather a straggle of veteran businesses that had survived Prohibition; their operators were evidently not making an independent living as winemakers but kept up the work as a sideline. It is no wonder that neither of the two books written about American wine in the decade following Repeal had anything material to say about Missouri wine. Frank Schoonmaker and Tom Marvel noted merely that of the once-numerous vineyards and wineries in Missouri, "only a few remain"; and Mary Frost Mabon could say only that Missouri, formerly one of "the top wine-producing states," would perhaps be one of them again.[64] There was little reason to think so: the state gave no encouragement to its wine industry, and most Missourians must have remained in ignorance of the fact that they had one.

At first glance, things seemed to be flourishing far more in Arkansas, where some 56 wineries operated in 1946. Almost all of them were in the northwestern corner of the state, the Ozark region, mostly clustered around the towns of Altus and Springdale. Winemaking there went back to the late nineteenth century, when the German-Swiss settlers around Altus and the Italians around Tontitown, near Springdale, had established the business. Some of the old names still survived: Doerpinghaus, Joerger, and Metz at Altus, Mantegani and Granata at Tontitown. The scale was usually very small: Richard Taldo at Tontitown had a 5,000-gallon winery, Charles Wagner at Subiaco had 4,000 gallons, Alphons Newman at Scranton had 5,000, and so on. Here, as elsewhere in the East, the production of grape juice paid the bills. Welch had built a juice plant in Springdale in 1922, with the result that the small vineyard acreage that had been all that was needed for the modest wine production of the state suddenly jumped by many thousands of acres, all of them planted to Concord grapes. After Repeal, Arkansas winemaking was essentially based on whatever grapes were left after Welch's requirements had been met, with the result that Arkansas wine was largely Concord wine.

Most wineries also made fruit wines from the apples, peaches, and berries of the region, and the market seems not to have made much distinction between grape wines and other fruit wines. As one patron of the old Van Gundy winery near West Fork recalled, "Van Gundy kept rhubarb, blackberry, raspberry, grape, strawberry and elderberry. . . . Whatever you wanted."[65] Whether made from grapes or from other fruits, most Arkansas wine was likely to be not only sweet but fortified as well, an intoxicating confection rather than a drink intended to enhance meals.[66] In the old days there had been wines from such grapes as the Cynthiana and Campbell's Early; there was a little of that left—mainly around

Altus—but not much. As one writer resignedly concluded, after reviewing the defects of the Concord as a wine grape: "The preference of Arkansas wine drinkers for the deep reddish-purple hue of Concord wine has been completely established and it is doubtful whether the other excellent American wines would catch on readily here. . . . So the Concord is king in most of Arkansas and will remain so in the foreseeable future."[67]

Arkansas winemakers operated behind the protection of trade barriers, like the winemakers of Michigan. Arkansas wines paid a 5 cent state tax on a gallon; all other wines paid 60 cents. If you wanted to sell out-of-state wines at wholesale, your license cost $650 more than a license to sell Arkansas wines; a retail license for out-of-state wines cost $375 more than one for Arkansas wines.[68] But there does not seem to have been much growth under this protection. In 1945, there was an extraordinary, anomalous production of 588,000 gallons of wine in Arkansas, followed by an equally anomalous production of 50,000 gallons the next year, but in the next four years production averaged 165,000 gallons without remarkable variation.[69] The giant of Arkansas winemaking was the Nelson Wine and Distilling Company of Springdale, founded in 1935. By 1946 it had a capacity of 300,000 gallons and a distillery to supply high-proof spirits for fortification. The two products were Concord wine and apple wine, both fortified to 24 percent! Among the labels used by the firm were Cocktail, Razorback, Eight Ball, and Pink Elephant—all suggesting the only kind of appeal such high-alcohol wines could have.[70] Like the Concord wines of Michigan, those of Arkansas were sold only within the state.

If they were protected by trade barriers, Arkansas winemakers nevertheless had plenty of obstacles within the state. The weather was one: spring freezes are a danger in the highlands of northwestern Arkansas. An unsophisticated market was another: the chances were not good that one could make a living by offering an expensive bottle of good Cynthiana wine to a man who wanted a bottle of Razorback 24 percent Concord. Worse, an outburst of prohibitionist zeal was a perennial possibility. Benton County, one of the two counties in which most of Arkansas's vineyards were concentrated, voted to go Dry in 1945, forcing the migration or closure of its several wineries. To defend themselves on the political side, the grape and fruit growers formed an Arkansas Wine Producers and Fruit Growers Association, which had a membership that included fifteen wineries in 1947.[71] The number of wineries operating in the state, however, declined steadily in the immediate postwar years, just as it did everywhere else. The fifty-six bonded wineries in 1945 had dwindled to thirty-three by 1950.[72]

Texas has seemed, not just to Texans but to many other observers, one of the places ordained to be winegrowing country. It has a wide variety of climates to go with its large spaces, from the semitropical lands along the lower Rio Grande to the high plains of the Panhandle, from the semiarid deserts of West Texas to the bayous of the east. Not all of it is grape-growing country, but much of it might be. In common with most of the rest of the country east of the Rockies, Texas abounds in native grapes: the Mustang *(Vitis candicans)*, for example, still to be seen vigorously overwhelming fences and hedges all over central Texas, or the Post Oak grape *(V. Lincecumii)*, now much diminished by the

grazing of cattle. *V. Berlandieri, V. Champini,* and *V. Monticola* appear to be uniquely Texan grapes, and most of the other native species grow there too: rupestris, rotundifolia, cordifolia, cinera, and so on. In response to the invitation of such abundance and variety, many pioneer efforts were made to develop viticulture in Texas; a few succeeded. The most notable was that of T. V. Munson (1843–1913), a nurseryman of Denison, Texas, with a passion for collecting, describing, and hybridizing native varieties of grapes. He was interested in winemaking but was not a significant producer himself. Most of the many new varieties of grape introduced by Munson still survive in historical collections, though few have any commercial importance and hardly any wine is made from them. But Munson is still remembered for his remarkable devotion to the cause of grape growing in America, and his practice of creating hybrids without making use of labrusca vines was prophetic.[73]

The fact is that Texas, though propitious to many native varieties, is—like most of the rest of the United States—hostile to vinifera.[74] Pierce's disease flourishes in the south-east of the state, cotton root rot attacks the vine in central Texas, and winter freezes it on the high plains. Many, many futile efforts were made to establish the European grape in Texas, but only the native grapes could be made to grow, and no large trade was ever established in Texas on that basis. There were, nevertheless, a good many scattered, small commercial wineries in business at one time or another in pre-Prohibition Texas, all dependent on native grapes. The Isleta Winery at El Paso continued the venerable wine-growing tradition of that region, which had flourished under the Spaniards but languished under Anglo rule; the Steinberger Winery at Windthorst showed the persistence of wine-making among the large German population of Texas; the Italians were represented by the Carminiti Winery and the Fenoglio Winery, both near Dallas. All of these, and a number of others, went under at the time of Prohibition.

When Repeal came, winegrowing in Texas had to start over again pretty much from the beginning. Despite the abundance of native grapes and despite the many hopeful efforts to establish winegrowing in nineteenth-century Texas, no significant wine tradition had ever been established there. Now, even after Repeal, more than the half the counties in the state remained Dry, a heavy discouragement to any winegrowing enterprise. One winery operated in 1934, two in 1935; by 1939 some twelve wineries were in business, all of them quite small.[75] They had also, perforce, to depend entirely on native varieties. The Texas Agricultural Experiment Station, reporting on the state's grape industry in 1940, acknowledged that there was almost no information available about suitable varieties and could only refer the grower who might want some guidance to the pre-Prohibition authorities, T. V. Munson and F. T. Bioletti.[76]

In this situation, without direction or purpose, the few wineries in Texas took whatever varieties they could get. The favored ones there were rather different from those that dominated in the other states east of the Rockies. They were old hybrids that had been grown in the American South since the beginning of the nineteenth century, such as the Herbemont and the Lenoir: both showed resistance to Pierce's disease. One of the few Texas wineries to be revived after Repeal was the Val Verde Winery of Del Rio, founded in 1883 by an Italian immigrant, Francis Qualia. It is still operating, making wines from native southern varieties including the Lenoir and the Herbemont from its own vineyards and vinifera wines from grapes purchased elsewhere in Texas.[77] The old German element was represented by the Niederauer Winery at Brenham and the Vorauer Winery at Fredericksburg, which operated in a small way into the 1950s; Vorauer grew some of the Munson varieties for its wine.[78]

In the 1950s, several large-scale growers of fruits and vegetables in the lower Rio Grande valley, where citrus culture had long been established, decided that they would enter the table-grape business; some experiments had been made from which they concluded that

FIGURE 34

Louis Gross in his Bernalillo, New Mexico, winery, 1962. (From *Westways* [September 1962]: 5; courtesy of Automobile Club of Southern California Archives.)

they could produce the earliest grapes in North America and so enjoy the profits that went with being first. They planted large acreages of the Thompson Seedless grape, a vinifera variety, apparently without consulting the authorities and without regard to the chancy record of vinifera in Texas. The vineyards were soon destroyed by cotton root rot and Pierce's disease, a result bad enough for the growers concerned but even worse for the fortunes of viticulture generally in Texas. The failure was so complete that it put an end to the viticultural research that had been carried on by Texas A. & M. University since the 1930s: why, the authorities asked, invest further in an enterprise that was doomed to fail?[79] Thus the state of winegrowing in Texas was, a generation after Repeal, worse than it had been at the beginning.

Things were not much better in New Mexico, where winegrowing on a small scale went back to the earliest settlement on the Rio Grande in the seventeenth century. In those days everything north of Mexico was "New Mexico," from Texas to California, so it is not easy to make clear statements about who was doing what where. In this discussion, *New Mexico* means the Rio Grande valley above El Paso. Although the winegrowing tradition there was a long one and was, besides, originally based on vinifera rather than on native American grape varieties, it had never had more than a local basis and used very primitive methods.[80] No one in New Mexico was studying varietal improvement or new technologies in fermentation. The old ways were the only ways, though native American grapes had shouldered aside most of the vinifera. New Mexico was remote from the major markets, its climate is severe, and its population was thin on the ground: all these conditions worked against the development of a prosperous wine-growing trade. It is not surprising, then, to find that in 1936 there were only two registered wineries in the state; ten years later there were ten, mostly of Mexican American identity: Aragon, Gutierrez, Nolasco, and the ambiguously named Agustin Wagner. But there were a couple of French producers, too: Louis Gross of Bernalillo and Louis Avant, of the La France Winery, also in Bernalillo. The production of New Mexico's wineries was 10,000 gallons in 1936; ten years later it had reached 18,000 gallons, but as this was divided among some ten wineries, the average was obviously very small indeed. The vineyard acreage was small too; it ran to approximately 1,000 acres in 1936 but sank to 700 acres in 1946. The rise in production between those two points means either that a larger proportion of the crop was being crushed for wine or that the wineries were using grapes and wine from other sources. Probably it was the latter, especially considering that the productivity of New Mexico vineyards was low, averaging under two tons per acre. One interesting thing about the tiny New Mexico industry was that it appeared to be mostly devoted to dry table wine at a time when the rest of the country was given over to sweet and fortified wines.

THE EAST COAST, NORTH AND SOUTH

Having reached Texas and New Mexico, this quick tour of winegrowing outside California may now return to its point of departure and head south from New York: it will not have much territory to cover in that direction. New Jersey, the Garden State, has always had a good reason to try viticulture and winemaking because of its nearness to the great market of New York City. Several fairly substantial enterprises and a number of smaller ones had succeeded before Prohibition, mainly around the southern New Jersey town of Egg Harbor City. Not far away, at Vineland (a temperance community despite its name), the teetotalling dentist Dr. Thomas Welch had succeeded in the mid nineteenth century in developing a pasteurized grape juice to supply the communion table of his Methodist church, and so introduced modern grape juice or, as he first called it, "unfermented wine." The difficulties of viticulture in New Jersey, where black rot and other fungal diseases flourish, had long since driven Welch to the shores of Lake Erie in western New York, leaving what remained of New Jersey's grapes to the wineries. The two oldest were H. T. Dewey and Sons, established in Ohio in 1857 before migrating to New Jersey, and L. N. Renault and Sons, founded in 1870. Both were in Egg Harbor City, and both survived Prohibition. Only a part of Renault's business was in New Jersey wine after Prohibition, for it dealt in California and imported wines as well.[81] Its specialty was a sparkling wine, which had national distribution. H. T. Dewey continued to produce New Jersey wines on a small scale; the firm's storage capacity was only 25,000 gallons in 1947. By 1950 the family began to weary of the work. William Dewey wrote to Will Widmer in 1950 saying that "we Deweys feel like letting some younger fellow take over": did Widmer know of any such fellow?[82] In 1952 the winery ceased to operate.

A few other, smaller wineries also reemerged after Repeal: the Herman Kluxen Winery at Madison, founded in 1865; the Tomasello Winery at Hammonton, founded in 1888; and the Miele Winery in Newark, founded in 1908. One interesting new venture was the Hopewell Winery near Princeton, founded by Peyton Boswell, editor of the *Art News*. Boswell, one of the legion who took up home winemaking under Prohibition, went commercial at Repeal with a small vineyard of native varieties such as the Sheridan, Ontario, and Adam Champagne, supplying a tiny winery of 2,000 gallons' storage. In his zeal Boswell published a book based on his experiences, *Wine Makers Manual: A Guide for the Home Wine Maker and the Small Winery*. He was prompted to perform this service, he wrote, because "practically nothing has been done by constituted authority to help the wine maker."[83] The little book had a respectable life, going through five printings down to 1952, but the little winery did not survive Boswell's death in 1936.

After the war, the condition of the wine business in New Jersey resembled that in the rest of the East: it was sliding into extinction. There were not enough grapes in New Jersey to sustain an industry. The average production in the first decade following Repeal, 1934–43, was only 2,540 tons; in the next decade it fell to 1,540 tons.[84] And of this small total, only a fraction was crushed for wine. Clearly, the wineries of New Jersey were not making much wine from New Jersey grapes, but depended on other eastern sources and on tank-car wine from California.

Pennsylvania, just across the Delaware from New Jersey, bulks large in the history of early experiments in American winegrowing, the list of hopeful experimenters being headed by William Penn himself. But in the first three-quarters of the twentieth century the state does not figure at all in the story of American wine. It *does* have a share in the great Grape Belt running along the southern Lake Erie shore from Buffalo to Sandusky, and although Pennsylvania's part of the belt is not large, it is productive. In the twenty years following Repeal, Pennsylvania produced an annual average of 17,000 tons of grapes, a figure that put it fourth in the table of eastern states (following New York, Michigan, and Ohio). Moreover, the trend of the production figures was upward: 24,000 tons in 1955, 33,500 tons by 1960. But Pennsylvania's grapes—almost exclusively Concords— went into grape juice, not into wine.

One of the main reasons for this situation was the state's decision, following Repeal, to adopt a system of state-owned liquor stores, which required large quantities of standard goods to keep its operations efficient. This arrangement effectively killed any hopes to establish small wineries, which would not be able to supply the state system but could have no other outlet. A few hardy souls made an attempt: according to Internal Revenue statistics, four licensed premises made a total of 8,000 gallons of wine in Pennsylvania in 1936; four years later the volume had risen to 11,688 gallons. And this pathetic figure was all that the most populous of eastern states after New York could manage to produce!

FIGURE 35
Peyton Boswell in his
winery at Hopewell,
New Jersey, in the 1930s.
(From Peyton Boswell,
Wine Makers Manual
[1935].)

Although Pennsylvania was not legally a Dry state, it was practically a desert as far as wine was concerned. The desiccating effects of public policy could hardly be better illustrated. After the war, though several large bottling firms held Pennsylvania bonded winery licenses, there was no producing winery in the state.[85]

South of Pennsylvania, across the Mason-Dixon line, wine had long been an exotic commodity: the first waves of the prohibition movement had rolled over the South, and much of the region had been Dry long before the Eighteenth Amendment. And if one did seek to find drink, what one found was bourbon or rye whiskey, or mountain moonshine. Table wine was essentially unknown except in the region's few large cities, notably the border city of Washington, D.C. There were, nevertheless, vineyards in the South, mostly of muscadine grapes, and wine of some sort was produced in small quantities, particularly in Virginia, North Carolina, and Georgia.

North Carolina was the largest producer of the three because it was the scene of Paul Garrett's activity in the 1930s. We have already seen how Garrett sought to extend plantings of muscadine vines throughout the South and how he proclaimed that he could use ten times the quantity of such grapes as were currently produced.[86] His enthusiasm had little if any effect. North Carolina had about 3,200 acres of grapes in 1935; immediately after the war, in 1946, the figure remained 3,200. Most of the yield from this acreage went to Garrett, who crushed the grapes in his Aberdeen, North Carolina, plant but then shipped the juice to his winemaking facility in Brooklyn. North Carolina thus made very little wine, though it furnished the grapes, which included other varieties of muscadine besides the Scuppernong—the James, Mish, and Flowers, for example. A few other wineries around the state produced wine, some of it from fruits other than the grape. One of these was the Tenner Brothers Winery, established in Charlotte in 1935 to make wine from muscadines and from blackberries, youngberries, and peaches. By 1949 it had reached a considerable size—some 600,000 gallons of storage capacity. Then, in 1953, it migrated over the border to South Carolina, lured by a preferential tax on wines made from South Carolina grapes and berries.

Georgia was also a source mainly of fruit wines, and especially of wines from the celebrated Georgia peaches. The Monarch Wine Company of Atlanta, founded in 1936, accounted for most of the production. Beginning with a storage capacity of 25,000 gallons for peach, blackberry, Scuppernong, and Concord wines, it had grown to a capacity of a million gallons by 1947.

Compared to the large quantities of fruit wines made in the South, not much muscadine wine was made; and there was hardly any wine made from the better-known grape varieties of the East. Virginia had some tradition of successful table-wine production from good varieties like the Norton, even though state Prohibition had arrived as early as 1916, and an interesting but unsuccessful effort was made to revive that tradition in the first years after Repeal. The Monticello Grape Growers Co-operative Association was formed in 1934 at Charlottesville. The organizer was a Virginian named Bernard Peyton Chamberlain, who, like Peyton Boswell in New Jersey and Philip Wagner in Maryland, was an amateur who had been compelled to become a winemaker by Prohibition. He too had written a book, somewhat preciously titled *A Treatise on the Making of Palatable Table Wines, Recommended to Gentlemen, Especially in Virginia for Their Own Use;* it was privately printed in an edition of four hundred copies in 1931. Now that wine might be made again commercially, the great need in Virginia (as everywhere else) was for suitable grapes. There were only 600 acres of vines in all of Virginia in 1935, and, as Frank Schoonmaker and Tom Marvel wrote, "hardly an acre of good wine grapes still remaining in the state."[87] The members of the Monticello co-op now undertook the slow process of repairing this defect by planting Norton grapes, the old Virginia variety long noted for its dark, astringent, nonfoxy wines capable of aging well. Paul Garrett helped by undertaking to buy and process what they grew.[88] But by 1940, six years after the beginning of the plan, the members of the co-op had only 20 tons of Nortons to sell. Further plantings apparently were not made, and so the effort lapsed.[89]

PHILIP WAGNER AND THE FRENCH HYBRIDS

The most promising development in the East during these years of stagnation and decline was the work of an amateur, as has so often been the case in the history of wine in America, both East and West. Philip Wagner was by profession a newspaperman; he had served abroad as a correspondent for the Baltimore *Sun* and later became an editor of the paper. During Prohibition he had made wine and, indeed, published the first good American book on winemaking for amateurs.[90] In 1932 he bought a property at Riderwood, Maryland, north of Baltimore, with a small, decayed vineyard of native eastern varieties on it; there he began his career as a viticulturist as well as winemaker. His goal was to find something better for eastern winemakers than what they had long been accustomed to—Catawba, Elvira, Noah, and the baleful Concord. With better grapes, there was no reason people in the East could not have good, inexpensive wine on a daily basis: this was always his unpretentious and civilized idea of the aim of his work.

Wagner was prepared to look anywhere for something better. He tried some of the non-labrusca hybrids created by T. V. Munson in Texas in the nineteenth century; he tried some of the new varieties developed at the Geneva Experiment Station in New York by Dr. Richard Wellington.[91] His most promising trials, however, were made with what have somewhat misleadingly come to be called French hybrids.[92] They were French in the sense that the people who created them were French, but the materials from which they were created were no more French than those in the uncounted thousands of hybrids that had been deliberately made since early in the nineteenth century. Controlled hybridizing of native American varieties with European varieties went back to the mid nineteenth century in America. Its aim was to create grapes with the resistance of the American varieties and the fruit quality of the European varieties, and so provide the basis for an American wine industry.[93] The phylloxera crisis of the 1860s and 1870s gave a powerful new stimulus to hybridizing: it was no longer a question of finding grapes for the United States, but of finding grapes for the winegrowing regions of the whole world.

While the official solution to the problem of phylloxera was to graft European scions to resistant American rootstocks, an unofficial alternative solution was to develop resistant hybrids of American and European vines that would grow on their own roots and produce an acceptable fruit. The French began with extant American hybrids, which were imported and planted in large numbers but were soon found to be unsatisfactory for one reason or another. These came to be called the old hybrids. Certain French experimenters then began to develop hybrids of their own, going beyond the simple primary hybrids (50 percent American, 50 percent European) they had started with to create complex hybrids.[94] The results of this work were described by the French themselves as direct producers—*producteurs directs*—because they grew on their own roots instead of having to be grafted to resistant roots as all vinifera were. Philip Wagner, when he began importing them, called them French hybrids to distinguish them from the old hybrids.

Such hybrids usually avoided or made but little use of the notorious labrusca species of native American grape, the species of the foxiest character among native grapes; they derived, rather, from such species as *V. Lincecumii, V. rupestris,* and *V. riparia.* They were not the creations of the research stations of France but typically were bred by devoted amateurs, whose names they bear: Baco, Couderc, Kuhlmann, Landot, Oberlin, Ravat, Seibel, Seyve-Villard. The usual method of identifying the French hybrids was by a combination of the breeder's name with a series number—Baco 1 or Seibel 4986 or Seyve-Villard 5247. Later, some of the more successful of the hybrids were given names under which they are now known: Chelois, Chambourcin, Seyval, and the like. Some of the named varieties have already disappeared for all practical purposes, and no doubt there will be many more new names. The list is open.[95] The *producteurs directs* were planted over very large acreages in France and elsewhere in Europe, but they have had to struggle against the hostility of the establishment. In 1975 all new planting of the hybrids for commercial wine production was forbidden in France, ostensibly in order to protect the reputation for quality of France's wine. Still, they persist.

Some of the older French hybrids were known in the United States before Prohibition, but only as curiosities.[96] Wagner first learned about them from his reading, and then sought information about them when he was based in London as a correspondent in 1936–37; on his return to this country he discovered that isolated plantings of them were already scattered around the United States.[97] From these sources, and from his own imports, he established a small nursery at Riderwood in 1941. He could now provide vines for his own experiments and to supply a growing number of interested amateurs; this was, he said, his "Johnny Appleseed operation." In 1945, finding himself with more grapes than he could use, Wagner bonded his Boordy Vineyard, not so much for commercial reasons as to show that decent wine could be made from grapes formerly unknown in this country and in places formerly untried or abandoned. An unsuspected bonus was the discovery that some of the French hybrids possessed not only superior fruit quality and disease resistance but cold hardiness as well; the French had not made this trait a special object in their breeding plans, but it was a point of first importance in the northeastern and midwestern American states.

Wagner's work, and the persuasiveness of his writing about that work, began to have their effect on the commercial winemakers as well as on the amateurs. The few people, amateurs and professionals alike, who knew about and took an interest in the French hybrids formed a sort of club for the exchange of information. They also held annual meetings at which the wines from the new grapes could be critically tasted. The promise of the French hybrids thus began to be known and to spread beyond the small group. Charles Fournier of Gold Seal Vineyards in the Finger Lakes, one of the club, planted the first commercial vineyard of French hybrids in this country beside Keuka Lake in 1944 from cuttings supplied by Philip Wagner. He was soon followed by the Canadian Bright's Vineyards at Niagara Falls. The experiment stations now began to pay attention too: "One by one, stations in Illinois, Ohio, Arkansas, Pennsylvania, Michigan, and Missouri and elsewhere became involved."[98] And then the point was reached at which some of the amateur growers who had planted vines from Philip Wagner's nursery began to think of commercial production, and so those new, small, different wineries that were to change the face of American winemaking began to appear. Here it is enough to say that without Philip Wagner and the French hybrids, this would not have happened in the eastern states. As Leon Adams, writing in 1973, put it simply: "Wagner and his hybrids have made possible most of the small winegrowing ventures that have started up in several eastern states since the Second World War."[99]

9

CHANGING WEATHER

THE BIG GET BIGGER

For many years after the war, the number of wineries in California continued its steady decline: there were 414 in 1945, 374 in 1950; not until 1970 was the decline arrested, then turned around.[1] Over the same period, there was a gradual but steady increase in production. California produced 116 million gallons of wine in 1945; ten years later the figure was 147 million. In these conditions, as the fish grew fewer and the pond grew larger, some of the fish became very large indeed.[2] The combinations put together during the war years by the distillers were still intact in the early '50s: National Distillers had Italian Swiss Colony and Lejon; Schenley had Roma and Cresta Blanca. But the co-ops dominated the production of California wine. The fact is a testimony to the continuing insecurity of the trade, for co-ops flourish when the market is troubled and tend to fade when it grows strong. Twenty-nine were operating in 1952, with a combined capacity of nearly 82 million gallons. Throughout the decade of the '50s, fresh mergers or talk of mergers went on among the co-ops and among the regular commercial wineries, as though bigness in itself were the only safe way to go.[3] The wine trade in California seemed headed toward oligopoly, if it was not already there.

During these years, the most sensational growth was shown by two enterprises that both reached astonishing proportions: the Allied Growers–United Vintners combination and the Gallo Winery. The competition between these giants for growth and market dominance makes the most obviously dramatic, if not perhaps the most significant, of the stories belonging to the two decades following World War II. That story also illustrates two very different methods of operation.

The Gallo Winery, started in Modesto at the end of 1933, on the eve of Repeal, by the brothers Ernest and Julio, had grown steadily but unobtrusively through the Depression and war years. Originally, it had followed the usual pattern of selling its wines in bulk to bottlers in and out of California—mostly out, for the eastern trade was the important one.[4] The brothers built a new winery in 1936 and had a storage capacity of 2 million gallons in the next year. In 1938 they began to bottle and label wine under their own name, and although there were some false starts in establishing the brand ("by golly, buy Gallo" was the slogan of one early sales campaign), they continued to expand production: the winery had more than 4 million gallons' capacity in 1940, 12 million in 1952. This was by no means the largest operation in California: in 1952 Roma had 30 million and Italian Swiss Colony 26 million, and some of the big co-ops had comparable capacity. Gallo was a major presence by 1950 but was not yet perceived as anything special. Later, when it came to be the overwhelmingly dominant power in the entire industry, stories were told about how it had exercised a controlling hand even in the early days. Ellen Hawkes, for instance, in her hostile account of the Gallo story, reports that the Gallos cornered 75 percent of the grape market in 1946 and so created the grape-buying panic of that year, to their vast profiting.[5] The story is fantastic, but thus are legends made.

Louis A. Petri (1912–80) had originally been destined for the medical profession but left school in 1935 to join the family winery. His grandfather Raphael and father, Angelo, had both been in the wine business in San Francisco before Prohibition, and Angelo went back into it after Repeal. Louis Petri started work as a barrel washer. In two years he was general manager; by 1944 he was president of the firm. The splendor of this meteoric rise is perhaps only a little dimmed by the fact that he was the boss's son. Petri proved to be a born entrepreneur, happiest when inventing and carrying out deals, restless and bored by merely routine business. If he were going to run the Petri winery, then he would make it run indeed.

The expansion of the already substantial Petri operation began before the war, when the Petris, who dealt entirely in bulk wines, bought out one of their big customers, Sunny Hill Wineries, a distributor in Chicago. During the war, when everyone was looking for additional supplies, they bought the Tulare Wine Company, a producing winery, and in common with the rest of the trade, began bottling under their own label. The first really sensational deal came in 1949, when Louis Petri bought the big Mission Bell winery in Madera, California, from the astute Krikor Arakelian.[6] This, at a stroke, gave the Petri wineries 20 million gallons of storage capacity, raising it to the third position in the state behind the big cooperative combinations, California Wine Association (29.5 million) and Guild Wineries (22 million).

Louis Petri now began to unfold a bold and original plan of operation. He set about organizing a large growers' cooperative, called Allied Grape Growers, consisting in its original form of some 240 members. He next organized a company called United Vintners, a family-held stock company, whose assets were the Petri wineries. United Vintners then sold its wineries to Allied Grape Growers; Allied Grape Growers, in turn, signed an exclusive marketing contract with United Vintners, which was now strictly a sales organization. The result of this dizzying sleight-of-hand, executed in 1951, was that Allied Grape Growers now possessed two large wineries and controlled the many thousands of acres belonging to its grower-members. United Vintners retained possession of its labels and its sales staff, and undertook to sell under those labels and with that sales staff the wines made from Allied grapes in Allied wineries. The scheme was a new twist on the idea embodied in the CWA and Guild. They were nonprofit marketing co-ops representing a collection of cooperative wineries. But United Vintners was a for-profit company, whose contract with Allied called for a fifty-fifty split of the profits between the contracting parties.

Petri and his family now had the money from the sale of their wineries and the prospect of half the profits from their continued operation. Petri fulfilled his part of the bargain. In the first year of the arrangement, United Vintners undertook to sell the produce of 30,000 tons of Allied grapes. Within a year it was 88,000 tons; two years later it was 108,000 tons. And that was only the beginning.

In 1953 Petri pulled off his most spectacular coup by buying Italian Swiss Colony from National Distillers, which was retreating from its venture into wine.[7] Italian Swiss Colony was then one of the two best-known, nationally advertised, nationally distributed brands (the other was Schenley's Roma brand), with a large business in franchise bottling—an arrangement by which the bulk wine shipped to private bottlers was put out under the Italian Swiss Colony label. Gallo had an option to buy the company but backed away from the deal, so Petri was able to get a bargain price from National Distillers, eager as it was to get out of the wine trade.[8] Petri's luck was still running: no sooner had he bought the company and all of its inventory than the California vineyards were hit by a black freeze, reducing the crop and sending up the price of Petri's huge new supply.[9]

With the purchase of Italian Swiss Colony and its 24 million gallons of storage, United Vintners now had a capacity of 44 million gallons, putting it well ahead of Roma and the CWA, each about 30 million gallons. It also had an array of well-known labels: Italian Swiss Colony, Gambarelli and Davito (popular in the Italian market of metropolitan New York), Lejon, and Mission Bell, in addition to the original Petri line.[10] United Vintners at once leased its new wineries to Allied Grape Growers, so that the separation of production from sales was maintained: Allied grew the grapes and made the wine; United Vintners sold it.

The process of acquisition and merger went on. In 1953, the same year that Petri made the Italian Swiss Colony purchase, he also acquired the Northern Sonoma Wine Company winery at Geyserville, a move that confirmed the growing importance of table wine in the company line. In 1956 the Larkmead Cooperative Winery merged with Allied, and in 1958, so did the Community Grape Products Cooperative at Lodi. In 1961 United Vintners acquired the Cella Winery and vineyards at Reedley. The process of acquisition had now reached its highest point: the Allied–United Vintners combination had a capacity of

FIGURE 36
Louis Petri. (Courtesy
of the Wine Institute.)

55 million gallons provided by big wineries at Fresno, Madera, Escalon, Reedley, Lodi, and Asti. It was calculated that Allied–United Vintners had 20 percent of the national market in 1957, and nearly 30 percent by 1967.[11] In order to feed this huge productive capacity, Allied Grape Growers had to expand. The 240 growers who formed the original cooperative in 1951 had increased to 1,500 a decade later, scattered over the whole length of grape-growing California, from Ukiah to Tulare.

Petri, while managing this remarkable enterprise, always kept his eye on other possibilities. In 1954 he offered to sell his business to an investment group but was unable to bring that off. In 1957 he talked of going public with United Vintners but did not bring that off either. But in 1959 he made a major move by selling United Vintners to Allied Grape Growers for $24 million. All operations were now concentrated in the new United Vintners, and Allied became the membership organization that received the profits from those operations. Petri, once again enriched by the sale of his properties to Allied, became an employee rather than an owner of United Vintners.

Petri's plan of acquiring properties only to deal them off exemplifies a principle laid down by another wine industry businessman, Morris Katz of Paul Masson: winemaking, Katz observed, is only doubtfully profitable because of the heavy capital investment required in vineyards and wineries, and because of the slow and uncertain returns. The prosperous people are the merchants, who don't own anything: "If you don't own anything," Katz said, "you're more apt to be profitable than if you do own something."[12] That seems to have been the wisdom guiding Petri's moves in the 1950s: he built an impressive business, he made many millions, and at the end of the process he owned nothing (or comparatively little)—by design.

One of Petri's novelties that especially caught the public imagination was converting a World War II tanker into a wine ship. The S.S. *Angelo Petri,* equipped with stainless steel tanks capable of holding 2.5 million gallons of wine, was commissioned in 1957 and served to carry wine from California through the Panama Canal to Texas and New York until 1975.[13] By this striking means—and the *Angelo Petri* was abundantly publicized—Petri evaded the control of the railroads and perhaps made a little money in the shipping business as well.[14] To operate the ship, with its vast load of wine, it was necessary first to build a storage depot at the port of Stockton, where the ship was loaded, and other depots at Houston, Texas, and Newark, New Jersey, where the ship delivered its cargo. Wine delivered to Newark was bottled there for distribution throughout the East. Wine delivered to Houston was transferred to barges that took it up the Mississippi and the Chicago Ship Canal to Chicago, where it was bottled for the midwestern trade. On its return voyages, the *Angelo Petri* carried cargoes of liquid sugar, grain neutral spirits, corn oil, molasses, and other liquid foods, as well as soda ash. Its ballast tanks, separate from the others, carried lubricating oil.

It had at least one close call in its career. At the beginning of a voyage in February 1960, loaded with wine, the *Angelo Petri* hit rough weather outside the Golden Gate. She lost her rudder, a wave shorted out the electrical system, and the ship was barely saved by her anchors from drifting onto the shore. The ship was then safely towed back into harbor, and the wine, after anxious inspection, was found to be undamaged.[15]

That wine had to be robust to withstand the treatment it got by this method of shipment. It was first pumped at the different United Vintners wineries into tank trucks that took it to Stockton, where it was pumped into tanks and stored. It was then pumped into the tanks of the *Angelo Petri.* On arrival at Newark it was pumped into storage tanks, and then pumped to the bottling line. If it was destined for Houston, it was pumped into storage tanks there, then pumped into barges that took it to Chicago, then pumped into storage, and then bottled. A wine that traveled thus from Madera to Chicago would have been pumped seven different times from receptacle to receptacle, quite apart from the handling it received in the process of manufacture. This practice would horrify contemporary winemakers, who seek to minimize the aeration inseparable from pumping; but if it troubled anyone at the time, the fact has not been recorded.

Petri had been among the first in the wine trade to advertise widely on the new medium of television; by 1960 the company had an effective national campaign exploiting the Italian Swiss theme through a "little old winemaker" in lederhosen surrounded by pretty young women in dirndls. Petri was also alert to the signs that table wine—and even superior table wine, not just the run-of-the-mill burgundies and sauternes that had largely defined the category since Repeal—was beginning to count for something. In 1952 he introduced a line of Signature wines chosen by a panel of recognized "gourmets"; they testified to the excellence of each bottle by putting their signatures on the label.[16] But it was difficult for Petri to carry the move toward table wines very far, working as he did for a co-op: the wineries for which United Vintners was the sales agent did not choose the grapes they would crush but accepted, perforce, what the grower-members offered them. Most of the crop was of standard varieties for fortified wine.

Petri's final flourish at United Vintners was made in 1964 when, to the general astonishment of the trade, he bought the patrician Inglenook Vineyards in the Napa Valley, one of the noblest among California's tiny group of aristocratic wineries. It was, people felt at the time, as though some vulgar, uncouth nouveau riche had carried off the king's daughter. But that was the last of Petri's exploits at United Vintners. He ceased to be president of the firm that year and retired offstage as chairman of the board.[17] Four years later, United Vintners was sold to Heublein and entered into a new phase of its history, a story that we need not follow here. Petri, who had held on to a piece of United Vintners before selling it separately to Heublein, was out of the wine business entirely by the beginning of the 1970s. United Vintners, at the moment it was sold to Heublein, had a storage capacity of 95 million gallons, so Petri had certainly succeeded in building an impressive operation, even by the large-scale standards of California. The elements out of which it had been constructed, however, were unstable, and the structure soon fell apart in different hands. Ernest Gallo's remark, that what Louis Petri was really good at was "buying and selling businesses" rather than building them up, seems fair enough.[18]

The history of the Gallo Winery's rise during these years of Louis Petri's inventive improvisations is rather different and much less dramatic: the story of the tortoise and the hare comes to mind. Petri loved the flamboyant gesture and the publicity that came with it; the Gallos sought to avoid personal publicity and, oysterlike, resisted all efforts to open them up. By 1950—to take that as a starting point—the Gallo Winery, which had begun to establish its own label in many markets around the country, had a capacity of approximately 10 million gallons. Now began a steady process of expansion, in part by purchase, in part by new building and new planting, and especially by agreeing to long-term contracts with other wineries. The latter scheme was the Gallos' equivalent of Petri's practice of letting someone else make the wine while he sold it. Thus in 1948 the Gallos contracted for all of the production of Frei Brothers, in the Dry Creek region of Sonoma County. Four years later, Gallo made a similar contract with the Napa Valley Cooperative, then by far the biggest producer in the valley; in 1954 it secured the production of the St. Helena Cooperative Winery, making Gallo much the biggest market for Napa Valley wine, controlling about 40 percent of the crop.[19] In 1953 Gallo signed five-year contracts with the Del Rey Winery co-op and the Modesto Cooperative Winery, both in San Joaquin County, to buy their annual production of 4.5 million gallons of wine.

But Gallo also grew through outright purchase: in 1954, a year after declining to take up its option for the purchase of Italian Swiss Colony, Gallo bought the bankrupt Las Palmas winery in Fresno from Cribari. This was a major facility, storing 6.5 million gallons of wine (forty years later it had been expanded to a capacity of 94 million gallons).[20] And Gallo also expanded its Modesto premises: a 2-million-gallon addition there in 1955 brought the storage capacity to 20 million gallons, up from 10 million in 1950. Two years later the figure stood at 32 million gallons; in 1960, it was 37 million.

The sales of Gallo wine kept pace with the productive capacity of the winery. In a well-known and doubtless apocryphal anecdote, Julio Gallo tells his brother Ernest, "I'll make all the wine that you can sell"; to which Ernest replies, "I'll sell all the wine that you can make."[21] Like many apocryphal stories, this one has its kernel of truth. Julio Gallo was the vineyard manager for the firm and the man who represented the winery in its relations with the many growers who sold their grapes to it; he was for many years directly involved in wine production too. And Ernest was emphatically the salesman, going back to the time when the Gallo brothers and their father sold fresh grapes to home winemakers during Prohibition. Ernest had learned how to spot an opportunity and how to exploit it when, as not more than a boy, he had sold grapes in the Chicago rail yards. It was not your ordinary twenty-year-old who bought a gun and made sure that anyone "suspicious" saw it when he was selling grapes in the Chicago rail yards: he carried much cash, and, as he said, "I was not going to let anyone take it away."[22] Now, as a partner in a steadily growing winery, he studied, as apparently no one else in the trade had studied, the possibilities of the complex—or, rather, chaotic—conditions that governed the trade in wine in the United States.

Any wine producer who hoped to have more than a local distribution had to work through the so-called three-tier system, in which the producer (usually in California) consigned its wine to a licensed wholesaler or distributor that did the work of selling to retail accounts. This system, which made it effectively impossible for a winery to sell directly to consumers outside the state of origin, reflected the deep suspicion in which the liquor trade was held at the time of Repeal. Most states, determined not to allow the producers to control the retailers, as had happened with the old saloon system, required distillers and winemakers (but not brewers) to sell only to licensed wholesalers. Thus a buffering wholesaler stood between the producer and the retailer and prevented any rapacious producer from controlling its markets. It occurred to Ernest Gallo that despite the obstacles, the producer might also be the distributor, through outright purchase of distributorships (where this was legal) or by acquiring effective financial control over ostensibly independent distributors.[23] He bought his first distributorship in 1939, and over the course of the years added a number of others. Once under Gallo control, a distributor would obviously promote Gallo wines to his retail customers. No doubt other wineries attempted to manipulate the awkward American market scheme after this fashion, but no one seems to have done it to such good effect as did Ernest Gallo: "We have built our company through paying close attention to our distributors," he said in his official account of the winery's history.[24] *Attention* in this context meant "control," one way or another.

As Gallo's distribution grew, Ernest decided that he "needed to have winery represen-tatives living in close proximity to our distributors. They would help to train the distribu-tors' sales forces, see that our point-of-sale material was used effectively, and so on."[25] How the "winery representatives" managed to impose themselves on the distributors is not ex-plained, but an anecdote told by Legh Knowles, who worked for Gallo, is suggestive:

> I started in Cincinnati. Ernest [Gallo] told me they take markets one at a time—"You go to Cincinnati; you be the distributor sales manager." He said to the distributor, "You don't know how to sell wine? I'll bring our sales manager in. You can hire him." He brings me in there, and the distributor says, "I usually hire all the people." Ernest says, "Fine. Hire this man."[26]

In later years, Gallo was to run into trouble with the Federal Trade Commission for "exclusionary marketing policies"—that is, for squeezing the competition out by what-ever means might be necessary. The main means, according to the FTC's complaint, was that of coercing distributors to sell Gallo wines exclusively. Faced with this complaint, Gallo decided to sign a consent order requiring the company to cease and desist from its long-established practices of financing wholesalers and then dictating their sales poli-cies.[27] Later, in the changed political climate of the Reagan administration, Gallo suc-cessfully applied to have the consent order rescinded before its original expiration date of 1986. Ernest Gallo was unrepentant about controlling his distributors: "I still think it is to the advantage of both our winery and the wholesalers for them not to take on com-petitive wine lines. . . . We simply will not accept any distributor treating our wines as an afterthought."[28] In his view, no Gallo distributor *needed* anything but Gallo wine: the com-pany made a complete line of products—sweet, dry, red, white, still, sparkling—as good as or better than anyone else's wine, or so Ernest Gallo seems seriously to have believed. Why should anyone need anything else?

It was not enough, however, to control the wholesalers and distributors: Gallo had to dominate the retail store as well. Ernest Gallo was himself indefatigable in visiting retail stores all over the country, at all seasons and at all times, to see how they operated and how what they did might be improved—or in plainer terms, how they might sell more Gallo wine. No detail was too small to escape Gallo's notice, and since he spent up to half the year not in his office but on the road, he saw many details. Even after his company had become the largest winery in the world, he would call on small mom-and-pop stores in the cities and on crossroads stores in the country. His observations were condensed into a few essential rules that his salespeople were trained to follow, thus:

> Talk to retailers about the advantages of carrying our product
> Obtain the most visible position at eye level for Gallo wines
> Trim shelves with colorful point-of-sale materials
> Use bottle collars to attract consumer attention

FIGURE 37
Ernest Gallo. (Courtesy of the Wine Institute.)

Rotate stock to ensure quality, and keep the Gallo shelves stocked

Dust our bottles to keep them bright and clean

Place counter displays in key traffic locations.[29]

It all seems transparently obvious, but it evidently worked—especially because of Ernest Gallo's close and demanding attention to the performance of his salespeople, who were trained, as the saying goes, to take no prisoners. The few essential rules for salespeople were in fact elaborated in a long training manual that gave instructions for all possible situations.[30] The aim behind such determined methods was not just to sell wine, but to sell more wine than anyone else in an ever-increasing volume; *total merchandising* was the Gallo term:

Ernest called it total merchandising. One time he asked thirty of us to define what we thought total merchandising was, and we all did it differently. Finally, there was one man from Ventura, California—his name was Conners—and he got up and said, "Ernest, I think what you mean is" (and this was supposed to be sarcastic) "if you have a great big supermarket, you open the door of that supermarket and you don't see any produce, you don't see any canned goods, you don't see any meat; all you see is Gallo wine." Ernest says, "*That's* total merchandising!"[31]

It was all very well to make a lot of wine and to sell it aggressively. But Ernest Gallo considered that the real key to success—that is, to dominating the market—was to give the public what it wanted. "The standards of wine should always be determined by the people to whom we hope to sell," Ernest Gallo told the American Society of Enologists in 1961, and in one form or another this was always the Gallo mantra.[32] It is not, perhaps, a particularly bold or original idea; "giving the people what they want" has always been standard business practice. But the wine business was a little different. The notion of good wine had a tradition behind it: certain types of wine, and certain exemplary wines in each of those types, defined a standard, and winemakers and wine buyers agreed that those standards were valid. Ernest Gallo did not. The only standard was what the public wanted, and since the public often said one thing but meant another, he was determined to find out the truth of the matter. If the public said that it wanted dry wines but in fact bought sweet wines, Gallo would make sweet wines. If it liked fizzy drinks—as the prodigious sales of soft drinks made manifest—then he would provide fizzy wines. If it wanted wines that tasted like strawberry soda or like sweet lemonade, Gallo would be glad to make them. The Concord-based wine called Gallo-ette, intended for a women's market that did not develop, has already been mentioned.[33] Paisano, a sweetened red wine designed to compete with the successful Vino da Tavola of Guild Wineries, soon after its introduction became the best-selling red wine in the country.[34] Gallo scored another big hit with a Grenache rosé, also slightly sweet. Then there was Pink Chablis, introduced in the early 1960s as part of a trio of "gourmet" wines—the other two being Hearty Burgundy and Chablis Blanc. Once the barriers were down, others rushed in to exploit the new possibilities: Italian Swiss Colony outdid itself by introducing not only its own Pink Chablis, but a Gold Chablis and a Ruby Chablis as well.[35]

All of these novelties, slightly sweetened red, pink, and white wines, were moves in a campaign to make wines that would suit what was imagined to be the American taste, notorious for its addiction to soft drinks. The steady growth in sales of such table wines was a new thing and inspired Ernest Gallo to prophecy. "When we consider these things," he wrote on the twenty-fifth anniversary of Repeal, "and realize that we are beginning to make wines more and more suited to the American taste, I leave to your individual imaginations the tremendous volume we are going to enjoy in the next few years. . . . Now in our 25th year, I believe we are at the turning point in our entire history."[36]

Following the growth of a market for "mellow" table wines, as they were called, the next big boom came after 1954, when the federal regulations were altered to allow the production of "special natural wines"—that is, wines to which various flavors had been added. Before the change, the only flavored wine that had been allowed was vermouth, which had originated in Italy in the late eighteenth century and had been widely imitated in the rest of the world, including California.[37] Any other flavored wine would pay a higher tax because it would be officially classified as the product of "rectification" rather than as a primary product, and it could be produced only in a rectifying plant, not in a bonded winery.[38] Now, under the altered regulations, wineries could compound their wines with any flavors they were bold enough to imagine: wine with cola, chocolate, cloves, gentian, rhubarb—you name it.

Who might have ventured first is not known, but the first big success in this line of goods belonged to Gallo. The Gallo sales staff in Los Angeles had reported that in stores with a large African American clientele, the owner often kept a bottle of concentrated lemon juice by his cash register. Customers would buy a bottle of white port and then, after they had paid for it, would open the bottle, take a drink, then hand the bottle to the owner to have a shot of lemon juice poured into it. Taking this hint, Gallo developed a lemon-flavored fortified wine called Thunderbird and put it on the market in 1957. It was an instant success, and there followed in its train a motley crowd of invented wines with neon names, some from Gallo and even more from the competition: Maverick, Gypsy Rose, Super Chief, Silver Satin, Golden Spur, Tom-Tom, Triple Jack, Red Rooster, Arriba, Swiss-up, Swiss Mist (sold in cans).[39] Guild even ventured onto the market with a cranberry-flavored Ocean Spray American Rosé. But as Ernest Gallo complacently remarked, none of these products "ever dented Thunderbird's success."[40]

Another change in the federal regulations led to the invention of other sorts of wines. These were unfortified but carbonated and, typically, had their sweetness complicated with a variety of fruit and other flavors: they included Bali Hai (pineapple, guava, and passion fruit), Spanada, Pink Pussy Cat, Tingle Pink, and many others. The Gallos again led in this market, first with a lightly carbonated sweet wine called Ripple, and then with a relatively plain and simple beverage called Boone's Farm Apple Wine in 1961.[41] Its huge success—it became for a time the biggest-selling "wine" in the country—led the Gallos into the apple orchard business on a large scale.[42] The market for these new wines—flavored or sweetened or carbonated, or all three—was large enough that many besides Gallo found room in it.[43] B. C. Solari, then head of United Vintners, told the members of the Los Angeles Advertising Club in 1962 that they were "wasting their time" on "new campaigns for Port, Sherry, Muscatel, Burgundy and Sauterne." Such wines belonged to the past; the future lay with the new wines.[44] So it may have seemed then.

The Gallo brothers, to their great credit, were always aware that making good wine was a precondition of selling wine. What is "good" is of course open to dispute, and there have been few to praise Gallo for such things as Ripple, Thunderbird, or Pink Chablis. But making sound table wine was always central to the Gallos' idea of their work, even though they were also prepared to give the public whatever it might want. They hired a professional viticulturist to supervise an experimental vineyard as early as 1946 and carried out varietal testing on a large scale when no other winery was apparently interested in such inquiry. Julio Gallo worked steadily on the difficult job of getting growers to plant better varieties and to follow better cultivation practices—*better* in this case meaning pretty much what any other winemaker would mean. In the course of time, the great growth of the Gallo winery and its immense purchasing power perhaps had as much or more to do with persuading growers to plant better varieties than all the arguments and demonstrations of the university experts. There is overwhelming testimony to the leading part that the Gallos had in improving the varietal basis of the California vineyards, especially those in the great Central Valley.[45]

The Gallo program for quality included the winery as well as the vineyard. In 1942 the Gallos hired a research chemist, Charles Crawford, as winemaker and encouraged him to develop a laboratory and experimental winery. "Ernest Gallo told me he wanted to improve his wines," Crawford recalled; "he wanted to make the best wine that could be made and sell it at a reasonable price."[46] Crawford, who remained with the winery until his death in 1999, entered wholly into the Gallo spirit. As he told one young winemaker, William Bonetti, when he hired him in 1949: "Look, here the work officially is forty hours a week. But we love our jobs so much that we stay as long as necessary."[47]

The outcome of all this determined effort in production and sales—most of it under the direct, personal supervision of the Gallo brothers themselves—was an astounding growth. By the 1960s, Petri and United Vintners had been overtaken and left behind. It was an advantage for Gallo that it was a private company, with the flexibility to move wherever the market might take it. United Vintners was a co-op of growers, mostly from the Central Valley, whose holdings were mostly in grapes for fortified wines; they were slow to see the coming shift to table wines and to the various new styles of wine.[48] Gallo had seen it, and had already developed sources outside the Central Valley for a supply of table wines; Hearty Burgundy, for example, was based on Durif (Petite Sirah) from Napa and Sonoma.

Gallo in 1966 moved into unchallenged first place among American winemakers, its various wineries then boasting a storage capacity of 100 million gallons. It was already well along in the process of vertical integration; ultimately Gallo was to have its own trucking firm, its own bottle factory, its own aluminum cap factory. Gallo wine was utterly consistent and reliable; it was sold almost everywhere that wine was sold in America; and it was inexpensive.[49] Americans, to the extent that they had any consciousness of wine at all, thought first of Gallo when they thought of wine. They might not think of it as anything more than undistinguished jug wine, but at least Gallo came first.

PLUS ÇA CHANGE

Despite such signs of prosperity as the growth of the Gallo enterprise, the dominant note in the wine industry through the '50s and into the '60s was one of anxiety and gloom over the instability of the trade. The old problems persisted: overproduction and the collapse of prices; the imbalance between supplies of raisin and wine grapes; the lack of a broadly based market. It is perhaps a little surprising to learn this, given the expansive character of the business in the past thirty years or more, but so it was.

How to cope with the surplus of grapes was the leading anxiety, as the long list of marketing orders and other "stabilization" devices that were debated and sometimes enacted makes plain. No other matter so occupied the industry: not new markets, not the problems of grape growing or winemaking, not the problem of making Americans conscious of wine but, over and over again, the problem of "stability" in the market. What had to be done was clear enough: the growers had to reduce overcropping and grow better varieties; and the wineries had to pay more for better grapes to the growers who would take the risk of growing them. But these were structural changes, and though there were plenty of authorities who counseled them, they were to be achieved only gradually. In the meantime, at repeated moments of crisis, emergency measures were repeatedly used.

At the end of chapter 7 we left the California scene in 1950, just when a crisis had been happily averted. A big crop in 1948 had driven prices down; a marketing order for winemakers and a marketing order for grape stabilization were passed in 1949 in order to avert disaster. A short crop that year relieved the market, and things went well in 1950, in part thanks to the Korean War. Such ups and downs were to be repeated throughout the decade and into the next. For instance, 1951 was a disaster: the crop that year was an all-time record, producing what was called a "ruinous surplus," along with a host of contending ideas of what to do about it.[50] The marketing order of 1949 was still in force and allowed some control over the quantity of wine that each producer could ship to the market. But everyone recognized that the order was a stopgap measure and that something more was needed. Three plans emerged.

One was for a grape quality grading program; this proposal was based on the suggestions of Professor Winkler at Davis, who had long argued that grapes should be graded for quality, just as, for example, apples, apricots, and avocados were. The standard for grapes would be based on the sugar and acid readings, and the winemakers would pay the growers according to the quality delivered. Through this simple measure, it was hoped, growers would cease overcropping their vines, quality would improve, and the surplus would disappear.[51] The second plan, called the Boragno Plan after Joe Boragno, a Selma grape grower who drafted the original proposal, provided that only wine grapes should be used in making wine, and that the varietal content requirement for wines bearing the name of a variety should gradually be increased to 80 percent from the current 51 percent. Raisin and table grapes would be used only for distilling high-proof brandy for fortification, for neutral blending wines, or for wines without varietal identification. The third proposal, called the Krum Plan, was for a set-aside of fortified wine to be controlled by a special administrative authority created by the marketing order.[52] All of these plans, and others, were hotly argued but never acted on, for the crop in 1952, though not small, was down from the year before. Sales picked up, and the emergency passed, as emergencies do.

People continued to worry, however, for the underlying causes had not changed.[53] In the next year, proposals were made for another marketing order to apply to the Central Valley—a sign, perhaps, that the North Coast had now managed to separate itself from the fortunes of the valley. The proposed order would create a promotional fund by assessment and would divert a part of production to a "stabilization pool" of fortified wines. Growers would be required to remove 12.5 percent of their crop before harvest by "green-dropping."[54] But again, the crop that year was below normal and the market was good, as it was again in the next year, 1954. Thus action on any and all of the proposals for regulating the market could be postponed. It also helped that the federal government continued to subsidize raisin exports.

The year 1955 brought a big crop but no crisis. The emphasis over the next several years was not on coping with surpluses but on obtaining standards of grape quality—that seemingly impossible goal—by means of marketing orders. Detailed proposals, endorsed by the Wine Institute, were put forward in 1957 and 1959 but failed to get much support.[55] And in 1961 the surplus question was back, but now in a slightly altered form. The crops in recent years had not been notably large, but the nation's drinking patterns were changing: table wine sales were going up, fortified wine sales were going down.[56] This was the first clear signal of the changes that were soon to transform the market, as will be set forth in the next chapter.

In the meantime, because the production of fortified wines required more grapes than did that of table wines, the decline in fortified wine sales troubled the grape market.[57] The makers of fortified wines and the growers combined to seek help, this time not from the state but from the federal authorities. They were led by the formidable Arpaxat "Sox" Setrakian, the leader of the California raisin industry and a longtime foe of the winemakers (though he was one himself).[58] The scheme presented to the U.S. Department of Agriculture early in 1961 called for a fixed quantity of grapes to be processed by the Central Valley winemakers: all production beyond that figure would be set aside to be held off the market and disposed of, if necessary, in some noncompetitive way (e.g., as industrial alcohol); and the wine (or high-proof alcohol or concentrate, as the grower might choose) thus set aside would belong not to the winemakers but to the growers whose grapes it was made from.[59] This step, it was thought, would raise the price of bulk fortified wine and allow the producers to pay the growers an adequate price for their grapes; and it would obviously make the growers think twice about how many grapes they would offer to the wineries. No one seems to have thought that raising prices would have a bad effect on sales.

The marathon open hearing held in Fresno in May 1961 to debate the measure turned out to be a Cave of Adullam where everyone with a complaint or a grievance, exacerbated through the long years of market instability, craved to be heard. The wine bottlers protested that they were being victimized; the Flame Tokay growers wanted to be exempt; the Thompson Seedless growers were asserted to be the cause of all the trouble; the raisin growers resented being put under new controls of any kind; all of the growers protested at being made responsible for the set-aside wine—and so it went. The complaint that wine is not an agricultural product, the crux of the legal case against the order creating the Wine Advisory Board in 1938, was heard again: "Wine," said one of the protesting bottlers, "is no closer to grapes than pajamas are to raw cotton" and so had no claim to the protection of a marketing order.[60] But the measure was approved, by a narrow margin, and passed into force as the Grape Crush Order, to operate for three years beginning with the crush of 1961.[61] It did have some success in raising prices; but grape acreage continued to expand in California, threatening to undo any effect of a marketing order, and there was talk of obtaining legislation to limit new plantings. The variety of interests opposed to the order was such that it was voted out in 1963.[62]

In 1965, at the risk of carrying this narrative beyond the limit of tedium, there was yet another record crop, creating another surplus and another round of arguments and proposals for market control, this time by the growers rather than the winemakers. The USDA was appealed to for a grape control order, but after some flurry of agitation, the effort lapsed. This failure was owing in part to the resistance of the wine-grape growers, who objected to the attempt to put them under the same controls as the growers of raisin grapes. Then the makers of fortified wine asked for a state order to set minimum prices, and got it.[63] They were reacting to the continued and disturbing fall in the sales of fortified wines. Not unnaturally, instead of cutting down on production they sought to fix prices, but without success: the order was terminated.

These were the last occasions on which the marketing order remedy was attempted in California. Before that time, however, a marketing order had been applied to a rather different affliction. In 1963 the raisin crop had been damaged by early rains. In order to keep the rain-damaged raisins out of the wineries (where they would be distilled into high-proof spirit for fortifying), the Wine Institute directed a campaign for a permanent order against the use of such material. It seems strange that any such measure might be needed, but the long tradition of treating the wineries as a salvage operation for the state's raisin crop was still intact. That things were now beginning to change was shown by the adoption of the measure over the loud protests of the raisin producers. The order was subsequently declared illegal, but that did not undo the shift in thinking that it had expressed.[64]

I have given so much attention to the repeated crises over surpluses in the California trade mainly in order to emphasize the extent to which the old problems persisted.[65] There was much that was now different in important ways from the bad old days just after Repeal, but too much that seemed not to have changed. The clamor for marketing orders also betrayed a sense among the growers and winemakers alike that the market they shared was fixed—or, worse, was shrinking—and that all they could do was to protect whatever stake in it they already had.

Among other old problems still persisting was that of the composition of California's vineyards. In general, not much had been done, as the repeated surpluses of Thompson Seedless grapes made plain. In the record vintage of 1951, for example, the proportion of raisin and table grapes in the crush was greater than it had been in 1938—not an encouraging statistic.[66] And when one turned to the subject of wine grapes, the report was not much better. Zinfandel was the most important red wine variety in 1952, followed by

Carignane, Alicante Bouschet, Mission (still!), and Grenache. Other red wine varieties—and these would include Cabernet and Pinot noir—had shown a decline in acreage over the ten years 1942–52. The leading white variety was Palomino, the acreage of which had more than doubled in the previous ten years; Burger, the next-most-planted white variety, had also increased its acreage; then came Sauvignon vert, French Colombard, and Sylvaner. All of these varieties had in common the characteristic of great productivity.[67] That trait tied in with another persistent problem—overcropping—which A. J. Winkler identified as the root of almost all the evils besetting the trade: surpluses, variations in crop sizes, reductions in wine quality.[68] Again, these were complaints that were heard just as loudly in the '30s as in the '50s. As Maynard Amerine told the Wine Institute in 1955, "What is needed is a regular supply of high quality grapes. This we do not have."[69]

Nor had ideas about wine among Americans risen much above a few elementary and largely mistaken notions, abetted, one must acknowledge, by the trade itself. Probably the most influential single account of California wine, contained in a series of handbooks issued beginning in 1943 by the Wine Advisory Board, instructed Americans that red wines were called Burgundy and Claret, white wines, Chablis and Rhine; "appetizer" wines were Sherry and Vermouth; "dessert" wines were Port, Muscatel, and Tokay. The "standard" wines of America were "higher in quality than those of any other country."[70] And, of course, every year was a vintage year in California: the Wine Advisory Board said so. The proposition that California made wine to a higher standard than any other place appears to have been an item of official faith: "The big volume of our production—the so-called standard wine—is far above the comparable wine of any other nation" is how one writer put it; another affirmed that "California's 'common' wines easily surpass the world's 'common' wines because of rigorous scientific controls and a high level of cleanliness and cost-saving mechanization."[71] Robert Benson calls this "the industry myth."[72] It is still frequently encountered.

Whether such simplifications and distortions were necessary adaptations to American ignorance, who can say? Perhaps they were. A survey commissioned by the Wine Advisory Board and carried out by Elmo Roper and Associates in 1955 produced some not particularly heartening results. Two-thirds of those polled drank alcoholic beverages, and about half of that group occasionally drank wine. Those who could name any wines at all named, in the order of decreasing frequency, "Port, Sherry, Kosher, Sauterne, Burgundy." Sherry and port were regarded by a large proportion of those who took wine with meals as mealtime wines. In general, wine was seen as unfamiliar, something that "Italians" drank, or as a drink for special occasions only; a large number never thought of wine at all.[73]

The familiar boasts about the superiority of California's "standard" wines conveniently overlooked the fact that there *was* no standard.[74] One of the encouraging signs of the period from the early '50s on was the rapid growth in the sale of table wines: in the four years 1950–53, table-wine sales in California alone rose by about 1.5 million gallons.[75] Some of this growth was in so-called premium wines, which were now doing better than at any point since Repeal. But on investigation it could be seen that most of the table wines contributing to this growth were either the sweetened Paisano or Vino da Tavola style of red wine (including the "kosher," or Concord-based, variant) or the sweetened rosé wines, led by those from Gallo and Italian Swiss Colony. The popularity of the sweet style even led the authorities to allow the use of Sweet Burgundy as a type.[76] As an ad for United Vintners' Bali Hai put it, there was now a "whole new world of dry wine. Dry wines that are made for the American taste. Dry wines that are sweeter." They were, in fact, "sweet dry wines."[77] Oxymoron has never troubled the advertising industry, and in this case at least it did not trouble the wine industry either.

All this was bad news for the grape growers of the North Coast counties, who still depended in large measure on bulk sales to the big wineries such as Petri and Gallo, which blended the northern wines into their traditional table-wine types. The new, sweeter wines could be made from cheaper valley grapes, since the sweetness masked defects of flavor and acid. In a report to the Wine Institute in 1954, Robert Mondavi saw this turn as a distinct threat to the North Coast:

> About ten years ago, practically all table wines were made from grapes grown in the north. Since then San Joaquin wineries have been using lower priced grapes from the Central Valley. . . . Coupled with this is the change in the palate of the consuming public from the Burgundy and Claret type of wines, which is full bodied and dry, to a lighter more mellow type wine. The large wineries, through their constant research work, have produced this mellow table wine which seems to meet the palate of the masses.

Probably, Mondavi thought, the North Coast producers should change their notions about what table wine is and "learn to produce wines according to the wishes of the public."[78] Mondavi took his own advice; varietal white wines from the Charles Krug winery with 2 percent to 3 percent residual sugar had a great success, as did a similar style of C. K. Mondavi generic red wines.

WESTWARD TILT

Other, far-reaching changes were being forced on the winemakers of California by the transformation of the state itself. Before the war, California was an underpopulated state: there were just under 7 million inhabitants in 1940 in its 158,000 square miles. By 1970 there were 20 million. Effectively, the population of the state had tripled in thirty years, and the shocks and confusions attendant on such a change were felt everywhere, including the wine industry. It was not simply the huge growth in population that troubled the state, though that was bad enough; it was the particularly American form of development that such growth took—not urban but suburban. While the population of the counties making up the Bay Area tripled, the population of San Francisco and Oakland, the established cities of the region, *declined*. By 1970, three-quarters of the Bay Area's people lived in suburbs that had been newly built to their demand and that had swallowed up thousands of acres of agricultural land.[79]

The most obvious and destructive change in this process was the loss of traditional vineyard regions under the tide of highways, shopping malls, and subdivisions. Among the earliest and the hardest hit was Santa Clara County, home to such old-line wineries as Paul Masson, Almadén, Mirassou, and Cribari; the 7,000 acres of vineyard spread over the Santa Clara Valley (also home to great orchards of plums and apricots) in 1938, just before the war, had shrunk to 2,600 acres by 1971, and the figure was continuing to dwindle.[80] Comparable dislocations occurred in Alameda and Contra Costa Counties, vulnerable as these were to the expansion of the East Bay region. Viticulture was not extinguished in these places, but it was certainly put in danger.[81] Napa and Sonoma Counties were under less pressure, but it was felt everywhere around the shores of San Francisco Bay.

In the south, the inundation of concrete and asphalt was even more sudden and extensive. Los Angeles County, the place where California winegrowing originated, still had some 4,700 acres of vineyard as late as 1940. But by 1956, a decade after the war, there were only 175 acres of vineyard in the entire county. To the east, in San Bernardino County, the Cucamonga district persisted for another generation, though on borrowed time. It had more than 32,000 acres of grapes just after the war, and twenty years later, in 1965, still managed to hang on to some 13,000 acres, despite the advance of the Los Angeles megalopolis from the west. There were even episodes of growth in a doomed region: the Cucamonga Winery undertook expansion programs in 1951 and again in 1956, including an upgrading of the vineyards. The Brookside Winery, based on the old Guasti property of the Italian Vineyard Company, developed a long chain of branch "wineries" (retail salesrooms) throughout Southern California beginning in the 1960s as a means of conducting its own retail sales.

Now, in the twenty-first century, only two winemaking enterprises still stubbornly persist in the Cucamonga district, regularly shrouded as it is in smog and increasingly covered by airports, freeways, warehouses, factories, housing tracts, and all the other material signs of commercial civilization. Curiously enough, Cucamonga Old Vines Zinfandel now enjoys a prestige value such as it never had before; but one wonders how secure a tenure on life those old vines can have.[82] There were 1,464 acres of grapes left in San Bernardino County in 2003, but there were only 45 nonbearing (i.e., recently planted) acres—a clear indication of approaching dissolution. The belated discovery of the outstanding quality of Cucamonga Zinfandel, just as it hovered on the verge of extinction, is one of those bitter ironies of which all history is full.

It was impossible not to despond in response to such an overwhelming change. Edmund Mirassou, writing in 1961, reviewed all the conditions of population increase, high taxes, diminishing acreage of suitable land, and rising costs, and sadly concluded that for the North Coast wine industry, "extinction appears imminent."[83] Louis Gomberg, looking at the same conditions, came up with a different, perhaps only partly tongue-in-cheek

FIGURE 38
The approaching end: a Cucamonga vineyard in the 1970s. (Photograph by George Rose.)

conclusion. The only viable future, he suggested, would be for the remaining vineyards to be devoted to the highest-quality grapes making the highest-quality wines at the highest prices. Anything less than that would be economically impossible.[84]

A different response, more practical and yet more creative than the despairing or the fanciful, was to open up some new regions to planting. Not much if anything had been done along that line since Repeal, for there had been no reason to do so. Now there was an urgent reason. Some tentative exploration had occurred as early as 1941, when Cella Vineyards made experimental plantings in the foothills of Fresno and Merced Counties; the results were good enough to encourage the belief that "the entire foothill area of the eastern edge of the state offers excellent possibilities."[85] Cella greatly expanded its vineyards in the region, but it does not seem to have been joined by others.[86]

The first extensive new vineyard development in postwar California outside the established regions was made by Almadén in 1956, when it bought a large property—2,200 acres—in San Benito County called the Paicines Ranch. It came into full production in the early 1960s, and in the exuberant language of Frank Schoonmaker, it was expected that the property would "produce more *vin rosé* than the whole French district of Tavel . . . nearly as much true Pinot Chardonnay as all the Grand Cru vineyards of Chablis put together . . . ; more Cabernet Sauvignon than any Bordeaux Chateau; twice as much Pinot Noir as Chambertin does, and far more Johannisberg Riesling than Schloss Johannisberg."[87]

In 1960 A. J. Winkler, of the University of California, surveyed the state and suggested, among other promising areas for consideration, the Carneros district in Napa County, Knights Valley in Sonoma County, the Anderson Valley in Mendocino County, and the terraces west of the Salinas River in Monterey County—an interesting list, since every item on it has since then been developed into a region of significant viticulture.[88] The first important response to this encouragement came from the Paul Masson and Mirassou Vineyards, both in the Santa Clara Valley, when they jointly planted a thousand acres of vineyard in the Salinas Valley, on land that had mostly been used for grazing cattle, in 1962. A whole range of varieties was planted, since no one was sure what would do best in the area.[89] Wente Brothers, in Alameda County, joined the move in 1963, planting 220 Salinas Valley acres to Pinot blanc, Riesling, Grey Riesling, and Pinot noir. The process of discovering what varieties would grow best in the available locations took some time, and some mistakes were inevitably made, but after a modest start the Monterey County venture was established.[90] In the early 1970s, an unhealthy outburst of speculative vineyard development distorted things: more than 25,000 acres were planted in Monterey County between 1972 and 1974. Since then a more orderly growth, and the establishment of a number of wineries large and small, have made the Salinas Valley a reliable part of California winegrowing. The southern end of the valley is also the site of the monster San Bernabe vineyard, where the Delicato Winery grows grapes on nearly 10,000 contiguous acres of vineyards.

One of the most significant effects of the Monterey development was to remind people that the wine map of California was by no means finally drawn. There is hardly any practicable part of California where vines have not been grown and wine made, but the ups and downs of history—economic depressions, Prohibition, wars, shifting populations, changing markets—have meant that in many places the early trials were not followed up or never came to anything much. But since the Mirassou-Masson move into Monterey in 1962, we have seen the creation of the Carneros region in Napa and Sonoma Counties, of the Sacramento–San Joaquin Delta region, of the Shandon-Estrella region and the Edna Valley in San Luis Obispo County, of the Santa Maria and Santa Ynez Valleys in Santa Barbara County, and the Temecula region in Riverside County, as well as the great expansion of vineyards in Mendocino County and the revival of extensive winegrowing in the foothill counties of the Sierra Nevada. If there was a positive side to the rampant urbanization (or, more accurately, suburbanization) of vineyard regions north and south, then this reopening of California to exploration and experiment was it. It would be wrong to suggest that there are still unknown regions waiting to be revealed in California; but it is also wrong to think that the current disposition is final or that the current assumptions cannot be challenged. How many, after all, of the state's possibilities have been adequately tested by people who were technically competent and economically sufficient? And by a market both sophisticated and open to new possibilities? And who can predict what the demands of the future will be?

Another, quite incalculable effect of the growth of California was something that came

FIGURE 39
New plantings in Monterey County: the Mirassou vineyard at Soledad, 1963. (From *Wines and Vines* 44 [February 1963]; reprinted with permission from *Wines and Vines*.)

to be called the California style—a heady promotional mix compounded of such things as California's scenery (ocean, mountains, desert), its natural wonders (redwoods, Yosemite, the Sierras), the glamour of Hollywood, its tourist attractions (Disneyland opened in 1955), its year-round sunshine, and its Pacific beaches. At its extreme, this style passed over into various forms of the bizarre and foolish, but those were the inevitable excesses of a style that encouraged openness and spontaneity. The newcomers who poured into the state naturally sought to acquire the signs of this style, and those who remained at home were kept well posted about it by the media. Wine participated in whatever benefits the diffusion of this California style brought with it. California was the wine state; the residents of California drank wine; therefore, wine was a part of the style. Some such association of ideas was perhaps an element in the dramatic rise of table-wine sales in California starting in the 1950s, and it may have helped in promoting the success of table wine in the other states starting in the 1960s. The argument is not of the sort that can be proved, but the power of image can hardly be ignored when one thinks about social change.

The success in the 1950s of three wineries devoted to the large-scale production of wines, especially of table wines, with some character and identity beyond that of the standard generic wines, showed the direction in which things were moving: these three were Almadén Vineyards, The Christian Brothers, and Paul Masson. Almadén, under the astute promotional guidance of Frank Schoonmaker, was making varietally labeled table wines familiar in many parts of the country.[91] The Christian Brothers, based in Napa Valley but with a big winery in the Central Valley providing fortified wines, had put their sales in the hands of the distributing firm run (with financing from Seagram's) by Alfred Fromm and Franz Sichel, who built a national market for the generic table wines, fortified wines, champagne, and brandies of the Brothers.[92] Unlike most of the other big wineries that provided complete lines of products, The Christian Brothers had large vineyards in Napa Valley as a source for their generic wines.[93] In 1945, while still working for The Christian Brothers, Fromm and Sichel—again with the backing of Seagram's—also took on the Paul Masson winery in Santa Clara County and built that into a major player in the growing game of table wine. In 1952 these wineries had combined sales of 190,000 cases of table wine; by 1967, when the tide turned toward such wines, their sales were 2,221,000 cases.[94]

In the early years Masson had no extensive vineyards of its own, but under the direction of its manager, Otto Meyer, it developed a respectable line of varietal wines, some of them bought from the neighboring Mirassou Winery or from Martini and Prati in Sonoma County.[95] Masson, now French in name only, prospered in German hands: Alfred Fromm, Franz Sichel, Otto Meyer, winemaker Kurt Opper, and champagne maker Hans Hyba. They were joined by the Italian American Leo Berti in 1955. In 1957 Masson began construction of a big new plant in Saratoga for the production of sparkling wine by the transfer process and for storing, finishing, and bottling its other wines. When it opened in 1959, the plant struck a note of glittering modernity quite unlike anything else among California wineries; under the name of Paul Masson Champagne Cellars it was effectively used as a tourist attraction. In 1961 Masson, as has already been noted, began the development of extensive vineyards in Monterey County, though it continued to depend on other producers for its supplies.[96]

These three wineries—Almadén, The Christian Brothers, and Paul Masson—found a niche between the vast, undifferentiated fortified-wine market dominated by the industrial producers of the Central Valley and the small, highly individual table-wine market belonging to the handful of prestige wineries mostly concentrated in Napa Valley—Beaulieu, Inglenook, Martini. And having found their niche, they worked not just to occupy it but to enlarge it, with marked success. Almadén, The Christian Brothers, and Masson were, if you like, compromise operations. Their wines cost more than those of the Central Valley but less than those of the prestige wineries; they promoted varietal wines of their own growth but dealt in bulk wines and sold large quantities of generically labeled wines as well; and they offered more or less complete lines to the trade: table and fortified,

sweet and dry, red and white, still and sparkling wines. They were highly necessary in-
termediaries in the process whereby the American public for wine was moved beyond
the level at which it had long lingered.

Of the three, Almadén was probably the most ambitious and influential. In 1950, with
backing in part of money from the Lucky Lager brewery, it began to modernize and enlarge its operations. It took the trouble to develop its own vineyards in new regions; it experimented with a solera sherry and a wide range of varietal wines: Gamay, Grenache
noir, Ruby Cabernet, Pinot blanc, Gewürztraminer, Grey Riesling, Sylvaner, Semillon. By
1952 Almadén had some 150 wholesalers across the country handling its wines, so one
might equally expect to find it in a restaurant in Texas or at a back-yard party in Connecticut (where I first encountered it in 1955). The attractively labeled bottles carried descriptions by Frank Schoonmaker telling drinkers in clear and emphatic prose about what
was in the bottle and, perhaps, making them a little more curious about wine than they
had been before. The costs of expansion were heavy, however, and Almadén's owner, Louis
Benoist, ultimately found that he could get no more credit.[97] Benoist was as well a spend-
thrift on a heroic scale, and his lavish expenditures seem to have been more than equal
to the company's growing income.[98] Almadén was sold to National Distillers in 1967, and
its role in California's wine industry was altered—not, however, before it had stirred up
a lively new interest in wine.[99] Much of what Almadén sold was hardly up to the level of
Schoonmaker's attractive prose, but the better wines did convey the idea that wines could
have distinct identities.

A fate like that of Almadén also overtook Paul Masson. In the years that Fromm and
Sichel directed it and Otto Meyer managed it, Masson, like Almadén, aimed at supplying good wines of a distinctive character. In 1971 Seagram's took over the company and
set out to make it a rival of Gallo in the competition for quantity, to the destruction of all
that its former directors had built up.

The cause of good table wine continued to attract a few, usually well-heeled newcomers to small-scale winemaking. In the '50s the most impressive of these enterprises by
far was the vineyard and winery begun in 1952 in Sonoma County by James Zellerbach,
the heir to a fortune in the paper industry.[100] Zellerbach's idea was to re-create as closely
as possible a Burgundian estate in California, and to this end he sought out the best opinions and spent whatever might be required. His Hanzell Winery, as he called it (compounded of his wife's name, Hana, and his own last name), was a reduced copy of the
Clos de Vougeot—a "millionaire's plaything," Leon Adams called it.[101] "One had a feeling," Roy Brady remarked, "that if a leaf were found on the drive when guests arrived
there would be floggings in the slave quarters." Its sixteen acres of terraced vineyards
yielded a first, token quantity of Chardonnay in 1956 and a commercial quantity of
Chardonnay and Pinot noir in 1957. The winemaker, R. Bradford Webb, had at his disposal stainless steel equipment throughout (including the crusher and the press) and had
aged the wine in French oak barrels: these were innovations in California practice that
were to have highly important consequences. The fermenting tanks for the Chardonnay

have been called the first temperature-controlled stainless steel tanks in California.[102] The wine, at an unheard-of price of $6 a bottle (only what Zellerbach figured it cost to produce), was greeted rapturously. Zellerbach died in 1963; the winery was briefly dormant, then sold; in 1975 it was sold again. The winery still enjoys a high prestige, but its real impact was in the '50s, when it revealed possibilities in California Pinot noir and Chardonnay that had hardly been suspected before.[103]

The wineries devoted to making good table wines in California began to grow restless about this time, as their numbers, their markets, and their confidence gradually increased. The wine then being produced in the state that might qualify as "premium" under one definition or another was estimated to be about 2 percent to 5 percent of the whole, but its sales were growing, and such wines brought in attractive returns.[104] In 1949 a plan was put before the Wine Institute for a program of aging wine under registration with the state: such wine could then be sold as "certified" with respect to variety and age: "The sponsors of this program believe that it will enable the industry, by passing on truthful information regarding the age and the variety of the wine in the bottle, to sell greater amounts of older and better wine for more money."[105]

The argument could hardly be put better than that, but the plan got nowhere; it was turned down by the board of directors the next month.[106] In the next year a group called the Association of Chateau Wine Growers was formed in another effort to get recognition for premium wines.[107] The *Chateau* in the name shows that things had not yet reached that point of confidence at which California winegrowers could boast of quality without a French association—indeed, that point is even now evidently still some years away. The plan was to raise the public perception of quality in California wine by making an annual selection from the wines produced by the members and identifying them by a special label. The wines would be varietals (with a requirement that 85 percent come from the variety named, instead of the 51 percent required by law), and they would be chosen by a committee of the Chateau Wine Growers themselves. The association lasted into 1952, when it seems to have quietly expired.[108]

A few years later another, more sustained public-relations effort was begun to promote the idea of quality in California table wines. Since World War II the Napa Valley Vintners Association had been modestly promoting Napa Valley wines by various local public-relations gestures. A suggestion by Robert Mondavi that the association hire a public-relations director led to an expansion of the idea: why not an association of all the eligible producers in the state, not just those in the Napa Valley, to push the idea of quality wine? It seemed a particularly good idea at the time because California's quality table-wine producers were nervous about the threat of imported wines: as long as good wine from California was not differentiated from the standard generic wines, it would have little chance in the competition against any wine that enjoyed the advantage of the word *imported*. Such, at any rate, was the general opinion. And it was this perceived threat from foreign competition that was the immediate stimulus for the formation of a new group. Once the suggestion for a statewide group had been put forth, the experienced wine-industry consultant Louis Gomberg was called in to develop the plan. After certain inquiries had been made and questions answered—mostly having to do with what was needed, who would join, and on what terms—the Premium Wine Producers of California was set up in May 1955.[109] The group faced two immediate questions: What should its relation to the Wine Institute be? And what *was* premium wine?

The first question was difficult because much of the impetus toward the formation of the association in the first place came from dissatisfaction with the Wine Institute's record of support—or rather, lack of support—for quality table wine from California. The advertising carried out by the Wine Institute as the agent for the Wine Advisory Board had been generic advertising. Some thought that such advertising did more harm than good: if an inquiring consumer, moved by an ad for California wine, bought a bottle of undistinguished California wine and was disappointed in it, he or she might never wish to go on to something better from California. And the weight in the Wine Institute was all on the side of the large producers of bulk and standard wine. So on this view, the Premium Wine Producers ought to go it alone. Against this view was the argument that as an element within the Wine Institute, the association might hope to get funding from the Wine Advisory Board. As James Lapsley puts it, "Money talked."[110] The Premium Wine Producers became a standing committee within the Wine Institute, and the Wine Advisory Board put up the money.

The second question—What *was* premium wine?—was even more vexed. Expensive wine? Prizewinning wine? Varietal wine exclusively? Estate-grown wine? Considering the very small number of wineries and the tiny quantities of wine that might qualify under any of these definitions, the course of prudence was to settle on a price qualification: anything costing more than a dollar a bottle (i.e., a fifth) was, for the purposes of the Premium Wine Producers Association, a premium wine.[111] As *Wines and Vines* observed, this arrangement meant that "it is the brand and not the firm which holds the membership in the premium group."[112] United Vintners was a major producer of standard wines, but its Signature label sold for the required price and to that extent it was a premium wine producer; so was the CWA, through its Ambassador line. The association did make one exclusion: no table wines from viticultural region V of the University of California classification system were eligible as premium wines. Thus no table wines from Fresno, Kern, Kings, Madera, or Tulare Counties—the lower part of the great Central Valley—could qualify. Otherwise, the association welcomed membership; the original nine had grown to twenty-eight member wineries by 1958.[113]

It was agreed that the campaign of the Premium Wine Producers was to be fought with the weapon of public relations rather than that of print advertising. The object to be achieved was the connection of the idea of quality with California wine. The standard moves of public relations were used: interviews with winemakers, mentions on TV and radio shows, magazine articles, events that would attract media notice. The main device employed was a program of comparative tastings. A selection of local citizens would be made—restaurant people, newspaper writers, any sort of celebrity who might be available—and a blind tasting arranged. Tasters were given a series of unidentified wines in pairs—one Californian, one European—and asked which they preferred. The results were noted down. At the end, the identity of the wines was made known, the prices given, and the scores revealed. The results showed a fifty-fifty split, and since the California wines were uniformly cheaper they came out ahead in the popular imagination. Such tastings, of which more than a hundred were held, generated a gratifying attention from the press, both local and national. As James Lapsley has observed, the results showed only the operation of the laws of probability rather than any defensible judgment of quality.[114] But the scheme undoubtedly gave California premium wines considerable publicity.[115]

It had also ruffled feathers within the Wine Institute membership. If the Wine Institute recognized a group of premium wine producers, what did that make the rest of them? Subpremium? Ernest Gallo was reluctant to admit that *any* wines were better than his, and no wine producer, whatever his private opinion about his wines might have been, liked to be excluded from the premium category. By 1958, resentment was sufficiently strong to compel some changes: the Premium Wine Producers Association was rechristened, awkwardly enough, as the Academy of Master Wine Growers. Two years later, the disgruntled producers excluded from the circle were mollified by the Wine Advisory Board's creation of a public-relations campaign for them under the name of the "popular wines" of California. This was not enough, however, to heal the rift, and at the end of 1964 the Wine Advisory Board ended the "fine" and "popular" programs. By that time, the growing sales of premium table wine softened whatever disappointment the Master Wine Growers may have felt. They continued in existence, but without external support.

GLAMOURIZING CALIFORNIA WINE

If the ordinary American had any notions about winemaking or winemakers in the 1950s, they were probably something like this: vineyards were native to Europe, where one might expect to meet brightly costumed natives singing and dancing at vintage time, especially if they were Italian; winemakers were sturdy peasants who might wear berets or lederhosen, according to the country in question. American winemakers—few outside California would ever have seen one—were farmers, perhaps owners of large vineyards, but still people of no particular sophistication, engaged in a relatively obscure trade of doubtful social value.

By the early 1960s all that was perceptibly changing, under the continued pressure of advertising and public relations. Wine began to acquire a certain glamour. I have already mentioned the growth of the idea of a California style as an element in the increasing appeal of wine. And there were other portents. One was tourism, a possibility that had been glimpsed immediately after Repeal. A speaker at the Conference of Vintners and Allied Interests at the Del Monte hotel in 1935 had urged "that visitors be invited to the wineries and vineyards, so they may be imbued with the lore of wine, and learn to know it."[116] The manager at Beringer Brothers, Fred Abruzzini, was ahead of this advice. He had opened the winery to the public at the time of the St. Helena vintage festival in 1934; he had continued to invite visitors thereafter and had opened a retail salesroom at the winery. By 1940 almost a third of Beringer's bottled-wine sales were made from the salesroom.[117] After the war, tourism in the wine country grew with the growth of tourism generally. Among the first after Beringer to grasp the public-relations possibilities of opening their winery to visitors were the Mondavis at Charles Krug, who hit on the idea of a tasting room in 1949. The Wine Institute helped by sending out winery guide maps and tour brochures; by 1954, the institute claimed, more than 250,000 people annually visited California's wineries.[118] This movement has never, since Repeal, met a reversal. The Paul Masson winery in Saratoga, built expressly to attract tourists, was receiving 200,000 annually by 1970.[119] By the end of the century, the volume of tourists through the various regions known as "wine country" in California, and preeminently Napa Valley, was beyond measurement. California was not the only place to develop wine tourism, however, and it may even have lagged behind some developments in the East. The big Finger Lakes wineries had elaborate hospitality rooms in the early '50s, and Taylor Wine Company at least was encouraging visitors as early as 1940.[120] In Ohio, Meier's Wine Cellars in Cincinnati had by 1954 a "Wine Stube" already "some years old."[121] And the wineries on the Lake Erie islands had a tradition of entertaining tourists that went well back into the nineteenth century.

As wineries became destinations for tourists, the next step was to make them attractive and interesting beyond the obvious purposes of business. Guided tours were, of course, soon hit upon, and these regularly led to a tasting room and retail salesroom where tourists could try the wines and buy any they might fancy. Other attractions were devised. One highly successful invention was the program called Music in the Vineyards, a series of outdoor summer concerts set up by Norman Fromm at the old Paul Masson winery in 1958 and kept going for many years. The Charles Krug Winery in Napa Valley began a series of August Moon concerts on the lawns of the winery in 1965, and Robert Mondavi, after leaving Krug to set up his own winery, took the idea with him; his summer festival began in 1970. In general, wineries that sought to attract tourists began to pay attention to architectural amenity—lawns, gardens, picnic areas, ramadas—so that wineries became pleasant places to hold wine tastings, barbecues, vineyard lunches, and the like for special-interest groups and tourists at large. The retail store might grow into an extensive gift shop. The public spaces might become galleries or small museums, or anything else that ingenuity might suggest. The development of the winery as hospitality center eventually made it difficult in some cases to decide when a winery was a winery and when it was something else, an issue that grew heated in Napa Valley in later years.[122] All of this was a far cry from the original notions of winery hospitality, when—as Roy Brady put it—the idea of the "winery as Taj Mahal lay in the future."[123]

Schoonmaker's *News from the Vineyards*, the quarterly newsletter that he wrote for Almadén, has already been mentioned. Other wineries gradually took up the idea; *Bottles and Bins,* edited by Francis Gould for the Charles Krug Winery, began publication in 1949

FIGURE 40

Not quite "the winery as Taj Mahal," but a good instance of the care for public appearance now taken for granted in California and elsewhere: Meridian Vineyards, Paso Robles. (Meridian Vineyards.)

and certainly did much to enhance the idea of wine among its readers.[124] The publication of a newsletter is now a familiar part of winery public relations, and the number and variety of such house publications have created a rich tradition.[125] Another variation on the idea of print was the creation, beginning in 1961, of the Napa Valley Wine Library. This was the child of three interesting people then resident in the valley: M. F. K. Fisher, the distinguished writer on things culinary and cultural; Mallette Dean, a St. Helena printer and artist; and Gould, the editor of Krug's *Bottles and Bins*. Apart from the library assembled at Davis to serve the Department of Viticulture and Enology, no institutional collection of the literature of wine seems at the time to have existed in California. The enthusiasm and energy of the founders was met by a corresponding enthusiasm among many other Napa Valley people, both in and out of the wine industry. With the assistance of the Friends of the Napa Valley Wine Library, a respectable collection, housed in the city library, was soon put together. It has continued to grow and has no doubt helped to teach the idea that wine is the cause of more intense appreciation, more argument, more study, and more publication than any other substance that we eat or drink. The Sonoma people were slower off the mark, but roused by the example of Napa, a small group formed in 1975 succeeded in opening the Sonoma County Wine Library in 1989; it has grown to be a worthy rival of—and collaborator with—the Napa Valley library.[126]

M. F. K. Fisher, beside her part in founding the Napa Valley Wine Library, helped to add another touch to the glamour of California wines. At some point in the 1950s, the University of California Press, recognizing the increasing importance of the wine industry in California and the increasing interest in it among the general public, determined to publish a lavish book about it. The book would be illustrated with photographs in black and white and in color by Max Yavno, a photographer of reputation who had already devoted some years to taking pictures of vineyards and wineries up and down the state. Fisher was asked by the press to write the text for this book, and after some hesitations and delays, the result appeared in 1962 as *The Story of Wine in California*.[127] No such splendid book about American wine had ever been published before. That it was possible both to imagine such a book and then actually to write it and publish it marked a new stage in public awareness of the subject. Yet it was, evidently, still a little premature: sales did not meet expectations.

The final seal upon California wine as a glamourous subject had, of course, to come from Hollywood. This was duly bestowed when a novel, *The Cup and the Sword* (1942), by Alice Tisdale Hobart, was filmed on location in Napa Valley with Rock Hudson and Jean Simmons in the leads; it was released as *This Earth Is Mine* in 1959. The film, loosely based on the life of Georges de Latour, the founder of Beaulieu Vineyards, was a fair success at the box office and surely did not lower the public perception of winemaking as a vocation.[128]

The distance traveled from the dark despair of 1947 to the early 1960s, a brief space of about fifteen years, appeared in retrospect to be immense. In 1947 an unregenerate industry stubbornly persisted in producing undistinguished, sweet fortified wines for an uninstructed and largely indifferent American public. At the beginning of the 1960s, that American public, now not quite the same as it had been, was beginning to become familiar with increasing quantities of decent table wine, distinctly identified. That was the essential thing; but it also helped to have such adjuncts as organized wine tastings, wine country tours, magazine and newspaper stories about wine, books about wine, and even movies about winemakers. The inexhaustible variety and interest of wine; the fascinating subjects of its growth, production, and maturing; the richness of its cultural, historical, and literary traditions; and the challenge of all this to the knowledge and judgment of connoisseurship were now at last beginning to be opened up in this country, and on a scale that meant something.

TECHNOLOGICAL CHANGES

As a coda to this chapter of transitions we may look briefly at some of the scientific and technical advances that went on quietly behind the façade. One of the most useful developments was called the Foundation Plant Materials Service (FPMS), established in 1952 at the University of California, Davis. It had long been known that the vineyard stock of the state was widely infected with viral diseases, and that many grape varieties were wrongly identified and confused with other varieties.[129] If nothing were done about these conditions, they would be entailed upon California's vineyards indefinitely. With the help of the Wine Advisory Board and under the supervision of the state Department of Food and Agriculture, the plant pathologists and viticulturists at Davis devised a program: selected varieties, including rootstocks, were planted in a foundation vineyard, tested for known viruses such as fanleaf, yellow mosaic, and leaf roll, and if found to be virus-free, certified as to health and variety. The stock thus selected was then, beginning in 1959, made available for sale to nurseries and other propagators in the state.[130]

The first experiments toward mechanical harvesting of grapes were also carried out in the 1950s. Mechanical pickers were already successfully at work on crops like tomatoes, and the importance of grapes among California's crops made them a logical candidate for mechanical handling. The earliest such machines, however, were developed in New York. One system developed at Davis was tried out in 1952 and tinkered with for some years thereafter: it worked by shearing the clusters with a cutter bar, like a grain combine, and could not handle short-stemmed varieties (such as Cabernet Sauvignon, Zinfandel, or Riesling) satisfactorily. There were other difficulties, too. A mechanical picker, whatever its principle, can't be selective in what it picks. It is also rough on the grapes, so that they may be broken or crushed at once and will need immediate processing. And it is likely to pick a good deal of stuff other than the grapes themselves—leaves, stems, cobwebs and the spiders that spin them, and anything else in the way. Such were the problems that needed to be met.

One response was to breed new varieties suited to mechanical harvesting, as the tomato growers had done. Another was to develop new methods of trellising to facilitate mechanical harvesting: the so-called Geneva double curtain method, now widely used around the world, came out of work on mechanical harvesting in New York. Another response was to design a harvester that shook the vines instead of cutting the clusters; such a machine was developed at Cornell University. Yet another was a machine that sucked up the grapes, vacuum-cleaner fashion: Gallo developed one on that principle. It worked, but it sucked up so many leaves that the "wine was green in color and tasted like alfalfa," and the machine "sounded like a banshee."[131] The principle eventually selected was that of beating the vines with mechanical "fingers," rods moving either horizontally or vertically within the vine canopy. But that came later.

Inside the winery, new designs began to replace the traditional wooden basket press. The new styles were preferred for several reasons: they could be automated; they were gentler and gave a superior press wine; and they were more efficient: the traditional figure of 150 gallons of wine from a ton of grapes could, with the new presses, be revised upward to 170 to 180 gallons per ton.[132] The Willmes press—a German design in which a bladder inside a perforated stainless steel cylinder is inflated by compressed air to press the grapes against the walls of the cylinder—was used in eastern wineries in 1955; it was soon widely adopted. The French Vaslin press, another horizontal cylinder press, used two opposed metal plates that were driven together to press the mass of grapes. The Vaslin press, like the Willmes press, was first used in this country by eastern wineries in 1957; it was the modern equivalent of the traditional basket press, now with two plates rather than one, and lying on its side instead of standing upright. There were other designs, some of them for continuous rather than batch pressing (e.g., the Garolla, from Italy), but the Willmes and the Vaslin became the presses of choice in the years after their introduction. The fact that they were both of European origin reminds us that technological developments in winemaking are international; no one country has any special claim to inventiveness or ingenuity, and many countries have contributed and continue to contribute to the creation of new methods and machines. The too frequently encountered notion that California is especially gifted in the matter of innovation is one of those provincialisms, like the proposition that every year is a vintage year in California, that will disappear only with maturity.

A new procedure that greatly improved the quality of California wines, especially white wines, was the use of temperature-controlled fermentation. The value of this procedure had long been recognized, but how to achieve it was the question.[133] Shortly after the war, André Tchelistcheff at Beaulieu, and the Mondavi brothers at the Charles Krug Winery, using stainless steel coils in wooden fermentors, showed what could be done to achieve greater fruitiness and freshness in white wines by slow fermentation at low temperatures. The results were so good that gradually wineries were prepared to make the costly investment in the necessary refrigeration equipment designed for the purpose. By 1949 cold fermentation was the standard practice in Napa Valley.[134]

In the production of red wines, a great step forward was made by the understanding and control of malolactic fermentation, the process whereby, after the primary fermentation, the malic acid in the new wine is broken down into the softer lactic acid and carbon dioxide. Following the studies carried out by Tchelistcheff in the 1940s, wineries learned how to control this fermentation, either to induce it where desired to soften the wine and help stabilize it, or to avoid it where it was not wanted.[135]

Two processes particularly useful to large wineries that were bottling vast quantities of wine to be distributed all across the continent were sterile filtration and centrifuging: by these means wine could be rendered absolutely stable (that is, free of any elements that might cause it to ferment, grow hazy, throw sediment, or otherwise misbehave). Centrifuging was an old principle, but a machine suited for the treatment of musts was not developed until the 1950s.[136] Sterile filtration was achieved with superfine filters, derived from German designs used to filter the fuel for buzz bombs.[137]

Sometimes there is nothing new about new introductions. A case in point is the use of French oak barrels for aging wine, already mentioned in connection with Zellerbach's Hanzell Vineyard. This had simply not been the California practice—partly because oak was not cheaply available on the West Coast but mostly because only a very little wine was aged at all, and if it was, then the rule was for large containers, tanks and ovals rather than barrels. The result that Hanzell got from barrel-aging its Chardonnays and Pinot noirs was so evident, and so different from what had been obtained with these wines in

California to that point, that its effect was immediate.[138] Barrel-aging in French oak, once a wholly alien and unknown practice, gradually became a standard method for those wineries that could afford it.[139] As barrel-aging (and later barrel fermenting too) entered into common practice, so too did arguments about the many refinements involved: What sort of oak? From what countries, or even what particular forests? Was American oak acceptable? How much "toast" did one want?[140] What proportion of new oak should be used? How much oak character was enough? And so on. Such questions about barrels would have seemed bizarre to any American winemaker from the innocent days, when a barrel was simply what you put the wine into before you shipped it. Now, as one authority puts it, "the subject of wood aging for wine has been elevated to a science."[141] It will remain an imperfect science, since what is in question is also a matter of taste, so the measure of what is the right touch of oak in a California wine is a question for time to settle.[142]

The flow of technological novelties into the practices of viticulture and winemaking in the first two decades after the war showed that attitudes had been altered. Before the war, the scientists of the University of California had had to struggle even to get the attention of winemakers, to say nothing of getting them to act on the good advice being given. That had now changed. There was a new confidence in the power of technology to deliver whatever result one might wish, and the wineries were eager to have the new methods and machines that were being invented. As Cornelius Ough put it, the researchers at Davis, of whom he was one, were "defining how wine should be made."[143] Or as William Bonetti recalled the spirit prevailing at Gallo when he was hired, the young technical men of the time felt that "we can do it all." What had taken Europe centuries to achieve might be done quickly here.[144]

Since then, there has been a reaction against such exuberant confidence—hubris, as some would have it. One sometimes feels now that an almost penitential renunciation of the old self-assurance has overcome American winemakers. Now we hear that wines are made in the vineyard, not the winery; that the old gravity-flow design is the best design; that wild yeasts make better wines than cultured ones; that wood is better than steel for fermentation; and so on through a long list of antitechnological reversions. The vogue for exalting the virtues of *terroir,* so conspicuous in recent years, is another form of this reaction, since the elements of *terroir,* however one may define them, are precisely those things about which nobody can do anything: soil, exposure, temperature, rainfall, and so on.[145] Instead of boasting about his power to manipulate his materials to any desired end, today's winemaker is likely to adopt a position of reverent fatalism: he can alter what he is given only for the worse.

No doubt a simple-minded conflict between the "scientific" and the "traditional" is the wrong way to think about the relations of old and new; there must be a complex and reciprocal adjustment instead. But there was a time when the scientists were sure that the future of wine was in their hands, and perhaps they had good reason to think so.

10

THE BIG CHANGE
California

A VERY SURPRISING TURN

In 1960 Julian Street's widow, Marguerite, was preparing a new edition of her husband's pioneering book, *Wines: Their Selection, Care, and Service,* originally published in 1933 for the instruction and guidance of an American public in its regained freedom to drink.[1] Julian Street had died in 1947, but his book continued to be read. His widow had prepared a second edition in 1948 and was now at work on a third. She wrote to her publisher, Alfred Knopf, that even though the job was a demanding one, it was a relief to think that at least the chapter on California would not need much revision: "The California picture," she said, "hasn't changed much."[2] That must have seemed true enough from the point of view of Connecticut, where Marguerite Street lived. But it seemed true in California, too, and not just to well-informed amateurs like Street but to distinguished professionals. Maynard Amerine and Vernon Singleton, writing in 1965 in *Wine: An Introduction for Americans,* ventured this prophecy:

> A number of small family wineries and wineries for local trade . . . still continue, and will probably survive on a local-pride basis for some time, but the future of the industry seems to lie with a few highly industrialized wineries producing wines at competitive prices and a few wineries specializing in high-quality wines.[3]

Amerine and Singleton had every reason to think this way: the number of wineries in California was still declining and had not yet bottomed out when they were writing, and the trend toward bigness exemplified by Gallo, United Vintners, and Guild Wineries seemed irreversible. By 1966 the concentration of things in California, a process that had been going on without interruption since Repeal, had reached the point at which 70 percent of the state's wine storage capacity was in the hands of twenty wineries.[4] At the same time, it would have been difficult for the most generous observer to have named more than two dozen wineries making fine wine.[5] Compared to the giants of the industry, the fine-wine producers were small, and their numbers did not appear to increase. On the contrary, the market share of those regions devoted to table wines had been steadily sinking, from 30 percent in 1938 to 14 percent in 1965.[6] And business fatalities were frequent. Louis Gomberg calculated that more than two hundred California wineries went out of business—"sold out, merged, or simply folded"—between 1952 and 1970.[7] They may not have been producers of particularly good wine, but the point is that the number of enterprises—good, bad, and indifferent—was shrinking. The processes of declining numbers and increasing consolidation that began shortly after Repeal were still going on; not much had changed.

The prediction that Amerine and Singleton naturally arrived at from such observations turned out to be sensationally wrong. Within a decade almost every significant feature of the California wine landscape had been altered out of recognition: small new wineries had greatly multiplied, the sale of fortified wines had gone into steep decline, the consumption of table wine had risen to levels undreamed of, and the big wineries were struggling to keep a hold on the market. To meet a surging demand, the vineyard acreage in the established table-wine regions had doubled, and vast new plantings of superior varieties had been made in vineyards formerly devoted to grapes for fortified wine. Marguerite Street would have been astounded by the changes that had, apparently without warning, burst out of what she took to be a quietly unchanging scene.

The quickest way to show what happened is by way of some contrasting figures.[8] We may take 1966, the last year in which the sale of fortified wines exceeded that of table wine, for the first half of our contrast. In 1966, then, there were 490,000 acres of grapes in California, of which 142,000 acres, or less than a third, were planted to wine grapes. The harvest of all these grapes was an unusually large 3.4 million tons. California made 165 million gallons of wine that year, divided between 85 million gallons of fortified wine and 80 million gallons of table wine. Apparent consumption (statistics for actual consumption don't exist) was 86 million gallons of fortified and 55 million gallons of table wine from California; add to that about 46 million gallons from other states and imports, and the national market for wine (including sparkling wines, vermouth, and flavored wines) was 187 million gallons.[9] California produced about 75 percent of that total.

Ten years later, the acreage of California's vineyards had leaped to about 660,000 acres, from which nearly 4 million tons of grapes were harvested—bigger, but not overwhelmingly bigger, than the harvest of ten years earlier. But wine production now was up to 332 million gallons, and of that total, nearly 300 million gallons were table wine; fortified wines had shrunk to 13 million gallons. In ten years the production of table wine in California had gone up by more than 200 million gallons—more than three times what it had been—and the production of fortified wine had fallen to less than one-sixth of the figure ten years earlier. Such a change was hardly a trend, but rather a transformation. The national market—the "apparent consumption"—of U.S. wine was 376 million gallons, approaching twice what it had been ten years earlier. Of this total (which includes imports), California produced 71 percent. More than a hundred more wineries were now operating in California than had been in 1966: 345 compared to 231—and the numbers were rapidly rising. As recently as the 1950s the appearance of a new winery had been a rare event; they now grew like mushrooms after rain. Most of the newcomers were relatively small, and they competed fiercely in the production of quality table wines.[10]

The changes in the vineyards were of the same order. The total acreage, as has been said, went up substantially, but far more significant was the change in the composition of the vineyards. Wine grapes had accounted for less than a third of the total in 1966; in 1976 the acreage of wine grapes had more than doubled and formed just over 50 percent of the total, a proportion not seen since Repeal. And of the 338,000 acres of wine grapes, 45,000 acres were nonbearing—that is, planted within the past three years. The regions regarded as best for the production of superior grapes for table wines had led the way in growth. In the ten years in question, acreage had gone from 12,000 to 23,700 in Napa, from 12,700 to 25,000 in Sonoma, and from 5,700 to 9,000 in Mendocino. Monterey County (where a particularly virulent outburst of speculative planting occurred) went from 1,090 to 33,000 acres. Other counties, too, came essentially from nowhere, though not quite as explosively as Monterey had: San Luis Obispo County went from 550 to 4,000 acres, Santa Barbara County from 100 to 6,000.

All of this remarkable growth was in wine grapes, and largely in superior varieties, at least by comparison to the standards that had prevailed for so long. The leading variety of red wine grape in 1966 was the Carignane, planted on 29,000 acres. Ten years later the leading variety of red wine grape was Zinfandel, planted on 30,500 acres. Carignane still occupied more than 27,000 acres, but other varieties now gave it a close run. Cabernet Sauvignon went from 2,500 to 27,000 acres; Barbera, which did not figure in the statistics for 1966, had 21,000 acres. Chenin blanc, also omitted from the earlier statistics, had 20,000. Pinot noir went from 1,700 acres to 10,000. Chardonnay, which did not figure in the statistics for 1966, had 11,500 acres in 1976. By the end of the decade, nearly 200,000 acres of wine grapes had been added to California's vineyards—for California wine, "the single most important occurrence in the decade of the 70s."[11]

As this somewhat breathless tour through the grosser statistics should make abundantly plain, the California trade had both changed direction and undergone a huge growth between, roughly, the middle of the 1960s and the middle of the 1970s. The reign of fortified wines from the Central Valley had been overthrown; table wine was now king, and its kingdom was more spacious than anything known before. The unquestioned dominance of varieties inferior or unsuitable for winemaking—particularly the Thompson Seedless—

FIGURE 41
In ten years the vineyard acreage of Monterey County went from 1,090 to 33,000 acres. Part of the reason was offers such as this one, from 1972. (From *Wines and Vines* 53 [April 1972]; reprinted with permission from *Wines and Vines*.)

now began to seem a strange anomaly, as better and more appropriate varieties were sought after for varietal winemaking.[12] In short, there had been a revolution, or at any rate a change so striking that people wondered what had happened.

WHAT HAD HAPPENED?

The precise moment at which the turn was taken can hardly be specified. One critical moment was certainly that at which the sales of table wine passed those of fortified wine in the American market; this occurred in 1967, thirty-four years after Repeal.[13] Another moment sometimes singled out for special remark was the founding of the Robert Mondavi winery at Oakville, frequently called the first new winery opened in Napa Valley since the war.[14] It was not: Stony Hill, Mayacamas, and Heitz, for example, were earlier. The Mondavi Winery was, however, the first big new winery to be built from the ground up in Napa since Louis Martini's winery in 1934, and its construction certainly marked the beginning of a new era of unrelenting, and highly successful, promotion for the region. But these things were the symptoms, not the causes, of a major change.

How had it come about? How had an industry that seemed inexorably sinking into the hands of a few large producers of standard wines, a process uninterrupted ever since Repeal, suddenly burst out in new and exciting directions? How had a market dominated by port, sherry, and muscatel suddenly been taken over by red and white table wines? And how had an American market largely indifferent to wine suddenly begun to take an alert and lively interest in wine in all its variety? There is, of course, no ready answer to these questions: like all really interesting historical questions, they will be answered according to the tastes and prejudices of the analyst quite as much as by anything resembling a demonstrable reason. But one is bound to try to answer.

From the stock of reasons that have been put forth by one authority or another we may take a small sample. Some say, for instance, that the age of jet travel made the difference. Many of the vast numbers of Americans who had toured Europe and encountered wine as a familiar part of daily life, so this argument runs, must have wanted to see wine on their own tables after they came home. When they began to buy table wine, things changed. Some say that increasing American affluence—of which international travel was merely one expression—allowed many people to afford what had before been thought of as a luxury.[15] Another form of this argument is the familiar baby boomer line: the postwar generation, fully permeated by the ethos of consumerism, wanted wine as unmistakable evidence of its status. In 1979, after a decade of the wine boom, it was found that more than half the table wine in the country was consumed by a relatively small group of people whose typical member—aged between twenty-five and fifty-four—had a college education and a good income, was probably a professional, and lived either in the Northeast or on the Pacific Coast. Not all of these were baby boomers, but the group supplied the model to which they aspired.[16]

There had also been a growing interest in good food and its sophisticated preparation. *Gourmet* magazine, a wholly isolated and unexpected phenomenon in publishing when it first appeared in 1941, had had a considerable effect by the 1960s and was now only one of several such publications. Julia Child's *Mastering the Art of French Cooking*, a landmark in the new consciousness of food and wine, came out in 1961 and sold in the millions. The large and growing number of Americans who knew *Gourmet*, Julia Child, or one or more of their ilk would have learned through them that wine was an essential part of any cuisine that aspired beyond meat loaf—and would also, if they were wise, have learned that it would transform meat loaf as well.

Some say that the gradual improvements in California winemaking began to win new markets. The long efforts of the University of California and other advocates of better viticultural and winemaking practices had at last had their effect. Wineries were beginning to pay more for better varieties of grapes—a highly significant turn. They were also beginning to use methods such as cold fermentation that dramatically improved the appeal of white wines, which now were fresh, aromatic, and fruity rather than flat and oxidized. Better practices at every stage of winemaking—picking, crushing, fermenting, pressing, filtering, and all the other basic processes—were now widespread.[17] Leon Adams thought that this production of "reliably palatable" wines made possible by technological control was the main reason for the new popularity of wine in America.[18] Then there was the cumulative effect of the advertising of the previous twenty years and more, along with the slowly widening influence of public relations. It has been said that allowing wine to be sold in grocery stores contributed to rising sales. That is no doubt true, but that movement did not begin until 1969, when the state of Washington switched wine from state stores to food stores. Since then a number of other states have followed suit.[19]

All of these reasons are no doubt valid, and of course their effect in combination was far more powerful than any one by itself could ever have been. At first glance, however, even in combination they do not seem sufficient to account for the extent of the change—an unprecedented expansion of vineyards, wineries, wine production, and sales, all of it devoted to table wine. All of the obvious movement up to this point had been toward the perpetuation and intensification of the patterns established after Repeal; but instead, those patterns had now been wiped out. As one puzzled commentator observed, "Something fundamental happened in America that caused wine consumption to explode in the 1970s"—but he gave no explanation.[20]

In thinking about change, historians must decide whether they are on the side of continuity or of catastrophe. Does the present grow out of the past in continuous fashion, or are there violent fractures in the process, suddenly turning things in new directions? In this particular matter I am on the side of the old-fashioned thinkers who argue for continuity. As I have tried to show in the preceding chapter, the sale of table wine had been on a long and unbroken rise; there had been much work toward the basic improvement of vineyards and winemaking; there had been much argument about quality in table wines and how to get it; and a small but influential group of winemakers devoted to the highest standards had set up in business. They in turn had seen a gradual but definite growth in a market interested in wine and prepared to pay for something better.

It must also be said that there had been a large growth in what may be called an uncritical market—the people for whom the "mod" wines, or "pop" wines, had been invented and who had responded by buying millions of gallons of such sweetened, flavored, and carbonated drinks. Some of these products were among the fortified wines, but even larger quantities counted as table wines in the official statistics. According to Louis Gomberg, sales of table wine rose at the "astonishing" rate of 12 percent annually in the years 1969–72. But half of that was in "special natural wines, apple and other fruit wines, Cold Duck, and miscellaneous other wines."[21] This fact greatly tempers any excitement one might feel over the remarkable statistics of the growth in "table-wine" sales in the 1960s: by far the greater part of the wines in question were flavored, sweetened, carbonated confections, not at all what one would choose to drink with meals. The sales of genuine table wine, though increasing, did so at a much more modest rate than those of the mod wines.

Americans were still far from taking sound dry table wines as the basis of their idea of wine. Nevertheless, they were drinking something other than fortified wine, and the consumption of genuine table wine continued to grow.

Among the table wines were two similar styles of light, fizzy wines from Europe: Lancer's and Mateus rosé wines from Portugal (the one imported by Heublein, the other by Schenley) had been popular since the late '50s. A little later they were joined by Lambrusco from the Italian province of Emilia-Romagna. All three became vogue wines, and were sold in huge quantities across the country.[22] They were easy to drink, presented no problem in selection, and yet carried the interest of a mildly exotic commodity: Lancer's came in an unusual terra-cotta bottle, Mateus in a *bocksbeutel*, a shape not used for any American wines. Lambrusco was clearly Italian. Such wines certainly helped to establish the idea that wine might be not only untroublesome but both interesting and agreeable— a big step.

It has also been argued that the early vogue for table wines was not for wine with meals—"table wines" in fact—but instead for white wines as an aperitif, a substitute cocktail; it no doubt also helped that white wine was served chilled.[23] It is the fact that for a time white wine eclipsed red wine, to the consternation of all those for whom the first duty of a wine is to be red, but this proved to be a temporary aberration. The aberration was powerful enough, however, to make some think that white wine was the future.[24] By 1976 the sales of white table wine had surpassed those of red, and they continued to grow even larger over the next few years.[25] The prices of white wine grapes rose sharply, and growers began grafting over red varieties to white.[26] They were overly hasty, however: by the early '80s the white wine boom had fizzled.[27] It was succeeded by the fashion for white Zinfandel, which is still with us.

But to return to the question: if it be objected that all these gradual steps cannot account for the changes that began to accelerate about the mid '60s, the response must be that in every process a point is reached at which that process turns into something else. That point, in the history of wine in America, was reached in or around the year 1965. On one side of that moment were the long years of preparation; on the other, the sudden-seeming, sometimes startling results. For a long time, no portents of change had been clearly visible, but all the while great changes had been under way:

> For while the tired waves, vainly breaking,
>   Seem here no painful inch to gain,
> Far back through creeks and inlets making
>   Came, silent, flooding in, the main.

These lines from Arthur Hugh Clough seem to fit this context quite as well as they did the very different one in which they were famously quoted by Winston Churchill.[28]

Whatever indicator one might select—the sales of table wine, the appearance of new wineries, the new winemaking practices, or something other than these—the moment of transformation no doubt occurred in the 1960s. But it is the privilege only of hindsight to see such things. It was not until about 1970 that the signs of change were visible to everyone, when talk of a wine boom became irresistible; and it will be convenient now to concentrate on the decade of the '70s in order to illustrate the new prevailing conditions.[29]

If one wants to narrow things more precisely, the "boom" was really heard in the five years 1968–72, when the wine industry—not just in California but across the nation—grew at annual rates of between 10 percent and 15 percent, and when wine consumption jumped from 213 million gallons to 337 million gallons.[30] After those golden years there were hiccups and stutters in the performance of the trade, but nothing to reverse the decisive turn that had already occurred.

As one winemaker, Charles Carpy, put it, three things were happening all at once:

1. Those who have been making good wine are learning to make more of it;
2. Those who may formerly have made so-so wines are learning to make a better product;
3. Newcomers are trying their hand at the game and doing the best they can.[31]

MORE AND BETTER

Let us take these simple propositions as a guide to the changes occurring, beginning with the expansion of vineyards and wineries in the counties around San Francisco Bay, where the makers of good wine were "learning to make more of it." For the established elite of the region—especially Beaulieu, Inglenook, Martini, and Wente—there was steady expansion and a more solid prosperity as demand increased and prices rose. Indeed, the well-placed wineries had to put their buyers on allocation.

Other well-established enterprises in the coastal regions were quick to expand as demand was felt. Sebastiani, in Sonoma, added a million gallons of storage in the decade after 1965 and maintained its position as the big winery in the Sonoma Valley; it successfully managed its conversion from a supplier of bulk wines to such accounts as the A&P grocery chain to the source of a nationally distributed wine under its own label. In Santa Clara County, the Mirassou Winery—which like Sebastiani had been for years a producer of bulk wines exclusively—also turned to selling under its own label, with results that typified the changes overtaking California. In 1960, Mirassou, still a bulk producer unknown to the general public, had a 400,000-gallon storage capacity; at the end of the 1970s, as a well-advertised producer of varietal wines under its own label, it had grown to 2.3 million gallons of storage capacity.[32] In Napa County The Christian Brothers began a building program in 1972 to add new crushing, fermenting, storage, warehousing, office, and laboratory spaces over a two-year period; by the mid '70s the company had reached a storage capacity of 20 million gallons, though a good deal of this admittedly came from the Central Valley, where it had large wineries at Reedley and Fresno for the production of brandy and of fortified wines.[33] In the Livermore region, the long-established Wente Winery added a million gallons of storage capacity and doubled its small cooperage in the decade 1967–77.[34] Almadén doubled its bottling capacity in 1973 and added a Central Valley facility in 1974 to stretch out its table-wine production; Masson expanded its red wine production capacity at Saratoga and its white wine production in Monterey Country by many millions of gallons.[35] At a lower level of quality, Franzia, in Ripon, jumped from 12 million gallons' capacity to 18 million in less than two years.[36] The days of "distress-priced bulk wine," as Louis Gomberg said, were now a thing of the past.[37] What had once been destined for jug wine at the low-profit end was now bottled in cork-finished fifths at very different prices.[38]

The rising prosperity of the wine trade generally, and the growing demand for wines that came from proper wine-grape varieties rather than from just any grape, at last established the price differential that was the essential precondition for growing better grapes. Winemakers, if they were to produce table wines of competitive quality, now had to have good wine grapes and had to pay accordingly. Growers could now take the kind of risk that in earlier days had not been worth taking. Before the 1960s it was generally not true that winemakers were willing to pay more for better grapes; now they were. North Coast grapes, recognized as superior to the produce of the Central Valley, at last began to command premiums that set them apart in price. They had always received a better price, but that price had stayed in close parallel with Central Valley prices. From the '60s onward, North Coast grape prices spiraled out of touch with those received in the Central Valley—touching new record highs almost every year from 1965, for example, when the top price for Cabernet Sauvignon was $200 a ton, and reaching $700 in 1971.[39] More meaningful, perhaps, are the *average* prices for this period. In 1968, to take that year as a starting point, the average price per ton of wine grapes in California was $71; a decade later, in 1978, it had tripled to $210. A little analysis of the average shows that real distinctions were being made: in 1968, Zinfandel from the southern San Joaquin Valley received an average price of $112 a ton; Zinfandel from Lodi, $185. But Cabernet Sauvignon from Napa Valley went at $485 a ton.[40]

The same pressure created new vineyards: the acreage of Napa vineyards grew from 11,800 in 1968 to 24,000 in 1978; in Sonoma, the figures were 12,400 and 26,600. A particularly interesting development was the expansion of vineyards into Los Carneros, a region running along the shores of San Pablo Bay at the southern end of Napa and Sonoma Counties. Los Carneros was not wholly new to vineyards: before Prohibition there had been good wine made there at the John Stanly's Riverdale Ranch and at James Simonton's Talcoa Winery. The region had not come back after Repeal, having been turned to pasture, though Louis Martini had bought a part of the Stanly Ranch in 1942; he was thus the first to begin the restoration of the area. Attracted by the possibilities of its cool growing conditions— it hovers between the region I and region II classifications—Beaulieu began to plant in Los Carneros with cool-climate grapes, notably Chardonnay and Pinot noir; its example was soon followed by others, including Krug and Buena Vista. The development was to lead, among other things, to new possibilities in the production of sparkling wine.

Another new region was the Delta, the low-lying region where the Sacramento and San Joaquin Rivers flow together east of San Francisco to create a maze of creeks, sloughs, and islands. This land, drained and protected by levees, had been wholly devoted to field and vegetable crops until 1959, when an experimental planting of grapes was made on Mandeville Island. The results were encouraging enough that significant planting followed. Now the Clarksburg Viticultural Area, as the main district is called, has about 5,000 acres of grapes; there is also a small Merritt Island Viticultural Area. Monterey County was another new development. These new areas were important, but so was the new activity in older regions: the old Sierra region was revived, as were the vineyards of Lake County.

There was much more new action among the second of Carpy's categories, the makers of "so-so wines," as they aimed at something better than, or at least different from, what they had been routinely making in the generation since Repeal. Mostly these were the producers in the Central Valley, now compelled by the market to take on the challenge of table wines. The first thing to be done was to alter, perhaps upgrade, the vineyards by planting varieties that could provide some character as well as volume. The turn toward wine grapes had begun earlier than is perhaps generally realized. In the mid 1950s wine grapes had made up only a little more than 13 percent of the new plantings in the Central Valley, but from that point on there was a steady and rapid rise in the proportion, until a decade later nearly half of the new plantings were of wine grapes. Clearly, the growers were responding to the new possibilities in the market.[41] In 1966 Fresno County had 149,000 acres of raisin grapes and 12,600 of wine grapes. A decade later the acreage of raisin grapes had declined a bit to 146,000, but that of wine grapes had nearly tripled to 35,000 acres, of which 5,000 were still nonbearing. There were comparable shifts in the two other major grape-growing counties in the southern part of the valley. Madera County had 27,000 acres of raisin grapes and 7,000 of wine grapes in 1966. By 1976 the figures were 29,000 and 28,000. In Kern County the 22,000 acres of raisin grapes did not change between 1966 and 1976, while the wine-grape acreage made a spectacular leap from 6,000 to 39,000 acres.

The Gallo brothers had for years taken the lead among the big producers in getting their growers to plant something better. In 1962 they hired the distinguished winemaker Philip Togni to head a varietal studies department to determine what varieties might work in the valley. In 1964 they established a grower relations department to advise and consult. In 1968 they offered the inducement of long-term contracts to growers in selected areas if they would plant the recommended varieties; Allied Grape Growers followed suit.[42] The varieties recommended were Sauvignon blanc, Ruby Cabernet, Barbera, Zinfandel, Chenin blanc, and French Colombard.[43] The planting of these varieties accordingly zoomed in the 1970s. In the five years from 1969 to 1974, for example, plantings of Barbera in the Central Valley went from 1,840 acres to 19,781; of Ruby Cabernet, from 1,920 to 16,455; of Chenin blanc, from 2,006 to 14,594; of French Colombard, from 5,461 to 22,962.[44] Such plantings made up a very large part of the total vineyard expansion in the whole valley, north and south.

The demand for grapes produced very large new plantings not only in the already developed parts of the San Joaquin Valley but also on the West Side, as it is called, until then a region almost entirely given over to pasture. Since the original irrigation works for the San Joaquin Valley drew water from the Sierra Nevada on the eastern side of the valley, the West Side went more or less unwatered. The construction of the California Aqueduct at the end of the 1960s changed that and opened up "virtually unlimited" land for vineyard expansion.[45] One expert prophesied at the end of the '70s that some 200,000 new acres of vineyards might be planted on the West Side.[46] The Southern Pacific Railway, which, surprisingly enough, still had West Side property left from the original federal land grants made to it in the nineteenth century, put in 2,200 acres of vineyard there and contracted with Almadén and Guild Wineries to supply grapes from the West Side.[47] Another West Side enterprise on a grand scale was the Blackwell Wine Company, making bulk wines from more than 3,000 acres of grapes near Lost Hills; this was the work of the Blackwell Land Company of Bakersfield.

The precipitous move away from fortified wines to table wines meant that the winemaking of the Central Valley must also change. Traditionally, the valley had been defensive about its "inability" to grow grapes suitable for table wine, and it had grown well accustomed to its role as the supplier of the nation's cheap fortified wines. Now it would have to show that it could make something else besides port, sherry, and muscatel.[48] The valley climate, most of it high region IV or region V on the University of California heat summation scale, means that grapes grown there suffer from the defects of hot-country grapes. They are typically low in acid, high in sugar, high in pH, and low in color; such grapes, without very skillful management in vineyard and winery, produce flat and uninteresting wines. Making decent wine from valley grapes was a serious challenge to viticulturists and enologists. If technology were to have an undisputed place in the production of wine, this would be the place—and not just technology in the winery, but in the vineyard. The situation called for new varieties and new methods.

To assist in the transformation of Central Valley winemaking, Fresno State University, which had long had a basic course in enology, added two new positions in 1974: "We think," the chairman said at the time, "that we can make even better table wines in the San Joaquin Valley than we do."[49] All would agree that the table wines needed improving, but not everyone was a believer in the valley's prospects in this regard. Harold Berg, then chairman of the Department of Viticulture and Enology at Davis, thought that the growers in the valley ought to "hold up" until Davis introduced new crosses especially adapted to their needs. They might plant Ruby Cabernet and French Colombard in the meantime. They should not plant the "best coastal varieties," he thought, for they would give very inferior wines under valley conditions: "We are concerned over the effect on the reputation of California wine if the San Joaquin started marketing these as varietal wines."[50] The university continued to be skeptical: an article titled "Grapes for Table Wines in California's Regions IV and V" expressed the fear that "San Joaquin Cabernet Sauvignon, Chardonnay, etc. . . . might weaken the public's confidence in California wines of these types." The authors concluded that only Ruby Cabernet and (sometimes) Barbera were capable of making good red wines in the valley; for white wine, only French Colombard and Chenin blanc.[51]

Two new grapes introduced by the university in 1972 and 1975—called Carnelian and Carmine—would, it was hoped, prove tailor-made for the new commerce of table wine in the valley. Their sponsors were enthusiastic: Carnelian, producing twelve tons to the acre at Fresno, was "light and pleasant"; Carmine, producing from four to seven tons in an unirrigated vineyard at Oakville, scored "higher than Cabernet in blind tastings."[52] Despite this promise, the varieties have never caught on.[53] Other new crosses designed for the heat of the valley included Ruby Cabernet and Calzin for red, Helena and Flora for white. It was certainly possible to make an interesting wine from Ruby Cabernet. "In some hands at least," Roy Brady wrote, "Ruby Cabernets from warm vineyards make very attractive wines, big, fruity, distinctive, and very drinkable at an early age."[54] Maynard Amerine, speaking in 1975, thought that Ruby Cabernet would "take its place among our better varieties" but that it was too often overcropped and therefore too low in acid. In consequence, "There are not as many good wines made from Ruby Cabernet as we think there could be."[55] In recent years the decline in the planting of Ruby Cabernet in the Central Valley has been reversed; the 6,600 acres in 1996 expanded to 8,000 in 2002. The one new University of California cross intended for the Central Valley that seems to have caught on is Rubired, which is used not as a source of varietal wine but to add color to Central Valley reds: there were 13,000 acres of it in 2002.

Now, after a generation of experience, it may be said that the varietal wines from the Central Valley have not raised the reputation of California wine in general, but neither have they disgraced it. The recommended varieties—Barbera, Chenin blanc, French Colombard—have not, as far as I know, produced any wines of notable quality. Nor has the monotonous demand for the fashionable varieties been helpful: when everyone, with one voice, called for Chardonnay and Cabernet Sauvignon (and later Merlot), who can wonder that growers, after dutifully making trials with the new University of California varieties, then planted Chardonnay and Cabernet Sauvignon (and later Merlot)? In 1985 there were 644 acres of Cabernet Sauvignon planted in the Central Valley counties, 1,600 of Chardonnay, and 70 of Merlot. Sixteen years later the figures were 24,400 of Cabernet, 32,000 of Chardonnay, and 18,000 of Merlot—nearly a third of all the Cabernet in the state, 30 percent of the Chardonnay, and 40 percent of the Merlot.[56] The winemaking methods now available allow for creditable standard wines to be made from such varieties, but not much more. Whether the appropriate methods of vineyard management have yet been established is an open question.

In an ideal world, the Central Valley would be known for wines—no doubt the result of long-studied blending practices—made from varieties happily adapted to the hot climate and capable of yielding wines of distinctive character. That has not happened yet.

The wine you tell lies about.

FIGURE 42
How Central Valley
Cabernet was advertised
in 1974. M. LaMont was a
brand name of the Bear
Mountain Winery in Kern
County, the first winery
to offer so-called valley
varietals. The text takes
for granted that French
wines are those to be challenged: that might not
be the case today. (From
Time [4 November 1974].)

Instead, the valley producers have tamely followed the market for the standard varieties. They might retort that they had no choice but were bound to follow what the market demanded; and in the meantime, the new varieties intended to provide table wines grown under valley conditions have not succeeded in imposing themselves. It will be slow work to establish what the valley can do best for the table wines of this country from its resources. And of course it has continued to supply unpretentious jug wines under the old names of burgundy and chablis, but now containing large quantities of French Colombard and Barbera as well as Thompson Seedless and Grenache. The valley continues to supply the demand for inexpensive fortified wines, too, but that is now a very small fraction of the trade and does not now show any signs of growing.

From the early '70s onward a parade of varietal wines issued from valley producers, including some of the biggest bulk-wine establishments. The old Di Giorgio winery, for example (now known as Bear Mountain), having planted the recommended wine grapes in the 1960s, was able to bring out its first varietal wines in 1972.[57] The Sierra Wine Corporation at Tulare—which in 1971 had swallowed up the 6.4-million-gallon winery of Cal-grape at Delano to make a 15-million-gallon combination ("America's largest bulk wine producer")—went into valley varietals, as they were called, though still as a bulk producer.[58] The California Growers Winery in Tulare County, created in 1936 by large-scale growers as an outlet for their surplus grapes, converted itself from a co-op to a corporation; planted large vineyards of Barbera, Chenin blanc, Colombard, and other varieties; more than doubled the winery's capacity; and went into the business of supplying varietals in bulk, for private-label bottling and under its own labels. The Giumarra Winery, a 10-million-gallon bulk producer farming 6,000 acres near Bakersfield, brought out valley varietals under its own label in 1975. These, and others, were all established bulk wineries that had now converted a substantial part of their production to varietal table wines.

A wholly new beginning was made by Angelo Papagni, a major grower of grapes and other fruits in Madera County, who built a big winery to process his own grapes for sale as varietal wines. The Papagni Winery started out in 1973 with a 3-million-gallon-capac-ity, air-conditioned winery building, which included plans for a "restaurant, service sta-tion, wine tasting room and retail room" that would make it, uniquely in the Central Val-ley, a tourist attraction.[59] Papagni made Barbera, Zinfandel, and Chenin blanc, in common with most other producers; he also made a varietal wine out of the despised Alicante Bouschet and managed to obtain some kind words for it.[60]

The big moment in all this activity, however, was the entry of Gallo into the field of not only varietals but "cork-finished" wines—an event that was widely felt as revolution-ary, the strongest possible confirmation of the fact that a great change had come to pass. Gallo was synonymous with vast quantities of standard wines and novelty wines sold in screw-cap bottles and jugs to a public innocent of critical judgment. Now Gallo, cautiously following rather than leading, confirmed as no other enterprise could the change in the market's expectations.[61]

NEWCOMERS

Carpy's third category in the division of our subject is "newcomers . . . trying their hand at the game and doing the best they can." Here is where the real revolution in California wine history is to be found, if we are to speak of a revolution at all: not in the mere ex-pansion of the material means, essential as that was, but in the establishment of an idea of excellence that would challenge the very highest standards, without apology or doubt. By and large, this was the ideal to which the newcomers were committed. Of course they were commercial, but they were commercial with a difference: high quality as well as profits was a primary consideration. As Roy Brady wrote in 1975, when the excitement of new ventures was still seething: "Great wine is not an accident of climate and geog-raphy. It is a creative act of men. California's greatest asset is a set of wine makers who want to make the finest wine in the world. They may succeed, and if they do they will in-evitably bring a new meaning to 'finest.'"[62]

Brady's extravagant words, at the time he wrote them, applied only to a few established wineries—Beaulieu, Wente, Martini. Mostly, he was thinking of the newcomers, people who had been attracted to winemaking in the preceding ten years and who took for granted that they were striving to make fine wine. Together, they had created a new set of expectations for California.

They were of all kinds and origins: a dermatologist (David Bruce), an architect (Pierre Lafond), a dancer (Rodney Strong), an engineer (David Bennion), an airline pilot (Joseph Swan), a food service executive (Donn Chappellet), a university lecturer (Warren Winiarski)—one might go on through a long list of professions and trades. Among other things, people of such origins at once lent a social distinction to the trade of winemaking that it had not had since the end of the nineteenth century, when winegrowing had attracted a notable group of professionals and men of wealth.[63] Maynard Amerine had long labored to create a respected professional standing for trained winemakers—enologists, that is; now the trade was mixed with people who did not, indeed, despise the technical training that Davis offered but brought very different skills and experiences to the job. Mingled among the crew of newcomers there were also, one is pleased to note, some professional wine men, not newcomers, who jumped at the chance to do something better: Robert Mondavi is the model instance, but there were others—Joseph Heitz of Heitz Wine Cellars and Justin Meyer of Silver Oak, for example—and the work of the new winemakers had to have its effect on all of the veterans as well.

The newcomers were sometimes investors only, but many were actual growers and winemakers. And the people who were attracted to working for them were often newcomers of diversified origins too. To take a personal view for a moment, three young people who entered the industry in the '70s and went on to distinguished careers as winemakers were all graduates of my institution, Pomona College, where they were trained for anything but winemaking: Tony Soter, in philosophy; Cathy Corison, in biology; and Patrick Campbell, in literature and religion.[64] They might stand as types of many of the newcomers who helped to transform winemaking. One thing that characterized most of them was a great reliance on their own energy and determination rather than on money. They had to have some money, of course; many supported themselves by weekday jobs that allowed them to devote nights and weekends to winemaking. Many started on a very small scale, working in garages or basements or old outbuildings. It might be years before such an enterprise became profitable—if it ever did—but the devoted people who did the work were not looking for quick and growing profits: they were making good wine, according to some ideal notion. They might not have been very sophisticated in these matters, but they were eager to learn and helped to teach one another. From the vantage point of the new century, the many brave beginnings made through the decade of the '70s now seem to have a legendary character. One wonders whether it would be possible nowadays to succeed on such slender foundations of capital, technology, and marketing savvy as they built on.[65]

To give some idea of the rate at which newcomers were appearing, we may look first at Napa Valley, where the strongest power of attraction seemed to lie. In the fifteen years from 1965 through 1979, 69 new wineries were established in Napa County, as compared with the half-dozen or so founded in the preceding thirty-odd years since Repeal. The peak years were 1972 and 1973, when 19 new wineries were founded, but there has continued to be a steady accession since then. By 2000 there were 233 wineries in the county— a spectacular gain from 35 in 1950, half a century earlier. And among those wineries of 1950, the small artisan sorts such as Pocai, Rossi, Varozza, and Carbone had long since disappeared, as had the big co-ops that for years processed the bulk of the valley's grapes: the Napa Valley Cooperative Winery and the St. Helena Cooperative Winery. Instead, there were such now such well-regarded wineries as Schramsberg (1965), Mondavi (1966), Chappellet (1967), Sterling (1969), and Trefethen (1969). There were also, of course, a number that did not last long.[66] The new wineries ranged in size from the large and well-capitalized Domaine Chandon to the almost domestic Alatera Winery.

Perhaps even more striking than the efflorescence of new wineries in Napa was the extent to which new wineries were spread across the state. Over the years in question, 1965–1979, new wineries were established in thirty-two of California's fifty-eight counties, from Humboldt in the north to San Diego in the south. The 227 wineries licensed in California in 1965 had shot up by 1980 to 380, and the number was climbing steadily. Sonoma came second to Napa with thirty-nine new wineries, including Joseph Swan, Dry Creek, and Chateau St. Jean. Eugene Seghesio's prophecy that winegrowing in Sonoma County was approaching extinction, made as recently as 1956, now seemed strange indeed.[67] Santa Cruz County had thirteen new wineries (e.g., Ahlgren, Devlin), Santa Clara County ten (Kathryn Kennedy, Mount Eden), Mendocino ten (Dach, Edmeades), Santa Barbara County ten (Firestone, Zaca Mesa), Monterey County seven (Durney, Jekel), and so on through a scattering of between one and six new wineries in other counties. The old Sierra region, once home to an extensive winemaking economy, came back strongly with some fifteen new establishments.

So-called new wineries might not be wholly new, in fact, but rather restorations and renovations of older wineries—perhaps an even better sign of renewed vigor than a wholly fresh beginning would be. The old Chateau Montelena (1882), Chateau Chevalier (1897), and Far Niente (1885) in Napa, for example, were brought back to life, as was Gundlach-Bundschu (1896) in Sonoma. Another possibility is represented by Kenwood Vineyards in Sonoma County. It grew out of the old-fashioned Pagani Winery, where bulk wine was made and where retail customers could buy a red or a white wine in half gallons or gallons. When new owners took over they developed the property into a large producer of premium wine, so that Kenwood grafts the new style of California winemaking directly onto the old stock—one of the relatively few cases of which this is true. It may also be noted here that the transformation of Pagani Winery into Kenwood exemplified the accelerating disappearance of simple, everyday wines in favor of wines aiming at the highest quality—and expense.

Most of the newcomers were small or medium-size wineries, though the days in which one might hope to set up a winery on a shoestring and sell a simple *ordinaire* to a local clientele directly from the cellar door were long gone.[68] The capital investment in land and equipment, the rising cost of materials, the expense of staying competitive in a rapidly changing market, and the burden of complying with all federal, state, and local regulations and fees ensured that the price of wine, and especially of premium wine, would rise steadily too. By 1976 one of the experts at Davis estimated that a well-built new winery for varietal wines would cost $45 for every gallon of capacity; for a small 25,000-gallon winery that works out to more than a million dollars.[69] That was all the more reason to aim at the highest level of quality.

The level of achievement attained by these new wineries was given international publicity in 1976, when the United States was rather casually celebrating the bicentennial of its founding. A young Englishman named Steven Spurrier, then a wine merchant in Paris, decided to exploit the occasion to his own advantage. He would stage a competitive tasting of certain grand French wines against some of the best that California could show and call the event Bicentennial USA. The resultant publicity, he argued, would be good for his business. Spurrier assembled his experts—all French—and set them to work judging six California Chardonnays against four white Burgundies, and six California Cabernets against four red Bordeaux. When the scores were added up it was found that California wines came in first: Chateau Montelena was narrowly preferred to Meursault-Charmes among the whites; Stag's Leap Wine Cellars Cabernet Sauvignon was narrowly preferred to Château Mouton-Rothschild. As all sober and judicious commentators have emphasized since, this unexpected result showed only that both the California wines and the French wines were very good; the margin of preference in any case was very narrow.[70] But such reasonable reflections could not diminish the astonishment at the precocious achievements of the Americans. Chateau Montelena had acquired its winery license only in 1969; Warren Winiarski's winning Stag's Leap Wine Cellars Cabernet Sauvignon came from young vines in a new vineyard and had been made in a winery founded in 1972!

The news of the judging results made only a mild stir in the California trade: *Wines and Vines* reported it without comment in a brief story.[71] But the public press had a field day with the "judgment of Paris," as it was inevitably called. There has been much argument since about what the tasting meant: Did it show that the Americans had learned traditional French techniques? Or that they had exploited their own technical and scientific advances? Such arguments are endless. But however one looked at it, there was no doubt about the results, or about the publicity: California wines had at last achieved recognition at the highest level of competition.

"GOLD IN THEM THAR GRAPES"

The blossoming of the California wine trade that began in the '60s and was visible to all by the early '70s inevitably drew excited prophecies from the experts. Bank of America, the biggest financial power behind California wine, forecast at the end of 1970 that annual wine consumption in the United States would rise from 250 million to 400 million gallons by the end of the decade.[72] In 1972, Wells Fargo Bank raised the level of expectation considerably: not 400 million but 490 million gallons of wine would be consumed annually in the United States by 1980.[73] In the next year, the prophecies were even more expansive: the Bank of America now declared—as a "reasonable estimate"—that the annual market for wine in the United States in 1980 would reach 650 million gallons.[74] Louis Gomberg, the private wine consultant, taking an even longer view, topped them all: by the end of the century, he thought, the U.S. market would be for a billion gallons of wine, 800 million gallons of it from California.[75]

With such heady prospects, investors of all kinds wanted in on the action. As *Time* magazine declared in a cover story on the American wine boom and the Gallo brothers' part in it, "There's gold in them thar grapes," and big, publicly held corporations were rapidly taking over wineries.[76] This was the new California gold rush. The individual investor could be accommodated through real estate syndicates or limited partnerships, aided and abetted by generous tax write-offs. There was a flurry of such activity in the early seventies, not always with happy results.[77] A few of the larger wineries went public at this time, a novelty in the wine industry: Taylor in New York, Franzia, and Almadén. The most publicized action was the movement of what the trade always regarded as outside interests into the wine business by way of purchase. To people whose memories went back that far, the times were now like those early war years when the big distillers were buying up California wineries—except that now it was not just the distillers (though they indeed came back) but a whole range of firms in the food and drink line. The first dramatic moves occurred in 1967, when National Distillers bought Almadén for $18 million; Heublein, a Connecticut firm of importers and distributors, decided that wine might be a good investment and entered the field in 1968 by buying 82 percent of United Vintners for $33 million. By 1970, according to Louis Gomberg, there were "more than 20" corporations listed on the New York Stock Exchange looking for opportunities to buy into California wine.[78] In 1972 Schlitz Brewery bought Geyser Peak Winery and Southdown Corporation bought control of San Martin. In 1973 there was a frenzy of acquisition: Beatrice Foods bought Brookside Winery (8.5 million gallons); the Los Angeles bottlers of Dr Pepper bought the Cucamonga Vineyard Company (Bonded Winery number 1); the New York bottlers of Coca-Cola bought Franzia (20 million gallons).[79]

By the end of the 1970s, many of the old names that had distinguished the California wine trade since Repeal, and in a few cases since before Prohibition, were the property of newcomers and "outsiders": both Beaulieu and Inglenook were Heublein properties, Almadén belonged to National Distillers, Beringer to Nestlé, Buena Vista to the German firm A. Racke.

Another interesting development was the movement of eastern wineries into California. The Canandaigua Wine Company, in the Finger Lakes district of New York, having grown prosperous through the sale of a sweet pink fortified wine called Richards Wild Irish Rose, became a California producer by buying the Bisceglia Winery in Madera (formerly the Yosemite Winery co-op) in 1974. Widmer's, long established in the Finger Lakes and now the property of the English firm of Reckitt and Colman, took a more original line: in 1969 it began developing a 500-acre vineyard near Healdsburg, in Sonoma County, so that an eastern winery became not merely an investor in but a grower of California wine. Some California varietals under the Widmer's Winery label reached the market in the '70s, but the venture was not a commercial success.[80] A third sort of east-west combination was the use of a well-established eastern name—Taylor—to sell California wine. The Coca-Cola Company had bought the Taylor Wine Company in 1977 and had immediately set about expanding production. Since there were severe limits to expansion in New York, the strategists for Coca-Cola invented a new label, Taylor California Cellars, and had the wine made by the big new Monterey Vineyard in the Salinas Valley, also just purchased by Coke.

The pattern in both the Widmer's and the Taylor ventures was a portent of the future: big, well-financed international companies exploiting a winery name, once associated with a particular place and product, as a brand to be applied wherever opportunity might lead. Brand promotion without regard to the identity of what came with the brand was not a forward step for American wine but a kind of regression. It was what the old bottlers had done for years after Repeal, putting their brands on wine of who-knows-what origin. Now, however, it was being done by well-practiced, well-heeled firms that prided themselves on their market savvy and that supplied not local but national markets. Coca-Cola and Heublein were particularly adept at this sort of game. It would be played by many others afterward.

A move from even farther east to west was made in 1973 when the house of Moët and Hennessy, the proprietors of Moët & Chandon Champagne, began buying land in Napa Valley for vineyards; their purchases included properties in Los Carneros, so they were among the early contributors to the revival of winegrowing there. The attraction of California for Moët and Hennessy was not merely that wine sales were surging in America but that expansion was impossible in France itself, owing to the strict delimitation of the Champagne region. They looked for new growth not only in California but in South America, South Africa, and Australia as well. In California they planted mainly Burgundian varieties, Pinot noir and Chardonnay. A new winery built at the southern end of Napa Valley went into operation in 1977; there experts imported from France supervised the production of wine according to the *méthode champenoise*. The result could not, of course, be called *champagne*, but went to market as California sparkling wine under the Domaine Chandon label. Domaine Chandon also contributed to the sophistication of the Napa Valley wineries as tourist destinations by opening a highly regarded restaurant at the winery in 1977.

Moët and Hennessy was followed by Piper Heidsieck in 1980, in a joint venture with Sonoma Vineyards. Since then four more French Champagne houses have set up California operations: Mumm, in partnership with Seagram's, in Napa Valley; Deutz, in partnership with Beringer, in San Luis Obispo County; Roederer Estate in Mendocino County; and Taittinger, as Domaine Carneros, in Napa County. Yet another firm, Pommery et Greno, instead of building its own winery, has taken over the former Scharffen-berger sparkling-wine operation in Mendocino County.

The French were soon joined by the Spanish producers of *cava*, as sparkling wine by the *méthode champenoise* is known in Spain: the house of Freixenet bought land in Sonoma County in 1983 and now produces sparkling wine there under the Gloria Ferrer label. Codorníu, the largest of the Spanish *cava* producers, came in 1989. These French and Spanish ventures were by no means the first European investments in California, which go well back into the nineteenth century. But they were certainly the most obvious European presences on the California scene, and no doubt the concentration on sparkling wine gave them an extra degree of glamour. They also contributed greatly to establishing the reputation of the Carneros region: Codorníu, Domaine Chandon, Freixenet, Mumm, and Taittinger now cultivate many hundreds of acres of Chardonnay and Pinot noir in Los Carneros.

These developments gave California a new credit outside the United States and helped to confirm its prestige within the country as well. Whatever might be said about the independent and progressive character of winemaking in California, it was a great boost to the self-confidence of the local producers to have the French, of all people, approve in so marked a manner what was being done there. But foreign investment was only one, relatively small element in the new prosperity of California wine.[81] Louis Gomberg estimated in 1974 that in the seven preceding years a total from all sources of more than $1 billion had been invested in the American wine industry, $750 million in vineyards and $250 million in new winery facilities: and these, he said, "are conservative figures."[82]

THE NEW CONSCIOUSNESS OF WINE

If a tourist had ventured across San Francisco Bay to the town of Napa at any time toward the end of the 1960s and made his way north into Napa Valley, he would have found a scene of pastoral tranquillity, where the fields were large and varied and the towns small and simple. If it were winter and a weekday, the traffic on Highway 29, the state road that bisects the valley from north to south, would be light and strictly local. A single-track railroad, the Northwestern Pacific, running parallel to the highway, was adequate for the shipping requirements of the valley's wineries: a daily train of a few cars only—the *St. Helena Rattler*, it was called—sufficed quite nicely. Vineyards began around Yountville and grew denser as one approached St. Helena, the center of things, but the vineyards by no means had the show to themselves: large orchards of plums (prunes, they were called), pears, and other fruits; here and there fields of grain; and many acres of pastureland mingled with the vineyards. St. Helena was unmistakably a farm town: the hardware store; the agricultural implement dealers; the office of the Production Credit Agency; and the feed, hay, and fuel store were prominent among the businesses that lined the main street. The importance of the town as a center of American winemaking was announced by a sign on the outskirts of town, welcoming the motorist to "this world famous wine grow-

Before: Freemark Abbey, St. Helena, in the 1950s, when Napa tourism was simple and direct. (Photograph by Max Yavno; courtesy of the Wine Institute.)

ing region." The message of that sign was confirmed by the few large wineries that lined the route into town from the south: Beaulieu, Inglenook, and Louis Martini notably. On the other side of town, the north end, Beringer and Krug, with their handsome buildings from the nineteenth century, were particularly well prepared for the reception of visitors. A handful of wineries were new, though the only one visible to the uninstructed tourist was the splendid Mondavi Winery, not far from Inglenook. More than balancing the signs of new activity were the many buildings standing empty or converted to other uses that had once been wineries: shuttered and derelict, occupied as commercial buildings, or re-modeled into private houses, they could be found in every corner of the county.[83]

If the tourist chose to eat in St. Helena, he would have found a place or two providing the unpretentious and uniform fare that one expects on the American road: nothing there aspired beyond the level of a café.[84] For entertainment, there was a movie theater; and for lodging, a couple of simple motels on the outskirts provided decent accommodation. That was the heart of Napa Valley in the 1960s.[85]

Visitors who now, at the beginning of the twenty-first century, drive to the valley find themselves, even before reaching the city of Napa at the southern end of the valley, so-licited by a series of expensive signs and billboards to visit historic wineries, to explore the wine country, to taste the area's "world-class" wines. The glittering promises are what one would expect from Reno or Las Vegas. As they move north on Highway 29 the traffic grows thick; if they are so ill-advised as to visit on a weekend in summer, the traffic does not move at all. On every side are vineyards in the monotony of monoculture: the prunes

FIGURE 43B

After: The Ferrari-Carano Winery, Dry Creek Valley, Sonoma County, created in the 1980s as a tourist destination. (Photo courtesy of Ferrari-Carano Vineyards and Winery.)

and the pears are long gone. The railroad is still there, but no daily freight runs on it; instead, a "wine train" carries tourists through the valley while they sip the local wines and eat in the detached comfort of an air-conditioned carriage.[86] Wineries rapidly punctuate both sides of the road, growing more frequent as one moves north toward St. Helena. Some are plain and unostentatious; others are more splendid, offering tours, tastings, picnic facilities, gift shops, art exhibits, restaurants, "culinary centers"; a few others hold themselves aloof, offering no encouragement to the tourist at all—a predictable development in a region where tourism threatens to overwhelm the daily life of the people who live and work there. St. Helena is no longer recognizable as a farm town: there are expensive wine shops, boutiques, bed-and-breakfast houses furbished in "period" style; the newsstand displays the *Wall Street Journal* and the *Financial Times;* the restaurants, which now abound on Main Street and on side streets as well, aim at the highest level of sophisticated cuisine and compete with one another in devising ever more precious menus. Scattered about in the more desirable locations are stylish and expensive new homes for rich professionals. Here and there rise large and opulent resort hotels offering every luxury. One may take limousine tours of the wineries, or balloon rides over the vineyards, or mud baths in a spa under the care of a skilled masseur.

The climactic event of the valley year is the wine auction held each June in aid of charity.[87] Here the very rich and fashionable compete with one another to astound the simple bourgeois by the extravagance of their behavior and their spending: as one headline describing this much-publicized event put it, the auction brings "astonishing bids and bacchanalian revelry" to the valley. Whether Bacchus ever had so much money may be doubted. In the year 2000, amid the swirl of catered parties, it cost each couple $2,000 merely to attend the auction; that year's high bidder paid half a million dollars for a six-liter bottle of Napa Valley wine. Such things make the extravagances of the *Satyricon* or the excesses of Tulipomania seem comparatively temperate and decorous amusements. That, no doubt, is the whole idea; and no doubt such competition for distinction in extravagance will, for a while at least, be sustained by its own momentum.

Our tourist of the 1960s, if transported to today's St. Helena, would look around him in complete bewilderment: what has happened to turn the unremarkable small farm town he once knew into this crowded Vanity Fair? These things are a fable. Napa Valley is, beyond doubt, the best known and most glamourous of all American wine regions, but—in their proper measure and according to their different natures—every established American wine-growing region has undergone a comparable change in the years since the wine boom began to be heard in the late 1960s; or, if it is a new region, it has been formed according to the new consciousness of wine as an attractive, sought-after commodity. Wine, which had been so long a neglected Cinderella in American culture, now comes forth in ball gown, glass slippers, and gilded coach. Without pausing to ask whether this development be a good thing, we may examine some of the steps by which the new condition was reached.

The first sign, apart from the figures of national consumption and the balance sheets of the wineries, was the appearance of wine magazines, a sure sign that the growth of a new market has been detected. The earliest ventures were short-lived: *The Bacchus Journal* (1966) was ahead of its time; *Vintage* (1970) did better but did not last. These tentative forays soon became a parade: *Wine World* (1971), *Grand Cru* (1971), *International Wine Letter and Digest* (1973), *California Grapevine* (1974), *Connoisseur's Guide to California Wine* (1974), and on through an ever-growing list. As the market grew, specialization could develop: hobbyists were served by magazines about winemaking, aspiring winegrowers by the *Vinifera Wine Growers Journal*, devoted to the cause of vinifera winegrowing in the eastern states. People attracted by the idea of wine as an investment had *Liquid Assets*, and reports on auction results appeared in *Decanter* and the *International Wine Review*. For the great mass of those eager to know what to buy, tip sheets and guides were provided in quantity: Robert Balzer's *Private Guide, Fred Cherry's Personal Wine Journal, The Pursglove Wine Letter,* and *Robert Finigan's Private Guide to Wines,* to name only a few. The possibilities of regional interests were exploited: the *Finger Lakes Wine Gazette*, the *Missouri Wine Country Journal*, the *Northwest Consumer's Wine Guide*.

Books, too, began to multiply, some of them quite solid, some of them too flimsy to stand up to any wear. Robert Balzer was a pioneer on the California scene: his *California's Best Wines* (1948)—a melange of anecdotes, descriptions, interviews, and recipes—was notable, if only for its assumption that California was worth writing about at all. The book was published in Los Angeles, for the New York publishers were not yet ready to add such an item to their lists. Balzer was followed by Idwal Jones, whose anecdotal (and highly unreliable) *Vines in the Sun: A Journey through the California Vineyards* appeared in 1949 and *did* have a New York publisher: Jones, unlike Balzer, was already an established writer. John Melville's *Guide to California Wines* (1955) announced a new stage of development, in which the reader was given a fuller and more systematic description of what was available; the assumption was that people now wanted to know about wines in detail and were seeking to buy.[88] The more sober University of California view, in which the "emphasis is on fact rather than fancy," was embodied in Maynard A. Amerine and Vernon L. Singleton's *Wine: An Introduction for Americans* (1965).[89] After that, the deluge: general guides and introductions (*Sunset Magazine's California Wine*, 1973), tour books (*Sonoma and Mendocino Wine Tour*, 1977), books of interviews (*Great Winemakers of California*, 1977), technical books (*A Practical Ampelography*, 1979), special-topics books (*Wines and the Art of Tasting*, 1974), biographies and memoirs (*My Life with Wine*, 1972), picture books (*The Treasury of American Wines*, 1973)—especially picture books, for wine is one of the most pictorial of subjects—and any other form of print that ingenuity might invent. As one can see from the samples noted here, practically the whole gamut of possibility was run in the decade of the '70s, from a standing start.

Newspapers, too, began to carry writing about wine, sometimes by a syndicated "expert," sometimes by local talent. The earliest such thing in California, according to Charles Sullivan, was written by Robert Mayock for the *San Jose News* in the early 1940s, but this was a premature bud.[90] Among the earliest of the postwar newspaper columnists were Hank Rubin, Bob Thompson, and Jefferson Morgan, all in the Bay Area, where wine was visible and where interest in it was concentrated as in no other part of the country. Some sort of milestone was reached in 1973, when the wine writers of the Bay Area organized as a professional group; with that development, one could say that the wine writer was now institutionalized. Outside California, wine writers were thinner upon the ground, but all told, a good many had cropped up—some "expert," some not, though not necessarily the worse for that. The *New York Times* inaugurated a regular wine column in 1972, but only on an experimental basis. As its author, Frank J. Prial, wrote on the first anniversary of his column, there had been many doubts at the beginning: "Was there enough going on to sustain a weekly column? Would there be any reader interest? No one was sure."[91] The doubts were quickly dispelled. The trade of writing about wine grew large enough to have a hierarchy, and it is to be noted that amid the swarm of writers some older voices took on a new prominence and authority: Frank Schoonmaker, Alexis Lichine, and André Simon now had audiences larger than ever, and their opinions were accorded the status of a master's.

The necessities of journalism—among others, the need for novelty, for variety, for conflict, for heroes and villains—have had predictable effects: exaggerated descriptive language; the regular, excited revelation on each successive publication date of newly discovered great wines; the invention of new fashions in wine; and the glamourizing of such figures as the winemaker. Brad Webb, the winemaker responsible for the first sensational Chardonnays from the Hanzell Vineyard, was out of a job when Hanzell shut down in 1963 and found it difficult to get another. "The prestige of a wine maker then," he said, "was about that of a restaurant cook."[92] Not now: as the new hero of wine journalism, the winemaker became a figure of power whose secrets were eagerly sought—Robert Benson's book called *Great Winemakers of California* (1977) conveniently embodies the new view. Winemakers—great or not—were so much in demand that they spent at least as much time on the road, making appearances before audiences of wine lovers, as they did in the winery, and their words were taken to offer privileged glimpses into the arcana of wine. Sometimes the journalist himself became the hero, the figure of power, whose revelations were accorded a semisuperstitious reverence. Or it might simply be the owner who was revered, presumably because to own a glamourous property is to be made glamourous oneself.

The new interest in wine, stimulated by the factitious excitements of journalism and worked on by eager tipsters with the latest information about what was best, or hottest, or next to be discovered, led a variety of sponsoring institutions to set up competitive wine judgings. For many years the only regular judgings had been those sponsored by the California State Fair in Sacramento and the Los Angeles County Fair in Pomona: these two were certainly adequate to accommodate such interest as there was in the generation after Repeal, and by the '60s many wineries had ceased to take part in them at all. Now the situation changed: wine judgings began to proliferate, not just in California but across the country. And as the tide of medals and ribbons swelled, it became almost a condition of self-respect to scoop in as many as would keep one up with the competition. Some of the new judgings had an attractive grassroots character: the Indiana State Fair, for example, in 1973 added "home made wine" to the list of domestic items eligible to compete for prizes at the fair.[93] More often, they had the hard, bright glaze of frankly commercial and promotional enterprises. The popularity of such events may be guessed at from the fact that in 2003 the magazine *Wine East* listed forty-four of them for that year, from the Florida State Fair International Wine Competition to the San Diego National Wine Competition and all points between.[94]

Wine judgings require only a limited number of judges, and after their decisions have been reported there is nothing more to do except to exploit whatever commercial advantages an award might offer. To supply more amusement to a more general public, what came to be known as the wine festival was invented and quickly spread to most parts of the country. It was not necessary to be in wine country in order to have a wine festival, nor did it have to be in the country at all: downtown would do as well. The International Wine and Cheese Festival opened in New York City in 1973. Anyone could create a festival: the sponsors were magazines, local charities, amateur wine societies, state or regional associations of wineries, or anyone with an interest in promoting such an affair—a hotel, a restaurant, a chamber of commerce. There was the Santa Barbara County Vintners' Association's Vintners' Festival, *Wine Spectator* magazine's California Wine Experience, Mendocino County's Winefest, the Central Coast Wine Festival, and the Russian River Wine Festival, to name a few in California. Outside California they were one of the most effective ways of letting people know that their own state or locality had some share in the making of that interesting commodity, wine, and the festival might be conveniently tied in with some other interest, commercial or cultural: the New Mexico Wine Festival, the Santa Fe Wine and Chile Fiesta, the Prosser [Washington] Wine and Food Fair, the Aspen/Snowmass Wine and Food Classic, the Great Tastes of Pennsylvania Wine and Food Festival, the Finger Lakes Wine Festival, the Colorado Mountain Winefest, or the simply named Wine Festival, sponsored by the Vinifera Wine Growers Association in Virginia, give an idea of the range. Some grew highly specialized—the International Pinot Noir Celebration at McMinnville, Oregon, for example—while others showed ingenuity in combination: the Paderewski Festival at Paso Robles, California, featuring (as the flyer promoting the affair put it) "music, history, food, and a celebration of Zinfandel."

Wine festivals might or might not include wine auctions, which also grew increasingly popular. The auction for charity, of which the Napa Valley Wine Auction is the type toward which all others aspire, was the most common form; the fact that the prices paid at such affairs counted as tax-deductible charitable contributions explains why they were typically so inflated. The simply commercial auction had a more restricted development. The English have carried on such auctions for years (with interruptions), but the incoherence of American wine law made them a difficult proposition here, even supposing that there had been an interested clientele for wine at auction. Most states require sellers of wine to post prices, but of course the whole idea of an auction is to find out what people are willing to pay. In 1969, however, a Heublein subsidiary, Vintage Wines Company, held an auction in Chicago, where no price posting rule obtained. The event received immense publicity and generated an excited response. Since then, other firms have entered the auction business, either live or, increasingly, on-line. The results are regularly reported in such publications as *Wine Spectator* and *Decanter*.

Another, curious development rising out of the new consciousness of wine was a vogue for home winemaking—not, as had been true during Prohibition and the Depression, because that was the only way to obtain a supply of wine, but because home winemaking was seen as a passport to an understanding of wine. The movement happened to coincide with the social restlessness of the late '60s, so it became mixed with the reaction against anything of "corporate" origin and with a new esteem for the authentic, the homely, the personal. Making wine at home was a way to be genuine. Home winemaking, on the widespread scale of the early '70s, turned out not to be a permanent shift but only a fad; yet for a time it looked solid enough.[95] Some local enterprises, such as the Berkeley firm called, in the style of the '60s, Wine and the People, attracted a large business, as did The Compleat Winemaker in Yountville, California. The Wine Art chain of stores, selling grape concentrate, yeasts, fermentation locks, corks, and other materials, had outlets in the smaller as well as in the great cities. Most remarkable of all, the giant retailer Sears Roebuck Company entered the action in 1973. Every store in the great national chain was to have a home winemaking section, just as there was a section for men's clothing, for garden tools, and for glassware. What could make the importance of home winemaking clearer than that? Sears even produced a series of illustrated, four-color catalogs, though this effort soon lapsed.

Such intense and widespread interest as I have been summarizing inevitably generated new organizations. The more dedicated home winemakers were an important part of the group that formed the American Wine Society in 1967; in its early days the society concentrated on wines from outside commercial sources, but it has gradually extended the range of its interests to include almost anything having to do with wine. Many other wine societies have been formed as a natural expression of the growing interest in wine among Americans. Some began in a more or less commercial way—that is, as a way to sell wine: Les Amis du Vin, for example, from the mid '60s offered a wine of the month through affiliated wine shops, but the many local chapters also arranged tasting programs that gave a good opportunity for members to try a variety of wines. Some were purely ornamental: The Knights of the Vine (1971) imitated such promotional groups as the Confrérie des Chevaliers de Tastevin of Burgundy and the Commanderie du Bontemps de Médoc et des Graves in Bordeaux, except that they had no regional affiliation or any social function to perform (apart from providing an excuse to dress in elaborate costume). There would be no point in noting such things except as they help to express what I have called the new consciousness of wine in America.

More solid, and better positioned for the long run, was the Society of Wine Educators, founded at a meeting on the Davis campus of the University of California in the summer of 1977. The initiative for the society came from the Wine Institute, which saw that the growing number of wine courses—and their teachers—would have to have help if they were to be made respectable. With the institute's assistance, a national organization was created and was soon on its own. The main aim was simple enough: "We wanted to set some standards," as one of the founders put it.[96] The society holds workshops, offers short courses, and administers a Certified Wine Educator Exam with the stated aim of professional development, though one need not be a professional.[97] The Enological Society of the Pacific Northwest, founded in 1975, is typical of the more general-interest style of group and may stand as a representative instance of a large category: it conducts tastings, gives dinners, sponsors talks by experts, arranges tours, and caters to the interests of its members in any other way compatible with amateurism.

The evolution of American wine societies has now been carried to a pretty high degree of specialization. There are societies for people who collect wine labels, wine books, or wine ephemera, or who are devoted to Zinfandel or to the promotion of wines from the grapes traditional along the Rhône valley. In some of these groups the public-relations flavor is pretty strong; in others it is wholly absent.

There are, beyond those named, a myriad of other wine-tasting societies and wine clubs, informal, local, and incalculably effective in assisting an interest in wine. There are also many clubs whose purpose is frankly commercial, all of them modeled on the wine-of-the-month idea in one form or another. The growing commerce in wine has additionally

FIGURE 44

The Wine Museum of San Francisco as it appeared during its brief, lamented life. (From "The Wine Museum of San Francisco: The Christian Brothers Collection" [n.d.].)

led to a trade in the accessories of wine, from corkscrews and decanters to elaborate and expensive temperature-controlled wine cellars; in the 1960s any enthusiast who wanted such things would have had to look very hard indeed to find them. Now they are familiar items, mostly through catalog sales or, increasingly, over the Internet.

Besides the many who were quick to seize on the commercial possibilities of the new wine consciousness, there were others who aimed to give it academic respectability. Extension courses in wine appreciation had been offered through the University of California at least from the 1950s, a very early point in the development of wine appreciation. A course on the geography of wine was offered at California State University, Northridge, as early as 1969, but the interest in such subjects was by no means confined to California. Cornell University was offering a course called "Introduction to Wine" in 1973, about the same time that the University of Michigan first offered one on the historical and aesthetic aspects of wine. Very likely there were other, earlier, such courses not on record; soon they had spread to colleges and universities across the country.[98] A laboratory course in winemaking was given at Allentown College, in Pennsylvania, in 1974, and practical instruction of that kind is now provided at a good many other places, more often than not in community colleges.

The academic and artistic side of the new wine consciousness found a notable expression in 1974 in the opening of the Wine Museum in San Francisco. Its basis was the collection of artworks, artifacts, and books formed by Alfred Fromm together with the collection of wineglasses formed by his associate, Franz Sichel: Fromm and Sichel, who were the national distributors of The Christian Brothers wines, called it The Christian Brothers Collection. The museum, in North Beach, was a stylish place and mounted highly interesting exhibits, but it did not survive the ups and downs of business life. After Fromm retired and his firm was sold, the museum had no support: Seagram's, which took over the collection, or some part of it, finally shipped it to its own museum near Toronto.[99] One hopes that the elegant and scholarly example so briefly provided by the Wine Museum will be remembered and will, sooner or later, inspire a successor.

By the end of the century there was a larger, more varied, and more prosperous wine industry in the United States than would have seemed imaginable a generation earlier, even to the most euphoric of optimists. It had also generated a large and varied production of wine magazines, wine books, wine clubs, wine courses, wine accessories, wine tourism, wine auctions, wine what-have-you—an epi-wine industry, or a para-wine industry, whose growth shows no signs of abating. Although almost all of this proliferation was purely commercial, some of it, at least, was the expression of a genuine and lasting interest. Altogether it was characteristically American—unstable in its exaggerations, gaudy, frequently vulgar, but always interesting.

11

A NEW DAWN (I)
The Northern and Central States

NEW YORK

At the beginning of the 1960s things had never been so good at the Taylor Wine Company. Founded in 1880 in the little town of Hammondsport at the foot of Keuka Lake, where winemaking began in New York, Taylor had survived Prohibition, the Great Depression, the war, and the postwar collapse of the wine market. Shrewd management and a good sales network now began to receive their reward as the sales of American wine started to grow. Taylor had always been a family business: the founder, Walter Taylor, had passed the winery on to his three sons, Clarence, Fred, and Greyton; they had run the business since Repeal, and now a third generation was at work in the winery. The Taylors were used to taking the lead among the winegrowers of the Finger Lakes: "innovators" and "pacesetters," Philip Wagner called them:

> They are the pacesetters on wages. They are the pacesetters on prices paid for grapes to independent growers and on premium payments for superior quality. They are the pacesetters in establishing Seaton Mendall's extension service for growers. They are pacesetters in assuming a large share of the chanciness in grape growing by buying vineyards and installing the former owners of them, as employees on salary, in their own homes. They are pacesetters in applying modern processing techniques to the ancient art of converting grapes into wine.[1]

Taylor was now, at the beginning of the '60s, by far the largest of the upstate New York wineries, and therefore by far the largest winery in the country outside California. Sales of Taylor wines had approached the 2.5-million-gallon mark in 1959, and the winery was poised for further growth.

Growth was rapid indeed. In 1961 it bought its close neighbor and longtime rival in Hammondsport, the Pleasant Valley Wine Company—the oldest of the Finger Lakes wineries, celebrated for its Great Western champagne. Growing sales matched growing capacity: in 1968 Taylor sold 6.6 million gallons of wine; four years later, in response to the general prosperity of that boom period, the sales had jumped almost 50 percent to close on 10 million gallons. The storage capacity of the winery had reached 14 million gallons, to which one could add Pleasant Valley's 3.3 million gallons.

All of this was the more astonishing because Taylor was making the sorts of wine it always had made. The technology in the winery was state-of-the-art, but the wines continued to be made from the native grapes that were still the almost exclusive basis of eastern winemaking: Isabella, Catawba, Delaware, Niagara, and, overwhelmingly, Concord. From these sources, Taylor conjured up a startling range of wines, mostly sweet and fortified, including two ports, three sherries, a "white tokay," a brut champagne, a very dry champagne, a pink champagne, a sparkling burgundy, and a list of what it called dinner wines: rhine, sauterne, claret, burgundy, rosé, and the proprietary Lake Country Red and Lake Country White.

How long Taylor might have been able to prosper on the basis of the old native grapes one can only guess, for now things changed. Clarence Taylor, the last of the three Taylor brothers, died in 1976, when the Taylor winery had reached a storage capacity of more than 22 million gallons. The next year the winery was sold to the Coca-Cola Company of Atlanta, Georgia, which had been watching the rising prosperity of the wine industry with an attentive and covetous eye. Coca-Cola saw that the wine people seemed to know little about promotion, whatever they might know about production, and decided that it was time for a veteran sales enterprise to take a hand. Coca-Cola wanted Taylor largely for its established name and its extensive distribution: Taylor, in short, was to be a brand that could be promoted on a national scale.[2]

There were not enough grapes in all of New York to feed an operation of the size that Coca-Cola now planned. Instead, Coca-Cola bought the big new Monterey Vineyard to supply the wine and invented a new label called Taylor California Cellars. Wine in unlimited supply could be provided by California, and the established name of Taylor would provide the necessary brand recognition.[3]

The transformation of Taylor from a historic winery inseparable from its Finger Lakes origins into a label for California wine seems in fact to have worked. Coca-Cola affirmed that its wine operations were profitable—but not profitable enough for a firm accustomed to better returns than the wine trade seemed capable of providing. After a brief six years of winemaking, Coca-Cola sold all of its wine properties in 1983 to the giant distilling firm of Seagram's. Four years later, Seagram's sold Taylor and its other wine interests to a newly invented firm called Vintners International, and in 1993, having failed to make a go of it, Vintners International sold Taylor to Canandaigua Wine Company, which was

FIGURE 45
Taylor Wine Company
of Hammondsport,
New York: "buildings
of a Victorian solidity
and amplitude."
(Author's collection.)

interested only in acquiring another label to add to its already large stock of well-known brands. In the sixteen years since its purchase by Coca-Cola, when its successes had seemed irresistibly attractive, Taylor had been sold and resold three times and finally extinguished as, apparently, no longer a commercially viable property. Taylor survives only as a name, with no more substantial meaning than any other name of convenience.

The stories of the two other independent old-guard Finger Lakes wineries are comparable. Gold Seal, the third of the Hammondsport wineries after Taylor and Pleasant Valley, was bought by Seagram's in 1979 and five years later was closed. Over on Lake Canandaigua, at Naples, the Widmer winery went through several sales and now, though still functioning, does so as a production facility having little or no relation to its historical identity.[4] But while the big, old-line firms were passing so rapidly from apparent prosperity into extinction, a fifth Finger Lakes winery—of no historic standing and no apparent interest in anything but the largest possible sales of the cheapest sort of wine—was quietly growing until at last it took over the properties of all its distinguished rivals. The story is the classic one of the unregarded outsider who in the end triumphs over the aristocrats who have scorned him.

Marvin Sands bought the Canandaigua winery, at the opposite end of Lake Canandaigua from Widmer's, in 1945, just after the war, and supplied bulk wine to bottlers.[5] In 1948 he was joined by his father, Mordecai: the elder Sands had had experience in a dubious sector of the wine trade as a partner in a Long Island City winery called Geffen Industries, which, according to Leon Adams, managed during the years after Repeal to turn out "copious" quantities of wine from "relatively few tons of fresh grapes."[6] In 1951 the elder Sands opened another winery, this one in Petersburg, Virginia, named Richard's Wine Cellars after his grandson, to make sweet muscadine wine from grapes grown mostly in the Carolinas. The Sands's operations were suddenly transformed in 1954 when Canandaigua Wine Company introduced a sweet, fortified pink Concord-based wine called Richards Wild Irish Rose.[7] The market for such wine has been described, according to the bland euphemisms supplied by political correctness, as "ethnic oriented," which is to say, wine for the mostly black ghetto, or for the wino wherever found.[8] The wine at once sold well and still, half a century later, sells well. The income from Wild Irish Rose allowed Canandaigua Wine Company to begin the process of expansion that was over the course of the next forty years to make it the largest wine producer in the United States after Gallo.[9]

The earliest moves, following up the start made in 1951 with Richard's Wine Cellars, took place in the South, a region otherwise neglected by the American wine trade. Canandaigua in 1956 bought the Mother Vineyard Winery of Manteo, North Carolina, and then in 1965 Tenner Brothers of Patrick, South Carolina, both producers of muscadine wine. In 1973 Sands obtained from the heirs of Paul Garrett the right to use the Virginia Dare label and so restored the connection between Virginia Dare and Scuppernong.[10]

In 1969 Canandaigua bought the Hammondsport Wine Company, specializing in sparkling wine, and Onslow Wine Cellars in North Carolina; with that, Canandaigua became the largest wine producer outside California, though still far smaller than several of the California giants.[11] In 1973 Canandaigua went public, and with the money raised, in the next year it ventured into the territory of the giants themselves, buying the Bisceglia Winery at Madera, California, a 4.5-million-gallon facility.[12] After an expensive and ultimately unsuccessful foray into the wine-cooler market in the '80s, Canandaigua returned to its policy of expansion through purchase. In 1986 it bought the Widmer winery, one of the old bulwarks of the Finger Lakes trade; in the same year it bought the Monarch Wine Company, makers of Manischewitz kosher wine in Brooklyn, and moved the Manischewitz operation to the Widmer plant. Thus Widmer, which under the Widmer family had been almost the lone champion of dry table wines from the better native varieties, became instead the source of sweetened Concord wine for the supermarket trade.

The storage capacity of the various Canandaigua properties now stood at 19.5 million gallons, to which were added, in 1991, the assets of Guild Wineries, the co-op that owned, among others, the Cribari, Roma, Cresta Blanca, and Cook's Imperial Champagne labels.

Two years later Canandaigua bought out the firm called Vintners International and so acquired, among other things, the Taylor, Great Western, and Gold Seal wineries.[13] Canandaigua now owned *all* of the big four wineries—or what was left of them—that had long dominated the Finger Lakes. Their existence henceforward was purely nominal: they were now mere labels, to be used on wines from any convenient source. Canandaigua was now not only the largest wine producer by far outside California, it was the second-largest wine producer anywhere—second only, of course, to Gallo.

The next major move in this process was the purchase of the Almadén-Inglenook properties, now much altered from their original form, from Heublein in 1994, which added yet another set of well-known labels to the growing army already assembled under Canandaigua's ownership.[14] It also added the huge Mission Bell winery at Madera, which had belonged at various times to Italian Swiss Colony, the California Wine Association, Krikor Arakelian, and Louis Petri. Canandaigua now consolidated its California production at Madera; by the end of the century, the capacity of the plant had grown to 55 million gallons. Canandaigua's purchase in 1999 of the Simi and Franciscan wineries, by comparison with earlier purchases, seemed almost an afterthought: both wineries were relatively small, but both were of high reputation. In 2001 Canandaigua bought Ravenswood, a highly regarded Sonoma winery specializing in Zinfandel, and it moved into the Pacific Northwest with the purchase of the Columbia, Covey Run, and Paul Thomas wineries in Washington and Ste. Chapelle in Idaho. In 2003, Canandaigua moved into expansion on an international scale with the acquisition of BRL Hardy, a large Australian consolidation with which it already maintained a joint venture called Pacific Wine Partners. The result of this combination was a wine-producing entity with greater capacity even than that of Gallo.

The process of acquisition had not been limited to wine properties. Canandaigua had an extensive trade in distilled spirits, both as producer and as distributor, and was in addition a distributor of beer. In recognition of this diversity, the holding company changed its name to Constellation Brands in 2000, but its wine operations continued to be managed as the Canandaigua Wine Company of New York. Since the name *Canandaigua* did not appear on any of its wines, and since it owned so large an array of historic labels, few among the public had ever heard of Canandaigua Wine Company, even as they bought its wines in increasing quantity.

Why was it, one may ask, that of all the big wineries of the Finger Lakes, only one— and that the least likely of them—survived into the twenty-first century? The simplest answer is that wines from the traditional native varieties, which were the main stock-in-trade of the Finger Lakes, could not sustain them. As the wine market grew, what was wanted was vinifera wine. The Finger Lakes wineries knew that they had to change: they were all experimenting with French hybrid vines from the 1950s and were cautiously growing vinifera in the 1960s, but this was all far too little too late. Widmer and Gold Seal both, as has been noted, established vineyards in California, but for whatever reasons they did not lead to successful commercial production. The Coca-Cola people converted Tay-

lor into a California brand, with some success. But back in New York, where the vineyards were still overwhelmingly planted to native varieties, the big wineries were fighting a rearguard action that was effectively over by the mid '80s. The Taylor winery in Hammondsport had been reducing its purchases of New York grapes since the '70s and by
the mid '80s had effectively stopped buying them. Canandaigua, on the other hand, had
made a successful adaptive move by buying the established Bisceglia Winery in California in 1974, so it could grow with the growing market as its Finger Lakes neighbors either did not or could not. Canandaigua also had Richards Wild Irish Rose, one of the few
large-selling wines still made from native grapes—though only in part from New York
State grapes.

As the dinosaurs of the Finger Lakes were shuffling off into oblivion, another, newer
breed was taking over: small wineries, family wineries, based on the French hybrids or
vinifera or both, selling to local or regional markets and capable of adapting more quickly
to changing conditions. Thus the economic development of the wine industry in New
York presented a perfect contrast: there was one huge operation—Canandaigua—grown
to gargantuan size by acquisition, and all around it were dozens and scores of small wineries, which, if they were to grow at all, would do so mostly by internal development.

The countermovement in New York owed a great deal in the beginning to the French
hybrids and to Philip Wagner. The earliest step in this new direction seems to have been
made by Everett Crosby, like so many pioneers an amateur without experience in grape
growing or winemaking. Crosby was a writer and director for radio working in New York
when he bought a property in Rockland County, on the western bank of the Hudson, thirty
miles upriver from Manhattan. Here he planted French hybrid vines obtained from Philip
Wagner's nursery in Maryland and bonded his High Tor Winery in 1952. Crosby persisted
for twenty years in making his two wines, called simply Rockland White and Rockland
Red, before selling out in 1972. By that time he was just beginning to have some company in the enterprise of small-scale, individual winemaking. Mark Miller, a commercial
illustrator, in 1957 had bought the Hudson River property, not far from Crosby's High
Tor, that was once the site of the experiments of Alexander Jackson Caywood, one of the
notable grape hybridizers from the heyday of the grape craze in mid-nineteenth-century
America.[15] Miller bonded his Benmarl winery in 1971, producing wine first from native
hybrid varieties and later from French hybrids. A few years earlier, in 1967, Walter Taylor began producing wines at his Bully Hill Vineyards in the Finger Lakes from French
hybrids: unusually, he was no amateur but a professional wine man, a son of one of the
Taylors who ran the Taylor Wine Company. Walter Taylor, too, had worked for the Taylor
winery, but he had ideas about how New York could do better and opened his own winery to demonstrate those ideas.[16]

Another, even sharper turn in the direction of New York winegrowing occurred in 1962
when Dr. Konstantin Frank, a Russian-born and Russian-trained German, who had managed large vineyard and winemaking enterprises in the Ukraine before the war, opened
a winery at Hammondsport, in the very center of the traditional New York wine indus-

try. Frank, who had been hired by Charles Fournier of Gold Seal in 1954 to carry out viti-cultural experiments, was a man with a mission. From his experience with cold-country viticulture in the Soviet Union he was convinced that vinifera grapes could be success-fully grown in such regions as New York. Undaunted by the 350-year history of failure to grow vinifera commercially (though not experimentally) in the East, he proceeded to ap-ply his methods and, in his own view at least, triumphantly succeeded. Frank would lis-ten to no cautions about the difficulty of growing vinifera, or to objections that the en-terprise was uneconomical, or to any other sort of warning, and he was outspokenly contemptuous toward all doubters and naysayers. He seems to have been vindicated: since Dr. Frank opened his Vinifera Wine Cellars, the spread of vinifera over some territories where it was previously thought impossible to grow has been, if not miraculous, certainly most impressive and exciting.[17]

What, then, had Frank done to bring about this startling change? It has already been mentioned that work with vinifera in New York and elsewhere in the East had never been abandoned.[18] But the scientists of the New York Agricultural Experiment Station could not be brought to say that growing vinifera was a commercial proposition. Some of the vinifera vines at Geneva went back to 1902, so it could hardly be said that vinifera would not grow at all; but whether it could be grown economically was the question. The main causes behind the general failure of vinifera were three: phylloxera, fungal diseases, and cold (and in the South, where cold was not a problem, Pierce's disease). The first two of these causes had not been understood by the hapless early settlers, but they could now be dealt with: grafting to native rootstocks controlled phylloxera; spraying with fungicides controlled mildew and black rot. The problem of severe winters remained. In too many years vinifera was seriously damaged by the winter cold; in some years the vines were killed to the ground. Even if it did not kill them, the cold might injure the vines in vari-ous ways and restrict production, and in the shortened growing season of the northern regions, the fruit—if there was fruit—might be difficult to ripen. How, then, could any-one responsibly advise the planting of vinifera when, though it might be kept alive, it would not yield a crop in some years, or even in most years, of each decade, and when the shocks and strains of successive winters might require extensive replanting of a vine-yard after only a short lifespan?

Frank's main idea was that properly selected rootstocks would contribute to solving the problem of cold resistance. Vines that had made the most vigorous vegetative growth, it was known, were the most vulnerable to cold because their abundant wood might not be fully mature before the first freeze. Vines that are fully mature—hardened off, as they say—will withstand severe cold. If a rootstock could be found that restricted vegetative growth and at the same time hastened the maturity of the vine, then that vine might be better prepared to stand up against the cold. Using *Vitis riparia* roots from the native stock in New York and some rootstock from the gardens of "a small convent in the Quebec province of Canada," Frank found candidates good enough to make a start with.[19] Find-ing the right rootstocks for the right varieties and for all possible variations in soil, exposure, and climate is of course a work of generations; still, a start was made. The earliest successes were with Riesling and Chardonnay.

The precise contribution of rootstocks to cold resistance still remains problematic and controversial, but the experimental work goes on.[20] There were other procedures, too, that would help the plants to cope against the cold, or that would diminish the effects of its inevitable damage. The old-fashioned, cumbersome, and expensive method was to bury the vines in winter, and more efficient ways of doing so were sought; one is by tilling a line of soil above the graft union of scion and rootstock. Vines could be trained to multiple trunks, so that if one were killed it could be removed without loss of production. Vines could also be allowed to keep some extra buds in the first pruning; if a sudden freeze should strike after growth had begun, some of the extra buds might survive to provide a crop, and if no freeze occurred, the extra buds could later be removed in a second pruning. The propagation of virus-free stocks, largely a postwar development, gave all vines, including vinifera, an improved chance of survival. And the careful selection of site was understood to be crucial: in a cold region, not all places are equally cold or exposed, as the growers in the Finger Lakes had long known.

The methods just described were enough to allow commercial planting of vinifera in the East to begin, and they have served to maintain and extend that planting in the succeeding half century. They are mostly palliative measures, not decisive solutions, and the ultimate role of vinifera in the economy of eastern winegrowing is not yet clearly determined; but it seems beyond doubt that there *is* a role.[21] So far, Riesling and Chardonnay, both relatively cold-hardy varieties, seem to have performed most reliably among the vinifera, though trials have been made and some successes achieved with many other varieties.[22] In discussing this subject it is helpful to keep in mind that *the East* is not really a very useful term. However it may be defined, "the vast area loosely called the East," in Philip Wagner's phrase, covers a lot of highly varied territory with a broad range of climates and conditions.[23] In some parts of this large space vinifera has been shown to be feasible; in others, the question remains open; in yet others, it seems clear that there is no place for vinifera.

The first commercial production of vinifera wine in the eastern United States was at Gold Seal in 1959, the firstfuits of the experimental work that Frank had carried out under the direction of Gold Seal's president, Charles Fournier.[24] Frank's own winery was established in 1962 and soon became an object of pilgrimage for would-be winegrowers from all over the eastern states. For the next generation, as small winemaking establishments were created everywhere east of the Rockies, it was usual to find that the founders— almost always people new to the business—owed a direct inspiration to Frank's example.[25] It was at Frank's home in 1967 that the American Wine Society was formed. In its original conception the society was a sort of declaration of American independence, intended to proclaim a new future for American wine now that the European vine had at last been made to grow: "the Society is not," so the constitution somewhat awkwardly read, "anti fine imported wines, but rather intends to emphasize that, by comparison,

FIGURE 46
Russian-born Dr. Kon-
stantin Frank, the un-
tiring worker in the cause
of vinifera in the eastern
United States. His Vini-
fera Wine Cellars in the
Finger Lakes region was
founded in 1962. (From
*American Wine Society
Journal* 17 [Fall 1985];
published with permis-
sion by the American
Wine Society.)

America can and is producing wines which are among the best in the world."[26] This was
the sort of thing that had already been heard in California, but it marked a distinctly new
consciousness in the eastern states. And it was thoroughly American in its readiness to
take promise as equivalent to performance.

The spread of new vineyards and new wineries in New York State reflected, in its own
way, the transformation that was going on in California. There was a new awareness of
wine, both domestic and European, and with it came a new imagination of possibilities:
things did not have to go on as they had but might be greatly changed and greatly improved. In the East, the success of the French hybrids and the promise of vinifera were
the special grounds of optimism. The changes were, at first, quite slow: High Tor, Benmarl,
Bully Hill, and Vinifera Wine Cellars were the only new wineries established over the
twenty-year span 1952–72. In 1973 another beginning was made at the eastern end of
Long Island, where Alexander Hargrave planted a small vineyard of vinifera. Yet evidently
something more was wanted if a more vigorous growth was to be achieved, and that something more was provided by the New York Farm Winery Act of 1976.

This legislation (inspired by the Pennsylvania Limited Winery Act of 1968, discussed below after note 35), by removing some of the obstructions and lightening some of the burdens that post-Repeal regulations had created in New York, encouraged many new beginnings.[27] The immediate pressure behind the Farm Winery Act was the fact that the big wineries of the Finger Lakes, relying more and more on California wine, had cut back their purchases of New York grapes, and the growers desperately needed new outlets. The new law greatly reduced the licensing fee for operating a winery, and in response the number of New York wineries jumped from thirty-nine to fifty-one in one year.[28] The first, tentative legislation was then extended to permit retail sales at the winery, to allow the opening of branch premises, and to allow tastings to be offered. Repeated efforts to break the hold of the retail liquor stores and to allow the sale of wine in grocery stores have so far failed in New York. Nevertheless, in the new climate of official support, wine-growing in New York has been greatly changed.

There were still plenty of problems. The stubborn fact was that most of the grapes in New York were Concords, and the wineries no longer wanted Concords. Grape growing is, after all, a very conservative business: one does not transform it at a stroke. So in 1985—a quarter century after the first, tentative experiments with better grape varieties began in earnest—there was still more Concord in New York than all other varieties put together: nearly 23,000 acres out of a total of 38,000.[29] The old-line native grapes—Catawba, Delaware, and the like—accounted for 7,500 acres. New hybrids, French and American (Aurora, Vidal, Seyval blanc, Cayuga, etc.), had 4,696 acres, and vinifera had 1,729, divided into 1,349 acres of white grapes and 380 of red, almost all of the latter being grown on Long Island. The figures might be disappointing or highly encouraging, depending on which end of things one looked at. But in the meantime, most grape growers were in trouble, caught between the old and the new.

To help themselves, the growers organized as the New York State Wine Grape Growers in 1981 and voted for a state marketing order to fund a program of research and promotion. The order was successfully challenged in the courts by the Taylor Wine Company, or rather by Taylor's owner, Coca-Cola Company, which saw no reason to pay an assessment that would go to help the New York industry in general. Taylor had already canceled contracts with growers and had cut the prices that it paid for grapes; now, by obstructing the marketing order, it had destroyed the growers' efforts to do something for themselves.[30] People in upstate New York were delighted to see Coca-Cola's retreat the next year, when it sold Taylor to Seagram's; but the hopes aroused by this change did not last long. Seagram's was quite unable to do anything about the rapidly shrinking market for the old-line New York State wines, and the situation only got worse. In 1984 Taylor, faced by a mounting inventory of unsold wines, announced that it would buy no more Concord grapes, and a few months later Gold Seal Winery was closed by its parent firm, Seagram's. New York's growers were, it was said, in desperate straits.

The state now acted to do what the growers had not been able to do through a marketing order: it created the New York State Wine and Grape Foundation with $2 million of public money to carry out research and promotion. The great hope of the wine industry in

New York has always been that someday, somehow, its wines would be sold in the state's grocery stores, and there was now a new push to bring about that much-to-be-desired condition—again without success. The creation of the Wine and Grape Foundation was a second-best result, but at least it was a thing that could be done.[31] The foundation has actively promoted New York State wines by all the means of advertising and public relations.

There are currently nearly 200 wineries operating in the state, scattered over its length from Lake Erie to the end of Long Island. The greatest concentration remains in the Finger Lakes region, the historic center of New York winemaking; it should be noted, however, that much activity has been shifted from the small Keuka and Canandaigua Lakes to the larger Seneca and Cayuga Lakes, since these larger bodies of water provide a more secure lake effect for the protection of vinifera. Seneca Lake has for that reason been called the Banana Belt of the Finger Lakes.[32] There has been some revival of winegrowing along the Hudson; even the Grape Belt along the Lake Erie shore south of Buffalo, where the Concord long reigned unchallenged, has seen a change. French hybrids and vinifera now begin to be seen there, though they are far from loosening the grip of Concord. At the opposite end of the state, the eastern tip of Long Island, vinifera is king in a wholly new winegrowing region. The original venture, Hargrave Winery, was soon followed by others.[33] It was found that red varieties—Cabernet Sauvignon and Merlot especially—did well on Long Island. New York State has always been thought of as white wine country, but Long Island has altered that notion, at least locally. Another surprise was the success of Long Island wines in the New York City market. The upstate winemakers have long lamented the indifference of their own metropolis to the wines of the state; Long Island reds changed that too. In the past few years the success of Long Island wines has attracted large capital, and a process of what may be called Napafication is under way. Wineries are changing hands at extravagant prices, and big investments have been made in glamourizing the winery properties as attractions for a large tourist traffic.[34] Altogether, things combined in the last quarter of the twentieth century to keep New York in its traditional place of leadership among the winegrowing states of the East, though now on quite a new basis.

THE PENNSYLVANIA STORY

The story of Pennsylvania from the '60s onward is very different from that of New York: instead of seeing an old industry dwindle and a new one grow up around it, Pennsylvania practically started from nothing. Wine was one of William Penn's original objects in establishing the colony, and there were many to follow him in repeated, futile efforts to grow vinifera grapes. After the eastern states turned to the native grapes, Pennsylvania had a few small enterprises that made wine, but nothing that amounted to much. The state seems effectively to have given up for a century or more, so that Prohibition found little to kill in Pennsylvania. After Repeal, as has already been observed, the state monopoly system adopted in Pennsylvania stultified any effort toward winegrowing that might have been entertained. At last, however, the new interest in wine that began to stir throughout the country in the 1960s was felt in Pennsylvania.

Pennsylvania already had vineyards in considerable measure; it produced nearly 50,000 tons of grapes in 1965, putting it fourth after California, New York, and Michigan. Almost all of the Pennsylvania vineyards were to be found in the northwestern corner of the state beside Lake Erie, a part of the historic Lake Erie Grape Belt running along the Ohio, Pennsylvania, and New York lakeshores. Practically speaking, all of Pennsylvania's grapes were Concords, grown not for wine but for juice and jellies. The grape-juice market was a narrow dependence, however, and some growers began to think that they might do better with wine grapes instead. When a bumper crop of Concords loomed in 1965, their plans for diversification became serious. They were joined by many of Pennsylvania's orchardists, whose own business was precarious and threatened from various directions. In this climate the state officials were prepared to listen to new proposals, even though they were hampered by the existence of the state liquor store system, a monopoly interest resistant to change.

In 1966 the state commissioned a ten-year feasibility study of the prospects for growing wine grapes in Pennsylvania, to be carried out at the agricultural experiment station operated by Pennsylvania State University in Erie County, in the Grape Belt.[35] In that year, too, the First Pennsylvania Wine Industry Conference was held on the theme of "What It Will Take to Develop This Industry," a sign that people were eager to move in this matter. There was no intention to wait ten years for results. Instead, in response to a campaign led by grape growers in Erie County, the state legislature passed the Limited Winery Act in 1968, which put the chances for winemaking in Pennsylvania on a brand new footing. Under the act, a winery might produce up to 50,000 gallons of wine annually—though as a protectionist measure, the wine had to be made entirely from Pennsylvania grapes. As its key provision, the act allowed a winery to sell its products directly to individuals and to restaurants rather than through the state stores; it might sell through the state stores, too, but it was not limited to that form of distribution. And it might offer wine tastings to its retail customers at the winery.

In the next year, 1969, two wineries started business: Presque Isle Wine Cellars and Penn Shore Vineyards, both, predictably, in Erie County, where grapes had long been grown and where there was already some familiarity with the old native American varieties and the newer French hybrids. These first responses to the Limited Winery Act were at opposite ends of the scale. At Presque Isle, Douglas Moorhead, who had headed the campaign to secure the act, was already established as a supplier of grapes, juice, and equipment for home winemakers and was interested in making only a fairly small quantity of superior varietal wine. Penn Shore was a wholly new business that wanted to make the largest possible quantity of wine from the grapes of the growers who backed it. It produced the legal limit of 50,000 gallons in its first year and succeeded in having the limit raised to 100,000 gallons in 1971. One should mention that even before the enabling act of 1968 there had been a lone pioneer in modern Pennsylvania winemaking. This was Melvin Gordon of

Birchrunville, in the southeastern part of the state, who bravely opened Conestoga Vineyards in 1963 and sold his small production through the state store system.

From its starting point in 1968, the growth of winemaking in Pennsylvania has been unspectacular but steady. Small vineyards have been planted, not just in Erie County but notably in the south-central and southeastern sections of the state, including the Pennsylvania Dutch country. The vines chosen are both such hybrids as Chancellor, Chelois, Vidal, and Seyval and a selection of vinifera varieties, more or less on the pattern of all the other eastern regions (with the exception of the all-vinifera region of Long Island). As Lucie Morton has observed, every new vineyard and winery in the East is, in effect, an independent research station in these early times of renewed winegrowing.[36] In its combination of enthusiasm, enterprise, and uncertainty, the situation resembles the days of agricultural pioneering in the nineteenth century and earlier, when the possibilities of a newly settled land were unproved and every sort of crop was tried in every sort of place. In such a situation, some failures are certain. But when a success is achieved, however small and tentative, it is invaluable in keeping alive the sense of possibility: the idea is everything, for without that nothing will be ventured.

By the end of the 1970s, only a decade after the new basis for winegrowing had been established in Pennsylvania, the state had two dozen wineries with a combined storage capacity of about 2 million gallons of wine. It had not yet found out what it might do best, nor could it be expected to. But it had acquired, relatively speaking, an enormous experience. That is a point that needs to be made generally about the new winegrowing enterprises in the states outside California. In absolute terms, the numbers are still small—the number of wineries, the size of the vineyards, the volume and variety of wines produced. But relative to the conditions when the big change began in the decade of the '60s, the change in the East is enormously greater than that in California, great as that has been. The citizens of Pennsylvania in 1960 lived in a state in which wine was merely one of the suspect fluids dispensed through cheerless state stores under the authority of the Pennsylvania Liquor Control Board, created in the wake of Repeal as a protection against the "return of the saloon," as the stock phrase had it. Grapes, they might perhaps know, were grown in that corner of the state farthest from the centers of population, but those grapes had nothing to do with wine. Most likely they had never seen a vineyard; certainly they had never heard of a Pennsylvania wine. There was no winery in the state, and no wine had been made there within living memory. By 1980, it was different: the state had blessed the development of a wine industry; the state university was engaged in viticultural experiment, and held an annual wine conference; new vineyards dotted the landscape in small but growing numbers; and new wineries sold their wines at the cellar door as well as in the state stores. Pennsylvania wine regularly figured on the wine lists of Pennsylvania restaurants. One enterprising journalist had even ventured to produce the *Pennsylvania Grape Letter* beginning in 1974 and had found an interested audience.[37] These developments were, as has been said, fairly small things in themselves, but relatively, they were immense.

Pennsylvania, in common with other eastern states, benefited from the new grape varieties now available, from new cultivation methods, and from new technology in the winery; but the essential step that enabled those things to be exploited was the passage of the Limited Winery Act of 1968. The act gave the idea to other states that they might do something for winegrowing too, and under one name or another comparable acts have been passed in many states: Indiana in 1971, Mississippi and New York in 1976, Connecticut in 1978, Alabama and Florida in 1979, Virginia in 1980, New Jersey and West Virginia in 1981, Georgia and Kansas in 1983. One's first response to this list might well be, So what? None of the states in question, with the large exception of New York and the smaller one of Virginia, has anything but a very local and limited wine industry. The importance of this development, however, lies more in the promise than in the actuality: it shows that winegrowing can be promoted as a valuable activity, worthy of encouragement by public authority, after long decades of neglect, repression, and obstruction. It is true that Mississippi, for example, remains a state with only one tiny winery and a per capita consumption of wine that puts it near or at the bottom of the list of states. But until 1966 Mississippi lay under statewide prohibition; it was, in fact, the last state to endure this condition. Just ten years after the demise of prohibition, the Native Wine Act was passed in Mississippi. Even before that, in 1972, Mississippi State University began a program of enological and viticultural research. The state that had been stubbornly Dry longer than any other was now giving official state support to vineyards and wineries.[38] The local response to such a startling turnaround was a dazed "Who'd believe it?"[39] The passage of the Mississippi act—and of the comparable acts in other states, most of them without any vital tradition of winegrowing or wine drinking—certainly testifies to a striking change of thought.

Leon Adams was the great propagandist and activist behind what has been loosely called the farm winery program. He was active in season and out in promoting the idea that "agriculture"—that is to say, winegrowing—could win over legislatures against the entrenched interests of state liquor commissions, liquor wholesalers, and the like; and he seems to have been right. The legislative means employed of course differed from state to state, according to differing conditions. In Pennsylvania the necessary legislation was to exempt wine from the state liquor monopoly; in Mississippi it was to reduce the license fees and the taxes on state-produced wine. It may be said that, allowing for differences from state to state, the usual plan was to reduce license fees to reasonable levels, allow winegrowers to sell directly at both wholesale and retail, permit wineries to offer free tastings, and give them the right to "stay open on Sunday because that is the day most people like to go on wine tours."[40] Official support might also entail a tax advantage for the state's own wines over those from other states. This practice was challenged in the courts, however, and a decision by the Supreme Court in 1984 declared it unconstitutional as a violation of the commerce clause.[41]

That special privileges seem to be needed in order to foster the growth of small wineries may suggest that they are, after all, only exotic plants, unable to survive without special care. But on reflection this view appears to be mistaken. The need for favorable special legislation is created only by the fact that the wine industry has suffered for years under hostile special legislation restricting what it can do and how it can do it: the power of life and death has been in the hands of the regulators, and only when that power is in some measure curbed can there be any confident growth. The sequence of farm winery laws that began in the 1960s is a beginning toward loosening a repressive regulatory power and is one of the most positive signs of changing attitudes.

One should keep in mind, too, that all such laws are still quite as restrictive as they are enabling. What the wineries would like to do is to sell their produce by the most direct means, but that simple end is not easily attained under the burdensome, arbitrary, and complex tangle of regulations that has grown up in the anarchy of states' rights since Repeal: the various farm winery acts often perpetuate such burdens or impose new ones of their own. Donating wine to charitable events is forbidden in some states; tasting wines at the winery is not allowed in others; direct sales from wineries to restaurants is sometimes not allowed. Many of the farm winery laws require that the state's wineries make their wine only from grapes grown in the state: Kansas wine, for example, must not come from Missouri grapes. Such a law has long been in force in California, but then California has more than enough grapes to supply all of its wineries. The case is quite different in most other states, so that such a rule is always having to be bent or adjusted when the crop is insufficient. In Connecticut the law requires that the winery itself must grow at least 51 percent of its grapes. Most of the farm winery laws strictly limit the amount of wine that may be produced: 100,000 gallons is the usual measure, and that must be of table wine only. And there are other restrictions: on the number of outlets permitted, for example, or on the hours of operation. New Jersey, in order to guarantee that a winery really *is* a winery, requires that it stand on at least three acres of ground having at least 1,200 vines. But perhaps the permissions rather than the restrictions are the most important things about farm winery legislation at this stage of history: such legislation has at least allowed a beginning where none was practicable before. More than 450 new wineries opened in the United States between 1978 and 1985, and much of the power behind that extraordinary growth certainly came from farm winery legislation.

NEW ENGLAND AND NEW JERSEY

The models of New York and Pennsylvania pretty much describe the forms that developed in the other states of "the East"—all that territory from the eastern slopes of the Rockies to the Atlantic. Either (as in New York) an established industry was transformed into something very different from what it had been, or (as in Pennsylvania) new enterprises grew up where none had been before. That last statement needs to be modified a bit, since there is *no* state without its history of winemaking, however tentative, experimental, and limited. Thus one can speak of historical winegrowing in Massachusetts, or Kentucky, or Kansas because if one looks closely at the record, *some* attempt at winegrowing, no matter where, may always be found. If I do not refer to the early trials in discussing some particular state, it is because we can take for granted that there *were* early trials in every state. But one must also keep in mind that only a few of the early efforts had even a limited success: most were isolated historical episodes without any practical consequences. Many of the states (both eastern and western) that now grow grapes and produce some wine make exaggerated—not to say simply false—claims for the historical continuity of the work. In fact, established winegrowing could have been found only in New York, Ohio, Michigan, Missouri, and, marginally, New Jersey in the northern tier of states. In the South, muscadine and fruit wines were made in substantial quantities in North and South Carolina and in Georgia. Arkansas had a small but persistent industry. And that, in effect, was it.

Massachusetts was at one time the great fountain of new grape varieties in this country, most of them derived from the species *Vitis labrusca,* the grape that the Pilgrims, the Puritans, and all the other New Englanders would have known. Some of the earliest experiments in breeding grapes in this country were carried out in Salem by John Fisk Allen and then by E. R. Rogers before the Civil War. Boston was the home of the influential Massachusetts Horticultural Society, whose exhibitions and publications were guides to grape growers all over the country; it was at an exhibition of the society in 1854 that the Concord grape was first put forward to the world. And as Charles Sullivan has shown, the Zinfandel grape was first known in this country in Massachusetts, where it was grown by fashionable amateurs who could afford to maintain greenhouses.[42] Massachusetts had never had a wine industry, however; nor has any other part of New England.

Generally speaking, the islands and coastal regions of southern New England have milder winter weather than the inland regions, and it was on an island that the new beginning was made. This was at West Tisbury, on the island of Martha's Vineyard, where the Chicama Vineyard opened in 1971 by the Mathiesen family as Massachusetts bonded winery number 1. The vineyards were of vinifera, planted with the advice of Dr. Frank, and their produce was supplemented with grapes from California. Chicama Vineyards is still operating more than thirty years after its founding, an unusual longevity among the small, pioneering wineries of the East. Something of the labor and the anxieties entailed is suggested by this account of the defensive measures required even in a region of relatively favorable climate: "Chicama vines are protected by sprinklers from frost, from birds by electronic bird-distress calls every thirty seconds, and from deer by fences eight feet high."[43] Chicama is the first Massachusetts winery; the biggest is Westport Rivers Vineyard and Winery at Westport, on the southern coast. Here the Russell family, beginning in 1982, has planted seventy-eight acres of vinifera and now makes estate-grown wines, including *méthode champenoise* sparkling wines.

Both Chicama and Westport Rivers conform to the pattern so familiar among new wineries in having been founded by people who came to winegrowing from wholly unrelated activities. George Mathiesen was a television executive; Robert Russell was a metallurgical engineer. Unusually, however, Mrs. Russell is the daughter of a man who owned an old Finger Lakes winery, Germania Cellars of Hammondsport, acquired by Great Western in 1941.

Massachusetts's Limited Winery Act of 1976 very sensibly does not limit the proportion of grapes from out of state that may be used by Massachusetts wineries. Several of the Massachusetts wineries, however, do without grapes altogether; instead, they make fruit and berry wines from apples, blueberries, and especially cranberries.

The softening effect of bodies of water on winter is felt everywhere in Rhode Island, the Ocean State. Three of the state's five currently operating wineries are in fact on islands; all of them grow vinifera, with some French hybrids as well. The big enterprise, founded in 1975, is Sakonnet Vineyards at Little Compton, which has been able to develop sales outside the state and so help to make the idea of Rhode Island wine known. In Connecticut, the last in this survey of southern New England states, wineries are scattered both along the shores of Long Island Sound and inland. The Connecticut legislature passed a farm winery bill in 1978, when the state had no operating winery—a good indication of the effect that propaganda for such legislation was beginning to have. The first of the new Connecticut wineries, Haight Vineyard at Litchfield, was planted in 1975 with a mix of vinifera and hybrid vines, and its first crush was in 1978. Since then sixteen more wineries have been founded, some eleven of which were still going at the turn of the century. Some are in the western part of the state, where an American viticultural area (AVA) called Western Connecticut Highlands was established in 1988: in this region hybrid vines are grown almost exclusively. The other Connecticut AVA, Southeastern New England (established 1984), is shared with Massachusetts and Rhode Island: here, near the shores of Long Island Sound, it is possible to grow vinifera. Two of the more expansive enterprises among Connecticut wineries—Crosswoods Vineyards (1984) and Hamlet Hill (1980)—were unable to survive, in part because of the uncertainties of the grape supply derived from vinifera. The people who have founded the new wineries show the usual mix of unrelated origins: in 1988 they included "a specialist in international law, a financier, a textile manufacturer, a tool and die maker, a former dairy farmer, a retired chef, an advertising executive, a businessman, a computer expert, and the Board Chairman of a noted jewelry and gift store [Tiffany and Company]."[44]

The state seems to have been more than usually encouraging toward Connecticut's small wine industry. The terms of the original farm winery bill were modified in 1987 to permit unlimited production of wine from Connecticut grapes—a permission more theoretical than real considering the slender supply of such grapes available to Connecticut winemakers. At the same time an official body called the Farm Wine Development Council was created to work with the Department of Agriculture in promoting Connecticut wine. In 2001 the state appropriated $4 million to be used for low-interest loans to people who would plant vineyards.[45] There were then only about 350 acres of vineyard in the state, a quarter century after the farm winery legislation had been passed; the Connecticut wineries, small though they were, were still heavily dependent on grapes from neighboring states, particularly New York.

New Jersey, to complete this circuit of eastern vineyards, is an old region rather than a new one. A number of high spots on the historical calendar belong to New Jersey, going back to late colonial days, when Edward Antill of Raritan Landing won the contest sponsored by the Royal Society of Arts for the largest vineyard north of the Delaware River. Antill did not manage to produce any wine, but he left his "Essay on the Cultivation of the Vine," published in 1771, one of the very earliest American contributions to the literature of wine. In the nineteenth century, New Jersey made some contradictory contributions: on the one hand, it is where the excellent native hybrid the Delaware grape was discovered, on the banks of the Delaware River in Hunterdon County; on the other, it is where Dr. Thomas Welch first developed pasteurized grape juice as a substitute for wine. In the latter half of the nineteenth century a fairly substantial wine industry developed there, based on a variety of native hybrids, and centered on the south Jersey town of Egg Harbor City.

Black rot and other diseases severely damaged the New Jersey wine trade, but a number of wineries persisted down to Prohibition and a few managed to survive it: H. T. Dewey, Herman Kluxen, Miele, Renault, Schuster, Tomasello. By the postwar era, however, very little remained and that little was badly decayed. The Dewey winery (1857) closed in 1952; Herman Kluxen (1865) went out of business in 1974. In 1977 there were only 351 acres of vines in the state. Nor was there any encouragement to take up winemaking. On the contrary, the state at the time of Repeal had decided to limit so-called plenary winery licenses to one per million inhabitants; that meant only seven such licenses for New Jersey's 7-million-plus inhabitants. With a plenary license one could use grapes from out of state for unlimited production and maintain multiple retail outlets. Alternatively, one could secure a limited license permitting production of up to 5,000 gallons a year exclusively from New Jersey grapes; no one ever applied for such a license.[46]

As more and more interested amateurs planted vineyards in New Jersey and more and more home winemakers developed their skills and ambitions, pressure to adjust the laws began to build up. The first new winery in New Jersey in many years, the Tewkesbury Winery, was bonded in 1979, but that came about because the owners had been able to buy a plenary license from an established winery that was going out of business. Others who hoped to enter the business could hardly hope to follow that example. Help came in 1981, when the state passed a farm winery bill on the model already familiar in many other states: low license fees, production of up to 50,000 gallons, tasting and retail sales allowed. New Jersey wine was also allowed a preferential tax rate.

In this new climate, a slow but fairly steady growth began. There were fifteen wineries operating in 1988, eighteen at the end of the century; some half-dozen or so other small wineries had come and gone in that time. Much of the activity was in a region not formerly exploited for wine, the Delaware Valley in northwestern New Jersey. Other wineries were in the sandy southern half of the state, where grapes had long been grown. Two AVAs have been recognized: one, the Central Delaware Valley, is shared with Pennsylvania; the other, Warren Hills, is a subregion within the larger Central Delaware Valley.

There was a determined effort to grow vinifera at first, but weather and prudence soon led to reliance on the French hybrids.[47] By 2003 there were nearly a thousand acres of vineyard, supporting twenty-two bonded wineries. The big (by New Jersey standards) wineries remained the old plenary ones, Renault and Tomasello; none of the new farm wineries produced more than 9,000 cases annually, and only one of them made that much. The wineries are organized as the Garden State Winegrowers Association and have been assisted in promotional work since 1985 by the New Jersey Wine Industry Advisory Council, funded by part of the state tax on wine sales.

OHIO, MICHIGAN, AND MISSOURI

Allowing for the many local differences, the story in these three states over the past generation is a version of the New York model. There was an established wine industry in each state, though only in Michigan did it seem to have much economic life.

As has been said earlier, by 1960 the Ohio industry seemed to be headed for certain extinction.[48] Since so many voices in the state were prophesying the end, it was a deliberate act of defiance when the Ohio Agricultural Research and Development Center (OARDC) set up a new experimental vineyard on the banks of the Ohio River, where winegrowing had been established at the beginning of the nineteenth century and from which it had long since been driven by the onslaught of pests and diseases. No vineyards had been seen in the southern part of the state for nearly a century. Now the state, in a deliberate effort to revive the industry, was planting a range of varieties, with special emphasis on the French hybrids.[49] This first step was soon followed by others. The OARDC set up an experimental winery at its headquarters in Wooster and in 1963 hired a viticulturist to conduct research and extension work; a little later, it added an enologist as well. Beginning in 1965 the OARDC, to make its vine trials in the Ohio valley more comprehensive, set up a series of one-acre experimental vineyards dotted over a three-hundred-mile strip along the river.[50] The promise of this work was such that in 1967 a new winery was opened in the Ohio River country of the state, the first new venture in many years: Tarula Farms in Clarksville, growing Niagara, Catawba, and a selection of French hybrids.

The official view in Ohio was that its viticultural future lay in the Ohio River valley, along the southern border of the state. That was why the experimental work was almost all carried out there, and that was why the official report of the state Department of Development recommended that the state promote the southern region rather than the small but established vineyard region along the Lake Erie shore. The northern Grape Belt, it was thought, would soon be completely taken over by urban and industrial development.[51] It has not so far worked out that way. The first small flurry of new wineries was in the south, obviously in response to OARDC's experimental work. That first response has not been sustained, and there are still more wineries in the central and northern sections of the state than in the south. And the next notable step in the re-creation of Ohio wine was taken in the old Concord grape territory of the far northeast.

Arnulf Esterer, an industrial engineer living in Ashtabula, was so interested in Konstantin Frank's experiments with growing vinifera in New York that he volunteered to work in a couple of Frank's vintage seasons. There, as Leon Adams puts it, Esterer "learned Frank's secrets of growing Vinifera in the East."[52] In 1968 Esterer planted nine acres of vinifera near Conneaut, and to make a long story short, he has successfully cultivated them (and some French hybrids) in the more than thirty years since. His Markko Vineyard is a source of highly regarded Cabernet Sauvignon, Chardonnay, and Riesling wines. Elsewhere in Ohio, not many have ventured to commit themselves to vinifera, though many have experimented with it. Henry Sonneman, for years the owner of Ohio's largest winery, Meier's Wine Cellars of Silverton, had made trials of vinifera on his Isle St. George vineyards from the early '60s. The OARDC, yielding to the persuasions of the believers, planted vinifera in the Ripley experimental vineyard in 1969; most were killed in the winter of 1972. Ohio wineries still depend on the old native varieties, especially the Catawba, and on the French hybrids—Vignoles, Vidal, Baco, and the like—for their wines. But vinifera persists, too, in fairly small plantings in carefully selected sites, and it seems certain to become of increasing importance.

The Ohio Wine Producers Association was formed in 1975 to represent the wine trade to the public. The state itself has been distinctly encouraging: the Ohio Grape Industries Program was created in 1979 to support research and promotion for the benefit of Ohio wine; in 1982 the legislature laid a tax on all sales of wine in the state to pay for the program.[53] The number of wineries in Ohio, in steady and rapid decline for many years, has been slowly growing since the 1970s.[54] So too has the vineyard acreage, which had climbed over 2,000 acres by the turn of the century. Much of that is still in Concords, but there is no doubt that the basis of Ohio wine is changing, and there is a far better understanding of what may be achieved than was true before.

Ohio was emphatically the home of the small winery. Yet it was also home to one large operation, Meier's Wine Cellars, which had since Repeal grown very large indeed. By 1965 Meier's had a storage capacity of 1.2 million gallons, and it distributed its wines over a large territory. The wines were what the market was then accustomed to: a complete line of labrusca-based wines (Catawba was the favored variety), bolstered by tank-car wine and fortifying brandy from California.[55] After the death in 1974 of Henry Sonneman, who had built the modest Meier's Grape Juice Company into the big winery, Meier's was bought by the Paramount Distilling firm of Cleveland, whose president, Robert Gottesman, surprisingly took a real interest in the wine business.[56] Under Gottesman, Meier's acquired three more of Ohio's older wineries—Mantey, Lonz, and Mon Ami—all in the Sandusky region. Mantey was later converted into a central processing center for the various Meier's properties under the name of Firelands Winery, and Gottesman made an effort to improve the line with some vinifera and French hybrid wines from the company's vineyards on North Bass Island.[57] The viticultural basis of the firm's wines, however, was not much changed.

In sharp contrast to the Meier's operation, most of Ohio's new wineries were small,

FIGURE 47
Ohio was once home
to many local wineries
and is so once again:
signpost in the Geneva
region of northeastern
Ohio. (Author's
collection.)

processing the yield from a few acres and selling the wine locally. This was the pattern long established in the state. Steuk Winery, for example, which went back to 1855, made a selection of native American wines from a mere four and a half acres of vines. What was different now was the influx of a new breed of winemakers, who—as in California and elsewhere—were not bred up to winemaking. They were engineers, doctors, advertising men, teachers, or computer technicians who had been attracted by the new sense of possibility that spread widely from the '60s onward. The French hybrid grapes were also new, though Ohio winemakers showed as well a leaning toward the out-of-the-way and oddball variety: one winery (Valley Vineyards) offered a wine from the table-grape variety developed in Missouri called Blue Eye; another (Steuk) made wine from a variety otherwise unknown to winemaking, Black Pearl, an Ohio hybrid from the nineteenth century.[58] One of the most successful of the new generation of Ohio wineries is Chalet Debonne, east of Cleveland, combining old and new. Starting from a basis of the old native grapes—Concord and Niagara—it has gradually increased the proportion of French hybrid and vinifera wines in a production that is now among Ohio's largest.

Michigan, despite its unfortunate history after Repeal, has in recent years made real progress.[59] The pattern of change resembles New York's: a few new, small wineries run by enthusiasts with new ideas opened up possibilities that the established wineries had not grasped or were not able to act on. The change began in 1971 when the Tabor Hill winery opened in the grape growing region of southwestern Michigan; until that moment, the few, large Michigan wineries had contented themselves with selling lightly fortified wines made almost exclusively from Concord grapes.[60] The backers of Tabor Hill planted vinifera and French hybrids, with mixed results (the vinifera plantings suffered severely in the winter of 1971) but with enough success to keep operating and to encourage others to enter the work.[61] A new region was exploited starting in 1974, when Chateau Grand Traverse was founded on Grand Traverse Bay, in northwestern Michigan. This was long-established fruit country, famous for its cherries; although it lies on the forty-fifth parallel, at the same latitude as Halifax, Nova Scotia, the region benefits from the regulating effects of the water in Grand Traverse Bay and Lake Michigan. There are now fourteen wineries around the bay, with a good reputation especially for white wines from Riesling, Chardonnay, Pinot gris, and other varieties. In the state generally the move away from the bad old days is most obviously shown by the decline in the proportion of Concord grapes used to make Michigan wine: in 1960 it was about 98 percent, but by 1980 it had declined to 40 percent.[62]

Michigan winemaking has been assisted by a research program at Michigan State University that began under the direction of Professor Stanley Howell just as the first new wineries were being established, about 1970. The program maintains several experimental vineyards around the state, and since 1972 a winery called Spartan Cellars at the campus in East Lansing. The main object of research is stated quite simply in one of the official brochures: "Because of the state's short growing season, harsh winters and spring frosts, research on cold hardiness of juice and wine grape cultivars is critical."[63] Since then several organizations and a series of legislative acts have helped to support the industry: the Michigan Grape Society (1978) is an industry group on the model of the Wine Institute; the Michigan Grape and Wine Industry Council (1985), a state agency, was created to carry out promotion with a budget financed by state licensing fees. The prominence of Michigan as a summer resort and tourist attraction for the whole of the Midwest has also been a boost to the winemakers, since they can count on large crowds of summer people for whom a winery is a novel attraction and wine an interestingly exotic commodity.

The gradual reemergence of a winegrowing industry in Missouri is a good illustration of the many and complex interests at work. Missouri is in some ways the most interesting and challenging of the central states—interesting because of its considerable historical contribution to the story of wine in America, and challenging because it combines what seem to be favorable conditions for the grape with particularly severe conditions. The historical contribution has to do mostly with the work done by German immigrants concentrated around St. Louis and in settlements upriver from St. Louis along the Missouri River, especially at Hermann.[64] The Missouri Germans made contributions to the scientific, practical, commercial, and promotional history of wine in this country beyond those of any other group. And their contribution was not limited to the United States. Missouri, thanks to the knowledge and experience of the Missouri Germans, supplied many of the native rootstocks that saved the vineyards of Europe (and America) after the phylloxera devastation.

Both the challenge and the opportunity of winegrowing in Missouri arise from its central position in the continental United States and from its great variety of climates and sites. The Missouri River crosses the state from west to east; the whole of the eastern boundary is formed by the Mississippi, so the state abounds in bluffs and coves and other riverine features. The topography varies from the Ozark Mountains in the south to the prairies of the north and west; there are limestone regions, corn regions, and great forests of hardwoods (Missouri oak is important in the production of American wine barrels). Missouri touches eight other states and seems to absorb a little of the varying characters of each—southwestern, prairie, southeastern. The state knows the extremes of continental climate: freezing winters and broiling summers with great humidity. It has an abundant supply of the diseases and pests from which the grape suffers in America: black rot, downy mildew, powdery mildew, dead arm, crown gall, grape berry moth, grape flea beetle, root borer, and of course phylloxera are all at home here. At the same time there are sites scattered about the state with privileged microclimates—sheltered, tempered by water against extremes, with prolonged ripening seasons, good exposure, and satisfactory soils. In some states—say, North Dakota or Wyoming—it is obvious that viticulture will never be possible except at the cost of wholly uneconomical care and expense; but in Missouri one is tempted to think that the grape is naturally at home. It is, and it isn't. That is the challenge. In this regard it is, perhaps, only exemplary of the country at large; but Missouri brings all these things into clear focus.

Prohibition, for whatever reason, seems to have hit the Missouri wine industry so hard that it was a long time getting back on its feet.[65] Grape growing continued but was almost wholly dependent on Concords for the grape-juice trade. By the 1960s this business was in steady decline; growers produced an average of approximately 3,000 tons of Missouri grapes a year, but only by increasing yields from a shrinking number of vineyard acres. A sign of the times was the closing of the American Wine Company, the only remaining winery of any size in Missouri, in 1954. The company's famous Cook's Imperial Champagne, produced since 1861 in St. Louis cellars, would now come from a big industrial facility in Fresno, California.

About the same time, though, the countermovement began. In 1965 a Missouri farmer who grew a few acres of grapes, James Held, took the bold step of buying the long-derelict Stone Hill Winery in Hermann; since Prohibition its cellars had been devoted to mushroom culture. With the winery building came a few old vines of Norton grapes, the variety on which the reputation of Hermann had anciently been established.[66] With these vestiges Held began his work. He was joined in 1968 by Lucian Dressel, who restored and reopened Mount Pleasant, the old Muench winery at Augusta. Both of these enterprises were historic renewals, bringing long-neglected wineries back to life, and it probably helped that despite Missouri's almost complete failure to revive after Prohibition, there were still some visible vestiges of the old German wine industry. It had not quite disappeared, and it had not quite been forgotten.[67] But there were precious few wine grapes in Missouri at the time; Held had some native American hybrids (Catawba, Niagara, and a scant few Nortons), while Dressel had planted French hybrids, something new to Missouri. This small renewed beginning, coinciding with the rising interest in table wine that now extended nationwide, was enough to change the direction of winegrowing in Missouri over the next decade. The Concord was to remain the dominant grape for some time, but it was clearly in decline. By the middle of the '70s, wine grapes nearly equaled the acreage of Concord, and a further blow was dealt to the Concord when the Welch Grape Juice people closed their Springdale, Arkansas, plant in 1978. This had been almost the entire market for the Concord crop in Missouri and neighboring Arkansas, and although Welch continued to accept grapes at Springdale, that was not going to go on indefinitely.[68]

The acreage of wine grapes in Missouri did not grow rapidly, but it did grow: there were 760 acres in 1976, 1,100 in 1991, and a few more than that by 2003.[69] Vinifera was found to be too chancy to be commercially practical; Catawba was the most widely planted among the native grapes, but the special pride of Missouri vineyards was the Norton or, as it might be called, the Cynthiana, Missouri law allowing winemakers to use either name.[70] Norton makes that rare thing: a good, well-colored, full-bodied, nonfoxy red wine from a native grape. Indeed, Norton-Cynthiana may be said to be the only native that can do so. A wide selection of French hybrids has been tried in Missouri, and these, together with Norton, dominate the vineyards there.

In the decade after Held and Dressel had given the first push, a number of others ventured: fourteen small wineries came into existence in the '70s, and by the end of that decade the state was prepared to enter into the action. The university had already begun studies of grape production in Missouri; in 1978, the governor appointed a task force to study the prospects of the business. Its optimistic report in 1979 held that Missouri's acreage of wine grapes—French hybrids were the recommended varieties—could be doubled by 1985 and that the state should create an advisory board to assist promotion.

The year 1980 was a watershed. The legislature raised the limits for a domestic winery (one using Missouri fruit) from 75,000 to 500,000 gallons, well beyond what the most sanguine projector could demand; the Missouri Wine Advisory Board was formed, and a state enologist, working out of the University of Missouri, was hired.[71] In the same year, the small region around Augusta, on the Missouri River, then home to just two wineries, was declared the first AVA in the federal authorities' new scheme of appellations.[72] The distinction was wholly nominal, but it seems to have done much for the morale of Missouri winegrowers. Far more substantial was the measure passed by the legislature in 1983 laying a special tax of 4 cents a gallon on all wine sold in Missouri to fund a grape and wine program under the state Department of Agriculture.[73] The program is devoted in part to extension work, in part to research, and in part to promotion. The promotional part of it is of course the most obvious, and it is no doubt the case that the legislature's interest in the wine industry had more to do with the idea of attracting tourism than with anything else. The newspapers of the state joined in the game to promote the new Missouri wineries as tourist destinations, and Missouri wineries have probably received—and have responded to—more ballyhoo than those of any other central state. There has been, in consequence, much exploitation of a pseudo-German style in the public behavior of the wineries; tourists are invited to visit the "Rhineland of Missouri" along the "Weinstrasse" for a "Wurstfest" or a "Kristkindl Markt," where the wines on offer might include a "Hermannsberger." Whatever one may think of such kitsch, the Grape and Wine Program has certainly given a public standing to winegrowing in Missouri such as it had never had before.

It has now been forty years since the renewal of Missouri winegrowing in 1965. As in other states, the hazards have been great: some forty-seven bonded wineries are now operating in Missouri, but at least another twenty-five have come and gone since 1965. The giant of the Missouri industry is Stone Hill Wine Company, producing 90,000 cases annually; after that the scale drops quickly, through the 25,000 cases produced at Augusta Winery to the 400 cases coming from La Dolce Vita Vineyard and Winery at Washington, Missouri. The annual production of wine in Missouri is currently about half a million gallons.[74]

THE THREE-I LEAGUE: INDIANA, ILLINOIS, AND IOWA

These three states—among the richest agricultural territories in the entire United States, abounding in corn and beans and pork and dairy products—are not very likely sites of viticulture. The bare-bones Protestant culture seems hostile to it, and the climate certainly is. The wish to grow wine, however, may prevail even against such conditions; if it does, it will certainly be slow work.

Indiana fits the Pennsylvania model very closely, but at the same time shows the difference between the prospects of winegrowing in the Midwest and those in the East. Like Pennsylvania, Indiana had grown grapes and made wine in the days of early settlement: indeed, there is reason to think that the very first successful commercial winemaking in the United States went on in Indiana.[75] That effort had not continued, however, and Indiana had long ceased to be thought of as a place where wine might be made. Nevertheless, the new imagination of possibility created by the wine boom set some enthusiasts in action. William Oliver, a professor of law at Indiana University, saw an opportunity in the Pennsylvania Limited Winery Act of 1968. He drafted a similar bill to enable farm winegrowing in Indiana and succeeded in having it passed by the legislature in 1971 as the Indiana Small Winery Act. It provided that wineries, for an annual license fee of $250, could produce up to 50,000 gallons of table wine from Indiana fruit and could sell it at retail.[76]

Indiana now had some fostering legislation, but it had no grapes to speak of, nor any knowledge of what to grow, where to grow it, or how to grow it. There were, even so, people prepared to venture. Treaty Line Wine Cellars opened in Brownsville, near the Ohio border, in 1971: it was operated by Dr. Donald MacDaniel, an optometrist who had worked with Oliver to secure the Indiana Small Winery Act. Professor Oliver himself opened his Oliver Wine Company near Bloomington the next year. Carl Banholzer, the son of a native of the Rheingau and a cofounder of Tabor Hill Winery in Michigan, migrated to Indiana and by 1973 had forty-four acres in vines and plans for a winery on property near the Lake Michigan shore. Ben Sparks, a retired naval commander, was developing a vineyard at Unionville. The more prudent of the pioneers planted French hybrids with reasonable success. Sparks, who began with vinifera, lost all his vines to winter cold in their second year. Banholzer, who succeeded in producing a Cabernet Sauvignon in 1975 to considerable publicity, saw his vineyards, vinifera and hybrids alike, nearly fail over the next three harvests.[77] The Oliver vineyard was severely set back in the winter of 1983. The vineyards that did best appeared to be, as they had been early in the nineteenth century, in the hilly country along the Ohio River at the state's southern border. This is limestone country, traditionally associated with bourbon whiskey; one observer has said that it is a "perfect site" for the production of sparkling wines, but that possibility has not been acted on.[78]

The struggles of the Indiana growers attracted a good deal of official sympathy. The state Agricultural Extension Service cooperated with Purdue University to offer its Grape-Wine Symposium in 1974, and this became a regular event. In 1975 the state obligingly reduced the tax on wine from Indiana farm wineries from 45 cents to 25 cents a gallon and in that year, when Banholzer opened his winery, the governor of the state and the mayor of Indianapolis attended the ceremonies: there and then, Indiana was officially declared to be "wine country."[79] In 1975 the Indiana Wine Grower's Guild was organized for the promotion and protection of the fledgling industry. Despite all this effort, growth was slow and irregular; by the end of the '80s only eight wineries were operating in Indiana. In 1989, recognizing this slow development, the state created the Indiana Wine Grape Council under the administration of Purdue University to assist the "profitability" of Indiana's winegrowing. The council was funded by receiving 5 cents of the 47-cent tax on every gallon of wine sold in the state, which produced a substantial revenue. One of the council's projects was to sponsor, with Purdue, a viticultural research program.[80] It also undertook promotional work.

At the end of the century, the vineyards and wineries of Indiana persisted but remained small. They had received favorable legislation: license fees and taxes had been reduced, and retail privileges granted. They had secured the assistance of the federal and state agricultural agencies. Research on their problems was carried on at Purdue; and an agency devoted to their promotion had been created by official action. Furthermore, Indiana is one of the few states in which the distribution of wine is not hampered by local prohibition. It would seem that relative to other American states, Indiana offers extremely favorable conditions for the development of a flourishing industry. Yet that has not come about, whatever the future might hold. Instead, as the Indiana vineyards have failed to prosper, more and more Indiana wine has been made not from grapes grown in the state, but from grapes brought in from neighboring states; or it might come from strawberries, or from honey—in short, not wine at all. Of the twenty-seven wineries operating in Indiana in 2003, only two had survived from the beginnings in the 1970s. Fourteen wineries had gone out of business, so the rate of failure in one generation came uncomfortably close to 50 percent. The acreage of wine grapes remained small—about 300 acres. Of the twenty-five wineries surveyed in the Butlers' *Indiana Wine* in 2001, eleven had no vineyards at all. Fourteen others did, the average size being a very modest 14 acres.[81]

Why was this? Midwestern suspicion of wine may be one reason, though there was plenty of public support expressed in Indiana. The hostility of the climate is doubtless a stronger reason. In that midwestern climate of humid summers and bitterly cold winters, corn and soybeans flourish mightily but grapes are not, to put it mildly, well suited. Money is certainly another reason: the sort of winery envisaged by farm winery acts is by definition small, perhaps too small to be economical in a state in which grape growing is only marginally economical at all. But after all, these are early times, and the effort continues.

Indiana, Illinois, and Iowa, despite many local variations, are essentially one place from the point of view of grape growing and winemaking. Indiana and Illinois both have southern borders on the Ohio River, Illinois and Iowa share a Mississippi River border, and Iowa's western border is the Missouri River: these river valleys were the historic places of grape growing in all three states. For the rest, they share the great central sweep of rich midwestern prairie, the home of John Deere's steel plow and McCormick's reaper but alien to Bacchus and his hillsides.

Illinois, agriculturally almost indistinguishable from Indiana, showed somewhat less enterprise in winegrowing at first but now seems to be making up for lost time. In wine, as in everything else, there is a sharp separation between urban Illinois—which means Chicago—and all the rest of the state, or "downstate." Chicago had been the site of the Mogen David Winery operation since 1933, processing large quantities of juice and concentrate from New York grapes into sweet kosher-style wines. The many millions of gallons of wine thus produced gave Illinois a misleadingly high standing in the table of winemaking states—misleading because outside of this one industrial-scale operation using New York grapes in downtown Chicago, the state made almost no wine.[82] A tiny production came from vineyards in the old Mormon town of Nauvoo on the Mississippi; other than that, nothing.

One brave new attempt began in 1966 when Bern Ramey, who had studied winemaking at Davis but had chosen to go into the marketing side of the business, opened the Ramey and Allen Champagne Vineyard winery in Monee with his partner, Joseph Allen. Improbably, they chose to concentrate on sparkling wine from their vineyards of French hybrids and made what was, by all reports, quite a good one. Philip Togni—a respected California winemaker—for one called it "a first rate wine" when he tasted it in 1966.[83] But

FIGURE 48
The Baxter Winery at
Nauvoo, Illinois. The
milk can to the left of the
door reminds one of the
dominant farming
activity of the Midwest.
(Author's collection.)

in 1968 the vines were poisoned by drifting clouds of 2,4-D, a weed killer then widely used in the sea of cornfields that surrounded the small vineyard.[84]

Despite such discouragements, there was a gradually growing number of small wineries in Illinois, based almost exclusively on the French hybrids and the old American types. The Illinois Grape Growers and Vintners Association was founded in 1987. In 1997 the state funded the Grape and Wine Resources Council to carry out research and promotional work, with provision for a state enologist and a state viticulturist. The University of Illinois surveyed the vineyards and wineries of Illinois in 1998 and found that there were at the time fourteen wineries but only about 180 acres of vines. Much of what was made in Illinois was from imported grapes and juice, or from various fruits other than grapes. The clear need was to encourage vine planting, and to further this end the university developed four different experimental vineyards around the state. As a result, by 2002 there were 800 acres of vineyard in Illinois and some thirty wineries, the majority of them founded in the past decade.[85] The leading varieties include Norton, Chambour-cin, Foch, Chardonel, and Vignoles. A very small acreage of vinifera is grown, essentially as an experiment at this stage.

Winegrowing in Iowa has an even more slender basis than in Indiana or Illinois. The Amana wineries, mentioned in chapter 8, are small enterprises whose stock-in-trade is fruit and berry wine sold to tourists in the Amana Colonies gift shops; the Council Bluffs vineyards, also mentioned in chapter 8, have not yet recovered, though there are efforts to bring that about. There are two pioneers currently producing table wines from native and French hybrids in Iowa: Summerset Winery near Des Moines and Tabor Home Win-ery in eastern Iowa. Both opened in 1997. The varieties currently favored include Foch, Vidal, and Catawba. The public authorities are more than sympathetic to this tiny infant industry. Iowa has a farm winery law, and wineries may do their own wholesaling as well as sell directly at retail. In addition, Iowa wines may be sold from premises such as gift shops that do not hold retail liquor licenses. Wineries are eligible for low-cost loans from the state's department of economic development.[86] And the state has formed not only an Iowa Wine and Grape Advisory Council but an Iowa Wine and Beer Promotion Board. All this apparatus for promotion and development shows a heartening change in the pub-lic attitude toward an activity once thought of as reprehensible, if it was thought of at all. At the same time, it seems grotesquely disproportionate to the 30 acres of producing vine-yard recorded in Iowa in the year 2000.

The same observation might be applied to Illinois and Indiana too: all three states seem to have quickly outraced the reality in their eagerness to promote the theme of wine-making in their states. To speak of "Iowa Wine Country" or of "exploring Illinois winer-ies" or of "experiencing Indiana wine," as is regularly done, seems more than a little strange when one considers that of the 93 million acres occupied by these three states, probably not more than 1,000 are vineyard. One cannot help thinking that the rich pro-vision of state boards, state associations, guides to the wine country, wine tours, wine judgings, and wine festivals that has been created in these states means that the cart has been put before the horse—or rather, that no real horse yet exists. Much hard work has gone into what has so far been achieved, however, and perhaps a little exaggeration will help to achieve the next step.

THE MARGINS OF THE MIDWEST

Four states on the margins of the Midwest—Kansas, Nebraska, Minnesota, and Wisconsin—have all shown a wish to participate in the new winegrowing in this coun-try, and of the four, the best organized and most active is, curiously enough, Minnesota, the coldest and most inhospitable to viticulture of them all. Or perhaps it is not so curi-ous: the sheer difficulty of viticulture in that region seems to have acted as a challenge; the general prosperity and the distinguished educational tradition of the state have also contributed to help things along. In any case, the interest of the work is out of all proportion to its scale, which is very small indeed and likely to remain so. Yet there is a Minnesota Grape Growers Association, formed in 1975; the legislature in 1980 passed a farm winery measure and in 1984 established a Grape Research Council and funded grape and wine research at the University of Minnesota.[87] The university, which has maintained a grape breeding program since early in the twentieth century, in 2000 opened an experimental winery at its Horticultural Research Center.

It will surprise most people to learn that seven bonded wineries operated in Minnesota in 2000, the oldest of them dating from 1976; three of them, it is true, specialize in fruit and berry wines, and all are quite small. If you grow grapes in Minnesota, as one of the veterans puts it, "You have two choices: either plan on taking your vines down off their trellis and covering them with soil each fall, or plant a local variety that is tough enough to tolerate −30°F."[88] The first choice entails labor and expense that makes it commercially uneconomical; the second means that you can't make a very good wine, since no variety yet known with sufficient hardiness to withstand such cold yields a very desirable juice. Accordingly, the object toward which all Minnesota grape breeding is directed is to develop a good wine grape with an unprecedented resistance to winter injury. A Wisconsin farmer named Elmer Swenson, who worked as an amateur breeder for many years before joining, late in life, the Horticultural Research Station of the University of Minnesota, has introduced a number of varieties tough enough to tolerate the cold; but the search continues. The Swenson hybrids, based on the native American species *Vitis riparia,* which flourishes in the northern states, include such named varieties as Edelweiss, Kay Gray, and St. Croix. French hybrids are also grown in Minnesota, notably Kuhlmann varieties, from Alsace, such as Foch and Millot: these, however, require to be buried in winter. The main region of planting is along the Mississippi River south and east of the Twin Cities, but it is not confined there.

Across the river in Wisconsin, only a few wineries producing wine from locally grown grapes have so far been founded (there are others using other Wisconsin fruits, notably cherries from the orchards on Lake Michigan). The best known is Wollersheim Winery in Prairie du Sac, on the Wisconsin River. This enterprise can claim, with some show of plausibility, to be the heir of Agoston Haraszthy's long-ago efforts to establish winegrowing in Wisconsin. At least it is known that Haraszthy planted grapes at the town he founded near Prairie du Sac before abandoning Wisconsin for California, where he eventually founded Buena Vista Winery, and perhaps the old cave on the Wollersheim property had some connection with Haraszthy's activity.[89] More to the point, Robert Wollersheim has been growing French hybrid grapes, under all the conditions of cold-country viticulture, since 1973 and has made a commercial success of the enterprise. He produces nearly 40,000 cases of wine—far more than anyone in neighboring Minnesota has managed, though not all of his production is from Wisconsin grapes. Wollersheim owns another, smaller winery in Cedarburg called Cedar Creek Winery. His example seems to be gradually having the effect of stimulating the founding of other wineries.

When we jump southwestward, from Wisconsin to Kansas, we encounter very different conditions. The first is cultural rather than climatic. Kansas was a Dry state from 1880, and it was Dry by constitutional provision. Everyone has heard of Carry Nation and Kansas, but Carry Nation was merely a bubble on the frothy surface of the state's deep tradition of Prohibition, established long before Nation was heard of and enduring long after her disappearance. After Repeal Kansas remained steadfastly Dry until 1948, when, grudgingly, it was allowed that those counties that voted to submit to Demon Rum could do so. Some did; many others did not. In this atmosphere, the effects of the new national interest in winegrowing were felt only faintly; still, they *were* felt.

In 1974 the Horticultural Research Center near Wichita operated by Kansas State University began trial plantings of grapes, including French hybrids and vinifera. Then Robert Rizza, a doctor of Sicilian descent who had set up practice in Kansas, planted a vineyard in 1978, including both native American varieties and a few of the French hybrids. From these innocent beginnings the idea began to grow that Kansas might make wine.[90] The experiments carried out at the Horticultural Research Center were quite promising: Kansas, one of the horticulturists reported, has "adequate sunlight, soils, water supply, and a favorable climate."[91] Kansas also has severe winters, hot summers, frequent drought, high winds, and a complete complement of pests and diseases. The vast fields of wheat that are the emblem of Kansas support a huge bird population. Birds are always a threat to grapes, but in times of drought in Kansas they may simply annihilate the crop.[92] The example of neighboring Missouri—a richer, more populous state on which Kansas has always cast a somewhat jealous eye—also had its effect. Grape growing and winemaking had suddenly begun to flourish in Missouri: why not in Kansas too? Rizza took the lead in agitating for a farm winery law, a first installment of which was passed in 1983. It reduced the state tax on locally produced wine (if there should be any) and allowed direct sales to retailers; but the annual license fee was set at $1,100, and no tastings were to be allowed at a winery, for did not the state constitution proclaim that "the open saloon shall forever be prohibited in Kansas"?[93] Kansas may have had a farm winery law, but it did not offer much of an invitation. No one yet ventured to open a winery, though Rizza spoke confidently of his intention to do so.

Meanwhile, some small-scale planting went on at scattered places throughout the state, and in 1987 the Kansas Grape Growers and Wine Makers Association was formed (as seems so often to have been the case, the organization anticipated the existence of anything to organize). In the next year the legislature amended the law to permit tastings and sales at wineries, except, of course, in Dry counties. Moreover, the state Department of Agriculture was authorized to establish an advisory program in viticulture and enology. That was the signal to begin at last. Kansas bonded winery license number 1 went to James Fair in 1988 for his property west of Topeka. Fair had some 15 acres under vines then, mostly French hybrids. He is no longer in business, but there are now seven small wineries producing wine from Kansas grapes. Dr. Rizza never achieved his ambition of opening a Kansas winery, but he was the great propagandist for the idea.

Nebraska is in some ways a more difficult territory than Kansas—rather colder, and in the west rather dryer. But it has not had to struggle quite as hard against an ingrained disposition toward prohibition. In fact the Nebraska legislature showed itself to be friendly toward wine even before there was any Nebraska wine to befriend by passing a farm winery law in 1985. Ed Swanson, a farmer near Pierce in the northeastern corner of the state, planted a vineyard that year, mostly of French hybrids, but with some Swenson hybrids such as St. Croix and La Crosse. Swanson opened his Cuthills Vineyard in 1994 and now has a storage capacity of 3,700 gallons. He has also begun a grape breeding program of his own, hoping to find the grape that will produce reliably even in fifty-mile-an-hour winds at −30 degrees Fahrenheit.[94] There are three other small wineries in Nebraska, and a Nebraska grape growers and wineries association as well. The Swenson hybrids dominate in the small vineyards scattered across the state, mixed with a few French hybrid varieties. Nebraska also relies on chokecherries, wild plums, apples, and honey to eke out its production of grapes for wine.

HOW MUCH HAS CHANGED?

A generation ago, the idea of surveying winegrowing in such states as Kansas or Mississippi or Massachusetts would have seemed merely a bad joke, like hunting for dodos or trying to buy left-handed monkey wrenches. Now nearly every state in the union has some sort of recent history in viticulture and winemaking, however small-scale, experimental, and restricted it may be. In some states, such as New York, Ohio, and Michigan, an existing industry has been transformed; in others, such as Pennsylvania, a substantial industry has been newly achieved. And in the others, such as Connecticut or Kansas, the idea that a winegrowing industry might be developed has at least been established. At the same time, the enthusiasts for the idea have learned that they need all the help that research, legislation, and experience can give them before they can reasonably expect a genuine success. Valuable beginnings have been made, but in most states they are only beginnings.

If we turn from the matter of winegrowing to that of wine drinking, the changes seem even more elusive and difficult to measure. Without question wine is known and available in places where before it did not, for all practical purposes, exist. But it remains a novelty, and a rather suspect novelty, for most—the very status of wineries as tourist attractions confirms that, and will probably perpetuate the bad idea.

After all of these cautious qualifications have been made, however, the fact remains that the prospect of winegrowing has been opened up again in most of the states of the union. Where no one thought about it for many years, there are now enthusiasts, both amateur and professional, eager to try what can be done. The state legislatures, unaccustomed for years to regarding wine as anything but an imported item available for taxation, have been taught to think that they might do something for winegrowing in their own states. The state universities and agricultural experiment stations have learned to take a serious interest in viticulture and enology as subjects for research and experiment. Newspapers and other media have been happy to promote local wines as proper subjects for local pride and interest. Altogether, these changes seem to mark a tremendous shift and the opening of new opportunity. How that opportunity will be exploited it is too early to say.

12

A NEW DAWN (II)
The South

MARYLAND AND VIRGINIA

Maryland, quite apart from anything else that might be accomplished there, will always have an important place in the modern history of American winegrowing as the scene of Philip Wagner's pioneering and deeply influential work.[1] Starting in the early '30s Wagner was the inspiration and the guide for countless enthusiastic grape growers and winemakers throughout the East. Wagner's own winery, Boordy Vineyards (established in 1945), was run on sound commercial lines and paid its own way, but it was never Wagner's ambition to make a lot of wine. On the contrary, he wanted more than anything to set an example of domestic winemaking, to show his countrymen that they might have good, sound wine of their own growing. As he put it strikingly: "The finest wines in the world are homemade wines"; and if he included the great château wines of France among the "homemade," he was at least technically right. "Wine," he said, "is made in the home, whether the home be a farmhouse, a peasant's cottage, or a great estate, and is made of grapes grown on the place."[2] His example inspired any number of others to try winemaking; the few who went into business did so, as Wagner would have wanted, on a very modest scale.

There are two notable constraints on winemaking in Maryland. One of them is the climate, described by Wagner as a rich compound of storms, wildly varying temperatures, floods, droughts, lethal winters, hail, and other afflictions: "Anything that survives in Maryland is worth trial anywhere this side of the Arctic circle."[3]

But with only a little modification, this description could be applied almost anywhere

in the East. Maryland had another set of obstacles in its regulations, complicated by local prohibition. One law restricted winery sales to "one bottle of one label to one customer
per year."[4] Tastings at the wineries were not allowed. It was of such restrictions as these
that Wagner was thinking when he wrote that "some few states have regulations so strin-
gent and arbitrary that they have you licked before you start."[5] A limited winery act was
secured in 1976, and its effect is visible in the fact that fourteen of the nineteen wineries opened in Maryland since Boordy was founded date from 1976 and later. There are
now several official bodies concerned with winegrowing: the Maryland Grape Growers
Association (1981), the Association of Maryland Wineries (1984), and the Maryland Winery and Grape Growers Advisory Board (1987) in the Department of Agriculture. But the
scale of the industry remains very small indeed: at the end of the century there were about
250 acres of wine grapes in the state, supplying twelve wineries whose sales ran to 100,000
gallons.[6] The first new winegrowers were faithful to Wagner's legacy and planted mostly
French hybrid vines; one of them, Hamilton Mowbray at Montbray Cellars, also planted
vinifera and had Riesling and Chardonnay to sell by 1971. Since then most of Maryland's
wineries have offered wines from both sorts of grapes—Cabernet franc has done well
among the vinifera, Chambourcin, Seyval, and Vidal among the hybrids. But about half
the crush in Maryland is of grapes grown in other states. Maryland wine can be very good,
but it is not yet made in very substantial quantities.

In 1946 a German named Urban Westenberger, from the great wine district of the
Rheingau, immigrated to Virginia and settled on the slopes of Massanutten Mountain
above the Shenandoah River in the northern part of the state. There were already a vineyard and a wine cellar on the property, and before long Westenberger, without troubling
the state and federal authorities for licenses and permits, had wine for sale—some 8,000
gallons of Virginia burgundy, rhine wine, and rosé by 1953. Two years later the revenuers
shut him down until such time as he could obtain a license and pay his taxes. This Westenberger managed to do, but he remained vulnerable to inspection and so was soon in
trouble again. When the inspectors analyzed samples of his Lorelei Vineyards wine taken
from store shelves, they found that it was unclean, cloudy, moldy, high in acetic acid, and
actively fermenting—a kind of dirty vinegar rather than a palatable wine. They closed
him down again, this time for good; Westenberger departed Virginia for Florida, the winery fell into decay, and the vineyards returned to scrub and weeds.[7]

As this story suggests, Virginia has always made wine of sorts, but not until recently
wine that many would be happy to drink. Since the beginning of settlement in 1607, Virginia has been the site of perhaps more distinguished, though futile, attempts to create
a winegrowing industry than any other state: it is enough to mention George Washington, Thomas Jefferson, James Madison, and James Monroe, would-be winegrowers all.
The region around Charlottesville was the scene of persistent efforts: there had been some
success with the Norton grape there in the late nineteenth century, and a renewed effort
was made there to establish winegrowing following Repeal. But the times were not propitious. The state of Virginia issued only twenty-two winery licenses in the first forty years

following Repeal, and only a handful of the licensees survived for any length of time. By 1970 there were four wineries in the state, one tiny operation in rural Clarksville and three good-size ones, making fruit wines and sweet fortified wines from muscadine grapes—grown not in Virginia but in the deeper South.[8] The production of Virginia wine from Virginia grapes had sunk so low that when Leon Adams was preparing the first edition of his *The Wines of America* (1973), he could find almost nothing to describe in the state. Since one of the purposes of that pioneering book was to show that winegrowing was an activity spread across almost every state of the country, Adams needed some Virginia instances and was glad to include, as evidence of commercial operation, the back-yard vines of Robert Hutton, a learned cataloguer of Japanese and Slavic books at the Library of Congress and a weekend viticulturist.[9]

Meanwhile, the preparations for change had been taking invisible shape. The growing interest in wine was felt in Virginia, too, and was responded to in what we may recognize now as the classic pattern, repeated all over the country. Scattered individuals, intrigued by the possibilities and seeing that the work would not otherwise be done, began to plant small vineyards and to think about making wine. They were of all sorts: civil servants, army officers, gentleman farmers, lawyers, teachers, almost anything except professional wine people, since these did not exist in the area. By the 1970s there were some score or more such vineyards in Virginia, and in 1974 the first of the new breed of winery opened. This was the Farfelu Winery of Charles Raney, a commercial pilot, and was based on a 12-acre vineyard of French hybrids that Raney had planted beginning in 1966 at Flint Hill, in northern Virginia.[10] Six more wineries opened in Virginia in the '70s, and then came the deluge: thirty-six new wineries were licensed in the '80s, and by the turn of the century Virginia had fifty-four wineries in operation with an aggregate storage capacity nearing 2 million gallons.

There were some distinctive elements in Virginia. One of them was foreign investment. The history of winegrowing in the eastern United States is littered with innumerable failures, and the new beginnings in Virginia were just as chancy as the old ventures had been. Nevertheless, Barboursville Vineyards, founded in 1976, was the property of a group of international investors, including the winemaking firm of Zonin from the Veneto in Italy. Another foreign investor was Dr. Gerhard Guth, a physician from Hamburg, who opened Rapidan River Vineyards in 1981. A French industrialist named Jean Leducq started Prince Michel Vineyards in 1983, and later bought Guth's operation. European money was accompanied by European winemakers. Barboursville brought in Gabriele Rausse, a graduate agronomist from the University of Milan; Guth hired Joachim Hollerith, a graduate of the Geisenheim school; a Belgian, Jacques Recht, came originally to work for the Ingleside Plantation Winery.

It was in part owing to this European presence that another distinctive element in Virginia winegrowing came about: the dominance of vinifera. Both Barboursville and Rapidan River Vineyards were planted exclusively in vinifera and trained, the former in Italian style, the latter in German. But the conviction that Virginia ought to be a region of vinifera antedated these experiments. In 1973 a retired State Department officer, R. de Treville Lawrence, who had a small vinifera vineyard at his Virginia home, helped to found something called the Vinifera Wine Growers Association, headquartered at The Plains, Virginia, and thereafter became an irrepressible propagandist for the cause of vinifera throughout the East. The association lobbied, sponsored awards and festivals, organized seminars and other meetings, and published the *Vinifera Wine Growers Journal,* which brought together reports and information about the winegrowing action in all of the states east of the Rockies. In the sacred cause of the vinifera faith, to which he had been converted by Dr. Konstantin Frank, Lawrence was an unsparing bigot, with the fanatic's clear, comprehensive view of things: all hybrids were inferior and of no account in comparison with vinifera, which alone was worthy of planting. No reports of failure, or loss, or difficulty could disturb this simple faith, which was preached through the eighteen years of the *Journal*'s lively existence. Others were less certain, but gradually the idea that vinifera was feasible in Virginia began to prevail, though always with the proviso that one should have some French hybrids to fall back on.[11] Virginia's weather is less extreme than that of the states lying to the north and south of it; as Lucie Morton puts it, it lies "north of Pierce's Disease and south of the deep freeze."[12] But the weather is troublesome enough and can be, in Wagner's word, "exasperating"; variable temperatures in winter can provoke budding followed by freezes; warm summers with abundant rain favor the fungal diseases.[13] Still, the thing can be done, under rules made increasingly clear by experience and research: careful site selection, careful choice of variety and of vine material, careful management. Chardonnay and Riesling are the white varieties most planted, Cabernet Sauvignon among the reds. The favored French hybrids include Seyval and Chambourcin. Together these varieties dominate the vineyards of Virginia, which mostly lie in the Blue Ridge foothills with Charlottesville more or less at the center, but may be found at points all over the state.

The state of Virginia has been particularly well disposed toward its new winegrowing industry and has provided a full complement of assistance and encouragement. As early as 1977 the Grape Growers Advisory Committee was appointed under the state Department of Agriculture to investigate the economic chances and to compile information. In 1980 the Farm Winery Act was passed, and its terms were more generous than in most such acts: there was no restriction on size, sales were permitted at wholesale and retail, and the very high state tax on bottled wine was removed from Virginian wines; the last provision, however, was soon overturned by a Supreme Court decision against such discrimination.[14] In 1984 the legislature created the Wine Marketing Program; in the next year the Winegrowers Productivity Fund, supported by the state wine tax, was set up and the Virginia Winegrowers Advisory Board created, with provision for a state enologist and a state viticulturist.[15] Since then a program of research and extension work has been established at Virginia Polytechnic Institute. As another official favor, the only wines sold in the state liquor stores are Virginia wines.[16] In 1988 the governor of Virginia, Gerald Baliles, made a three-day official tour of Virginia vineyards and wineries, an act unprecedented in Virginia or anywhere else in the United States and a striking illustration of a new willingness on the part of a high public official to show that he thought wine-growing a thing to be encouraged.[17]

Virginia appears to be among the more prosperous of the new winegrowing states. The number of wineries is considerable (more than seventy), and the failure rate among them is distinctly lower than in many other states.[18] The help of the state has been considerable. So has the great growth of Washington, D.C., which provides an interested and relatively sophisticated market not available, say, to wineries in southern Indiana or West Texas. But in return for such a market, Virginia has had to make reasonably good wines. The small scale of Virginia's production and the high costs of cultivating vinifera in difficult conditions made the wines expensive—another reason why they had to be good. In the early days, when winemaking was a seat-of-the-pants operation, there were many dubious moments. The presence of the several trained Europeans already mentioned, the steep learning curves of the successful pioneers, and the assistance of the state experts have brought Virginia winemaking to a high level of technical competence, a level far removed indeed from that of Westenberger's Lorelei Vineyards.

THE SOUTHEASTERN STATES

The semicircle of states whose coasts form the southeastern outline of the United States—the Carolinas, Georgia, Florida, Alabama, Mississippi, and Louisiana—are a special case in the grape-growing world. This is the home of Pierce's disease, a mortal enemy to most grapes; it flourishes especially in the warm lowlands, so grape growing—with one exception—is largely barred in those regions. The exception is *Vitis rotundifolia,* which appears to have reached an accommodation with Pierce's disease in some long-ago botanical age.[19] Florida is, in effect, all low-lying, warm, humid land; so is much of Louisiana. In both states viticulture is practically limited to the species rotundifolia.[20] The rest of the southeastern states all have more or less of highland territory, and in those regions more conventional viticulture may be carried on.

North Carolina illustrates the pattern clearly, beginning with the fact that the climate is difficult for the grape. In the hot summers there is not much cooling at night, a condition unfavorable to grapes; so, too, are the rain that falls during the summer and the very high temperatures that are likely to occur just at harvesttime. Warm spells in wintertime encourage the vine to grow, and then to suffer from spring frosts. And almost the entire range of diseases and pests in which the North American continent abounds is at home in North Carolina: phylloxera, nematodes, Pierce's disease, black rot, powdery mildew, bitter rot, ripe rot, grapevine root borer, and grape scale. But as experience with the selection of varieties, sites, and rootstocks, as well as with cultivation and management practices, grows, these problems can be dealt with more or less successfully; North Carolina is in this respect perhaps not much worse off than most of the eastern United States. It has also the advantage of a long east-west dimension, rising as one moves westward from the coast through the Piedmont to the Appalachians. On these higher grounds the possibility exists for what is called, in the South, bunch grape cultivation—*bunch grapes* being a southern term to distinguish the grapes that all the rest of the world knows simply as grapes from the native rotundifolia, which grows in loose clusters of a few berries each.

Prohibition, persisting long after Repeal, is another condition shared by North Carolina and other southern states; the state had gone Dry in 1909, and after Repeal local prohibition persisted. The consequence was that the state was largely without wineries. It grew considerable quantities of muscadine grapes in vineyards on the coastal plain, but these were shipped north to Virginia or south to South Carolina, where they were processed by large wineries specializing in sweet wines for the southern trade.

The North Carolina legislature looked with a friendly eye on grapes because the state had long sought to alter its dependence on tobacco and cotton. North Carolina State University had undertaken a program of breeding new varieties of muscadine at the beginning of the '60s, and the legislature had supported this effort with a research grant in 1965.[21] At the same time the farmers of the state were encouraged to plant more muscadines by the demand for them at the wineries: Richard's Wine Cellars in Virginia offered free cuttings and five-year contracts at $200 a ton.[22] For a few years, muscadine grape growing prospered, but the seemingly inevitable condition of oversupply soon overtook it. The acreage of grapes moved up from about 500 at the end of the '60s to more than 2,000 by the mid '70s, when prices dropped to levels that made grape growing uneconomical.[23] Meanwhile the legislature, in a move to encourage the development of winegrowing, reduced winery license fees and cut the tax on native wines.[24]

Taking advantage of this arrangement, a group of growers formed a joint enterprise called Duplin Wine Cellars, at Rose Hill in the southeast of the state. The wines were entirely from muscadine grapes—the variety called Carlos was the mainstay—and ran through the whole gamut of types: red and white, table and fortified, still and sparkling. As long as the operation was protected by preferential taxation it had a surprising success. Duplin Wine Cellars produced 140,000 gallons of muscadine wine in 1982, and production was near 200,000 gallons the next year, when the state's attorney general ruled the preferential tax unconstitutional.[25] Duplin Wine Cellars, in consequence, nearly foundered: sales dropped like a stone in water, and by 1986 production was a mere 10,000 gallons.[26] Growers began to give up on their vineyards, a trend greatly accelerated by a devastating freeze in 1984 followed by two years of drought. By 1987 the state's vineyards had shrunk to 750 acres. Duplin Wine Cellars recovered and now operates (as Duplin Winery) at a more modest level of production, restricted by the diminished supply of muscadines. The state compensated for the lost tax differential on North Carolina wines by diverting some of the now-higher taxes to a fund to support research and promotion in aid of the state's grape and wine industry.[27]

About the time that the Duplin venture was begun, another, very different sort of beginning was made near Asheville, at the opposite end of the state, high in the Blue Ridge. Here the heirs of the Vanderbilt who had created the lavish Biltmore Estate at the end of the nineteenth century (a 250-room house on a 125,000-acre property) began to plant a vineyard in 1971. The idea was to add yet another attraction to the estate as a tourist destination. The first vines were French hybrids, but by the 1970s the possibilities of vinifera in the East had been reconsidered, and given the French-château style of Biltmore it seemed more appropriate to try vinifera. The estate hired a French winemaker, Philippe Jourdain, converted the old dairy barn into a winery, and opened it to the public in 1985. The swarms of tourists who pass through the Biltmore Estate each year buy more wine than the 77 acres of vineyard can supply; in order to meet the demand and to provide wines that North Carolina can't produce (such as Zinfandel), a good deal of the wine made at Biltmore comes from juice shipped in from California and Washington State.[28] The winery itself, an expensive establishment of modern equipment in a sort of Petit Trianon setting, is one of the major attractions of the Biltmore tour.

Biltmore is too extravagant and exotic a place to serve as a model for other wineries, but there has been some other experimentation with French hybrids and vinifera, by growers in the Piedmont region especially: small wineries such as Germanton (1981), Westbend (1988), and Hanover Park (1999) produce wines from Seyval, Vidal, Chardonnay, Chambourcin, and Cabernet Sauvignon. The last two of these wineries are in the Yadkin Valley, in the northwestern corner of the state, which became North Carolina's first American viticultural area (AVA) in 2003.

To assist in promotion and research, the state founded a North Carolina Grape Council in 1986, funded by the state tax on wine. According to the council, there were twenty-five wineries operating in North Carolina in 2002, producing 600,000 gallons of wine from 1,100 acres of vineyard. The two extremes in this scene are the Biltmore winery, producing vinifera wine in the western mountains, and Duplin Wine Cellars, producing muscadine wine in the eastern coastal plain. The remainder, all small, lie scattered between. They have all been assisted by legislation passed in 2001 that creates some valuable new privileges: wineries may now hold tastings in grocery stores, open multiple outlets, sell wine by the glass, and hold a wholesaler's license. In addition, a wine producer's permit allows a grower to have wine made for him and then to sell it from his farm— even in a Dry county. These are measures far more generous than is usual among the states, and it will be interesting to see what economic effect they have.

As one moves south from North Carolina, the landscape of wine becomes even emptier; here and there a scene of hopeful activity develops from time to time, but then falters and disappears. The ferment of new interest in winemaking that took hold in the '60s spread to those states that had long been compelled by climate to produce only fruit wines or wines from the native muscadine. The results have been almost uniformly disappointing, as a few episodes will show.

South Carolina has always had grapes but few wineries. For years the only one was the Tenner Brothers Winery, which processed large volumes of wine from muscadine grapes at Patrick, a few miles over the border from North Carolina.[29] Two enterprises that began in the mid '70s had almost opposite inspirations but came to the same sad end. In 1975 Richard Leizear, who grew muscadine and native hybrid grapes in the Piedmont region at

Woodruff, decided to organize the growers of the district to develop their own winery. Leizear—who was, incidentally, a teetotaler—already had a considerable plant at his Oakview Farm for the production of grape juice. He now decided that since the outlets for South Carolina grapes were so few and so uncertain, the growers would have to rely on themselves and produce their own wine. With the aid of large loans Leizear's grape juice plant was transformed into a 600,000-gallon winery, supplied by 260 acres of vineyards. The new venture, christened Oakview Plantation, would be, according to Leizear, "dedicated to promoting American grapes, American names. . . . Contrary to the opinion of wine snobs the Southern Vitis rotundifolia is a varietal grape of real merit if properly merchandised and vinted. The Concord is a great grape and the Catawba even greater."[30]

How a teetotaler arrived at such judgments, who can say? Oakview Plantation produced wines under the brand names of Golden Scuppernong and American Beauty Rose, but the conditions were not right. The South Carolina tax on table wines was high, and the law that required all wine to be sold through a distributor kept Oakview from developing its own markets by direct sales.[31] In 1979 Oakview was closed and then sold; reopened as the Foxwood Winery, it operated through the '80s, making fruit wines as well as grape wines. In the early '90s it shut down for good.

At the same time that the Oakview Plantation venture was getting started, a wine-smitten dentist in the South Carolina low country opened a winery on a very different basis: no muscadine or labrusca here, but French hybrids and vinifera. Dr. James Truluck had done a tour of duty with the air force in France, and after his return to his hometown of Lake City he dreamed of opening a winery in that hot, humid region of tobacco fields to provide, as he said, "a touch of France in the Old South." He put in his first vines in 1972 and opened the winery in 1976. The first wines were all from French hybrid grapes, but as the vineyards grew so did the number of vinifera varieties. Truluck was a tireless experimenter in the vineyard—at one point he had more than three hundred varieties on trial—and to show that he kept an open mind, they included many old-line American hybrids, including a large selection of the varieties developed by T. V. Munson in the nineteenth century.[32] Truluck's business received a welcome assist in 1980 when the legislature lowered the tax on wine produced in South Carolina from 57 ½ cents a gallon to 5 cents. Truluck Vineyards operated through the '80s but closed early in the '90s, just as Foxwood Winery did. Shortly thereafter Tenner Brothers closed, and so the three substantial wineries in South Carolina were all gone, leaving only one or two (the number varies) small farm wineries to carry on winemaking. It is not clear whether anything useful has been learned—except, perhaps, that South Carolina currently will not support anything more than the most modest scale of winemaking.

For a long time, *wine* in Georgia meant a drink made from peaches rather than grapes. The big winemaking enterprise—in fact the sole enterprise—was the Monarch Wine Company in Atlanta, founded in 1936 to process the abundant peach crop for which the state is famous as well as the rotundifolia grapes native to Georgia.[33] The state gave a liberal advantage to Georgia wines, which paid a tax of 40 cents per gallon while all others paid

Truluck
Vineyards
A Touch of France
In The Old South

FIGURE 49
The transplantation
of France to the Old
South did not take, but
it showed some new
possibilities. (Author's
collection.)

$1.50, but this incentive did nothing to encourage winemaking in the state. It was not until the beginning of the 1980s that some tentative experimentation with the possibilities began. The fall line in Georgia, which runs diagonally across the state from the northeast to the southwest, marks a division between two kinds of grape culture: below the line, the conditions of the Cotton Belt South prevail: hot summers, warm nights, high humidity, warm episodes in winter, and the full range of diseases all mean that the only safe choice is the muscadine. To the north of the fall line in the highlands, it is possible to think of other species of grape. Here at the beginning of the 1980s three small vineyards of vinifera and French hybrids were established: Split Rail, Stonepile, and Apalachee. At the same time, the University of Georgia began research into wine grapes.

In 1982, to the general surprise, a large-scale venture called Château Élan was set in motion—"surprise" because the region was untested, the market undeveloped, and all the questions about the choice of varieties, the methods of cultivation, the problems of production unanswered. Headed by a successful manufacturer of pharmaceutical products, Donald Panoz, Château Élan, located at Braselton northeast of Atlanta, was to include not only a vineyard and winery but a convention center, hotels, restaurants, golf courses, and other amenities that would, taken together, make a destination for tourists. The plans for the wine element were expansive. The aim was to have more than 500 acres of vineyard, all of vinifera, by 1985; 125 were planted in 1983, and ground was broken on what was supposed to be a 500,000-gallon winery. To manage this enterprise, the company brought in Ed Friedrich, a native of the Mosel Valley trained in Germany, who brought California credentials as well: he had been winemaker at Paul Masson and general manager at San Martin. Now he would preside over the creation of distinguished wines from Georgia—the "top of the line," he promised, as good as or better than anything made in California or Europe.[34]

It did not work out that way. By the end of the 1980s Château Élan had 200 acres of vineyard and a 200,000-gallon-capacity winery, but things got stuck at that point. Friedrich died in 1986, and that must have diminished the élan behind the Château. In 2004 production was at 20,000 cases, a small fraction of what had been imagined at the beginning. Nor had the wines achieved any particular reputation. Vinifera continued to be produced, but it was supplemented by sources from out of state (read California); Château Élan also made muscadine wines, since that was what Georgia had in ready supply. The resort aspect of the undertaking was a different story: restaurants, hotels, and golf courses were understood in Georgia quite as well as they were in other states, and they flourished at Château Élan even if the winemaking as originally planned did not.

Small-scale winemaking in Georgia, encouraged by a farm winery act passed in 1983, remained very small scale: between 1983 and the end of the century, seven little wineries appeared, making wines for local sale from vinifera, French hybrids, and native American varieties.[35] There was not yet any organization of growers or winemakers.

The boast of Florida is that in a region in which grape growing has always been challenged by a host of formidable enemies, nowhere is it more difficult than in Florida. The state has no high country: all is flat and low-lying. Pierce's disease is rampant; the soil is infertile, the rainfall uneven, the insects voracious, the weeds tough and vigorous, the temperatures high, the atmosphere humid.[36] Under the circumstances, it has seemed easier to make wine from citrus fruits, which prosper in Florida as the peach does in Georgia. Yet the indomitable wish to make good wine still struggles on in Florida. There has been a Florida Grape Growers Association since 1923, which may make it the oldest such group in America. The University of Florida has carried on research in viticulture and grape breeding since even before Repeal and has introduced a number of hybrids and crosses, in part based on the wild bunch grapes that manage to grow vigorously in "Florida's nematode-infested, coarse-textured sands": the search for resistance to Pierce's disease has been the main object of the work.[37]

Limited commercial winemaking has also persisted in Florida. The vicissitudes of the work are well illustrated by the fortunes of Bartels Winery in Pensacola. Founded by a German immigrant in 1910 in southern Alabama on Perdido Bay, the winery depended on muscadine grapes. Renewed after Repeal in 1937, it migrated over the state line, just across Perdido Bay, to the neighborhood of Pensacola, Florida, in 1940. The vineyards remained behind in Alabama but the wine was now made in Florida, where the aviators at Pensacola Naval Air Station gave it a market it would otherwise never have had among the hard-shell Baptists of the Florida panhandle. John Weaver—the grandson of Herman Bartels, the founder—was experimenting with new grapes for his vineyards in the 1970s and had good hopes of the bunch grape called Lake Emerald, bred for white wine by the university in 1954, but the promise did not come to much.[38] Bartels Winery, which made about 10,000 gallons of muscadine wine a year, most of it sold through its own restaurant, lasted longer than most Florida winemakers but went out of business in 1979. So have most of the other Florida wineries: the state has issued nearly half a hundred winery licenses in the years since Repeal, but at the turn of the century only seven were operating, making wine from crosses bred for Florida, from muscadines, and from other fruits and berries, including pineapple, tomato, and watermelon.

The oldest winery at that time went back only to 1985, though there had been a flurry of interest and enterprise earlier, beginning in 1979 when the legislature passed a farm winery act. Alaqua Vineyard (established 1981) was the first to start up under the new legislation, which exempted farm wineries from the state's exorbitant wine tax, the highest in the nation. The Florida Heritage Winery also opened in 1981, followed by Lafayette Vineyard and Winery and Wines of St. Augustine in 1983. None of these firms survived. Their successors, the few wineries currently operating in Florida, are all small.[39] The current leader is the combination of San Sebastian and Lakeridge Vineyards, both under the same ownership and producing together an annual 40,000 cases. A good deal of wine is drunk in Florida, mostly by the tourist traffic, but not much of it comes from Florida, nor does it seem likely that it soon will. The state legislature diverted some of the taxes paid on native wines sold in Florida to fund the Viticulture Trust Fund in 1988; the way the money is spent—on promotion, marketing, or research—is determined by the Viticulture Advisory Board.

The story in two other Gulf states, Alabama and Mississippi, is the same as in the other southeastern states, with only local variations. In recent years there has been enthusiastic activity among small growers and amateurs, legal and administrative help from the lawmakers, and technical help from the universities and experiment stations. Nature and the market remain largely unmoved. In 1972 James Eddins, who had been tending a small vineyard in Maryland, returned to his home territory in southern Alabama and began growing muscadine grapes there. For a time he sold his crop to Bartels, across the line in Florida, but when that market disappeared Eddins went to work with a sympathetic representative in the state legislature. In 1979 they succeeded in obtaining the passage of the Alabama Farm Winery Act. At first there had been opposition from the Alabama liquor wholesalers, who feared that giving the farm winemaker the right to sell produce directly would undercut them. A little sober reflection soon persuaded them that they had nothing to fear; anything that might help to educate the people of Alabama about wine could only be good for everyone in the trade, and the chances of a large volume of wine moving to market independently of the wholesalers were remote indeed.

In 1980, the year after passage of the Farm Winery Act, Eddins opened his Perdido Winery as Alabama bonded winery number 1 and was soon followed by a few others scattered across the state from north to south. Two or three experimented with French hybrids as well as with the reliable muscadines. Winemaking in Alabama, though it generated a good deal of publicity, has remained an exotic and marginal business. Only ten bonded winery licenses have been issued since 1979, and of the ten licensees only three survived to the end of the century. One of them was Eddins's Perdido Vineyards, which is now past its twenty-fifth anniversary and continues to produce a substantial quantity of muscadine wine.

The late conversion of Mississippi from a Dry state to one in which a wine industry is the object of official support was touched on in the preceding chapter. It must be admitted here that the value of that conversion has, so far, been more symbolic than actual as far as the production of wine is concerned. The farm winery act of 1976 was followed the next year by the opening in Merigold of Mississippi's first modern winery, The Winery Rushing, which—despite the French syntax of its name—was firmly grounded in native muscadine grapes. The next to open, Thousand Oaks, across the state from Rushing at Starkville, had some French hybrids to experiment with. The most interesting fact about the third, Almarla Vineyards at Matherville, in the southeast of the state, is that it was founded by a man who before retirement had been the chief chemist for the Bureau of Alcohol, Tobacco and Firearms. Altogether, nine winery licenses have been issued in Mississippi in the quarter century since the Native Wine Law, as it is called, was enacted. The mortality rate has resembled that in neighboring Alabama: only one was operating in 2004. The program in viticulture and enology set up with high hopes at Mississippi State University in the 1970s had been severely cut back by the beginning of the '90s and absorbed into a food-science program. By the mid '90s, a writer could state flatly that as far as winemaking was concerned, "Alabama and Mississippi have all but given up."[40]

THE BORDER STATES:
TENNESSEE, KENTUCKY, AND WEST VIRGINIA

Among the border states of the South, Tennessee appears to have done better in creating a small winegrowing industry than most of the others. The beginnings were greatly assisted by Judge William Beach of Clarksville, a home winemaker who looked forward to running a small winery in his retirement. To that end he and some friends organized as the grandly named Tennessee Viticultural and Oenological Society in 1973. In 1977 they secured state legislation in the form of the Grape and Wine Law, and the first commercial winery was launched in 1980. Since then some twenty-four wineries have been opened in regions all across the state, from the cotton flatlands in the west around Memphis to the mountains of eastern Tennessee; of those twenty-four, some nineteen are still operating, a very high survival rate. Judge Beach realized his dream in the Beachaven Winery, opened in 1987. Tennessee is indubitably a southern state—high heat, high humidity, and all the accompanying diseases—but its hills and valleys provide a great diversity of terrain, so that in some places not only the native muscadine but other sorts of grapes grow: the old native hybrids, French hybrids, and even some vinifera. The economics of grape growing, however, are not very encouraging, and Tennessee's wineries depend on grapes purchased out of state as well as on local ones.

To encourage its new industry Tennessee created an official body in 1985 called the Viticulture Advisory Board to operate within the Department of Agriculture; the state also supplies some help through extension programs in grape growing and winemaking. Opposing these helpful efforts is an obstructive piece of legislation passed in 1983: it prohibits anyone who has not been a resident of Tennessee for two years to own or invest in a Tennessee winery. This strange restriction was attributed to the liquor wholesalers of Tennessee, who feared anything that might affect their entrenched position.[41]

One would not expect Kentucky, the home of bourbon whiskey, to show much disposition toward winegrowing, nor has it. Neither would one suppose that Kentucky, where the mint julep is practically a state religion, would still be strong on prohibition. But it is; two-thirds of its counties are legally Dry.[42] These two forces, the whiskey interest on one side and the Drys on the other, have so far succeeded in holding back almost all efforts to make wine in Kentucky. Under pressure of the new national interest in wine, the legislature authorized the creation of small wineries in 1976, but only grudgingly: a winery could not sell wine to stores or restaurants except through the established wholesalers, and it could sell individuals only one bottle a year! Such legislation was a grimly satirical joke rather than a genuine permission. It has since been altered, but only to the extent that an individual may now buy a case annually. How this restriction is monitored I do not know. Even under such farcical regulation, wineries have somehow managed to function. There were ten very small wineries licensed in 2004, though not much Kentucky wine came from Kentucky grapes.

The history of renewed winegrowing in West Virginia was also marked by political difficulties but seems to have worked out well in the end. The state is in the popular imagination the home of moonshine, a place where hillbilly distillers and revenue men still struggle to outwit each other in the remote hills and hollows. Whatever the truth of that may be, the connection between alcohol and illegality is deeply ingrained in West Virginia. After Repeal, wine was available only through state stores; and when the wine revolution began to cause stirrings there, the governor, Jay Rockefeller, vetoed a farm winery bill not once but four times on the grounds that it would be an "abuse of public office to foster the consumption of alcohol."[43] On the fourth occasion, in 1981, the legislature overrode the veto by a record margin, and at the same time delivered wine from the bondage of state stores by allowing its sale in groceries and other shops. The West Virginia Farm Winery Act requires that 75 percent of the grapes be from West Virginia; it also permits tastings and sales at the winery, and a production of up to 50,000 gallons. The pioneers in winegrowing in West Virginia include Robert Pliska, who organized the West Virginia Grape Growers Association in 1979, and Wilson Ward, who was instrumental in pushing through the Farm Winery Act and opened the state's first bonded winery, Fisher Ridge, in 1979, in anticipation of its passage.

Development since then has remained intensely local. There are several hundred acres of grapes, mostly French hybrids with a scattering of vinifera, planted at locations all over the state. The rugged terrain of West Virginia offers a great variety of sites; the state Department of Agriculture has established demonstration vineyards at six different locations around the state to help determine what the many variations mean for viticulture. Some fourteen wineries have been opened since Fisher Ridge, and more than half of them have survived into the twenty-first century. None has more than a few thousand gallons of storage capacity, so they may quite correctly be called farm wineries. A good deal of fruit wine and mead is also produced.

ARKANSAS, TEXAS, AND OKLAHOMA

Arkansas presents a paradox. It has a long history of established winegrowing, but as the interest in (and the sales of) wine has grown nationwide, the number of wineries in Arkansas has steadily diminished—despite the fact that the state has had an active program of research and teaching at the state university and has made other efforts to encourage winegrowing. The University of Arkansas program in viticulture and enology goes back to 1967 and emphasizes the whole sequence of winemaking operations from vine to bottle; it maintains an experimental vineyard for varietal testing and has done much work in the breeding and introduction of new varieties especially suited to the South. It also offers graduate instruction in enology. The state for many years made its contribution with a preferential tax on Arkansas wines; when that was repealed following the Bacchus decision the legislature, to soften the blow, directed that a part of the new, higher tax be used to support the research program at the university. Despite all of these efforts, Arkansas, which had fifty-six wineries in 1946, had only ten in 1973, and since 1997 has had only five—all but one of them founded *before* the wine boom hit the United States.

Two of these wineries are long established and large: Wiederkehr Wine Cellars (capacity 750,000 gallons) and Post Familie Vineyards (400,000 gallons). Both are in Altus, in the high country overlooking the Arkansas River valley; both claim 1880 as a founding date; both were founded by Swiss settlers; and both remain in family ownership. Wiederkehr has been a pacesetter in modern methods of production, in promotion, and in the introduction of new varieties and of vinifera. Post has clung to the more traditional style in Arkansas, which means wines from the old American hybrids, though wines from French hybrids are produced as well.

The other three Arkansas wineries are small: Mount Bethel, the property of another member of the Post family and also in Altus, produces wines from American grapes; so does the even smaller Cowie Wine Cellars at Paris, on the other side of the river from Altus.[44] The fifth winery, Chateau aux Arc (!) Vineyards, was founded in 2001, which may be a hopeful sign; it, too, is at Altus and makes wine from vinifera grapes. In every other state in which winegrowing might be imagined to have a plausible chance there were, from the 1970s on, people who planted vineyards and built wineries where none had been before. But hardly anyone seems to have been attracted to Arkansas, where they might have benefited from both proven sites and considerable theoretical and practical work. Dr. Justin Morris, who presides over the work in grapes and wines at the university, thinks that the Altus region is the best site for vinifera in all the states east of the Rocky Mountains.[45]

Why, then, has no one ventured? And why has there been no renewal of winemaking in the old Tontitown-Springdale region, where grapes have been grown since well back in the nineteenth century? There were, indeed, two new wineries bonded in the 1980s, Cotner at Fayetteville and Concert Vineyards at Lakeview, but they quickly expired.[46] The fact that more than half of the state's counties are Dry is a consideration, no doubt; but in that matter Arkansas is hardly different from any other southern state. Nor is the weather any more of a challenge—indeed, the Altus region enjoys very attractive conditions, by southern standards. Land costs are not greater than elsewhere in the South and are lower than in many parts of the country. The failure of Arkansas to attract substantial new enterprise in winemaking over the past generation remains a mystery.[47]

Texas is too large to belong to one region. West of the Pecos it is definitely southwestern—mountainous, semiarid, given over to mesquite and cactus. The Panhandle is high plains country, while the low spine (the Balcones Fault Zone) running from north to south between Dallas and San Antonio is a more temperate and fertile country, as the chain of cities that has developed there shows. To the east and south the land is as humid and overgrown as the western part is dry and barren, the soils acid rather than alkaline. Winegrowing in Texas thus has a confusing variety of conditions to deal with, so that both the problems and the possibilities are multiplied.

As in other states, enthusiastic amateurs had a lot to do with renewing the interest in winegrowing in Texas; but, rather exceptionally, such institutions as the University of Texas, Texas A. & M., and the state's agricultural experiment stations were among the pioneers too. To take some of the amateurs first: In 1958 an experimental vineyard at Texas Technological University at Lubbock, on the high plains, was uprooted in order to make way for a highway. Robert Reed, a horticulturist at the university, saved a few vines from destruction and planted them in his back yard in 1958. There they grew well. When a chemist named Clint McPherson, an amateur winemaker, joined the faculty at Texas Tech, he and Reed combined to carry out experimental work in varietal testing on their own, including native American, French hybrid, and vinifera vines. They called their vineyard "'Sagmore' because their trellis wires sagged more than anyone else's."[48] Later they were joined by another Texas Tech chemist, Roy Mitchell. By 1965 they were making wine good enough to venture something a little larger, a fifteen-acre plot. The deliberation with which McPherson and Reed carried out their work is notable. Instead of rushing headlong into enthusiastic production, they took their time. The long history of failure with vinifera made them rightly cautious, and the lack of local experience with the French hybrids meant that they would have to make their own experiments. The work attracted some investors in a project to build a winery, and in 1976 the Llano Estacado Winery was bonded.[49] Support also came from Texas Tech, which funded an experimental winery directed by Mitchell in 1973.

While the amateur work that led to Llano Estacado was quietly in progress, other more public agencies were taking up the cause of grapes and wine in Texas. By far the most impressive was the University of Texas itself, which since its founding in the nineteenth century has had as part of its endowment a vast holding of land—more than 2 million acres—in West Texas. Though originally thought to be fit only for grazing, and not for much of that, the property had produced abundant revenues from oil and gas production since the 1920s. Oil and gas, however, are nonrenewable resources, and the university was concerned to find alternative uses for its lands to supplement its declining revenues. Grapes were one possible crop (others were almonds, walnuts, olives, jojoba, and peaches), and in 1970 the university, working in cooperation with Texas A. & M., Texas Tech, and the Agricultural Extension Service, began a grape demonstration project. Using such sophisticated high-tech means as infrared scans from polar-orbiting satellites, the university team surveyed its huge territories to find suitable sites for vineyards.[50] The first to be planted was in 1975, near Van Horn in West Texas, and it was followed by others in West Texas, on the high plains, and in the center.

The work in these vineyards and others around the state showed that grapes could be an economically viable crop; even more exciting was the revelation that vinifera would grow, even though, in West Texas at least, the fruit might ripen in July. As one of the people concerned in the demonstration, George McEachern, wrote, "It was this discovery that stimulated the almost revolutionary expansion of the new industry" in central, western, and northern Texas.[51] All sorts of things were happening at once in the '70s. The Texas Agricultural Experiment Station carried out an independent feasibility study of the viticultural prospects in vineyards near Lubbock and El Paso.[52] In 1973 McEachern at Texas A. & M. began planting demonstration vineyards all across the state, from east to west and from north to south, in cooperation with private growers. Many of these small plantings died, but others prospered, and so across the state people began to learn about vinifera in Texas. As McEachern said, "There were many successful vineyards across the state: Bobby Smith, Clint McPherson, Ed Auler, The A&M Cooperatives, University of Texas, the Experiment Stations; all the early boys did the same thing, learned with the industry, and grew one step at a time."[53]

In 1977, confirming the new interest in grapes, the Texas Grape Growers Association (later called the Wine and Grape Growers Association) was formed, and in the same year the Texas legislature passed a bill to permit the production of wine in Dry counties, of which Texas still has an inconvenient number.[54] Subsequent legislation authorized tastings at the winery; if, as is frequently the case, the winery is located in a Dry county, it can't offer tastings but it can sell directly to retailers.

While all this ferment was going on, and as vineyards continued to develop, a handful of new wineries came on the scene: Fall Creek, La Buena Vida, Glasscock Vineyards.[55] But this was Texas, and what was wanted was someone who would think *big*. That someone turned out to be the University of Texas. In 1980 the regents of the university toured their West Texas vineyards and sampled wine from the harvests of 1978 and 1979.[56] The result was an enthusiastic decision by the regents to expand the university vineyard from 20 acres to 1,000 acres, concentrating especially on Riesling, French Colombard, and Chenin blanc. The West Texas vineyard near Bakersfield, at an elevation of 2,400 feet, was chosen as the site of development, and extensive planting began in 1981. They did not intend to go into the wine business but rather to demonstrate that large-scale grape growing was economically practical in Texas and so to attract an investor who would take over the work and pay the university a royalty on sales.[57] And of course the regents hoped that others would be found to develop new vineyards and wineries on the university's land.

Gallo and Paul Masson were rumored to be among the first to show an interest in the project, but in 1983 a deal was made with a group of French and Texan investors. The Gill-Richter-Cordier Corporation combined a French winemaking and distributing firm, Cordier; a French vineyard development company, Richter S.A.; and a Texas investment banker, Richardson Gill, who already had a share in the Llano Estacado Winery and thought well of the future of Texas wine. Their agreement with the university, to be reviewed after five years, provided that if all went well an additional 2,000 acres would be planted, so that by 1993 there would be 3,000 acres of grapes under cultivation yielding a projected 5 million gallons of wine.[58] The winery—called Ste. Genevieve—that now went up some miles east of the small West Texas town of Ft. Stockton was as impressive as the vineyards that surrounded it. Of French design and construction, the building has walls forty feet high and is visible for miles as it rises in the midst of its drip-irrigated green vineyards—a surreal vision in that dry, stony land, unrelated to anything around it.

After all these grandiose provisions, the results were not what had been hoped for. Two years after the opening of the winery in 1985, the venture in its original form ended; Bank of America, which had loaned the money for the construction of the winery, took back its property and then accepted an arrangement with only one of the original partners, the Cordier firm. Now, nearly twenty years later, the vineyards are still there, and Ste. Genevieve is still producing; but the vineyards and the winery remain as they were originally established instead of tripling in size, as the plan called for. The elevation of the vineyards means that late spring frosts are a threat; that problem has been met Texas style, with a battery of natural gas heaters and "a flock of helicopters" to drive warm air pockets down onto the vines.[59]

Yet the Texas achievement has been on the whole quite remarkable. Winegrowing has been established all over the state, in sharply varying conditions; much has been learned

FIGURE 50
The University of Texas's
West Texas land as it was
before the vines went in.
(From *American Wine
Society Journal* 7 [Fall
1975]; published with
permission by the
American Wine Society.)

about the choice of varieties, about rootstocks, about cultivation practices. Vinifera has established itself in some regions, but in others the French hybrids or a mix of vinifera and hybrids are the rule. Some growers have succumbed to the devastations of hail and frost, but others have contrived to survive. Lucie Morton, surveying the prospects in 1980, thought that these and other hazards would always keep Texas winemaking on a small scale. To hail and frost one must add, from different parts of the state, saline water, erratic rainfall, cotton root rot, Pierce's disease, high winds, gophers, mockingbirds, wild pigs, and salt marsh caterpillars, to make only a selection from the available diseases, hazards, and pests; but she concluded that if Texas could not manage to make large quantities of bulk wine at economical prices, it might still make smaller quantities of very good wines.[60] That prediction seems generally to have been borne out. At the end of the '80s a survey of winegrowing in Texas concluded that although "the Texas grape and wine industries are small, highly specialized, and financially weak," they continue to "grow and develop."[61]

At the end of the century there were thirty-four wineries in operation, producing more than 1 million gallons of wine annually; twenty-five years earlier, the figures had been five wineries and 14,000 gallons. This is certainly a remarkable achievement. The first detailed survey of Texas vineyards, made in 2001, showed 2,900 acres of grapes producing 9,300 tons, putting Texas fifth among the wine-producing states, after California, Washington, New York, and Oregon.[62] The major producing region is the plains area around Lubbock, where cotton root rot and Pierce's disease are not threats, the climate is dry, and the nights are cool. Grapes from this region supply not merely the local wineries but others across the state.

Unfortunately, the Texas industry has already institutionalized the conflict between smaller and larger wineries—always a threat anywhere, though so far avoided in such newly developed winegrowing states as Oregon and Washington. The smaller wineries are organized as the Texas Wine and Grape Growers Association and are committed to a policy of local development through tasting rooms and sales at the winery; four of the larger wineries are organized as the Associated Wineries of Texas and naturally aim at a wider distribution through the three-tier system.[63]

Texas winegrowing has, by the way, a remarkably academic character. Apart from the institutional presence of the University of Texas, it was three Texas Tech faculty members who got things running with the Llano Estacado Winery in 1976; Sanchez Creek Winery was founded by the chairman of the Department of Anthropology at Southern Methodist University, and Cypress Valley Vineyard by a professor of engineering at the University of Texas at Austin. The medical profession is perhaps even more prominent: among the pioneers were Dr. Henry McDonald (Chateau Montgolfier), Dr. John Anderson (Schoppaul Hill), Dr. Arthur Bieganowski (Bieganowski Cellars), Dr. Bobby Smith (La Buena Vida), and Dr. Antoine Albert (Bluebonnet Hill). But such elements, though striking, are essentially similar to those in all the other states where winegrowing has been reestablished and transformed in the last generation.

Texas is among those fortunate states allowing the sale of table wine in grocery stores (if they aren't in a Dry county), and that is where most Texas wine is bought. Texas is also among the most unfortunate states for the complexity and arbitrariness of its liquor regulations: every individual precinct in the state may choose whether it is to be Wet or Dry, and the result is a confusion almost impossible to describe.[64] As in most of the other new wine-producing states (Oregon and Washington are the exceptions), its wines do not yet circulate beyond the boundaries of the state but depend on a local market.

The brief annals of winegrowing in Oklahoma make a cautionary tale. Not until 1970 did the state issue its bonded winery license number 1, to a hardy soul who made wines from grapes that he bought in neighboring Arkansas.[65] The sound of the wine boom was heard in Oklahoma, however, and it caught the ear of an official of the Office of Economic Opportunity, an agency created by the Great Society of Lyndon B. Johnson and extinguished by Richard Nixon. One of its objects in the brief years of its existence was to get people off welfare and into productive work. Why not put needy families on the land and have them grow grapes for wine? When this idea was put forth in 1972, the state had but one winery, only two years old, and no recent experience in growing grapes; but no matter.

The yields that people were getting in other states, and the prices that were being paid for grapes, created an attractive arithmetic: a ten-acre vineyard, it was calculated, would produce within a few years an income of $7,000 a year in a region where the average per capita income in 1972 was $1,384.[66] The plan originally proposed was to settle three hundred families on three thousand acres of land; they would prepare and plant the land, and in return would be given title to it.[67]

The plan actually carried out was far more modest. The state horticulturist recommended a site in the southeastern corner of the state, near the Texas border, in a Dry county. Cuttings of French hybrid grapes sufficient to plant thirty acres were secured, with some difficulty, in the spring of 1972; ten families, selected from the five thousand that applied, arrived in May and were housed in surplus army trailers, without plumbing or power. While they went to work cultivating the new vineyard, the local hard-shell Baptists prayed that the wicked work would fail and petitioned the governor to put a stop to it.[68] He did not need to interfere. Whether it was God, or nature, or human weakness that was responsible, the Oklahoma grape project soon failed.[69] In the early days of settlement on the prairies it used to be said, as a serious meteorological proposition, that "rain follows the plow." Of course it does no such thing: the idea is the purest wishful thinking, disproved over and over again by bitter experience. The plan for creating a wine industry by resettling welfare families in Oklahoma was perhaps not as fantastic as the notion that rain follows the plow, but it had an equally strong element of the wishful in it.

By 1975 only one family remained at the vineyard; there was a crop to sell, but not surprisingly, there was no one to buy it. Two years later, when the property was sold and the venture ended, the vineyard was "overgrown with wild vegetation."[70] The new owners, who came from Napa Valley, restored the vineyard and in 1983 opened a winery under the name Cimarron Cellars. In 1986 the state allowed Cimarron to sell wine at retail, though not to give tastings.

Since good authorities think that there are many sites around the state that would be well suited to viticulture, there are undoubtedly possibilities for Oklahoma wine. Whether and how they will be realized remains to be seen. So far, it must be admitted, the bacchic impulse has been feeble indeed in Oklahoma, but it seems to be growing stronger. Since Cimarron Cellars opened, several new wineries have been established in Oklahoma, more than half of them in recent years; in 2004 there were nine in operation, all of them very small.

As this survey of the old Confederacy and its bordering states must have shown, wine-growing remains a problematic activity there. In the low country of the Atlantic and Gulf states, "bunch grapes"—whether native American, French hybrid, or vinifera—are still, as they have always been, difficult to grow, and the new introductions created by plant breeders have not yet become established. The indigenous muscadine remains the dominant grape, and its wines have no following outside the South. Generally speaking, the regional preference remains for sweet wines rather than dry table wines. And generally speaking, the prohibitionist spirit remains strong throughout the region. Yet the scene has changed from what it was; where there once seemed mere impossibility, there is now some sort of promise. At the eastern and western limits of the old South—Virginia and Texas—the basis for a prosperous industry has been laid. In between, all sorts of interesting experiments have been carried out, and if things remain precarious, one must still admire the persistence and energy of the experimenters.[71] Who knows what may yet develop in Kentucky, say, or in Georgia?

13

THE WEST WITHOUT CALIFORNIA

WASHINGTON

Washington and Oregon, the two states that complete the Pacific Coast of the United States between California and Canada, are both schizoid territories. The Cascade Range runs north and south like a spine through both states, about a quarter of the way along their west-to-east dimension. On the western, maritime side, where the ocean is cooled by the Japan Current, it rains—a fact that provides for many well-worn jokes about the weather. The Coast Ranges and the parallel Cascade Range are heavily forested. In the well-watered valleys the trees grow large and the grass is green. On the Olympic Peninsula of Washington may be found the only rain forest in the United States. But on the eastern side of the mountains it does not rain.[1] The Cascades, which rise as high as 14,000 feet, make an effective barrier to the wet weather coming in off the Pacific, so the whole of eastern Washington and eastern Oregon alike lies in a rain shadow. Much of the country is essentially desert. It is nevertheless fruitful desert, if one can bring water to it; eastern Washington, since the carrying out of the Columbia Basin project for power and irrigation, has water. The hills that lie athwart the Columbia River in the southern-central part of Washington run east and west, so they present many gentle south-facing slopes providing good air drainage (important protection against frost) and excellent exposure to the sun in this northern latitude. The soil is a sandy loam or silt loam allowing deep root penetration; it is hostile to phylloxera, so the vines can grow on their own roots. Summer temperatures may rise over 100 degrees Fahrenheit; winter temperatures may sink below –10 degrees, so winter damage is a constant threat to the vine. Yields are high—twice what one might expect in California's North Coast region.

It has long been known that vinifera will grow in Washington State. Small plantings were made around Walla Walla, Yakima, and Wenatchee in the late nineteenth century, where some small-scale winemaking was carried on as well but did not long persist.[2] In the early twentieth century, after water was supplied to the Yakima Valley from the Cascades, new vinifera plantings were made and, again, some wine was made as well. In 1914 one of the notable pioneers in Washington vinifera, William Bridgman, planted a vineyard in Sunnyside. Bridgman's vineyards expanded during the Prohibition years; immediately after Repeal, when he had some 165 acres of vinifera, he opened the Upland Winery to produce vinifera wines. The winery, in one form or another, operated until 1972. For many years the manager at the Upland Winery was Erich Steenborg, a native of Germany, who had been trained at the great wine school at Geisenheim and had worked as a winemaker on the Mosel.[3] In his enthusiastic judgment, eastern Washington was destined to make great wines: "The irrigated regions of eastern Washington," he wrote, "are wonderfully adapted to the production of excellent wine grapes, probably equaling any other region that may be found either in America or Europe."[4] In 1938 Steenborg, through the friendly offices of his old school at Geisenheim, had imported half a million cuttings of German varieties into eastern Washington, including Gutedel, Riesling, Sylvaner, Blue Portuguese, and Müller-Thurgau.[5]

While it was thus quite clear that Washington could grow vinifera, it was also true that it could profitably grow native American grapes as well. On the western, maritime side of the state, they were the only choice. A labrusca variety known locally as Island Belle had been the basis of a small grape-growing industry along Puget Sound going back to the late nineteenth century. After Repeal, the first newly bonded winery in Washington, the St. Charles Winery on Stretch Island in Puget Sound, began making wine from Island Belle grapes; it was soon joined by two more wineries and by two grape-juice processors as well, all using the Island Belle.[6] Over the mountains, in eastern Washington, the planting of native American varieties went back to the beginnings, so both native and vinifera varieties were grown; there was no clear disposition to favor the one sort over the other. When irrigated farming on a large scale began to develop in the Yakima Valley early in the twentieth century, the Concord grape entered the scene and soon dominated. The Concord could supply not only the winemakers but the much more active grape-juice trade as well. Moreover, the Concord flourished more powerfully in the conditions of eastern Washington than it ever had back in its native East, producing well-ripened crops of great abundance. Concord quickly became king in Washington, as indeed it still is.[7]

The received myth in Washington (and in Oregon as well) is that when the enthusiasts who revived and transformed winegrowing there in the '60s and '70s consulted the California experts about growing vinifera, they were told that "it couldn't be done."[8] The truth of the matter is quite different. Martin Ray wrote in 1940 that "Washington has every pos-

sibility for successful grape growing in its eastern valleys" and gave Maynard Amerine as his authority.[9] Frank Schoonmaker, writing in 1941, affirmed that although Washington winemaking was in its "embryonic" state, Washington sooner or later "will produce fine wines and will rank among the best viticultural regions of the United States."[10] Amerine, writing in 1942 to describe American wine for an English readership, casually remarked that "proper varieties of *V. vinifera*, planted in the cooler districts of California (or in similar regions of the Pacific Northwest), and vinified properly, will produce fine table wines."[11] From the point of view of 1942, the future of Washington was just as promising as that of California: neither state had yet really shown what it could do. The real question is why, when such opinions were held and when practical experience had shown the success of vinifera in Washington, did nothing substantial develop? Why, when vinifera would grow, was Concord grown instead? Such was the puzzle presented by Washington.

Part of the answer is historical. Prohibition, by making commercial wine illegal, had given a powerful boost to the production of Concord grapes, which had a booming market in grape juice. Because of the conservative nature of grape growing, the Concord vineyards once established would not readily be given up, certainly not when they continued to be profitable. Another part of the answer is political. After Repeal, the state of Washington adopted a monopoly system of liquor distribution, setting up a Washington State Liquor Control Board, which oversaw the whole trade. As an encouragement to domestic industry, the act imposed a high markup on all wines imported into the state and a much lower one on Washington wines. It also permitted wineries using Washington fruit exclusively to sell directly to wholesalers and taverns, while all other wines could be sold only through the stores operated by the board. Because Washington already abounded in Concord grapes, in apples and cherries, and in berries—loganberries, boysenberries, marionberries, youngberries, raspberries, gooseberries, currants, strawberries, huckleberries—the line of least resistance in this protected market was to produce sweet wines made from Concords, apples, and berries. A system of "high fermentation" designed to secure high levels of alcohol in fruit and berry wines was obligingly worked out by two University of Washington scientists. In this method, using a yeast tolerant of a high level of alcohol, the winemaker ameliorated his must by feeding it a steady diet of sugar until the wine reached nearly 17 degrees. The point of this process was to provide the equivalent of a fortified wine without actually fortifying it. At the end of Prohibition Washington produced no brandy, so it would have had to import it from California. But because the law said that wines must be made exclusively from Washington fruit in order to enjoy a protected market, no California brandy could be used. High fermentation was the solution.[12] Later, Washington produced its own brandy; by 1943 half of all the wine made in the state was fortified.[13]

Still another part of the answer was climatic. Vinifera vines certainly grew in eastern Washington, but they did so under the threat of killing winter temperatures. In most years the vines might come through in good shape, but too often for comfort, a winter of severe cold would come along with lethal effect. Such an episode would not have to be repeated very often before a grower might decide that some other crop would offer more security. Thus the uncertainty of the weather put a severe restraint on the expansion of vinifera planting. Vinifera vines, it is true, could be defended against the cold by burying them at the end of every growing season, but that practice was uneconomical on any large scale.

Another part of the answer was cultural. The residents of Washington were no more sophisticated in the matter of wine than those of any other state. They had little experience of table wines and now, in the protected Washington market, they had little opportunity to learn. Sweetened, high-alcohol wines made of Concords, fruits, and berries were now in effect officially encouraged by the state, and they are what determined the idea of wine in Washington. Even the Upland Winery, the lone producer of vinifera wine in the state, depended on its ports and sherries—blends of vinifera and labrusca wines—in order to make a living. It may also be noted that the geography of the state helped to inhibit a knowledge of wine. The overwhelming majority of the population lived on the western side of the Cascades, around Puget Sound, but the grapes grew, invisibly to most people, miles away across the mountains to the southeast.

In the generation after Repeal the wine industry of Washington went on pretty much as it had begun, enjoying a modest prosperity. Labrusca wines continued to be made around Puget Sound; Concord and vinifera wines came from eastern Washington; fruit and berry wines might be made anywhere. Several producers of fruit and berry wines set up shop in and around Seattle, where the market was. They could also buy Concords in the Yakima Valley and transport them to Seattle for processing. By 1937 there were forty-two wineries operating in Washington, after which the number began slowly to decline.[14] The big players were the Pommerelle Company and the National Wine Company, both founded in 1934. They divided the Washington wine world between them, Pommerelle making fruit wines, including (as its name suggests) apple wine, and National (Nawico) making various styles of Concord wine, including blends in which vinifera might figure. The Washington Wine Producers Association was established in 1935; like their Michigan contemporaries, the members of the association directed an industry that was for all practical purposes confined within their own state.

In 1937 the Irrigated Agricultural Research Extension Center of Washington State University at Prosser, in the Yakima Valley, hired a young horticulturist named Walter Clore to carry out experimental work on crops suited to irrigated farming, grapes among them. This appointment came in anticipation of the great expansion of agricultural opportunities about to be created by the Grand Coulee Dam and the flood of irrigation water it would provide. The demands of Washington's wine industry were not then very urgent: Clore did no work on wine grapes until 1941, and it was another quarter century before research into wine began. In the meantime, the basis for further experimental work was quietly laid as the vineyard at Prosser developed.

Before anything very creative could happen, it was necessary that some things should change. One change came about in 1954 when the two big wineries, Pommerelle and National, merged to become American Wine Growers. Pommerelle had bought National some years earlier, but the two firms had continued to operate in competition. Now they were made one, and the new company began some small plantings of vinifera in response to declining sales of the standard Washington wines: it produced no varietal vinifera wines yet, but at least it was preparing for the possibility.[15]

In 1964 an important new move was made when Washington State University initiated its Wine Project, involving researchers at the university and at the Irrigation Experiment Station in Prosser; the immediate motive was the likelihood that the Washington wine industry would soon lose its protected status and would have to be refounded on a new and better basis.[16] Support for the Wine Project was provided in the first instance by the Washington Wine and Grape Growers Council and afterward by a number of other agencies. With Walter Clore's vinifera plantings as a basis, the Wine Project undertook to find out what sorts of wines might be made in the state. The director was Charles Nagel, a food scientist at Washington State University, whose link to wine was that his father had been a cellarmaster for Louis M. Martini in Napa Valley. The Wine Project made it possible for the authorities to make recommendations to the increasing number of people now inquiring about the prospects of winegrowing in Washington. The firstfruit of the work was a report on ten years of trials published in 1976.[17]

Another change, this one of fundamental importance, took place in 1969 when the law protecting Washington wines was set aside: wines from all sources could now be sold outside the state liquor stores, although those stores retained their monopoly on spirits and continued to sell wine too. Washington wines were now on the same footing as wines from California and elsewhere.[18] The immediate result was the death of the old Washington wine industry: by the end of 1969 only three wineries remained in the state.

The movement away from wines made from Concords, fruits, and berries and toward an industry based on vinifera had already begun in a small way. The tentative moves of American Wine Growers in this direction have already been mentioned. A firmer commitment to vinifera was demonstrated by an interesting group of University of Washington professors who had been making wine at home for some time from vinifera grapes purchased in the Yakima Valley. They then made the mistake of showing the growers what good wines they, the amateurs, had made from Yakima grapes; according to Lloyd Woodburne, the founder of the amateur group, the growers "cut off the grape supply because they decided to make the good wine themselves."[19] It probably didn't happen quite that way (they had sources in California, too), but in any case the group decided to develop its own vineyard: that way the members would have a guaranteed supply to sustain their home winemaking.

What they started soon outran their expectations. They bought a 5.5-acre property near Sunnyside in 1962 and planted it to such varieties as Riesling, Chardonnay, Semillon, and Cabernet Sauvignon. Having incorporated in order to buy the vineyard property, they decided to go commercial under the name of Associated Vintners, with the aim of making fine wines such as no commercial winery had yet produced in Washington. To do so they set up a small winery in Kirkland, a Seattle suburb. The first significant crop was harvested in 1967; the first wines, a Riesling and a Gewürztraminer, were released in 1969 and greeted rapturously in Seattle. The winery grew steadily thereafter, moving from smaller to larger to yet larger premises. By the time of a big expansion in 1980, new management had taken over. In 1983 Associated Vintners became the Columbia Winery, the name under which it now operates, its origins in amateur winemaking no longer apparent.[20] It is, nevertheless, an impressive testimony to the power of amateur enthusiasm. The work of Associated Vintners was of crucial importance in the modern history of wine in Washington.

This, however, is getting ahead of our story. Throughout the decade of the 1960s, a slow process of preparation was going on, of which the growth of Associated Vintners was a part. The Wine Project at Washington State University was another. Yet another was the emergence of American Wine Growers—the result of the amalgamation of the Pommerelle Company and the National Wine Company in 1954—as a producer of vinifera wines. Its first such wine was a Grenache rosé put on the market in that year, when the company also began planting vinifera at Grandview, in the Yakima Valley. Semillon and Grenache were the first varieties, followed by Pinot noir, Cabernet Sauvignon, and Riesling.[21] But it was another ten years before American Wine Growers committed itself to vinifera table wines, when it guessed that the market for such wines had now arrived.

In 1967, in confirmation of its new aim to produce good table wines, American hired André Tchelistcheff, the esteemed winemaker at Beaulieu in Napa Valley, to serve as a consultant.[22] The often-told story is that Tchelistcheff, on a visit of inspection to Seattle, found nothing to encourage him in the wines made by American Wine Growers. Then by chance he was offered a bottle of Gewürztraminer made at home by Dr. Philip Church, one of the Associated Vintners group, and that at once excited him: "I was just shocked by the quality of this wine—just unbelievably shocked. It was one of the best Traminers then that I tasted in America." If a home winemaker can make such wine as this from

Washington grapes, Tchelistcheff thought, then "there is definitely hope in Yakima Valley."[23] He agreed to consult for American Wine Growers. Three years later two of the wines made under Tchelistcheff's direction, a Semillon and a Riesling, were presented at the conference of the American Society of Enologists (as it then was) in San Diego. "Everybody," Tchelistcheff recalled, "was just shocked by the extreme quality of those two wines."[24] The rise of Chateau Ste. Michelle Vineyards, the name under which American Wine Growers marketed its wines, had begun.

The end of protection for Washington wine in its home state, which came in the late '60s when the old law was taken off the books, was as much the result of the California wine interest's lobbying power as of anything else.[25] But it may also be seen as the end of the beginnings for the new Washington wine industry. The era of fruit and berry wines was now over; when the dust of that collapse had cleared, a scattering of new vineyards and wineries became visible. New plantings on a substantial scale began to be made: Sagemoor Vineyards at Pasco, Veredon Vineyards near Plymouth in the Horse Heaven

Hills, Stewart Vineyards at Granger, and others up and down the Yakima and Walla Walla Valleys now put a wide range of vinifera varieties to practical, commercial trial. Between 1969 and 1971, about 500 acres of vinifera were planted in Washington.[26] The dominant notion at this stage was that white varieties were the preferred choice. Everyone had Riesling, Chenin blanc, Chardonnay, Semillon; Gewürztraminer and Sauvignon blanc were also familiar. But the reds were not neglected: Cabernet Sauvignon, Merlot, Zinfandel, Pinot noir, and such unfamiliar varieties as Lemberger were all part of the mix. All were planted on their own roots, since phylloxera had not yet been found in Washington.[27]

There was a boundless confidence at work in Washington in the early '70s as plantings grew rapidly. "We're going to be number 2" was the rallying cry then (behind California but ahead of New York). Even the cautious Walter Clore made bold predictions: "We will not need to take a back seat," he said. "We have something unique. We can compete with the rest of the U.S. and even with Europe."[28] The Washington State Department of Commerce and Economic Development sponsored the first Pacific Northwest Wine and Grape Seminar in 1973. In 1974 the Society of Washington Wine Producers and Winegrowers was formed.

New wineries were, however, rather slow to appear. American Wine Growers and Associated Vintners had the show pretty much to themselves. In 1971 an interesting variation arrived. Seneca Foods Company, a large processor based in New York, announced that it was building a new winery at Prosser in the Yakima Valley, where the company already made grape juice and applesauce. Now it would make wine too. The novelty was that the wine would come not only from vinifera but from French hybrid varieties as well. Two years earlier, Seneca had made a deal with Philip Wagner, of Boordy Vineyards in Maryland, to use his winery's name on the produce of a new winery that Seneca had built in Westfield, New York, in the heart of the Concord belt. The idea was to exploit the substantial new plantings of French hybrid grapes that had been made in the region; Wagner, as the high priest of the French hybrid in this country, was the obvious choice to sponsor the enterprise. Now Seneca was extending the idea from New York to its Washington territory; the wines made there, in the new 200,000-gallon-capacity winery, would also be labeled Boordy Vineyard. There were already some plantings of French hybrids in the Yakima Valley, a hedge against the uncertainties of vinifera in a region where much was still new and untested.[29] The idea was to use a mix of hybrids and vinifera to make inexpensive blends.[30] The plan did not work out. The wines were not liked, or at any rate they did not sell. Wagner's insistence on unpretentious simplicity may have been a contributing reason: in addition to a Pinot Chardonnay (as it was then called), the first Boordy wines from Washington were called simply Yakima Valley Red, Yakima Valley White, and Yakima Valley Rosé.[31] The Seneca-Boordy operation in Washington closed in 1976.[32]

This misstep did not damage confidence in Washington. On the contrary, new investment began to come into the state about this time. In 1970, in the early days of the national wine boom, a venturesome investment manager for an insurance company in San Francisco, Wallace Opdyke, concluded that Washington wine was a good bet and organized a group to buy American Wine Growers, whose original owners and managers were beginning to die out. The deal was closed in 1972; this move seems to have excited a wider interest in Washington wine, for in 1973 the United States Tobacco Company of Greenwich, Connecticut, which had a lot of money and a good reason to wish to diversify its interests, bought the winery, now known as Chateau Ste. Michelle. U.S. Tobacco was prepared to spend large sums of money on its new acquisition and at once proceeded to do so. A 500-acre vineyard was newly planted at Cold Creek in the Yakima Valley, and the existing winery at Grandview was expanded. Plans were made for a new winery in the Seattle area. It materialized in 1976 as the splendid Chateau Ste. Michelle in Woodinville, fifteen miles north of Seattle. Built in the French provincial style on a large property that had once been a prosperous lumberman's estate, it houses the headquarters of the company and a winery with a storage capacity of nearly 3 million gallons. It is now one of the tourist attractions of the Seattle region.[33]

The Ste. Michelle operation, sustained as it is by a large capital source, has grown steadily. It dominated Washington wine production even in the days when it was American Wine Growers; it dominates now. Indeed, the contrast between the Washington giant and all the other wineries of the state is more overwhelming than that between Gallo and the rest of California. In 1981 Ste. Michelle began to build a big new winery at Paterson, Washington, in the Horse Heaven Hills above the Columbia River, where they had made extensive new plantings. The new facility, now operated as a separate winery called Columbia Crest, was a $25 million affair. Its current storage capacity is over 6 million gallons. In 1991 Ste. Michelle established a big new vineyard called Canoe Ridge Estates and added a winery there in 1993. The company had along the way (1986) been renamed Stimson Lane Vineyards and Estates (after the address of its Woodinville headquarters), though it remained a property of the U.S. Tobacco Company. It made another large acquisition in 1991 when it bought the bankrupt Snoqualmie Winery, founded in 1983 and the second largest winery in the state. In 1986 and 1987 Stimson Lane expanded in a new direction for a Washington winery by buying two well-known wineries in Napa Valley, Villa Mt. Eden and Conn Creek. By 1990 nearly four-fifths of all the wine sold by Washington wineries came from Stimson Lane properties.[34] Ernest Gallo might well envy such a command of the market.

Not until 1974 did small new winemaking ventures begin to appear in Washington. Two opened that year, Mont Elise at Bingen and Puyallup Valley Winery; both were outside the main regions of development. The next year passed without any new foundations, but there were three in 1976, one in 1977, and three in 1978. This spasmodic progress at last hit high acceleration in the '80s: twelve new wineries opened in 1982, eight in 1983, ten in 1984, and so on.[35] Washington currently has more than two hundred wineries, and production from the 29,000 acres of wine grapes has hit 13 million gallons. This is by far the greatest growth to be found in any of the states that shared in the new winemaking movement that began in the 1960s. The boast that "we're going to be number 2" has been fulfilled.

The new wineries also opened up new regions. The Yakima Valley was the navel of winegrowing, from Yakima down to the Yakima River's junction with the south-flowing Columbia at the Tri-Cities (Richland, Kennewick, and Pasco). There had been some vineyard planting on the Wahluke Slopes, north of that point on the Columbia, and some more along the Columbia after it makes its right turn and heads west for the ocean. All of this is now a part of the huge Columbia Valley American Viticultural Area (AVA), which contains the Yakima Valley AVA as well. A tributary is the Walla Walla AVA, along the valley of the Walla Walla River to the east of the Columbia near the Oregon border. In recent years this has been one of the hot spots of growth. The number of wineries there has almost doubled, and some of its wine has earned high acclaim—though much of that wine comes from grapes grown not in the Walla Walla but in the Yakima Valley. The process of devising new AVAs within the old ones, as particular regions become identified, has now begun: the small Red Mountain AVA at the lower end of the Yakima Valley was approved in 2001, the Horse Heaven Hills have applied for approval, and others will no doubt follow.

In 1995 an AVA was created for Puget Sound, where the cool and wet climate had not been thought fit for the cultivation of vinifera. The region includes not just the land bordering the sound but the many islands and the western foothills of the Cascade Range. There is a good number of small wineries in the region—about thirty—but no large vineyards. Their production is not likely to grow much, because this is where people live in Washington. One of the pioneers in the area was Bainbridge Island Winery, which planted Chardonnay and Riesling in 1976 and has since planted Müller-Thurgau, Pinot noir, and Pinot gris. The Neuharth Winery opened in Sequim, on the Olympic Peninsula, in 1979 (but using grapes from eastern Washington). One winery operates on Lopez Island in the San Juans, another on San Juan Island. The Mount Baker winery is at the northern edge of the Puget Sound AVA, near Bellingham. At the northwestern corner of the state, near Vancouver, an isolated outpost called Salishan Winery opened in 1982. The map of Washington now shows wineries dotted about at many points, including the cities of Seattle and Spokane, where they naturally depend on bringing in grapes from vineyards elsewhere. This pattern of putting the winery far from the vineyards but close to the centers of population, unusual elsewhere, is well marked in Washington.

Most Washington wineries are on the small side, emphasizing the contrast between the relatively many small and the very few large. They range from the 100-case annual production of Marchetti Wines in Olympia to the 6-million-gallon storage capacity of Columbia Crest, with a great many operating at 10,000 cases of annual production or less: Animale Cellars (200 cases), Bunchgrass (400), Fox Estate (1,500), Page Cellars (500), Vashon (600)—the list of such modest enterprises is long. One reason that such small wineries can survive is that many do not own vineyards and so do not struggle under that capital cost. Such is the case with the cluster of wineries in and around Spokane, for example: Robert Karl Cellars, Knipprath, Latah Creek, Caterina, Arbor Crest. All of these and a good many others buy their grapes from elsewhere in the state, and some of them manage to produce quite highly regarded wines.

Conversely, if the wineries are often small, the vineyards are often large. This circumstance has much to do with the conditions of irrigated agriculture; just as in California's Central Valley, a farm in eastern Washington is likely to be big. Grapes may be but one crop among others in what can only be called corporate farming. Such was the case with Hogue Cellars, which grew to be the largest in the state after Ste. Michelle, with a winery storage capacity of 1.3 million gallons supplied by 600 acres of vines.[36] But grapes were only a part of the farm's crops, which included hops, spearmint, potatoes, and asparagus; the Hogues raised cattle too on their 2,000 acres. Balcom and Moe, at Pasco, have 110 acres in vineyards as part of a 3,000-acre property. The Red Willow Vineyard at White Swan occupies 120 acres on a 2,200-acre farm. The vineyards called Sagemoor, Bacchus, and Dionysus developed by Alec Bayless and his associates beginning in 1972 are not part of a diversified farming operation but are a corporate enterprise in themselves: the property of the Vineyard Management Company, they cover more than a thousand acres in the Yakima Valley. There seems to be a sharp division of labor in Washington, after the industrial model, in which one set of proprietors grows the grapes and another set makes the wine. The division is not complete by any means, nor need it be permanent.

Recognition of the new wines made in Washington came very quickly, when there were only two wineries in the state. The first to notice was the food columnist for the *Seattle Post-Intelligencer*, Stan Reed, who was powerfully smitten by the first commercial offerings of Associated Vintners, a Riesling and a Gewürztraminer, in 1969, and told his readers that, overnight, Washington wine had undergone a revolution.[37] This was an important moment, for it is with wines as with prophets: they are often without honor in their own country. The Finger Lakes region in upstate New York has sought in vain for generations to win the respect of the New York City market; Texas wines are still regarded as curiosities in Dallas and Houston; the table wines of California were neglected in their own state until the eastern establishment took them up. The new vinifera wines from Washington, however, were received with enthusiasm by the Washingtonians, and there has been a happy harmony between the producers and their in-state admirers ever since. In 1974 a Washington Riesling in a judging organized by Robert Lawrence Balzer for the *Los Angeles Times* took top honors in a competition of Rieslings from around the world: the excitement created by this triumph was so great in Washington, according to one writer, that it marked the turning point in the growth of the wine industry.[38] In 1983 *Time* magazine took favorable notice of Washington: "It has the climate, soil and available land to become a wine region of world repute."[39]

The figures for production and distribution confirm that Washington wines had more than a local success. In 1981 about a quarter of Washington's production of approximately a million gallons was shipped out of state—by no means a contemptible figure. Ten years later, 44 percent of the wine that Washington produced was exported: 2.6 million gallons out of a total production of 6.4 million gallons. At the turn of the new century, 75 percent of Washington's sales were out of state.[40]

What sort of wines Washington was destined to make best could not, of course, be known at the beginning of its new affair with vinifera. The general opinion, as has been said, inclined toward white varieties: Riesling, especially, was regarded as the grape of choice; Gewürztraminer, Chenin blanc, Sauvignon blanc, Semillon, and Chardonnay were also early favorites. Chardonnay, predictably, now leads all other varieties in the state, but that has more to do with the rigid expectations of the American market than with any special distinction in Washington Chardonnay. In 1982, there were 6,000 acres of white wine varieties to only 1,500 of red.[41]

The prospects for red wines were not as clear because, as André Tchelistcheff put it, "they need more aging, more know-how, more sculpting by the wine maker."[42] But the red wines of Washington have come on strong in recent years. The current disposition of things in Washington's vineyards shows a clear preponderance of red over white varieties.[43] Merlot is the most-planted red variety, followed by Cabernet Sauvignon: the wines from both varieties are highly esteemed. Syrah has come from nowhere to a respectable presence in the past few years. A Washington specialty—one would like to see more of such things in addition to the standard varieties—is a variety popular in Austria and Hungary called, in Washington, Lemberger (elsewhere Limberger, or Blaufränkisch, or Kékfrankos), a favorite of Dr. Clore at the Research and Extension Station. A few wineries now make wine from it in fairly substantial quantities.[44]

The Washington wine industry has generated a good number of trade and official organizations. The first, already mentioned, was the Washington Wine Producers Association, organized in 1935; this was a trade association, whose main object in the early days was simply to maintain the protected status of the Washington winemakers. In 1938 the association rechristened itself the Washington Wine Council; later, in the time of expansion, it became the Washington Wine and Grape Growers Council. In 1974 the Society of Washington Wineproducers and Winegrowers, or the Washington Wine Society for short, was organized not only as a lobbying group but to support research.[45] The Wine Institute, whose members are producing wineries, was formed in 1982 as a lobbying group. The growers organized as the Washington Association of Wine Grape Growers in 1983. The state has also signaled its support in various ways. The Wine Marketing Advisory Council under the Department of Agriculture was formed in 1983 with a grant from the legislature. In 1985 the legislature voted a grant for the promotion of wine, and this support was translated into permanent form in 1986 by an act creating the Washington Wine Commission, paid for by levies on the sale of grapes and wine in Washington. The Wine Institute and the Wine Commission merged in 1988; the Commission-Institute is now the main agency for the promotion of Washington wines.

A program in viticulture and enology at Washington State University is now in the planning stage. In the meantime, such work is offered at Walla Walla Community College, and students at Washington State can get a bachelor of science degree in agriculture with emphasis on viticulture and enology.

The happy relation between Washington winemakers and Washington wine drinkers is exemplified in the Enological Society of the Pacific Northwest, an association of amateurs of wine founded in 1975 and creatively active since then. It has blossomed into eight chapters in Washington and Idaho. It offers monthly dinners, an annual wine competition, a fall festival of wine, organized tours, and short courses. The Prosser branch of the society founded a wine library as a part of the local public library.[46]

Washington's is the outstanding success story among the new winegrowing states. That success owed a little bit, perhaps, to the beginnings made after Repeal, but Island Belle and Concord wines would never have achieved much, nor had anything notable been done with the small acreage of vinifera grown in the state. In common with other states, Washington had first to wait for the wine boom in California before its own transformation could take place. When that moment came, the change was swift and far-reaching; it was so, in large part, because Washington could benefit from the complete winegrowing establishment already in place to the south in California. The cuttings with which to plant the new Washington vineyards came from California nurseries. So did the viticulturists to tend them: Dr. Wade Wolfe, vineyard manager for Ste. Michelle; John Pringle, in charge of the Sagemoor Vineyard. So did the winemakers who taught Washington how to make its wines: Joel Klein at Ste. Michelle, Brian Carter at Paul Thomas, David Lake at Columbia Winery, Mike Conway at Hogue Cellars, and Mike Marcil at Quail Run, to name but a few, were all California-trained. Alan Shoup, the strategist behind the great growth of Ste. Michelle and a leader in the affairs of the industry, is an alumnus of Gallo Winery. This is not to say that Washington did not have its own conditions, or to deny that plenty of important pioneering work was carried out by Washingtonians themselves; but it is certain that the ready supply of materials, of knowledge and experience, and of trained workers from California made a big difference.

The effect of the California model is apparent in other ways too. Washington wineries quickly learned from their California counterparts to exploit tourism as a profitable adjunct to winegrowing: Tom Stockley's *Winery Trails of the Pacific Northwest* appeared in 1977 and has had many successors to instruct tourists. The imposing château winery of Ste. Michelle, designed with tourist traffic in mind, opened in 1976. So elaborate and expensive a monument could hardly be widely imitated, but the idea that it suggested was not lost on other Washington wineries; most of them, after their own fashion, encourage the idea of the winery as a place of public resort. Public relations and the cultivation of the media were soon under way; the flourishing growth of such work was confirmed by the formation of the Washington Wine Writers Association in 1985. The Tri-Cities Northwest Wine Festival began in 1979, the Tacoma Wine Festival in 1983, the Spokane Wine Festival in 1985, and the Western Washington Wine Fair in Puyallup in 1986. The first World Vinifera Conference was held in Seattle in 1989. It can hardly be said that Washington has been backward in the matter of promoting its wines. It has also, no doubt inevitably, begun to find its equivalents to the dubious phenomenon of the cult winery that emerged in California toward the end of the century—that is, the small, select winery of rigidly limited production whose wines, through the power of advertising, the excitement of competition for a scarce commodity, and the acquisitive passion among the rich, are eagerly bid for at prices having no relation to any intelligible or defensible standard. It would be invidious to name any names, for the wineries in question are probably innocent of any intention to create so absurd a situation. The point is that it has occurred in Washington alone (as far as I know) of the winemaking states outside California.

OREGON

Oregon is often supposed to be a sort of country cousin to Washington, sharing a comparable heritage but not making so much of it from a worldly point of view. Perhaps so. More to the point, however, is the fact that although it shares the same division into well-watered west and arid east, it does not have a Columbia River running through its eastern wastes. Its winegrowing is therefore mostly on the western side of the Cascades. This is one striking difference from Washington. Another is that winemaking in Oregon is on a much smaller scale than that in Washington: there are, as in Washington, one or two firms much bigger than all the rest, but on nothing like the Washington scale of disproportion. Another difference is that Oregon has its own favorite varieties, Pinot noir and Pinot gris chief among them, that are not much favored at all in Washington. In short, although Oregon and Washington are conveniently lumped together as the Pacific Northwest, they need to be discussed separately as winegrowing states, for the differences are probably more striking than the resemblances.

It had long been known that vinifera would grow in Oregon as it does in Washington. Small plantings of such varieties as Zinfandel and Riesling, obtained in California, were planted in both southern and northern Oregon by German settlers at the end of the nineteenth century.[47] If a little wine was made from these and other plantings, it was only a little. During Prohibition there was a flurry of new planting of vinifera in southern Oregon, but these were of table varieties such as the Flame Tokay.[48] There were also a few vineyards near The Dalles, on the Columbia River. In the Willamette Valley, the agricultural heart of Oregon, only native American varieties were grown.

After Repeal, the son of one of the original German growers near Roseburg opened a winery that operated until 1965: this was Doerner Winery, the sole product of which was red table wine, a blend of several varieties. A few other wineries made wine from grapes in Oregon, but entirely from Concords and other labrusca types. The main business in Oregon, as in Washington, was in wines made from Oregon's fruits and berries: apples, loganberries, blackberries, cherries. By the end of the '30s the high point of this development was reached: there were twenty-eight wineries in Oregon in 1938, producing just over a million gallons of fruit and berry wines.[49] One reason that so large a number of establishments could exist was that Oregon had a farm winery category requiring only a $25 license fee; with this license, a grower could have wine made from his fruit at another facility and then sell it himself at retail. Thus Oregon had, for example, the Thomas and Elsie Forrest Winery at Broadbent with a storage capacity of 4,000 gallons, and the Kraemer Winery at Milwaukie with a capacity of 5,000 gallons. The big player among the small fry was Hood River Distillers of Hood River, with a capacity of 350,000 gallons.

After 1938, competition from California, the effects of the war years, and no doubt changing tastes as well, all helped to send the Oregon wine industry into decline. By the beginning of the 1960s, Honeywood Winery in Salem, producing fruit and berry wines, was the only large winemaking enterprise left in Oregon; it was accompanied by a handful of small farm wineries. No one then would have predicted any future for winegrowing in the state.

By the sort of dramatic irony familiar in these stories, the low point was also the turning point. In 1960 Richard Sommer, who came from an Oregon family but had trained as an agronomist at the University of California, Davis, bought a small property near Roseburg in the Umpqua Valley. Sommer had a definite idea in mind: he would plant vinifera vines and make wine from them. All agree that this was the moment—and it is unusual to be able to specify a critical moment so precisely—at which the modern Oregon wine industry began. Sommer's first small planting, of Riesling and Chardonnay, was made in 1961. His Hillcrest Winery was bonded in 1963, and the first wines were put on the market in 1967: they were then regarded as the only "grape wines," as the local press innocently called them, being made in Oregon.[50]

Sommer's example persuaded Paul Bjelland to make the next venture in the Umpqua Valley; he began to plant 19 acres of grapes on a 200-acre property near Roseburg in 1968. A few Umpqua Valley farmers also undertook to plant grapes in order to supply the two wineries now operating, but no other new developments took place there for some years. In the meantime, the focus of Oregon's small new winegrowing enterprise was about to shift. The Umpqua Valley, in the southwestern quarter of the state, is warmer and drier than many other sites on Oregon's Pacific slope: that is what attracted Sommer to the region in the first place. But vigorous development, beginning about the time that Sommer had his first wines for sale, took place in a less likely region, the Willamette Valley. The Willamette River runs from south to north over a course of some 180 miles before it flows into the Columbia at Portland. The valley that it drains has been the heart of Oregon's settlement and agricultural production since the early days of the state. Most of Oregon is either high or dry, or both: the forested coastal mountains, the Cascades, and the high, dry rangeland east of the Cascades are not suited to agriculture. The Willamette Valley is. Some sixty miles broad at its northern end, it gradually tapers to less than ten at its southern end. It is a region of low hills, which offer many attractive sites for vineyards, but it is also humid and verdant, after the fashion of western Oregon. It would seem to be rather wetter and cooler than ideal country for the vine is thought to be, but it is here that winegrowing began to flourish.[51]

FIGURE 53

"Nothing fancy" is the Oregon watchword: Richard Sommer's Hillcrest Winery, where modern Oregon winemaking began. (Author's collection.)

The beginning was made by Charles Coury, who bought property near Forest Grove in the northern part of the Willamette Valley in 1965 with the purpose of planting grapes and making wine. Coury had written a thesis at Davis on the relations of climate and grape variety and had concluded that the Willamette Valley would be a place where grapes adapted to the northern European regions—Burgundy and Alsace—might flourish. Against considerable skepticism, he acted on his educated guess by planting Riesling and Pinot blanc. His Charles Coury Vineyards never got beyond a very small production and did not survive the decade of the '70s.[52] Nevertheless, Coury is acknowledged as the first of the modern Willamette pioneers. He was closely followed by David Lett, who had been at Davis with Coury and had, through Coury's theories, gotten "all fired up about Pinot noir."[53] He bought land in 1966 at Dundee, near McMinnville, and began to plant Pinot noir. His Eyrie Vineyards released its first Pinot noir in 1970, and with that Oregon found what was very quickly identified as its signature wine.

It may be noted that the three men who were first on the Oregon scene in the 1960s—Sommer, Coury, and Lett—were all trained at Davis. So too was William Fuller of Tualatin Vineyards, who followed in 1973.[54] But other newcomers were a mix of all sorts: Richard Erath (his winery was established in 1972) was an engineer, as was Richard Ponzi (1970); David Adelsheim (1971) has a degree in German literature; Ronald Vuylsteke of

Oak Knoll (1970) worked for Tektronix in Portland; Susan Sokol was a history professor and her husband, William Blosser, a land-use planner before they combined to launch Sokol Blosser Winery in 1971; and Myron Redford of Amity Vineyards (1976) was a population researcher at the University of Washington.

Following this sequence of beginnings, Oregon wineries proliferated rapidly, especially in the northern Willamette Valley. Only a decade after Richard Sommer had put in his first Riesling vines in the Umpqua Valley, there were thirty-four wineries in Oregon. More than half of them were in the northern Willamette, which soon began to develop distinctive subregions: Tualatin Valley, Chehalem Ridge, Dundee Hills, Eola Hills. By far the densest concentration of vineyards and wineries is in Yamhill County in the neighborhood of Dundee (population 1,700). This dominance is largely owing to the proximity of Portland and to the topographical fact that the region offers a series of south-facing hillsides. Yamhill County is, above all else, the home of Oregon Pinot noir. As one moves to the warmer, southern end of the Willamette Valley, the wineries grow fewer: there is a cluster around Salem and a string running down to Eugene. Two of the largest wineries in Oregon are both in the south Willamette: Willamette Valley Vineyards, near Salem, and King Estate Winery, Eugene. Pinot noir is the leading variety in the south as well as the north of the Willamette Valley.

The Willamette Valley was granted the status of an AVA in 1984, and there will be a further subdivision of the region when current applications have been approved.[55] A little later in 1984, the same recognition was granted to the Umpqua Valley. Since then growth in the Umpqua AVA has been slow. There were five wineries within the AVA when it was formed; today there are eleven. The reason given for this relative backwardness is the isolation of the area; it is two hundred miles south of Portland, the nearest large city. As in most of Oregon's vineyards, Pinot noir is the leading variety in the Umpqua; there are those who think the region might in fact be better suited to Cabernet Sauvignon and other Bordeaux varieties, but this thought has not yet been acted on.[56]

Farther south yet are the Rogue River and Applegate Valley AVAs, and here, indeed, Cabernet Sauvignon and Merlot take precedence over Pinot noir. The Rogue River AVA is in fact two separate valleys blocked off by a jumble of mountains: the Illinois Valley, around Cave Junction, is closest to the ocean and grows Pinot noir. The main valley, running east from Grant's Pass to Ashland, is warmer and grows a large acreage of Cabernet Sauvignon and Merlot. Applegate Valley, lying between the two parts of the Rogue River AVA and originally a part of it, is now a separate AVA. The pine-forested Rogue River region—in summer a place of high temperatures on dry hills—would seem to most people more like nearby California than Oregon. People were growing vinifera grapes here successfully during the Prohibition years—for the table, not for wine.[57] But as in the Umpqua Valley, and perhaps for the same reason, the new winegrowing has not yet taken off. The first new winery was Valley View (1978), which clearly deviates from the Oregon standard by producing Syrah, Merlot, and Cabernet Sauvignon wines. At the turn of the century there were six active wineries in the Rogue River AVA and seven in the

Applegate, all small. In all three southern AVAs there is also a good deal of experimentation with different varieties—Tempranillo, Syrah, Cabernet franc—as the region attempts to discover a means of distinguishing itself from the dominant Pinot noir culture to the north. In the early years of the winegrowing revival in Oregon, vines were planted on their own roots, since phylloxera was not yet known in the state. It appeared in 1990, and since then plantings have been made on various resistant rootstocks. Some parts of the state are as yet unaffected, but their immunity is not likely to be permanent.[58]

Not all Oregon wine comes from the Pacific slope, just most of it. In this it is the exact mirror image of neighboring Washington, which grows a lot of wine in the east and not very much in the west. Across the Cascades in Oregon, to the east, one tiny winery—Mountain View—makes wine in the remote town of Bend, where one does indeed get a splendid mountain view of the Three Sisters. North, along the Columbia River, Oregon has a small share in the huge Columbia Valley AVA, most of which lies across the river and extends far to the north in Washington. A few hundred acres of grapes grow in Hood River and Wasco Counties, in Oregon's section of the Columbia Valley AVA, but only two wineries operate in the area, Hood River Winery and Flerchinger Vineyards. In the northeastern corner of the state, the Walla Walla AVA—mostly on the Washington side of the Columbia—extends into Oregon (AVAs are geographical, not political, so they regularly disregard political boundaries), and here for a time the Seven Hills Winery produced wine from irrigated vineyards. The winery has now migrated to the Washington side, but the vineyards remain.

One Oregon anomaly may be mentioned. Serendipity Cellars Winery at Monmouth, in the northern Willamette Valley, made a success of a wine produced not from vinifera but from the French hybrid known as Maréchal Foch (Kuhlmann 188–2), a grape with Pinot noir, Gamay, and the American riparia in its ancestry. It is adapted to cool-country, short-season conditions. The owner of Serendipity, who got his Foch grapes from a neighbor's vineyard, found that the wine he made from it was his most popular wine. He paid $1,000 a ton to the grower, and since the variety produced six tons to the acre rather than the average three tons for Pinot noir, the grower was making more money per acre than any other grower in Oregon. Since it has good color and Pinot noir often does not, it is legal to add up to 5 percent Foch to Oregon Pinot. Foch does not yet appear as a separate category in the statistics of Oregon grape acreage, but its virtues may allow it to survive, despite the recent closing of Serendipity Cellars. Philip Wagner was much pleased to learn of this modest success of one of the hybrids that he had so devotedly promoted.[59] He would also have been interested in the fact that the Girardet Winery in the Umpqua Valley lists a Baco noir, another French hybrid, among its top varietals, and that the winery uses DeChaunac, Chancellor, and other hybrids in its inexpensive Vin Rouge and Vin Blanc. And Wagner would have enthusiastically approved the reason for this practice: to provide good, sound, inexpensive wines for everyday drinking.[60] It is perhaps significant that Girardet's proprietor is a Swiss, accustomed to thinking of wine as an excellent thing for daily, unpretentious use, rather than as an earth-shattering experience of the ultimate. Would that we had more like him. But it is unlikely that the French hybrids will continue to generate much interest in Oregon unless there should be an unexpected shift in the public's notions.

Oregon seems to have had a reasonably enlightened government to work with in the development of its winegrowing industry. Self-help had to come first: the Oregon Wine Growers Association was formed in 1969. The association originated with the wineries of the Umpqua Valley; a little later the Willamette people formed their own group, the Wine-growers' Council of Oregon, but the two were soon merged (1978) under the original name. One valuable piece of work accomplished by the organized winegrowers was to secure a set of strict labeling regulations for Oregon wines in 1977. A varietal wine—and most of Oregon's production is so labeled—must contain 90 percent of the variety named rather than the 75 percent required by federal regulation; and generic names such as chablis, burgundy, and rhine are forbidden on Oregon wines. All labels must show the region of origin, and the grapes must all come from that region. Other state regulations include a ban on importing anything but virus-free vines and restrictions on the use of pesticides.

The usual promotional events were quickly established. The Oregon Wine Festival was first held in 1970, when there were only about nine wineries in the state.[61] In 1974 a wine judging was held for the first time at the state fair. About 1970 Oregon State University began experimental work in viticulture and now offers courses in viticulture and fermentation science, though it does not yet have a full-fledged program in viticulture and enology. A two-year institution, Chemeketa College in Salem, is beginning such a program and has plans to build a viticulture center, including a winery.

By 1983, when Oregon had some thirty-three wineries and had begun to make an impression on the rest of the country, the state, following the recommendation of the Oregon Winegrowers Association, established the Oregon Wine Advisory Board as part of the state Department of Agriculture. It provided for research and promotion by diverting part of the tax on wine to the board and by an assessment on grapes split between the grower and the buyer.[62] And to show its goodwill, the state created an official Oregon State wine cellar in 1986.[63] The most recent legislation in assistance of the wine industry allows the creation of joint facility wineries, in which several bonded winery license holders can pool resources to build a winery at the disposal of all of them. The first of these new establishments, the Carlton Winemakers' Studio, opened in 2002.

Oregon Pinot noir enjoyed a spectacular promotional success in the very infancy of the industry. In the summer of 1979 Gault-Millau, the publishers of the respected *Nouveau Guide* to food and wine, organized a wine *olympiade* in which some 330 wines from thirty-three countries were judged. Two Oregon Pinot noirs, from The Eyrie Vineyards and Knudsen-Erath Winery, outscored some distinguished Burgundian names, but the showing of the California wines involved got most of the publicity in this country; there was, as well, a good deal of skepticism about the methods of the competition. The event did, however, have a surprising consequence. Robert Drouhin, an important proprietor and *négociant* in Burgundy, refused to credit the results of the Pinot noir section in the Gault-Millau judging. He therefore set up a judging of his own, early in 1980; this time Drouhin Chambolle-Musigny 1959 came in first, but second was The Eyrie Vineyards 1975—ahead of Drouhin's Chambertin Clos de Bèze 1961. This affair *did* get publicity, and David Lett at Eyrie found himself besieged by enthusiasts eager for a bottle from his slender stock of winning wine.[64] As for Drouhin, he needed no more convincing. He came to Oregon to survey this interesting new source of rivalry, bought land near Dundee, and created his own winemaking estate devoted to Oregon Pinot noir: Domaine Drouhin Oregon.

Drouhin's venture into Oregon, which began in 1987, was not the only outside investment in the state. California investors soon made an appearance: the Benton-Lane Winery (1992) is owned by two Napa Valley winegrowers; Van Duzer (1998) is owned by William Hill of Napa, and Archery Summit (1993) by Pine Ridge Winery of Napa. The attractive power of Oregon was well shown when in 1997 Tony Soter, one of the most highly regarded winemakers and consultants in California (Chappellet, Etude, Spottswoode, Viader, Moraga), chose to relocate to the northern Willamette to grow Pinot noir and Chardonnay. The Australians arrived with the founding in 1987 of Dundee Vineyards by Brian Croser, the noted owner and winemaker at Petaluma in the Adelaide Hills of South Australia, and Cal Knudsen, once the partner of Richard Erath in Knudsen-Erath Winery before its reversion to the original Erath name. Dundee, which puts out its wine under the Argyle label, has made sparkling wine its main object and so has added a new dimension to Oregon winemaking. The most expensive development so far among Oregon wineries is the King Estate, the creation of a family originally from Kansas City grown wealthy in the aircraft electronics business. On the King Estate, southwest of Eugene, a 250-acre vineyard supplies a 400,000-gallon-capacity winery, designed to be a showpiece as well as a working facility.

Oregon, obviously, is not immune to the forces operating in the wine world elsewhere, particularly in California—the forces that come together as the corporate takeover. But Oregon wineries have consciously sought to hold on to a distinctive Oregon style. In the stereotype, they would be small, family affairs, aiming at a rustic rather than a sophisticated character: no Napa Valley glitz, but rather a down-home kind of rural simplicity. The proprietor would favor blue jeans and a checked woolen shirt, and he could be found with his dog in the vineyards or hoisting barrels in the winery. The winery buildings themselves would be unpretentious and functional—converted farm buildings, for choice. "Nothing fancy" would be the watchword. The work in vineyard and winery would be a family responsibility: husband and wife, and children if there were any, would participate directly in a hands-on operation. But the winemaking would be of the highest standard, the result of personal attention to every step of the process, from planting the vine to bottling the finished wine, supported by the latest technical knowledge.

How much of the simple, rustic image cultivated by Oregon winemakers really describes their lives and how much belongs to the Oregon myth is a question that we need not decide. The fact is that some, at least, of the newer Oregon wineries represent quite large investments, and some energetically apply all the sophisticated public relations and promotional devices developed in Napa and elsewhere. But it is also the fact that the consolidations and unchecked corporate growth that characterize California and, to some extent, Washington have not yet overwhelmed Oregon, where genuinely small, family-run wineries abound. Of the 153 Oregon wineries listed in the *Wines and Vines Directory* for 2004, 81—or more than half of the total—produced fewer than 5,000 cases of wine annually.[65] Only one (Bridgeview) produced as much as 100,000 cases; a sprinkling were over 25,000 cases, but the overwhelming majority were at 25,000 cases or less, most of them clustered between 5,000 and 10,000 cases.

Wineries of this size would be considered hardly viable in California. So how is it possible to keep alive in Oregon? One reason is land cost, which is much lower than in California. Another reason is that many Oregon winemakers do not depend wholly on their wine business to keep them going. Some wineries are parts of diversified farms; some are part-time enterprises. It helps, too, to have a local clientele to whom one can sell directly without dividing the profits with wholesaler and retailer. Almost every Oregon winery sells at retail, and although Oregon wines have a fairly wide distribution outside the state, most of the production is consumed by loyal Oregonians. The proximity of the wineries of the northern Willamette to the big city of Portland gives them a ready-made large market. And a final reason may be that in Oregon, as elsewhere among the winemakers of America, there are a good many people who accept that they will not make a lot of money as long as they continue to make wine.

L'affaire Drouhin sealed, as nothing else could have done, the idea that Oregon was Pinot noir country. As one writer puts it, "All anyone in Oregon wine talks about, thinks about and prays for is Pinot noir."[66] Yet there have been doubts about the wisdom of staking everything on so chancy a proposition as Pinot noir. Uncertain harvests, low yields, problems in handling a variety notorious for its unpredictable behavior, and as a consequence the necessarily high cost of the wine, are troubles that seem inevitably to afflict anyone seeking to make Pinot noir even in regions that suit the habits of the grape. In 1981 William Blosser, himself a maker of Pinot noir, declared that growing Pinot noir in Oregon was simply "uneconomical."[67] Moreover, the very fine wines of a good year may be followed by quite poor wines the next, and innocent buyers, unfamiliar with vintage years and the unreliability of the variety, can find themselves opening an expensive disappointment. But for now, at any rate, Pinot noir remains the unchallenged king in Oregon. The state's claim to be the spiritual home of Pinot noir is bolstered by the International Pinot Noir Celebration, held on the campus of Linfield College in McMinnville since 1987. This has become so popular an attraction, open to people both in and out of the trade, that participation (which requires a healthy fee) is now determined by lottery.

And after all, Oregon grows other grapes too. In the early days, Riesling was tagged as the grape of choice: that is what Richard Sommer first planted, and others followed his lead. Riesling, as it grows in America, has never had the qualities that it displays in the favored German sites—the sprightly, fresh, acid character, the apple and honey flavors that one finds in the great wines of the Mosel and the Rhine. Although it may make a good wine here, it is not like what it is in Germany; and in any case, it has not caught on here, though Oregon Riesling has been highly praised. A variant on the Riesling theme is offered by the Müller-Thurgau variety, which a number of Oregon growers have taken up; though there were only 94 acres of it in 2003, some sixteen wineries had joined to promote it.

Chardonnay of course was planted at once in Oregon, and there is still a large acreage of it there—some 900 acres in 2003—but that acreage is declining. Oregon Chardonnays are more acidic than those of California, and the style has not been greatly popular.[68] Growers looking for a different white grape, and thinking of the success of Pinot noir, not unnaturally concluded that they might find what they wanted within the pinot family, in Pinot blanc or Pinot gris. And so it has proved. The true Pinot blanc, often confused with Melon or Chenin blanc in California, is in fact a mutation of Pinot noir. The Oregon growers affirm that theirs is the real thing, the genuine Pinot blanc, first brought in by Charles Coury when he made his plantings of northern grapes in 1967.[69] There are currently 180 acres of Pinot blanc planted, and an association of wineries has formed to promote the wine. There is even more excitement about Pinot gris in Oregon. This grape—known variously as Tokay d'Alsace, Pinot grigio, Rülander, and yet other names—is, like Pinot blanc, a mutation of the unstable Pinot noir. David Lett, at Eyrie, began making Pinot gris in a small way in the 1970s; in 1981 he decided to graft over his Riesling vines to Pinot gris, hoping to improve his cash flow.[70] It was soon discovered that Pinot gris and Oregon salmon paired beautifully, and the synergy of this combination has propelled Pinot gris to preeminence among Oregon whites. There are now 1,797 acres of Pinot gris in Oregon. Added to the 7,300 acres of Pinot noir and the 180 of Pinot blanc, the three pinots occupy more than 9,000 of the state's 13,400 vineyard acres.[71]

THE MOUNTAIN WEST

It is an historical-cultural accident that has identified California as the wine land of the west; we should recognize a vast viticultural area extending over 26 degrees of latitude from Mexico to Canada including all the coastal states and western parts of Idaho. . . . California should be conceived as part of it, the historical center but perhaps not forever dominant.[72]

So it seemed to Roy Brady, who had given the subject much thought. The establishment of Oregon and Washington as important winegrowing states certainly confirms the idea. Brady doubtless included Idaho, even though it is three hundred miles from the nearest coast, because the state has had an intermittent history of grape growing since the nineteenth century. Irrigated regions in the Snake River valley near the Oregon and Washington borders are the historic home of grape growing in Idaho, especially in the region of Lewiston, just across the border from Clarkston, Washington. But if Idaho had grapes in its past, it also has some formidable obstacles. There is first the threat of killing winter cold; all of Idaho is high ground—it is hard to find anything below 2,000 feet elevation— and it is, if anything, colder even than eastern Washington and Oregon.[73] The ruggedly mountainous character of the state also limits the likely places for viticulture. Then there is the fact that a large part of the population is Mormon and so not merely indifferent to wine but actively hostile to it. The state also allows local prohibition. For the limited part of Idaho's not very large population that might be interested in wine, a further obstacle lay in the fact that after Repeal the state adopted a system of state stores. These were the only places where one could buy wine, and only from such stock as the state might choose to provide. The predictable result was that Idaho residents drank very little wine—312,000 gallons in 1970, which put it forty-ninth out of the fifty states (only North Dakota, with a smaller population, drank less).

A change began to be felt at the end of the '60s, when there was a move to allow wine to be sold in grocery stores as well as in the state stores. This was accomplished in 1971, and the paltry 312,000 gallons drunk in 1970 jumped to more than a million in 1972, putting Idaho ahead of Alaska, Delaware, Montana, South Dakota, Utah, West Virginia, and Wyoming—as well as of North Dakota—in the wine consumption sweepstakes.[74] Now that wine had escaped from the bondage of the state stores, people in Idaho began once again to think about making it as well as buying it. A small venture called Idaho Wine and Grape Growers, established near the university town of Moscow in 1970, turned out to be premature; it went out of business in 1975.

Scattered plantings of grapes continued, however. Conditions in Idaho provide high daytime temperatures in the short growing season, but cool nights. Riesling has been from the first the preferred variety, and most Idaho wineries make a specialty of it. The favored region was not, as it had been in the nineteenth century, the neighborhood of Lewiston on the Washington border but the valley of the Snake between Boise and the Oregon border, many miles to the south of Lewiston. The first successful new winery, which has since grown to be overwhelmingly the largest of Idaho wineries, was Ste. Chapelle Winery, founded in 1976 at Emmett by William Broich. Broich was using fruit grown on the Symms ranch, at Sunny Slope near Caldwell, and in 1978 he and the Symms family agreed to move the operation to the ranch. The Symms ranch had long been a producer of fruit such as apples, cherries, pears, and peaches. Planting of wine grapes on the ranch began in 1971, so when Ste. Chapelle migrated to Caldwell there were vineyards ready to supply it.

Ste. Chapelle has had a startling growth from its small beginnings. By 1980 it was producing more than 100,000 gallons and had secured wide distribution outside Idaho— an essential condition considering the small size of the Idaho market. The vineyards at the Symms ranch had grown to more than 170 acres, and the winery had contracts for the grapes from several hundred acres of vines owned by independent growers. In 1998,

FIGURE 54
Ste. Chapelle Winery, Idaho: a remote echo of France in the Snake River valley. (Photograph
by Charles L. Sullivan.)

when it had a storage capacity of half a million gallons, Ste. Chapelle was sold to Corus
Brands of Washington, owners of, among other properties, the Columbia Winery at Woodinville. Corus, in turn, sold Ste. Chapelle to the Canandaigua wine group in 2001. The
extent to which Ste. Chapelle dominates winemaking in Idaho may be measured from
the fact that its current production comes from 209 acres of its own vineyards and from
a further 240 acres of contracted vineyards—out of a total of only 750 acres in the entire
state. The other wineries operating in Idaho remain small and local. The oldest of the
surviving wineries, after Ste. Chapelle, is the tiny Weston Winery (1982), also at Caldwell;
other small wineries in the valley of the Snake in southern Idaho are Hell's Canyon Winery (1989), Indian Creek (1987), Koenig (1995), Sawtooth (1988), and Vickers (1992).

Apart from the legislative act in 1971 that allowed wine to be sold outside state liquor
stores, the state does not seem to have done much for its wine industry. There is no farm
winery law, or state-supported body engaged in promotion, or state-supported research
into the viticultural and enological questions peculiar to Idaho conditions. The purchase
of Ste. Chapelle Winery by Canandaigua, and of Sawtooth by Corus Brands, shows that
large corporations think well of the prospects of wine in Idaho. But the small fry left on
the outside are perhaps a little dispirited. They formed an Idaho Grape Growers and Wine
Producers Commission in 1992, and its current assessment of the situation is by no means
confident. "The future," so the commission says on its Web site, "is far from assured."

Only a small percentage of the state's population can be counted as likely wine drinkers. Not much is being done to develop markets outside the state, and within the state Idaho wine is not promoted by hotels and restaurants. On a very optimistic estimate, some 50,000 acres are available as suitable sites for viticulture in Idaho, but fewer than a thousand acres have in fact been planted. Idaho looks with a sad and jealous eye on neighboring Washington, where vineyards and wine production are expanding vigorously, while growers in Idaho, whose product is in no way inferior, are forced to "sell off a sizeable portion of their yield each year" to the "burgeoning markets" of Washington, where their grapes disappear anonymously into a flourishing rival's wines.[75]

It is perhaps a sign of malaise that Idaho, almost alone of the significant wine-producing states, has as yet no AVA. Texas has seven, Oregon six, New Mexico three, Colorado two, and Arizona one, but Idaho none.

Unlike that of Idaho, Colorado winemaking has enthusiastic local support, both official and unofficial. Accustomed to tourism, well supplied with resorts, hotels, and restaurants, and unhampered by a state liquor monopoly, Colorado has welcomed its new wine industry. Like virtually every state in the union, Colorado had some grape growing and winemaking in its past, but only on a small scale and in scattered locations; it was quickly stifled when the state went Dry in 1916, three years before the Eighteenth Amendment was passed.[76] No sign of renewal occurred until 1968, when a Denver dentist, Dr. Gerald Ivancie, opened Ivancie Wines in Denver. This was necessarily a compromise operation. Ivancie bought his grapes in California but made the wine in Denver: some 8,000 gallons in the first year.[77] The hobby enterprise quickly outgrew hobby limits, and Ivancie sold the winery in 1972. The new owners aspired to make Colorado wines from Colorado grapes and began to cooperate with a few growers in western Colorado on experimental plantings of vinifera in 1973. Ivancie went out of business in 1975, but the work it had started was carried on by others.

The Four Corners Regional Commission, created by federal legislation for the four states—Colorado, New Mexico, Arizona, and Utah—whose right-angle boundaries meet at an imaginary point in the southwestern desert, began a study in 1970 of the feasibility of grape growing in the region and concluded that cautious beginnings could be recommended.[78] In 1974 Colorado State University began experimental viticultural work at its station in Orchard Mesa, near Grand Junction. Grand Junction, on the western slope of the Rockies at the spot where the Gunnison River, coming up from the south, flows into the Colorado River on its way southwest, has long been a region of irrigated fruit farming. The altitude is even dizzier than Idaho's: Colorado's vineyards lie at elevations from 4,000 to 7,000 feet, and viticulture is feasible only because some sites along the Colorado and the Gunnison are sheltered against the prevailing cold and wind and offer privileged microclimates. The names of the wineries are expressive of the character of the country: Canyon Wind, Cottonwood Cellars, Creekside, DeBeque Canyon, Rocky Hill, Stoney Mesa, Terror Creek, Trail Ridge. They are mostly clustered in Grand Valley, just east of Grand Junction, or along the Gunnison in Delta County some miles to the south.

This concentration is recognized in the two AVAs so far established in Colorado: Grand Valley and West Elks, in Delta County.

The state of Colorado did its part in 1977 by passing a farm winery law to encourage an industry that, at the time, consisted of only a few acres of grapes and no wineries at all. The state's invitation got a response the next year, when Colorado Mountain Vineyards opened at Golden, near Denver. In 1984 Pike's Peak Vineyards opened near Colorado Springs, and in 1985 Plum Creek Cellars at Larkspur (both Colorado Mountain and Plum Creek later migrated to the Grand Junction area, at Palisade on the Colorado River, where the vineyards were). Since then another twenty or so small wineries have opened. The Pike's Peak vineyards are anomalous by Colorado standards in being located on the eastern slope of the Rockies, the Front Range as it is called, and in producing wines from French hybrid as well as vinifera grapes. More like the Great Plains than like the mountains, the slopes of the Front Range are more exposed to cold and variable weather than are the protected spots in the west where the main Colorado development is. The Pike's Peak vineyards were planted in 1969 with Chancellor, Ravat, Aurora, and other hybrids from Philip Wagner's nursery, as well as with such vinifera as Riesling and Chardonnay.[79]

The state's winemakers organized in 1982, calling themselves the Rocky Mountain Association of Vintners and Viticulturists. In 1990 the state confirmed its support for the industry by creating the Colorado Wine Industry Development Board to carry out research and promotion. The scale of operations remains small in Colorado. At the turn of the century there were 650 acres of vineyard, 65 percent in the Grand Valley region and most of the rest in Delta County. The most-planted variety is Merlot; Chardonnay is second, and so on through some half-dozen other varieties. White grapes slightly outweigh red. The wineries all remain small: there is no one giant among them, for only one winery produces as much as 11,000 cases in a year. The industry, on this small scale, appears to be more than ordinarily stable. Only a few of the forty or more wineries set up since 1978 are not still in business.

Winegrowing in New Mexico faces, as it does in the other mountain states, the two problems of winter and water—too much of the one and too little of the other. The state has, however, the distinction of being the site of the oldest winegrowing activity in the United States, even though that activity survived into the twentieth century only in the most vestigial way.[80] Indeed, the scene in 1970 would have given little reason to prophesy much of a future. There were then eight small operations in the state—"eight little roadside wineries selling inexpensive table wines in gallon jugs," as Leon Adams described them.[81] The giant among them was the Gross Winery at Bernalillo, on the Rio Grande a few miles upriver from Albuquerque. Louis Gross, whose father came from France, opened his winery in 1939 and made wine from his 25-acre vineyard of vinifera vines. At the other end of this small scale was the Joe P. Estrada Winery at Mesilla, downriver toward the Texas border, where the proprietor made 600 gallons a year of wine from his two acres of Mission grapes to sell to his neighbors. Everything else in New Mexico fell between these two limits. Rico's Winery, in Albuquerque, pursued another tack by making wine from grapes brought in from the Cucamonga district of Southern California.

Efforts to move the industry in new directions began in the 1970s. New Mexico participated in the Four Corners Regional Commission plan to develop winegrowing, which, it was said, "helped greatly in generating enthusiasm."[82] One sign of the new enthusiasm was the formation of the New Mexico Vine and Wine Society in 1974. The society was an amateur organization created by two physicists, John Lilley and Baron Brumley, with the purpose of promoting "enology and viticulture in the Land of Enchantment."[83] The society made an effort to get a farm winery bill from the legislature in 1977, but the politicians were not yet ready to recognize wine as a cause to support. New developments in the '70s came so slowly as to be almost invisible. Only two new wineries were founded in the decade: La Viña in 1977, the hobby of Clarence Cooper, a professor of physics at the University of Texas, El Paso; and Viña Madre Winery in 1978, near Roswell, not along the Rio Grande but in the Pecos Valley. At the end of the '70s there were only four wineries in New Mexico, most of the "little roadside wineries" that Leon Adams had seen having gone out of business.

Some quiet development went on around Belen, on the Rio Grande south of Albuquerque, and in the high country north of Santa Fe. At Belen, beginning in 1977, a retired air force veteran named Don Spiers planted French hybrid grapes as the answer to the problem of New Mexico's dry, cold winters. Encouraged by the results, three years later he and his partners planted 135 acres of such varieties as Vidal blanc, Seyval, and Chancellor. They did well enough that in 1983 they were joined by other investors who together brought the total planting up to 300 acres.[84] Spiers and his partners were then ready to build a winery; it was bonded in 1985 as Rio Valley Winery, at Bosque Farms, with a storage capacity of 60,000 gallons.[85] Another, much more modest winery, also based on a vineyard of French hybrid vines, opened in Belen in 1982—Chiavario Vineyards, whose owner, Richard Chiavario, was one of the legion who followed the advice of Philip Wagner in planning his vineyard.[86] Between Taos and Santa Fe, at an elevation of 6,000 feet in the valley of the Embudo River, La Chiripada Winery was founded in 1982. It manages to produce wines from ten acres of French hybrids such as Léon Millot, de Chaunac, Seyval blanc, and Baco. The general estimation of the French hybrids is probably no higher in New Mexico than it is elsewhere, but the opinion of one authority is worth quoting: "The northern portion of the state makes some of the finest French-American wines in the nation. Both red and white wines are generally soft, fruity, delicately scented, and are very pleasant on the palate."[87]

All of these undertakings certainly made sense: the growers of French hybrids were consulting New Mexico conditions prudently and making haste slowly in the development of a market. New Mexico at the beginning of the '80s was still not producing as much as 25,000 gallons of wine annually. Then some quite fantastic things began to happen. Where the idea began, and who took the lead in spreading it, I do not know; but about 1980 sev-

Unmistakably southwestern, but the winery, at an elevation above 6,000 feet, specializes in wine from French hybrid grapes. (Author's collection.)

eral groups of investors—French, Swiss, German, Italian, and Spanish—were persuaded that New Mexico could immediately be developed into a major source of wine. The excitement of supplying the still untapped American market, combined with the unexplored possibilities of New Mexico, made a heady mix that some found impossible to resist. One group—the French Winegrowers Association, headed by a Swiss named Jean Zanchi—bought 8,000 acres of land near Truth or Consequences on the Rio Grande seventy-five miles upriver from Las Cruces. Zanchi had water rights from the City of Albuquerque, which had prudently accumulated such rights in excess of its requirements. Zanchi began experimental plantings of vinifera in 1981. By 1983 the acreage planted had grown to 285, and it was announced that planting would continue till the 8,000 acres were complete. At that point, it was hinted, the group might exercise an option on yet another 8,000 acres.[88] A "20-million bottle winery" was planned for completion in 1984. When the greenhouse that was to be the nursery for the vast plantings opened in 1983, the interest was such that the governor and a U.S. congressman attended the ceremonies.[89]

Another group of French investors committed themselves to the entirely untested lands around Lordsburg in southwestern New Mexico, on the other side of the Continental Divide from the Rio Grande valley. Calling themselves the San Andres Corporation, they planted 210 acres of Chardonnay in 1983 and planned another 200 of mixed varieties as well as a small winery. The first wines were to be sold in the New Mexico market, but they looked to worldwide distribution as the enterprise grew.[90] Back over the Continental Divide, between Lordsburg and Deming, two other big new developments were planned. A Canadian-Swiss group called the Luna County Development Corporation put in 171 acres of grapes in 1983 on a 3,440-acre property. The intention was to plant the entire property within two or three years and to build a 10-million-gallon winery in Deming by 1985 to supply a national market.[91] A second group at Deming, a Swiss-Italian combination called Uvas Farming Corporation, planted 400 acres in 1983; 600 more were planned for 1984. A million-gallon winery, designed for expansion to 3 million gallons, was under construction. At the same time, it was reported that three groups of German investors were scouting for land in the Rio Grande valley, one of them reportedly negotiating to buy 10,000 acres.[92]

What was one to make of this? It was, as one writer said, "a flood of foreign cash" that "seemed to come overnight."[93] The proposed scale of operations was immense: it was seriously proposed that about 18,000 acres of grapes be planted in just a few years to feed wineries not yet built for a market ignorant of wine. The plans were expansive indeed. At a very modest computation, the acres of vines to be planted would yield some 7.5 million gallons of wine in a state that had not yet managed to produce 25,000 gallons. It was no wonder that so grandiose a structure on so pitiably small a base soon toppled.

The people behind the Uvas Farming Corporation actually completed their winery at Deming, though on a smaller scale than originally planned. Still, it was by far the largest winery in the state when it went into operation in 1984 as St. Clair Winery; the next year it produced 200,000 gallons, a remarkable figure considering that the vineyards were only in their third year.[94] Two years later the winery filed for bankruptcy.[95] Over at Lordsburg, the San Andres Corporation opened its Blue Teal Winery in 1985 and produced 80,000 gallons of wine; then a combination of root rot in the vineyards and a shift in the value of the dollar put an end to the business. Elsewhere the grandiose schemes of the early '80s splintered and dwindled in the effort to carry them out. Jean Zanchi's vineyards did not get beyond their early stages; for a number of years he sold grapes to other wineries, and in 1993 he opened a winery under the name of Duvallay. It is no longer in business. There were troubles in the vineyards as well as in the marketplace. Winter damage, spring frosts, cotton root rot, and other afflictions soon showed that development had gone on in reckless disregard of actual conditions.

The main survivor in the general wreck was Hervé Lescombes, who had originally come to New Mexico to work for the Zanchi group but had subsequently joined the San Andres Corporation in Lordsburg. After that collapsed, he kept the Blue Teal label and acquired the St. Clair and Mademoiselle de Santa Fe interests as well. By the turn of the century his New Mexico Wineries at Deming was among the biggest wineries in the state, though its annual production of 30,000 cases bore no relation to the expansive plans that had excited the investors of the early '80s.

Perhaps in recognition of the difficulties that had laid low the foreign investors in the

'8os, the state legislature created the New Mexico Winegrower's License in 1988. To qualify, a winery must get at least 50 percent of its grapes from New Mexico; in return it could sell directly to wholesalers and at retail, provide tastings, sell wine by the glass, maintain two off-site sales locations, and conduct Sunday sales except where local option prohibited it.[96] These were privileges designed, of course, for the small winery, and since the delusory excitements of the days of foreign investment, new wineries in New Mexico have all been small. Legislation also permits New Mexico wineries to sponsor festivals at which they may offer free tastings and sell their wines by glass or bottle; these events have become effective promotions for the trade.

The mortality rate among New Mexico wineries has been high. The oldest winery now operating dates only from 1977; of the thirty-eight wineries founded since 1977, half are now out of business.[97] These odds have not deterred new enterprise, however, for nine new wineries have been set up in the past decade. Nothing remains of the old Mexican American tradition of little roadside wineries that were all that Leon Adams found in New Mexico in 1970.

Arizona has more vinifera grapes than all of the other mountain states put together: some 2,400 acres in 2003. Most of these grapes, however, are table grapes, grown in irrigated low-desert lands for the early market: they ripen even before the earliest California grapes and so enjoy a special advantage. Wine grapes are quite another matter. Arizona, with a large Mormon element in what was then a small population, passed a prohibition law in 1913 that surpassed almost all others then known in the severity of its proscriptions: even medical and industrial uses of alcohol were prohibited. There had been stirrings of interest in winemaking before that time, but they were so completely stifled that even when it was possible to think of a return to winegrowing, the thought seems not to have occurred to anyone.

So it remained until the beginning of the 1970s, when the University of Arizona began to participate in the grape research project sponsored by the Four Corners Commission. Gordon Dutt, a soil scientist, and Eugene Mielke, a horticulturist, led the work of experimental vine planting. The difficulties were familiar enough: on very high ground, winter kill; everywhere else, the main problems were inadequate water and the presence of cotton root rot. Taking soil temperatures as a guide, Dutt and his associates concluded that the valleys and plains of southeastern Arizona in Cochise and Santa Cruz Counties, at elevations ranging from 2,500 to 5,000 feet, would permit the cultivation of well-flavored vinifera grapes yielding good wines. They hoped that high elevation would inhibit root rot, but were disappointed: the answer lay in grafting to resistant rootstock. Water, as always, was a crucial difficulty, but one of the motives behind the Four Corners Grape Project was the fact that grapes do not take as much water as cotton or alfalfa and so are suited to regions not otherwise open to agriculture. It was shown that with careful cultivation practices, the water available in southeastern Arizona was adequate for vineyards.[98]

The first grapes from the university's experimental vineyards, planted in 1971, were made into wine at the laboratory winery in Tucson in 1974. This first step in the revival of winemaking in Arizona was noticed in *Wines and Vines,* but there was no precipitate rush to plant in the state.[99] Gordon Dutt himself, with a group of partners, began planting a vineyard on property near the university's experimental plot in 1979 with the intention of making wine. But before his vines were bearing, the first post-Prohibition winery in Arizona was opened by a Tucson businessman in 1980: the R.W. Webb Winery, which got its grapes not from Arizona but from Mexico and California.[100]

Since then the development of the Arizona wine industry has been gradual and small-scale. One impediment is that it may take more water to operate a winery than it does to grow a vineyard. There was some talk in the early days of the possibility that big-money investment and large-scale development might be just around the corner, but that did not materialize. The failures in New Mexico no doubt helped to dampen enthusiasm for such ventures. Instead, a modest succession of small wineries appeared, almost all of them in the southeastern corner of the state: San Dominique (1983), Sonoita (1984), Arizona Vineyards (1985). The viticultural basis was equally modest. By the end of the '80s there were about 300 acres of wine grapes in Arizona, about half of which were Cabernet Sauvignon, Sauvignon blanc, and Pinot noir.[101] Things have not changed much since.

At the beginning of the twenty-first century, some fourteen small wineries had been founded in Arizona since the first one in 1980, and of that number eleven were still in business—a very good record indeed, and evidence that if growth has been slow, it has been prudent. It has been helped by a farm winery law that authorized production of up to 75,000 gallons, wine tasting, and direct sales. The Arizona Wine Growers Association was formed in 1982, and in 1984 the state received its first AVA, Sonoita. Nothing like the wine boom that swept over New Mexico has been heard in Arizona, nor is it likely that it ever will. But grapes make sense as an Arizona crop, and one may expect winemaking there to go on in an unspectacular but steady way.

In this survey of the West beyond the borders of California, I have so far failed to mention Montana, Wyoming, Utah, Nevada, Alaska, and Hawaii, just as in my survey of the states east of the Rockies I failed to mention North and South Dakota, Vermont, New Hampshire, Maine, and Delaware. As it happens, *all* of these states have had, or do now have, wineries at work, just as in the nineteenth century there was *no* state that did not make trial of grapes and wine as the early settlers experimented with all the possibilities.[102] But just as it was in the nineteenth century, so in some cases is it now, new technologies notwithstanding. Some of these states are not likely, barring climate change, to achieve a genuine winegrowing industry. Others perhaps may, but their experience is yet too restricted. They may produce exotic specialties: milk wine in Alaska, pineapple wine in Hawaii, sacramental nectar in Utah. But they may also produce genuine wine in one way or another, as do the four wineries currently operating in Utah, the two in Hawaii, the two in Montana, the two in South Dakota, the two in Wyoming, and the one in North Dakota (the last state to be heard from in this connection). It may well be the happy task of later historians to take some or all of these states into serious account.

In the meantime, winegrowers in the West outside California deserve much credit for their accomplishments in the last generation. Settlement in the West is not new, but viticulture and winemaking there, having long been neglected, are in effect quite new activities. The winegrowers have had to face the hazards of mountainous and arid sites, and to do so with little experience to rely on. They have had to work in places almost wholly without any tradition of wine, often among populations actively hostile to it and in states that had to be educated into helpfulness; they have had to face the competition of well-established California for the custom of the relatively few who drink wine. Altogether, the people who have created the wine industry of the West have shown remarkable energy and enterprise.

14

CALIFORNIA TO THE PRESENT DAY

THE STATISTICS OF RECENT HISTORY

Since the revolution occurred in American wine, the wine industry's road in California has often been bumpy and difficult, but never enough to turn back a steady movement of growth. A comparison of the figures from 1970, when the revolution had clearly begun, with those from the end of the century in 2000 shows the direction quite clearly.[1]

To start in the vineyards: In 1970 the acreage devoted to grapes of all kinds in California was 479,000; in 2000 it was 852,000. For wine grapes, the numbers were 157,000 in 1970 and 480,000 in 2000, so that there are now more than three times as many wine grapes in the state as there were thirty years earlier.

As the scale of plantings was transformed, so too was the composition of the vineyards. The leading red variety in 1970 was Carignane, with 27,000 acres; French Colombard led the whites at 18,000 acres. By 2000 Cabernet Sauvignon had become the leading red variety, with 69,000 acres (up from 7,000 acres in 1970); Chardonnay was not only the most planted white variety, it was far and away the most planted of all wine varieties: 103,000 acres, up from 3,000 acres in 1970.

The established regions of grape growing, except for those devastated by urban and suburban development, all showed powerful increases: Napa County went from 15,000 to 41,000 acres, Sonoma from 15,000 to 52,000, Mendocino from 6,500 to 16,000. But there were also large plantings in places formerly not much developed, especially in the three counties making up the Central Coast region: Monterey went from 6,600 acres to 41,000, San Luis Obispo from 800 to 20,500, and Santa Barbara from 258 to 16,000.

The quantitative growth in these regions was accompanied by an increasing recognition of qualitative growth as well. In the foothills of the Sierra Nevada, where winegrowing went back to the Gold Rush but had languished for many years, Amador County went from 500 to 2,700 acres of grapes, El Dorado County from 34 to 1,100.

As the acreage increased so did wine production, from 212 million gallons in 1970 to 565 million in 2000. The proportion of table wine in this total continued to grow at the expense of fortified wines, as did the proportion of legitimate wine grapes in the total tonnage crushed. California wineries still used many tons of raisin and table grapes in the crush of 2000, but much of the juice went into grape concentrate (used commercially for sweetening) or into high-proof brandy. California continued to dominate the nation's wine production; its share has never fallen below 82 percent in any year.

In 1970 there were 240 wineries in California, out of a national total of 435; in 2000 the figure was 847, out of a total of 1,800. Napa County led all the rest, with the improbable figure of 259 wineries operating in 2000, up from 27 in 1970.[2] Sonoma came next with 202 (also 27 in 1970). But growth was relatively greater elsewhere: Mendocino went from 2 to 35, Monterey from 1 to 24, San Luis Obispo from 3 to 63, Santa Barbara from 1 to 54.

A final category in this quick statistical review is that of exports. In 1970 exports of American wine were so small that the figures, whatever they were, do not appear in the statistics. By 1980, however, exports had reached the considerable sum of nearly 8 million gallons and were growing fast—a 53 percent increase took place in the single year from 1979 to 1980. By 2003 exports—effectively all of it California wine—had reached 74 million gallons: the major customers were, in order, the United Kingdom, Canada, Japan, the Netherlands (as a point of distribution rather than as a destination), and Belgium.

TRENDS IN THE MARKET

Many novelties and fads have excited the market since the 1970s: Cold Duck, the various pop wines and mod wines, Lambrusco, wine coolers, white Zinfandel, and most recently, low-alcohol wines flavored with fruit juices and sold as varietal wines. Some of these—Cold Duck, for example—have faded into oblivion. Wine coolers were a different story. Compounded of artificial fruit flavors, water, carbon dioxide, and wine at less than 7 percent alcohol, the coolers came on the market in a small way about 1981. By 1984 nearly 37 million gallons were being shipped annually; by the end of the decade it was 90 million. Soon the market was crowded with competing coolers jostling for shelf space: Vino Coolada, Sausalito Sling, and Calvin Cooler were among the sixty-plus on the market by 1985. The parade was led, soon after its introduction, by Gallo's Bartles and Jaymes brand. The vogue for coolers then began to fade, and as it did so the manufacturers increasingly switched from a basis of cheap wine to even cheaper malt liquor, which could be flavored just as readily. The coolers are still around, but they are not *wine* coolers.

White Zinfandel, introduced about 1975, seems to have some irresistible advantages going for it from the standpoint of the producer.[3] It is made from grapes not yet fully ripe, so that one need not be anxious about proper maturity and thus can use fruit from the Central Valley, which is abundant and inexpensive. It is regularly doctored with inexpensive concentrate to sweeten it, and a little gas may be added as well. It requires no aging, so that it may be moved to the market almost at once. Finally, Americans love it. White Zinfandel has effectively killed the domestic production of other rosé wines; it shows few signs of losing popularity, and it may prove to be that long-sought-after commercial ideal, the wine equivalent of the American soft drink. The fact that only Americans drink it seems to confirm that idea.

Nonalcoholic "wines" were introduced in 1985 under the Ariel brand by J. Lohr Winery and have gained a modest place in the market.[4] Because they have undergone fermentation, they are no longer merely grape juice; but since their alcohol has been removed (effectively if not entirely), can they be wine? At least they are straightforwardly identified, so that customers know what they are getting. That could not be said of the so-called formula wines that appeared in 1997, when Almadén converted its bag-in-box California Chardonnay to California Chardonnay with Natural Flavors. This turned out to be a mixture of about half wine with water, sweeteners, and flavorings, called "natural" after the permissive formulas of our authorities in such matters. Since only half was wine, and since only 75 percent of that wine needed to be Chardonnay for it to be considered "varietal," the presumption was that the product contained roughly 37 percent Chardonnay. What Almadén had begun was soon widely copied, and these bogus "varietal" wines were widely sold for the next few years. Beginning in 2001 a change in regulations put an end to the deception.

What goes into the package is evidently open to a good deal of manipulation. And so is the package. Wine bottle sizes went metric in 1974, in part because the change would assist an export program.[5] Repeated attempts to establish wine in cans have so far failed; so have trials of plastic bottles for wine. It perhaps says something about the American perception of wine that although plastic containers are standard for inexpensive wine in Europe, they don't go over here: wine is still considered too special for ordinary packaging. Bag-in-box containers, however, *have* caught on. Developed in Australia, this container uses a pouch of plastic or metal foil to hold the wine. The pouch is enclosed in a protective cardboard box. A spigot in the pouch can be pulled through an opening in the box and the wine drawn off through it. As the wine is withdrawn, the light plastic or foil of the pouch collapses and so reduces the air space above the wine. Introduced in this country in the mid '70s, the bag-in-box was quickly adopted by the restaurant trade to handle large quantities of wine—five, ten, even twenty liters—in a way far more convenient than any bottle could be.

In response to charges that they were a health hazard, lead capsules (the capsule is the sheath over the bottle neck covering the top of the cork) were made illegal in 1992. They were replaced by capsules made of plastic or tin, or in some cases not replaced at all. Instead, some wineries chose to use a bottle with a wide-flanged lip. The cork, which by law must be covered, was protected by a disk of wax and paper or plastic fitted snugly to the top of the cork. Corks themselves have come in for heavy troubles in recent years because of the frequency with which wines are spoiled by being "corked"—that is, contaminated by corks infected with trichloroanisole (TCA). A number of synthetic cork materials have been tried and sold in all wine-producing countries. A bolder step has been taken by some wineries, which have decided to put at least a part of their production—including some very expensive wines—into bottles closed with metal screw-caps, long associated with cheap jug wine but thought to be the most secure, neutral closure available.

As for labels, the old days of the stock label, chosen from an array of preprinted blanks offered by the printer's sales rep, are now quite unimaginable. The marketers and the students of consumer psychology have, of course, made their contributions to label design, always seeking the magic combination that will jump off the shelf and into the customer's shopping basket.[6] The printers have done their part by providing new technology for embossing, laser cutting, and otherwise shaping and ornamenting paper, while the makers of labeling machinery have designed machines that will handle labels of any size or shape and put them precisely where they may be wanted: neck, shoulder, body, front, or back.

The general tendency in labeling has been toward greater particularity. In the old days a bottling company might put its name on the label and let it go at that. Now one may get a chemical analysis of the wine, a history of the vintage season, and a set of suggestions about food and wine combinations. Another development has been to treat the label as a work of art. Baron Philippe de Rothschild is given credit for the concept, beginning in 1924 when he commissioned Jean Carlu to make a special design for the label on that year's Château Mouton-Rothschild. Since then, and especially in the past thirty years, any number of notable artists and printers have been enlisted to produce labels. The paper wine label as we know it did not enter into general use until after the mid-nineteenth century. Now the splendid, varied abundance of wine labels has attracted collectors just as passionate as those who pursue stamps, menus, theater playbills, timetables, bus tickets, matchbooks, or any other paper ephemera. Ours is the golden age of the wine label.

As for what is in the bottle, Americans continued in 2000 to prefer Cabernet Sauvignon and Chardonnay. In the '50s these names would have been known only to the most sophisticated of American connoisseurs. By the '60s they were beginning to be more widely recognized but were still regarded as alien and difficult names; by the '70s they had triumphed, and they remain what would be called in computer jargon the default wines of the American market: unless otherwise specified they are what you will get. Cabernet and Chardonnay have so dominated the idea of premium wine in America that they inevitably inspired a reaction: ABC—"anything but Cabernet" or "anything but Chardonnay"—became a slogan for the rebellious. So far, the main alternative has been Merlot, a grape that has had a simply meteoric rise in favor during the past decade. In 1990 there were 7,500 acres of Merlot in California; in 2003 there were 52,000 acres.

The Merlot boom has by no means put an end to the search for different and interesting grapes in California. Some winemakers, particularly those participating in the Meritage scheme, have encouraged the planting of minor Bordeaux varieties: Petit Verdot (1,096 acres in 2003), Malbec (1,065 acres), and Cabernet franc (3,500 acres) have now achieved a substantial presence in California.[7] Others have bet on the Rhône varieties: Mourvèdre (anciently known in California as Mataro), Carignane, Counoise, Grenache, Cinsaut, and Syrah among the reds, and Viognier, Rousanne, and Marsanne among the whites. Most of these were already known in California, but they were now reexamined with a new interest: perhaps something special might be done with them. The two varieties that have stood out among the rest are the red Syrah and the white Viognier.[8] A group calling itself the Rhone Rangers, with some 120 winery members, has been organized to promote the fortunes of California "Rhone" wines.

Another group, arguing from the popularity of Italian wines, has invested in such varieties as Nebbiolo, Freisa, Sangiovese, Aglianico, and Dolcetto. They have formed a Consorzio Cal-Italia of some fifty wineries, making "Cal-Ital" wines from such varieties. Barbera, which has always had a large acreage in California, is still well ahead of all other Italian varieties: 9,000 acres to 177 of Nebbiolo, 90 of Dolcetto, 135 of Freisa, 2,600 of Sangiovese. As the numbers show, Sangiovese is the clear leader among the "new" Italian varieties, but its wines have not yet inspired much enthusiasm. Among Spanish varieties, Tempranillo, long known in the state as Valdepeñas, has aroused some interest: there are currently some 760 acres of it. There has also been some experimentation with Portuguese varieties such as Touriga Francesa, Tinta Madeira, and Souzão for use in fortified wines. Other exotica (at least from a California viewpoint) that may sometimes be met with by the more determined seekers include the French Tannat and Pinot Meunier, the South African Pinotage, and the German Scheurebe. Whether any of the varieties mentioned will ever catch on permanently, who can say? Perhaps some variety yet unheard of, or yet unconstructed by the genetic engineers, will be the future. Meanwhile, the fact that so much testing of so many varieties is currently going on bears testimony to the spirit of openness among California winegrowers.

The long slide of fortified wines from their position at the top still shows no signs of stopping: in 2003 the sales of wine in the United States were 627 million gallons, of which 558 million were table wine, 28 million sparkling wine, and 41 million fortified wine.[9] Clearly table wine, whose sales rose in value from $2.5 billion in 1991 to $6.8 billion in 2003, is now the undisputed king of the American market—but the term includes so many things that it has to be broken down if it is to mean anything. The rough-and-ready classification of table wine most frequently encountered is a simple division by price. At the bottom of the scale are the jug wines, made in huge volume and often sold in 1.5- or 3-liter bottles or in boxes. For some years now the sales of jug wines have been flat: that is, they have not risen in proportion to the increase among other categories of wine. Accordingly, this high-volume, low-margin section of the business has not attracted new entrants. Instead, the wineries whose labels contend in this market have grown fewer and fewer and bigger and bigger. These producers are also the source of the various flavored wines on the market.

After the jug and flavored wines, most of the rest of the table wines are known as premium wines of one sort or another. There is an indeterminate category of wines costing between $4 and $7 that expands in times of oversupply—fighting varietals, they are called. Anything costing $7 a bottle or more—with no upper limit—is called premium. The trade abounds in subdividing terms for these wines: *fighting varietals* at the bottom, followed by *premiums, super premiums,* and *ultra premiums;* or *popular premiums* and *classic premiums;* or, to vary things, *luxury, mid-luxury,* and *super luxury* wines.[10] When, after the boom years, the consumption of wine in this country began to decline, as it did from 1986 until 1992, the market analysts discovered the interesting fact that although overall sales of wine were going down, the sales of premium wine were rising. The American public, it was now said, was "drinking less but better."[11] The moral was not lost on the winegrowers, who concentrated on producing wines that would, by whatever means, qualify as premium. The almost exclusive focus on price as the measure of status had the unfortunate, if predictable, effect of stimulating a competition in prices—not to lower them, but to raise them. Some conservative wineries, unwilling to charge what they considered unwarranted, exorbitant prices, suffered in the marketplace in consequence. It was a disadvantage to be "underpriced."

The willingness of the American wine-buying public, or at least the most affluent part of it, to accept price as a sufficient measure of value was shown by the emergence of the so-called cult wines in the decade of the prosperous '90s. These wines, mostly from Napa Valley, were made in tiny quantities, offered to a restricted clientele, and priced at levels previously unheard of: it was the old Martin Ray method, but now applied to a market filled with eager bidders. The original asking prices, high enough in all conscience, were forced up to stratospheric levels in the heated competitions of auction sales: single bottles changed hands at prices in the hundreds or even thousands of dollars.[12]

Even at less-fevered levels than those of the cult wines, the prices of sought-after California wines are still high. A list of "Classic-Scoring California Cabernets and Blends," published at the beginning of 2002 by the consumer magazine *Wine Spectator,* gives some idea. The average price for a bottle of one of the ninety-one wines listed, from the years 1990 to 1998, was $226; the extremes were $33 for a 1991 Flora Springs Napa Valley Reserve Cabernet and $1,208 for a 1994 Screaming Eagle Napa Valley Cabernet.[13] Admittedly, these prices are for wines thought to be the very best that California can produce; but at the same time, with the exception of the few cult wines included in the list, they are commercial wines designed for the American marketplace. No one is compelled to buy such wines, and no winemaker can be blamed for probing the market to discover how much the traffic will bear. But such prices make it evident that the wines that carry them are no longer regarded as foods, or as adjuncts to food, but as jewels or trophies.[14]

The extravagances notwithstanding, the price of wine in general has not been out of line. Moreover, the standards of winemaking by the end of the century were so high and so reliable that "bad" wine in the old sense had virtually disappeared. This change was an international phenomenon, not only a Californian one. There was plenty of wine that was not particularly exciting, but it was sound and drinkable. The ordinary wine drinker (if there is such a creature) is well served at the beginning of the twenty-first century; indeed, there is every reason to think that sound, inexpensive wine has never before been as abundant and reliable as it is now. California has done its part in bringing that about.

BUSINESS DEVELOPMENTS

The most marked business trend is the increasing acquisition of smaller properties by larger—the process of purchase, merger, and consolidation known as the corporate takeover. The process is no doubt a local expression of the consolidation of business that is going on globally, but it has particularly troubling implications for the wine industry, where rightly or wrongly, small-scale operation and individuality have always been prized.

One of the earliest instances of the process was the entry of the Heublein Corporation into the California wine industry. Heublein, a Connecticut-based distributor and importer of food products, had grown rich after the war when the craze for vodka swept the country and its Smirnoff brand dominated the market. The firm moved into California in 1968 by buying up most of United Vintners from the Allied Grape Growers Cooperative. This gave Heublein at one stroke the Italian Swiss Colony, Petri, Mission Bell, Lejon, and Inglenook brands, together with eight wineries in the North Coast region and the Central Valley. In the next year Heublein startled the wine country by buying Beaulieu from Georges de Latour's daughter.

Beaulieu continued to operate in its own character, but Heublein's treatment of the Inglenook winery was a different matter. The management determined that the name would now be used as the label for a line of nationally distributed wines, and *Inglenook* appeared on half-gallon bottles of generic wine labeled burgundy, rosé, and chablis. Heublein's Italian Swiss Colony property was also transformed. The historic name was brightly truncated to Colony and the label used on the inexpensive varietal wines that the big new plantings in the Central Valley were now making possible. The degradation was not as striking as that which had been imposed on Inglenook, but it was severe enough. Italian Swiss Colony had made sound and reliable table wines from Sonoma vineyards; Colony was anonymous bulk wine.

In 1982 Heublein, which had bought and merged so many properties, was itself bought by R. J. Reynolds Industries, a tobacco firm busily re-creating itself by means of acquisitions. Now the real carnage began. United Vintners disappeared into a new Heublein Wine and Spirits Company; Italian Swiss Colony ("Colony") was shut down; wineries at Asti, Escalon, Lodi, and Reedley were sold back to Allied Grape Growers, from which Heublein had originally acquired them, along with the Italian Swiss Colony, Petri, and Lejon labels. In 1987 Heublein acquired the big Almadén winery, proceeded to sell off its assets, and moved all production to the Mission Bell winery at Madera. And then, within a few days of its Almadén purchase, Heublein itself was sold by Reynolds (now called RJR Nabisco, the creation of yet more mergers) to the giant Grand Metropolitan Ltd., a London-based international conglomerate.

The process of acquisition, recombination, and divestment continued. In 1989 Heublein bought the moribund Christian Brothers, largely for the sake of its brandy business. Beaulieu, the one Heublein property that had managed to operate more or less independently, was now brought under the same administration as the Inglenook and Christian Brothers brands. Then, in 1994, Heublein sold its Almadén and Inglenook brands, as well as the giant Mission Bell Winery, to Canandaigua. Heublein had in the meantime bought the M. G. Vallejo and Glen Ellen brands, which it now kept, along with the Christian Brothers name; it also developed a new brand called Blossom Hill (in allusion to an old Almadén property) and made wine in what had been an Almadén winery at Paicines, San Benito County. To underline all these changes, Heublein wines disappeared into a new organization called United Distillers and Vintners and so came to an end as a distinct property. It now operates as a part of the huge international combine known as Diageo.

This sinuous history is difficult to follow, but the trail of wreckage is clear enough. After twenty-five years of purchases and sales involving hundreds of millions of dollars; after wholesale movements of executives from Connecticut to California and back; after resignations, downsizings, plant closures, lawsuits, tangles with federal regulatory agencies, and vast volumes of advertising, what was the net effect?[15] Italian Swiss Colony, Petri, Lejon, and The Christian Brothers were gone or reduced to mere labels, shared out among big conglomerations.[16] Inglenook had been degraded to a mere parody of what it had once been. Beaulieu, many think, is on the same path. Other properties had been dealt off and transformed, with dubious results. It is hard to say who or what had been benefited by all this disruption; and it is hard to believe that such properties as Inglenook and Italian Swiss Colony could not have been maintained in their integrity and made to prosper if only management had been willing to see it happen. Instead, the most up-to-date business methods had been applied to the destruction of the firms they exploited. It is interesting to note that none of the wineries and brands that Heublein started with in 1968 or subsequently acquired, with the sole exception of Beaulieu, has survived.

Heublein was only the most prominent of the disturbing forces at work in this turbulent period. Many other large firms bought into California: Schlitz, Coca-Cola, Nestlé, Norton Simon—the list might be continued. One of the victims of the changing times was the cooperative winery, once so imposing a part of the California industry. The co-ops were already moribund, partly because of changes in the tax law but also because of the changing character of the market. Eventually they were either bought up by corporations or, having grown obsolete, went out of business. The last surviving cooperative winery in California—East-Side, in Lodi—ceased to operate as a co-op in 2002.

There were other instabilities. By 1974 the vast new plantings of the years immediately preceding had brought California's vineyard acreage to an all-time high of 650,000 acres, and the effects of overproduction were felt for the next several years, particularly in the Central Valley.[17] There was also much anxiety about competition from cheap imports at this time, and certainly with good reason, as far as the numbers went: imports had nearly tripled in volume from 1965 to 1973. Some of the players who had been attracted to the wine game now began to want out. Pillsbury, which had bought Souverain in 1973, disposed of it in 1976; John Hancock Life Insurance pulled out of its Monterey Vineyards investment that year; the Scottish and Newcastle Breweries, after taking some heavy losses on the Simi Winery, which it had bought in 1974, sold it in 1976.

These vicissitudes did not stop the continued expansion of the wine business overall in California, nor did they check the movement toward bigness: from comparatively small beginnings such firms as JFJ Bronco, Canandaigua, Mondavi, and Kendall-Jackson all grew large during the '70s. Since then a number of large international firms have bought and combined properties in California: Diageo, Foster's, Allied Domecq, Vincor. By the turn of the century the California wine industry displayed some sensational contrasts of scale—the huge, increasingly international conglomerations at one end and the tiny cult wineries at the other. Between such extremes it appears to be more and more difficult to make a living. In 1965, it may be remembered, Maynard Amerine and Vernon Singleton predicted that California winemaking would soon be almost entirely in the hands of a few wineries as their numbers diminished and the survivors grew larger.[18] It would be easy to make the same prediction now, when the pace of acquisition and merger is hotter than it ever has been and the drive toward globalization in every sort of commodity is unremitting. But Amerine and Singleton turned out to be wrong, even though they had good evidence on their side, and the same may be true of current predictions. Despite all the difficulties and risks confronting such enterprises, some sixty-one new, small wineries were bonded in California in the year 2001 alone.

One reason among many for a winery to want to be big is the continuing crisis in the system of wine distribution in the United States. The three-tier system, so called, had been devised originally to forestall the development of monopoly practices by the producers.[19] What had not been foreseen was that the system would eventually create monopoly conditions for the wholesalers. Under the system, producers are not allowed to sell directly to retailers but must work through a wholesaler—mandated middlemen, they have been called. Over the course of time their numbers have dwindled and the survivors have grown big. The more than 10,000 wholesalers operating in the 1960s had shrunk to about 300 by the end of the century; the five largest control a third of the market.[20] This sort of giantism is particularly bad news for the small winemaker, who does not make enough wine to interest the big wholesaler, which already has more accounts than it needs or wants; and so the little winery cannot gain entry into those states that require a producer to work through a wholesaler.

The frustrations of this situation have been intensified by the development of the Internet. Now a consumer, no matter where he might live, can—in theory at least—make his selection from a world of wine. Entrepreneurs were quick to grasp the new, infinitely expanded possibilities offered by Internet sales (the first in the field was Virtual Vintners in 1994), but just as quickly they ran into the walls created by the Twenty-first

Amendment. The states, and the wholesalers within their boundaries, were not about to give up their control over the movement of alcoholic drinks, wine among them. State governments were determined to guard the revenues; the wholesalers were even more fierce in defending their profits. Direct shipping, particularly of wines bought over the Internet, was a violation of the states' right to control the liquor traffic within their borders and would not be tolerated.

Under pressure from the wholesalers, several state legislatures, led by Florida's, passed laws making it a felony to ship wine directly into their states. Conviction could mean death to a winery, since the Alcohol and Tobacco Tax and Trade Bureau (TTB) will allow no felon to hold a bonded winery license. The shipping companies, led by the United Parcel Service, announced that they would have nothing to do with shipping wine, even to those states where it was legal to do so—so great was the fear of legal action. In response, a number of consumer and trade groups brought suit to force open the barriers: now that one might have access through the Internet to all the wines of the world, they argued, the obstacles created at the time of Repeal seemed intolerably out of date.

The situation is currently obscured in a cloud generated by suits and countersuits, pressure groups, public campaigns, legislative proposals, and other rich sources of confusion and discord.[21] A series of court decisions has sometimes confirmed the consumer's right of access, sometimes the right of the state to bar that access. The issue was scheduled to reach the Supreme Court late in 2004.[22] The conflict brings into play almost every issue that has ever troubled the history of alcoholic drink in this country and so does not seem likely to reach a satisfactory end anytime soon: guarding the underage from access to liquor, perpetuating the system of distribution and the vested interests that profit from that system, protecting the rights of the states to control alcoholic drink as provided in the Twenty-first Amendment, protecting the revenue, maintaining the Brandeis decisions, fulfilling the prohibitionist wish to obstruct the "traffic"—all these and no doubt many other long-familiar causes are tied up in the Gordian knot known as the direct shipment question.

Under these various conditions favoring bigness, an old practice adapted to new purposes has been found to serve the small winemaker—the system of custom crushing. It has always been possible for a fully equipped winery to produce and store wine not on its own account but for some other party—a grower or a merchant who supplies the grapes and keeps title to the wine produced from them. It was a familiar practice in times of surplus and still is. But there is now a different idea about custom crushing.

As the capital costs of winemaking continue to rise, custom crushing has become a way to support the high costs of a winemaking facility and at the same time cater to a variety of customers and their different purposes; and, preeminently, it is a way for a small enterprise to make wine without capital costs. A holder of a winery license can buy grapes and send them to a custom-crush facility, where they are made into wine according to the winery's instructions or even under the winery's step-by-step supervision, then stored, and finally bottled before being sold under the label of the commissioning winery. Some custom crushers extend their services further by locating a source of grapes to be used as well as performing all the other steps from grape to bottle and beyond—they may even ship the wine and help to sell it. Another custom-crush scheme is designed to help wineries that buy grapes from vineyards located far from the winery. The grapes—instead of being trucked a long distance to the winery, with all the risks that entails—can be sent to a custom-crush facility and then shipped either as juice or as finished wine. The custom-crush plant thus becomes a satellite winery.

A refinement of the idea came into being in 1991 when the TTB made available a new license for so-called alternating proprietors.[23] The alternating proprietorship gives the license holder all the privileges of a winery—conducting tastings, offering samples, and so on—even though the licensee may own no part of the facilities where the wine is produced.[24] Some facilities have been built expressly for custom crushing, but more often the work is done at established wineries with extra capacity that they are glad to use for the purpose. It is an interesting fact that some of the most prestigious of the cult wines rely on custom crushing, a scheme well suited to their small production. The Laird Family Estate winery, owner of one of the largest vineyard acreages in Napa Valley, makes little wine of its own but does custom crushing for such clients as Colgin, Lewis, Cornerstone, and Aubert, all small and sought-after labels.[25]

The evident hazard for a winery without vineyards and without its own winemaking equipment is that it must take its chances of finding a supply of grapes and must accept the charges that the custom crusher sets; it has no control over either end of things. But these risks apart, custom crushing seems to have worked out well so far and is virtually certain to become of increasing importance not just in California but elsewhere.

SOME SOCIAL ISSUES

One of the most protracted and publicized conflicts in California wine history began in 1965 when the United Farm Workers union, led by César Chávez, struck against the grape growers of the Delano region, in the southern section of the San Joaquin, and the call went out to boycott grapes.[26] The UFW, which was poor, could not sustain a long strike, but the device of a boycott could be kept up indefinitely, and was. Chávez also led a march of workers from Delano to Sacramento, the state capital, 250 miles away, to great publicity.

Chávez began to get results; in 1967 the UFW signed contracts covering its field workers with The Christian Brothers, Almadén, and Paul Masson, three of the biggest wineries in the country, and then with Gallo, the biggest of them all (though the number of its field workers was not great). The Gallo contract was renewed in 1970, but when the time came for the next renewal Gallo objected to certain UFW practices and signed with the rival Teamsters instead. Chávez called for a boycott of Gallo wines, and although the Gallos protested that they were the innocent victims of a turf war between rival unions, the general public seems to have sided with Chávez. He led another march, this time not to Sacramento but to Modesto and the Gallo winery, where Chávez promised the Gallos that he would call off the boycott if the company would let its workers choose which union

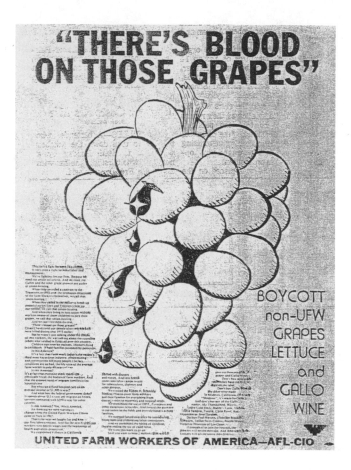

FIGURE 56
One notable item from
the long boycott of Gallo
wine by the United Farm
Workers. (From *Los
Angeles Times*, 11 October
1976.)

would represent them. The UFW followed up the march on Modesto with sensational full-page ads in the *New York Times* and other papers. "Don't buy Gallo wines," they said; one proclaimed that "there is blood on those grapes"; another showed a migrant mother and father standing next to their residence, a dusty station wagon filled with children.[27]

The conflict dragged on until in 1977 the Teamsters agreed to a truce with the UFW and withdrew from the farm labor field. This seems to have satisfied Chávez, who declared an end to the Gallo boycott on 1 February 1978, almost five years after it had begun. That outcome might be regarded as a victory for Gallo, which had suffered, no doubt, in its public relations but had not had to make much of a change in its operations. No one pretends that the problems of farm labor have been settled, but there has been nothing in recent years to match the drama of the Chávez-Gallo conflict.

A different and positive development in the labor force was the employment of women in responsible positions at every level of the wine industry. There was no tradition, as far as I know, of rooted opposition to women in the trade, as there is said to have been in some European communities; women simply were not employed, except as pickers in the vineyard or workers on the bottling lines. Women, it is true, had long been owners of wineries, but almost always in virtue of widowhood, as with the *veuve* Cliquot in France. The beginning of a new opportunity for women may be dated to 1965, when Mary Ann Graf became the first woman to graduate with a degree in fermentation science from the University of California, Davis. What was surprising was that by her own account, she had no trouble getting jobs, first with Gibson Winery and then with Italian Swiss Colony, Sonoma Vineyards, and Simi. This entry through the technical side seems to have been of strategic importance. Graf was followed at Davis by Zelma Long, who then worked at the Robert Mondavi Winery, becoming chief enologist there before migrating to Simi. These two women did not exactly precede a deluge, but by 1985 a quarter of the students in the enology program at Davis were women, and by that time women were winemakers at Firestone Vineyard, Buena Vista, Domaine Chandon, Chappellet, Sebastiani, and others.[28] Outside California, women were to be found in charge of winemaking at wineries in New York, Oregon, Washington, and elsewhere. Since then the presence of women in all phases of winery operation and management has become well established.

Another public question that arose early in the '70s was the prelude to a whole series of conflicts that troubled the wine industry throughout the decade of the '80s under the general heading of neoprohibitionism. It began in 1972 when an organization called the Center for Science in the Public Interest petitioned both the Food and Drug Administration (FDA) and what was then the Bureau of Alcohol, Tobacco and Firearms (BATF) to require all alcoholic beverages to carry a list of ingredients on their labels. The BATF produced a set of regulations that satisfied no one, and then another set, and then gave up the question. The FDA thereupon declared that it would take over the job and decreed that ingredient labeling would be required as of January 1977. The liquor interests challenged the authority of the FDA in this field and secured a court ruling giving the BATF exclusive jurisdiction over the labeling of alcoholic beverages.[29] The BATF then tried a third time to devise regulations and again gave up the struggle. The matter next went to the courts, where in 1986 a U.S. Circuit Court of Appeals ruled against such labeling.

The inconclusive struggle over ingredient labeling was only a beginning. The National Institute of Alcohol Abuse and Alcoholism (NIAAA), an agency created by Congress in 1970, was the institutional embodiment of a growing anxiety at this time about alcohol and "other drugs." The NIAAA announced in 1977 that pregnant women should not drink if they wished to avoid giving birth to mentally retarded or physically deformed babies.[30] The FDA then called for a warning label about fetal alcohol syndrome, and the BATF, under pressure, agreed to consider such a thing. The struggle over ingredient labeling had, in effect, been renewed, only now the object was not to inform but to frighten. The leader of the campaign in Congress was Senator Strom Thurmond of South Carolina; he succeeded in getting Senate approval of warning labels in one form or another in 1979, in 1980, and again in 1986, but on each occasion the measure went no further. A minor victory came in 1987, when sulfite warnings were required on wine bottles. The FDA had declared in 1985 that sulfites were a health hazard, and the BATF, in dutiful support of the FDA, ruled in 1986 that wine labels must state that the wine contains sulfites.[31]

MADE FROM GRAPES, DEXTROSE,
WATER, SUGAR AND YEAST
WITH SULFUR DIOXIDE AS A
PRESERVATIVE.

HEBLEY'S

NEW YORK STATE

PORT

Bottled by
HEBLEY WINE COMPANY
Ft. Union, New York

1 QUART

ALCOHOL 20 % BY VOLUME

This wine should be chilled
before serving.

ALCOHOL 12% BY VOLUME

Made from Grapes and Yeast with Sulfur
Dioxide Added as Preservative.

Produced, Bottled and Distributed by
Attleby Vineyards, Attleby, California

FIGURE 57
Sample wine labels devised
by the Food and Drug Ad-
ministration in 1976 to show
ingredients. (From *Wines and
Vines* 57 [July 1976]; reprinted
with permission from *Wines
and Vines*.)

Senator Thurmond's long campaign for warning labels succeeded with the passage of the Alcoholic Beverage Labeling Act of 1988. This required the following message to appear on every container of alcoholic drink, whether domestic or imported:

GOVERNMENT WARNING: (1) According to the Surgeon General, women should not drink alcoholic beverages during pregnancy because of the risk of birth defects. (2) Consumption of alcoholic beverages impairs your ability to drive a car or operate machinery, and may cause health problems.

The warning was a much-diminished version of Senator Thurmond's original scheme, which called for five different texts that would be used in constant rotation and that warned against mental retardation and other birth defects, impaired ability to drive, hypertension, liver disease, cancer, and alcohol addiction.[32]

The campaign for warning labels was accompanied by a series of related attacks on alcoholic drink. A coalition group called SMART, encouraged by the ban on the broadcast advertising of tobacco, sought to ban liquor advertising on television and radio; it managed to get congressional hearings on the question in 1985, but no legislation followed. Another campaign, particularly associated with the group MADD (Mothers against Drunk Driving), succeeded in raising the legal age for drinking in many states through the passage of the National Minimum Drinking Age Act of 1984. Increasing taxes—not for revenue but for deterrence—was another line of attack: the Center for Science in the Public Interest proposed to increase the tax on wine from 17 cents a gallon to $11.37.[33]

In 1986 California passed Proposition 65, a ballot measure that purported to aim at protecting the state's drinking water but in fact took in much more territory. The act required the governor to draw up a list of all chemicals "known to the state" to cause cancer or to result in reproductive harm and then to see that the public was warned against such substances. Wine, because it contains alcohol and ethyl carbamate (urethane), made the list, along with all other alcoholic beverages.[34] The law requires that the following warning notice be prominently displayed wherever alcoholic drink is sold:

WARNING: Drinking distilled spirits, beers, coolers, wine and other alcoholic beverages may increase cancer risk, and, during pregnancy, can cause birth defects.

What effect, if any, this measure has had on the wine-drinking public I do not know, nor, one may suspect, does anyone else. But it was certainly evidence of the growing tendency to aim at prohibition in the name of health.

In the first half of the 1980s, the increasingly vigorous attack on alcohol did not seem to affect the winemakers: shipments of wine continued to show steady growth, and adult per capita consumption of wine reached an all-time high in 1986. Then the decline set in. Sales did not go up in 1987, and then for the next four years they moved sharply downward: California shipped 424 million gallons to market in 1987 but only 375 million in

1991. It was no doubt an exaggeration to speak, as *Newsweek* did, of a "moderation craze" and of a "rampaging sobriety" sweeping through the country, but the winemakers now had good reason for anxiety and began to think about how to defend themselves.[35]

An early effort to "promote the well-being of wine in the United States" by means of an organization called Americans for Wine was made in 1979 but soon disappeared. The Winegrowers of California held seminars in 1985 and 1987 to discuss the whole neo-prohibitionist agenda from an ostensibly detached and objective viewpoint.[36] Robert Mondavi made a well-publicized move by announcing a "Mission" to defend wine as "part of the civilized way of life." The Mission was soon turned over to an organization called the National Wine Coalition, which hoped to emphasize the *National* in its name but was in fact the creature of the Wine Institute and was hampered accordingly. The coalition never succeeded in establishing itself as genuinely national in the eyes of its potential supporters but continued to be seen as a California enterprise. It was shut down for lack of funding in 1995. A rival effort took shape in the form of a group called AWARE (American Wine Alliance for Research and Education), dedicated to creating a "balanced, comprehensive view" of wine in the United States—an admirable goal indeed. AWARE continues to operate under the umbrella of the American Vintners Association, a trade group that includes some California wineries but largely represents the non-California interest.

There were other groups dedicated to the defense of alcoholic drink by direct or indirect means: The distillers created the Century Council in 1991, piously devoted to opposing "every sort of alcohol abuse and misuse."[37] The Licensed Beverage Information Council (1979) was ostensibly meant to represent the whole spectrum of alcoholic-beverage producers and their belief that "education is the best method available to address alcohol abuse."[38] Then there were the National Vintners Association, the Winegrape Growers of America, the Women for Wine Sense, and the Wine Industry National Education System (WINES), not to mention state and local organizations by the score. As one official put it, there were "many disparate groups with numerous chiefs, few Indians and little money."[39]

It is not clear what effect all these defensive exercises in public relations may have had. But things turned around in startling fashion at the end of 1991 through quite another means. In November 1991 the CBS weekly program *60 Minutes* presented, as one of its segments, some interviews with experts who wondered why it was that the French, who ate more fats than the Americans, nevertheless had a lower incidence of heart disease. The solution to this "French paradox" might be, it was suggested, the healthful effects of drinking red wine![40] That was all that the health-conscious American public seemed to need, at least for a time: the demand for red wine immediately soared. In the supermarkets, sales went up by 44 percent in the month following the television program. Gallo's Hearty Burgundy, it was said, was put on allocation.[41] The effect continued through the next year, when the sales of table wine from California rose by 20 million gallons and prices for some red wine grapes went up by 50 percent.[42] The neoprohibition movement was in no way extinguished by this sudden shift, but the atmosphere had been changed in a dramatic way.

The excitement generated by this turn of affairs led to some predictable excesses; wine, one now read, might help to resist cancer, or Alzheimer's disease. No responsible person talked that way, but the winemakers were emboldened to think that they might advertise the healthful effects of wine, perhaps even on the same labels as carried health warnings. That was the absurd contradiction into which things had now been driven; and when doctors disagree, as they so blatantly did, who shall decide? In this case the BATF did, holding fast to the line laid down by its charter that such claims, "irrespective of falsity," could not be allowed. And after all, would it really be a step toward a "balanced, comprehensive view of wine" to have people eagerly drinking it as a "free ticket to longevity" instead of shunning it as a general hazard to health?[43] The one extreme seems quite as perverse as the other.

SOME NEW RULES AND RULERS

In 1976, in part because of its struggles with the FDA over ingredient labeling and in part because of the difficulties that had arisen in defining winegrowing regions, the BATF announced that it would make a general overhaul of its labeling regulations.[44] The proposed changes were positive, aiming at higher standards of identity and clearer information for the public. What finally emerged, after long and contentious hearings, were a rule raising the minimum varietal requirement in a varietally labeled wine from 51 percent to 75 percent and a new provision for the establishment of American viticultural areas. The new varietal requirement was on the whole welcomed by the industry, and the idea of officially defined American viticultural areas (AVAs) was regarded as at least worth a trial.

Up to this point in American wine history the only officially defined place-names were all political divisions: United States, California, Sonoma County. It was now provided that "any interested party" (not just a grape grower or winemaker) could file a petition with the BATF to ask for official recognition of a viticultural area whose identity would be geographical rather than political. The petitioner had to show that the name in question was a recognized one, that there was historic evidence for the boundaries proposed, and that there were geographic features peculiar to the region that distinguished it from surrounding areas. There was no requirement that any grapes be grown in the area proposed or any wine made there: the BATF was prepared to allow the grape growing and the winemaking to be wholly prospective. Nor is anything said about cultivation practices, permitted varieties, maximum yields, or methods of production and handling—in short, all those things that are inseparable from European principles of *appellation contrôlée* or *denominazione controllata* or *denominación de origin*. In many cases, then, the new viticultural areas would be essentially empty categories, viticultural areas waiting for viticulture to happen. In other cases, there *was* a history of winegrowing, and drawing the boundaries of such areas could be a hotly disputed business. "Napa Valley" is an obvious example, and there were others—though not many—in which there were financial reasons to fight for the use of a name.

There are now some 148 AVAs, all of them created since 1978, and the list continues to grow. It is important to understand that the only things officially recognized in an AVA are the name, the geographical description, and the boundaries: the designation has nothing to do with the grapes or the wine, if in fact any grapes or wine actually come from the area in question. It is certain that many Americans do not understand the limitations of the term but regard it as an official stamp of approval. It must also be said that the scheme of the AVA has lent itself to exploitation by marketers, who have succeeded in obtaining AVA designations that have little to do with the actual disposition of things but much to do with attractive naming: the San Francisco Bay AVA is a clear instance. The recent, unsuccessful effort to obtain a California Coastal AVA for most of the state's wine-growing regions outside the Central Valley is another.

The creation of AVAs rescued the term *estate bottled:* there had been no definition before, and the BATF wanted to get rid of it. Now, with the creation of AVAs, an estate bottling could be defined as a wine that came from a winery in a particular AVA where it grew the grapes and made the wine. In a very large AVA, *estate bottled* cannot mean much, but in the very small ones it can. Yet another change in the new labeling rules was the permission to allow statements about the aging of wine. Ever since the labeling rules had first been set forth in 1935, the federal government had sternly forbidden any hint about aging. Now, on the grounds that truthful statements that were neither disparaging nor misleading should be allowed, it was permitted to state that a wine had, for example, been "aged in American oak for 18 months."

The BATF had been threatened with extinction under the budget-cutting program of the Reagan administration, but the threat had passed, partly owing to opposition from the wine industry itself. In 2002, however, as one of the crowd of unpredictable changes that followed the terrorist attacks on the World Trade Center and the Pentagon, the BATF did disappear—or, rather, was remodeled. The work having to do with criminal law enforcement was transferred to a new agency under the Department of Justice called the Bureau of Alcohol, Tobacco, Firearms and Explosives (ATF). The regulatory and tax-gathering functions of the alcohol and tobacco section remained with the Treasury Department, but the office was rechristened the Alcohol and Tobacco Tax and Trade Bureau, or TTB for short. The rules under which this newly named agency worked remained unchanged.

There were signs in the course of the 1980s of a growing friendliness toward wine on the part of Congress. The Wine Equity and Export Expansion Act was passed in 1984 to reduce barriers against the export of American wine. Wine was one of the commodities included in the Market Promotion Program, a scheme designed to assist exports. In 1989 Congress approved funds for the National Grapevine Importation Facility, to be maintained at the University of California, Davis, which, if not a move directly in support of wine, was close enough.[45] The House Agriculture Committee began to take an interest in wine after a long period of neglect, testimony to the fact that winegrowing had spread to an increasing number of states and was therefore of increasing political importance. Representative Eligio de la Garza (D-Texas), the chairman of the committee, proposed in

1989 that the supervision of the wine industry should be moved from Treasury to the Department of Agriculture (USDA) in recognition of the fact that it was a "food beverage."[46] The proposal got nowhere, but it was evidence that the old tradition of federal assistance to winegrowing was not wholly forgotten.

De la Garza and the committee took a new tack in 1990 by adding an amendment to the Farm Bill of that year directing the USDA to conduct a study to determine how it might best assist the American wine industry.[47] The study was never performed—there were no funds for it—but again a point had been made. The next year the Agriculture Committee held hearings on the subject of how the USDA might help American wine, and the participation in these hearings suggested how the wine interest was becoming a political presence outside California: congressional representatives from Virginia, West Virginia, New York, Missouri, Washington, and Oregon as well as California asked to be heard.[48] In 1995 and 1996 Congress made appropriations of $500,000 for research in enology and viticulture to be shared by Cornell University and the University of California, Davis; the Agricultural Appropriations Bill of 1997 directed the USDA to report on the long-term research needs of American viticulture.[49]

There is not yet a wine bureau in the vast structure of the USDA, nor has the TTB lost its grip on the regulation of wine. It would be fair to say, however, that the idea of official encouragement had been revived and perhaps a bit strengthened by these friendly attentions paid to the wine trade by a Congress that was at the same time lavishly funding antialcohol programs. In 1993 Congress passed a joint resolution declaring the period 21–27 February to be American Wine Appreciation Week: this was one of those gestures that cost nothing to make, but it was hard to imagine that it would have been made just a few years earlier.

INDUSTRY QUARRELS AND TROUBLES IN THE VINEYARDS

One of the victims of the expansive days of the 1970s was the Wine Advisory Board. When the board prepared for its customary three-year renewal vote at the beginning of 1975, it was told by Governor Jerry Brown's administration that it must limit its contracts with the Wine Institute (which had done much of the board's work from the beginning), plan to give up its lobbying activities, and accept a "consumer representative" on its board. Rather than submit to these conditions, the board voted itself out of existence at the end of June 1975. Whether such a move would have been made if the times had not been so prosperous for the industry may be doubted.

When efforts were made after a time to renew the sort of work that had been done by the Wine Advisory Board before its suicide, the divisions within the industry made it hard to get cooperation. Proposals for a California Wine Grape Commission got nowhere in 1981, but in 1984, over much opposition, a marketing order of the kind that had created the original Wine Advisory Board was passed and the Winegrowers of California came into being. It lasted only three years, for its board of directors was made up of equal numbers of winemakers and grape growers, and they could not agree. The winemakers then voted to establish something called the California Wine Commission, excluding the grape growers. This, too, lived only a three-year span: in 1990 a long-smoldering conflict between the big producers and the not-so-big flared up, with the result that the commission was voted out of existence. Since that time there has been no state-supported promotional program for the wine industry of California. The history of this failure to renew the work of the old Wine Advisory Board seemed to show clearly enough that the growers could not work with the winemakers and that the big wineries could not work with the smaller ones. Whether it showed any reason to hope that these different interests could ever work together remains to be seen. Perhaps a little adversity—such as lay behind the Wine Advisory Board originally, and such as began to threaten in the early years of the twenty-first century—might bring them together.[50]

These conflicts were underlined in 1990 by the resignation of some eighteen wineries from the Wine Institute, led by Kendall-Jackson.[51] The dissenting wineries were those that had led the fight to kill the Wine Commission; now they set up their own organization, called the Family Winemakers of California—*Family* in this context being a polemical term meant to assert that the group would not be controlled by big business (even though there were big businesses among its members). Over the next two years about seventy-five wineries resigned from the Wine Institute, including, in 1992, the Robert Mondavi Winery.[52] Since there were now two rival groups, and since some wineries belonged to neither, no one could claim to speak for a united industry.

Meanwhile, a single-minded pest was at work in the vineyards. California vineyards, especially in the established North Coast regions, are mostly grown not on their own roots but on rootstocks selected for their resistance to phylloxera. This practice has been standard since the phylloxera onslaught at the end of the nineteenth century.[53] In California, the favorite rootstock had long been Rupestris St. George, a native American variety; in 1958, however, the University of California issued a report on phylloxera-resistant rootstocks that recommended a different choice for the table-wine regions of California.[54] Tests showed that a rootstock known as AxR#1, originally developed in France in the nineteenth century, consistently outperformed Rupestris St. George: it rooted easily, took grafts well, and gave high yields of well-developed fruit—exactly what a grower would want. The report recognized that AxR#1, a cross between a resistant rupestris vine and a very nonresistant vinifera variety, the Aramon, had "only moderate phylloxera resistance" but concluded that it was nevertheless "the nearest approach to an all-purpose stock."[55] The authority of the university in this matter seems to have been decisive: AxR#1 became the rootstock of choice for California's nurserymen and for the growers whom they supplied, and this happened just as the great expansion of the California vineyards was about to begin.

There were skeptics: Lucie Morton, who knew that the French had long since concluded that vinifera-rupestris crosses had low resistance to phylloxera and had ceased to use them, wondered why the Californians were using AxR#1. Her doubts were published in the trade

journal *Wines and Vines* in 1979, but no troubles had yet shown up, so her question went unheeded.[56] The first signs of a new phylloxera infestation were picked up at two places in Napa and Sonoma Counties in 1983 on vines grafted to AxR#1 rootstock, and soon more and more reports of phylloxera in Napa and Sonoma began to pile up.[57]

At first it was said that a new strain of phylloxera must be responsible: biotype B, it was called. There may well have been one, since phylloxera is genetically variable. What has once been effective against it may not always be. But the simpler—and correct—conclusion was that AxR#1 rootstock was not, after all, resistant and that the French had been right about it. A program of replanting to resistant rootstock now had to be undertaken, on a scale not seen since the phylloxera devastation in the northern counties at the end of the nineteenth century. In the natural course of things a vineyard must be replanted, but that is a gradual and orderly process. This one would have to be sudden and very, very expensive: to the cost of removing old vines and planting new ones must be added the loss of crop over the several years it takes for a new vine to produce. The figures that statisticians produce to measure such expenses are perhaps more poetic than actual, but there is no doubt that the misguided practice of using AxR#1 stock was costly.[58] In 1993 it was calculated that 22,000 of Napa Valley's 34,000 acres of vines were on AxR#1 rootstock; not all of these vulnerable acres would have to be replanted at once, and many would be replanted without regard to phylloxera. But some 3,600 acres had already been taken out for one reason or another, and it was expected that several thousand more would be taken out annually until the conversion to more resistant rootstock was complete.[59]

Those whose temperament leads them to find the bright side of things have since maintained that extensive replanting in Napa and Sonoma Counties was a Good Thing. It gave growers a chance to plant better varieties, they said, or better clones of approved varieties; they could experiment with new forms of vine training and new patterns of planting, particularly the denser planting long practiced in certain European wine regions. Moreover, the rising demand for wine at a time when vineyard acreage was not increasing sent up the price of grapes. No doubt all this was true, but if phylloxera produced such good results it was still a bad cause. Who was to blame? The university, knowing that growers wanted a productive rootstock, had recommended the productive AxR#1 despite the knowledge of its weak resistance to phylloxera; the growers, wanting a productive rootstock, were happy to accept the recommendation, though the weakness had not been concealed from them. It would seem to be a case of mutual seduction.

A new—or renewed—affliction hit California when an outbreak of Pierce's disease occurred in the Temecula region in 1998. The disease has always been latent since it destroyed the Anaheim vineyards in the 1880s. It was only in fairly recent years that some understanding of this lethal infection had been reached: the cause was not, as had been thought, a virus, but a bacterium with the elegant name of *Xylella fastidiosa,* which works by blocking the water supply of the vine and so causing death. It was also known that it was mainly carried by insects known as sharpshooters and that these insects used certain plants as hosts. The new outbreak was connected to a carrier—a vector, in the jargon of the biologists—called the glassy-winged sharpshooter, newly introduced into California and, unluckily, bigger, adapted to a greater variety of host plants, and more mobile than the native insects. It could thus spread the disease farther and faster than had been known in the state before.

No outbreak of the disease comparable to that in the Temecula region has since occurred in California, but the glassy-winged sharpshooter has shown up in many different parts of the state—often on shipments of nursery stock—and this development has generated great anxiety. The official response was to throw money at the problem: within a year's time the state had appropriated $7 million, the federal government $29 million to support research and control. Probably the recent troubles with phylloxera had made both the trade and the public particularly edgy, so that the response to the threat of Pierce's disease was unusually strong and quick. There is not much that can be done yet about bacterial infection once it is established, so research and control have concentrated on dealing with the sharpshooter by preventing its spread and by finding chemical or biological means to kill it. There is active work on breeding vines that will resist Pierce's disease, but no one expects that to succeed any time soon. In the meantime, the disease remains a threat.[60]

The devastations of phylloxera and Pierce's disease are only the most notable of recent attacks by pests and diseases: nature always has more in store. At the beginning of the new century, growers in California also have to worry about eutypa dieback, fanleaf degeneration, oak root fungus, young vine decline ("black goo"), vine mealybugs, nematodes in great variety, leafhoppers, thrips, mites, orange tortrix, and twig borer—to keep the list short. There are also troubles consequent on new methods. Drip irrigation, for example, confines the root development of the vine to a very restricted space and so allows root-feeding pests a much more convenient system to work on. One does not "conquer" nature; the process of adjustment and readjustment to shifting conditions is perpetual.

GRAPE GROWING AND WINEMAKING IN THE NEW CENTURY

Both viticulture and winemaking are deeply conservative: we grow ancient varieties of grapes in our modern vineyards, and the essential items of traditional winemaking—crusher, fermenting vat, press, storage barrel—are still the essential items of modern winemaking. But the sorts of care that go into grape growing and winemaking, and the means devised to assist the grape grower and the winemaker in their traditional tasks, show many changes and novelties. The array of technical means now available is formidable in scope and complexity, and it is the product of genuinely international work.

Those who set out to plant a vineyard today might begin by studying infrared photographs taken from satellites in order to find a promising territory. Once the land is chosen, they can of course have detailed soil analyses carried out by experts who specialize in the work. They can also install portable, solar-powered weather stations at various points to record such variables as temperature, relative humidity, precipitation, solar radiation, wind speed, and a whole list of other conditions, so that the property's weather and climate are known in detail. The grapes that they choose to plant will probably be from the rather small group of varieties traditionally held to be superior, but the planting stock may have been multiplied by mist propagation, it will have been heat-treated against viral infection, and it will be selected from a variety of available clones.[61]

In time, perhaps, scientists will be able to modify the genetic systems of the traditional grape varieties so that they resist phylloxera, Pierce's disease, nematodes, and mildew while retaining their character for wine. That has not happened yet, so new vineyardists must decide how they want to control diseases and pests. The indiscriminate use of chemical pesticides and fungicides is now no longer thinkable. At the opposite extreme is the organic method; what this entails has yet to be clearly defined, but it means at a minimum that one uses no fungicides, no synthetic fertilizers, no herbicides, and no fumigating agents. Between these extremes is the approach called sustainable agriculture, which aims to alter the land as little as possible and makes use of such practices as Integrated Pest Management; this works by providing a habitat for the common pests' natural predators through planting of cover crops and other means and thus diminishes the reliance on chemical sprays.

Laying out the vineyard (nowadays done by laser devices) raises a question: how close should the vines be set? In days not very long ago, that had not seemed to be in question. The space between rows had to be wide enough to allow the passage of a standard farm tractor, and the space between vines big enough to allow row plowing, eliminate crowding, and improve the exposure to light. The standard recommendation of the university experts for vineyards in the coastal counties was for spacing six feet by twelve feet or eight feet by twelve feet, which translated to 540 or 410 vines per acre. The main consideration was cost: wide spacing allowed efficient cultivation and management without reducing production.

In recent years this practice has been repeatedly challenged, in part because of the influence of European models. Narrower spaces between rows and between vines in the row would allow the number of vines per acre to be doubled, or even tripled or more, over the standard California measures. Crowded vines that had to compete against close neighbors would produce smaller, more intensely flavored berries (so it was said); and with more vines per acre, each vine could be permitted to carry only a small crop better suited to its capacity. So how close should they be? As one authority has put it, "Nobody really knows what the proper spacing is . . . it's all theory."[62] But dense planting is increasingly the rule.

The new vineyard today will demand a lot of water, if it can get it. Drip irrigation, developed in Israel in the '60s, is now widespread in newly planted California vineyards. A narrow, flexible water line is strung from grape stake to grape stake and from trellis post to trellis post, and an emitter, or "dripper," is set into the line over each vine. Water drips slowly through the emitter in measured quantities, irrigating each vine in the most economical manner that has yet been devised. To make control even more precise, moisture sensors that record the status of soil water and plant water may be spotted around the vineyard, and information is relayed from them to the computer that controls the irrigation system. If there is a good water supply, a system of overhead sprayers might well be installed as frost protection: when a freeze hits, the water is turned on and forms ice on the vines. The release of latent heat as the water freezes protects the vine, even though it is covered in ice.

A generation ago, when a new California vineyard went in, it would have had no trellising arrangements. Instead, the vines would have been trained as low-growing, self-supporting bushes: head pruning, this technique was called. The young vines were supported by redwood grape stakes in their first years, but the mature vine stood by itself on a short trunk while the stake it had once leaned on slowly rotted away. That has all changed. Canopy management, the manipulation of the leaf cover in order to obtain the best exposure of the fruit to sunlight, has become the subject of intense study and argument.[63] The trellis is the key to the canopy: should it be horizontally divided? Vertically divided? Undivided but vertically trained? How does one get the best spotted sunlight, as it is called? The answers depend on what one is growing, and where: cool climates are one thing, hot climates quite another; vigorous vines need one sort of treatment, weaker vines another. Some trellising systems are more labor-intensive than others; some are designed to produce more fruit, some less.

By and large, growers in California use the double-cordon, spur-pruned system of training. The vine is allowed to form a trunk up to the first wire strung between trellis posts; two canes are then trained horizontally, to the right and left of the trunk along the wire, to make a T-shape. In time these horizontal canes become arms, called cordons. A few short spurs along each cordon are left by the pruning, and from these each year the fruiting canes grow out. Another two wires above the level of the cordon, called catch wires, give the young shoots support. As the season goes on, the mass of canes and leaves spills out into the rows on either side of the vine—the California sprawl, it is called. But there were many variants, in growing numbers: lyre trellises, vertical trellises, Geneva double curtain trellises, and so on.

During the growing season the vines may have some of their leaves removed from around the developing bunches to get the best exposure. Workers may also go through the vineyards to do cluster thinning—cutting off bunches of grapes in order to lighten the vine's load and allow the remaining fruit to ripen better. When the crop is ripe it may very well be machine-harvested, though harvesting by hand continues to be regarded as preferable. It is more selective and gentler, and it allows whole clusters to be picked—important if one is doing whole-cluster pressing or fermenting. If a crop is harvested by machine, the grapes will to some extent be broken and bruised, and oxidation may quickly set in. To counter this problem, a system of field crushing has been developed. Instead of being sent back to the winery for crushing, the harvested grapes are crushed by a mobile crusher in the vineyard and the must kept in closed, wheeled tanks that can then be hauled to the fermentation vats at the winery.

What does all this cost to develop? The direct expenses include such things as land preparation; trellis material; rooted, grafted cuttings from the nursery; the drip irrigation system, including pumps, motors, and filters; and the ongoing machinery and labor costs of cultivation—plowing, weeding, spraying, fertilizing, pruning. To these must be added such overhead costs as property taxes, insurance, maintenance, and depreciation. Estimated costs for the first three years—the time it takes to bring a new vineyard into production—range from $6,000 up to $40,000 per acre, depending in large part on the cost of land to start with. By any estimate, the figure is likely to be large.

New technologies are, if anything, more striking in the winery than in the vineyard. There are modern devices to attend to every stage of the winemaking process, beginning with the delivery of the grapes to the crushpad. To handle the grapes at the beginning, one may see mechanized sorting tables, chilling tunnels, finely adjustable crusher-stemmers, must chillers, and presses of every size and principle of design: pneumatic drum presses, electrically powered hydraulic basket presses, progressive-draining continuous presses, self-cleaning bladder presses, jacketed presses for temperature control, closed presses to prevent oxidation, open membrane presses, tank presses. The juice for white wine may then go to settling tanks or dejuicers made of stainless steel and fitted with various sorts of screens; here the solids settle out before fermentation. Alternatively, for the same purpose one might use a desludging or decanting centrifuge.

The must now being ready for fermentation, a whole array of containers awaits it. Stainless steel, temperature-controlled fermentors are the popular choice. They can be controlled by computer, so that every step in the fermentation process is precisely monitored, every stage recorded. If something goes wrong, the computer sounds the alarm. The fermentors may be equipped for punching down (that is, for breaking up by mechanical means the cap of seeds, stems, and skins that forms at the top of a fermenting vat), or they might be equipped for pumping over (that is, leaving the cap intact but circulating the fermenting wine over it by pumping). Another choice is the rotary fermentor, a stainless steel tank mounted on its side and mechanically rotated; a variant design is a stationary, side-mounted tank equipped with revolving paddles inside to agitate the mass of skins and seeds.

A cultured yeast, selected for its specific properties, is introduced, and the fermentation begins. The stainless steel, temperature-controlled fermentor now makes many variations possible. By setting the temperature low, especially for white wines, the fermentation can be prolonged over many days. For red wines, a high proportion of uncrushed grapes may go into the vat, the must sulfited and cooled to delay fermentation, and then allowed to sit and soak for one or two days—a process of maceration known as cold soak, intended to extract as much color and flavor as possible from the skins before fermentation. In another method, after fermentation has begun, part of the juice—about 10 percent—is drawn off in order to concentrate the juice that remains; the fraction drawn off is kept and sold as a rosé. This is an old French practice, called *saignée,* now more and more imitated in California. A generous provision of tanks also allows for another technique, called rack-and-return: in this step, when fermentation has pushed the cap to the top, the tank is drained and the fermenting juice temporarily transferred to another tank. The cap falls to the bottom of the tank, where the seeds—the source of the most astringent tannins—are captured by a special screen and removed. The juice is then returned to the tank and the fermentation continues. The aeration of the juice created by this movement early in the fermentation also helps soften the tannins in the resulting wine. Yet another possibility is extended maceration at the end rather than at the beginning of fermentation; the new wine is kept on the skins for many days—from ten up to forty—after fermentation is complete to assist the further extraction of color and the softening of tannins.

Another novelty is the prevailing use of stainless steel tanks not only for fermentation but for storage. In barrel maturation, the softening of a wine's tannins is attributed to the effect of the oxygen that finds its way through the wood. Stainless steel tanks do not allow any oxygen to enter; to compensate, a process of so-called micro-oxygenation has been developed to feed measured quantities of oxygen into wine kept in stainless steel. Induced malolactic fermentation—a secondary fermentation, carried out not by yeast but by bacteria, in which the harsher malic acid is transformed to the softer lactic acid—is now a standard procedure in California, for wines in which it is desirable. The process, formerly little understood and wholly spontaneous, is now precisely managed. The processes of filtering and fining, employed before the wine is bottled, have also undergone remarkable technological development, including sterile filtration.

Some of the most impressive technology has been applied to what might be called the correction of mistakes, particularly the problem of high alcohol. In California the warm climate readily produces high sugar in the grapes, and this natural condition is abetted

FIGURE 59

A spinning cone installation: very high technology for those who want it. (From *Wines and Vines* 76 [June 1995]; reprinted with permission from *Wines and Vines*.)

by the current practice of allowing the fruit a long hang time to produce a full (some say overfull) maturity. The frequent result is a wine of 14 percent alcohol or even higher. Such wines pay a higher tax than those under 14 percent, and there is some resistance to wines of so high an alcoholic content on the part of buyers. Thus there are good reasons to want to cut down a too-high alcohol level. One method of doing so is called reverse osmosis, employing osmotic pressure to separate a solution of low concentration from one of higher concentration. This process requires expensive machinery. So does another method, the use of a spinning cone column employing centrifugal force in a vacuum at low temperature. This device can separate a liquid into various components with great precision, and can be used to remove unwanted flavors as well as an excess of alcohol.

At the same time as the ingenious and sophisticated developments brought by technology to the vineyard and winery are more numerous and impressive than ever before, a strong tendency may be noted to revert to the old ways. Part of the reason may be a simple reaction against the control of the technicians, but another part of the reason is that modern scientific analysis has sometimes confirmed the value of traditional methods. Mixed up with these things is the widespread feeling that we have gone too far in manipulating nature and should now encourage its restoration. In the winemaking world, all of these impulses are expressed in the idea that wine is made in the vineyard and that the winemaker's role is only that of an attentive midwife.

The dense planting of vineyards is one example of the new traditionalism: the practice is wholly European and flies in the face of all that Californians had formerly believed. In some vineyards, particularly of Zinfandel, the new methods of trellising are rejected in favor of the old-fashioned head pruning, which is said to suit the nature of the variety better. Some winemakers ignore modern methods of measurement to determine ripeness and the moment of harvest in favor of their own empirical judgment: when the grapes taste "right," it is time to pick, never mind what the refractometer says. The ideal winery now, some say, should resemble those that were built in the old days, innocent of electric pumps and mechanical conveyors; instead, it should be built on a downhill slope so that grapes, must, and wine may move by God's own force of gravity. If possible, winemakers should do without sulfiting the must, and instead of employing one of the many pure strains of cultivated yeasts, they should rely on wild native yeasts alone. They want not stainless steel fermentors but wood ones, and they may cheerfully allow the fermentation temperatures for red wine to run higher than is allowed in a temperature-controlled stainless steel tank. Storage and maturation of course are carried out in wood: the overwhelming acceptance of oak-barrel aging in California in the past generation is without question the most notable instance of a traditional method rediscovered, reexamined, and enthusiastically promoted. Finally, reactionary winemakers are skeptical about fining and filtration as a way to clarify wine, holding that these practices may rob the wine of important elements in the process of making it bright and clear.

The contemporary winemaking scene is thus a rich mixture of methods and traditions and attitudes, and the one certain conclusion to be drawn is that there is no settled way of winemaking here. Kipling said of poetry, "There are nine and sixty ways of constructing tribal lays, / And—every—single—one—of—them—is—right!" We might say something like that of winemaking in this country. More than one student of the subject has tried to calculate the number of choices that a winemaker must navigate in the process from grape to bottle; the results are always formidable—two hundred or two thousand, it hardly matters which. The basic outline of winemaking might be simple enough, but it is accompanied by a complex array of options generated by all the variables of the work and of the means provided. A time may come when the various winemaking regions across the country establish clear, fixed rules for their own territories—what grapes to grow, how to grow them, and how to make wine out of them—but we are far from that point now. Meanwhile, American winemakers are free to go their own way, a freedom that includes the freedom to go wrong, of course, but also the freedom to try new things and new ways.

WAGNERIANS AND MARTIANS

The wine industry in the United States, though it has met plenty of obstacles, has now grown to a great size. But can it be said that the United States has become a wine-drinking country? Does it even show signs that, one day, it might be? One may doubt. There are now more acres of vineyard than ever before; there are more wineries, in more states, than ever before, making more wine in greater variety than has ever been known before. There is now no doubt that the country can make good wine over a large expanse of its territory, and sometimes great wine in certain privileged places. The wine trade flourishes today on a scale far surpassing anything known in the past. Indeed, the United States is the fourth-largest producer of wine in the world, after Italy, France, and Spain. And yet, for all that, wine is still far from an everyday, familiar creature for most Americans. Most Americans, in fact, have nothing to do with it and never think of it.[64] They are abetted in this ignorance by the fact that in many places the status of wine remains problematic—put in question by legal restrictions and moral disapproval. And it cannot be too often or too strongly stressed that as long as the second part of the Twenty-first Amendment remains in force, wine will always have a difficult time in America.

When we turn to the fraction of the population that *does* drink wine, we find all too frequently a set of ideas, attitudes, and practices that seems almost as retrograde as anything at the time of Repeal. There is an obsession with prices (the higher the better), an obsession with ratings, a touching dependence on the judgments of the supposed wine experts, and an obsession with having only the best, accompanied by an anxious display of knowingness and a corresponding fear of revealing ignorance. No doubt these things are inseparable from human weakness and will show up in our behavior toward anything in which we take an interest. But wine seems, in America, peculiarly liable to inspire affectation and artificiality.

The prominence of the idea that wine is an investment rather than something to drink is symptomatic of the trouble; so too are the ideas of wine country as a sort of agricultural Disneyland and of the winery as a tourist amusement; and so too is the publicity given to the fashionable antics on display at wine auctions or other forms of celebration and promotion. The press seems unable to describe the wines of a region without extravagant statements about the triumphs they have achieved at international judgings or the acclaim they have received from paid enthusiasts. Most of these distortions and exaggerations are foolish rather than wicked, but that is just the point. Little of it would go on in a genuine wine-drinking country.

The tendency of all this folderol is to exclude wine from a place in everyday life and to isolate it in a special sphere open only to a privileged elite, or, worse, to tourists on a spree. Philip Wagner devoted his work as viticulturist and winemaker to fostering the idea that every man could have a daily supply of good, sound wine, to be enjoyed with hamburger quite as much as with *caneton à la Montmorency*. Let us call the people who take this view of wine's role the Wagnerians. Wagnerians are always delighted to have a bottle of superlative wine, but their happiness does not depend on it, nor are they so foolish as to think that only the superlative is fit to drink. Their happiness *does* depend on having wine each day, normally with the evening meal, for they know what an agreeable enhancement to food of any sort it provides. If the wine is sound and appropriate to the food it accompanies, they are content to ask no more for the moment. Of course they are always looking for the best possible wine within the limits of their budget, but good sound wine will not only suffice, it is a necessary part of the daily regimen.

The opposite view is conveniently embodied in Wagner's contemporary, Martin Ray, whose idea of wine was that anything less than the superlative was unworthy, that no price could be too high, and that the enjoyment of wine required rigorous preparation. Let us call the people who think thus the Martians. For them, everything else at a meal—

food, conversation, flirtation—must yield to an intense concentration on the wine and its qualities and to a comparison of judgments. The defects that are discovered loom large, and the poor boobs who are unable to detect them are made to feel their unworthiness. Practically speaking, these two groups may be so far apart that they are unaware of each other: the well-satisfied purchaser of a five-liter bag-in-box of supermarket chablis has probably never heard of the eager cultist happily possessed of a $2,000 bottle of Napa Cabernet. There is no doubt room for both Wagnerians and Martians, and a great deal of room in between for a variety of views. But in this country, which is the dominant side?

When one begins to inquire into the *idea* of wine in America, it looks as though the Martians have it mostly their way and the Wagnerians have been overwhelmed. The people who write about wine in the popular press largely appear to be Martians, who take for granted that anything under $20 a bottle is a "bargain" wine and who routinely review for their middle-class readership wines costing $30, $40, $50, and up. Even in affluent America such wines can hardly be a part of the daily supper. They enforce the idea that wine must be something special—a matter of display, or of costly indulgence. That idea is strongly reinforced by the price of wine in restaurants, where a not particularly distinguished bottle routinely costs two or three times the price of the most expensive entrée on the menu. No wonder that so many people view wine as an investment rather than an attractive drink. No wonder—and this is perhaps the worst effect of all—that the ordinary American, unable to understand how a natural fruit product (as wine undoubtedly is) can be sold for $50 or more a bottle, sensibly decides to have nothing to do with the mystery.

Opposed to all these Martian influences one can hardly hear a Wagnerian voice. The California wine trade at one time mounted an advertising campaign for generic wine—that is, wine without any frills—but this program ended with the death of the old Wine Advisory Board, and nothing of the kind has been heard since. Instead, the dominant style in the advertising of wine is what has been called tuxedo marketing—the assiduous cultivation of "an image of exclusivity."[65] The idea that wine not only can be but should be inexpensive, plentiful, and good rather than costly, rare, and indescribably complex seems in danger of disappearing from American consciousness, where, it must be admitted, it has never had a secure lodging. And this when the supply of inexpensive, plentiful, and good wine is greater than ever before in the history of wine.

Leon Adams, writing in 1978, thought that within a decade the per capita annual wine consumption in America would rise to five gallons: young people, he thought, would account for this increase, and they would be free of the snobbery that has long afflicted wine in this country. "The wine revolution," Adams declared in confident contemplation of his vision, "has only begun."[66] More than twenty years later, at the end of his survey of the fortunes of American wine, Paul Lukacs reluctantly concluded that none of Adams's predictions had yet come true: "Table wine still has little to do with daily home life in much of the country. In this regard, the wine revolution still has only just begun."[67] As long as the Martians make the loudest noises, as long as the idea of wine is inseparable from the worst forms of conspicuous consumption, a wine revolution such as Leon Adams thought he saw on the near horizon will have to remain a distant prospect.

Nevertheless—and this must be emphatically said—much has been accomplished, and it seems right to conclude this history on a positive note. If the United States is not yet a wine-drinking country, it is indisputably a country in which much good and interesting wine, in growing volume, is produced and consumed. It is all the more remarkable in view of the fact that the entire industry has been re-created in the space of a mere two generations since Repeal. The general sense of achievement among winemakers was nicely expressed by the veteran Edmund Mirassou, of the Mirassou Winery, on the fiftieth anniversary of Repeal at the end of 1983. Mirassou, who was old enough to remember the blight of the Prohibition years and the struggles that continued for a generation afterward, could speak with special fervor. "Thank God," he said, "for the entrepreneurs, and the universities—and the banks that had the courage to lend us money—it has worked out well."[68]

NOTES

CHAPTER 1. FORMS OF LIFE IN A DRY WORLD

1. Public Law no. 66, *U.S. Statutes at Large* 41 (1921): 305–23. Before the constitutional amendment had been ratified, Congress had passed a wartime prohibition act on 21 November 1918—an act already rendered pointless by the end of the fighting and then superseded by the Eighteenth Amendment. The Volstead Act enforced both wartime and constitutional prohibition, and Wilson argued that only the second was proper: see Charles Merz, *The Dry Decade* (Garden City, N.Y.: Doubleday, Doran, 1931), pp. 41, 49. The wartime prohibition act, prohibiting the manufacture of intoxicating beverages, took effect on 1 July 1919 but does not seem to have been generally enforced before the Volstead Act came into force on 16 January 1920.

2. Justin Steuart, *Wayne B. Wheeler: Dry Boss* (New York and Chicago: Fleming H. Revell, 1928), pp. 150–51.

3. Norman H. Clark, *Deliver Us from Evil: An Interpretation of American Prohibition* (New York: W. W. Norton, 1976), p. 131.

4. "The Yale Club, with prophetic insight, laid down enough bottles to last out fourteen years" (Andrew Sinclair, *Prohibition: The Era of Excess* [London: Faber and Faber, 1962], p. 194). A few states prohibited the private possession of alcohol (Andrew Barr, *Drink: A Social History of America* [New York: Carroll and Graf, 1999], p. 105).

5. H. L. Mencken put this idea with his usual distinctness: "Big Business was in favor of Prohibition, believing that a sober workman would make a better slave than one with a few drinks in him" ("Breathing Space," *Baltimore Evening Sun*, 4 August 1924, in Marion Elizabeth Rodgers, ed., *The Impossible H. L. Mencken* [New York: Doubleday, 1991], p. 285).

6. J. C. Burnham, "New Perspectives on the Prohibition 'Experiment' of the 1920's," *Journal of Social History* 2 (1968): e.g., p. 60. David Musto says that death rates from cirrhosis of the liver "plummeted" in the Prohibition years (*New York Times,* 16 March 1986).

7. Taft had opposed the Eighteenth Amendment as ill-advised sumptuary legislation, but once it was ratified he was prepared to see it enforced with more rigor than some of his fellow justices approved (Allen E. Ragan, *Chief Justice Taft* [Columbus: Ohio State Archaeological and Historical Society, 1938], pp. 90–99).

8. Wesley Jones (1863–1932), a senator from Washington and a special champion of the Drys, gave his name to the act, which was in fact the work of Bishop Cannon of the Anti-Saloon League (Mark Edward Lender, *Dictionary of American Temperance Biography* [Westport, Conn.: Greenwood Press, 1984], *s.v.* "Jones"). The Jones Act, by making the sale of alcohol a felony, also had the effect of making the buyer subject to prosecution for misprision of a felony. Before this, as has been said, no penalty attached to buying alcohol—only to selling it.

9. David E. Kyvig, *Repealing National Prohibition* (Chicago: University of Chicago Press, 1979), p. 66.

10. Burnham, "New Perspectives," p. 58. One state, Maryland, steadfastly refused to pass any concurrent legislation at all, giving a new dimension to the term *Maryland Free State.*

11. This was, allegedly, less than the alcohol content of sauerkraut (Sinclair, *Prohibition,* p. 421).

12. Kyvig, *Repealing National Prohibition,* pp. 128–29.

13. Ibid., p. 61.

14. E.g., the fourth volume of Ernest Hurst Cherrington, ed., *Standard Encyclopedia of the Alcohol Problem* (Westerville, Ohio: American Issue Publishing, 1924–30), a sort of summa of Dry faith and knowledge, affirmed in 1929 that "despite continued activity among the wets, and insidious misrepresentation, both at home and abroad, as to the ineffectiveness of the Volstead Act, leaders in every branch of American activity bear overwhelming testimony as to Prohibition's benefits" (p. 2214, *s.v.* "Prohibition").

15. Burnham, "New Perspectives," p. 65.

16. One account of the organization holds, simply, that the members of the AAPA sought repeal solely in order to get rid of the income tax! See Fletcher Dobyns, *The Amazing Story of Repeal: An Exposé of the Power of Propaganda* (Chicago: Willett, Clark, 1940). Among the influential directors of the AAPA were Henry Joy, president of the Packard Motor Car Company; John J. Raskob, treasurer of the E. I. du Pont du Nemours Company; his boss, Pierre du Pont; former senator James Wadsworth; and philanthropist Edward S. Harkness (Kyvig, *Repealing National Prohibition,* p. 1).

17. Kyvig, *Repealing National Prohibition,* p. 97.

18. The eleven commissioners included Newton D. Baker, former Secretary of War; Roscoe Pound, dean of the Harvard Law School; William S. Kenyon, a judge of the U.S. Circuit Court of Appeals; and Ada Comstock, president of Radcliffe College.

19. Franklin P. Adams, "Conning Tower," *New York World* (February 1931): quoted in Sean Cashman, *Prohibition: The Lie of the Land* (New York: Free Press, 1981), p. 210.

20. Kyvig, *Repealing National Prohibition,* p. 128.

21. The Crusaders published a magazine called *The Hot Potato,* in reference to what the Prohibition issue had become for the politicians.

22. But Kenneth Rose says that the main argument of the Women's Organization was home protection, by which it effectively took the Woman's Christian Temperance Union's position away from it (*American Women and the Repeal of Prohibition* [New York: New York University Press, 1996], pp. 2, 90).

23. Kyvig, *Repealing National Prohibition*, pp. 122–23. Among the officers of the Women's Organization were Gladys Harriman, wife of a Brown Brothers Harriman partner; Mrs. Archibald Roosevelt, daughter-in-law of Theodore Roosevelt; Alice du Pont, wife of the chairman of the board of du Pont; and others of comparable standing (Rose, *American Women and the Repeal*, p. 80).

24. *Time* (18 July 1932): 9.

25. Kyvig, *Repealing National Prohibition*, pp. 131–32.

26. The political character of the AAPA is vividly demonstrated by the fact that it could not bring itself to endorse Roosevelt, even though his was the party of Repeal (Sinclair, *Prohibition*, p. 412).

27. Prohibition lasted for thirteen years, ten months, and nineteen days.

28. *Time* (10 April 1933): 32.

29. Kyvig, *Repealing National Prohibition*, p. 186.

30. Ruth Teiser and Catherine Harroun, *Winemaking in California* (New York: McGraw-Hill, 1983), p. 160.

31. Louis A. Petri, *The Petri Family in the Wine Industry*, interview by Ruth Teiser, Berkeley: Regional Oral History Office, Bancroft Library, University of California, 1971, p. 3.

32. Philip M. Wagner, *American Wines and How to Make Them* (New York: Knopf, 1933), p. 95.

33. Horace O. Lanza, *California Grape Products and Other Wine Enterprises*, interview by Ruth Teiser, Berkeley: Regional Oral History Office, Bancroft Library, University of California, 1971, pp. 5–7.

34. U.S. Department of the Treasury, Bureau of Prohibition, *Statistics Concerning Intoxicating Liquors, April, 1928* (Washington, D.C.: GPO, 1928), table 24.

35. Lanza, *California Grape Products*, p. 10.

36. The high point was 1924, when 2,944,764 gallons of sacramental wine were shipped. After 1926, the figure was greatly reduced and never again reached a million gallons (U.S. Department of the Treasury, Bureau of Industrial Alcohol, *Statistics Concerning Intoxicating Liquors, December 1932* [Washington, D.C.: GPO, 1932], table 23). The drop is explained by a ruling made in 1926 that reduced by half the quantity of sacramental wine allowed for use in the home—a measure prompted by the great number of self-styled priests serving homemade religions who had cropped up under Prohibition and had secured permits to obtain sacramental wine (Ruth Teiser and Catherine Harroun, "The Volstead Act, Rebirth, and Boom," in *The University of California/Sotheby Book of California Wine*, ed. Doris Muscatine, Maynard A. Amerine, and Bob Thompson [Berkeley: University of California Press, and London: Sotheby Publications, 1984], pp. 54–55).

37. U.S. Department of the Treasury, Bureau of Industrial Alcohol, *Statistics Concerning Intoxicating Liquors, December 1931* (Washington, D.C.: GPO, 1931), table 7. Wine was also distilled into brandy, and that, if it could not be sold directly, could easily be stored or used in fortifying wine for permitted purposes.

38. It appears that much of the wine made in California during Prohibition was made "not from choice, but as a matter of expediency in salvaging grapes that had become unfit for transportation to Eastern destinations. . . . The result is that much dry wine in California at the present time is not what might be considered commercially sound. . . . Quite a large bulk of the dry wines in the state run excessively high in volatile acids, which means the beginning of vinegar development" (*California Grape Grower* 5 [August 1924]: 8).

39. Bureau of Industrial Alcohol, *Statistics Concerning Intoxicating Liquors, December 1932*, table 86.

40. U.S. Department of the Treasury, Bureau of Prohibition, *Statistics Concerning Intoxicating Liquors, January 1930* (Washington, D.C.: GPO, 1930), table 39.

41. U.S. Department of the Treasury, *Report of the Commissioner of Internal Revenue, 1920* (Washington, D.C.: GPO, 1920), p. 35.

42. U.S. Department of the Treasury, Bureau of Industrial Alcohol, *Statistics Concerning Intoxicating Liquors, December 1933* (Washington, D.C.: GPO, 1933), table 59.

43. Ibid., table 69. There are other, much higher, estimates of production for this period.

44. Ibid. Large quantities of wine were used as distilling material, and smaller quantities were converted to vinegar. Losses were also considerable: 15 million gallons between 1921 and 1933 (ibid.). When these items are taken into account, the quantity of wine produced grows even greater.

45. Philip Wagner reports that "many" wineries "sold their equipment intact to the great *bodegas* of the province of Mendoza in Argentina" (*American Wines and How to Make Them*, p. 96).

46. The following account is drawn from the papers of the Hammondsport Wine Company, now in Cornell University's Kroch Library.

47. The following account of Widmer's winery through Prohibition is drawn from the Widmer papers, now in Cornell University's Kroch Library.

48. There were at least twenty different permits dispensed by the Prohibition authorities, at least thirteen of which might apply to winery operations: see U.S. National Commission on Law Observance and Enforcement, *Enforcement of the Prohibition Laws: Official Records* (Washington, D.C.: GPO, 1931; hereinafter referred to as the *Wickersham Report*), vol. 2, p. 301n.

49. In this history I use capital letters for genuine Port, Sherry, Madeira, and other wines but lowercase letters for wine of those names made and so labeled in this country.

50. This discussion of California wineries under Prohibition is largely drawn from the records of the Bureau of Alcohol, Tobacco and Firearms (though it was not called that at the time), now deposited in the Department of Special Collections of the Shields Library at the University of California, Davis.

51. So, at any rate, it is stated in the inspector's reports in the BATF papers at Davis. According to Charles Sullivan, who interviewed people who worked for Masson at the time, Masson sold wine openly throughout the Santa Clara Valley (personal communication, 18 June 2000).

52. Much of the old To-Kalon vineyard is now the property of the Robert Mondavi Winery. Mondavi is reviving the To-Kalon name.

53. Salmina's wine, by the time of Repeal, had a volatile acidity content above the legal limit and had to be blended with new wine to reduce the acidity: see chapter 5, at n. 60.

54. "Passing of Andrew Mattei," *Wines and Vines* 17 (May 1936): 24.

55. Philip Hiaring, "Sebastiani Vineyards: The Name of the Game Is Growth," *Wines and Vines* 58 (September 1977): 18.

56. Teiser and Harroun, *Winemaking in California,* p. 180; Beaulieu brochure (ca. 1934; copy in the Wine Institute Library).

57. Harry Baccigaluppi, who managed the Colonial Grape Products bonded warehouse in New York, remembered traffic of up to 400 barrels of wine a week (*California Grape Products and Other Wine Enterprises, Part II,* interview by Ruth Teiser, Berkeley: Regional Oral History Office, Bancroft Library, University of California, 1971, p. 84).

58. U.S. Department of the Treasury, *Report of the Commissioner of Internal Revenue, 1923,* p. 28. One of them was the Theodore Gier Vineyard Company, with properties in Oakland, Napa, and St. Helena; shortages were found in the inventory, and it was claimed that the missing wine had been bootlegged to a clientele in wealthy Piedmont (*San Francisco Chronicle,* 19, 21 May 1922).

59. Leon D. Adams, *Revitalizing the California Wine Industry,* interview by Ruth Teiser, Berkeley: Regional Oral History Office, Bancroft Library, University of California, 1974, p. 8; Charles L. Sullivan, *Like Modern Edens: Winegrowing in Santa Clara Valley and Santa Cruz Mountains, 1798–1981,* Local History Studies 28 (Cupertino, Calif.: California History Center, 1982), p. 128.

60. Everett Crosby, *The Vintage Years: The Story of High Tor Vineyards* (New York: Harper & Row, 1973), p. 2.

61. Sylvia Bargetto Nolan, interview in Charles Sullivan, *Wines and Winemakers of the Santa Cruz Mountains: An Oral History* (Cupertino, Calif.: D. R. Bennion Trust, 1995), p. 180.

62. Sullivan, *Wines and Winemakers,* p. 449.

63. U.S. Department of the Treasury, *Report of the Commissioner of Internal Revenue, 1923,* table 82. The Wickersham Commission reported that nearly 8 million gallons of wine (including some unspecified quantities of "cider, mash and pomace") were seized in the years from 1920 through 1929 (*Wickersham Report,* vol. 5, p. 348, table 1). The quantity of spirits seized in any year was usually larger than that of wine.

64. A story in Eleanor Ray and Barbara Marinacci, *Vineyards in the Sky: The Life of Legendary Vintner Martin Ray* (Stockton, Calif.: Heritage West Books, 1993), pp. 146–48, implicates federal authorities in extorting wine from Paul Masson during Prohibition. Corruption among the Prohibition authorities was taken for granted, and one may suppose that they had a part in any illegal movement of wine from licensed wineries. But it is not easy to measure what quantities may have been involved.

65. Mabel Walker Willebrandt, "Memorandum of the Interpretation of Section 29, Title II, of the National Prohibition Act," *Wickersham Report,* vol. 5, p. 29.

66. F. T. Bioletti and W. V. Cruess, "Possible Uses for Wine-Grape Vineyards," Bulletin 14, State Board of Viticultural Commissioners (Sacramento: State Printing Office, 20 May 1919).

67. Not during the early years of Prohibition, at any rate. Later, when the crop exceeded the demand, new uses were again investigated.

68. The trade in fresh grapes for home winemaking had been growing in anticipation of Prohibition for several years before the actual passage of the Volstead Act, but no one supposed that it would grow to the extent that it did (John R. Meers, "The California Wine and Grape Industry and Prohibition," *California Historical Society Quarterly* 46 [1967]: 27). In 1921, growers reported that they were getting four times as much for their grapes as they ever had before (*New York Times*, 13 February 1922).

69. Carl Wente, "A Look Backward at the 'Dark Days,'" *Wines and Vines* 43 (December 1962): 17.

70. U.S. Tariff Commission, *Grapes, Raisins and Wines*, Report 134, 2nd ser. (Washington, D.C.: GPO, 1939), table 13.

71. Ibid. The advertising pages of the *California Grower* in the first years of the '20s are dominated by railroad ads offering speedy shipment of grapes.

72. The myths about Prohibition continue to obscure the reality. Since the vineyards *ought* logically to have declined under Prohibition, it was assumed that they had in fact done so. An article in the September 1976 issue of *Wines and Vines*, for example, states that without the small demand for altar wine, "the few vineyards [in California] that survived might have been pulled up" (p. 22). So also James Laube, writing in 1989, says that in California "most of the vineyards were either abandoned or replanted to other agricultural products" (*California's Great Cabernets* [San Francisco: Wine Spectator Press, 1989], p. 29). The fact is that vineyards flourished as never before. One estimate of the activity in new vineyard planting is that "approximately $100,000,000 of new money was invested in vineyard properties in a period of three years (1920–23)" (Jessie Schilling Blout, "A Brief Economic History of the California Wine-Growing Industry" [San Francisco: Wine Institute, 1943], p. 7).

73. U.S. Department of Agriculture, Bureau of Agricultural Economics, Crop Reporting Board, *Fruits and Nuts Bearing Acreage, 1919–1946* (Washington, D.C.: GPO, 1949), p. 29; "California's Grape Production since 1919," *California Grower* 11 (September 1931): 5. Figures in this report differ from those in other sources, but not critically.

74. *California Grower* 7 (February 1926): 6; Robert Schick, "The Arkansas Wine Industry," *Wine Review* 14 (June 1946): 12. Much of this growth was in Concord grapes for the pasteurized grape juice trade. In 1924, H. G. Swartout reported that in Missouri, "thousands of acres of vineyards have been planted during the past two or three years and as a result the State may regain the position of importance it once occupied in the grape growing industry" (*Grape Growing in Missouri*, Bulletin 208 [Columbia: University of Missouri, College of Agriculture, Agricultural Experiment Station, January 1924], p. 3).

75. C. C. Wiggans and E. H. Hoppert, "Grape Growing in Nebraska," Extension Circular 1257 (Lincoln: University of Nebraska, Agricultural College Extension Service, June 1925), p. 3.

76. U.S. Department of Agriculture, *Fruits (Noncitrus): Production, Farm Disposition, Value, and Utilization of Sales, 1889–1944* (Washington, D.C.: GPO, 1948), pp. 67, 77. Winegrowers in the Finger Lakes district were getting more than twice the pre-Prohibition price per ton for their grapes by 1922, and the volume sold had doubled each year (*New York Times*, 27 August 1922).

77. Cashman, *Prohibition*, p. 39.

78. See Philip Wagner's prefatory remark in *American Wines and How to Make Them*, pub-

lished in the last months of Prohibition: "Wine has enjoyed increasing popularity throughout the period of prohibition. I have even heard it suggested that if prohibition were to continue in force for another decade, we might reasonably expect the United States to become a wine-drinking nation."

79. *Wickersham Report*, vol. 1, p. 128. Clark Warburton, *The Economic Results of Prohibition* (New York: Columbia University Press, 1932), pp. 37–38, puts the figure by one method of estimating at an average of 86.5 million gallons for the years 1921–31; by another method, 107 million gallons. The Wine Institute's estimate for the years 1927–33 is an average of 67 million gallons (see Ralph B. Hutchinson, "The California Wine Industry" [Ph.D. diss., University of California, Los Angeles, 1969], p. 193). No doubt the great volume of home winemaking was in part owed to the fact that it was easier to make a decent wine at home than it was to make a decent beer.

80. National Prohibition Act, Section 29, Title II.

81. Alterations in the Volstead Bill with the same intent as Section 29 were, however, introduced in the House without success: see Willebrandt, "Memorandum on the Interpretation of Section 29, Title II," p. 26.

82. See the debate in *Congressional Record*, 66th Congress, 1st session, 4 September 1919, vol. 58, pt. 5, pp. 4847–48.

83. Willebrandt, "Memorandum on the Interpretation of Section 29, Title II," p. 11.

84. Paul Garrett (1863–1940) was the most successful producer and promoter of wine in the eastern United States before Prohibition. Starting with the family winery in North Carolina, he ultimately had properties in Virginia, New York, and California devoted to the production of his Virginia Dare wine, the most popular wine in the country. He was a leader in the fight against Prohibition and was recognized as a spokesman for the industry. During Prohibition he had a major part in the creation of the Fruit Industries enterprise.

85. Paul Garrett, "The Right to Make Fruit Juices," *California Wine Grower* 4 (July 1923): 2.

86. U.S. Congress, House of Representatives, Judiciary Committee, *Hearings on Proposed Modification of the Prohibition Law to Permit . . . 2.75 Per Cent Beverages, Part 1* (Washington, D.C.: GPO, 1924), 21, 22, 30 April; 14, 21 May 1924, p. 519.

87. Ibid., *Part 2:* 4 June 1924, p. 548; Volstead's account was cited by John Philip Hill from hearings held before the House Rules Committee, 10 June 1921.

88. *Wickersham Report*, vol. 5, p. 20. The phrase *nonintoxicating in fact* was used in the Senate debate on Section 29.

89. The formula was 2.75 percent alcohol by weight or 3.45 percent by volume. This would mean something for beer but not for wine.

90. *New York Times*, 19 September 1924.

91. *New York Times*, 11, 12, 13 November 1924.

92. *New York Times*, 13 November 1924.

93. Those who did typically bought them in flat boxes called lugs, containing from 22 to 26 pounds each, from which a gallon to a gallon and a half of wine might be made (Wagner, *American Wines and How to Make Them*, p. 133).

94. See the company's ad, e.g., in *California Grape Grower* 7 (May 1926). Italian Swiss Colony also had a trade in frozen grape juice and in frozen grapes (ad in *California Grower* 10

[July 1929]: 18), and shipped fresh grapes as well. According to Edmund Rossi, Italian Swiss Colony grapes were always accompanied by packets of sulfur dioxide to help achieve clean fermentations and so enhance the reputation of the grapes (*Italian Swiss Colony and the Wine Industry,* interview by Ruth Teiser, Berkeley: Regional Oral History Office, Bancroft Library, University of California, 1971, p. 30).

95. The account that follows is drawn from the papers of the George Lonz Winery, now at Bowling Green State University, Bowling Green, Ohio.

96. The nature of the clientele for juice and concentrate during Prohibition is confirmed by Harry Baccigaluppi, who worked for one of the major suppliers: "There was a tremendous amount of business of that kind done, and . . . for the most part done with the first families of the nation . . . doctors, dentists, lawyers, engineers, stock brokers— that's the kind of people they sold this product to" (*California Grape Products and Other Wine Enterprises, Part II,* p. 95).

97. The price per ton for California grapes was about $60 in 1926; in 1928 it was $17 (U.S. Tariff Commission, *Grapes, Raisins and Wines,* pp. 55, 59).

98. John A. Parducci, *Six Decades of Making Wine in Mendocino County, California,* interview by Carole Hicke, Berkeley: Regional Oral History Office, Bancroft Library, University of California, 1992, p. 19.

99. Ibid., p. 10.

100. U.S. Tariff Commission, *Grapes, Raisins and Wine,* table 158.

101. Ibid., table 15.

102. California Vineyardists Association, "Form of Organization, Purposes, and Functions of the California Vineyardists Association," undated brochure ([San Francisco?]: ca. 1926), copy in the Wine Institute Library; H. F. Stoll, "Plans of the California Vineyardists' Association," *California Grape Grower* 8 (July 1927): 1–2. The CVA was largely concerned with what we would call, but what it could not call, the wine-grape sector of California viticulture: there were separate organizations concerned with table grapes and with raisin grapes.

103. Donald D. Conn, "The California Vineyard Industry: Five Year Report" (San Francisco: California Vineyardists Association, 25 April 1932), p. 7. What may have been a general suspicion of the CVA is expressed in a flyer of 1927 addressed to "California Grape Growers" and warning them against signing up with the CVA, claiming the organization was a railroad plot intended to bind them to any shipping scheme the railroads might want (California State University, Fresno, Library). Conn was a former railway man. Leon Adams says that the efforts of the CVA to regulate shipments were "a pretty hot subject" among California grape growers (*Revitalizing the California Wine Industry,* interview by Ruth Teiser, Berkeley: Regional Oral History Office, Bancroft Library, University of California, 1974, p. 20).

104. "Salvaging Our Grapes," *California Grape Grower* 8 (September 1927): 14.

105. The name reflects the fact that the purpose of the enterprise was to process not just grapes but fruits of all sorts: "The corporation has been made a co-operative agency for the processing, storing and distribution of all fruit products withheld from the market as surplus from this territory" (H. O. Lanza, "The Grape Products Consolidation," *California Grower* 10 [July 1929]: 8). I have no evidence that Fruit Industries ever processed anything but grapes, despite its name.

106. For Conn, see Teiser and Harroun, "The Volstead Act," pp. 61–66. The Di Giorgio Fruit Company, the largest fruit producer in California, had joined the combination by July 1929 as a contributor though not as a wholly owned part (*California Grower* 10 [July 1929]).

107. Adams says that the plan to promote concentrate was Garrett's idea (*Revitalizing the California Wine Industry*, p. 22).

108. Circular 488, 6 August 1929 (*Fruit Products Journal* 9 [September 1929]: 12). Dr. James M. Doran (1885–1941), who had been a chemist with the Bureau of Internal Revenue, was Commissioner of Prohibition, 1927–30, and following the reorganization of Prohibition enforcement, Commissioner of the Bureau of Industrial Alcohol, 1930–33. Upon Repeal he switched sides and became the technical director of the Distilled Spirits Institute.

109. *California Grower* 10 (August 1929): 9. The Bureau of Prohibition seems to have thought that a single, dominant source of supply for the country's home winemakers would make supervision much easier.

110. Dorothy M. Brown, *Mabel Walker Willebrandt: A Study of Power, Loyalty, and Law* (Knoxville: University of Tennessee Press, 1984), pp. 181–82.

111. Ibid., pp. 182–83.

112. Ibid., pp. 181, 185.

113. Vine-Glo was not alone in offering such a service. A pamphlet dated 1931 put out by Italian Swiss Colony describes directions for "sherry type beverage" and "Burgundy type beverage" and adds, "Should you desire, reliable service men are available at your house for the proper refinement of your beverage" (copy in the Wine Institute Library). And see the account of the service offered by the Lonz Winery, above.

114. Brown, *Mabel Walker Willebrandt*, p. 187.

115. About a million gallons of Vine-Glo were converted by Fruit Industries into brandy. Fruit Industries paid off its loans from the Farm Board after World War II (ibid., p. 296, n. 37). The government's reversal of position and Conn's protest against this change are documented in Conn, "The California Vineyard Industry," pp. 51–60.

116. Norbert C. Mirassou and Edmund A. Mirassou, *The Evolution of a Santa Clara Valley Winery*, interview by Ruth Teiser, Berkeley: Regional Oral History Office, Bancroft Library, University of California, 1986, p. 8.

117. *California Grower* 13 (October 1932): 3; strictly speaking, one should say the Bureau of Industrial Alcohol. By the Prohibition Reorganization Act of 1930, the enforcement of Prohibition was assigned to the Department of Justice and a new agency of the Treasury Department, the Bureau of Industrial Alcohol, took over the business of licensing and monitoring production. Among the wineries that went back into production in 1932 were Italian Swiss Colony in Sonoma, the Guasti Winery and the Mission Winery in Cucamonga, the Mokelumne Winery in Lodi, and Beringer Brothers in Napa (undated press release [ca. November 1932] of Grape Growers League of California; copy in the Wine Institute Library).

118. *California Grower* 14 (March 1933): 4.

119. The *California Grape Grower* 14 (September 1933) published an article by A. E. Bagshaw on "How to Secure a Winery Permit" for the many who were then interested. The trickle of restored wineries in 1932 became a flood in 1933.

120. BATF records, University of California, Davis, Shields Library, Gallo file. In the East, Will Widmer reported to members of the Finger Lakes Wine Growers Association in September 1933 the statement by the Bureau of Industrial Alcohol that it had "no intentions of handicapping the operations of wineries this fall" (Finger Lakes Wine Growers Association file, box 5, Widmer papers, Cornell University, Kroch Library). The situation was evidently wide open to unrestricted production, despite the fact that Prohibition was still in force.

121. Adams, *Revitalizing the California Wine Industry*, p. 31.

122. Leon D. Adams, *The Wines of America* (Boston: Houghton Mifflin, 1973; 4th ed., 1990).

123. The league was formed by eight growers who each put in five hundred dollars to promote wine as a "temperate beverage" (Wine Institute, "The First Twenty Years of the Wine Institute: A Report to Members at the Twentieth Annual Meeting" [San Francisco: Wine Institute, 8–9 March 1954], p. 1).

124. "Grape Growers League of California," *California Grower* 13 (December 1932): 9. Among the officers of the league were Sophus Federspiel, F. Cribari, Georges de Latour, Edmund Rossi, Lee Jones, and L. M. Martini, winemakers all.

125. U.S. Congress, House of Representatives, Committee on Ways and Means, *Prohibition: Modification of Volstead Act, Hearings, Dec. 7–14 1932* (Washington, D.C.: GPO, 1932).

126. Advertisement for Pelton Water Wheel Company, *California Grower* 14 (February 1933): 7.

127. Cashman, *Prohibition*, p. 239. The Bureau of Prohibition in the Justice Department was abolished in August 1933.

128. Edmund Rossi, quoted in *New York Times*, 14 January 1933, 7.

129. Adams, *Revitalizing the California Wine Industry*, p. 53; and idem, *The Wines of America*, p. 27.

130. U.S. Congress, House of Representatives, Committee on Ways and Means, *Legalization of Wine: Hearings, 8 June 1933* (Washington, D.C.: GPO, 1933), p. 12.

131. To Marvin H. McIntyre, 18 April 1933 (Roosevelt papers, Roosevelt Library, Hyde Park, New York). Charles Sullivan attributes the provision limiting wine to 3.2 percent alcohol to the ignorance of southern senators (*Like Modern Edens*, pp. 133–34). Evidently a number of different influences contributed to the outcome.

132. H. F. Stoll, "3.2 Per Cent Wines Make Their Appearance," *California Grower* 14 (May 1933): 3. All of the 3.2 wines appear to have been diluted with water and then sweetened and carbonated in order to add some interest to their otherwise pallid character. One formula (from *California Grape Grower* 14 [June 1933]: 9) is as follows:

    i. 100 gals. of red wine of 10% alcohol content
    ii. 90 pounds cane sugar
    iii. 11.4 gals. of Malaga concentrate
    iv. 6 pounds citric acid

    The *New York Times* reported that the winegrowers of Germany, though eager to reopen their American market, refused to make a 3.2 wine (18 June 1933).

133. *California Grape Grower* 14 (July 1933): 13. The editor was Horatio F. Stoll (1873–1947), who had been advertising manager for Italian Swiss Colony and a member of the Board of Viticultural Commissioners formed in 1913. He edited *California Grape Grower*

through the years of Prohibition and, after its transformation into *Wines and Vines,* continued to edit it until 1939.

134. Sales could not have been large. Congressman Buck reported that in the first month of the new dispensation, the government collected $8.8 million in taxes on 3.2 beer and $900 on 3.2 wine (Committee on Ways and Means, *Legalization of Wine, Hearings, 8 June 1933,* p. 25).

135. In 1933, the last year of Prohibition, there were about 695,000 acres, 500,000 of which were in California (U.S. Department of Agriculture, Bureau of Agricultural Economics, Crop Reporting Board, *Fruits and Nuts Bearing Acreage 1919–1946,* p. 29).

136. Andrew Barr has suggested, perhaps fancifully, in his account of the drinking habits of the American Indians that this was the style of drinking in America from the outset (*Drink: A Social History,* pp. 6–7).

137. U.S. Department of the Treasury, Bureau of Industrial Alcohol, *Statistics Concerning Intoxicating Liquors, December 1933,* table 59.

CHAPTER 2. THE RULES CHANGE

1. Tugwell (1891–1979) was assistant secretary of the Department of Agriculture in August 1933, and undersecretary (a newly created post) from 1934. He was associated with some of the New Deal's boldest enterprises, including the Agricultural Adjustment Administration and the Resettlement Administration. He thus attracted some of the most intemperate hostility from the enemies of the administration, who called him a subversive ("Rex the Red") and anything else that might occur to them. He was forced out of Washington in 1936; later he became governor of Puerto Rico. He ended his days as a fellow of the Center for the Study of Democratic Institutions in Santa Barbara, where, one hopes, he was pleased to see the many new small wineries developing in California's Central Coast region.

2. See, for example, the discussions of Dufour in Indiana, of the French in Alabama, of the work of the U.S. Patent Office, and other instances of federal support for winegrowing in Thomas Pinney, *A History of Wine in America: From the Beginnings to Prohibition* (Berkeley: University of California Press, 1989).

3. Rexford Guy Tugwell, "Wine, Women and the New Deal," 5 February 1934; reprinted in *The Battle for Democracy* (New York: Columbia University Press, 1935), p. 184.

4. Jefferson's efforts to establish winegrowing in this country are well known: "We shall yet see [the United States] a country abounding in wine and oil" is a typical comment (R. de Treville Lawrence III, ed., *Jefferson and Wine,* 2nd ed. [The Plains, Va.: Vinifera Wine Growers Association, 1989], p. 239). The official encouragement of winegrowing of course went back to the beginnings of settlement in America. Jefferson was merely the most prominent and most eloquent of public men on the subject.

5. Rexford G. Tugwell, *Roosevelt's Revolution: The First Year—A Personal Perspective* (New York: Macmillan, 1977), p. 303. The codes were temporary because they were originally set up under the National Recovery Administration only in anticipation of the time when the federal and state governments would legislate permanent codes for the regulation of the liquor traffic: see chapter text, after n. 25.

6. This account of the USDA's plans for research is taken from the uncataloged USDA Wine File in the National Agricultural Library, Beltsville, Md. The papers in the file were saved from destruction by Dr. John C. McGrew, formerly a research plant pathologist at the Beltsville station.

7. Memo to R. G. Tugwell, 27 November 1933, p. [11]: USDA Wine File, National Agricultural Library, Beltsville, Md.

8. The Oakville station, on the property of the old To-Kalon Vineyard, had been established in 1903 to carry out work against phylloxera in an experimental vineyard. It had been closed down at the end of 1933 as an economy measure. Tugwell visited the place in the summer of 1934 on a visit to California's wine regions, no doubt in connection with the department's plans for research (*Wine Review* 2 [August 1934]: 22). The property has now been made over to the University of California, Davis.

9. "Memorandum Relative to Wine Work," 5 July 1935: USDA Wine File, National Agricultural Library, Beltsville, Md.

10. C. A. Magoon, "Memorandum for Dr. Auchter," 15 August 1934: USDA Wine File, National Agricultural Library, Beltsville, Md. Eugene C. Auchter was principal horticulturist in the Division of Fruits and Vegetables, Bureau of Plant Industry.

11. It is on record that the crusher, specially designed by the manufacturer, was made by the Healdsburg Machine Shop and shipped on 10 August 1935 (*Wine Review* 3 [September 1935]: 34).

12. "Wine Investigations in the Bureau of Plant Industry, Soils and Agricultural Engineering," 30 June 1950: USDA Wine File, National Agricultural Library, Beltsville, Md.

13. Leon D. Adams, *The Wines of America* (Boston: Houghton Mifflin, 1973), p. 30.

14. E. C. Auchter to J. H. Gourley, 9 February 1935; F. D. Richey to Clarence Cannon, 23 February 1935: USDA Wine File, National Agricultural Library, Beltsville, Md. Cannon was willing to allow himself to be photographed with a group of fellow congressmen all drinking a farewell toast to near-beer on the occasion of the passage through the House of the bill legalizing beer (*New York Times*, 16 March 1933, 3); this suggests that he cannot have been a determined prohibitionist.

15. *Bulletin of the Plant Industry Employees' Association* [Beltsville] 10 (June 1956): 1. The building intended to house a winery at the Meridian, Mississippi, agricultural experiment station was also built but suffered the same fate as the one at Beltsville.

16. The department did, however, continue its research on grapes and grape breeding, particularly in the experimental vineyard near Fresno. Until 1932 this project was directed by George C. Husmann, the son of pioneering nineteenth-century nurseryman, winegrower, and writer George Husmann; the son thus carried on his father's work well into the twentieth century.

17. This condition is comically illustrated by the behavior of the Library of Congress; even after Repeal it consigned books on wine to the special section (Delta Collection) of indecent books to be kept from the public (Robert W. Hutton, "Wine at the Library of Congress," *American Wine Society Journal* 10 [Fall 1978]: 40).

18. U.S. Senate, Committee on Finance, *Hearings on the Liquor Tax Administration Act*, 13, 15, 16 January 1936 (Washington, D.C.: GPO, 1936), p. 134.

19. This account of the muscadine project is taken from the records of FERA, National Archives, RG 69.

20. 29 June 1934: Office of Secretary of Agriculture, General Correspondence 1906–70: RG 16, PI 191, E.17, box 2002, USDA records, National Archives.

21. Clarence Gohdes, *Scuppernong: North Carolina's Grape and Its Wines* (Durham, N.C.: Duke University Press, 1982), p. 77n. The name *Scuppernong* is properly that of one variety of the species muscadine, but it is often used loosely, especially in the South, to mean muscadine generally. There are in fact many muscadine varieties.

22. Undated memorandum [October 1934?]: FERA Old General Subjects Series, box 64, National Archives.

23. Gohdes, *Scuppernong*, p. 78.

24. Gohdes suggests that the Dry forces put an end to the enterprise (ibid., p. 80), and Leon Adams says that "Dry Congressmen forbade" the work (*The Wines of America*, p. 46); neither writer gives any authority.

25. C. Auchter to Senator Bulkeley, 1 December 1937: Secretary of Agriculture, General Correspondence, 1906–70: RG 16, E.-17, box 2669, USDA records, National Archives.

26. Memo, Jerome Frank to H. A. Wallace, 10 November 1933: RG 16, Liquors 1933, Secretary of Agriculture General Correspondence 1906–70, USDA records, National Archives.

27. Raymond B. Fosdick and Albert L. Scott, *Toward Liquor Control* (New York: Harper and Brothers, 1933).

28. In 1862, during the Civil War, table wine was taxed at 5 cents a gallon; the tax was abolished in 1866. In 1898, during the Spanish-American War, table wine was taxed at 8 cents a gallon, the tax being withdrawn in 1902. In 1914, the first of a series of emergency taxes was imposed on wine. These were not withdrawn before Prohibition ended the regular commerce of wine. The rate for table wine at the moment of Prohibition was 18 cents a gallon (Wine Institute, "Historical Wine Tax Summary: Wine Laws, Regulations and Interpretations," rev. ed. [San Francisco: Wine Institute for the Wine Advisory Board, 1 May 1949]).

29. Liquor Taxing Act of 1934, public 83, 73rd Congress.

30. U.S. Congress, House of Representatives, Committee on Ways and Means, *Legalization of Wine, Hearings, 8 June 1933* (Washington, D.C.: GPO, 1933); U.S. Congress, *Tax on Intoxicating Liquor: Joint Hearings before the Committee on Ways and Means, House of Representatives and the Committee on Finance, United States Senate, December 11 to 14, 1933* (Washington, D.C.: GPO, 1934).

31. *California Grape Grower* 15 (January 1934): 19; the new taxes followed the recommendations of the Wine Producers Association.

32. Wine Institute figures. U.S. Congress, House of Representatives, Committee on Ways and Means, *To Amend the Revenue Act of 1918, as Amended,* Report 1817 (Washington, D.C.: GPO, 17 August 1935), p. 2, gives an even lower figure: 21 million gallons. The Ways and Means committee had hoped for $10 million in wine tax revenue in the first year, but in fact only $4 million came from this source (*Congressional Record: House of Representatives,* 73rd Congress, 2nd session, 4 January 1934, p. 101; U.S. Tariff Com-

mission, *Grapes, Raisins and Wines*, Report 134, 2nd ser. [Washington, D.C.: GPO, 1939], table 181, p. 394).

33. The 50 million gallon figure is from U.S. Tariff Commission, *Grapes, Raisins and Wines*, table 119, p. 289.

34. Philip M. Wagner, *Wine Grapes: Their Selection, Cultivation, and Enjoyment* (New York: Harcourt Brace, 1937), p. 5.

35. Robert D. Rossi, "Post-Repeal Wine Consumption," *Wines and Vines* 16 (January 1935): 3.

36. U.S. Tariff Commission, *Grapes, Raisins and Wines*, table 179, p. 391.

37. Ibid., p. 287. S. W. Shear and R. E. Blair, *California Fruit Statistics and Related Data*, Bulletin 763 (Berkeley: University of California, California Agricultural Experiment Station, 1958), put the average production of homemade table wine from 1934 to 1938 at 32,599,000 gallons, as against an average for commercial table wine in the same period of 19,655,000 gallons (grapes table 17).

38. Lucius Powers, *The Fresno Area and the California Wine Industry*, interview by Ruth Teiser, Berkeley: Regional Oral History Office, Bancroft Library, University of California, 1974, p. 50.

39. U.S. Congress, Senate, Committee on Finance, *Hearings on the Liquor Tax Administration Act*, p. 95. A representative of the Ohio industry proposed that there should be no tax, "in the interests of temperance." So did Paul Garrett.

40. U.S. Congress, Senate, Committee on Finance, *Hearings on the Liquor Tax Administration Act*, p. 104.

41. U.S. House of Representatives, Committee on Ways and Means, *To Amend the Revenue Act of 1918*, pp. 2, 13. Since the wine market was now overwhelmingly dominated by fortified wines, the argument for temperance was hollow.

42. Wine sales (including imports) were 45 million gallons in 1935, 60 million in 1936, and 67 million in 1937 ("Third Wine Industry Statistical Survey," *Wines and Vines* 20 [July–August 1939]: 16).

43. Federal revenues from domestic wine were $8,313,000 in 1936 but only $5,425,000 in 1937. The 1936 level was not reached again until 1941, when war prosperity and rising prices lifted revenues to $11 million (U.S. Congress, Senate, Judiciary Committee, *Liquor Industry: Hearings, 10, 16, 17 December 1943* [Washington, D.C.: GPO, 1944], exhibit 19).

44. *Public Papers and Addresses of Franklin D. Roosevelt*, vol. 2: *The Year of Crisis 1933*, ed. Samuel I. Rosenman (New York: Random House, 1938), p. 512.

45. Ibid., p. 513.

46. Since Congress was not then in session, the device of the executive order was used to fill what would otherwise have been a vacuum.

47. Leonard V. Harrison and Elizabeth Lane (*After Repeal: A Study of Liquor Control Administration* [New York: Harper and Brothers, 1936], p. 24) called FACA

> the outstanding oddity among the emergency organizations of the New Deal. Although it was established under an act designed to stimulate industry, it was nevertheless conceived as an instrument for holding the liquor business in check. It possessed powers of life and death over the industries whose codes gave it life. . . . Although dependent for its existence upon codes governing private industries, it was a wholly independent

governmental agency responsible only to the President. It was at once a parasite of the liquor industry and its sovereign.

48. See the discussion of eastern conditions in chapter 8.

49. U.S. Federal Alcohol Control Administration, *Code of Fair Competition for the Wine Industry* (Washington, D.C.: GPO, 1934). Harry A. Caddow, "Code of Fair Competition and What It Means to the Wine Industry," *California: Journal of Development* 24 (December 1934): 18, 51.

50. Public Law 401, 74th Congress, 29 August 1935.

51. U.S. Congress, House of Representatives, Committee on Ways and Means, *Federal Alcohol Control Bill*, Report 1542 (Washington, D.C.: GPO, 17 July 1935), p. 3. Cullen, a Democratic congressman from New York, had sponsored the bill that legalized 3.2 beer and wine before the advent of Repeal in 1933 (see chapter 1, after n. 127).

52. Jefferson E. Peyser, legal counsel for the Wine Institute, recalled of his work on federal legislation, "Some of those federal people could never understand. They never quite got over the fact that Prohibition had been repealed, and they did treat the industry for a number of years just like bootleggers" (*The Law and the California Wine Industry*, interview by Ruth Teiser, Berkeley: Regional Oral History Office, Bancroft Library, University of California, 1974, pp. 13–14).

53. Gilman G. Udell, comp., *Liquor Laws* (Washington, D.C.: GPO, 1978), p. 164.

54. See the critical account of the system of label review by Robert W. Benson, "Regulation of American Wine Labeling: In Vino Veritas?" *UCD Law Review* 11 (1978): 190–95.

55. Advertising file, box 2; U 1950–51 file, box 14, Widmer papers, Cornell University, Kroch Library.

56. John E. O'Neill, "Federal Activity in Alcoholic Beverage Control," *Law and Contemporary Problems* 7 (Autumn 1940): 597. The FAA was made independent of the Department of the Treasury by the Liquor Tax Administration Act of 1936. It was then abolished by the Reorganization Act of 1940 and its functions taken over by the Alcohol Tax Unit of Treasury in 1940. In 1972 its regulatory functions were transferred to a new Bureau of Alcohol, Tobacco and Firearms. As of 2003, that agency had been dismantled and the parts reassigned. A criminal enforcement division, including supervision of firearms, is assigned to the Justice Department. The supervision of the wine industry remains with Treasury under the newly named Alcohol and Tobacco Tax and Trade Bureau (TTB). The regulations affecting the wine industry are compiled in U.S. Department of the Treasury, TTB, part 1, chap. 1 of Title 27, *Code of Federal Regulations*, a work that in its current form requires nearly a hundred pages to list the regulations specifically affecting wine.

57. James T. Lapsley, *Bottled Poetry: Napa Winemaking from Prohibition to the Modern Era* (Berkeley: University of California Press, 1996), p. 88.

58. U.S. Federal Alcohol Control Administration, *Legislative History of the Federal Alcohol Administration Act* (Washington, D.C.: GPO, 1935), p. 73.

59. Liquor Tax Administration Act, 1936, in Udell, *Liquor Laws*, p. 207.

60. James Seff and John F. Cooney, "The Legal and Political History of California Wine," in *The University of California/Sotheby Book of California Wine*, ed. Doris Muscatine, Maynard A. Amerine, and Bob Thompson (Berkeley: University of California Press, and London: Sotheby Publications, 1984), p. 441.

61. *Congressional Record: House of Representatives,* 74th Congress, 2nd session, 15 June 1936, p. 9440.

62. U.S. Tariff Commission, *Grapes, Raisins and Wines,* pp. 323n., 343.

63. David E. Kyvig, *Repealing National Prohibition* (Chicago: University of Chicago Press, 1979), p. 186. Kyvig's study particularly emphasizes the important role of the states' rights doctrine in bringing about Repeal.

64. The Wet states in December 1933 were Arizona, California, Colorado, Connecticut, Delaware, Illinois, Indiana, Louisiana, Maryland, Massachusetts, Montana, Nevada, New Jersey, New Mexico, New York, Oregon, Pennsylvania, Rhode Island, Washington, and Wisconsin. Iowa, Michigan, Missouri, and Ohio soon joined.

65. As Repeal drew near, there was a flurry of public interest in practical and theoretical schemes of liquor control. The model of state monopoly in Scandinavian countries was much discussed, and a study paid for by John D. Rockefeller Jr. reported in favor of the monopoly plan (see Fosdick and Scott, *Toward Liquor Control*).

66. The illustrations of the law in 1936 are taken from the summary in Harrison and Lane, *After Repeal,* pp. 229–82.

67. "Forever" turned out to be until 1948, when the state voted to go Wet (though permitting local options on a county basis).

68. U.S. Congress, *Tax on Intoxicating Liquor: Joint Hearings,* pp. 304–46.

69. *Public Papers and Addresses of Franklin D. Roosevelt,* vol. 2, p. 512.

70. E. M. Sheehan, "The Marketing of California Wines," *California Grape Grower* 15 (June 1934): 3.

71. U.S. Tariff Commission, *Grapes, Raisins and Wines,* table 92, p. 247.

72. "Gossip, Distilled and Blended," *Wine Review* 2 (December 1934): 23. New legislation permitted retail sales from bulk containers in Wisconsin, Ohio, Florida, and Georgia in 1935 (Harry Caddow, "Quality Enforcement Extended into the Winery," *Wines and Vines* 16 [August 1935]: 24).

73. Leon D. Adams, *California Wine Industry Affairs: Recollections and Opinions,* interview by Ruth Teiser, Berkeley: Regional Oral History Office, Bancroft Library, University of California, 1990, pp. 1–2: he says about 1935, but that is a mistake. The legislation was the Swing Act of 17 July 1945.

74. U.S. Tariff Commission, *Grapes, Raisins and Wines,* p. 276.

75. Ibid., pp. 315–16. The new tariff arrangements, by putting a higher tariff on inexpensive bulk wine than on more expensive bottled wine, inverted the traditional scheme. The domestic producers knew that they were competing only against the lower level of the import market and were therefore happy to see it crippled.

76. Anthony M. Turano, "The Comedy of Repeal," *American Mercury* 39 (October 1936): 173.

77. Udell, *Liquor Laws,* p. 213.

78. U.S. Congress, House of Representatives, Judiciary Committee, *Liquor Law Repeal and Enforcement Bill,* Report 1258, 74th Congress (Washington, D.C.: GPO, 18 June 1935).

79. See Ralph B. Hutchinson and William Dunn, "The Constitution, Interstate Commerce and Wine," *Wines and Vines* 48 (April 1967): 20–26.

80. See *Premier-Pabst Sales Co. v. Grosscup et al.,* 298 U.S. 226 (1936); *State Board of Equalization of California et al. v. Young's Market Co. et al.,* 299 U.S. 59 (1936); *Mahoney, Liquor*

Commissioner, et al. v. Joseph Triner Corp., 304 U.S. 518 (1938); *Indianapolis Brewing Co. v. Liquor Control Commission et al.*, 305 U.S. 391 (1939); *Joseph S. Finch & Co. et al. v. McKittrick, Attorney General, et al.*, 305 U.S. 395 (1939).

81. Jefferson Peyser, the longtime counsel for the Wine Institute, says that Brandeis was opposed to "the use of alcoholic beverages" but gives no evidence (*The Law and the California Wine Industry*, p. 2). I do not find the subject discussed in the biographical literature about Brandeis.

82. The federal regulatory system is not a clear or simple structure. Authority over questions of advertising and labeling is theoretically confused by the fact that more than one agency has responsibility. The Federal Trade Commission has powers over advertising, and the Food and Drug Administration over labeling. Either or both might interfere with the BATF or (more recently) TTB, but neither seems to have done so in a determined way. Conflict can, however, occur: the BATF and the FDA disagreed over the issue of ingredient labeling in 1975; see Iver P. Cooper, "The FDA, the BATF, and Liquor Labeling: A Case Study of Interagency Jurisdictional Conflict," *Food Drug Cosmetic Law Journal* 34 (July 1979): 370–90; and the brief discussion in chapter 14, after n. 28.

83. One of the institutional results is that a small library is now required simply to record the various regulations: nine volumes of the Commerce Clearing House *Liquor Control Reporter*—"which presents, summarizes, annotates and updates alcoholic beverage laws and regulations in each of our 50 states and at the federal level"—are now the necessary reference for anyone working in this branch of the law. "Each volume of this series contains over 1,000 pages" (John Manfreda and Richard Mendelson, "U.S. Wine Law" [mimeographed manuscript, 1988], p. 1).

84. Carl Bundschu, "Distribution Rules Protested," *Wine Review* 5 (April 1937): 10.

CHAPTER 3. THE DISMAL '30S

1. Wine was defined by federal regulation as the product of the normal alcoholic fermentation of the juice of sound ripe grapes that contained not less than 7 percent or more than 16 percent alcohol by volume; the regulation also specified limits for volatile acidity and for the sugar content of dry wines, but not much else (U.S. Department of Agriculture, Food and Drug Administration, "Definitions and Standards for Food Products for Use in Enforcing the Food and Drugs Act," Service and Regulatory Announcements: Food and Drug 2 [Washington, D.C., August 1933]). This follows the FDA regulations of 1906, circular 19.

2. A few titles from 1934 include *Wining and Dining with Rhyme and Reason, Bacchus Behave!, What to Do about Wines,* and *What Everybody Wants to Know about Wine.*

3. Frank Schoonmaker, "New Decalogues of Drinking," *Saturday Review of Literature* 11 (3 November 1934): 253, 260–61. Schoonmaker (1905–76) was one of the most important influences on the development of wine in America after Repeal through his writings, his business as a wine merchant and winemaker, and particularly his work in establishing varietal labeling.

4. Ibid.

5. Frank Schoonmaker and Tom Marvel, *The Complete Wine Book* (New York: Simon and

Schuster, 1934); Julian Street, *Wines: Their Selection, Care, and Service* (New York: Knopf, 1933); Philip M. Wagner, *American Wines and How to Make Them* (New York: Knopf, 1933). One might add Allan Taylor, *What Everybody Wants to Know about Wine* (New York: Knopf, 1934), which has the distinction of being illustrated with reproductions of labels drawn from the collection of H. L. Mencken.

6. Maynard Joslyn, at the University of California, recalled "an interesting experience in 1934" when a "lady from Santa Rosa brought in a sample of beautiful tawny port." This, it seems, came from a winery that she inherited. The wine—originally a red port—had after eighteen years of unobserved aging become a yellow-brown wine, "the most mellow thing I had ever tasted" (*A Technologist Views the California Wine Industry,* interview by Ruth Teiser, Berkeley: Regional Oral History Office, Bancroft Library, University of California, 1974, p. 23). Such a thing was, it need hardly be said, quite exceptional. Much more typical was the experience of the Petri family when they bought the Alba Winery in Escalon after Repeal: the several hundred thousand gallons of wine in storage at the winery were "real bad and unsaleable" and "had to be dumped down the sewer" (Louis A. Petri, *The Petri Family in the Wine Industry,* interview by Ruth Teiser, Berkeley: Regional Oral History Office, Bancroft Library, University of California, 1971, p. 11).

7. Quoted in "The Long Memories of Prohibition," *Wines and Vines* 64 (September 1983): 36.

8. "The Wines of the U.S.," *Fortune* 9 (February 1934): 118. *Fortune* thought that fine wines, when and if they should appear in America, would come from the East, not from California.

9. Julian Street, "Wine: Cinderella of Repeal," *Scribner's Magazine* 98 (September 1935): 151.

10. Burke H. Critchfield, "The Status of California Wine in Eastern States," *Fruit Products Journal* 14 (July 1935): 326; Meigs Russell, "Wise and Far Seeing Policies the Need of American Wineries," *Fruit Products Journal* 13 (March 1934): 198.

11. Harry Caddow, "Wine Institute Activities," *Wines and Vines* 16 (May 1935): 12. The problem persisted even after California passed wine quality standards: the state Board of Health issued some 744 citations against dealers of substandard wines in 1937 and confiscated some 1.67 million gallons of such wine in that year (*Wines and Vines* 19 [March 1938]: 12).

12. Transcript of hearings, Federal Alcohol Control Administration, San Francisco, 31 August 1934, p. 29 (Alcohol and Tobacco Tax and Trade Bureau Library, Washington, D.C.).

13. "Do you remember all those stuck vats of red grapes?—in some cases whole fermentation rooms of them! High sugar, of course, in some cases prevented complete fermentation but the usual cause was hot fermentations" (A. J. Winkler, "Grape Varieties for Dry Wines," *Wine Review* 4 [May 1936]: 12).

14. Maynard A. Amerine, "Dessert Wine Production Problems of California Grapes, IV: Muscat of Alexandria," *Wines and Vines* 33 (April 1952): 61. This disaster coincided with the early use of cans for wine; one result was that most of the cans shipped from one winery "contained masses of a substance that appeared to be cotton—'Fresno Mold,' it was called" (Leo Berti, "Canned Wine: Past Experience and Future Possibilities," *Wines and Vines* 31 [December 1950]: 22).

15. "Notes on Wine Meetings at Berkeley," *Wines and Vines* 16 (June 1935): 24.

16. *Wine Review* 2 (August 1934): 8.

17. H. H. Marquis, "The Menace of Second-Hand Barrels," *Wine Review* 3 (May 1935): 19. Maynard Amerine adds that the same objections applied to tank cars: "When you got the tank car it might have had olive oil in it the day before, or it might have had petroleum in it the day before; and in many cases they were not really lined tanks, they were just metal tanks, so there was a huge pick-up of metal as they went East" (*The University of California and the State's Wine Industry*, interview by Ruth Teiser, Berkeley: Regional Oral History Office, Bancroft Library, University of California, 1972, p. 15).

18. Chapter 2, at n. 32.

19. U.S. Tariff Commission, *Grapes, Raisins and Wines*, Report 134, 2nd ser. (Washington, D.C.: GPO, 1939), p. 293, table 122. The national per capita figures reported by the Wine Institute are 0.421 in 1934, 0.580 in 1935; 0.755 in 1936; and 0.825 in 1937 (*Annual Report* [San Francisco: Wine Institute, 1956–57]). The figures at least move upward, though the quantity is small.

20. Judge Marion De Vries, cited in Jessie Schilling Blout, "A Brief Economic History of the California Wine-Growing Industry" (San Francisco: Wine Institute, 1943), p. 15.

21. W. V. Cruess, "Pasteurization and Closures," *Wine Review* 2 (September 1934): 8.

22. Berthe Porchet, *La Vigne et le vin en Californie* (Lausanne: Imprimerie Vaudoise, 1937), p. 38. *Sweet wine* is a term favored by the California winemakers in place of *fortified wine*. In 1938 they persuaded the Federal Alcohol Administration (FAA) to ban the use of *fortified* on wine labels and in advertising, a ban that remains in force today. The argument was that *fortified* suggested intoxicating power and injured the wine industry's efforts to establish wine as a drink of moderation (Harry Caddow, "FAA Regulations and Amendments," *Wines and Vines* 19 [September 1938]: 3; Leon D. Adams, *Revitalizing the California Wine Industry*, interview by Ruth Teiser, Berkeley: Regional Oral History Office, Bancroft Library, University of California, 1974, pp. 96–100). But the term is, as Frank Schoonmaker observed, "a regrettable California localism" ("The Merits of California Wines," *Wines and Vines* 16 [March 1935]: 5).

23. See, e.g., Selden Clark, *California's Wine Industry and Its Financing* (New Brunswick, N.J.: Graduate School of Banking, American Bankers' Association, Rutgers University, 1941), p. 41.

24. Amerine, *The University of California and the State's Wine Industry*, p. 16.

25. The names *angelica, madeira, marsala,* and *malaga* were also used, the last three apparently not very widely. California does not appear to have made much effort to develop fortified wines of any distinctively Californian character or to have ventured many new names. One may mention, however, the blends of sherry and port sold by Colonial Grape Products soon after Repeal: these were called Sher-po and Po-sher. Such names were later (in 1942) banned by revised California regulations, which forbade labels that indicated a mixture of standard types.

26. H. H. Marquis, "Wine in the Hotels of America," *Wine Review* 3 (October 1935): 8. There was, it appears, a regional pattern in the preferences for fortified wines, on the east coast at any rate: port dominated in the north, sherry in the south (Legh F. Knowles, *Beaulieu Vineyards from Family to Corporate Ownership*, interview by Lisa Jacobson, Berkeley: Regional Oral History Office, Bancroft Library, University of California, 1990, p. 28).

27. "You never went to Mr. Jones and asked him for a raise. . . . Because if you stood around and talked to him . . . you got talked out of it before you knew what you were doing" (Myron Nightingale, *Making Wine in California, 1944–1987*, interview by Ruth Teiser and Lisa Jacobson, Berkeley: Regional Oral History Office, Bancroft Library, University of California, 1988, p. 13).

28. "Without a doubt, he was the finest winemaker of his day" (ibid., p. 15). A student of Bioletti's before World War I, Brown was the first graduate in enology from the University of California (Elie C. Skofis, *California Wine and Brandy Maker*, interview by Ruth Teiser, Berkeley: Regional Oral History Office, Bancroft Library, University of California, 1988, p. 7) and was chairman of the Wine Institute's Technical Advisory Committee in 1951. His middle name, it should be noted, was McSherry.

29. Ruth Teiser and Catherine Harroun, *Winemaking in California* (New York: McGraw-Hill, 1983), p. 180; Leon D. Adams, *The Wines of America* (Boston: Houghton Mifflin, 1973), p. 291; Meigs B. Russell, "Shewan-Jones Plant a Model of Efficiency," *Fruit Products Journal* 14 (December 1934): 104. For an amusing account of how a winery operating under Prohibition came to have such splendid equipment, see Joslyn, *A Technologist Views the California Wine Industry*, p. 46.

30. Veteran winemaker Charles Ash called Lachman "the greatest wine man we have ever had in California. . . . He could go through a hundred samples like lightning and classify them with uncanny accuracy. . . . He was the first to break away from using foreign labels on California wines" ("Reminiscences of Pre-Prohibition Days," *Proceedings of the American Society of Enologists* 3 [1952]: 42).

31. But there are always dissenters to such reputations: "I've tasted wine with Morrow both at the State Fair and at other tastings, and I don't think his sense of taste was particularly acute or discriminating" (Joslyn, *A Technologist Views the California Wine Industry*, p. 40). Ash put it perhaps more reasonably: "[Morrow] was a good taster but not comparable to Lachman, either in speed or accuracy, but who was or is?" ("Reminiscences," p. 42).

32. "Italian Swiss Colony," *California Grape Grower* 14 (December 1933): 20. Leon Adams describes how he arranged this "festival" with girls from the local high school in $90 worth of rented costumes (*Revitalizing the California Wine Industry*, p. 56).

33. Adams, *Revitalizing the California Wine Industry*, pp. 65–66. The people in the wine industry who were indifferent to wine were either new investors or among the table grape and raisin growers, for whom the wineries were just another "outlet."

34. Construction began in July 1933. Martini at first meant it only as a source of dry wine for his Kingsburg operation, but it became his main enterprise after 1940 (Louis M. Martini and Louis P. Martini, *Wine Making in the Napa Valley*, interviews by Ruth Teiser and Lois Stone, Berkeley: Regional Oral History Office, Bancroft Library, University of California, 1973, p. 3).

35. Cal Growers was organized as a co-op whose chief members were Arpaxat Setrakian, Harry Hitzel, H. B. Leonard, and Charles Clapp: "Each . . . has extensive grape holdings in his control and the winery is supplied with grapes from that source" ("Wahtoke Winery Operating," *Wine Review* 2 [June 1934]: 34).

36. Adams, *The Wines of America*, p. 176.

37. James T. Lapsley, *Bottled Poetry: Napa Winemaking from Prohibition to the Modern Era* (Berkeley: University of California Press, 1996), p. xi.

38. "Resumé of the Number of Wineries That Have Given Up Their Bonds since the Repeal of Prohibition," Wine Institute memo dated 22 June 1942, copy in the Wine Institute Library. See also Lapsley, *Bottled Poetry,* chapter 2.

39. U.S. Tariff Commission, *Grapes, Raisins and Wines,* p. 39, table 10.

40. That increase in yield was no doubt evidence of overcropping (i.e., allowing the vine to carry more fruit than it can ripen), an irresistible practice when prices were sinking; since overcropping diminishes the quality of the fruit, it added to the problems of California wine.

41. U.S. Department of Agriculture, *Agricultural Statistics* (Washington, D.C.: GPO, 1936–38). Bearing acreage of vines in California declined from a peak of 647,000 in 1926 to a low of 468,000 in 1936, after which it began to climb again. The proportion of wine grapes to the whole remained around 25 percent in these years (U.S. Tariff Commission, *Grapes, Raisins and Wines,* pp. 37–40).

42. The analysis that follows is drawn from figures supplied by the Giannini Foundation of Agricultural Economics and published in *Fruit Products Journal* 13 (November 1933): 80.

43. At Repeal, Napa County, for example, had nearly two-thirds of its 11,000 acres of vineyard planted to two varieties: Petite Sirah (Durif) and Alicante Bouschet (H. H. Marquis, "The Valley of the Crushed Grape," *California Wine Review* 2 [August 1934]: 10). Lapsley thinks it "doubtful" that more than a hundred acres of either Pinot noir or Cabernet could be found in the Napa Valley at the time of Repeal (*Bottled Poetry,* p. 43).

44. William C. Ockey, "The Cost of Producing Wine Grapes," *Wine Review* 3 (March 1935): 24, table 7.

45. Lapsley, *Bottled Poetry,* p. 46. The figures on average prices for grapes are taken from the same source, p. 45.

46. From the records of shipments of white juice grapes from California, it appears that muscats were the overwhelmingly dominant varieties among white grapes. In 1932 California shipped 6,191 carloads of muscat grapes, 236 of Malaga, 47 of Thompson, 16 of Burger, and 64 of "Other White" ("California's Grape Shipments," *California Grower* 14 [January 1933]: 11). The name *muscat* without further qualification typically means in California the Muscat of Alexandria, a raisin grape.

47. Porchet, *La Vigne et le vin en Californie,* p. 20. According to Leon Adams, the last Catawba vineyard in California, in the Uvas Valley, Santa Clara County, persisted until 1969 ("Historical Note," in California State Vinicultural Association, *Grapes and Grape Vines of California* [New York: Harcourt Brace, 1981], n.p.).

48. This is not to imply that our view from the twenty-first century is the final wisdom: one may easily imagine a time when the current dominance of Cabernet Sauvignon and Chardonnay will seem to have been an aberration.

49. Of the 1,861,000 tons crushed in the years 1933–35, 930,000 tons were table and raisin grapes (S. W. Shear and R. E. Blair, *California Fruit Statistics and Related Data,* Bulletin 763 [Berkeley: University of California, Division of Agricultural Sciences, California Agricultural Experiment Station, 1958]).

50. The fact that the wineries were prepared to use surplus raisin grapes arose in part from the shortage of white wine grapes created by Prohibition.

51. L. K. Marshall, "The Wine Problem," in *California Department of Agriculture Bulletin* 26 (January–March 1937): 59. Marshall (1887–1957) was the organizer and general manager of the Bear Creek Vineyard Association, a cooperative winery at Lodi; he had a long and important career in the California industry. In 1935 he organized the group of cooperatives eventually known as Guild Wineries. In fairness to Marshall, one may note his article in *Wines and Vines* 24 (August 1943): 14, recanting his earlier position. Immediately after Repeal, he explains, all efforts were concentrated on "the best methods of making wine. In the search that ensued, the opinion became widespread that a good winemaker could make a good wine from any material." He later saw that good grapes were the only way to good wine, and that winemakers should be prepared to pay for good grapes. Marshall himself, who had been trained in agronomy at the University of California, maintained an experimental vineyard and cooperated with A. J. Winkler's viticultural work at Davis.

52. Maynard A. Amerine and Maynard Joslyn, *Commercial Production of Table Wines*, Bulletin 639 (Berkeley: University of California, College of Agriculture, Agricultural Experiment Station, 1940), p. 4.

53. Walter Richert, "Recent Grape Plantings: The Trend Is Backwards," *Wine Review* 7 (December 1939): 7.

54. According to Cornelius Ough, the clone of Chardonnay then grown in California was defective and yielded only about a quarter ton to the acre, a good reason not to grow it. Work on clonal selection by H. P. Olmo changed that (Cornelius Ough, *Researches of an Enologist, University of California, Davis,* interview by Ruth Teiser, Berkeley: Regional Oral History Office, Bancroft Library, University of California, 1990, p. 40). Philip Hiaring, writing about Olmo's work, says that there were only 1.5 acres of Chardonnay in California in 1940 ("Harold P. Olmo: A Vineyardist Is Wine Man of the Year," *Wines and Vines* 69 [March 1988]: 16). Frank Schoonmaker and Tom Marvel, *American Wines* (New York: Duell, Sloan & Pearce, 1941), p. 46. In 1940 the wine grape varieties in California vineyards were divided between 159,500 acres of red varieties and 15,500 acres of white. The leading varieties among the reds were Zinfandel, 53,000 acres; Carignane, 31,000 acres; Alicante Bouschet, 29,000 acres; and Mission, 11,000 acres. Among the whites, they were Palomino, 4,000 acres; Burger, 3,000 acres; and Sauvignon vert, 1,600 acres (Maynard A. Joslyn and Maynard A. Amerine, *Commercial Production of Dessert Wines,* Bulletin 651 [Berkeley: University of California, College of Agriculture, Agricultural Experiment Station, 1941], p. 9). Martin Ray, writing in 1940, said that there were almost no true Pinot noir grapes outside his own small vineyard, from which he might get 10 tons a year (to Julian Street, 15 January 1940, Julian Street papers, Princeton University, Firestone Library). Ray was inclined to exaggerate things in his own favor, but in this case he may have been right enough.

55. Schoonmaker and Marvel observed that even seven years after Repeal, one could still see many hillside vineyards in the coastal counties abandoned in favor of more productive plantings on the valley floors (*American Wines*, pp. 31–32)—and that was in the *good* regions.

56. For the introduction and slow dissemination of the French hybrids in the eastern United States, see chapter 8.

57. *California Grape Grower* 14 (August 1933): 15; 15 (January 1934): 12; 15 (October 1934): 16–17. The Tulare Winery named a new 63,000-gallon tank the "President F. D. Roosevelt" in honor of the chief executive's work "in behalf of the repeal of the eighteenth amendment" (*Sacramento Bee*, 1 September 1934).

58. U.S. Tariff Commission, *Grapes, Raisins and Wines*, pp. 61n., 225; Charles H. West, "Are Winery Facilities in California Adequate for the Present Requirements of the Wine Industry?" *Wines and Vines* 16 (March 1935): 4.

59. John B. Cella II, *The Cella Family in the California Wine Industry*, interview by Ruth Teiser, Berkeley: Regional Oral History Office, Bancroft Library, University of California, 1986, p. 9.

60. Philo Biane, *Wine Making in Southern California and Recollections of Fruit Industries, Ltd.*, interview by Ruth Teiser, Berkeley: Regional Oral History Office, Bancroft Library, University of California, 1972, pp. 51–52.

61. Antonio Perelli-Minetti, *A Life in Wine Making*, interview by Ruth Teiser, Berkeley: Regional Oral History Office, Bancroft Library, University of California, 1975, p. 84.

62. Ernest Gallo and Julio Gallo, with Bruce B. Henderson, *Ernest and Julio: Our Story* (New York: Times Books, 1994), p. 69.

63. U.S. Tariff Commission, *Grapes, Raisins and Wines*, p. 225. The ten largest wineries in 1936 were as follows: Roma Wine Company (now at Fresno), 8.2 million gallons' capacity; Italian Swiss Colony, 6.75 million; Petri Wine Company, 4.75 million; Bisceglia Brothers, 4.25 million; Italian Vineyard Company, 4 million; Cribari, 3.1 million; California Grape Products Company, 3 million; Bear Creek Vineyard Association, 2.5 million; Community Grape Corporation, 2.25 million; Sebastiani Winery, 2.21 million ("American Winery Directory," *Wine Review* 4 [August 1936]). By 1939 the calculation was that 53 wineries in California were responsible for 90 percent of the state's wine production ("Community Winery Holds Annual Meeting," *Wine Review* 7 [July 1939]: 33).

64. W. V. Cruess, *The Principles and Practice of Wine Making*, 2nd ed. (New York: Avi Publishing, 1947), p. 69.

65. As L. K. Marshall, the manager of the (cooperative) Bear Creek Vineyard Association, put it, "As most men in the wine field know, the majority of the co-operatives owe their existence to the low grape prices prevalent in the first few years of Repeal" ("The Position of the Co-ops," *Wines and Vines* 25 [December 1944]: 31). The means whereby the California cooperatives were financed are outlined in E. A. Stokdyk, "The Case for Cooperative Wineries," *Wine Review* 4 (February 1936): 15–16; Stokdyk reports that in the first two years following Repeal more than $3 million had been advanced through the farm credit agencies to California cooperative wineries.

66. Julio Gallo says simply that Lodi was the birthplace of the co-op movement because there "the growers got fed up with John B. Cella, who had started Roma Winery there upon repeal. Cella was always trying to drive the grape market down" (Gallo and Gallo, *Ernest and Julio: Our Story*, pp. 145–46).

67. The German element was strong in and around Lodi: in addition to Bauer, the names

associated with the Lodi co-ops include Baumbach, Beckman, Mettler, Kurtz, Weiden-rich, and Volbrischt ("The Co-operatives at Lodi," *Wine Review* 2 [July 1934]: 18).

68. The cooperatives continued to grow until, by 1946, they accounted for a third of California's wine production; their numbers peaked at twenty-nine in 1953. Since then, there has been a steady decline in their numbers and importance. In 1980 there were only eight co-ops left of the forty-four that had been established between 1934 and 1975; by 2002 all were gone. One reason for their disappearance was the loss of the right to maintain a tax-free reserve fund by the Revenue Code revision of 1951 (Irving H. Marcus, "California's Cooperative Wineries," *Wines and Vines* 34 [March 1953]: 9). Co-ops do not pay taxes on corporate profits, which are returned to members as earnings.

69. H. H. Marquis, "The Vagaries of the Wine Market," *Wine Review* 4 (January 1936): 13.

70. The original members of the group were Bear Creek Vineyard Association, Lodi; Del Rio Winery, Lodi; and Muscat Growers Cooperative Winery, Kingsburg ("California Wine Sales Is New Sales Co-operative," *Wine Review* 5 [November 1937]: 27). They undertook marketing because "they are convinced that such marketing associations are the salvation of the cooperative winery" ("Cooperative Marketing Agency Organized," *Wine Review* 5 [December 1937]: 25). Fruit Industries was also a marketing co-op, but its members were not themselves cooperative wineries.

71. The account of this process is given in fascinating detail by Lapsley in *Bottled Poetry*.

72. Martin Ray's renewal of the Paul Masson Winery in 1936 was too small to have any general effect; Almadén did not begin its recovery until the 1940s.

73. "Wine Districts of the Central Valley," *Wines and Vines* 17 (September 1936): 10.

74. The blame for this strange practice has been put on the wholesalers of wine rather than the producers; ultimately, the blame no doubt lay with the consumers, who knew nothing about the conditions of wine production. If a consumer bought a bottle of X claret and found it good, he naturally supposed that X made an equally good sherry or rhine wine, and would expect to get such things from his dealer. Accordingly the wholesale dealers required the wineries to deliver a complete line of wines to meet these expectations. Brand identity was the informing idea.

75. As late as 1962, the Beaulieu Winery—a large but not an industrial-scale operation—had forty varieties of wine in its line (Knowles, *Beaulieu Vineyards from Family to Corporate Ownership*, p. 29).

76. U.S. Department of the Treasury, *Report of the Commissioner of Internal Revenue* (Washington, D.C.: GPO, 1938).

77. Because neither Colorado nor Hawaii can have had any significant grape production, these operations presumably depended on grapes from California, if in fact they produced wine at all. By no means all of the bonded wineries listed in the *Report of the Commissioner of Internal Revenue* were actually producing wine: some simply held licenses to do so and awaited a favorable opportunity.

78. There was, however, some new investment: the Knobview Fruit Growers Association erected a new 200,000-gallon winery, and the Rosati Winery, another co-op, was built at a cost of $10,000 in 1934 (*Wine Review* 2 [October 1934]: 40).

79. A Widmer's brochure from 1959 shows sixty different varieties of wine bottled under the Widmer label, including White Tokay, Haut Sauternes, Extra Sweet Grape Wine,

Rhine Wine, and Chablis, as well as the standard burgundy, sherry, and port. Widmer's, to its credit, also offered a notable series of varietals from the traditional native hybrids: Catawba, Delaware, Diana, Dutchess, Elvira, Isabella, Moore's Diamond, Salem, and Vergennes. No other eastern winery made so full a range of native varietals. In 1996 Widmer's (now one of the many properties of the Canandaigua Winery) still offered an array of twenty-six wines, but—alas for the historically minded—the only native grape still bottled as a varietal was the inferior Niagara.

80. For a full discussion of the history of experiment, failure, and limited success with wine-growing in the eastern United States, see Thomas Pinney, *A History of Wine in America: From the Beginnings to Prohibition* (Berkeley: University of California Press, 1989).

81. See chapter 8 for a description of eastern winemaking methods.

82. A sugar-deficient must could, however, be corrected by the addition of grape concentrate instead of the direct addition of sugar. And a wine deficient in alcohol could be brought up to strength by the addition of grape spirit.

83. The Michigan formula of 16 percent was enacted into law. *Wine* in Michigan was defined as having not more than 16 percent alcohol: anything over that was classified as "distilled spirits," paid taxes accordingly, and could be sold only through state stores. This rule put up an effective barrier to the fortified wines of California and New York (Greyton H. Taylor, "Trade Barriers Are a Major Obstacle to Wine Distribution," *Wine Review* 8 [April 1940]: 7).

84. F. W. Fabian, "Michigan," *Wine Review* 11 (August 1943): 54–56.

85. U.S. Tariff Commission, *Grapes, Raisins and Wines*, pp. 324–25; Harry E. Goresline and Richard Wellington, "New York Champagnes," *Wines and Vines* 17 (December 1936): 5. The complexity of this blend may be suggested by the fact that Catawba and Delaware are pink grapes, Elvira and Duchess are white, and Isabella and Eumelan are black. Catawba, however, seems always to have been the dominant element.

86. U.S. Tariff Commission, *Grapes, Raisins and Wines*, table 135, p. 330.

87. The Charmat process came to North America during the Prohibition years: Canadian Wineries Ltd. began production using Charmat's method and equipment about 1928. After Repeal, the company built a plant in Lewiston, New York, opened in 1935 ("How the Charmat Process Came to the U.S.," *Wines and Vines* 50 [June 1969]: 48).

88. The annual production of grapes in all states other than California averaged 251,000 tons from 1934 through 1940.

89. For early experiments with vinifera in the East and for the introduction of the French hybrids, see chapter 8.

90. But Garrett, like the other large eastern producers, depended heavily on wine from California; he had large wineries at Healdsburg in Sonoma County and at Cucamonga in San Bernardino County.

91. In 1860 Ohio produced 568,000 gallons of wine to California's 246,000; Ohio's share of national production in that year was 35 percent. Within a decade it had sunk to barely 7 percent (Susan Sifritt, "The Ohio Wine and Grape Industries" [Ph.D. diss., Kent State University, 1976], p. 400). According to Charles Ash, whose experience in the wine industry went back to 1898, Ohio wines toward the end of the nineteenth century were notorious for adulteration: "No place in our country and perhaps the world made a more

adulterated wine than was made in Ohio at that time. They were made from dried apple pomace and glucose. They were colored by aniline dye and preserved by benzoate of soda" (Ash, "Reminiscences of Pre-Prohibition Days," p. 40). The Sweet Valley Wine Company was prosecuted for making an "Ohio Claret Wine" from pomace (John D. Garr, "A Survey of American Wine Laws," *Food Drug Cosmetic Law Journal* 16 [June 1961]: 337).

92.   "Ohio's 3000 Acres of Grapes," *Wine Review* 3 (September 1935): 30. There were other exotica in Ohio: M. Hommel was reported to make a Barbera and something called a Persian Nectar (Margaret Kelly, "The Wine Industry in Ohio," *Wine Review* 7 [January 1939]: 16).

93.   At first, an Ohio wine might be blended with 60 percent of out-of-state wine and still be labeled *Ohio!* In 1939 this measure was reduced to 40 percent ("Ohio Wine Bill Passed," *Wine Review* 7 [July 1939]: 32), and later to 25 percent. Part of the reason for these allowances was the shortage of suitable grapes. At the time of Repeal it was estimated that only half of the pre-Prohibition acreage of wine grapes remained in the prime areas of the state around Sandusky and on the Lake Erie islands ("The Wine Grape Crop in Ohio," *Wine Review* 2 [July 1934]: 15).

94.   Schoonmaker and Marvel, *American Wines*, pp. 179–80. Mary Frost Mabon also noted that "Ohioans make a fetish of lengthy age in wood, and prefer their wines round and rather amber-colored" (*ABC of America's Wines* [New York: Knopf, 1942], p. 191).

95.   Paul Cross Morrison, "Viticulture in Ohio," *Economic Geography* 12 (1936): 71. The 1940 census reported grapes on 47,341 Ohio farms ("State of Ohio," *Wine Review* 11 [August 1943]: 74), but most of these must have been simply domestic plantings.

96.   In 1940, the head of horticulture at Ohio State University reported that the average yields for grapes in Ohio ranged from 2.2 tons for Concord down to 1.4 for Catawba and 1.2 for Delaware. Grape berry moth was the leading pest of the vineyards, reported in 77 percent of them (unidentified clipping, ca. September 1940, copy in the Sandusky Library).

97.   The largest wineries were those clustered around Sandusky: John G. Dorn, Engels and Krudwig, M. Hommel, Mon Ami, and Sweet Valley; Meier's Winery at Silverton (near Cincinnati) and Lonz on Middle Bass Island in Lake Erie were also large producers. The figure of 112 wineries comes from the reports of the Internal Revenue Service and would include all establishments holding a license. The *American Winery Directory* for 1935, however, lists only forty-five wineries for Ohio, probably much closer to the number actually producing wine in that year.

98.   Sifritt, "The Ohio Wine and Grape Industries," p. 218.

99.   Ibid., pp. 407, 434–35.

CHAPTER 4. MAKING AND SELLING WINE IN THE '30S

1.   Stralla (1901–81) had been a newspaperman before his venture into wine; he operated the Krug Winery as the Napa Wine Company until 1940, and then moved operations to Oakville, where he continued until selling out in 1947. Stralla helped to organize the Napa Valley Vintners' Association.

2.   Lou Stralla, interview by James Beard in *History of Napa Valley: Interviews and Reminis-*

cences of Long-Time Residents (St. Helena, Calif.: Napa Valley Wine Library Association, 1979), vol. 2, p. 305.

3. W. V. Cruess, *The Principles and Practice of Wine Making* (New York: Avi Publishing, 1934), p. 70.

4. Amerine to Julian Street, 20 October 1940 (box 15, Julian Street papers, Princeton University, Firestone Library).

5. As late as 1966, more than half of the wineries in California owned no vineyards at all (Ralph B. Hutchinson, "The California Wine Industry" [Ph.D. diss., University of California, Los Angeles, 1969], p. 66).

6. U.S. Tariff Commission, *Grapes, Raisins and Wines,* Report 134 (Washington, D.C.: GPO, 1939), p. 42.

7. W. V. Cruess, "Notes on the Use of Concrete in Wineries," *Wines and Vines* 18 (January 1937): 14. In hearings before the state Department of Public Health in January 1942, the director said, in reply to the question about whether dirt floors were allowable under the rules, "As long as those dirt floors are kept clean and orderly that's good enough" (California Department of Public Health, Bureau of Food and Drug Inspection, *Wine Standards Hearing, 12 January 1942* [Sacramento, 1942], p. 51: transcript in the Wine Institute Library). Myron Nightingale remembered that there were dirt floors in the fermenting room at the Shewan-Jones winery in the 1930s, a winery noted for its up-to-date equipment and arrangements (*Making Wine in California, 1944–1987,* interview by Ruth Teiser and Lisa Jacobson, Berkeley: Regional Oral History Office, Bancroft Library, University of California, 1988, p. 16).

8. These were borrowed from the practice of the French in Algeria (Cruess, "Notes on the Use of Concrete in Wineries," pp. 14–15), though they had been seen in California as early as 1911, at the Lachman and Jacobi wine cellar in Petaluma. The first to make extensive use of them was reportedly the Roma winery; one tank for storage at Roma was rated at 120,000 gallons ("Roma's Concrete Wine Storage Tanks," *Wine Review* 3 [April 1935]: 28–30). The very first recorded use of concrete for storage in California was the famous 500,000-gallon cistern built at Italian Swiss Colony, Asti, in 1897.

9. If they were not properly lined, some of the cement would dissolve into the wine, with undesirable effect; an inadequately lined rough concrete surface was also difficult to clean. And if not properly reinforced, they would crack. In consequence, some authorities did not recommend concrete tanks, and experience has confirmed their suspicions: such tanks, regarded as the state of the art in the 1930s, are no longer in general use, though a good many of them survive. Philip Wagner, visiting a nameless California winery "of excellent reputation" in 1949, was shown their lined concrete fermentors and asked about the lining. "'Nothing to it,' said the proprietor, strolling around it. 'We just slap on a coat of roofing tar and touch it up once a year'" ("California Thirty Years Ago," *Wine East* 9 [November 1981]: 14).

10. F. T. Bioletti, "A New Wine Cooling Machine," Bulletin 174 (Berkeley: University of California, College of Agriculture, Agricultural Experiment Station, 1906). The machine in question was developed by Bioletti and Robert Jordan at Jordan's Mount Veeder winery; it was adopted by a number of wineries before Prohibition. E. H. Twight, who entered the California wine industry in 1900, reported that "The Italian Vineyard Company at

Guasti, and other concerns, were using refrigeration long before the prohibition period. In 1910 the writer was using a 90-ton ice machine at Guasti to cool the fermentation during the vintage and to refrigerate the wine after the vintage" ("Winery Methods Are Not New," *Wine Review* 4 [April 1936]: 15).

11. Berthe Porchet, *La Vigne et le vin en Californie* (Lausanne: Imprimerie Vaudoise, 1937), p. 29. "In very hot weather with thoroughly ripe grapes and where no other means of cooling is at hand, it is sometimes justifiable to add blocks of ice direct to the vats" (W. V. Cruess, "Rules for Sound Fermentations," *Wine Review* 5 [September 1937]: 18). André Tchelistcheff says that this was the practice at Beaulieu in the '30s (*Grapes, Wine, and Ecology*, interview by Ruth Teiser and Catherine Harroun, Berkeley: Regional Oral History Office, Bancroft Library, University of California, 1983, p. 82).

12. L. K. Marshall credits the invention of this method to Adolph Bauer of Lodi, before Prohibition ("Wine Growing in the Lodi District," *American Journal of Enology and Viticulture* 6 [January–March 1955]: 34).

13. Supposing that a winery had any means at all of providing cold water, it was likely to be a cooling tower rather than refrigeration machinery. Air circulation was the primary means for cooling in the tower method, but ice might be added.

14. In an address to winemakers in 1937, George L. Marsh of the University of California's Fruit Products Division observed that "a few of you are now cooling during fermentation, but often in a hit or miss manner and only for the purpose of obtaining a complete fermentation. It is doubtful whether very many of you realize that cooling is perhaps your most important tool for improving quality" ("Cool Fermenting Must," *Wine Review* 5 [May 1937]: 13).

15. James T. Lapsley thinks that the Martini Winery at St. Helena, newly built in 1933, was probably the first in California to employ mechanical refrigeration (*Bottled Poetry: Napa Winemaking from Prohibition to the Modern Era* [Berkeley: University of California Press, 1996], p. 59). H. K. Hensley, in "The Practice of Refrigeration" (*Wine Review* 2 [July 1934]: 11–13), reported on refrigeration units installed at the Novitiate of Los Gatos, Tulare Winery, St. George Winery, Pacific Coast Winery, Mt. Tivy Winery, and B. Cribari and Sons. These appear to have been used primarily for clarification rather than to control fermentation, though some systems could perform both functions.

16. Instruction in these methods was readily available before Prohibition in such works as Frederic Bioletti, "The Principles of Wine-Making," Bulletin 213 (Berkeley: University of California, College of Agriculture, Agricultural Experiment Station, 1911), and, immediately upon Repeal, in W. V. Cruess, *Principles and Practice of Wine Making*.

17. In some places, instead of being sulfited (treated with sulfur dioxide), the must might be pasteurized by steam coils inside the tanks (Marius Biane, "How Quality Can Be Controlled," *Wines and Vines* 19 [April 1938]: 20). And in some places, sulfur dioxide either was not used at all or was used carelessly, without exact measurement.

18. According to Cruess, overripe grapes were often diluted with water at the crusher "by ear"—that is, without measurement (*Principles and Practice of Wine Making*, 2nd ed. [New York: Avi Publishing, 1947], p. 122).

19. This practice, which had been well established before Prohibition, was evidently not generally understood at the onset of Repeal. A particularly vivid illustration of the elemen-

tary level at which winemaking recommenced in California is an unidentified newspaper clipping in a letter from Carl Bundschu to Rexford Tugwell, 21 August 1934, notifying Napa Valley winegrowers of a demonstration to be held at Inglenook Winery: a representative from the University of California would "demonstrate the use of SO-2 and metabisulphite in wine making, and the preservation and increase of pure yeast cultures. Any wine maker desiring a start of pure yeast may bring a clean gallon jug and take away enough for a start" (RG 16, Liquors 1934, USDA records, National Archives). Lapsley concludes, after a review of the evidence from Napa County, that the use of pure yeast was a novelty not much practiced (*Bottled Poetry*, p. 56).

20. According to Leon Peters, stainless steel began to be used for winery equipment in California about 1938 ("Protect Your Stainless Steel," *Wines and Vines* 29 [October 1948]: 34). But there were scattered earlier instances. Cameo Vineyards, for example, had four stainless steel tanks in its bottling room as early as 1935 (O. M. Shelton, "Cameo Vineyard Company's Model Plant," *Wine Review* 3 [May 1935]: 15).

21. According to Martin Ray, the only press at Inglenook Winery was a continuous screw press, "unfit for anything but making brandy" (Ray to Julian Street, 16 May 1940, Julian Street papers, Princeton University, Firestone Library).

22. Or sometimes they were not pressed at all, in which case only the juice released by crushing was fermented. In some wineries, the crushed white grapes, after the juice was run off, might be added to the tanks of fermenting red grapes (W. V. Cruess and Maynard A. Joslyn, "Crushing and Fermenting White Wine," *Wine Review* 2 [December 1934]: 12).

23. The settling step was often omitted, according to Lapsley, *Bottled Poetry*, p. 60.

24. Cruess and Joslyn, "Crushing and Fermenting White Wine," p. 12: but instead of such manipulations, the authors observed, "it is much better to carefully watch the maturing of the crop and pick the grapes at the proper sugar content."

25. Walter S. Richert and Ben H. Cummings, "Improved Winery Construction," *Wine Review* 5 (May 1937): 9.

26. "Join for Quality Wine," *Wine Review* 4 (June 1936): 31. The group of twelve wineries called itself the Sonoma County Wine Improvement Association.

27. Maynard Amerine recalled that Julius Fessler, of the Berkeley Yeast Laboratory, "did a thriving business" in the early years following Repeal "doing very simple analysis for wineries just to keep them out of the clutches of the government" (*The University of California and the State's Wine Industry*, interview by Ruth Teiser, Berkeley: Regional Oral History Office, Bancroft Library, University of California, 1972, pp. 53–54).

28. In 1943 there were seventy-six licensed brandy distilleries in California; the number then was probably pretty much what it had been through the 1930s (U.S. Senate, Judiciary Committee, *Liquor Industry: Hearings 10, 16, 17 December 1943* [Washington, D.C.: GPO, 1944], exhibit 2, pp. 59–60).

29. W. V. Cruess, "Research in Enology," *California Journal of Development* 24 (December 1934): 10. The use of Bentonite was originally recommended by L. G. Saywell of the University of California, both for clarification and for stabilization. The Bentonite (hydrous alumina silicate) used in the California wine industry is mined in Wyoming.

30. "Centrifugal Clarification of Wine," *Wine Review* 2 (December 1934): 17. The experimental work was done by L. G. Saywell.

31. Cruess, *Principles and Practice of Wine Making*, 2nd ed., pp. 32–33.

32. Ibid., pp. 199–200.

33. Robert Hughes, "Metallurgy, Metals, and the Winery," *Wine Review* 3 (April 1935): 12.

34. L. K. Marshall, "The Wine Problem," *California Department of Agriculture Bulletin* 26 (January–March 1937): 60–61.

35. Writing in 1940, Martin Ray said that most California wines were pasteurized, including those of Beaulieu, Inglenook, and Wente: "I cannot name one wine maker I am sure does not pasteurize in California" (to Julian Street, 2 May 1940, Julian Street papers, Princeton University, Firestone Library). Even after allowing for Ray's usual exaggeration, one may suppose that the practice was common enough.

36. Maynard A. Joslyn and Maynard A. Amerine observed in 1941 that many California sweet wine musts were exaggeratedly low in acidity, the result of using table and raisin varieties, of late picking, and of excessive cropping (*Commercial Production of Dessert Wines*, Bulletin 651 [Berkeley: University of California, College of Agriculture, Agricultural Experiment Station, 1941], p. 13).

37. E. H. Twight, "Sweet Wine Making in California," *California Grape Grower* 15 (October 1934): 4–5; idem, "Port Wine Making in California," *Wines and Vines* 17 (May 1936): 5; Porchet, *La Vigne et le vin en Californie*, pp. 34–35. Port and muscatel might also be produced by fermenting the wine dry and then adding fortified concentrate to bring up the sugar and alcohol content (E. H. Twight, "Improving Sweet Wines," *Wine Review* 18 [June 1937]: 14).

38. But it need not have contained any muscat at all until 1949, when the government determined that the name *muscatel* was varietal, not generic. It was feared at the time that there might not be enough muscat grapes available in California to meet the new requirement that anything called muscatel must contain not less than 51 percent of wine made from muscat grapes.

39. The winemaking there was supervised by E. H. Twight, one of the generation whose careers spanned both the pre-Prohibition and the post-Repeal eras in California. Maynard Amerine thought that the muscat wine Twight produced in 1935 was "one of the best produced in the state since Repeal" ("Edmund Henri Twight 1874–1957," *Wines and Vines* 38 [May 1957]: 29).

40. Cruess, *Principles and Practice of Wine Making*, 2nd ed., p. 244.

41. Ibid., p. 206.

42. About 1,000 acres of Palomino grapes grew in the Central Valley in the '30s, enough for only a fraction of the sherry produced.

43. Cruess, *Principles and Practice of Wine Making*, 2nd ed., p. 205. Two of the earliest sherry makers in the Napa Valley were both Portuguese—one actually from Madeira—and it may be that they aimed at a Madeira character in their sherry, as Portuguese may be supposed to do: see Charles L. Sullivan, *Napa Wine: A History from Mission Days to the Present* (San Francisco: Wine Appreciation Guild, 1994), pp. 43, 64.

44. E. H. Twight, "Sweet Wine Making in California, Part II," *California Grape Grower* 15 (November 1934): 4; idem, "California Sherry Making," *Wines and Vines* 17 (April 1936): 5, 15; E. M. Sheehan, "California Sherry Wine," *California Grape Grower* 15 (May 1934): 3; Maynard A. Amerine and E. H. Twight, "Sherry," *Wines and Vines* 19 (May 1938): 3–4.

For a state-of-the-art baking room in this era, see "The Hot Room at Cresta Blanca," *Wine Review* 3 (May 1935): 21. If the winemaker so desired, he might label his sherry wine *marsala* or *madeira* to indicate that it was sweet rather than dry (California Department of Public Health, *Wine Standards Hearing, 12 January 1942*, p. 31, transcript in the Wine Institute Library).

45. H. H. Marquis, "California Sherry Production," *Wine Review* 4 (June 1936): 6.

46. W. V. Cruess began experiments with *flor* yeast in 1937: "Experiments in Sherry," *Wines and Vines* 24 (October 1943): 21. Ten years later he had *flor* sherries available for test tasting: *Wines and Vines* 28 (May 1947): 21. The baking method remained standard, however, though it grew to be better understood and more sophisticated: see Myron S. Nightingale, "California Methods of Baking Sherry," *Wine Review* 14 (May 1946): 8–9.

47. Cruess suggests that it may have been flavored with angelica root and so have acquired its name, but he gives no evidence (*Principles and Practice of Wine Making*, 2nd ed., p. 243).

48. Maynard A. Amerine, "The Composition of California Wines at Exhibitions, Part Three: Dessert Wine," *Wines and Vines* 28 (March 1947): 23; Frank Schoonmaker and Tom Marvel, *American Wines* (New York: Duell, Sloan & Pearce, 1941), p. 221. Amerine adds that there were "almost as many methods of producing tokay as there are producers."

49. W. V. Cruess, "Tests on Unfortified Sweet Wines," *Wine Review* 4 (February 1936): 20–21.

50. It is only fair to quote what Dr. Berthe Porchet has said about California sweet wines in the '30s: "The sweet wine industry requires techniques and a precision of operation that can be provided only by a specialized and conscientious personnel. The making of these wines is one of the specialties of which the California industry can be proud" (*La Vigne et le vin en Californie*, p. 38). Porchet, of the Station fédérale d'essais viticoles et arboricoles at Lausanne, had spent the season of 1936 in California studying wine production. I have drawn extensively on her descriptions in my account of California winemaking.

51. W. V. Cruess, *Wines and Vines* 16 (June 1935): 23. Later Cruess put his remarks even more strongly. Writing in 1944, he recalled that "during the first vintage following repeal many inexperienced persons and companies undertook to make wine. Losses by stuck fermentations and 'Tourne' bacteria were appalling to say the least. One cellar made an entire cellar, 200,000 gallons, of spoiled wine!" ("Wine and the Fruit Products Laboratory," *Wines and Vines* 25 [December 1944]: 39). The Sciarone Winery in Escalon had a similar disaster: after 220,000 gallons of wine turned to vinegar, the owner sued his winemaker, claiming that he "did not know his business" (*Wine Review* 2 [June 1934]: 35).

52. W. V. Cruess, "Suggestions for Increasing Consumer Interest," *Wines and Vines* 18 (November 1937): 6.

53. In 1938, for example, most of the 25,000 gallons of bottled wines sold by Beaulieu to a New York distributor the previous year were returned, spoiled, to the winery; Beaulieu then found that almost half of its inventory was spoiled, fit only for distillation. This was at a winery always known for the highest standards in the California industry (Lapsley, *Bottled Poetry*, p. 39; Tchelistcheff, *Grapes, Wine, and Ecology*, pp. 49–50, 62).

54. Edmund Henri Twight (1874–1957), a graduate of the Sorbonne and of the agriculture school at Montpellier, had worked at a number of wineries in California before Prohi-

bition and was the first professorial appointment in viticulture at the University of California. After Repeal he was hired at Davis expressly to tutor the staff in wine, no one there having any expertise in the matter. He thus played an important part in maintaining some continuity in the wine knowledge of California. See Maynard A. Joslyn, *A Technologist Views the California Wine Industry,* interview by Ruth Teiser, Berkeley: Regional Oral History Office, Bancroft Library, University of California, 1974, p. 22.

55. Maynard A. Amerine and E. H. Twight, "Claret," *Wines and Vines* 19 (January 1938): 24; E. H. Twight and Maynard A. Amerine, "Port Wine," *Wines and Vines* 19 (February 1938): 6; Maynard A. Amerine and A. J. Winkler, "Angelica," *Wines and Vines* 19 (September 1938): 24; idem, "Burgundy," *Wines and Vines* 19 (November 1938): 5–6.

56. See chapter 3, at n. 20.

57. "New claret" from bulk containers sold at *retail* for 30 cents a gallon in San Francisco in 1934 (*Wine Review* 2 [October 1934]: 9).

58. H. H. Marquis, "Selling Wine Out of a Barrel," *Wine Review* 2 (October 1934): 8. So also the *Wine Review* stated in December 1934 that "most of the wine in California" was "sold in jug lots from original barrels" (p. 23).

59. See the discussion of barrel wines in chapter 2, after n. 70. Wisconsin and Louisiana joined California in allowing sales from the barrel. No state now allows the practice. It was ended in California in 1945 by the Swing bill. A "last legitimate barrel house"— Mazzoni, in San Francisco's North Beach—was reported as closing in June 1968 (Charles van Kriedt to Roy Brady, 20 May 1968, Roy Brady papers, University of California, Davis, Shields Library).

60. Frederick Koster, quoted in W. V. Cruess, "California Wine Industry Conference," *Fruit Products Journal* 13 (June 1934): 294. A writer for the *Wine Review* in 1935 stated that it cost at least 15 cents more for a quart of wine in bottle than in bulk (Stratford Enright, "Conditions in the Wine Barrel Store," *Wine Review* 3 [July 1935]: 16).

61. *Wines and Vines* 17 (December 1936): 13, reporting that Beaulieu was "one of the most important bottle-wine firms in the land." *Wine Review* 3 (October 1935): 18 cautiously recommended the practice of bottling "fine" wines at the winery as a means of enhancing the general prestige of the industry.

62. Louis Gomberg estimated that there were about fifteen hundred of these bottlers across the country (*Analytical Perspectives on the California Wine Industry, 1935–1990,* interview by Ruth Teiser, Berkeley: Regional Oral History Office, Bancroft Library, University of California, 1990, p. 48). The first insulated steel tank cars built especially for wine were put into service by the California Wine Association before Prohibition (Louis S. Wetmore, "Will Post-War Wine Shipments Be Made in Tank Steamers?" *Wines and Vines* 24 [March 1943]: 17). The average shipping charge for wine sent by rail tank car from California to eastern and midwestern markets was 10 cents a gallon (Stuart F. Leete, "California Wine Moves to Market," *Wine Review* 4 [December 1936]: 11).

63. Roy Brady, in an unpublished MS, dated 14 January 1992: Roy Brady papers, University of California, Davis, Shields Library. In 1945 *Business Week* reported that California wines were sold across the country "under 75,000 to 100,000 labels" ([17 November 1945]: 42).

64. The system was also open to a variety of abuses. Since there was no identification of the

wine's origin, the same wine could be sold under different labels at different prices by the same bottler: see the letter from L. S. in *Wines and Vines* 20 (December 1939): 23, complaining of this practice in Chicago. Wine sold from the barrel was subject to the same abuse. Louis J. Foppiano recalled that at his family winery's retail store "we had three barrels—forty-five cents, sixty or seventy cents, and ninety-five cents or a dollar. It was all the same wine" (*A Century of Winegrowing in Sonoma County, 1896–1996*, interview by Carole Hicke, Berkeley: Regional Oral History Office, Bancroft Library, University of California, 1996, p. 46).

65. W. N. McDonald, "The Sales Story of 'Eastern,'" *Wine Review* 8 (September 1940): 9.

66. Tom Marvel, letter to the editor, *California Grape Grower* 15 (September 1934): 18.

67. Perhaps just as well: one of the trial brands was called Vin-Tin-Age (*Fruit Products Journal* 16 [November 1936]: 75). Much of the wine sent out in cans became cloudy or corroded the cans. After these problems were corrected, the sale of canned wine persisted at least into 1939: see Leo A. Berti, "Canned Wine; Past Experience and Future Possibilities," *Wines and Vines* 31 (December 1950): 22. The idea appears to be perennial: Yosemite Winery introduced canned wine ("Kan-O-Wine") in 1954 (*Wines and Vines* 35 [December 1954]: 10); "Swiss Mist," introduced by United Vintners in 1962, was canned; Geyser Peak and Villa Bianchi were selling wine in cans in 1981 (*Wines and Vines* 62 [April 1981]: 16), and Coca-Cola's Wine Spectrum was test-marketing the idea at the same time (*New York Times*, 26 December 1982, III, 21).

68. *California Grape Grower* 15 (October 1934): 14; *Wines and Vines* 16 (October 1935): 5. According to *Fortune* magazine, even the experts were confused by such names: "It is told that at a recent California State Fair one Livermore winery was awarded an honorable mention for its Moselle, but that a gold medal went to another firm that had bought ten barrels of the Moselle and labeled it 'hock'" ("Great Wine Boom," *Fortune* 23 [May 1941]: 122; the anonymous article was written by Philip Wagner).

69. These names are drawn from the collection of catalogs and lists at California State University, Fresno. California had no monopoly on such offenses: in the '30s Widmer's in New York State had wines called Hochheimer, Niersteiner, and Deidesheimer, as well as Hungarian Style Tokay (label file, box 6, Widmer papers, Cornell University, Kroch Library). By 1937 the Federal Alcohol Administration had disallowed such proper names as Yquem and St. Julien on the grounds that they had not been in established general use before Prohibition.

70. Copy at the California State University, Fresno, Library.

71. Richard Paul Hinkle, "Foppiano at the Century Mark," *Wines and Vines* 77 (September 1996): 20. *Barberone* was a name invented to suggest some sort of Barbera wine after the regulations required that at least 51 percent of a varietally named wine be made of the variety named (H. A. Caddow, "Learning the New Label Rules," *Wine Review* 4 [December 1936]: 9); Barberone could be anything.

72. They analyzed 399 samples of white table wine, 282 of red table wine, and 488 of dessert wine.

73. Maynard A. Amerine, "The Composition of California Wines at Exhibitions," *Wines and Vines* 28 (February 1947): 25.

74. Ibid., p. 26.

75. These descriptions were widely circulated: my text is from the *California Journal of Development* 26 (September 1936): 64.

76. A few small steps were taken toward definition. In California, by regulation of the Department of Public Health in 1942, "dry sherry" had to have a sugar content of less than 2.5 percent, and "sherry" a sugar content of between 2.5 and 4.0 percent. Before that, Amerine had found "dry" sherries with a sugar content of 7 percent and "sherries" with as little as 0.88 percent ("The Composition of California Wines at Exhibitions, Part Three," p. 23).

77. Louis A. Petri, "Wine Quality and the Advertising Program," *Wine Review* 7 (June 1939): 8.

78. A copy of Mrak's letter, undated but evidently from June 1936, is in the USDA Wine File at the National Agricultural Library, Beltsville, Md. Mrak (1901–87), then a microbiologist studying such things as metal contaminants in wine, succeeded Cruess as chairman of the Division of Food Technology in 1948 and later became chancellor of the University of California, Davis, at the time of its great expansion (1959–69). The administration building at Davis is named for him.

79. All these items are in the collection at the California State University, Fresno, Library. A comparably bleak picture is given in H. H. Marquis, "Wine in the Hotels of America," *Wine Review* 3 (October 1935): 8–10. Of course, if one lived in California, the chances were better: the Palace Hotel in San Francisco had wines from Cresta Blanca, Italian Swiss Colony, Beaulieu, Almadén, Concannon, Beringer, and Garratti on its list in 1934 (*California Grape Grower* 15 [August 1934]: 12). But outside San Francisco such a range must have been very rare indeed.

80. Fougner (1884–1941), a New York newspaperman with experience in England and France who then became a publicity agent, was one of the self-appointed experts who guided Americans in the world of wine after Repeal. Fougner, who wrote much under the name Baron Fougner, wrote a column in the *New York Sun* called "Along the Wine Trail."

81. Box 1, Julian Street papers, Princeton University, Firestone Library. The St. Regis took on the wines of Martin Ray and Inglenook in 1940, when the war compelled a search for new sources of supply (Julian Street to Martin Ray, 16 July 1940, 17 September 1940, Julian Street papers, Princeton University, Firestone Library).

CHAPTER 5. COUNTERCURRENTS

1. See chapter 1, at n. 121.

2. Louis M. Martini claimed to have been instrumental in forming the California Sweet Wine Producers Association (Louis M. Martini and Louis P. Martini, *Wine Making in the Napa Valley*, interview by Ruth Teiser and Lois Stone, Berkeley: Regional Oral History Office, Bancroft Library, University of California, 1973, p. 40). If so, the connection was an ironic one, in view of Martini's later move to the Napa Valley and the production of dry wines. Lucius Powers names Arthur Tarpey and Arpaxat Setrakian among the founders (*The Fresno Area and the California Wine Industry*, interview by Ruth Teiser, Berkeley: Regional Oral History Office, Bancroft Library, University of California, 1974, p. 24).

3. See chapter 2, after n. 48.

4. W. V. Cruess, "California Wine Industry Conference," *Fruit Products Journal* 14 (June 1934): 293–94, 308, 311; *California Grape Grower* 15 (July 1934): 14–15.

5. The members of the committee included A. R. Morrow, Sophus Federspiel, Arthur Tarpey, E. M. Sheehan, Edmund Rossi, H. O. Lanza, Lee Jones, and a number of others of the old guard (*California Grape Grower* 15 [July 1934]: 15).

6. Statewide Vintners' Committee, "Important Notice to Every Wine Producer in California," 16 October 1934 (form letter in the Wine Institute Library). Leon D. Adams says that he arranged this meeting and wrote the program for it (*Revitalizing the California Wine Industry*, interview by Ruth Teiser, Berkeley: Regional Oral History Office, Bancroft Library, University of California, 1974, p. 59).

7. The number is not certain. There are fifty-six names on a memo titled "Wineries Believed to Have Attended the First Meeting of the Wine Institute"; the memo is dated 25 November 1958 (Wine Institute Library).

8. "Program Wine Producers Meeting," 20 October 1934 (mimeographed sheet, Wine Institute Library).

9. The number thirty-two is given in the *California Grape Grower* 15 (November 1934): 18. In the report titled "The First Twenty Years of the Wine Institute: A Report to Members at the Twentieth Annual Meeting" (San Francisco: Wine Institute, 8–9 March 1954), the number is stated to be forty-eight.

10. Because Morrow had been head of the California Wine Association before Prohibition, when the CWA had a near-monopoly control over the wine market, there was some suspicion among grape growers that the institute was a device to reestablish that control.

11. Caddow (1899–1957), a Scotsman, was already a veteran of the campaign for wine, having been an assistant to Donald Conn of the California Vineyardists Association, secretary of the Grape Growers League, and secretary of the Wine Producers Association. Peyser (1899–1989) served as legal counsel to the Wine Institute for forty-one years. Most of the directors of the institute were simply taken over from the directorate of the Wine Producers Association, so that the connection went directly back through the association to its predecessor organization, the Grape Growers League of 1932.

12. Later the Wine Advisory Board had its offices there too: the building was sold in April 1946 (*Wine Review* 14 [April 1946]: 86).

13. *California Grape Grower* 15 (November 1934): 18.

14. Celler (1888–1981), a longtime member of Congress from New York City, had supported his family after the death of his father as a wine salesman while working his way through college; Celler says little about this experience in his autobiography (*You Never Leave Brooklyn* [New York: John Day, 1953]), but he remained a friend of the industry (Jefferson Peyser, *The Law and the California Wine Industry*, interview by Ruth Teiser, Berkeley: Regional Oral History Office, Bancroft Library, University of California, 1974, p. 27).

15. Ruth Teiser and Catherine Harroun, *Winemaking in California* (New York: McGraw-Hill, 1983), p. 192.

16. "Report of the Secretary to the Annual Meeting of the Membership of the Wine Institute, August 16, 1935" (typescript in the Wine Institute Library).

17. Memorandum from W. M. Platt to Leon Adams, 10 March 1942 (Wine Institute Library). The figures for large wineries were 120 out of 194; for small wineries, 21 of 244; the

total membership of the institute was thus only 141 out of 438 establishments, or 32 percent.

18. *California Grape Grower* 15 (November 1934): 18. In its twenty-year report, the institute calculated that it had cost its members an average of only a seventh of a cent per gallon of wine ("The First Twenty Years of the Wine Institute," p. 8).

19. Harry Caddow, "Annual Meeting of the Wine Institute," *Wines and Vines* 16 (September 1935): 12. Whether the recommended prices made any difference in the market I do not know. The recommendations were well below what the growers had hoped for.

20. "Report of the Secretary to the Annual Meeting of the Membership of the Wine Institute August 16, 1935."

21. See chapter 3, n. 1.

22. Leon D. Adams wrote that the Department of Public Health standards were a "reissuance" of earlier ones (*The Wines of America* [Boston: Houghton Mifflin, 1973], p. 33); later he said that in fact they were written by him, at the Wine Institute (*California Wine Industry Affairs: Recollections and Opinions,* interview by Ruth Teiser, Berkeley: Regional Oral History Office, Bancroft Library, University of California, 1990, pp. 12–13). But the Western Wine Producers Association also contributed: their recommendations were made in August 1934 ("The Standards for California Wine," *Wine Review* 2 [August 1934]: 20–21). Carl Bundschu, the manager of Inglenook Vineyards and a director of the Wine Institute, is also identified as "one of those who led in the efforts of the Wine Institute to establish quality standards in 1934" (*Wines and Vines* 28 [October 1947]: 44). The main provisions, apart from those discussed in the text, included a minimum alcohol content of 10 percent for white table wine, 10.5 percent for red, and 19.5 percent for fortified wine; a maximum volatile acidity of 0.12 gram per 100 cc for red table wine and 0.11 for white; and a requirement that varietal wine had to contain 51 percent of the variety named. When federal standards were established in 1936, they allowed a lower minimum alcohol content and a higher volatile acidity content, as well as permitting the addition of sugar and up to 25 percent of wine from sources not part of the appellation shown on the label: see U.S. Federal Alcohol Administration, *Regulations No. 4, Labeling and Advertising of Wine* (Washington, D.C.: GPO, 1935). Julius Fessler, writing in 1946, thought that the limit set by the state on volatile acidity was "the most constructive step" taken since Repeal toward "the production of sound wines" ("Stability in Wine," *Wine Review* 14 [October 1946]: 28).

23. Harry Caddow, "Wine Institute Activities," *Wines and Vines* 16 (May 1935): 12. The *Wine Review* reported in May 1935 that already "more than 300 establishments have been visited, 167 samples have been analyzed and 90 lots of wine have been quarantined" (p. 30). The chief of the state Department of Public Health wrote that "at the beginning of the enforcement program approximately two-thirds of the samples taken were found to be substandard" (Milton P. Duffy, "Wine Standardization Progress," *Wines and Vines* 19 [March 1938]: 12). By the end of 1936, nearly 2 million gallons of wine in California had been "libeled or quarantined by the Department of Public Health" ("California Quality Enforcement," *Wine Review* 5 [February 1937]: 16).

24. Harry Caddow, "Quality Enforcement Extended into the Winery," *Wines and Vines* 16

(August 1935): 12; Milton P. Duffy, "Enforcement of California Wine Quality Standards," *Fruit Products Journal* 15 (August 1936): 355.

25. The Federal Alcohol Control Administration had published standards of quality and identity at the end of March 1935, but the agency had then been abolished when the National Industrial Recovery Act was declared unconstitutional in May 1935 (see chapter 2, at n. 50), and its regulations had never gone into force. The successor to FACA, the FAA, published its regulations for wine (*Regulations No. 4*) at the end of 1935, to take effect from 1 March 1936. Other important provisions in these regulations, which covered labeling as well as official standards, were the requirement that varietally labeled wines contain at least 51 percent of the named variety and that vintage-dated wines be 100 percent of the year listed and entirely from the region named. Neither varietal naming nor vintage dating was anything but rare in the trade at this time, but the provisions proved important in the future. California had even tougher regulations for vintage-dating: they required a sworn statement to be filed with and approved by the Department of Public Health, and no vintage date could appear on a container of more than one-gallon capacity ("California Quality Enforcement," p. 15). A few years later the rules were made even tougher ("Vintage Wine Regulations," *Wine Review* 8 [April 1940]: 4; [July 1940]: 30). One supposes that there had been much fraud in the matter.

26. Louis A. Petri, "Wine Quality and the Advertising Program," *Wine Review* 7 (June 1939): 7.

27. Harry Caddow, "FAA Regulations and Amendments," *Wines and Vines* 19 (September 1938): 3. Petri thought that no national program of advertising for California wine would have been possible before this regulation, guaranteeing that wines advertised as Californian were in fact genuine ("Wine Quality and the Advertising Program," p. 7).

28. This arrangement lasted until 1950, when all enological and viticultural work was consolidated at Davis. The division of labor had never been exact: enological work as well as viticultural work was carried on at Davis, soon more extensively than at Berkeley, which specialized much less in wine ("New Division of Fruit Products at University of California," *Fruit Products Journal* 14 [August 1935]: 373; "Grape Growing and Winemaking Taught at the University Farm at Davis," *Wines and Vines* 18 [July 1937]: 22). In the original division, W. J. Cruess headed the Department of Fruit Products, A. J. Winkler the Department of Viticulture.

29. A major work, however, is F. T. Bioletti, "Outline of Ampelography for the Vinifera Grapes of California," *Hilgardia* 11 (1938): 227–93, which appeared in the year before his death.

30. Cruess (1886–1968) was an indefatigable worker who "was into everything; he had a very inquiring mind" (Charles M. Crawford, *Recollections of a Career with the Gallo Winery and the Development of the California Wine Industry, 1942–1989*, interview by Ruth Teiser, Berkeley: Regional Oral History Office, Bancroft Library, University of California, 1990, p. 43). See W. V. Cruess, "A Few Reminiscences," *Wines and Vines* 33 (December 1952): 17–18, for some account of pre-Prohibition winemaking.

31. The book first appeared serially in the *Fruit Products Journal* between November 1933 and June 1934. Cruess's book, much altered and expanded, is the basis of Maynard A. Amerine and W. V. Cruess, *The Technology of Wine Making* (Westport, Conn.: Avi Pub-

lishing, 1960; 4th ed., 1980). One may also mention the pamphlet got out in 1934 by Cruess and Maynard Joslyn, presumably for wider circulation than one could expect from a book: this was "Elements of Wine Making," Circular 88 (Berkeley: University of California, College of Agriculture, 1934).

32. According to Maynard Joslyn, who was one of the team, Cruess and his assistants visited "every one of the 650 wineries" then operating in California (*A Technologist Views the California Wine Industry*, interview by Ruth Teiser, Berkeley: Regional Oral History Office, Bancroft Library, University of California, 1974, p. 16).

33. W. V. Cruess, "Wine and the Fruit Products Laboratory," *Wines and Vines* 25 (December 1944): 39. The annual wine conference held at Berkeley under the auspices of the Division of Fruit Products was the most important professional meeting for California winemakers in the '30s.

34. In 1937, to take a single early year, the Fruit Products Division under Cruess was investigating sweet wine mold, oxidation in sherry, wine cooling, *flor* yeast in sherry, utilization of pomace, the effects of metals on wine, concrete tank surfaces, the vitamins of grapes and wines, clarification and filtration, and fermentation methods (*Wines and Vines* 18 [November 1937]: 10).

35. Quoted in Teiser and Harroun, *Winemaking in California*, p. 190, from a speech of 1958; see also Ernest Gallo and Julio Gallo, with Bruce B. Henderson, *Ernest and Julio: Our Story* (New York: Times Books, 1994), pp. 55–56. One of the pamphlets was probably F. T. Bioletti's "Principles of Wine Making," Bulletin 213 (Berkeley: University of California, College of Agriculture, Agricultural Experiment Station, 1911). The latter is "the only publication of the College of Agriculture that was ever withdrawn from circulation"—the reason, of course, being Prohibition (A. J. Winkler, "Eighty-Five Years of Work in Viticulture and Enology," undated typescript [ca. 1965], p. 6 (copy in the Wine Institute Library).

36. The coincidence of their given names concealed very different origins. Joslyn (1904–84) was born in Russia. He was a professor in the Department of Food Technology at Berkeley. Amerine (1911–98) was born in San Jose and grew up near Modesto; after taking a Ph.D. at Berkeley in plant pathology, he joined the Department of Viticulture at Davis, where he eventually became professor of enology and chairman of the department. He was for many years the best-known and most articulate member of the California wine scientists, with a long and distinguished list of publications for both professional and popular audiences. But it is interesting to know—and typical of the state of things in those days—that Amerine, at the time he was hired at Davis, "had no personal knowledge of grapes or wine making" (Joslyn, *A Technologist Views the California Wine Industry*, p. 22). Amerine himself said that he knew something about grape growing (*The University of California and the State's Wine Industry*, interview by Ruth Teiser, Berkeley: Regional Oral History Office, Bancroft Library, University of California, 1972, p. 4)— but there wasn't any wine field to know about.

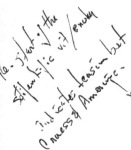

37. Maynard A. Amerine and Maynard A. Joslyn, *Commercial Production of Table Wines*, Bulletin 639 (Berkeley: University of California, College of Agriculture, Agricultural Experiment Station, 1940); Maynard A. Joslyn and Maynard A. Amerine, *Commercial Production of Dessert Wines*, Bulletin 651 (Berkeley: University of California, College of Agri-

culture, Agricultural Experiment Station, 1941); idem, *Commercial Production of Brandies,* Bulletin 652 (Berkeley: University of California, College of Agriculture, Agricultural Experiment Station, 1941). These were "prepared as a guide to the California wine industry in improving the quality and stability of wines and brandies" (idem, *Dessert, Appetizer and Related Flavored Wines: The Technology of Their Production* [Berkeley: University of California, Division of Agricultural Sciences, 1964], p. v). The bulletins on table wines and dessert wines formed the basis of later book-length treatments of their subjects. According to Joslyn, the collaboration between him and Amerine was a way of reconciling the conflicts between the Department of Fruit Products at Berkeley (where Joslyn worked) and the Department of Viticulture at Davis (where Amerine worked): the one emphasized the importance of controlled fermentation; the other, of varieties (Joslyn, *A Technologist Views the California Wine Industry,* pp. 26, 89).

38. "New Home for Wine Research," *Wine Review* 7 (June 1939): 910. A. J. Winkler suggests that the decision to provide the building was influenced by A. P. Giannini, then a trustee of the university. Winkler and Burke Critchfield, of the Bank of America, had called on Giannini to explain the need for new facilities (Winkler, *Viticultural Research at University of California, Davis, 1921–1971,* interview by Ruth Teiser, Berkeley: Regional Oral History Office, Bancroft Library, University of California, 1973, p. 20).

39. "Sixteen Hundred Wine Types! Marvellous Collection of Wines at University Farm," *Wines and Vines* 19 (June 1938): 23.

40. Maynard A. Amerine, *Wine Bibliographies and Taste Perception Studies,* interview by Ruth Teiser, Berkeley: Regional Oral History Office, Bancroft Library, University of California, 1988, p. 26. Amerine, according to Martin Ray, was particularly hurt by the indifferent response to *Table Wines: The Technology of Their Production in California,* published with Maynard Joslyn (Berkeley: University of California Press, 1951; Martin Ray to John Melville, 17 March 1956, Martin Ray papers, University of California, Davis, Shields Library). Amerine wrote that the disappointing sales of the book meant that there was "little technical interest" in California ("Report to the Wine Institute Technical Advisory Committee Meeting, May 13, 1955," mimeographed text "not for publication": copy in the Roy Brady papers, University of California, Davis, Shields Library).

41. As Amerine said, the people at Davis took the view that "winemaking is a branch of biochemistry, and grape growing is a branch of genetics and plant physiology. And if you don't know anything about plant physiology, you don't know anything about grapes. If you don't know biochemistry, you don't know anything about wine" (Amerine, *Wine Bibliographies and Taste Perception Studies,* p. 22). It is not surprising that such a view might be resented. It is a version of the popular fallacy that only a cook can tell whether the cake is good. But it is good advice for the cooks.

42. See E. W. Hilgard, *Report of the Viticultural Work during the Seasons of 1883–4 and 1884–5* (Sacramento: James L. Ayers, Superintendent of State Printing, 1886), and subsequent reports. What Hilgard began was carried on by F. T. Bioletti: his "Grape Culture in California: Its Difficulties; Phylloxera and Resistant Vines," Bulletin 197 (Berkeley: University of California, College of Agriculture, Agricultural Experiment Station, 1908), specified six different regions for grape growing in California: North Coast, South Coast, Intermediate Central Valley, Sacramento Valley, San Joaquin Valley, and Hot Desert.

43. Winkler (1894–1989) was chairman of the Department of Viticulture at Davis from 1935 until his retirement in 1962. His major work is *General Viticulture* (Berkeley: University of California Press, 1962). A heroic, pergola-trained vine of the Mission variety, the original grape of California winemaking, is his memorial at Davis. It tells much about the conditions that Winkler and other Davis scientists worked under to know that Mrs. Winkler was the head of the Davis chapter of the Woman's Christian Temperance Union (Lynn Alley, Deborah Golino, and Andrew Walker, "Retrospective on California Grapevine Materials Part I," *Wines and Vines* 81 [November 2000]: 151).

44. Amerine, *The University of California and the State's Wine Industry*, p. 12.

45. Maynard A. Amerine and A. J. Winkler, "Composition and Quality of Musts and Wines of California Grapes," *Hilgardia* 15 (February 1944): 553–54. A revised edition of this important report is idem, *California Wine Grapes: Composition and Quality of Their Musts and Wines*, Bulletin 794 (Berkeley: University of California, Division of Agricultural Sciences, Agricultural Experiment Station, 1963).

46. Walter Richert recommended to growers in 1939 that they should consult the experts at Davis "more frequently" about the choice of varieties than in fact they did ("Wanted: More Wine Grapes," *Wine Review* 7 [April 1939]: 21).

47. See, e.g., A. J. Winkler, "Factors Determining Wine Quality," *Wine Review* 5 (September 1937): 8–11.

48. A. J. Winkler, "Grape Varieties for Dry Wines, Part 1," *Wine Review* 4 (May 1936): 7.

49. Amerine and Winkler, "Composition and Quality," p. 515.

50. Ibid., p. 664. In *California Wine Grapes,* Amerine and Winkler relegate the Malbec to the category of the "nonrecommended."

51. H. P. Olmo, "Breeding New Grape Varieties," *Wine Review* 7 (April 1939): 8–10, 32; idem, "Selecting and Breeding New Grape Varieties," *California Agriculture* 34 (July 1980): 23–24.

52. A list of the more successful new introductions for wine, with the year of their introduction, would include Ruby Cabernet (1948), Emerald Riesling (1948), Rubired (1958), and Royalty (1958).

53. There were 13,208 acres of Rubired and 8,098 acres of Ruby Cabernet planted in California in 2002; 817 acres of Rubired were nonbearing, 174 of Ruby Cabernet. Other Olmo varieties were not extending their position in the California vineyard. There were about 25,000 acres of Olmo varieties in 1980 and 24,000 acres in 2002: the gains for Rubired and Ruby Cabernet were more than offset by the decline in the figures for other varieties (California Agricultural Statistics Service, *California Grape Acreage* [Sacramento: California Agricultural Statistics Service, 1980, 2002]). These figures are anything but negligible, but they perhaps do not correspond to the expectations originally held out for the Olmo introductions.

54. *California Grape Grower* 15 (October 1934): 14.

55. W. V. Cruess, "Grading, Scoring and Classifying Wines," *Wine Review* 3 (May 1935): 13, 18. Cruess offered a tentative hundred-point score card for discussion and revision as a first step toward a system of classification. The latter-day versions of such a system are presumably ignorant of this ancestor.

56. Dr. F. E. Gladwin, of the Fredonia, New York, Experiment Station, carried out work on

wine grape breeding even before Repeal ("New Grape Varieties in New York," *Wine Review* 2 [December 1934]: 31). For a further discussion of research in New York, see chapter 8, "Winegrowing in New York."

57.   André Tchelistcheff recalled that he was "amazed" by the "primitiveness" of the Beaulieu operation when he was introduced to it in 1938 (*Grapes, Wine, and Ecology,* interview by Ruth Teiser and Catherine Harroun, Berkeley: Regional Oral History Office, Bancroft Library, University of California, 1983, pp. 42, 82).

58.   George Deuer, interview by Bernard Skoda, 1974, in *History of Napa Valley: Interviews and Reminiscences of Long-Time Residents* (St. Helena, Calif.: Napa Valley Wine Library Association, 1979), vol. 2, p. 109. At Beaulieu, too, sales of case goods were "very limited" (Tchelistcheff, *Grapes, Wine, and Ecology,* p. 47). The Gallos were purchasing wine in bulk from Beaulieu into the 1950s: Gallo and Gallo, *Ernest and Julio: Our Story,* p. 157.

59.   James T. Lapsley, *Bottled Poetry: Napa Winemaking from Prohibition to the Modern Era* (Berkeley: University of California Press, 1996), p. 16.

60.   Ibid. Larkmead did continue to bottle some wines under its own label, with good results.

61.   Ibid., p. 32.

62.   Tchelistcheff, *Grapes, Wine, and Ecology,* p. 47.

63.   Unless one admits *Wine of California,* thirty-five pages of pictures and text put out by the Santa Fe Railway Company in 1937, as a genuine book. Frank Schoonmaker and Tom Marvel's *American Wines* (New York: Duell, Sloan & Pearce) appeared in 1941. The winemakers so resented Schoonmaker and Marvel's critical remarks that they commissioned Mary Frost Mabon, of *Harper's Bazaar,* to undo the damage. The result, her *ABC of America's Wines* (New York: Knopf, 1942), is now historically interesting, but its treatment of the subject is uniformly complimentary.

64.   I do not know of any substantial collection of winery promotional material. It would be highly instructive about the state of public wine knowledge in the first years after Repeal.

65.   Simon (1877–1970) was born in Paris and lived in England from 1902. He published more than a hundred books and pamphlets on wine and food; formed a great library of books on those subjects; helped found the Wine Trade Club, the Saintsbury Club, and the Wine and Food Society; and edited the society's quarterly journal, *Wine and Food,* from the beginning. Symons (1900–41) was a bibliographer, collector, calligrapher, and biographer, as well as the founder of the First Editions Club and cofounder of the Wine and Food Society.

66.   See Patrick Morrah, *André Simon: Gourmet and Wine Lover* (London: Constable, 1987), pp. 120–24.

67.   André Simon, "First American Impressions," *Wine and Food* 5 (Spring 1935): 7.

68.   Idem, "Californian Wines," *Wine and Food* 6 (Summer 1935): 7–12; the immediate job, he wrote, was "bettering the beverage wines of California without delay."

69.   The list of wines, accompanied by an introductory note by Philip Wagner, is a fascinating conspectus of what qualified as good wine from American producers in 1935 (*Wine and Food* 8 [Winter 1935]: 77–83). See also "American Wines Face the Jury," *Wine Review* 3 (November 1935): 11–12.

70.   *Wine and Food* 12 (Winter 1936): 86.

71. See chapter 7, after n. 68, for further discussion of new wineries dedicated to quality in California. It says much about the market for distinctive wines from California that before 1940 Martini sent his Napa Valley wines to his Kingsburg winery to be added to the bulk wines from that source (Lapsley, *Bottled Poetry*, p. 22).

72. The *Wine Review* reported that toward the end of the season in 1935, grapes were being bought at prices from $3.50 to $8 a ton (4 [January 1936]: 13). Harry Caddow, "Possibilities of Stabilization," *Wine Review* 4 (May 1936): 10, spoke of "ruinous" prices.

73. The vineyard acreage had gone not up but down: the total acreage in California in 1934 was 499,000; in 1938, it was 489,000. The proportion of wine grapes in these totals remained almost unchanged at approximately 35 percent. There must have been widespread overcropping of the vines.

74. Jessie Schilling Blout, "A Brief Economic History of the California Wine-Growing Industry" (San Francisco: Wine Institute, 1943), p. 18.

75. "Resumé of the Number of Wineries That Have Given Up Their Bonds since the Repeal of Prohibition," memo dated 22 June 1942, copy in the Wine Institute Library.

76. Blout, "A Brief Economic History," pp. 18–19, notes that the rules for collecting the federal tax on brandy also contributed to the crisis. Since the tax on the brandy used in fortifying wine—and most of the wine made in California was fortified—had to be paid within a stated time regardless of whether the wine had been sold, wineries were forced to dump their wines on the market in order to pay the tax gatherer, which further depressed prices. The government changed the rule in 1938, collecting the tax at the time of the sale of the wine rather than at the time of processing.

77. Ibid., p. 19.

78. "Although we may produce more grapes than we know what to do with, there is no overproduction of real wine grape types—nor is there an over-production of quality wines made from these varieties. If there is any over-production, it is of non-wine grapes that go into wines" (Richert, "Wanted: More Wine Grapes," p. 11).

79. H. H. McPike to President Roosevelt, 9 November 1938 (Roosevelt papers, Roosevelt Library, Hyde Park, New York). According to Leon Adams, the main architects of the prorate scheme were Burke Critchfield of the Bank of America and Walter Taylor, head of Fruit Industries (*Revitalizing the California Wine Industry*, p. 71). Both were associated with the large-scale segment of the wine industry.

80. Burke H. Critchfield, *The California Wine Industry during the Depression*, interview by Ruth Teiser, Berkeley: Regional Oral History Office, Bancroft Library, University of California, 1972, pp. 15–16. In Sonoma County the vote was 591 against and 60 for the measure; in Mendocino, 162 against and 66 for; in Napa, curiously, things were reversed: 118 yes and 58 no ("Prorate Grape Plan Approved by Growers," *Wines and Vines* 19 [August 1938]: 5). Some growers and wineries refused to participate despite the law ("The Prorate Reports," *Wine Review* 7 [July 1939]: 15).

81. U.S. Tariff Commission, *Grapes, Raisins and Wines*, Report 134, 2nd ser. (Washington, D.C.: GPO, 1939), pp. 67–68; "The Prorate Reports," p. 15.

82. Memo from A. A. Brock, California State Department of Agriculture, 17 November 1948 (copy in the Wine Institute Library).

83. Peter Valaer, "California Brandy Production," *Wine Review* 10 [November 1942]: 10.

84. Amerine, *The University of California and the State's Wine Industry*, p. 19. Amerine also gives an interesting account of how the brandies submitted were tested before being accepted for the prorate program (ibid., pp. 18–19).

85. James Riddell, "Brandy Production: Past, Present, Future," *Wines and Vines* 49 (January 1968): 19.

86. Joslyn, *A Technologist Views the California Wine Industry*, p. 59.

87. Otto E. Meyer, *California Premium Wines and Brandies*, interview by Ruth Teiser, Berkeley: Regional Oral History Office, Bancroft Library, University of California, 1973, p. 8. Joslyn says that to make a "smoother" product, The Christian Brothers added to the prorate brandy "invert syrup, glycerin, and other components" (*A Technologist Views the California Wine Industry*, p. 59).

88. The coastal growers organized at the end of 1938 into the Coastal Dry Wine Producers Association to defend themselves against the prorate steamroller (*Wine Review* 7 [January 1939]: 26). They succeeded in obtaining a bill from the legislature before the vintage of 1939 "specifying that no such program could ever apply to their grapes again" (Adams, *The Wines of America* [1973 ed.], p. 175; *Wine Review* 7 [April 1939]: 25).

89. Jefferson Peyser says that "several suits" were instigated under this act (*The Law and the California Wine Industry*, p. 50).

90. "Wine Industry Acts to Prevent Sales below Cost," *Fruit Products Journal* 17 (August 1938): 372; *Business Week* (9 September 1939): 42.

91. The crop turned out to be 2,228,000 tons, less than the crops of 1937 and 1938 but well above the average for the decade.

92. The wineries involved in the scheme were the Earl Fruit Company and Wallace Wineries, Delano; Tulare Winery, Tulare; Alta Winery, Dinuba; St. George Winery, San Joaquin Winery, Fresno Winery, California Winery, and Crestview Winery, Fresno; Morello Winery, Kerman; Franzia Brothers Winery, Escalon; Bisceglia Brothers Winery, Wahtoke; Frasinetti Winery, Florin; Acampo Winery and Da Rosa Winery, Lodi; and Colonial Grape Products, Elk Grove ("Central California Wineries Expand," *Wines and Vines* 21 [March 1940]: 27).

93. See Lapsley's analysis in *Bottled Poetry*, p. 113. The Bank of America had made loans totaling more than $7 million to the wine industry by 1937; in 1938 it loaned nearly $3 million to help pay for the prorate scheme; and in 1939 it provided most of the $4 million needed to pay for the operation of Central California Wineries (Marquis James and Bessie Rowland James, *Biography of a Bank: The Story of Bank of America* [New York: Harper and Brothers, 1954], pp. 403–05).

94. Critchfield (1888–1970) had been the main link between the Bank of America and the wine trade, having been loaned by the bank earlier to help in the formation of the Wine Institute, to carry on lobbying in Washington in the interest of the wine trade, and to develop the prorate program of 1938. He remained with Central California Wineries until 1941. Critchfield recalled that A. P. Giannini, though directing his bank to support the growers and winemakers of California, had no high opinion of the people who controlled the industry: "they're just a bunch of bootleggers," he said, though he excepted the Wentes—one of whom, Carl, later became head of the Bank of America. See Critchfield, *The California Wine Industry during the Depression*, pp. 15, 23, 36, 38.

95. The California Cooperative Wineries was incorporated in January 1940 "to facilitate the balancing of wine inventories between member wineries and to act as a clearing house for the exchange of information" ("Cooperatives Unite," *Wine Review* 8 [February 1940]: 5).

96. "We've Turned the Corner," *Wine Review* 7 (November 1939): 5. Later the *Wine Review* praised the formation of Central California Wineries as the dawn of a "new theory of banking practice," by which the Bank of America had attacked the "fundamental problems of the entire wine industry" rather than restricting itself to "conservative commercial loans" (8 [March 1940]: 43, 48).

97. Central California Wineries estimated that their operation had been worth an extra $10 million to California growers in 1939 ("Stabilization Program Brings Ten Million to Growers," *Wine Review* 8 [January 1940]: 29).

98. In February 1940, for example, Central California Wineries bought more than a million gallons of wine from three Lodi wineries that lacked "established outlets for their products" ("Stabilization Measures," *Wine Review* 8 [February 1940]: 4).

99. "Central California Wineries Expand," *Wines and Vines* 21 (March 1940): 26–27. The marketing work of Central California Wineries was in the hands of a subsidiary called the Central Winery, Inc., formed in 1940. In 1941 Central California Wineries contracted with Louis Golan to sell wine under the GoLan label, which was then heavily but not very successfully promoted. Golan, a former vice president in charge of sales and advertising for Schenley, later bought the old American Wine Company of St. Louis and its famous Cook's Imperial champagne.

100. According to Ruth Teiser and Catherine Harroun, this move outraged the chairman of the grand jury, the dean of Hastings College of Law, who alleged that the attorney general was obstructing justice ("The Volstead Act, Rebirth, and Boom," in *University of California/Sotheby Book of California Wine*, ed. Doris Muscatine, Maynard A. Amerine, and Bob Thompson [Berkeley: University of California Press, and London: Sotheby Publications, 1984], p. 77). Louis Gomberg, however, maintained that all was straight and aboveboard; he and two others had persuaded the attorney general to desist (*Analytical Perspectives on the California Wine Industry, 1935–1990*, interview by Ruth Teiser, Berkeley: Regional Oral History Office, Bancroft Library, University of California, 1990, pp. 47–48). Carl Wente said that the case against Central California Wineries had been brought by people "jealous" of its success ("A Look Backward at the 'Dark Days,'" *Wines and Vines* 43 [December 1962]: 18).

101. Harry Caddow, "Advertising California Wines," *Wines and Vines* 19 (November 1938): 3.

102. Leon Adams considered the Thompson agency to be "ignorant of wine" and yet unwilling to listen to the Wine Institute people (*Revitalizing the California Wine Industry*, pp. 85–86).

103. *Wines and Vines* 20 (September 1939): 3. The first Wine Week coincided with the outbreak of war in Europe, to the dismay of the wine industry. In California it was accompanied by local celebrations in San Francisco, the Livermore valley, Lodi, Cucamonga, and Escondido ("Vintage Festivals," *Wine Review* 7 [August 1939]: 13).

104. Lapsley, *Bottled Poetry*, p. 86.

105. The Martini and Gallo wineries were notable dissentients to the marketing order. Martini was sued by the state in 1939 for refusing to pay his assessments (Martini and Martini, *Wine Making in the Napa Valley*, p. 43). Gallo settled without legal action. The technical issue on which Martini contested the order was whether wine was an agricultural product.

106. Julius Jacobs, "Jeff Peyser: The Man of the Year," *Wines and Vines* 64 (March 1983): 24. See also Peyser, *The Law and the California Wine Industry*, p. 10. The advertisements of the Wine Advisory Board were identified as sponsored by the "Wine Growers of California."

107. "Marketing Order Wins," *Wines and Vines* 21 (February 1940): 3 (table of contents page). In 1941 the California Marketing Act was amended to provide specifically for wine as an agricultural commodity.

108. Amerine and Joslyn, *Table Wines: The Technology of Their Production*, 2nd ed. (1970), p. 130.

109. Adams, *The Wines of America*, pp. 174–75; idem, *Revitalizing the California Wine Industry*, pp. 128–30.

110. There were 374 bonded wineries in California in 1950, 342 in 1952. The decline continued until the mid 1960s: see chapter 9.

111. "The California Wine Temple," *Wine Review* 7 (March 1939): 40.

112. There were no surprises among the winners, which included Wente, Beaulieu, Masson, and the like ("International Awards for California Wines at Treasure Island," *Wine Review* 7 [October 1939]: 7). The grand prize was won by a Beaulieu Cabernet entered, after the fashion of the time, as a burgundy. Maynard Amerine, who was chairman of the judging committee, thought it the "best tasting that we'd had in California," one that "actually meant something" and had "a really lasting influence" (*The University of California and the State's Wine Industry*, pp. 38, 79). The exposition may have had good effects within the industry itself without being a very successful public promotion.

CHAPTER 6. WINE IN THE WAR YEARS

1. Harry Caddow told the annual meeting of the Wine Institute that the "potential export markets" opened up to California by the war totaled 17 million gallons (*New York Times*, 20 February 1941, 34).

2. The Wine and Brandy Export Association of California was, however, formed in June 1941, under the direction of the Wine Institute: it aimed especially at the South American and Caribbean markets ("California Wine for the World," *Wine Review* 9 [July 1941]: 10–11).

3. By far the biggest customer—taking half of the entire quantity of exports—was the French army in Indochina, whose supplies from France had been cut off (*Wine Review* 9 [March 1941]: 20; John S. Pyke, "Wine and National Defense," *Wine Review* 9 [October 1941]: 9). In 1941, U.S. exports of wine rose to 575,000 gallons (*Wine Review* 10 [March 1942]: 21).

4. *Business Week* (15 July 1944): 42. In 1944, more than 8 million gallons of wine were imported, by far the largest figure since Repeal (*Wines and Vines* 26 [August 1945]: 11).

Three-quarters of this wine came from Spain and Portugal, with significant additions from Chile and Argentina. The greater part of it was fortified wine: in 1944, 6,764,000 gallons of fortified wine, 791,000 gallons of vermouth, 531,000 gallons of table wine, and 87,000 gallons of sparkling wine were imported (U.S. Tariff Commission, *Grapes and Grape Products,* War Changes in Industry Series, Report 24 [Washington, D.C.: GPO, 1947], pp. 62, 66, 70).

5. With France out of the picture, "producers here believe that they have the best chance they have ever had to build up demand for American wine in this market" ("Plan Liquor Promotion," *New York Times,* 23 June 1940, III, 7). The next year *Fortune* magazine, in a survey (anonymously by Philip Wagner) titled "The Great Wine Boom," called the situation "a great challenge and a great opportunity for the upper bracket of the U.S. wine industry" (23 [May 1941]: 89).

6. Park and Tilford had contracted with Beaulieu in 1937 to distribute its wines in the East, but the first shipment, as has been noted earlier (chapter 4, n. 53), had to be returned as spoiled.

7. Frank Schoonmaker had been advising the Sherry Wine and Spirits Company since 1937, and his hand is evident throughout the catalog, which indeed acknowledges his assistance (p. 19, copy in the author's collection). Other long-established dealers offering American wines included Bellows and Company (Martin Ray and Inglenook wines), S. S. Pierce, M. Lehmann and Company, and W. A. Taylor. The major importing firm of Julius Wile and Company inquired about taking on the Widmer line of New York State wines in 1940, but Schoonmaker had been there first (Julius Wile file, box 3, Widmer papers, Cornell University, Kroch Library).

8. *Wine and Food* 27 (Autumn 1940): 228–29. Ray wrote at the time that this development illustrated the proposition that "wars have played a major role in the introduction of many great wines into new and lasting markets. It looks like this will be my war" (to Julian Street, 9 April 1940, Julian Street papers, Princeton University, Firestone Library). It should be noted that the Californians did not take up Ray's wines until Julian Street, an Easterner, had praised them in the right quarters.

9. When Horatio F. Stoll, the editor of *Wines and Vines,* attempted to rebut Schoonmaker's arguments for better labeling in 1935, he was reduced to mere impertinence ("The Merits of California Wines," *Wines and Vines* 16 [March 1935]: 5, 26). Another point of view was expressed by an Ohio winemaker who said, when the varietal idea was put to him, "Cripes, I make everything out of Catawbas. I'd only have one wine to sell" (*Fortune* 23 [May 1941]: 129).

10. Frank Schoonmaker, "The Case Is Presented for Varietal Names," *Wines and Vines* 21 (November 1940): 8–9.

11. Another reason California was reluctant to adopt varietal labeling was the widespread practice of field blending: that is, the intermixture of different varieties in a single vineyard. There was no way to separate them in picking. But I suppose that this was only a minor argument.

12. According to Maynard A. Amerine, Schoonmaker, on this fateful visit to California, showed the California winemakers "that it was possible to go into a winery and pick out the good and bad wine. That was a very important contribution, because a lot of the

winemakers in California just assumed that their wines were good automatically. . . . He was not interested in dessert wines. That was his second contribution" (*Wine Bibliographies and Taste Perception Studies,* interview by Ruth Teiser, Berkeley: Regional Oral History Office, Bancroft Library, University of California, 1988, pp. 39–40). *Wines and Vines* 20 (December 1939) reported that Schoonmaker had traveled "over one thousand miles" in Northern California, "tasting more than five hundred wines," and that he hoped to be able to sell ten thousand cases of his California selections ("Importer Now Sells California Wines," p. 8).

13. To the wineries already named Schoonmaker soon added Masson, Beaulieu, Korbel, Martini, Beringer, Cresta Blanca, and the Novitiate of Los Gatos (Sherry Wine and Spirits Company catalog, 1941). By 1941 the catalog of Charles L. Richardson and Company of Boston listed forty-two different wines under the heading "Schoonmaker American Wines." Scatena Brothers wines were also among Schoonmaker's early selections. He had intended to feature the wines of Martin Ray, but the two men had quarreled and Ray had been dropped from the list (Eleanor Ray and Barbara Marinacci, *Vineyards in the Sky: The Life of Legendary Vintner Martin Ray* [Stockton, Calif.: Heritage West Books, 1993], pp. 226–27). Frank Schoonmaker and Company in 1941 became majority stockholders in the revived Almadén Wines ("The Almaden Vineyards," *Wines and Vines* 22 [December 1941]: 14) and so became not merely merchants but producers of California wine.

14. Vintage-dating was rarely included. The rules for this practice were unclear and restrictive, the result of an effort to prevent fraud in the matter after Repeal.

15. The currency of the term *varietal* has led to a grammatical anomaly. *Varietal,* the adjective, has displaced *variety,* the noun, in American wine language. One reads of "the choice varietal Cabernet Sauvignon," or the "superior varietals Chardonnay and Pinot noir" when they are of course not varietals but varieties. All varieties of grapes will obviously have varietal characteristics, but the term is now generally understood to mean "a variety having superior or distinctive qualities." Although a wine made from Thompson Seedless grapes would be a varietal, it would be thought strange to produce such a thing. This anomaly has led to further confusions, as in the writer who speaks of the "generic Criolla grape" grown in Argentina (*Wine Spectator* 27 [30 April 2002]: 108): if the opposite of *varietal* is *generic,* then an unworthy grape must be generic! The main point, however, is that *varietal* has driven out *variety* in American winespeak, though I have not followed the practice in this work.

16. Quoted in "Importer Now Sells California Wines," p. 21. Not all agreed with Schoonmaker's description of his wines as "sound, properly made, honestly labeled." Martin Ray wrote, "You and I know that his Pinot Noir is not Pinot Noir; that his Cabernet is not Cabernet-Sauvignon; that his white wines are filled with sulphur; that his Sherries are not Sherries; that his Sauternes are doctored wines." But, Ray added, Schoonmaker *had* "bought the best available and, to this extent, he cannot be blamed" (to Julian Street, 4 April 1940, Julian Street papers, Princeton University, Firestone Library). Ray was always unwilling to admit that any wines but his were any good, but Schoonmaker's American wines could not have been any better than the standards of American winemaking then allowed.

17. See, e.g., B. B. Turner, "Our Wines' Reputation," *Wine Review* 9 (July 1941): "Certain importers," Turner declared, though reduced to selling American wines, were "keeping the market open for the absent foreign wines" by labeling the "California wines they handle with grape variety names, even though such names are unintelligible to the consumer" (p. 9). Turner was general manager of Roma, then the largest American winery. The *Wine Review* supported him editorially: "A major effort has been made to convince the wine consuming public that wine labeling in this country is dishonest, thereby accusing United States growers and vintners of what amounts to fraud" (9 [July 1941]: 7); the magazine then published a series of articles as a "defense program for U.S. wines" against the criticism of American labeling practices.

18. The *New Yorker,* writing on the introduction of Schoonmaker's American varietal wines, remarked that the new scheme of nomenclature "is no more than everybody with an ounce of intelligent interest in our native wines has known all along should be done, but it remained for Mr. Schoonmaker to do it, and he deserves the gratitude of all patriotic wine-drinkers" ([24 February 1940]: 65).

19. The law was approved 7 March 1887 and repealed in 1911. Inglenook Winery, for at least one example, advertised that the purity of its wines was "guaranteed by the Pure Wine Stamp" (*San Francisco Merchant* [11 November 1887]).

20. H. A. Caddow, "Permanent Wine Labeling Regulations," *Wines and Vines* 17 (February 1936): 10.

21. FACA hearings, San Francisco, 31 August 1934, on proposed regulations for labeling, standards of identity, standards of fill, and standards of quality (transcript in the TTB library, Washington, D.C.); *Wine Review* 2 (September 1934): 11.

22. See chapter 2, after n. 57. The federal regulations went into force in 1936; by the end of that year no wine could be sold under labels that had not been officially reviewed and approved—a requirement that created a serious procedural bottleneck when thousands of labels had to be approved each week to meet the deadline. The major changes required were in clearly specifying the place of origin in conjunction with the name of the wine type ("California Sherry"; "New York State Port") and in stating who had made or bottled the wine ("bottled by"; "produced and bottled by"; "blended and bottled by"; "bottled at the winery"). To help California wineries, some of which had had labels in use for fifty years, to comply with the new regulations, the Wine Institute prepared a series of specimen labels to illustrate what was required (Harry A. Caddow, "The New Wine Labeling," *Wines and Vines* 17 [December 1936]: 18).

23. Meigs B. Russell, "Why Masquerade American Wines under Foreign Names?" *Fruit Products Journal* 13 (October 1933): 35–36. French, German, Spanish, Italian, and Portuguese producers were, of course, steadily opposed to the American use of European names and protested in whatever ways were open to them. The stubbornness of the problem may be suggested by the fact that the situation today is just what it was in 1936, as far as the law is concerned.

24. See chapter 2, at n. 3. The same point had been made before Prohibition by Harvey W. Wiley, the head of the Pure Food and Drug Administration. He thought that the growth of the American wine trade had been seriously held back by "the mistaken notion that wines could only be sold if labeled with the names of foreign wines." American wines

had distinct characters, so that "it is the part of wisdom to adopt for these distinctive types of wines in each locality, names by which they may be known and recognized in the trade" (*Beverages and Their Adulteration* [Philadelphia: P. Blakiston's Son, 1919], p. 188).

25. The point needs emphasizing because it is often misunderstood or ignored. Patrick Matthews tells a quite circumstantial story in which Schoonmaker and the Wentes sit around a table "brainstorming" in search of a new kind of name and come up with the varietal idea: "So the first varietally-named wine in the western hemisphere was Wente Brothers' 1932 Sauvignon Blanc" (*The Wild Bunch: Great Wines from Small Producers* [London: Faber and Faber, 1997], p. 154). The statement is so sensationally wrong that one fears its very audacity may compel belief among the innocent.

26. "California's Bottled Wines," *California Grower* 14 (February 1933): 14.

27. There does not seem to have been any law governing the composition of wine with varietal labels before 1936. *Riesling*, for example, was often understood to be a generic name and was used accordingly (when it was later declared to be a varietal name, *Riesling* was replaced by *Rhine*). The new labeling regulations imposed by the FAA in 1936 specified that a wine carrying the name of a grape on the label must contain not less than 51 percent by volume of wine from the grape in question. At the time, Harry Caddow of the Wine Institute thought that this rule would "greatly reduce the quantity of Cabernet and several other wines on the market, because the acreages of certain of these grapes are limited." Nor was he sure that such wines could command higher prices ("The New Wine Labeling," p. 18). Furthermore, as W. V. Cruess noted, "a chemist cannot prove that a given wine has or has not 51 percent of the variety declared on the label" (*Principles and Practice of Wine Making*, 2nd ed. [New York: Avi Publishing, 1947], p. 183). The 51 percent minimum of wine from the named variety was never felt to be adequate. Schoonmaker argued at hearings in 1942 for a minimum of 65 percent to 75 percent (California, Department of Public Health, Bureau of Food and Drug Inspection, *Wine Standards Hearing, 12 January 1942* [Sacramento, 1942], transcript in the Wine Institute Library, p. 47). The law was not changed until 1983, when 75 percent was the formula legislated; see chapter 14, at n. 44.

28. The people at the University of California, Davis, for example, were in favor of varietal names as a way toward establishing wine quality: see, e.g., A. J. Winkler, "Grape Varieties for Dry Wines, Part 1," *Wine Review* 4 (May 1936): 7. Wente had a Sauvignon Blanc available as early as 1936 (*Wine and Food* 12 [Winter 1936]: 41). An informative record of varietal labeling both before and after Prohibition is Maynard A. Amerine and Paul Scholten, "Varietal Labeling in California," *Wines and Vines* 58 (November 1977): 40–41.

29. Thomas Pinney, *A History of Wine in America: From the Beginnings to Prohibition* (Berkeley: University of California Press, 1989), p. 226.

30. Jancis Robinson declares that variety is the overwhelmingly important determinant of wine quality: "the grape alone determines perhaps 90 percent of the flavour of a wine, and shapes its character by regulating the intensity, weight, acidity, longevity and potential" (*Vines, Grapes and Wines: The Wine Drinker's Guide to Grape Varieties* [London: Mitchell Beazley, 1986], p. 6). Perhaps so, especially if one is thinking of the difference between those varieties highly suitable for wine and those varieties quite unsuitable— the difference between Cabernet Sauvignon and Mission, for example. But among the

highly suitable varieties, that 10 percent of flavor and character not determined by variety but by soil, climate, cultivation practices, and winemaking methods looms very large—the difference, say, between a Cabernet from Kern County and a Zinfandel from Sonoma.

31. Writing in 1949, in the still-early days of varietal labeling, Maynard A. Amerine observed that "the differences in color, aroma or flavor between wines with the same [varietal] label are so great in some cases as to make it impossible to believe that wines were derived wholly, or even partially, from the variety named." Amerine concluded that much of this variation came from irregular (mostly bad) practices in grape growing and winemaking, and from the confused identity of the grapes grown in California vineyards ("Wine Production Problems of California Grapes, Part I," *Wine Review* 17 [January 1949]: 18, 20).

32. Thirteen is the traditional number permitted in Châteauneuf-du-Pape, though practically the wine is largely based on Syrah and Grenache.

33. "American Books," *Wine and Food* 32 (1941): 204.

34. James M. Seff, "An Analysis of the Gesell Decision," *Wines and Vines* 61 (January 1980): 32–34.

35. Proprietary names for Meritage wines include Harmonie, Camaraderie, Cardinale, Trilogy, Magnificat, Beritage, Opus One, Insignia, Rubicon, Vendimia, Quintessa, Synergy, and Legacy.

36. In August 1942, the Wine Institute estimated that "the number of European-trained wine and brandy men now in California probably exceeds 100" (*Wall Street Journal,* Pacific Coast edition, 18 August 1942).

37. Otto E. Meyer, *California Premium Wines and Brandies,* interview by Ruth Teiser, Berkeley: Regional Oral History Office, Bancroft Library, University of California, 1973, pp. 8–9.

38. *Wine Review* 8 (July 1940): 16; *Wines and Vines* 54 (February 1973): 12.

39. This was the San Luis Brandy Company, Manteca, purchased in September 1938.

40. Wagner, "The Great Wine Boom," p. 89.

41. "California Invasion," *Time* (8 February 1943): 73. The "invasion" was not wholly confined to California. National Distillers bought the Sweet Valley Wine Co. in Ohio in 1943 ("National Distillers Buy Ohio Winery," *Wine Review* 11 [September 1943]: 23).

42. The Central California Wineries people were glad to sell out to Schenley as a profitable way of ending the threat of an antitrust action that hung over them (see chapter 5, at n. 100). The Cella family was persuaded to sell the Roma Wine Company by the uncertainties of the grape supply. Roma owned few vineyards and largely relied on independent growers—who, if they had wine grapes, now enjoyed a seller's market and if they had raisin grapes, were required to turn them into raisins (Harvey W. Martin, "Schenley Buys Roma and CWI," *Wines and Vines* 23 [November 1942]: 9); the selling price for the winery was $6,400,000 (John B. Cella II, *The Cella Family in the California Wine Industry,* interview by Ruth Teiser, Berkeley: Regional Oral History Office, Bancroft Library, University of California, 1986, p. 31).

43. E. B. Wienand, "The Big Four and the Facts," *Wines and Vines* 25 (February 1944): 11.

44. "The Big Wine Deal," *Fortune* 25 (September 1943): 256 (written anonymously by Philip Wagner). Rosenstiel, who knew nothing about wine, hired Leon Adams to educate him

(Leon D. Adams, *Revitalizing the California Wine Industry*, interview by Ruth Teiser, Berkeley: Regional Oral History Office, Bancroft Library, University of California, 1974, p. 92).

45. "California Invasion," p. 74. Myron Nightingale, who worked for Schenley at Cresta Blanca, thought that "the big corporations, with few exceptions, have done nothing but good for the California wine industry." But as far as the wine business was concerned, he added, "their heart just wasn't there" (*Making Wine in California, 1944–1987*, interview by Ruth Teiser and Lisa Jacobson, Berkeley: Regional Oral History Office, Bancroft Library, University of California, 1988, pp. 26, 34).

46. Eric Strutt, "Let's Look at Radio," *Wines and Vines* 23 (February 1942): 10. The article examines some of the difficulties that had to be met for national broadcasting: some states did not allow women to appear in wine advertising; others forbade mention of prices, or any wine advertising during daytime hours (ibid.).

47. Cresta Blanca's main operations were moved from the original Livermore property to the big Greystone Winery in St. Helena, now renamed Cresta Blanca Winery ("Greystone Remodeled, Renamed," *Wines and Vines* 24 [March 1943]: 40). Nightingale said that Cresta Blanca "was running wine in the back door, and it was going out the front door by the gallons—to such an extent that it was far more than the yield from the grapes or the area from which it was supposed to be coming" (*Making Wine in California*, p. 65).

48. Leon D. Adams, *The Wines of America* (Boston: Houghton Mifflin, 1973), pp. 246–47. The combination of wartime shortages and wartime ceiling prices meant that every producer sold at the highest allowable price: see chapter text after n. 72. Cresta Blanca was thus doing only what every other company was doing, or would do if it could. Perhaps it did so more effectively, which would be a reason for resentment.

49. "There is more than a little evidence to show that during the war years the trade and consumers were under pressure to buy tremendous volumes of wine, in part because of tie-in procedures" ("The Brighter Side," *Wines and Vines* 28 [April 1947]: 31). André Tchelistcheff says that Park and Tilford, the importing firm representing Beaulieu, required dealers to buy ten cases of wine in order to get one case of whiskey (*Grapes, Wine, and Ecology*, interview by Ruth Teiser and Catherine Harroun, Berkeley: Regional Oral History Office, Bancroft Library, University of California, 1983, p. 73). See also Adams, *Revitalizing the California Wine Industry*, p. 86, and idem, *California Wine Industry Affairs: Recollections and Opinions*, interview by Ruth Teiser, Berkeley: Regional Oral History Office, Bancroft Library, University of California, 1990, pp. 22–23.

50. U. S. Congress, Senate Judiciary Committee, Subcommittee, *Liquor Industry; Hearings, December 1943 and January 1944* (Washington, D.C.: GPO, 1944), pp. 348–49, 353–54, 418, 508. Tie-in sales were no doubt common. But the practice would not have been confined to the distillers whenever, as the distillers did, the seller had both what the buyer wanted and what the buyer did not much want. The resentment of the distillers' presence in the wine industry continued after the war: the House Judiciary Committee, investigating the "concentration of economic power in the hands of large industry" in 1949, heard the distillers charged with "controlling the price of California wine grapes, raisins and table grapes" ("Boo!" *Wines and Vines* 30 [August 1949]: 7).

51. Seagram's, which had never done much with its California properties, sold them in 1945, the Mount Tivy Winery going to The Christian Brothers, and Paul Masson to Fromm

and Sichel, the distributors of Christian Brothers wines (though Seagram's retained an interest). Schenley sold Greystone to The Christian Brothers in 1950; National Distillers sold Italian Swiss Colony to United Vintners in 1953; Hiram Walker leased its Valliant property to Almadén in 1955. Further disposals continued into the 1970s, when the tide turned and buying California properties again seemed a thing to do.

52. Maynard A. Amerine, *The University of California and the State's Wine Industry,* interview by Ruth Teiser, Berkeley: Regional Oral History Office, Bancroft Library, University of California, 1972, p. 21.

53. The federal excise tax on table wine went from 6 cents to 8 cents a gallon in October 1941; to 10 cents in November 1942; and to 15 cents in April 1944; the rate on fortified wines changed thus: 1936, 10 cents; 1938, 15 cents; 1940, 18 cents; 1941, 30 cents; 1942, 40 cents; 1944, 60 cents. Fortified wines were a far more productive tax cow than were table wines, as the sixfold increase in the tax rate indicates.

54. S. W. Shear and R. E. Blair, *California Fruit Statistics and Related Data,* Bulletin 763 (Berkeley: University of California, College of Agriculture, Agricultural Experiment Station, 1958), table 5, p. 164. Some "raisin" grapes were unfit for raisins; some matured too late; and some, no doubt, were simply sold without regard to the order.

55. "Commenting on the News," *Wines and Vines* 23 (August 1942): 13.

56. James T. Lapsley, *Bottled Poetry: Napa Winemaking from Prohibition to the Modern Era* (Berkeley: University of California Press, 1996), p. 100.

57. *Wines and Vines* 24 (January 1943): 28 reported that the entire pool of prorate brandy had now been disposed of, the loans paid off, and the growers compensated, but this was not quite the case: see chapter 5, at n. 82.

58. *Wines and Vines* 24 (October 1943): 9. "No other major farm crop in the United States skyrocketed so much as did grapes for crushing" (Martin Lefcourt, "Should Prices Be Lower?" *Wine Review* 13 [September 1945]: 14). According to Charles Bonner, the temptations of high prices were irresistible to some raisin-grape growers, who were legally excluded from the market: "As the war continued, patriotism wore a little thin in certain areas. 'Wetting down' of good raisins to make them ferment and spoil was a well-known trick. By spoiling the raisins, it was then possible to sell them to a winery at a much higher price" (*A Rocky Road: The Pilgrimage of the Grape,* ed. John G. Taylor [Fresno: Pioneer Publishing, 1983], pp. 90–91).

59. It was, in fact, slightly larger: 2.5 million tons as opposed to 2.3 million in California. Outside California, the production averages for the same years are 207,000 tons in the war years as opposed to 203,000 in the three years before the war.

60. There was even some new development: Italian Swiss Colony made experimental plantings on 120 acres in the Anderson Valley in 1944 ("Swiss Colony Plants Vineyard," *Wines and Vines* 25 [March 1944]: 33). And new planting accelerated in 1945 and 1946.

61. The total wine production in the three years 1939–41 was 289,934,000 gallons; in the three years 1942–44, it was 233,556,000, a net decrease of about 56 million gallons.

62. U.S. Congress, Senate Judiciary Committee, *Liquor Industry: Hearings, 10, 16, 17 December 1943* (Washington, D.C.: GPO, 1944), p. 406. The original membership of the committee is listed in *Wine Review* 10 (April 1942): 9; it included bottlers and suppliers as well as winemakers from California, Ohio, and New York. For the eastern winemakers, the sup-

ply of sugar for amelioration was maintained: the member wineries of the Finger Lakes Wine Growers Association used 1,456,000 pounds in 1942 and 1,860,000 in 1943 (Finger Lakes Wine Growers Association file, box 1, Widmer papers, Cornell University, Kroch Library).

63. It was at this time that the fifth supplanted the quart as the standard bottle measure for wine, to the great resentment of the European-born clientele of the eastern bottlers ("On the New York Wine Front," *Wine Review* 12 [March 1944]: 66).

64. Giles B. Cooke, "Cork Culture in Arizona," *Wines and Vines* 24 (June 1943): 18–19. Six bottles of Beringer champagne were sealed with Napa Valley cork in 1943, a symbolic first that seems to have had no second ("Cork in California," *Wine Review* 11 [October 1943]: 32). In the next month restrictions on cork were removed ("Cork Situation," *Wine Review* 11 [November 1943]: 32). Nevertheless, it was stated that 150,000 cork oak trees were planted in California in the years 1941–45; a large distribution of cork oak acorns was also made in the Gulf states ("Cork Oak Program Launched in the South," *Wine Review* 13 [May 1945]: 22). The search for acorn supplies revealed the interesting fact that California already had more than 5,000 mature cork oaks (George Greenan, "Cork: California Trees Produce a Million Acorns," *Wine Review* 13 [July 1945]: 14).

65. *Wines and Vines* 23 (August 1942): 5, 13; 24 (June 1943): 28. For a description of the rules governing tank car use, see "Tank Cars," *Wine Review* 10 (November 1942): 5.

66. California had had a tartrate industry before Prohibition; Georges de Latour used the money he had made dealing in cream of tartar to found the Beaulieu Vineyard at the turn of the century. For wartime uses of tartrates, see H. A. Caddow, "War and the Wine Industry," *Wines and Vines* 23 (May 1942): 15–16. Some 2 million pounds of tartrates were recovered in 1942 (Wine Institute, "Brief Outline of Important Economic Developments in the California Wine Industry, 1942–1943," processed document [San Francisco: Wine Institute, September 1943).

67. "Why Move California's Stills to the East?" *Wines and Vines* 23 (May 1942): 18; "Interview with MacNamara," 25 (June 1944): 32. The Wine Institute estimated that about 20 percent of California's brandy distilling capacity was involved ("Brief Outline of Important Economic Developments"). The move probably wasn't necessary, but such ill-considered decisions were common enough in time of war and needed no conspiracy theory to explain them. By 1943 some of the stills left in California were producing industrial alcohol from Hawaiian molasses (ibid.), which ended up as antifreeze on the Russian front (Louis A. Petri, *The Petri Family in the Wine Industry,* interview by Ruth Teiser, Berkeley: Regional Oral History Office, Bancroft Library, University of California, 1971, p. 16).

68. "Worries in Wine," *Wines and Vines* 24 (May 1943): 8.

69. Robert M. La Follette Jr., "Never Prohibition Again," *Atlantic Monthly* 171 (January 1943): 37. Senator La Follette actively opposed all the attempts at Dry legislation.

70. Sheppard's bill was introduced in February 1941. It was resurrected by Senator Josh Lee of Oklahoma (Senator Sheppard having died in the meantime) as an amendment to the Draft Bill in October 1942, when it was sent back to committee (*New York Times,* 23 October 1942, 1).

71. It was introduced by Congressman Joseph Bryson of South Carolina in March 1943. A flood of petitions in support of the bill forced the House Judiciary Committee to give it

a hearing in January 1944, but the hearing lasted only a day and the bill was then buried in committee (*New York Times*, 3 December 1944, IV, 10). An editorial in the *New York Times* deplored the furor over the bill as a frivolous waste of time and money in wartime (6 January 1944, 22).

72. General Maximum Price Regulation, 11 May 1942. The price of grapes for raisins was fixed, as was that of grapes sold in interstate commerce. The latter condition meant that in effect no grapes left California.

73. Ray and Marinacci, *Vineyards in the Sky*, p. 298.

74. At the time of the 1943 vintage, for example, the highest price allowed for red table wine in bulk was 40 cents a gallon; but the same wine could be sold for $4.03 for a case of fifths, or the equivalent of $1.68 a gallon (*Wines and Vines* 24 [October 1943]: 11). The Wine Institute estimated that bulk shipments out of California in 1943 were less than 40 percent of the volume sold, half of the figure for the preceding year ("Brief Outline of Important Economic Developments").

75. Charles M. Crawford, *Recollections of a Career with the Gallo Winery and the Development of the California Wine Industry, 1942–1989*, interview by Ruth Teiser, Berkeley: Regional Oral History Office, Bancroft Library, University of California, 1990, p. 58.

76. "Mont La Salle and the Fine Wines of The Christian Brothers," *Wine Review* 7 (December 1939): 14. Alfred Fromm, *Marketing California Wine*, interview by Ruth Teiser, Berkeley: Regional Oral History Office, Bancroft Library, University of California, 1984, pp. 11–15.

77. "Picket California Wine in New York," *Wine Review* 7 (May 1939): 28; *New York Times*, 1 June 1939, 3.

78. Anonymous, "Safeguarding the Profit Margin," *Wine Review* 10 (August 1942): 12. The Wine Institute estimated that before the war 80 percent of California wine was shipped out in bulk. By the end of 1943 the figure was reversed: 80 percent of California wine was now shipped as "cased goods"—i.e., bottled ("From Bulk to Package Shipments," *Wine Review* 12 [June 1944]: 6). The figure may be too high, but a decisive turn had no doubt been made. According to a report in *Wines and Vines*, the bottling capacity of the big wineries more than doubled during the war years; at Petri, for example, the bottling line that handled 4,500 cases a day in 1941 handled 17,500 by 1945 ("Bulk Shipments to Increase," 26 [November 1945]: 15).

79. Irving H. Marcus, "Independent Bottler Faces Tough Times," *Wines and Vines* 27 (April 1946): 71.

80. See the summary of the OPA's effects in Irving Marcus, "Give the Devil His Due," *Wines and Vines* 27 (December 1946): 17. Herman Wente, speaking as president of the Wine Institute, acknowledged that wartime price controls had placed "a dollar-and-cents premium on quality wines in a more definite way than had been known before" ("Wine Moves Ahead!" *Wine Review* 14 [February 1946]: 9).

81. *New York Times*, 25 February 1943, 31.

82. *Wines and Vines* 24 (February 1943): 9.

83. *New York Times*, 2 April 1943, 29.

84. It was also said that some firms did not mind taking losses because their taxes were already so high (*Fruit Products Journal* 23 [December 1943]: 118).

85. Ibid.

86. As a release from the Wine Institute dated 21 July 1944 put it, the new terms for bulk wine "should result in increased sales of bulk wine and resumption of other peacetime production and marketing practices"—i.e., that the bottlers would be back in business (copy in the Widmer papers, Cornell University, Kroch Library).

87. *Wines and Vines* 25 (September 1944): 15. The new ceiling for bottled fortified wines was $5.81 a case, up from $4.82; for red wine, $4.27, up from $3.88; for white wine, $4.52, up from $3.99. Varietal wines were allowed higher prices under "special" pricing categories.

88. U.S. Tariff Commission, *Grapes and Grape Products,* p. 8.

89. Arvin Wine Company and California Products Company files, box 12, Widmer papers, Cornell University, Kroch Library). Custom crushing was made illegal before the 1944 crush.

90. "Ownership Changes," *Wines and Vines* 24 (May 1943): 7; "Garden Vineyards Purchased," 24 (June 1943): 28; "Larkmead Winery Changes Hands," 24 (August 1943): 28. The Larkmead transaction was a complicated one, but essentially it was meant to supply bulk wine to a bottler: see Lapsley, *Bottled Poetry,* pp. 123–24.

91. Gibson bought the Acampo Winery from Cesare Mondavi, who used the money to buy the Charles Krug Winery in Napa Valley in 1943 and so started the Mondavi family career in that region.

92. "Renault Buys Wineries," *Wines and Vines* 24 (February 1943): 19.

93. Harvey W. Martin, "Control of Guasti in New Hands," *Wines and Vines* 24 (September 1943): 12. The Italian Vineyard Company was sold again in early 1945, this time to Garrett and Company.

94. Prices were also driven down late in the season by rain in October; this damaged the raisin crop, part of which then went to the wineries for salvage (Felix Butte Jr., "The 1945 Grape Season," *Wines and Vines* 26 [December 1945]: 23).

95. The price of wine at retail reached its highest level in the early months of 1945, at approximately a dollar a fifth for standard table wines. Considering the greatly inflated prices that the wineries had paid for grapes, "the wonder is," Irving Marcus wrote, "that the war-time price of wine to the consumer was only approximately twice that of the last pre-war year" ("Wine Price Bugaboo," *Wines and Vines* 26 [November 1945]: 11).

96. An editorial in *Wines and Vines* urged the winemakers to avoid a price war and to trust in the strength of the market; at the same time it admitted that the outlook was thoroughly confusing (26 [August 1945]: 11). In November, in the face of continued drops in prices, *Wines and Vines* urged the trade not to panic but to hold prices "in proper relation to production cost" (26 [November 1945]: 11).

97. Quoted in "The Road Ahead," *Wine Review* 13 (August 1945): 25.

98. See, for example, Edmund A. Rossi, "The Coming Expansion of the Table Wine Market," *Wines and Vines* 25 (December 1944): 29.

99. M. F. K. Fisher, "Through a Glass Darkly," *Atlantic Monthly* 174 (November 1944): 109. I do not think her remark will bear analysis, but it testifies to a new optimism about American wine.

100. Frank Schoonmaker, "The Future of Quality Wine," *Wines and Vines* 26 (December 1945): 21, 37.

101. "Wine Institute Meeting," *Wine Review* 13 (March 1945): 30. This, of course, had been the whole burden of Maynard A. Amerine and A. J. Winkler's "Composition and Quality of Musts and Wines of California Grapes," *Hilgardia* 15 (February 1944): 493–673.

CHAPTER 7. POSTWAR DISAPPOINTMENTS

1. "Winery Construction in for Boom," *Wines and Vines* 26 (July 1945): 19.

2. Herman L. Wente, "Wine Moves Ahead!" *Wine Review* 14 (February 1946): 8. The writer of the speech was probably Leon D. Adams, who says that he wrote all the official public utterances of Wine Institute officials (*Revitalizing the California Wine Industry,* interview by Ruth Teiser, Berkeley: Regional Oral History Office, Bancroft Library, University of California, 1974, pp. 57, 80).

3. "Construction at Record Level," *Wines and Vines* 28 (January 1947): 16–17. In the next month *Wines and Vines* revised its estimate of new capacity upward to 50 million gallons (28 [February 1947]: 33).

4. *Wine Review* 14 (May 1946): 28; "Construction at Record Level," p. 17; *Wines and Vines* 28 (May 1947): 31. The Bisceglia winery had a capacity of 3 million gallons and planned for expansion to 10 million; the Liberty Winery had a million-gallon capacity; the Di Giorgio winery, supplied by 13,000 acres of company grapes, had a capacity of 9.5 million gallons.

5. "Sunnyside Winery Resumes 1944 Expansion Program," *Wine Review* 14 (February 1946): 32; "New Fresno Winery," *Wine Review* 15 (February 1947): 32.

6. "Fresno Activity Booms!" *Wine Review* 14 (November 1946): 26; "Construction at Record Level," p. 17.

7. These and yet more wonders are described in "Production Pattern at Di Giorgio Winery," *Wines and Vines* 32 (July 1951): 18–20. The Di Giorgio winery had some 50-gallon barrels for experiments in aging sherry, but they were unusual. The *smallest* cooperage at the new Del Rey winery, built in 1946, was two 5,000-gallon tanks (Barton Boni, "New Wineries Designed for Efficiency," *Wines and Vines* 28 [February 1947]: 34).

8. Quoted from "Production Pattern at Di Giorgio Winery," p. 20.

9. "Di Giorgio Presentation," *Wine Review* 13 (January 1945): 34.

10. When the Arvin civic center, where the Di Giorgio bust originally stood, was demolished and rebuilt, the bust was transferred to the Di Giorgio school, where it stood next to the school trophy case until 2000. In that year it was formally transferred to the new Agricultural Pavilion in Bakersfield. Then it disappeared. My efforts to trace its present whereabouts have been unsuccessful. The bust is, I think, a unique tribute to a California winemaker, even though Di Giorgio cared nothing about winemaking.

11. Quoted in Ruth Teiser and Catherine Harroun, *Winemaking in California* (New York: McGraw-Hill, 1983), p. 212.

12. Robert Di Giorgio and Joseph A. Di Giorgio, *The Di Giorgios: From Fruit Merchants to Corporate Innovators,* interview by Ruth Teiser, Berkeley: Regional Oral History Office, Bancroft Library, University of California, 1986, p. 132.

13. Horace O. Lanza, *California Grape Products and Other Wine Enterprises,* interview by

Ruth Teiser, Berkeley: Regional Oral History Office, Bancroft Library, University of California, 1971, p. 47, states that Di Giorgio did not drink wine.

14. Adams, *Revitalizing the California Wine Industry,* p. 70.

15. In all fairness to the Di Giorgio winery, one must note that its Angelica received an honorable mention in the wine judging at the California State Fair in 1948. Perhaps Louis M. Martini had something to do with that achievement. He had been hired during the war years to market Di Giorgio's wine: "In addition, he was really the expert who assisted our winemakers in producing quality wine" (Di Giorgio and Di Giorgio, *The Di Giorgios,* p. 149).

16. "Construction at Record Level," p. 16. On winery bottling, see chapter 6, after n. 74.

17. "St. George Makes Additions," *Wine Review* 14 (May 1946): 28; "Alta Vineyards Construction," *Wines and Vines* 27 (June 1946): 35, and 28 (January 1947): 17. The Guild plant made it possible for this union of different cooperative wineries to centralize and control blending, bottling, and distribution.

18. See the enumeration of new equipment purchased or on order in "Wineries Busy in Building and Buying," *Wines and Vines* 26 (September 1945): 17, 40.

19. "Vai Brothers Purchase Cucamonga Vineyard," *Wine Review* 13 (February 1945): 16; "Cribari and Sons Acquires New Gilroy Property," *Wine Review* 14 (March 1946): 28. Some of the Mira Loma property was in vines that went back to the late nineteenth century as part of the holdings of the Charles Stern and Sons Winery; Stern had been one of the pioneers of the California wine trade.

20. André Tchelistcheff, *Grapes, Wine, and Ecology,* interview by Ruth Teiser and Catherine Harroun, Berkeley: Regional Oral History Office, Bancroft Library, University of California, 1983, p. 73. Stelling was not alone in his commitment to superior varieties: see James T. Lapsley, *Bottled Poetry: Napa Winemaking from Prohibition to the Modern Era* (Berkeley: University of California Press, 1996), pp. 128–29.

21. "Cordelia Acquisition Announced by Butte," *Wine Review* 14 (February 1946): 34; "Eastern Acquires Waterford," *Wine Review* 14 (May 1946): 19, 28.

22. "I.V.C. to Garrett's," *Wine Review* 13 (April 1945): 50.

23. "Madera Vineyardists Organize First County Cooperative," *Wine Review* 14 (February 1946): 34; "Fresno Activity Booms!" p. 26; Irving H. Marcus, "New Coops Under Way," *Wines and Vines* 27 (February 1946): 16–17; "Yosemite Cooperative Winery," *Wines and Vines* 28 (May 1947): 27; Irving H. Marcus, "California's Cooperative Wineries," *Wines and Vines* 34 (March 1953): 10–11. In its first year of operation, the Del Rey Winery made 1 million gallons of muscat wines and 237,000 gallons of port and sherry ("Del Rey Crush Told," *Wine Review* 15 [May 1947]: 29). The Yosemite Cooperative made only fortified wines.

24. "Whether American consumers will continue this unusual preference for sweet wines or, as they again become better acquainted with wines, will revert to the more usual preference for table wines is an important question affecting the future consumption of grapes" (U.S. Tariff Commission, *Grapes and Grape Products,* War Changes in Industry Series Report 24 [Washington, D.C.: GPO, 1947], p. 34).

25. "Never before in the post-Repeal history of the California wine industry has wine flowed out of the wineries at such a rate as during the first third of this year" (Irving Marcus, "Record Crush Still Looms as Good Possibility," *Wines and Vines* 27 [July 1946]: 11).

26. Irving Marcus, "Independent Bottler Faces Tough Times," *Wines and Vines* 27 (April 1946): 23, 71; idem, "Bulk Dessert Wine," *Wines and Vines* 27 (September 1946): 19.

27. See the summaries of current research published in 1944 by W. V. Cruess on enology ("Wine and the Fruit Products Laboratory") and by A. J. Winkler on viticulture ("The Work of the Division of Viticulture"): *Wines and Vines* 25 (December 1944): 39–45. At Davis, all regular instruction was stopped and classes wholly given over to various military programs. Research work, however, continued with a much-diminished staff.

28. The work on varietal testing and rootstock resistance was aided by the university's acquisition of a twenty-acre vineyard at Oakville in Napa County to supplement the sites at Davis. The Napa property was part of the old To-Kalon vineyard, now owned by Martin Stelling ("Vineyard Station Started," *Wine Review* 15 [May 1947]: 29; C. B. Hutchison, "Viticultural and Enological Research Projects at the University," *Wines and Vines* 28 [December 1947]: 9).

29. *Wine Review* 11 (June 1943): 24; J. H. Freitag, N. W. Frazier, and W. B. Hewitt, "Pierce's Disease of Grapevines: Vectors, Hosts and Control," *Wine Review* 13 (February 1945): 18, 20, 22, 28. The Anaheim disease, also called the California vine disease, was not named Pierce's disease until 1941: the name acknowledges the work done by pathologist Newton B. Pierce in studying the original outbreak in the nineteenth century (M. W. Gardner and W. B. Hewitt, *Pierce's Disease of the Grapevine: The Anaheim Disease and the California Vine Disease* [Berkeley and Davis: University of California, Department of Plant Pathology, 1974], p. 166).

30. *Wines and Vines* 28 (December 1947): 33.

31. Pierce's disease is thought to be native to the southeastern United States, particularly the gulf coast, which is also the home of the only grape species known to show resistance to it, the native American *Vitis rotundifolia*. For the serious recurrence of Pierce's disease in California, see chapter 14, before n. 60.

32. *Wine Review* 14 (April 1946): 84. Plantings of grapes by the Horticulture Department at UCLA in 1929, when the university was founded, had succumbed to Pierce's disease within a few years, evidence that the disease so long established in the region was still virulent there. This experience suggested the idea of making experimental plantings there in 1946 to see what might survive (*Wine Review* 14 [July 1946]: 18). According to H. P. Olmo, the experimental plot at UCLA, at the corner of Sunset Boulevard and Veteran Avenue, was the "most expensive" piece of agricultural land in California (*Plant Genetics and New Grape Varieties*, interview by Ruth Teiser, Berkeley: Regional Oral History Office, Bancroft Library, University of California, 1976, p. 46).

33. Gardner and Hewitt, *Pierce's Disease*, p. 197. The bacterium is named *Xylella fastidiosa*.

34. The first class of enologists since before Prohibition graduated from the University of California, Berkeley, in 1940: its members were Charles Crawford, Ze'ev Halperin, Louis P. Martini, Myron Nightingale, and Aram Ohanesian, all of whom had notable careers in the industry.

35. Elbert M. Brown, "The TAC—Its History and Its Aims," *Wines and Vines* 32 (May 1951): 21. Louis Gomberg, then with the Wine Institute, says that it was on his initiative that the TAC was founded (*Analytical Perspectives on the California Wine Industry, 1935–1990*, interview by Ruth Teiser, Berkeley: Regional Oral History Office, Bancroft Library, Uni-

versity of California, 1990, p. 30). In 1951 the subcommittees of the TAC were devoted to such subjects as consumer taste preference, stillage disposal and winery sanitation, wine stability, wine tasting, wine type specifications, brandy quality, oxidation of white wines, and fining (Brown, "The TAC," p. 21). In Charles M. Crawford's version, the TAC grew out of an effort to gain professional respect for winemakers through the formation of a union; the Wine Institute then deflected the movement into the TAC (*Recollections of a Career with the Gallo Winery and the Development of the California Wine Industry, 1942–1989,* interview by Ruth Teiser, Berkeley: Regional Oral History Office, Bancroft Library, University of California, 1990, pp. 47–48). This is confirmed by Elie C. Skofis, *California Wine and Brandy Maker,* interview by Ruth Teiser, Berkeley: Regional Oral History Office, Bancroft Library, University of California, 1988, p. 50.

36. "Winemakers' Professional Group Formed: American Society of Enologists," *Wines and Vines* 31 (January 1950): 26. In 1984, in recognition of its expanded scope, the organization was renamed the American Society for Enology and Viticulture; in recognition of the differing regional conditions, there is an eastern section as well, holding its own meeting and publishing its own journal.

37. The first person in California, as far as I know, to call himself an enologist was the interesting figure of John Ignatius Bleasdale (1822–84), an English-born, Portuguese-trained Catholic priest of scientific leanings who had been a leader in the development and promotion of the Australian wine industry during his twenty-seven years' residence there. In 1878 he migrated to California, where he served as the first secretary of the State Board of Viticultural Commissioners. In his translation of Villa Maior's *The Viniculture of Claret* (San Francisco: Payot, Upham, 1884), Bleasdale identifies himself as an "Organic Chemist and Oenologist."

38. Edmund A. Rossi Jr., *Italian Swiss Colony, 1949–1989: Recollections of a Third-Generation California Winemaker,* interview by Ruth Teiser and Lisa Jacobson, Berkeley: Regional Oral History Office, Bancroft Library, University of California, 1990, p. 19.

39. Charles Holden, "Welcoming Remarks," *Proceedings of the American Society of Enologists* 1 (1950): 2.

40. Leon Adams states that the ASE was set up in competition with the TAC in order to establish an organization independent of the Wine Institute (*Revitalizing the California Wine Industry,* p. 126). For Maynard A. Amerine's views, see "The Professional Status of Enologists," *Wines and Vines* 40 (August 1959): 31, and idem, *The University of California and the State's Wine Industry,* interview by Ruth Teiser, Berkeley: Regional Oral History Office, Bancroft Library, University of California, 1972, pp. 28–29. The achievement of professional standing for enologists was a primary object of Amerine's work. The TAC came to an end in June 1973.

41. But it was perhaps not as advanced as was sometimes claimed—for example, by the writer who announced in 1946 that "technologically the California wine industry leads the world": the reason, he thought, was that at Repeal, since there were no old winemakers left to reimpose a tradition, "an entirely new generation of technically trained men came into the industry to run it as a science" (Walter S. Richert, "A Research Program for the Wine Industry," *Wines and Vines* 27 [September 1946]: 13). If only the process were so neat and simple.

42. Among the confusions about varietal identity, Chenin blanc was known for years after Repeal in the Napa Valley as White Pinot or Pineau de la Loire, and it was sometimes spoken of as White Zinfandel; Chardonnay was always called Pinot Chardonnay in California; and the grape called Gamay Beaujolais was in fact a clone of Pinot noir. There were other such confusions.

43. H. P. Olmo, "Introduction, Improvement and Certification of Healthy Grape Varieties," *Wines and Vines* 32 (July 1951): 9.

44. California Crop and Livestock Reporting Service, *California Fruit and Nut Crops 1908–1955,* Special Publication 261 (Sacramento: California Department of Agriculture and U.S. Department of Agriculture, 1956).

45. California Crop and Livestock Reporting Service, *Acreage Estimates, California Fruit and Nut Crops 1919–1953, by Counties,* Special Publication 275: Supplement (Sacramento: U.S. Department of Agriculture and California Department of Agriculture, 1956).

46. California Crop and Livestock Reporting Service, *Acreage Estimates, California Fruit and Nut Crops as of 1950* (Sacramento: U.S. Department of Agriculture and California Department of Agriculture, 1951), p. 23.

47. A. J. Winkler, "Grape Varieties and Vineyard Expansion," *Wine Review* 14 (April 1946): 72–78. Winkler gives these figures for the leading wine varieties in California in 1944 (bearing acreage): Zinfandel, 49,000 acres; Carignane, 31,000; Alicante Bouschet, 25,000; Mission, 10,000; Mataro, 7,600; Petite Sirah, 7,400; Palomino, 4,200. The only white varieties apart from Palomino to be listed were Burger, 2,600; Colombard, 1,400; and Sylvaner, 500.

48. To be precise, the 1951 total was 499,951 (California Crop and Livestock Reporting Service, *Acreage Estimates, California Fruit and Nut Crops 1919–1953,* p. 6).

49. A. J. Winkler, "Grapes for a Single Purpose," *Wines and Vines* 32 (April 1951): 67.

50. Philip M. Wagner, "California Thirty Years Ago," *Wine East* 9 (November 1981): 14.

51. "As if sugar point was the only factor in wine production," as Winkler remarked disgustedly ("Grapes for a Single Purpose," p. 68). The practice neglected all other quality considerations and might very well reward bad grapes. "The practice of paying a premium for grapes of over 22 Balling for producing table wines is fundamentally unsound. The raisined, rotten grapes (from some vineyards) which pass for Zinfandel should not be accepted by the wineries" (Maynard A. Amerine, "Wine Production Problems of California Grapes, Part III," *Wine Review* 17 [March 1949]: 11).

52. Maynard A. Amerine, "An Historical Note on Grape Prices," *Wines and Vines* 27 (October 1946): 28. The average prices paid per ton for grapes to be crushed for wine at the end of the 1950s were as follows: raisin grapes, $52; table grapes, $42; wine grapes, $51 (Ralph B. Hutchinson, "The California Wine Industry" [Ph.D. diss., University of California, Los Angeles, 1969], pp. 128–29).

53. James Lapsley sees this turn of things as the crisis in the fortunes of the Napa Valley (*Bottled Poetry,* pp. 130, 135).

54. Hutchinson, "The California Wine Industry," p. 110.

55. Eugene Seghesio, "Grape Growing in Sonoma County," *American Journal of Enology and Viticulture* 7 (April–June 1956): 77. The decline in Sonoma County was quite real. The vineyards had been stable at approximately 22,000 acres for many years but after the

war fell into a steady decline: from 22,000 acres in 1945 to 16,000 acres in 1950 and to a low of 11,000 in 1960 (Ernest Peninou, assisted by Gail G. Unzelman and Michael M. Anderson, *History of the Sonoma Viticultural Districts: The Grape Growers, the Wine Makers and the Vineyards,* History of the Viticultural Districts of California 1 [Santa Rosa, Calif.: Nomis Press, 1998], p. 48). A comparable decline occurred in Napa County, where acreage fell to a low point of 9,623 in 1960 (Lapsley, *Bottled Poetry,* p. 176).

56. H. P. Olmo, "Breeding New Wine Grape Varieties," *Wine Review* 18 (February 1950): 8. New plantings of wine grapes were being made in California but not at the same rate as those of raisin grapes: in consequence, the bearing acreage of wine grapes fell from 33 percent of all grapes in 1946 to 27 percent in 1965 (Hutchinson, "The California Wine Industry," p. 88).

57. See Olmo's arguments for combining "good yield with high quality" in "Wine Grape Varieties of the Future," *Proceedings of the American Society of Enologists* 3 (1952): 45; idem, "Our Principal Wine Grape Varieties Present and Future," *American Journal of Enology and Viticulture* 5 (1954): 20.

58. See California Crop and Livestock Reporting Service, *California Grape Acreage* (Sacramento: annual), for the relevant years.

59. The acreage in 2003 for Ruby Cabernet is 7,472.

60. Charles L. Sullivan, *Napa Wine: A History from Mission Days to the Present* (San Francisco: Wine Appreciation Guild, 1994), p. 247.

61. Maynard A. Amerine, "Wine Production Problems of California Grapes, Part I," *Wine Review* 17 (January 1949): 18–20. A. J. Winkler gave a detailed analysis of the effects of overcropping: delayed maturity of the crop, low-acid grapes, reduced vine growth, irregular production, and consequent disruption of prices. The practice he attributed to the war years, "when anything resembling a grape could be sold at a profit." The solution was to impose quality standards at the wineries ("Effects of Overcropping," *American Journal of Enology and Viticulture* 5 [1954]: 4–12).

62. Amerine, "Wine Production Problems of California Grapes, Part I," p. 22; idem, "Wine Production Problems of California Grapes, Part II," *Wine Review* 17 (February 1949): 10; idem, "Wine Production Problems of California Grapes, Part III," p. 11.

63. Maynard A. Amerine, "Wine Production Problems of California Grapes, Part VI," *Wine Review* 17 (July 1949): 19.

64. Maynard A. Amerine, "The Response of Wine to Aging, Part IV: The Influence of Variety," *Wines and Vines* 31 (May 1950): 30.

65. Ibid. In 1939 Martin Ray wrote that according to a survey of the industry made by the bottle manufacturers, no winemaker in California aged wines in bottle for more than five months, and even that was an exceptional practice. Probably the practice had not much changed in the intervening ten years (Martin Ray to Julian Street, 18 December 1939, Julian Street papers, Princeton University, Firestone Library).

66. Wagner, "California Thirty Years Ago," pp. 12–13.

67. Ibid.

68. To Martin and Eleanor Ray, 12 February 1953, Martin Ray papers, box 6, University of California, Davis, Shields Library. Philip Wagner recalled of a visit to California in 1949 that "there were surprisingly few students at Davis. The Davis faculty was out beating

the bushes for competent, superior people to enter this industry, they were so dubious about the future of the industry" ("Keynoter Philip Wagner," *American Wine Society Journal* 18 [Winter 1986]: 125).

69. See the informed discussion of this subject in Sullivan, *Napa Wine*, pp. 241–45.

70. A hoary, and rueful, joke among winemakers runs: "If you want to make a small fortune in the wine business, start with a large one."

71. There are many other, and more hostile, epithets to be found in the accounts of Ray, of which *rascal* and *scamp* are mild instances. See Roy Brady, "Martin Ray," in *The Brady Book: Selections from Roy Brady's Unpublished Writings on Wine*, ed. Thomas Pinney (Santa Rosa: Nomis Press, 2003), pp. 68–76.

72. See the detailed account of vineyard and winery practices at Paul Masson under Martin Ray in John J. Besone, "Wine Making Traditions Survive at Paul Masson," *Wine Review* 9 (April 1941): 8–11. Besone, a graduate in enology from Berkeley, was employed at Masson.

73. "Not in the accustomed one dollar to two dollar price range, but bottles at four dollars and up"—and this in 1939 (Eleanor Ray and Barbara Marinacci, *Vineyards in the Sky: The Life of Legendary Vintner Martin Ray* [Stockton, Calif.: Heritage West Books, 1993], p. 223). Ray's table wines went to market in champagne bottles because, he claimed, no other bottle available in California had a neck interior straight enough to hold a two-inch cork tightly. He sold his wines in a variety of ways, all calculated to enhance the idea of scarcity: one method was the futures system, 50 percent payment in advance and delivery several years later; see Charles L. Sullivan, *Like Modern Edens: Winegrowing in Santa Clara Valley and Santa Cruz Mountains, 1798–1981*, Local History Studies 28 (Cupertino, Calif.: California History Center, 1982), p. 141.

74. Ray to Julian Street, 12 February 1940, Julian Street papers, Princeton University, Firestone Library.

75. Ray and Marinacci, *Vineyards in the Sky*, p. 210. The figure is fantastic, but that it should be set down as historical truth suggests the larger-than-life impression that Martin Ray made. He certainly knew good wine. In 1940 he wrote to Bellows and Company, the New York importers, asking them to find him Romanée-Conti '34, Richebourg '34, Haut-Brion '29, Yquem '28, and Johannisberger '21, among many other wines of comparable quality (list in Julian Street papers, Princeton University, Firestone Library).

76. Ray to Julian Street, 15 January 1940, Julian Street papers, Princeton University, Firestone Library.

77. The state of California had built a home for delinquent women on the property in the 1920s but was now getting rid of it. Only a single, overgrown acre of Zinfandel vines survived from Haraszthy's vineyards, and these the Bartholomews did not know about until some time after their purchase (Frank H. Bartholomew, *Bart: Memoirs of Frank H. Bartholomew* [Sonoma, Calif.: Vine Brook Press, 1983], pp. 113–15).

78. According to Frank Bartholomew, it was A. J. Winkler, of the University of California, Davis, who first identified their new property with Haraszthy's Buena Vista and encouraged the idea of restoring it to winegrowing (Bartholomew, *Bart*, pp. 114–15). This casts doubt on Leon D. Adams's claim to have provided this information first (*The Wines of America* [Boston: Houghton Mifflin, 1973], p. 186).

79. Bartholomew, *Bart,* pp. 117–18; see also idem, "'These Are Amiable Wines, Made by Amiable Men,'" *Wines and Vines* 60 (January 1979): 44–45.

80. "The Almaden Vineyards," *Wines and Vines* 22 (December 1941): 14, identifies Frank Schoonmaker and Company as holding the "majority interest" in Almadén; *Wine Review* 10 (February 1942): 17 says that the "head of Almaden Wines, Ltd., is Frank Schoonmaker and Co., Inc." After Schoonmaker went into the army the affairs of Frank Schoonmaker and Company fell into disarray and Schoonmaker's Almadén stock, some 348 shares of a total 795, was bought back by Benoist (Widmer papers, Schoonmaker and Company file, box 11, Cornell University, Kroch Library). Schoonmaker apparently did not have a financial interest in Almadén thereafter but was active as a consultant to the firm after the war.

81. Sullivan, *Like Modern Edens,* p. 146. "Nobody knew what a rosé was until Frank Schoonmaker mentioned it to Louis Benoist one year when there was a terrific surplus of Grenache. Grenache clicked in Frank's mind, and he said, 'Well, why not make a Grenache rosé?' And Louis Benoist asked, 'What is a rosé?' That's what the wine industry was like then. Nobody really knew what a rosé was" (Wagner, "California Thirty Years Ago," p. 14).

82. The new Krug varietal wines were not ready for market until 1947 (Lapsley, *Bottled Poetry,* p. 189).

83. Eleanor McCrea, *Stony Hill Vineyards: The Creation of a Napa Valley Estate Winery,* interview by Lisa Jacobson, Berkeley: Regional Oral History Office, Bancroft Library, University of California, 1990.

84. George Remington, "The Sherries and Ports of Solera Cellars," *Wines and Vines* 29 (November 1948): 54.

85. The Ficklins did make much-admired table wines from Ruby Cabernet and Emerald Riesling vines, but they were for sale only at the winery (Adams, *The Wines of America,* p. 317).

86. Mayacamas, Stony Hill, Souverain (now Burgess), and Ficklin are still flourishing. Hallcrest has been revived (1989) by John Schumacher.

87. Eleanor McCrea, "Insider's Story of Stony Hill," *Wines and Vines* 63 (November 1982): 52; reprinted from *Napa Valley Wine Library Association Report.*

88. "Premium Wine Program Under Way," *Wines and Vines* 30 (May 1949): 14. For further discussion of this movement and its successors, see chapter 9, after n. 108.

89. "Fireworks in Fresno," *Wines and Vines* 30 (June 1949): 7.

90. Mark Holliday, "California's Premium Wines," *Wine Review* 17 (September 1949): 6. James Lapsley puts the proportion of premium wine in California for the thirty years after Repeal at 1 percent (*Bottled Poetry,* p. xv).

91. S. W. Shear and R. E. Blair, *California Fruit Statistics and Related Data,* Bulletin 763 (Berkeley: University of California, College of Agriculture, Agricultural Experiment Station, 1958). The second-largest crush had been only the year before: 1,170,000 tons in 1945, almost half a million tons less than in 1946. The wine produced in California in 1946 totaled 152 million gallons.

92. "Wine Price Headache Continues," *Wines and Vines* 28 (March 1947): 13. On the eve of the vintage, Harry Caddow, secretary and manager of the Wine Institute, reported that

inventories were not adequate to meet current demands, and that the grape crop might not be as large as the preceding year's ("Wine Industry in Strong Position," *Wine Review* 14 [July 1946]: 14).

93. Skofis, *California Wine and Brandy Maker*, p. 15, says that at the Italian Swiss Colony plant in Clovis, "we crushed ten thousand tons of Emperors into dessert wine at $115 a ton!" Roma, he adds, "contracted with many of the wineries in the area to make wine for them at two dollars a gallon. Two dollars a gallon for dessert wine!"

94. John B. Cella II, *The Cella Family in the California Wine Industry,* interview by Ruth Teiser, Berkeley: Regional Oral History Office, Bancroft Library, University of California, 1986, p. 36. Louis A. Petri recalled that Schenley and National Distillers had losses of $11 million and $9 million, though he did not remember which firm had what figure (*The Petri Family in the Wine Industry,* interview by Ruth Teiser, Berkeley: Regional Oral History Office, Bancroft Library, University of California, 1971, p. 22). Ernest Gallo took the prudent course of declining to compete in the rush to buy grapes but instead sold most of his inventory of bulk wine at the moment of highest prices (Crawford, *Recollections of a Career with the Gallo Winery,* pp. 61–62).

95. "Statistical Review 1946," *Wines and Vines* 28 (April 1947): 51. All of this bounty reflects the expansiveness of the postwar boom stimulated by the government's inflationary policy.

96. Louis Gomberg, "Gomberg Sees Long Range Wine Grape Surplus Program," *California Grape Grower* (December 1973): 35. The collapse was not confined to California. In the Finger Lakes region of New York, Marvin Sands entered the wine business after the war by contracting for half a million gallons of wine to be paid for at the current rate of $1.60 a gallon. Prices then dropped as low as 25 cents a gallon. The note Sands had signed took eight years to pay off instead of the two originally stipulated (Hudson Cattell, "Wine as Commitment at Canandaigua," *Wine East* 9 [March–April 1982]: 8).

97. "The Brighter Side," *Wines and Vines* 28 (April 1947): 31; Leon D. Adams, *California Wine Industry Affairs: Recollections and Opinions,* interview by Ruth Teiser, Berkeley: Regional Oral History Office, Bancroft Library, University of California, 1990, p. 23; Myron S. Nightingale, *Making Wine in California, 1944–1987,* interview by Ruth Teiser and Lisa Jacobson, Berkeley: Regional Oral History Office, Bancroft Library, University of California, 1998, pp. 20, 27; Skofis, *California Wine and Brandy Maker,* p. 11; Ernest Gallo and Julio Gallo, *Ernest and Julio: Our Story* (New York: Times Books, 1994), p. 144.

98. Harry Baccigaluppi, "The Outlook for Wine," *Wines and Vines* 28 (April 1947): 33.

99. See "Producers Least Affected by Slump," *Wines and Vines* 28 (September 1947): 6. But no one was immune. The Charles Krug Winery lost $370,000 when eastern distributors broke their contracts for bulk wine (Jay Stuller and Glen Martin, *Through the Grapevine* [New York: Wynwood Press, 1989], p. 242). Harold Berg, then at Cresta Blanca, recalled that their shipments "went from 180,000 cases a month to from 3,000 to 5,000 cases—in six months' time" ("'Hod' Berg Wins A.S.E. Merit Award," *Wines and Vines* 55 [March 1974]: 18).

100. John B. Cella II recalled that Schenley in 1946 had paid "$1.25, $1.50, any price. Which at that time was a tremendous price" (*The Cella Family in the California Wine Industry,*

p. 36). *Wine Review* 16 (February 1948): 8 reported that table wine sold as low as 28 cents a gallon, dessert wine for 38 to 40 cents at the end of 1947. A brief prepared by the wine and spirits trade for the House Committee on Ways and Means estimated that the loss on wine inventory owing to declining prices was over $70 million (file copy dated 20 April 1948, Wine Institute Library). See also Harry Baccigaluppi, *California Grape Products and Other Wine Enterprises: Part II,* interview by Ruth Teiser, Berkeley: Regional Oral History Office, Bancroft Library, University of California, 1971, p. 100, recording the fall of bulk wine prices from $1.40 to 50 cents at the beginning of 1947.

101. Brother John's offer to Widmer would also be in violation of The Christian Brothers' contract with their distributor, Fromm and Sichel, which enjoined the company from shipping in bulk or bottling under another label (Ed Everett, "The Christian Brothers New Focus," *Wines and Vines* 62 [February 1981]: 55).

102. Brother John to Will Widmer, 7 August 1947 (Widmer papers, C file, box 10, Cornell University, Kroch Library). Widmer declined the offer, saying that his cellar was full.

103. "Grape Crop Developments and the Wine Market," *Wine Review* 15 (July 1947): 9.

104. On Kearney, see "Cooperative Winery Incorporated," *Wines and Vines* 28 (September 1947): 42.

105. The California statistics for 1947 are these: grape crop, 2,836,000 tons; tonnage crushed, 966,000 tons; wine produced, 94,522,000 gallons: "Statistical Survey of 1948," *Wines and Vines* 30 (April 1949): 27.

106. Shear and Blair, *California Fruit Statistics and Related Data.* In 1946, 747,000 tons of a total of 1,644,000 tons of raisin grapes had been crushed for wine; in 1947, only 319,000 of a total of 1,699,000 tons. The production of raisins rose from 772,000 tons in 1946 to 1,224,000 tons in 1947, an increase almost exactly balancing the decrease in the quantity used by the wineries.

107. "The Grape Crop and the 1947 Wine Market," *Wine Review* 15 (June 1947): 11. The same editorial declared that the situation was "a grape-grower problem. Further, it is a raisin-variety problem, not one involving wine-type grapes." See also *Wines and Vines* 28 (July 1947): 11.

108. Charles Crawford says that this was proposed to the Wine Institute by the TAC (*Recollections of a Career with the Gallo Winery,* p. 35).

109. Louis Viney, letter to the editor, *Wines and Vines* 28 (May 1947): 6. A memo dated 26 June 1947 by Louis Gomberg in the files of the Wine Institute summarizes some of the proposals about how to meet the crisis, including asking "all the grocery stores, hotels, restaurants, railroads, etc., to give away surplus Thompsons in a grand, national gesture to help out the grape growers."

110. "Raisin Group Proved Right," *Wines and Vines* 28 (November 1947): 9. The Commodity Credit Corporation bought 120,000 tons of raisins and shipped them to Germany.

111. Harry A. Caddow, "The Present Wine Market," *Wine Review* 15 (October 1947): 11, 24.

112. The inventory of California wine went down by 13 million gallons, and shipments went up by 7 million gallons (Shear and Blair, *California Fruit Statistics and Related Data,* table 16).

113. Raisin grapes made up 575,000 tons of the whole crush; there were 107 million gallons of fortified wine to 22 million of table wine: Shear and Blair, *California Fruit Sta-*

tistics and Related Data, tables 4, 5, 16. In the next year, as the ratio rose even higher, *Wines and Vines* speculated about the causes of the anomalous American preference for fortified wines but found no answer. The article concluded that table wines would probably never take the lead in this country ("The Dessert Wine Boom," *Wines and Vines* 30 [December 1949]: 12).

114. See "Raisin Marketing Program Asked," *Wines and Vines* 29 (April 1948): 15, 39; "Wine Marketing Program Moves ahead Rapidly," *Wines and Vines* 29 (May 1948): 9; "The Inventory of Hope," *Wines and Vines* 30(January 1949): 8; John A. Margolis, "Grapes Need a Holiday for Stability of California Grape and Wine Industry," *Wine Review* 16 (September 1948): 6–7, 29; Marketing Order Files, Wine Institute Library.

115. "The Inventory of Hope," p. 8. It got even worse before it got better: "As low as 30 cents per gallon" was reported for some bulk dessert wine in August and September 1949, before the short harvest changed things (*Wines and Vines* 30 [December 1949]: 11).

116. General John R. Deane, "A Newcomer's Impression of the Wine Industry," speech at National Wine Week Banquet, Fresno, 11 October 1949, copy in the Wine Institute Library. The average price for grapes in 1949 was $33 a ton.

117. "Big League Stuff," *Wines and Vines* 30 (October 1949): 3. As the names suggest, these wines were aimed at what was imagined to be a woman's market.

118. *Wines and Vines* 31 (April 1950): 34. In 1949 Philip Wagner, on his first visit to California, to serve as a wine judge at the state fair in Sacramento, recalled being driven to Sacramento by Leon Adams: "Our entire conversation from San Francisco to Sacramento had to do with, believe it or not, the horrible and dangerous surplus of grapes existing in California at that time" ("Keynoter Philip Wagner," p. 125).

119. Ralph Hutchinson calls this "the most complex order in the history of the wine industry" ("The California Wine Industry," p. 220). The scheme allowed a winery to sell between 30 June 1949 and the end of February 1950 only a quantity of wine equal to its inventory on 30 June. For the remaining four months of the fiscal year it could sell without limit: "Marketing Order Likely," *Wines and Vines* 30 (March 1949): 9; 30 (June 1949): 6. It is hard to see how such a scheme would produce orderly marketing.

120. "Proposed Fair Trade Regulations," *Wine Review* 16 (November 1948): 8–9, 30–32; "Fair Trade Bill for Wine," *Wine Review* 17 (June 1949): 5.

121. Walter S. Richert, "$3,000,000: How Should It Be Spent?" *Wines and Vines* 30 (November 1949): 11. Louis Gomberg called the plan a "half-baked effort to create a fund of money during normal conditions and times, so that when adverse conditions and times occurred growers could be paid from this grape stabilization fund" (*Analytical Perspectives on the California Wine Industry,* p. 64). Gomberg's summary is not quite accurate: the stated purpose of the fund was to buy up any surpluses in order to dispose of them via "non-competitive channels" ("New Marketing Order in Vintners' Hands," *Wines and Vines* 30 [August 1949]: 13). What such channels might be is discussed in "Report on Conference with Alcohol Tax Unit on Removal of Surplus Wine—Tax Free," 26 September 1949 (copy in the Wine Institute Library). The possible methods of handling the surplus include "dumping as is," dumping after dilution with water, distilling, export, or denaturing by boiling. In the event, no action was taken, and the money raised by assessment was returned to those who had paid it.

122. Additionally, in 1949 a raisin marketing order was issued, providing for the diversion of some 90,000 tons of raisins.

123. The leading fortified wine types in 1949 were, as they had been since Repeal, the following, listed in order of their importance with each type's percentage of the total production in parentheses: port (31.30 percent); sherry (21.11 percent); muscatel (18.30 percent); angelica (10.77 percent); white port (8.74 percent); and tokay (2.23 percent). Muscatel had slipped a bit in consequence of having been ruled a varietal rather than a generic wine. This ruling meant that at least 51 percent of the wine had to be from muscat grapes, and the muscat crop was short in 1949 ("Wine Types," *Wines and Vines* 31 [April 1950]: 41).

CHAPTER 8. BACK EAST

1. Robert Schick, "The Arkansas Wine Industry," *Wine Review* 14 (June 1946): 8.

2. See the summary of eastern wine history in chapter 3, "The Eastern Scene."

3. There were small plantings of vinifera grapes in Washington State, but the potentialities of this fact had hardly yet been grasped. There were also small plantings of vinifera in New Mexico.

4. For an eloquent presentation of the difficulties under which eastern winegrowing is carried on, see Philip M. Wagner, "Grapes and Wine Production in the East," in *Wine Production Technology in the United States*, ed. Maynard A. Amerine (Washington, D.C.: American Chemical Society, 1981), pp. 192–224.

5. I am describing the practice after Repeal; the rack-and-cloth press is now a thing of the past.

6. According to W. V. Cruess, heating the juice to extract color and fermenting off the skins were practiced for red wine in North Africa and "in California at one time" (*The Principles and Practice of Wine Making* [New York: Avi Publishing, 1934], pp. 69–70).

7. Perhaps it would be more precise to say "prefers to" rather than "must." According to Harvey W. Wiley, the first head of the Food and Drug Administration, eastern winemakers could make better wines without added sugar and water than with those things added; his attempt in 1909–10 to establish an official definition of wine that excluded the addition of sugar and water was defeated by the protests of the winemakers (*Beverages and Their Adulteration* [Philadelphia: P. Blakiston's Son, 1919], pp. 191, 252–53).

8. See the official provisions regulating these practices in U.S. Department of the Treasury, Alcohol and Tobacco Tax and Trade Bureau, "Wine," *Code of Federal Regulations, Title 27, Part 1, Chapter 1*, 2004 rev. (Washington, D.C.: GPO, 2004).

9. The origin of the term is not known: see appendix A in Thomas Pinney, *A History of Wine in America: From the Beginnings to Prohibition* (Berkeley: University of California Press, 1989).

10. Eastern grapes do not have a sufficient sugar content to make raisins, nor does the country east of the Rockies have a sufficiently dry summer to produce a raisin, even supposing the grapes were of the right kind.

11. The figures for the production of grapes and wine are drawn from the annual reports

of the Internal Revenue Service and the annual *Agricultural Statistics* of the U.S. Department of Agriculture.

12. A hybrid is properly a cross between two different species, an "interspecific" cross. A cross between two varieties of the same species is not a hybrid, but is usually spoken of as a cross.

13. Greyton H. Taylor, "New York Wines: Their Place in the Market," *Wines and Vines* 35 (November 1954): 29.

14. The winemaker at Gold Seal Winery, for example, candidly told the TAC that "it is clear that there is a definite need for new varieties in the East" (Alexander Brailow, "New York—Finger Lakes Region Champagne," *Wines and Vines* 33 [October 1952]: 13).

15. "Cross Native and European Grapes," *Fruit Products Journal* 18 (September 1939): 22. It should be said that the New York breeding program was mostly directed toward developing varieties for use as table or juice grapes. Not until 1964 did wine varieties get priority, when grants from state and industry supported a program for research on wine grapes (P. J. Chapman and E. H. Glass, *The First Hundred Years of the New York State Agricultural Experiment Station at Geneva, N.Y.* [Geneva: New York State Agricultural Experiment Station, 1999], pp. 134–35).

16. The varietal chart published by *Wines and Vines* 83 (December 2002) showed 28 wineries still producing Catawba, 14 producing Delaware, 5 producing Diamond, and 2 producing Ives.

17. Philip M. Wagner, *A Wine-Grower's Guide* (New York: Knopf, 1945), p. 207.

18. See Jancis Robinson, *Vines, Grapes and Wines: The Wine Drinker's Guide to Grape Varieties* (London: Mitchell Beazley, 1986), p. 262; the popularity of the hybrid in Japan is, she writes, "something of a mystery."

19. Fresh grape juice, which depends on pasteurization for its preservation, was commercially developed by a teetotal Methodist dentist in New Jersey named Thomas Welch, beginning in 1869.

20. See Frank Schoonmaker and Tom Marvel, *American Wines* (New York: Duell, Sloan & Pearce, 1941), pp. 162–67, for a litany of imaginary American wines—Wiscasset, Chicopee, Cape, Housatonic, Pocomoke, and so on.

21. From U.S. Department of the Treasury, *Report of the Commissioner of Internal Revenue* (Washington, D.C.: GPO, annual).

22. R. D. Anthony, "Vinifera Grapes in New York," Bulletin 432 (Geneva: New York Agricultural Experiment Station, 1915). Some of the vines from the 1902 plantings were still alive in 1960 (Keith H. Kimball, "Another Look at Vinifera in the East," *Wines and Vines* 42 [April 1961]: 63).

23. J. R. Magness and I. W. Dix, "Vinifera Grapes in the East," mimeographed report (Washington, D.C.: U.S. Department of Agriculture, March 1934). The USDA collection was mostly of table grapes but included Zinfandel, Cinsaut, Valdepeñas, Chasselas, and Blauer Portugieser.

24. Tressler (1894–1981) later was president of Avi Publishing, which specializes in books on food processing technology; his list included some important books on winemaking.

25. Charles M. Crawford, who was later in charge of winemaking for Gallo, helped to install the Tressler process in New York state wineries in 1940; he recalled that the process

made a "good, very nutty" sherry (*Recollections of a Career with the Gallo Winery and the Development of the California Wine Industry, 1942–1989*, interview by Ruth Teiser, Berkeley: Regional Oral History Office, Bancroft Library, University of California, 1990, p. 15). Maynard A. Amerine and Vernon Singleton refer to the process as an "old French treatment" (*Wine: An Introduction for Americans* [Berkeley: University of California Press, 1965], p. 271).

26. Philip M. Wagner, "Eastern Wine-Growing: Problems and Prospects," *Pennsylvania Grape Letter and Wine News* 6 (February 1979): 1.

27. A number of these bonded wineries were in fact the premises of California producers that had bottling and warehousing facilities around New York City, or of eastern bottlers that held winery licenses: Bisceglia Brothers, the Eastern Wine Corporation, and Garrett and Company, among others, all held New York winery licenses in 1949, though they made no wine there.

28. Olan D. Forker and Bennett A. Dominick Jr., *Toward the Year 1985: Fruit Production and Utilization*, Special Cornell Series 7 (Ithaca: New York State College of Agriculture, 1969), table A-1.

29. See the account of New York practices before the 1950s in Seaton C. Mendall, "The Man Who Made It Happen: 1.5–4.5 T/A," *Eastern Grape Grower and Winery News* 5 (February 1979): 12–13.

30. Berton Roueché, "Breathing through the Wood," *New Yorker* 23 (29 November 1947): 72–87. Although the Bolognesi family sold it in 1970, the Hudson Valley Wine Company persisted into the 1990s.

31. Based on the figures for 1946; by 1949 the figure was up to about 4.5 million.

32. Summarized from U.S. Department of the Treasury, *Report of the Commissioner of Internal Revenue*, for the years in question. The number of sparkling-wine producers is somewhat inflated by the inclusion in the federal statistics of bonded storerooms and field warehouses as well as wineries. Figures in *Wines and Vines* 30 (September 1949): 42 give an average production between 1940 and 1948 of about 450,000 gallons for California and 607,000 for New York.

33. "Minutes of a Meeting of the Eastern Wine Industry," 20 July 1936, typescript, box 5, Widmer papers, Cornell University, Kroch Library.

34. "Wine Conference of America," *Wines and Vines* 28 (March 1947): 22.

35. Wine Institute, "The First Twenty Years of the Wine Institute: A Report to Members at the Twentieth Annual Meeting" (San Francisco: Wine Institute, 8–9 March 1954), p. 8. Jefferson E. Peyser says that the conference was "allowed to die" when it was "infiltrated" by wholesalers, importers, and others so that "it just got to be something that wasn't what we wanted it to be" (*The Law and the California Wine Industry*, interview by Ruth Teiser, Berkeley: Regional Oral History Office, Bancroft Library, University of California, 1974, p. 28).

36. Scott Clemens, "Making Premium Kosher Wine," *Practical Winery and Vineyard* 16 (March–April 1996): 6.

37. A way exists around the strict requirement that only a Sabbath-observant Jew can handle a wine that is to be kosher. If the must is pasteurized, it is regarded as *mevushal* ("cooked"); it, and the wine made from it, may then be handled by anyone as long as

the rabbinical staff oversees the various steps of production. Such wine may also be served by anyone and remain kosher, which is not true for non-*mevushal* wines (ibid., pp. 8–9).

38. J. Myron Bay, quoted in John Hutchinson, "Sacramental and Kosher Wines: An Industry Godsend in More Ways Than One," *Wines and Vines* 57 (September 1976): 20.

39. Clemens, "Making Premium Kosher Wine," p. 5.

40. "Kosher Wine Only," *Wines and Vines* 26 (July 1945): 23. Monarch sold the property to Roma in 1950, which sold it in turn to the Eastern Wine Corporation ("Roma Buys Monarch Wine Company of California," *Wines and Vines* 31 [March 1950]: 30; "Martin Lefcourt Buys Monarch," *Wines and Vines* 31 [May 1950]: 34).

41. "Mogen David Is Moving," *Wines and Vines* 51 (November 1970): 32.

42. "Milwaukee Popularity Poll," *Wines and Vines* 30 (May 1949): 7; "The Case for Mogen David," *Wines and Vines* 33 (July 1952): 11.

43. William Chazanof, *Welch's Grape Juice: From Corporation to Co-operative* (Syracuse, N.Y.: Syracuse University Press, 1977), pp. 248–49.

44. The major wineries in the first years after the war were Dorn, Engels and Krudwig, Hommel, and Sweet Valley in Sandusky, and Meier's in Silverton.

45. Susan Sifritt, "The Ohio Wine and Grape Industries" (Ph.D. diss., Kent State University, 1976), pp. 219–23.

46. Ibid., p. 225. William Steuk, who operated a very small winery near Sandusky, began experimenting with French hybrid vines after the war, but not on a scale to affect the industry in the state generally (Henry Sonneman, "Ohio State Wines," *Proceedings of the American Society of Enologists* 3 [1952]: 20).

47. F. W. Fabian, "Michigan," *Wine Review* 11 (August 1943): 54. Edwin Haynes remembered that when, about 1960–62, he tried to interest growers in Michigan in the French hybrids, no one responded: "All they wanted to grow was Concords and Niagaras" ("45 Years in Wine," *Wine East* 11 [September–October 1983]: 26).

48. One—the St. Julian Wine Company of Paw Paw—went back to 1921, but as a Canadian enterprise, one of the four wineries set up at Windsor, across the river from Detroit, in order to use Michigan grapes: see Leon D. Adams, *The Wines of America* (Boston: Houghton Mifflin, 1973), p. 156.

49. Fabian, "Michigan," p. 55.

50. Ibid., pp. 54–56.

51. W. C. Geagley, "Michigan Wine Industry," *Wine and Liquor Retailer* (September 1940): 3; Adams, *The Wines of America*, p. 156. Adams attributes Geagley's ideas about 16 percent wine to the influence of Dr. Harvey Wiley, first head of the Food and Drug Administration (*Revitalizing the California Wine Industry*, interview by Ruth Teiser, Berkeley: Regional Oral History Office, Bancroft Library, University of California, 1974, p. 98). That may well be: Circular 13 of the Food and Drug Administration, dated 20 December 1904, defines wine as containing "not less than seven (7) nor more than sixteen (16) per cent of alcohol by volume." It is more than likely that Geagley found his formula there. But why did he set his standard for the alcoholic content of wine at the high end? That figure is roughly the upper limit of alcohol that can be produced by unaided

fermentation before the yeast are killed. But no Concord grape can come close to such a level, and all that Geagley had in mind was the Concord grape.

52. William Geagley, "Let's Extol Michigan Wines," *Michigan Beverage Man* (April 1961): 13. One can only wonder whether this extraordinary idea expressed a genuine delusion or was a conscious untruth.

53. Geagley, "Michigan Wine Industry," p. 5.

54. The list of wine types in Michigan Department of Economic Development, "A Report on the Michigan Wine Industry" (manuscript; Lansing, 1949, copy in the Wine Institute Library), is as follows: port, sherry, tokay, muscatel, blackberry, cherry, American Red, American White, and sauterne. Blackberry and cherry indicate Michigan's status as a fruit-growing state; "American" wines are those containing less than 51 percent of Michigan produce. They were a small fraction of the total, which was presumably limited to the types named.

55. "Michigan Plans New Winery Laws," *Wines and Vines* 28 (October 1947): 46.

56. "Always Something New," *Wines and Vines* 30 (December 1949): 6; the winery was Michigan Wineries.

57. *Benton Harbor News Palladium,* 20 April 1951.

58. Fabian, "Michigan," p. 55; Michigan Department of Economic Development, "A Report on the Michigan Wine Industry," appendix F.

59. Roy Brady, MS tasting notes, 10 July 1948 (Roy Brady papers, University of California, Davis, Shields Library).

60. "Michigan's Wine Industry Comes of Age!" *Wine Review* 14 (December 1946): 36.

61. See George Kraus, *The Story of an Amana Winemaker,* as told to E. Mae Fritz (Iowa City: Penfield Press, 1984).

62. "Other than standard" is one of those euphemisms of which the TTB is so fruitful: formerly the category was called "substandard."

63. See chapter 1, before n. 50, for a suggested explanation.

64. Schoonmaker and Marvel, *American Wines,* p. 183; Mary Frost Mabon, *ABC of America's Wines* (New York: Knopf, 1942), p. 214.

65. *Springdale Observer,* 22 February 1990. The Van Gundy winery ceased operations in 1945.

66. In 1945, for example, of the 234,000 gallons of Arkansas wine entering the market, 158,000 gallons were fortified (U.S. Department of the Treasury, *Report of the Commissioner of Internal Revenue* for 1945, table 93).

67. Schick, "The Arkansas Wine Industry," pp. 12, 18. He might have added that "Arkansas wine drinkers" managed to drink only 0.15 of a gallon per capita in 1945, tying Arkansas with Kentucky for next-to-last place among the American states, followed only by Tennessee at 0.08 of a gallon.

68. Ibid., p. 18; *Wines and Vines, Yearbook of the Wine Industry 1946,* p. 54.

69. The figures are from U.S. Department of the Treasury, *Report of the Commissioner of Internal Revenue.* I cannot explain the figures for 1945 and 1946 except as mistakes.

70. Information from the Nelson Wine and Distilling Company papers, Shiloh Museum, Springdale, Arkansas. J.O. Nelson, the founder and proprietor, died in 1948, and the business of the firm was wound up in 1950.

71. Ibid.

72. U.S. Department of the Treasury, *Report of the Commissioner of Internal Revenue*. The decline in the number of wineries in Arkansas has continued: only five operated in 2004, though the standards of winegrowing had greatly improved.

73. T. V. Munson's monument is his *Foundations of American Grape Culture* (Denison, Tex.: T. V. Munson & Son, 1909).

74. Vinifera had indeed grown in the Rio Grande valley around El Paso in the eighteenth century and afterward, but the vineyards had long ago effectively disappeared.

75. Figures from the annual directory of the *Wine Review*.

76. E. Mortensen and U. A. Randolph, "Grape Production in Texas," Circular 89 (College Station: Texas Agricultural Experiment Station, 1940), p. 16.

77. One Texas winery, at least, actually offered a wine from the indigenous Mustang grape: this was the Southern Pride Winery of Brenham, which also made wine from the Herbemont as well as from the Munson variety called Carman, derived in part from the Post Oak grape (*Wines and Vines Directory of Wineries*, 1947).

78. Roy E. Mitchell, "Texas Wine History" (n.p.: Texas Wine and Grape Growers Association, 10 November 1993).

79. Sarah Jane English, *The Wines of Texas: A Guide and a History*, rev. ed. (Austin: Eakin Press, 1986), pp. 20–21. Three "very large research vineyards" were pulled out in the early 1960s ("Lone Star on the Rise," *Eastern Grape Grower and Winery News* 8 [December 1982]: 16).

80. The vinifera variety of colonial New Mexico appears to have been the same as that in California, the so-called Mission grape, and to have originated from the same sources in Mexico.

81. Renault had bought both the St. George Winery in Fresno and the Montebello Wine Company in San Francisco during the war.

82. W. H. Dewey to Will Widmer, 10 February 1950, Widmer papers, box 14, Cornell University, Kroch Library.

83. Peyton Boswell, *Wine Makers Manual: A Guide for the Home Wine Maker and the Small Winery* (New York: Orange Judd Publishing, 1935), p. 5. Boswell also edited a short-lived magazine called *Wine and Good Living*, evidently before the time for such a thing had arrived in this country.

84. U.S. Department of Agriculture, *Agricultural Statistics*, 1946, table 235; ibid., 1955, table 245.

85. As late as 1969, the "wine industry" in Pennsylvania was described as consisting of "six licensees who bottle finished wines from other states" (*Control States Review* [March 1969]: 29).

86. Chapter 2, after n. 17.

87. Schoonmaker and Marvel, *American Wines*, p. 184.

88. Edward D. C. Campbell Jr., "Of Vines and Wines: The Culture of the Grape in Virginia," *Virginia Cavalcade* (Winter 1990): 115.

89. Chamberlain survived long enough to see the revival of the Virginia wine industry in the 1970s. He presented a bottle of post-Repeal Norton claret to the Jeffersonian Wine Grape Growers Society on its formation in 1981 ("Historic Wine to Jeffersonians," *Eastern Grape Grower and Winery News* 8 [April–May 1982]: 7).

90. Philip M. Wagner, *American Wines and How to Make Them* (New York: Knopf, 1933); see chapter 3, at n. 5.

91. Philip M. Wagner and Jocelyn Wagner, "Testing Direct Producers in the East," *Wines and Vines* 24 (September 1943): 16.

92. The name was given to them by Wagner when he began importing them; as he says, they came from France, and the name was "short and simple" (Philip M. Wagner, "Wagner's Question: Better Name for Hybrids?" *Wines and Vines* 59 [May 1978]: 54). Since there have been additions to them from German and American sources, the term is now a misnomer, but it remains convenient.

93. See Pinney, *A History of Wine in America*, pp. 203–15, for a summary of these experiments.

94. Albert Seibel (1844–1936) began tentatively in 1874, more determinedly in 1886. The life dates of some other distinguished hybridizers will give an idea of the periods in which they worked: Baco (1865–1947); Couderc (1850–1928); Kuhlmann (1858–1932); Landot (1900–42); and Seyve-Villard (1895–1959).

95. The original list of twenty-five names was drawn up by the French government; since then the joint Canadian–U.S. Great Lakes Grape Nomenclature Committee has been created to select names ("The Numbered Days of Numbered Wines," *Wines and Vines* 52 [October 1971]: 6; "Seibel 9549 Becomes 'De Chaunac,'" 53 [October 1972]: 6).

96. Philip M. Wagner, "The French Hybrids," *American Journal of Enology and Viticulture* 6 (1955): 16. A letter from Richard Wellington of the Geneva Station states that they had Seibel 2 at Geneva by 1906 (Philip Wagner papers, box 4, file 43, Cornell University, Kroch Library).

97. For this history, see Philip M. Wagner, "The East's New Wine Industry," *Wines and Vines* 60 (March 1979): 24–26. Curiously enough, Wagner's first direct encounter with the French hybrids was not in France but at the British agricultural station in East Malling, Kent (Hudson Cattell, "Philip Marshall Wagner, 1904–1996," *Wine East* 24 [January–February 1997]: 4). One of the early experimenters in this country was Dr. Robert Dunstan of Greensboro, North Carolina, beginning in 1938 ("Robert T. Dunstan Dies in Florida," *Wine East* 15 [January–February 1988]: 5). The New York Agricultural Experiment Station at Geneva had a number of them under test by 1937 (Philip M. Wagner, *Wine Grapes, Their Selection, Cultivation, and Enjoyment* [New York: Harcourt Brace, 1937]: 279).

98. Wagner, "The East's New Wine Industry," p. 25.

99. Adams, *The Wines of America*, p. 63.

CHAPTER 9. CHANGING WEATHER

1. The low point was 226, in 1967 and 1969. These are numbers for winery licenses: not all holders of licenses were actually making wine.

2. By 1954, the four largest wineries had 41 percent of the California crush (Ralph Hutchinson, "The California Wine Industry" [Ph.D. diss., University of California, Los Angeles, 1969], p. 29).

3. The California Wine Association and Guild Wineries, both large marketing co-ops,

planned to merge in 1954. If this plan had come off, it would have produced by far the biggest winemaking enterprise in the state.

4. The Gallos were unusual, however, in producing nothing but table wine in the first years. Not until 1937 did they erect a still and enter the market for fortified wines (Ernest Gallo and Julio Gallo, with Bruce B. Henderson, *Ernest and Julio: Our Story* [New York: Times Books, 1994], p. 83; Charles M. Crawford, *Recollections of a Career with the Gallo Winery and the Development of the California Wine Industry, 1942–1989*, interview by Ruth Teiser, Berkeley: Regional Oral History Office, Bancroft Library, University of California, 1990, p. 26).

5. Ellen Hawkes, *Blood and Wine: The Unauthorized Story of the Gallo Wine Empire* (New York: Simon and Schuster, 1993), p. 166. She credits the story to "several 'oldtimers' in Napa and Sonoma." See chapter 7, after n. 91, for a very different account of the events of 1946.

6. Arakelian (1871–1951), born in Turkish Armenia, came to Fresno at the age of twelve and gradually developed a large business in fruit and melons. During Prohibition he was an important supplier of grapes, and on Repeal he entered the wine business. The Mission Bell property once belonged to Italian Swiss Colony; it was sold to the CWA in 1915, and Arakelian then bought it about 1925. It is now the property of Canandaigua and the source of wines labeled Masson, Almadén, The Christian Brothers, etc.

7. National had determined to invest in petrochemicals as more profitable than wine (Elie C. Skofis, *California Wine and Brandy Maker*, interview by Ruth Teiser, Berkeley: Regional Oral History Office, Bancroft Library, University of California, 1988, p. 16).

8. Ernest Gallo states that he informed Petri of the chance to buy Italian Swiss Colony and that Petri got it "for the figure I had hammered out in my negotiations" (Gallo and Gallo, *Ernest and Julio: Our Story*, p. 165). The reported price was $16 million (*Time* [27 April 1953]: 102).

9. Skofis, *California Wine and Brandy Maker*, p. 20.

10. Its leading wine in New York, called Fior d'Italia, was a mixture of a "dry port" of 23 degrees of alcohol produced in Fresno with red table wine from Sonoma County, making a 13-degree wine with some residual sugar. This was the formula for "Italian-style" or "mellow" wine: "high-alcohol, very slightly sweet, heavy red wine" (ibid., p. 13).

11. "Allied-Heublein Deal in Works," *Wines and Vines* 49 (August 1968): 15.

12. Morris Katz, *Paul Masson Winery Operations and Management, 1944–1988*, interview by Ruth Teiser, Berkeley: Regional Oral History Office, Bancroft Library, University of California, 1990, p. 30.

13. The ship, 530 feet long and 58 feet in beam, made seven round trips a year. A laboratory on board allowed a technician to monitor the wines en route. The idea of a wine ship was not wholly new: the Waterman Line offered in 1953 to outfit a ship with stainless steel tanks for the shipment of wine but does not seem to have had any takers (*Wines and Vines* 34 [July 1953]: 5). In pre-Prohibition days, shipment by water to eastern markets was common: the great Winehaven plant of the CWA, built on the shores of San Pablo Bay, shipped cargoes of 50,000 gallons at a time after the building of the Panama Canal (Antonio Perelli-Minetti, *A Life in Wine Making*, interview by Ruth Teiser, Berkeley: Regional Oral History Office, Bancroft Library, University of California, 1975, p. 91).

14. "The railroads really were making life miserable for all of us," Petri recalled. The success of the S.S. *Angelo Petri* was such that the rail rates for wine fell to less than half of what they had been (Louis A. Petri, *The Petri Family in the Wine Industry*, interview by Ruth Teiser, Berkeley: Regional Oral History Office, Bancroft Library, University of California, 1971, pp. 26, 27).

15. The *Angelo Petri* was sold in 1975, registered under the Panamanian flag, renamed the *Sea Chemist*, and employed in the liquid bulk cargo trade (*New York Times*, 14 November 1976, 63).

16. They were Harold H. Price, a San Francisco lawyer and member of the Wine and Food Society; Russell S. Codman, a Boston wine merchant; and Morrison Wood, a Chicago journalist who published a series of cookbooks featuring wine. Just what these experts chose from is not made clear, but presumably all the wines in question were Petri wines.

17. According to William Andrew Beckstoffer, there was a "palace revolt" and Petri was "kicked out" (*Premium California Vineyardist, Entrepreneur, 1960s to 2000s*, interview by Carole Hicke, Berkeley: Regional Oral History Office, Bancroft Library, University of California, 2000, p. 27).

18. Gallo and Gallo, *Ernest and Julio: Our Story*, p. 165.

19. James T. Lapsley, *Bottled Poetry: Napa Winemaking from Prohibition to the Modern Era* (Berkeley: University of California Press, 1996), pp. 175–76.

20. "Gallo Buys Cribari Winery, Inventory," *Wines and Vines* 35 (May 1954): 8; Gallo and Gallo, *Ernest and Julio: Our Story*, p. 161.

21. Or, in the version given in "How Gallo Crushes the Competition," *Fortune* 68 (1 September 1986): 27, "Julio's goal is to make more wine than Ernest can sell, Ernest's to sell more than Julio can make."

22. Gallo and Gallo, *Ernest and Julio: Our Story*, p. 28.

23. See Hawkes, *Blood and Wine*, pp. 183–85.

24. Gallo and Gallo, *Ernest and Julio: Our Story*, p. 270.

25. Ibid., p. 132.

26. Legh F. Knowles, *Beaulieu Vineyards from Family to Corporate Ownership*, interview by Lisa Jacobson, Berkeley: Regional Oral History Office, Bancroft Library, University of California, 1990, p. 25.

27. *Wall Street Journal*, 20 May 1976; *Wines and Vines* 57 (July 1976): 18. For Ernest Gallo's account of the episode, see Gallo and Gallo, *Ernest and Julio: Our Story*, pp. 268–71.

28. Gallo and Gallo, *Ernest and Julio: Our Story*, p. 271.

29. Ibid., p. 103. Knowles says that he wrote the first Gallo sales manual: its principle was "If you can't see it, you can't buy it" (*Beaulieu Vineyards from Family to Corporate Ownership*, p. 25).

30. It is described in "How Gallo Crushes the Competition," p. 29; it then ran to sixteen chapters in three hundred pages.

31. Knowles, *Beaulieu Vineyards from Family to Corporate Ownership*, pp. 25–26.

32. As the Gallo marketing manager, Howard E. Williams, put it, "This company aims to supply wines Americans will readily like, instead of only trying to teach them what we vintners think they ought to like, as our industry has been content to do for the past 24 years" ("Prestige Promotion and Thunderbird," *Wines and Vines* 38 [November 1957]: 41).

33. See chapter 7, after n. 116.

34. Vino da Tavola, according to Julio Gallo, was "a common Valley red wine sweetened with port" (Gallo and Gallo, *Ernest and Julio: Our Story*, p. 156). Compare the formula for Fior d'Italia in note 10, above. Paisano, by contrast, was said to be "almost all North Coast Zinfandel" (Crawford, *Recollections of a Career with the Gallo Winery*, p. 39).

35. *Wines and Vines* 51 (May 1973): 14. Richard Peterson, who was with Gallo at the time, says that Gallo's Pink Chablis was a fifty-fifty blend of the company's standard rosé with a muscat-flavored white wine called Rheingarten. Peterson sweetened and carbonated the mixture; the result, he maintained, "by the standards of the market that Gallo was in . . . was an excellent wine" (Dr. Richard G. Peterson, "Self-Interview, 1976," in *History of Napa Valley: Interviews and Reminiscences of Long-Time Residents*, vol. 2 [St. Helena, Calif.: Napa Valley Wine Library Association, 1977], p. 160).

36. Ernest Gallo, "Outlook for a Mature Industry," *Wines and Vines* 39 (June 1958): 28. By the end of the 1970s, these "mellow" wines are said to have had 80 percent of the table-wine market (Lapsley, *Bottled Poetry*, p. 200).

37. Retsina (pine resin–flavored) and May wine (woodruff-flavored) were also produced, but in negligible quantities. The new regulations also allowed the addition of sugar to flavored wines—a practice otherwise forbidden in California—and one reason the production of flavored wines in bonded wineries was opposed.

38. Richard L. Ryan, "How the ATTD Laboratories Keep Their Eye on You," *Wines and Vines* 42 (July 1961): 21.

39. The flavored wines pursued a course from high-alcohol fortified wines (e.g., Thunderbird) to mid-alcohol wines to low-alcohol wines at approximately 9 percent alcohol (e.g., Annie Green Springs, introduced in 1973). The low-alcohol wines—given funky names to attract the hippie and dropout crowd of the late '60s and '70s—were known as "pop" or "mod" wines. They had a meteoric success, streaking from 3 million gallons in 1969 to 7.5 million the next year ("A Wineman Tells It Like the Market Is," *Wines and Vines* 52 [March 1971]: 17), but as quickly faded. *Time* magazine noted that such wines "added a pleasant extra dimension to the effects of pot" (24 May 1971). Then there was Cold Duck, a sparkling wine with some Concord juice added for special flavor. Such things were succeeded by the wine coolers, slightly alcoholic fruit drinks with a low-alcohol wine base.

40. Gallo and Gallo, *Ernest and Julio: Our Story*, p. 178.

41. The change in regulations, made in 1958, authorized the retention in still wines of as much carbon dioxide as would not result in the production of an "effervescent wine" (Excise Tax Technical Changes Act of 1958).

42. Gallo and Gallo, *Ernest and Julio: Our Story*, pp. 216, 231–32.

43. Four years after their introduction, the special natural wines sold more than 13 million gallons (Irving H. Marcus, "What the New Wine Types Have Accomplished," *Wines and Vines* 44 [January 1963]: 16).

44. B. C. Solari, "And Deliver Us from Glamour," speech to Los Angeles Advertising Club, 23 October 1962, copy in the Wine Institute Library.

45. André Tchelistcheff makes the surprising remark that the prosperity of the Gallo Winery "liberated" the California wine industry from the control of the Bank of America:

"Gallo, in expansion of purchasing power, restored the industry" (*Grapes, Wine, and Ecology*, interview by Ruth Teiser and Catherine Harroun, Berkeley: Regional Oral History Library, Bancroft Library, University of California, 1983, p. 71). The same prosperity made it possible to pay more money for better grapes—the essential prerequisite for progress that had been missing since Repeal.

46. Crawford, *Recollections of a Career with the Gallo Winery*, p. 53. R. Bradford Webb, who worked for Gallo in 1951, confirms this claim: "Gallo was offering technologists the freedom of making better wine and it was a rare opportunity" (*Brad Webb: Innovator*, interview by William Heintz, 1988 [Healdsburg, Calif.: Sonoma County Wine Library Oral History, 1991], p. 32). For the development of the Gallo research laboratory and its contributions, see Arthur Caputi Jr., "Fifty Years of Research at the World's Largest Winery," *Practical Winery and Vineyard* 22 (November–December 2000): 5–15, 78.

47. William Bonetti, *A Life of Winemaking at Wineries of Gallo, Schenley, Charles Krug, Chateau Souverain, and Sonoma-Cutrer*, interview by Carole Hicke, Berkeley: Regional Oral History Office, Bancroft Library, University of California, 1998, p. 24. Bonetti adds that he was encouraged to experiment. Webb recalled that "the boss was there before you got there in the morning and was still there after you left" (*Brad Webb: Innovator*, p. 25).

48. See the remarks of Richard Oster, head of United Vintners, in "A Conversation with Dick Oster," *Wines and Vines* 54 (February 1973): 40.

49. "It's a religion with us that we give the consumer the same wine that we've given him in the past and that we want to give him in the future," Charles Crawford told an interviewer (Hudson Cattell, "Gallo: The Little Winery That Got Bigger," *Pennsylvania Grape Letter and Wine News* 7 [March 1980]: 6).

50. The expression was used in a mimeographed notice of an organization meeting for a "Grower-Vintner Grape Quality Grading Program," 9 June 1952, copy in the Wine Institute Library.

51. A. J. Winkler, "Grape Standardization," *Wines and Vines* 33 (June 1952): 11.

52. Kenneth Knapp, "Why I Am for the Boragno Grape Stabilization Plan," *Wines and Vines* 33 (February 1952): 15–16; "Under Consideration: Three Roads to Stability," *Wines and Vines* 33 (March 1952): 5.

53. These causes included not just grape surpluses but a standard of winemaking that did nothing to increase interest in wine. As Maynard A. Amerine observed in 1952, it was not a good time to ask the industry to adopt better practices, yet "it may very well be asked whether the continued production of large quantities of relatively poor quality dessert wine is not an important cause of the poor economic condition" ("Dessert Wine Production Problems of California Grapes, I: Introduction," *Wines and Vines* 33 [January 1952]: 15).

54. "Grower Meeting Backs Order," *Wines and Vines* 34 (April 1953): 28. Green-dropping is the removal of unripe fruit from the vine in order to limit the crop and to enhance its quality.

55. "Proposed Marketing Order Would Set Quality Goal," *Wines and Vines* 38 (September 1957): 13; "New Mkt. Order Likely," *Wines and Vines* 40 (January 1959): 15; "Fading Market Order," *Wines and Vines* 40 (March 1959): 15. In 1957, heavy rains at harvesttime damaged late-ripening varieties such as Zinfandel and reduced the crop.

56. Sales of fortified wine had slipped only slightly between 1960 and 1961 but dropped by 9 million gallons in the next year; table wine went up by 4 million gallons in the same period (*Wines and Vines* statistical issue [April 1963]). Over the period 1952–63, sales of table wine went up by 70 percent. By 1961 sales of table wine in the California market equaled those of fortified wine ("The 'Impossible' in Table Wine Is about to Happen," *Wines and Vines* 42 [August 1961]: 16; "What the New ATTD Director Thinks about the Wine Industry and Its Relations with Government," *Wines and Vines* 45 [September 1964]: 21).

57. The reason more grapes are required is that they are also used to make the brandy that is added to a fortified wine.

58. "Corpus Delicti," *Wines and Vines* 44 (September 1963): 4. Setrakian was one of those winemakers who did not himself drink wine (Robert Setrakian, "Recollections of A. Setrakian," in A. Setrakian, *A Leader of the San Joaquin Valley Grape Industry*, interview by Ruth Teiser, Berkeley: Regional Oral History Office, Bancroft Library, University of California, 1977, p. 70).

59. "Stabilization Order Highlights," *Wines and Vines* 42 (May 1961): 16.

60. "Who Said What at Stabilization 'Hearing,'" *Wines and Vines* 42 (June 1961): 25. For the dispute over wine as an "agricultural commodity" in 1938, see chapter 5, after n. 105.

61. For an account of the hearing and the terms of the order as passed, see ibid., pp. 21–25; "How Washington Acted on Marketing Order," *Wines and Vines* 42 (July 1961): 17; "Crushing Order Now Operative," *Wines and Vines* 42 (September 1961): 15. The quantity set aside from the 1961 crush was the equivalent of 27 million gallons of fortified wine. Many wineries greatly increased their storage capacities in consequence; the United Vintners winery at Madera doubled its crushing capacity (Robert Rossi Jr., "United Vintners Expands Its Madera Premises," *Wines and Vines* 43 [September 1962]: 25).

62. "Day of Decision: August 14," *Wines and Vines* 44 (August 1963): 15. The opposition of Allied Grape Growers was an important reason for the defeat of the order. Wine prices went up under it, but grape prices did not (Hutchinson, "The California Wine Industry," pp. 222–23). Werner Allmendinger, who supervised the order for the USDA, recalled that under it some 475,000 tons of grapes were diverted from the wineries in 1961 and 1962: "Most of it went into industrial alcohol" ("'Al' Allmendinger to Retire," *Wines and Vines* 64 [May 1983]: 70).

63. "Marketing Order for Bulk Dessert Wine Now a Fact," *Wines and Vines* 47 (July 1966): 14. This was called the Marketing Order for Bulk Dessert Wine; it was later (November 1966) extended to cover bulk grape concentrate and bulk high-proof brandy for fortifying. Its legality was challenged in the courts, and it lapsed in 1967; see Hutchinson, "The California Wine Industry," pp. 225–30.

64. The Court of Appeals ruled that the state had no right to limit the use of raisins: "Order Dead; Crush Very Live," *Wines and Vines* 45 (September 1964): 13.

65. Louis Gomberg summarized his idea of the period between 1947 and 1968, when things at last turned upward, as "one continuing series of depressed pricing, punctuated only by temporary respites due to war (Korea—1950) or short crops (1967—for example)": "Gomberg Sees Long Range Wine Grape Surplus Program," *California Grape Grower* (December 1973): 35. Robert Mondavi called the years 1933 to 1968 the "over-supply era" ("A Plea for Generic Promotion," *Wines and Vines* 63 [January 1982]: 36).

66. Edgar Millhauser, "Quality Wine—Why Not Specific Categories?" *Wines and Vines* 33 (May 1952): 6.

67. H. P. Olmo, "California's Principal Wine Grape Varieties, Present and Future," *Wines and Vines* 36 (May 1955): 28–29.

68. A. J. Winkler, "Effects of Overcropping," *American Journal of Enology and Viticulture* 5 (1954): 11.

69. Maynard A. Amerine, "Some Facts and Fancies about Winemaking and Wines," Report to the Wine Institute Technical Advisory Committee Meeting, 13 May 1955, copy in the Roy Brady papers, University of California, Davis, Shields Library.

70. From "The Story of Wine and Its Uses," 5th ed. (San Francisco: Wine Advisory Board, 1967). The handbook series was written by Leon D. Adams, who boasted that the categories he invented for the purpose ("dessert," "appetizer," and so on) "subsequently achieved legal status in government regulations." He also adapted the handbook series into a "Wine Study Course" that more than a quarter of a million people had signed up for by 1958 (*The Commonsense Book of Wine* [New York: David McKay, 1958], p. 20).

71. "'Time' Reviews Wine Competition," *Wines and Vines* 28 (October 1947): 11; *San Francisco News*, 19 December 1950.

72. Robert W. Benson, *Great Winemakers of California* (Santa Barbara, Calif.: Capra Press, 1977), p. 15.

73. "What the U.S. Public Thinks about Wine," *Wines and Vines* 36 (October 1955): 20–22. Louis Gomberg thought that the conduct of the survey was "flawed" because the staff knew little about wine (Jay Stuller and Glen Martin, *Through the Grapevine* [New York: Wynwood Press, 1989], p. 68).

74. Occasionally one heard a less boastful note: Antonio Perelli-Minetti, commenting in a 1969 interview (copyrighted in 1975) on the prospects of export for California wine, said, "We haven't got good wines to send over there. The only wine that we could send over there would be wine from Napa-Sonoma Counties. The rest of the wine that we produce now, dry wine, is like the Algerian wine, and some parts of Europe they won't take it" (*A Life in Wine Making*, p. 136).

75. Irving A. Marcus, "The Seven Fat Years of Table Wine Sales in California," *Wines and Vines* 35 (October 1954): 21.

76. Amerine says that the name was not widely used but that "the practice of making burgundy sweet has occurred" ("Some Facts and Fancies about Winemaking and Wines"). As for rosé (or pink wines of one sort or another), Louis Gomberg estimated that it was the largest-selling wine category in the country by 1970 ("The Pink Wine Revolution," *Wines and Vines* 51 [September 1970]: 56).

77. *Wines and Vines* 51 (November 1970): 21.

78. Robert Mondavi, "Plan for Grape and Winegrowing for the Future," Report to the Wine Institute Technical Advisory Committee, 3 December 1954, copy in the Wine Institute Library. Elbert M. Brown also noted the rising use of inexpensive Central Valley and Cucamonga reds at the cost of North Coast wines in the popular "mellow" table wines and suggested that the North Coast people would have to change their style ("The Clarification and Stability of Wines in the Pre-Prohibition Era," *Proceedings of the American Society of Enologists* 4 [1953]: 4).

79. Stephanie S. Pincetl, *Transforming California: A Political History of Land Use and Development* (Baltimore: Johns Hopkins University Press, 1999), p. 145.

80. By 2000 the figure was 1,412, concentrated in two areas: the upper foothills of the Santa Cruz mountains on the west, and the southern area around Gilroy. The old vineyard region had found a new identity as Silicon Valley.

81. In 1945 Alameda County had sixteen wineries; in 1960, only nine. The comparable figures for Contra Costa County are eight and four; for Santa Clara County, forty-six and thirty-four.

82. Firestone, Norman, and Geyser Peak wineries all offered old-vines Zinfandel from Cucamonga in 2000, at prices ranging from $10 to $25.

83. Edmund Mirassou, "Are North Coast Grapes Expendable?" *Wines and Vines* 42 (February 1961): 18.

84. Louis Gomberg, "California—Land of Great Wines Only?" *Wines and Vines* 43 (January 1962): 24.

85. "New Viticultural Region?" *Wines and Vines* 31 (September 1950): 11.

86. The Gallos bought land in the region in 1970 but planted apples rather than grapes (Gallo and Gallo, *Ernest and Julio: Our Story,* p. 257).

87. Frank Schoonmaker, "Almaden's Great New Vineyard," *Wines and Vines* 41 (August 1960): 21.

88. "Winkler Measures New Acreage for Premium Grapes," *Wines and Vines* 42 (January 1961): 27. The survey was undertaken at the request of the Wine Institute (A. J. Winkler, *Viticultural Research at University of California, Davis, 1921–1971,* interview by Ruth Teiser, Berkeley: Regional Oral History Office, Bancroft Library, University of California, 1973, p. 40).

89. Some seventeen varieties, red and white, were planted: "Birth of a New Vineyard Area," *Wines and Vines* 44 (February 1963): 19.

90. One mistake, unfortunately widely imitated in the extensive plantings throughout California that followed in the subsequent years, was to plant vines on their own roots rather than on phylloxera-resistant rootstocks. The argument was that new regions need not worry about phylloxera, but this was to take a very short view indeed.

91. The illustrated newsletter put out by Schoonmaker for Almadén called *News from the Vineyards* was widely circulated from its first issue in 1951; it had a press run of 750,000 by 1969 and must have introduced many people to a more intelligent level of talk about wine than they could easily have found elsewhere at the time.

92. See chapter 6, at n. 37, for Fromm and Sichel. The combination of a Catholic winery with Jewish distributors was a happy ecumenical arrangement.

93. The Christian Brothers were slow to adopt varietal labeling, even though they had the grapes to support the practice. They eventually paid for their slowness: their generic wines lost ground when generic labeling no longer had the respect of the market, and The Christian Brothers wines, even when rechristened with varietal names, never regained the ground lost. In 1989 the Brothers determined to get out of the wine business and sold out to Heublein.

94. Lapsley, *Bottled Poetry,* p. 182.

95. Katz, *Paul Masson Winery Operations and Management,* pp. 23, 31.

96. Katz estimated that Masson's vineyards never supplied more than 22 percent of its needs (ibid., p. 39).

97. William Dieppe, *Almadén Is My Life*, interview by Ruth Teiser, Berkeley: Regional Oral History Office, Bancroft Library, University of California, 1985, p. 45.

98. At one point Benoist owned "seven houses, two airplanes, and a 110 foot yacht" (Charles L. Sullivan, *Like Modern Edens: Winegrowing in Santa Clara Valley and Santa Cruz Mountains, 1798–1981*, Local History Studies 28 [Cupertino, Calif.: California History Center, 1982], p. 148).

99. It was, predictably, greatly expanded: sales were about 2 million cases in 1969; they were 12 million in 1980 ("Bill Dieppe Retired," *Wines and Vines* 63 [January 1982]: 46).

100. Zellerbach (1892–1963) was ambassador to Italy, 1956–60.

101. Leon D. Adams, *The Wines of America* (Boston: Houghton Mifflin, 1973), p. 188.

102. James Halliday, *Wine Atlas of California* (New York: Viking, 1993), p. 188. Webb recalled that he had applied several techniques new to California winemaking: "stainless steel, inert atmosphere, pure culture malolactic, French wood aging, sterile sampling, spray fining, etc." (*Brad Webb: Innovator*, p. 42). Or as another writer put it, "More than anything, Webb wanted to make wine using the scientific method" ("Jake Lorenzo," "Tribute," *Practical Winery and Vineyard* 21 [May–June 2000]: 74).

103. The Chardonnays of Stony Hill and Mayacamas in the 1950s also helped to show the way.

104. Mark Holliday, "California's Premium Wines," *Wine Review* 17 (September 1949): 6; Lapsley says that in the 1950s only 1 percent of the table wine sold was varietal wine, and that the premium wineries accounted for less than 5 percent of all table wine produced (*Bottled Poetry*, p. 170).

105. "Premium Wine Program under Way," *Wines and Vines* 30 (May 1949): 14.

106. "Fireworks in Fresno," *Wines and Vines* 30 (June 1949): 6.

107. The members were Souverain, Los Amigos, Buena Vista, Hallcrest, Mayacamas, Ficklin, Stony Hill, Shangri La, and Kew (*San Francisco News*, 19 December 1950).

108. There was talk of reviving it in 1957 (*Wines and Vines* 38 [January 1957]: 12).

109. The core group of wineries at the beginning was Almadén, Ambassador District Wines, Asti Vineyards, Beaulieu, Beringer, Buena Vista, The Christian Brothers, Cresta Blanca, Hallcrest, Inglenook, Korbel, Charles Krug, Paul Masson, Signature Vintners, Weibel Champagne Vineyards, and Wente Brothers (Lapsley, *Bottled Poetry*, p. 258). Martin Ray was asked to join but, characteristically, declined to be part of an enterprise not based on his own ideas: the wineries in the group should, he wrote, be more concerned with raising their own standards than with the competition from imports (Martin Ray to Louis Gomberg, 20 April 1955, copy in the Roy Brady papers, University of California, Davis, Shields Library).

110. Lapsley, *Bottled Poetry*, p. 151.

111. It should be noted that $1 in 1955 was roughly equivalent to $8 in 2004.

112. "Wise and Otherwise," *Wines and Vines* 36 (August 1955): 16.

113. Lapsley, *Bottled Poetry*, pp. 151–52.

114. Ibid., p. 153.

115. Robert Mondavi said that the program "marked the turning point in the recognition

of California wines versus imports" ("A Plea for Generic Promotion," p. 36; one suspects that the author of the piece, originally given as an address to the Wine Institute, was in fact Leon Adams).

116. "The Conference at Del Monte," *Wine Review* 3 (October 1935): 12.

117. Lapsley, *Bottled Poetry*, pp. 81–82.

118. Wine Institute, "The First Twenty Years of Wine Institute: A Report to Members at the Twentieth Annual Meeting" (San Francisco: Wine Institute, 8–9 March 1954), p. 3.

119. Otto E. Meyer, *California Premium Wines and Brandies*, interview by Ruth Teiser, Berkeley: Regional Oral History Office, Bancroft Library, University of California, 1973, p. 42.

120. A Taylor brochure, dated 1940, includes an "invitation . . . to visit The Taylor Winery at Hammondsport in the beautiful Finger Lakes Region of New York State. Thousands of visitors from all over the country have been our guests" (copy in the author's collection).

121. "Ohio Winery Steps Out," *Wines and Vines* 35 (December 1954): 28. Max Goldman, writing as a Californian transplanted to New York, was struck by the treatment of visitors at New York wineries: "hospitality . . . is supreme" ("The New York State Industry as It Appears to a Former Californian," *Wines and Vines* 40 [May 1959]: 18).

122. See the discussion of this question in Charles L. Sullivan, *Napa Wine: A History from Mission Days to Present* (San Francisco: Wine Appreciation Guild, 1994), pp. 349–52.

123. Roy Brady, *The Brady Book: Selections from Roy Brady's Unpublished Writings*, ed. Thomas Pinney (Santa Rosa, Calif.: Nomis Press, 2003), p. 30.

124. *Bottles and Bins* may claim to be the first of the post-Repeal newsletters, but the history of the subject is not settled; the newsletter put out by Mayacamas is perhaps the second.

125. Chateau Montelena, Mayacamas, Domaine Chandon, Foppiano, Sebastiani, and Simi— to name only a few—have or have had interesting newsletters.

126. The founders included Joseph Vercelli, Mildred Howie, John Hutchinson, and Bo Simons.

127. The Premium Wine Producers of California contributed to the expenses of the book. One result was that no identification of the subjects of the photographs was given, for fear of seeming to provide free advertising to individual wineries at the expense of the Wine Advisory Board.

128. For an account of the genesis of the film, see Louis Gomberg, *Analytical Perspectives on the California Wine Industry, 1935–1990*, interview by Ruth Teiser, Berkeley: Regional Oral History Office, Bancroft Library, University of California, 1990, pp. 54–56. It had at least one predecessor before the war, the film version of Sidney Howard's *They Knew What They Wanted* in 1940.

129. A. J. Winkler, "A Proposed Program for the Introduction, Improvement, and Certification of Healthy Grape Varieties," *Wines and Vines* 32 (July 1951): 7–9.

130. Curtis J. Alley, "Certified Grape Stocks Available," *Wines and Vines* 40 (February 1959): 30.

131. Paul Osteraas, "The Gallo Vacuum Grape Harvester," *Wines and Vines* 47 (April 1966): 50; H. P. Olmo, *Plant Genetics and New Grape Varieties*, interview by Ruth Teiser, Berkeley: Regional Oral History Office, Bancroft Library, University of California, 1976, p. 103.

132. Zelma Long, "Enological and Technological Developments," in *The University of California/Sotheby Book of California Wine,* ed. Doris Muscatine, Maynard A. Amerine, and Bob Thompson (Berkeley: University of California Press, and London: Sotheby Publications, 1984), p. 179.

133. The Germans led the way. In this country, Rudolf Jordan Jr.'s *Quality in Dry Wines through Adequate Fermentations . . . A Manual for Progressive Winemakers in California* (San Francisco: Pernau Publishing, 1911) presented the case for cool fermentation.

134. Lapsley, *Bottled Poetry,* p. 163.

135. Ibid., pp. 167–68.

136. Crawford, *Recollections of a Career with the Gallo Winery,* p. 42.

137. Ibid., p. 45.

138. Zellerbach is said to have insisted on Burgundian barrels not for any enological reason but only because he liked their looks.

139. Beaulieu's celebrated Georges de Latour Private Reserve Cabernet Sauvignon, one of the few wines to be barrel-aged in post-Repeal California, was always held in American oak.

140. Barrel staves are assembled over a fire, which assists in bending them into the required shape. As a result, the inner sides of the staves are lightly charred, or "toasted." The degree of toasting desired is specified by the buyer.

141. Norman S. Roby and Charles E. Olken, *The New Connoisseurs' Handbook of California Wines,* 3rd ed. (New York: Knopf, 1995), p. 23. A leader in experimentation with all the varieties of oak and its application in varying measures was Robert Mondavi: see Stephen Brook, *The Wines of California* (London: Faber and Faber, 1999), p. 215.

142. In the first enthusiasm over the possibilities of oak aging there were no doubt many excesses committed; at the same time many of the old guard refused to have anything to do with the fashion. As one of them put it, "If I want wood, I can chew a toothpick." More judicious was the response of Justin Meyer: oak character in a wine was not necessarily a virtue, he noted, and even if it were, some winemakers (Meyer among them) might prefer American oak. Or they might prefer to emphasize varietal character rather than wood ("Values of Diversified Cooperage in the Wine Industry," *Wines and Vines* 51 [April 1970]: 57).

143. Cornelius Ough, *Researches of an Enologist, University of California, Davis,* interview by Ruth Teiser, Berkeley: Regional Oral History Office, Bancroft Library, University of California, 1990, p. 42. Ough had been a member of the Department of Viticulture and Enology at Davis since 1958.

144. Bonetti, *A Life of Winemaking,* p. 29.

145. There is also a plain commercial reason for promoting the idea of *terroir;* anyone can grow a Chardonnay, but only one Chardonnay can come from a particular spot. Whether that spot produces a distinguished Chardonnay is another question.

CHAPTER 10. THE BIG CHANGE

1. See chapter 3, at n. 5.

2. A. I. M. S. Street to A. A. Knopf, 23 April 1960, Alfred A. Knopf papers, University of

Texas, Harry Ransom Humanities Research Center. Marguerite Street rewrote the introductory discussion of California wines for the third edition of the book but made almost no change in the list of wineries included for discussion: Los Amigos, Hallcrest, Cribari, and Italian Swiss Colony were dropped and Masson added.

3. Maynard A. Amerine and Vernon Singleton, *Wine: An Introduction for Americans* (Berkeley: University of California Press, 1965), p. 287.

4. Calculated from *Wines and Vines Directory* by Ralph B. Hutchinson ("The California Wine Industry" [Ph.D. diss., University of California, Los Angeles, 1969], p. 22).

5. Such a list would certainly have included these names: Beaulieu, Buena Vista, Concannon, Chalone, David Bruce, Ficklin, Hallcrest, Hanzell, Heitz, Inglenook, Kornell, Krug, Martini, Mayacamas, Mirassou, Robert Mondavi, Novitiate of Los Gatos, Martin Ray, Richert, Ridge, Souverain, Stony Hill, Wente, and Woodside.

6. Calculated from Wine Institute statistical surveys by Hutchinson ("The California Wine Industry," pp. 72–76).

7. Louis Gomberg, "Lest We Forget," *Wines and Vines* 52 (November 1971): 24.

8. The information that follows is mostly derived from the annual statistical issue of *Wines and Vines*, supplemented by the annual summary of *California Fruit and Nut Crop Acreages* of the California Crop and Livestock Reporting Service.

9. The official figures show the quantities of tax-paid wine for each year, but there is no way to know how much of it was actually sold at retail. The presumption is that most of it did finally reach consumers' hands, but when that occurred is not on record.

10. New wineries were not confined to California but began to appear all over the country in the decade of the '70s; the process reached a high point in 1980, when 107 new wineries were opened ("A Record 107 Wineries Opened," *Wines and Vines* 62 [May 1981]: 63).

11. A. Dinsmoor Webb (chairman of the Department of Viticulture and Enology at the University of California, Davis), "A Wine Scholar Looks to the '80s," *Wines and Vines* 61 (February 1980): 20.

12. This does not mean that the superseded varieties disappeared from California vineyards. There were 268,000 acres of Thompson Seedless in California in 2000, but the Thompson Seedless, apart from its use as a fresh or dried fruit, was more and more used to produce such things as high-proof brandy, grape concentrate, or fresh grape juice.

13. The figures were 87,666,558 gallons of table wine versus 78,937,439 for fortified wine (*Wines and Vines* 49 [April 1968]: 28). Irving Marcus, the editor of *Wines and Vines*, proclaimed 1967 "a millenium [*sic*] year" ("Millenium," *Wines and Vines* 48 [October 1967]: 4). Charles Sullivan calculated (not very seriously) that the moment must have come on 24 March 1967 ("March 24, 1967," *Wines and Vines* 48 [June 1967]: 68).

14. In the three years following the opening of the Mondavi Winery, these wineries were founded or refounded: Chappellet, Chateau Montelena, Freemark Abbey, Martin's Spring Mountain Cellars, Nepenthe Cellars, Napa Valley Wine Cellars, Spring Mountain Vineyards, Mount Sterling, and Swan Vineyards ("Action along California's North Coast," *Wines and Vines* 50 [October 1969]: 17).

15. This shift was attributed in part to more women in households going to work, and in

part to inflation; whatever the real net gain in income might have been, all seem agreed that there was a genuine rise in disposable income among Americans.

16. The specifications are from a survey carried out for Coca-Cola's Wine Spectrum: Peter Sealey, "Inside Taylor California Cellars," *Wines and Vines* 62 (December 1981): 44.

17. A survey of winery practices made in 1967 concluded that the people making varietal table wines in California "are very much aware of advances in wine technology and are quick to adapt applicable advances to their operation" (G. M. Cooke and H. W. Berg, "Varietal Table Wine Processing Practices in California, I: Varieties, Grape and Juice Handling and Fermentation," *American Journal of Enology and Viticulture* 20 [1969]: 6).

18. Leon D. Adams, "Who Caused the Wine Revolution," *Wines and Vines* 60 (February 1979): 38, repeating the argument he had made in "The Wine Revolution in America Cannot Be Over-Emphasized," *Wines and Vines* 55 (September 1974): 68. Adams notes that one well-known technologist told him, "Since I began making good table wine I've begun drinking it myself."

19. The states that followed Washington in switching from state monopoly to food stores are Idaho, Iowa, New Hampshire, Maine, Alabama, West Virginia, and Montana. Some other states, of course, had long allowed the sale of wine in food stores.

20. Sealey, "Inside Taylor California Cellars," p. 42. The "Francophile" atmosphere of the Kennedy years has been given as yet another contributing reason for the wine revolution (Paul Lukacs, *American Vintage: The Rise of American Wine* [Boston: Houghton Mifflin, 2000], p. 187).

21. Louis Gomberg, "Is Consumer Scarcity the Industry's Main Woe?" *Wines and Vines* 57 (September 1976): 30.

22. The importers of the leading brand of Lambrusco, Riunite, began with a shipment of 100 cases in 1967; in 1983 they sold 11 million cases, "more wine than all of the French and German imports combined" (Larry Walker, "Villa Banfi Winery Is Dedicated," *Wines and Vines* 65 [November 1984]: 93).

23. Andrew Barr, *Drink: A Social History of America* (New York: Carroll and Graf, 1999), p. 121. Frank Prial makes the same argument in his "Wine Talk" column, *New York Times*, 6 March 1985, III, 13: most table wine drunk in the United States was then white wine, and "white wine is, in this country, more of a substitute for liquor than it is a companion to food."

24. Kirby S. Moulton, "Will Red Wine, Not White Wine, Be the Wine of Tomorrow?" *Wines and Vines* 58 (September 1977): 36. The sales director for Coca-Cola's wine interests declared in 1981 that "the white wine phenomenon is fundamental and long term. White wines are here to stay" (Sealey, "Inside Taylor California Cellars," p. 44).

25. In the six years 1974–79, sales of California red table wine remained fairly steady at approximately 50 million gallons. Sales of white table wines in the same period rose from just under 40 million gallons to about 110 million ("The First Color Breakdown of Table Wine Marketings," *Wines and Vines* 60 [December 1979]: 28).

26. The acreage of Chardonnay in California jumped from 2,500 in 1970 to 16,000 in 1979, of Chenin blanc from 5,600 to 27,600, of French Colombard from 13,000 to 35,800, of Sauvignon blanc from 834 to 6,200, of Semillon from 773 to 2,750, and of Riesling

from 1,400 to 9,500 (California Crop and Livestock Reporting Service, *California Grape Acreage* for the relevant years).

27. Jon Fredrikson, "The '80s Didn't Deliver as Forecast," *Wines and Vines* 71 (June 1990): 33.

28. My belief in the continuity of the history of California wine is greatly reinforced by the fact that the only two historians who have made a serious study of the period in question are on the same side. James T. Lapsley, though his focus is on Napa Valley alone, sees the transformation of the 1960s as the "harvest" of long years of preparation (*Bottled Poetry: Napa Winemaking from Prohibition to the Modern Era* [Berkeley: University of California Press, 1996], p. 1 and chap. 11). Charles L. Sullivan, also writing about Napa, uses a similar organic metaphor: "the seeds of the coming revolution were germinating as the fifties wound down" (*Napa Wine: A History from Mission Days to Present* [San Francisco: Wine Appreciation Guild, 1994], p. 254).

29. Depending on the style of the writer, one spoke of a wine "boom" or of a "revolution," "craze," "mania," or "explosion." I have not seen other terms.

30. Joseph L. Swarthout, "The New York Wine Industry: Continued Prosperity," *Wines and Vines* 56 (September 1975): 62.

31. Charles A. Carpy, "Freemark Abbey: A Napa Valley Winery Is Reborn," *Wines and Vines* 50 (September 1969): 19.

32. Mirassou began to develop its own brand in the late '50s at the winery; in 1966 it moved into general distribution of its brand ("Mirassou Starts Brand Business," *Wines and Vines* 47 [September 1966]: 6).

33. For the new Napa County facility, see "The Christian Brothers Build Big St. Helena Wine Complex," *Wines and Vines* 53 (March 1972): 12.

34. *Wines and Vines* 56 (February 1975): 12.

35. Almadén: *Wines and Vines* 54 (March 1973): 22; "Big New Names in Central Valley," *Wines and Vines* 55 (March 1974): 17. Masson: "Masson Adding 2.1 Million," *Wines and Vines* 52 (July 1971): 11. Masson also, against the trend, made a large investment in new facilities for sherry production in Madera County (*Wines and Vines* 55 [March 1974]: 17).

36. "Franzia Brothers . . . on the Move," *Wines and Vines* 52 (October 1971): 30; 54 (March 1973): 22.

37. Louis Gomberg, "Gomberg Sees Long Range Wine Grape Surplus Program," *California Grape Grower* (December 1973): 34.

38. In the early years of the wine boom—before the new plantings of superior varieties could come into production and as demand rose—winemakers inevitably went in for "stretching." A. J. Winkler, in 1971, thought that "our wines are not as good right now as they were five or ten years ago because they are being stretched to a degree with ordinary varieties" (*Viticultural Research at University of California, Davis, 1921–1971*, interview by Ruth Teiser, Berkeley: Regional Oral History Office, Bancroft Library, University of California, 1973, p. 84).

39. Irving Marcus, "Blame," *Wines and Vines* 52 (November 1971): 4.

40. Figures from California Crop and Livestock Reporting Service, *California Grapes, Raisins, and Wine: Production and Marketing* (Sacramento, 1968–78). The difference between the prices paid for grape varieties at the bottom and at the top of the scale is immense:

as John McGrew has observed, "No other agricultural crop has such a wide price spread" ("Why Try to Improve on Perfection?" *Wines and Vines* 54 [May 1973]: 22).

41. Hutchinson, "The California Wine Industry," table 2.6, p. 114.

42. Allied offered three-year contracts renewable at the grower's option; Gallo offered a fifteen-year contract. Both were tied to the going market prices (Ron Berryhill, "A Grower Looks at Contract Agreements between Wineries and Growers," *Wines and Vines* 49 [February 1968]: 28–29).

43. "Varietal Table Wines Bow in Cork Finish at E. & J. Gallo," *Wines and Vines* 55 (November 1974): 21. These recommendations substantially agreed with those of the University of California.

44. Figures are from the California Crop and Livestock Reporting Service.

45. "Vineyards on West Side?" *Wines and Vines* 51 (October 1970): 23.

46. A. Dinsmoor Webb in "U.C.'s Webb: 200,000 New Acres?" *Wines and Vines* 60 (May 1979): 22.

47. *Wines and Vines* 53 (December 1972): 16.

48. The Central Valley wineries had in fact been producing an increasing quantity of table wine since about 1950, but without any significant change in the composition of the vineyards (Hutchinson, "The California Wine Industry," pp. 37, 40).

49. "Fresno State Beefs Up Enology," *Wines and Vines* 55 (February 1974): 46.

50. Quoted in *Wines and Vines* 51 (December 1970): 21. A report by Maynard A. Amerine and Douglas Fong on the results of added acid and controlled temperatures in fermenting Cabernet Sauvignon and Pinot noir from region IV grapes was not encouraging: one might get an improvement in color but not in flavor ("Further Studies on Making Wine of Varieties Grown in Region IV," *American Journal of Enology and Viticulture* 25 [1974]: 44–47).

51. Curtis J. Alley, C. S. Ough, and Maynard A. Amerine, "Grapes for Table Wines in California's Regions IV and V," *Wines and Vines* 52 (March 1971): 20–22. Region IV means San Joaquin, Stanislaus, and Merced Counties; region V is Madera, Fresno, Tulare, and Kern Counties.

52. "Davis 'Short Course' Draws 200-Plus," *Wines and Vines* 56 (May 1975): 35.

53. The first Carnelian wine, a Carnelian Nouveau, was released by Franciscan Vineyards in 1976, when some 2,000 acres had been planted. By the end of the decade, further planting had effectively ceased. Only 102 acres of Carmine were reported in 2000, and it has since disappeared from the list of varieties reported by the California Agricultural Statistics Service.

54. Roy Brady, "Letter from California: Whither Californian Wine?" *Wine and Food* 127 (Autumn 1965): 60. Brady was thinking of the Ruby Cabernet produced by the Ficklin Vineyard in Madera County.

55. Maynard A. Amerine, in "Davis 'Short Course' Draws 200-Plus," p. 35.

56. California Agricultural Statistics Service, *California Grape Acreage*, 1985 and 2001. By far the greater part of these plantings is in San Joaquin County: nearly 34,000 acres.

57. The varieties first offered, under the M. LaMont label, were Ruby Cabernet, Barbera, Zinfandel, French Colombard, Chenin blanc, Emerald Riesling, and Grenache rosé.

These were at least a defensible selection for the conditions of region V, in which the Bear Mountain winery lay. Five years later, Bear Mountain introduced what it called the first San Joaquin Chardonnay ("M. LaMont Lays Claim to First San Joaquin Chardonnay," *Wines and Vines* 58 [August 1977]: 12).

58. In 1963 the entire production of Sierra was of fortified wines; by 1981 it had more than tripled in size and fortified wines made up only 2 percent of production. Instead, it offered some twenty varietal table wines, including Feher Szagos, Peverella, and Ugni blanc ("Sierra: A Bulk Winery Making Top Table Wine," *Wines and Vines* 62 [April 1981]: 35).

59. "Papagni Has First Crush at New Winery at Madera, Calif.," *Wines and Vines* 54 (November 1973): 17. Papagni took the interesting view that his new winery was a reversion to the pre-Prohibition days, when the Central Valley produced wines with a "style and quality" after which he "would fashion his own wines" (*Papagni Press* [newsletter] 1, no. 1 [Autumn 1976]).

60. Papagni, in legal and financial difficulties, filed for bankruptcy in 1986; the winery he built is now devoted to the production of grape concentrate.

61. Gallo's cork-finished varietal wines were introduced in 1974 ("Varietal Table Wines Bow in Cork Finish," p. 21). Unlike other Central Valley producers, Gallo already had large sources outside the valley.

62. Preface to a MS on California wine dated 18 October 1975, Roy Brady papers, University of California, Davis, Shields Library.

63. See chapter 7, at note 69.

64. Soter, after making wine for Chappellet and others and while consulting for a number of wineries, founded Etude Wines, which he recently sold to Beringer Blass; he continues as Etude's winemaker and has his own winery in Oregon. Corison also made wine for others before establishing Corison Winery in St. Helena. Campbell has been vineyardist, winemaker, sales manager, and everything else at his Laurel Glen Vineyard on Sonoma Mountain.

65. The fullest and most interesting account of this era in California winemaking that I know of is Charles L. Sullivan's series of interviews with the generation of winemakers working in and around the Santa Cruz mountains from the 1960s onward: *Wines and Winemakers of the Santa Cruz Mountains: An Oral History* (Cupertino, Calif.: D. R. Bennion Trust, 1995).

66. The wineries founded in Napa in the 1970s were Alatera, Beckett Cellars, Buehler Vineyards, Burgess, Cakebread, Carneros Creek, Cassayre-Forni, Caymus, Charles F. Shaw, Chateau Chevalier, Chateau Montelena, Clos du Val, Conn Creek, Cuvaison, Diamond Creek, Domaine Chandon, Evensen, Field Stone, Flora Springs, Forman, Franciscan, Green and Red Vineyard, Grgich Hills, Joseph Phelps, Long Vineyards, Markham, Mount Veeder, Napa Vintners, Napa Wine Cellars, Oak Knoll, Pecota, Pine Ridge, Pope Valley, Raymond, Ritchie Creek, Riverbend, Robert Keenan, Roddis, Round Hill, Rutherford Hill, Rutherford Vintners, St. Clement, S. Anderson, Sattui, Shafer, Silveroak, Smith-Madrone, Spotteswoode, Stag's Leap Wine Cellars, Stags' Leap Winery, Stonegate, Trefethen, Tudal, Tulocay, Villa Mount Eden, Vose, Whitehall Lane, William Hill, Yverdon, and ZD Wines.

67. See chapter 7, at n. 55.

68. Louis Gomberg notes, apropos of the steady decline in the number of mom-and-pop wineries in the '70s, "The wine business is quite different, and far more demanding, than the grape business; . . . wine calls for technical, management and marketing skills, continuing capital outlays for facility maintenance and expansion, inventory buildup and market development, and above all, a degree of capital intensity considerably exceeding that of basic farming operations" ("The Five-Faced Winery Picture," *Wines and Vines* 61 [September 1980]: 40).

69. A. Dinsmoor Webb reported in "It Costs a Million Dollars for a Small Winery," *Wines and Vines* 57 (December 1976): 14. If something more than a small winery were wanted, then costs might be anything. André Tchelistcheff guessed that between 1972 and 1979 Thomas Jordan had spent $50 million on the Jordan estate and winery (*Grapes, Wine, and Ecology*, interview by Ruth Teiser and Catherine Harroun, Berkeley: Regional Oral History Office, Bancroft Library, University of California, 1983, p. 181).

70. The best account I know is Gerald Asher, "The Judgment of Paris Revisited," *Gourmet* 57 (January 1997): 24, 97–99. The complete list of the wines in the tasting is as follows: *California Chardonnay:* Spring Mountain '73, Freemark Abbey '72, Chalone '74, Veedercrest '72, Chateau Montelena '73, and David Bruce '73. *French white Burgundy:* Meursault-Charmes Domaine Roulot '73, Beaune Clos des Mouches '73, Bâtard-Montrachet '73, and Puligny-Montrachet, Premier Cru Les Pucelles '72. *California Cabernet:* Clos du Val '72, Mayacamas '71, Ridge Vineyard Mountain Range '71, Freemark Abbey '69, Stag's Leap Wine Cellars '73, and Heitz Cellars Martha's Vineyard '70. *Bordeaux:* Château Mouton-Rothschild '70, Château Haut-Brion '70, Château Montrose '70, and Château Léoville-Las-Cases '71.

71. "Californians Defeat French Wines in Paris Tasting," *Wines and Vines* 57 (August 1976): 18.

72. John A. Knechel, "Bank of America Lays It On the Line; It's a Rosy 10 Years ahead for Wine," *Wines and Vines* 51 (September 1970): 34. The bank said that a rising disposable income and the arrival at drinking age of "forty million young adults" during the decade were major items in its calculations.

73. G. Michael Oberst, "The California Wine Industry," industry report (San Francisco: Wells Fargo Bank, September 1972). In fact, consumption reached 480 million gallons in 1980: as Lapsley says, "The Wells Fargo economists deserve a prize" (*Bottled Poetry*, p. 270).

74. Philip E. Hiaring, "World's Largest Bank Sees 650-Million-Gallon Market for Wine in U.S. in 1980," *Wines and Vines* 54 (September 1973): 21. The *New York Times* remarked of this report that "its tone is almost rhapsodic" (22 September 1973, 16).

75. Louis Gomberg, "Supplying a Demand of 1-Billion Gallons," *Wines and Vines* 53 (February 1972): 22.

76. *Time* (27 November 1972).

77. One of the most heavily promoted limited partnerships, Oakville Vineyards—which had bought the old Inglenook ranch and house (but not the winery) from the John Daniel estate—went bust in 1976, a victim of the recession that hit the wine trade in 1973–74. A number of other wineries changed hands in these years. The riskiness of such ventures for those looking for quick results was clearly set forth in "The Grapes of Wrath," *Dun's Review* (July 1972): 35–37, 82.

78. "Vintage Years for California Wineries," *Business Week* (19 September 1970): 48.

79. At the end of the decade of the 1970s, the tally of the more important outside interests stood thus: National Distillers owned Almadén; Labatt Brewery (Canada) owned Bear Mountain; Heublein owned Beaulieu, Italian Swiss Colony, Inglenook, and United Vintners; Nestlé owned Beringer; Beatrice Foods owned Brookside; Coca-Cola of New York owned Franzia; Schlitz owned Geyser Peak; Seagram's owned Masson; Coca-Cola of Atlanta owned Monterey and Sterling; Norton Simon owned San Martin; Schiefflin and Company owned Simi; and Renfield Importers owned Sonoma Vineyards.

80. Widmer's sold the vineyard in 1979. Gold Seal Vineyards, Taylor's neighbor on Lake Keuka, developed large vineyards in Monterey and Tulare Counties in the early 1970s, but no wine seems to have come to market from them under the Gold Seal name (*New York Times*, 18 April 1973, 76; *Wines and Vines* 56 [July 1975]: 20; "New York Is No Stranger to 1975 Vintage Uncertainties," *Wines and Vines* 56 [October 1975]: 27).

81. Foreign investment continued to grow in California: by 1985 it was estimated that "more than 40 wineries, vineyards, or wine-related businesses in California are foreign owned or financed" (Walter Vornbrock, "The Lure of California Land," *Wines and Vines* 66 [November 1985]: 20).

82. Louis Gomberg, "Analyst Sees 5–6% Annual Growth Rate," *Wines and Vines* 55 (October 1974): 27. Gomberg repeated this figure in 1979, noting that the capital came from "all sources—banks, insurance companies, distillers, importers, private investors, and others. Three quarters of that money went for vineyards, the remaining quarter of a billion for capital improvements" ("To Interpret Statistics Know Which Wines You're Talking About," *Wines and Vines* 60 [August 1979]: 24).

83. In her survey, published as late as 1980, Irene W. Hayes found sixty-five of these "ghost wineries," as she called them (*Ghost Wineries of Napa Valley: A Photographic Tour of the 19th Century* [San Francisco: Sally Taylor and Friends, 1980]).

84. "I am in a dismal little restaurant in the Napa valley. Since it is the only eating place for miles, the policy is to charge the famine price for hamburgers. You order them rare; they come charred" (Hugh Johnson, "The Wines of California," *Gourmet* 30 [October 1970]: 16).

85. Philip M. Wagner described it even more bleakly in 1949: "Napa Valley was a shabby place. . . . Everything needed paint. There was only one place where you could get edible food. . . . Everybody was in debt to the Bank of America" ("Keynoter Philip Wagner," *American Wine Society Journal* 18 [Winter 1986]: 125).

86. The quarrel over permitting the wine train to operate was extraordinarily bitter; the residents of the valley evidently considered it the last straw in the burden of tourism that had been piled on them. The train is not allowed to stop at any wineries along the way.

87. One might doubt that charity would have anything to do with it were it not for the fact that the regulations require some such object in order for an auction to be held at all.

88. Roy Brady, reviewing the literature of California wine in 1984, says of Melville's "bland" book: "Rereading the book today, the most startling thing is that a good 40 percent of the wineries are no more, and almost as many survive in little but name" (in Doris Muscatine, Maynard A. Amerine, and Bob Thompson, eds., *The University of California/ Sotheby Book of California Wine* [Berkeley: University of California Press, and London: Sotheby Publications, 1984], p. 310).

89. Ibid.

90. Charles L. Sullivan, *A Companion to California Wine: An Encyclopedia of Wine and Wine-making from the Mission Period to the Present* (Berkeley: University of California Press, 1998), *s.v.* "Grau and Werner." Wine journalism was not wholly unknown in the United States, but it was unusual. G. Selmer Fougner had written a column called "Along the Wine Trail" in the *New York Sun* from 1933 to 1941, but it was long before he had any successors. According to Hudson Cattell, the first regular newspaper column on wine by an American was by Ruth Ellen Church in the *Chicago Tribune*, 1962 ("Ruth Ellen Church—In Memoriam," *Wine East* 19 [March–April 1992]: 5).

91. Frank J. Prial, "Wine Talk," *New York Times*, 7 July 1973, 16.

92. R. Bradford Webb, *Brad Webb: Innovator*, interview by William Heintz, 1988 (Healdsburg, Calif.: Sonoma County Wine Library Oral History, 1991), p. 73. Webb did not foresee the transformation of the restaurant cook into the figure of the master chef, rivaling the winemaker for prestige.

93. *New York Times*, 5 October 1975, 64.

94. *Wine East* 30 (January–February 2003): 42–45.

95. I do not mean to say that home winemaking has disappeared: far from it. There is probably a more accomplished group of home winemakers at work than ever before, but the brief fashion has passed.

96. Harriet Lembeck in the *New York Times*, 8 January 1976, XIII, 6.

97. See Charles L. Sullivan, *The Society of Wine Educators: A History of Its Inception and the First Ten Years* (Princeton, N.J.: Bob Levine, 2000).

98. The *New York Times* reported in 1976 that there were then "wine courses at 600 colleges around the country every year" (8 January 1976, XIII, 6).

99. *Wines and Vines* 65 (May 1984): 16.

CHAPTER 11. A NEW DAWN (I)

1. Philip M. Wagner, "Vintage in the Finger Lakes," *Wine East* 26 (May–June 1998): 14; the article was written in 1963.

2. The same thing was happening to the other big Finger Lakes wineries. Gold Seal signed a marketing agreement with Seagram's in 1975, and four years later was bought out by Seagram's. Widmer's was bought by the R. T. French Company, itself a part of the British Reckitt and Colman Company, in 1971. All of these businesses had been greatly expanded since the beginning of the '60s.

3. Wines from the native hybrids continued to be produced by the Taylor Winery at Hammondsport, but there was to be no more expansion in that quarter: the energies behind Taylor were now diverted to California.

4. It is now the site at which Manischewitz kosher-style wines are made.

5. Sands (1924–99) presided over a great expansion of his firm's activity before his death, including dealings in imported beers, distilled spirits, cider, and bottled waters.

6. Leon D. Adams, *The Wines of America* (Boston: Houghton Mifflin, 1973), p. 58.

7. The name of the winery is Richard's, but that of the wine is Richards, without the apostrophe.

8. *Wines and Vines* 55 (April 1974): 16. The word *wino*, meaning an "alcoholic, particularly one who drinks cheap domestic wine," is of American origin (Eric Partridge, *Dictionary of Slang*, 8th ed.). The earliest entry for the word in the *Oxford English Dictionary* is from 1915.

9. With the acquisition of the Australian firm BRL Hardy in 2003, the total capacity of Canandaigua-Constellation's wine properties surpassed that of Gallo, but not all of that production was American.

10. Adams, *The Wines of America*, p. 59: Adams points out that Sands used the label not just for a Scuppernong but for a whole line of wines, including fruit wines.

11. The storage capacities were 5 million at Canandaigua, 2 million at Richard's, 500,000 at Tenner Brothers, 50,000 at Onslow, and 400,000 at Hammondsport.

12. *Wines and Vines* 55 (April 1974): 16. Bisceglia Winery was originally the Yosemite cooperative, founded in 1946.

13. "Done Deal," *Wines and Vines* 74 (October 1993): 15.

14. At the end of the decade of the '90s, Canandaigua's brands included Almadén, Bisceglia, Cook's, Cresta Blanca, Cribari, Deer Valley, Dunnewood, Estancia, Franciscan, Guild, Inglenook, Gold Seal, Great Western, Henri Marchant, Italian Swiss Colony, Manischewitz, Masson, Mateus, Roma, Simi, Taylor California Cellars, Taylor New York, Virginia Dare, and Widmer. In 2001 Canandaigua added six more labels by purchase from Sebastiani: Vendange, Talus, Heritage, Nathanson Creek, La Terre, and Farallon. As these were only brand names to start with, rather than actual wineries, they did not have the same significance as the older labels in this multifarious gallery. It has since been much added to.

15. Caywood (1819–89) is best known for his introduction of the variety called Dutchess.

16. Taylor (1931–2001) was outspoken in his belief that New York wines depended too much on ameliorating and on blending with California wine (tank-car wine) and was fired from the Taylor Wine Company for his imprudent expression of this belief. After Taylor was sold to Coca-Cola in 1977, Walter Taylor was successfully sued to prevent his use of the Taylor name on the wines from his Bully Hill Vineyards. His protracted court fights with Coca-Cola over this issue, and his use of cleverly altered labels, generated much publicity for Bully Hill.

17. In any comprehensive discussion of the establishment of vinifera in the East, many others besides Dr. Frank would have to be mentioned. The first modern commercial trial of growing vinifera in eastern North America, for example, was by T. G. Bright and Company in Ontario in 1946 (Keith H. Kimball, "Another Look at Vinifera in the East," *Wines and Vines* 42 [April 1961]: 63). Bright's first vinifera wines were made in 1955.

18. See chapter 8, at n. 22.

19. Charles Fournier, "Birth of N.Y. State Pinot Chardonnay," *Wines and Vines* 42 (January 1961): 32. Fournier says that between 1953 and 1961 Frank made "over 250,000 grafts representing thousands of combinations of 58 rootstocks with 12 V. vinifera varieties and many clones of each of them in 9 soil conditions" ("A Scientific Look at Vinifera in the East," *Wines and Vines* 42 [August 1961]: 27).

20. "In trials [of vinifera] conducted by the Geneva Station, the various rootstocks did not differ in affecting the winter cold hardiness of the vines" (Nelson Shaulis, John Einset,

and A. Boyd Pack, "Growing Cold-Tender Grape Varieties in New York," Bulletin 821 [Geneva: New York State Agricultural Experiment Station, 1968], p. 10). This is still the official view of the question.

21. Frank's vineyards at Gold Seal and on his own property were seriously damaged by the cold winters of 1962 and 1963: "Some varieties were completely wiped out, others were damaged though not totally ruined" (Jim Gifford, "Vitis Vinifera in the East: Its Booming Future," *American Wine Society Journal* 15 [Fall 1983]: 68). And that is only one episode.

22. In 1996 there were 914 acres of Chardonnay and 385 acres of Riesling in New York (New York Agricultural Statistics Service, *Survey of Orchards and Vineyards, 1996* [Albany: New York State Department of Agriculture and Markets, 1996]).

23. Philip M. Wagner, "Grapes and Wine Production in the East," in *Wine Production Technology in the United States*, ed. Maynard A. Amerine (Washington, D.C.: American Chemical Society, 1981), p. 204.

24. The relationship of Frank and Fournier has been described as "fruitful but stormy" (*New York Times*, 18 April 1973, 49). It must also be acknowledged that by 1980 Gold Seal had concluded that vinifera grapes in the Finger Lakes were uneconomical (John P. Tomkins, "Comments on East Coast Viticulture," *Vinifera Wine Growers Journal* 8 [Summer 1981]: 78).

25. They more often than not owed a direct debt to Philip Wagner and his nursery of French hybrids as well. Largely owing to Frank's intransigent style, there grew up a factitious conflict between the Frankophiles and the Wagnerites, but Wagner himself was too judicious to participate in it.

26. Constitution of the American Wine Society, Article IIb. In later years the xenophobic note was diminished. Article II in the 1988 revision gives the society's purpose as promoting "the appreciation of wine, especially American wine."

27. The act reduced the license fee from $625 to $125; a New York farm winery could produce up to 50,000 gallons a year and could sell at wholesale and retail. Later legislation allowed a winery to operate an on-site restaurant and to open branch outlets.

28. The first farm winery license issued was to Mark Miller of Benmarl Vineyards in recognition of his efforts in securing the legislation (Mark Miller, *Wine—a Gentleman's Game: The Adventures of an Amateur Winemaker Turned Professional* [New York: Harper & Row, 1984], p. 180).

29. The figures are supplied by the New York State Wine and Grape Foundation. A decade later, when the total acreage had declined owing to the removal of unprofitable vineyards, Concord occupied 20,000 of the state's 31,000 acres (New York Agricultural Statistics Service, *Survey of Orchards and Vineyards, 1996*).

30. The average prices paid for New York wine grapes, largely determined by the big Finger Lakes wineries, fell from $305 a ton in 1981 to $182 in 1985, too low to cover the costs of production (George L. Casler, "New York's Vineyard Industry," *Wines and Vines* 68 [March 1987]: 26–27).

31. As a special concession to the grape growers, the state permitted wine coolers (low-alcohol mixes of wine and fruit juices) made from New York State grapes to be sold in New York grocery stores for two years, on an experimental basis (*New York Times*, 2 September

1984, IV, 6); the plan was quickly declared to be an illegal discrimination (*New York Times*, 27 February 1985, III, 13).

32. By Nelson Shaulis (Hudson Cattell, "Celebrating Riesling with History and a Tasting," *Wine East* 29 [July–August 2001]: 24).

33. There were 31 wineries on Long Island in 2004. Hargrave Winery, founded as the first on Long Island in 1973, was sold by Alexander Hargrave in 1999 for $4 million.

34. "Major Investments Spur Long Island Wine Growth," *Wine East* 28 (September–October 2001): 24–29.

35. *Pennsylvania Grape Letter and Wine News* 7 (April 1980): 1. The work was paid for by state funds collected from harness racing; it included experimental vineyards and, later, an experimental winery. Research on grapes had been carried out at the Erie County Station since 1937.

36. "Each vineyard and winery is a mini-research station generating information—ecological, economic, and enological data adding up to the present and pointing to the future" (Lucie T. Morton, *Winegrowing in Eastern America: An Illustrated Guide to Viticulture East of the Rockies* [Ithaca, N.Y.: Cornell University Press, 1985], p. 16).

37. This was Hudson Cattell's *Pennsylvania Grape Letter and Wine News,* from which grew the valuable magazine called *Wine East.* Cattell did not found the publication, but he took it over at an early stage.

38. One should note, however, that trials of grape varieties and rootstocks had been conducted at the USDA station at Meridian, Mississippi, since 1934. Meridian, it may be remembered, was where the USDA planned to build an experimental winery after Repeal: see chapter 2, at n. 8.

39. Morton, *Winegrowing in Eastern America,* p. 120, quoting Louis D. Wise, the Mississippi State University administrator instrumental in establishing the school's wine program.

40. Adams, *The Wines of America,* 3rd ed. (New York: McGraw-Hill, 1985), p. 536.

41. *New York Times,* 30 June 1984, 48. The case, usually referred to as the Bacchus case, is 468 U.S. 288 (1984).

42. Charles L. Sullivan, *Zinfandel: A History of a Grape and Its Wine* (Berkeley: University of California Press, 2003), chap. 2.

43. Adams, *The Wines of America,* 2nd ed. (New York: McGraw-Hill, 1978), p. 168.

44. Elizabeth Lincoln, "Grapes and Wine in the Nutmeg State," *American Wine Society Journal* 30 (Fall 1988): 85.

45. "Connecticut Legislation to Boost Grape Production," *Wine East* 29 (January–February 2002): 6–7.

46. James R. Williams, "Diary of a Farm Winery Bill," *American Wine Society Journal* 16 (Spring 1984): 22.

47. The Tewkesbury Winery, which had committed itself to vinifera, went out of business in 1992 because, as the owner said, "in the northern part of New Jersey it doesn't work to grow vinifera" (*New York Times,* 22 November 1992, XIII, 6).

48. See chapter 8, after n. 43.

49. According to Hudson Cattell, it was Henry Sonneman of Meier's Wine Cellars who had lobbied for this work to be done (*Wine East* 19 [January–February 1992]: 4).

50. The extent to which interest in research was growing in the state is shown by the fact

that the experimental vineyards were supported not only by the OARDC but by the Ohio Bankers Association and the Ohio Farm and Power Equipment Retailers' Association (Susan Sifritt, "The Ohio Grape and Wine Industries" [Ph.D. diss., Kent State University, 1976], p. 244).

51. Ohio Department of Development report, 1 January 1965, cited in Sifritt, "The Ohio Grape and Wine Industries," p. 243.

52. Adams, *The Wines of America*, 2nd ed., p. 98. The fact that Frank made "secrets" of his methods is one of the reasons his work was not accepted by the scientific establishment. Because he was unwilling to allow his work to be put to the test of replication, Frank could hardly have expected any other response.

53. Originally set at 3 cents a gallon and later raised to 5 cents, it provided nearly a million dollars annually by 1990.

54. The low was twenty-seven wineries in 1963; some fifty-two new wineries were founded between 1965 and 2000. By 2003 there were eighty-six bonded wineries and several more in the planning stage.

55. A brochure from this period, in support of the proposition that "there is a Meier's wine for every purpose and occasion," lists twenty-five different wines, including three burgundies, four ports, and three champagnes (copy in the author's collection).

56. He is credited with helping to initiate the Ohio Grape Industries Program.

57. See Eleanor Heald and Ray Heald, "Firelands Winery—Showcase for Ohio Vinifera Wines," *Practical Winery and Vineyard* 14 (November–December 1993): 44–46.

58. Ulysses Prentiss Hedrick, *The Grapes of New York* (Albany, N.Y.: J. B. Lyon, 1908), says that Black Pearl is probably a seedling of the Clinton grape, an old New York variety.

59. For that history, see chapter 8, after n. 46.

60. One should note, however, that the Bronte winery, one of the big Michigan wineries, began experimenting with French hybrids in 1953 (Adams, *The Wines of America*, 2nd ed., p. 213). This effort was apparently too little, too late: Bronte went out of business in 1984.

61. Tabor Hill's founder was forced to sell the winery in 1978, but it remained in business producing vinifera wines.

62. Kirk Heinze, "The Michigan Grape Industry: Transition, Progress, and Challenge," Special Report 8 (East Lansing: Michigan State University, Agricultural Experiment Station, 1983), p. 9. Concord continued to dominate all plantings, but proportionately less of it went into Michigan wine.

63. Ibid., p. 4.

64. See the discussion in chapter 8, after n. 62.

65. For one suggested explanation of this delay, see chapter 8, after n. 63.

66. The Norton vines are said to have been planted in 1868 (Bruce I. Reisch et al., "The Relationship between Norton and Cynthiana, Red Wine Cultivars Derived from *Vitis aestivalis*," *American Journal of Enology and Viticulture* 44 (1993): 441.

67. See the excellent study of German architectural and decorative work in Charles Van Ravenswaay, *The Arts and Architecture of German Settlement in Missouri* (Columbia: University of Missouri Press, 1977).

68. When Welch finally ended its contracts with Missouri Concord growers in 1991, they

covered only seventeen growers on 184 acres (*St. Louis Post Dispatch*, 2 September 1991).

69. William D. Heffernan and Paul Lasley, "Missouri Grape Industry Past, Present and Future" (Columbia: University of Missouri, Extension Division, 1977), p. 7; information from the Missouri Grape and Wine Program.

70. There is a long controversy over the relationship of these two names, some holding that Norton and Cynthiana are the same grape, others that they are quite distinct. See the discussions in Hedrick, *The Grapes of New York*, pp. 228–29 and 366–68. See also Reisch et al., "The Relationship between Norton and Cynthiana."

71. He was Bruce Zoecklein, from Fresno State University in California; in 1981 he was joined by Larry Lockshin as extension viticulturist. Lockshin had been trained at Cornell University, so that East and West met in Missouri.

72. For this development in the federal regulations, see chapter 14, after n. 44.

73. This tax was raised to 6 cents a gallon in 1988 and to 8 cents in 1998. The Department of Agriculture consults with the Missouri Wine Advisory Board on the allocation of the Grape and Wine Program budget.

74. Information from the Missouri Grape and Wine Program.

75. See Thomas Pinney, *A History of Wine in America: From the Beginnings to Prohibition* (Berkeley: University of California Press, 1989), p. 131, and the full account in James L. Butler and John J. Butler, *Indiana Wine: A History* (Bloomington: Indiana University Press, 2001).

76. The license fee is now $500, and the production limit is 500,000 gallons.

77. The 1975 Cabernet sold for $21.20 a bottle. A writer in the *Chicago Sun-Times* politely described it thus: "very light in color; fruity, berry nose; lots of spritz; mouthfuls of fruit, but very short on tannin and I do not predict a long life" (25 March 1976).

78. John J. Baxevanis, *The Wine Regions of America: Geographical Reflections and Appraisals* (Stroudsburg, Penn.: Vinifera Winegrowers Journal, 1992), p. 176.

79. Philip E. Hiaring, "A Vinous Tour of Indiana, the Hoosier State," *Wines and Vines* 57 (June 1976): 37.

80. "Viticulture Research in Indiana," *Wines and Vines* 74 (February 1993): 11. The university was conducting grape trials at four horticultural research farms in 2002.

81. Butler and Butler, *Indiana Wine*, pp. 155–205.

82. Illinois stood third among wine-producing states for many years. Mogen David moved from Chicago to Westfield, New York, in 1980; when it did, wine production in Illinois fell from 1,442,880 gallons in 1980 to 5,412 in 1981 ("Behind U.S. Wine Production Stats . . . A Few Surprises," *Eastern Grape Grower and Winery News* 8 [June 1983]: 12).

83. Togni to Roy Brady, 19 July 1966, Roy Brady papers, University of California, Davis, Shields Library.

84. The winery and vineyard were sold in 1969 to Dr. John Thompson, who restored the vineyard after securing promises from his neighbors to give up 2,4-D.

85. Imed Dami, "Illinois," *Wines and Vines* 84 (February 2003): 46.

86. Jim Rink, "Field of Dreams in Jackson County," *American Wine Society Journal* 33 (Spring 2001): 15.

87. For a full summary of these and earlier developments, see Penelope Krosch, "Grape Research in Minnesota," *Agricultural History* 62 (Spring 1988): 258–69.

88. Birger Johannessen, Minnesota Grape Growers Association brochure, 1987.

89. See Brian McGinty, *Strong Wine: The Life and Legend of Agoston Haraszthy* (Stanford, Calif.: Stanford University Press, 1998), pp. 120–21, for a discussion of the evidence.

90. In the nineteenth century Kansas had made some wine, in common with every other state, but the time that elapsed before any renewal took place was unusually long.

91. Dr. Thomas J. Schueneman, "The Grape in Kansas: Poised for a Winegrowing Comeback?" *Vinifera Wine Growers Journal* 9 (Winter 1982): 227.

92. At the Horticultural Research Center "the entire crop in 1980 was consumed by hordes of birds seeking relief from the record drought" (Schueneman, "The Grape in Kansas," p. 228).

93. *Vinifera Wine Growers Journal* 11 (Spring 1984): 68.

94. Millie Howie, "Cuthills Vineyard: A Winery in Pierce, Nebraska," *Wines and Vines* 81 (January 2000): 113.

CHAPTER 12. A NEW DAWN (II)

1. See chapter 8, "Philip Wagner and the French Hybrids."

2. Philip M. Wagner, *Wine Grapes: Their Selection, Cultivation, and Enjoyment* (New York: Harcourt Brace, 1937), p. 3.

3. Philip M. Wagner, "The East's New Wine Industry," *Wines and Vines* 60 (March 1979): 24.

4. Lucie T. Morton, *Winegrowing in Eastern America: An Illustrated Guide to Viticulture East of the Rockies* (Ithaca, N.Y.: Cornell University Press, 1985), p. 100.

5. Philip M. Wagner, "Philip M. Wagner. Federal Aid, Private Research, State Experiments, State Laws, and the Winery," *Vinifera Wine Growers Journal* 2 (Fall 1975): 18. See also Wagner's account of his struggles to ship wine to Texas: "More Trouble Than It's Worth," *Wines and Vines* 48 (March 1967): 29.

6. Information from the Association of Maryland Wineries.

7. The story of Westenberger is told by Hank Burchard, "Lorelei Vineyards of Luray: A Cautionary Tale," *Vinifera Wine Growers Journal* 4 (September 1977): 336–43.

8. The four were the Woburn Winery at Clarksville (storage capacity 5,000 gallons), notable for the fact that it was the property of an African American, John Lewis (see Lucie T. Morton, "An Update on Virginia Viticulture," *Wines and Vines* 62 [October 1981]: 48); Dixie Wine Company in Richmond (600,000 gallons); Laird and Company in North Garden (700,000 gallons); and Richard's Wine Cellars of Petersburg (2 million gallons). From these came such wines as Rustic Arbor, Southern Queen, Ramblin' Rose, and Old Mr. Mack.

9. Information from Robert Hutton, 2001.

10. *Farfelu,* according to *Larousse,* means "bizarre, extravagant, fantasque," which says a great deal about how winegrowing was then regarded in Virginia.

11. Elizabeth Furness at Piedmont Vineyards is credited with planting Virginia's first modern vinifera vineyard in 1973: see Lucie T. Morton, "Elizabeth Furness: Virginia's Wine Pioneer," *Eastern Grape Grower and Winery News* 5 (October 1979): 55.

12. Morton, "An Update on Virginia Viticulture," p. 47.

13. "The sometimes exasperating climate of Virginia" (Philip M. Wagner, "A Misleading Impression," *Wines and Vines* 59 [January 1978]: 50).

14. In the Bacchus case, 468 U.S. 288 (1984).

15. The board's purpose is "to increase the productivity of the grape and wine industry, provide for its orderly growth, and engage in research and publicity/promotion to improve marketing" (*Vinifera Wine Growers Journal* 13 [Spring 1986]: 12).

16. This is not as great an advantage as might be supposed. The state liquor stores are the only place where spirits may be purchased in Virginia, and that is what people go to them for. Wine of all sorts and origins may be freely bought in grocery stores and other shops.

17. "A Governor Tours Wine Country," *Wine East* 15 (July–August 1988): 8–11.

18. I calculate that about twenty-five have gone out of business since 1950.

19. See the discussion of *V. rotundifolia* in chapter 8, before n. 20.

20. Resistant "bunch grapes" (i.e., grapes other than rotundifolia) have been bred in the southern states but are not yet economically significant.

21. A main aim in the breeding program was to create varieties that would yield good red and white table wines. Such improved varieties of the muscadine grape as Magnolia, Carlos, and Noble, now widely grown in the South, came from the North Carolina State University program, led by Carlos Williams and William B. Nesbitt (Jean-Pierre Chambas, "The Growth of the Southeastern Vineyard," *The Sandlapper* [Clemson University; July 1981]: 31).

22. Clarence Gohdes, *Scuppernong: North Carolina's Grape and Its Wines* (Durham, N.C.: Duke University Press, 1982), p. 88.

23. The price for muscadines fell from $325 a ton in 1972 to $150 in 1976 (*Charlotte Observer*, 1 November 1983).

24. The annual winery license fee was set at $100. The tax on native wines was 5 cents per gallon; others paid 60 cents (Gohdes, *Scuppernong*, p. 90).

25. This ruling came in advance of the judgment in the Bacchus case but must have been affected by the probable outcome.

26. Pamela Watson, *Carolina Wine Country: The Complete Guide* (Greenville, N.C.: Woodhaven Publishing, 1999), p. 55.

27. *Wine East* 15 (January–February 1988): 4.

28. The ambitious scale of the original planning for the Biltmore Winery has not been reached. There were to have been 600 acres of vineyard and a winery capacity to match— say, 400,000 gallons—by 1994 (*Vinifera Wine Growers Journal* 12 [Summer 1985]: 85). According to the *Wines and Vines* 2004 directory, Biltmore then had 77 acres of vines and a storage capacity of 224,000 gallons. Much of the wine, as has been noted, is made from imported juice.

29. Tenner Brothers had originally been in North Carolina: see chapter 8, after n. 86.

30. Richard L. Leizear, "S. C. Muscadine Winery Denounces Technology," *Vinifera Wine Growers Journal* 2 (Spring 1975): 47.

31. It is said that the South Carolina wholesalers, under pressure from the wineries that supplied them, refused to handle Oakview wines and so compelled it to go out of busi-

ness (H. C. George, "Behind the Scenes . . . How Alabama's Farm Winery Law Came to Be," *Wines and Vines* 60 [December 1979]: 37).

32. James J. Cox, "A Bit of France in South Carolina," *Wines and Vines* 62 (March 1981): 50.

33. See the account of Monarch's origins in Leon D. Adams, *The Wines of America* (Boston: Houghton Mifflin, 1973), pp. 50–51.

34. *New York Times*, 23 August 1982, 15.

35. According to the National Agricultural Statistics Service, Georgia had 1,100 acres of vineyard in 2002.

36. According to R. P. Bates, professor of food science, University of Florida, "More than any other state Florida is plagued by serious impediments to grape growing" ("The Emerging Florida Wine Industry," *American Wine Society Journal* 17 [Summer 1985]: 44).

37. John A. Mortensen, "Developing Florida's Grape Industry from the Breeder's Viewpoint," *Vinifera Wine Growers Journal* 15 (Fall 1988): 184. One such hybrid is a white grape called Blanc de Bois, introduced in 1987.

38. Robert D. Shaw Jr., "The Grapes of Hope," *Vinifera Wine Growers Journal* 1 (Spring 1974): 13–14.

39. In 2003 there were eight: Chautauqua, Three Oaks, Dakotah, San Sebastian, Lakeridge, Florida Orange Groves and Winery, Rosa Fiorelli, and Eden Vineyards.

40. *Wall Street Journal*, 30 June 1995, A, 14.

41. William O. Beach letter, *Eastern Grape Grower and Winery News* 9 (August–September 1983): 41.

42. The South is particularly rich in such contradictions. The county in which the famous Jack Daniels whiskey is distilled in Tennessee is Dry, so no whiskey may be sold there: distilled, yes; sold, no. Such things are comic, no doubt, but grotesquely so.

43. "Ready for a West Virginia Wine? It's Coming," *Wine East* 8 (July 1981): 17.

44. Robert Cowie, who takes an interest in the history of winegrowing in Arkansas, has opened a museum devoted to the subject at his winery.

45. Author's interview, 1994.

46. The plan of the Cotner Vineyard was to concentrate on the Cynthiana, the aestivalis variety that is regarded as Arkansas's own (*Wines and Vines* 68 [May 1987]: 17).

47. There were 1,500 acres of vineyard in Arkansas in 2001, tenth place among the states.

48. Sarah Jane English, *The Wines of Texas: A Guide and a History*, rev. ed. (Austin: Eakin Press, 1986), p. 23.

49. The name, meaning "staked plain" in Spanish, is supposed to come from an episode in Coronado's futile search for the cities of Cibola: in order not to get lost on the featureless plains, he ordered stakes to be driven to mark a route.

50. Jim Hicks, "Space Age Technology to Develop Yellow Rosé of Texas," *American Wine Society Journal* 7 (Fall 1975): 37.

51. "History of the New Texas Wine Grape Industry," in English, *The Wines of Texas*, p. 185.

52. "Texas Talks of Growing Wine Grapes," *Wines and Vines* 60 (August 1979): 35; Leon D. Adams, *The Wines of America*, 2nd ed. (New York: McGraw-Hill, 1978), pp. 203–04.

53. Quoted in English, *The Wines of Texas*, p. 24.

54. The bizarre complexities of liquor regulation in this country are well shown by the state of the laws in Texas. There are 184 counties in which distilled spirits are legal, but in

parts of some of those counties they are not legal. Five counties will not permit spirits but allow beverages under 14 percent alcohol. Eleven counties allow only beer of less than 4 percent. And fifty-four counties are wholly Dry.

55. The Guadalupe Valley Winery, bonded in 1975, was the earliest of all the "new" Texas wineries, but it began as a bottling rather than a producing enterprise.

56. These wines were made at an experimental winery in Midland that the university operated until 1991.

57. *New York Times,* 23 July 1980, III, 14.

58. Carolyn Bobo, "University of Texas Is Fostering Wine Production," *Wines and Vines* 64 (November 1983): 46.

59. Louise Owens, "Ste Genevieve," in *The Oxford Companion to the Wines of North America,* ed. Bruce Cass (New York: Oxford University Press, 2000), p. 206.

60. According to Jim Kamas, "The single greatest risk to growing *Vitis vinifera* cultivars [in Texas] is Pierce's disease" (*Growing Grapes in the Texas Hill Country* [Fredericksburg: Texas Agricultural Extension Service, ca. 2000], p. 1). Lucie T. Morton, "The Prospects for Texas Wine," *Wines and Vines* 61 (October 1980): 26–33. Another lurking problem for Texas is phylloxera. Most of the new vineyards have been planted on their own roots and will be vulnerable when the pest shows up.

61. Charles O. McKinney and John E. Crosby, "Vineyards in Texas—Past and Present," *Wines and Vines* 71 (June 1990): 57.

62. Figures on wine production from the Texas Wine Marketing Research Institute; on acreage, from the Texas Department of Agriculture.

63. Louise Owens, "Texas," in *The Oxford Companion to the Wines of North America,* ed. Cass, p. 234.

64. See ibid., pp. 235–36, for a summary.

65. This was the Schwarz Winery in Okarche; it managed to operate until 1989. There had been at least one pre-Prohibition winery, near Oklahoma City, founded when Oklahoma was still a territory, but when Oklahoma was given statehood in 1907 it entered the Union as a Dry state: see Thomas Pinney, *A History of Wine in America: From the Beginnings to Prohibition* (Berkeley: University of California Press, 1989), pp. 410–11.

66. Homer Bigart, "Welfare Clients Tend Oklahoma Vineyard," *New York Times,* 26 June 1972, 35.

67. *Wines and Vines* 53 (March 1972): 18.

68. *New York Times,* 26 June 1972.

69. According to Adams, the cause was a change in the state administration (*The Wines of America,* 2nd ed., p. 197); no doubt that contributed.

70. Terri L. Darrow, "Winegrowing in Oklahoma," *Wines and Vines* 69 (October 1988): 42.

71. *The Wine Spectator* 27 (31 May 2002): 142–44 published an interesting report on 117 wines tasted from wineries in the southern states, including Georgia Merlot, North Carolina Shiraz, Maryland Cabernet franc, and a Bordeaux blend from Virginia. The average bottle cost was $20, with a range from $9 to $35; the highest score, on the magazine's 100-point system, was 86 for a Virginia Bordeaux blend, a Virginia Syrah, and a North Carolina Chardonnay.

1. There is, of course, *some* rain: the Yakima Valley averages 7.5 inches annually.

2. Judy Peterson-Nedry, *Washington Wine Country* (Portland, Oreg.. Graphic Arts Publishing Center, 1999), pp. 23–24; Ronald Irvine with Walter J. Clore, *The Wine Project: Washington State's Winemaking History* (Vashon, Wash.: Sketch Publications, 1997), p. 428.

3. Steenborg (1903–91) had come to the United States in 1926 and worked as a draftsman for a utility company. When Repeal came he was "the only trained winemaker in the Pacific Northwest," and his services were eagerly sought after. He made wines from native American varieties at the St. Charles Winery before moving to the Upland Winery (Irvine, *The Wine Project*, p. 134).

4. Erich Steenborg, "Wine Grapes in the State of Washington," *Wine Review* 7 (October 1939): 12.

5. *Wine Review* 7 (October 1939): 13.

6. "Winery Expands," *Wines and Vines* 21 (February 1940): 27. The Island Belle grape is in fact the variety known as Campbell Early, a blue labrusca-vinifera hybrid introduced in 1892.

7. In 2002 there were nearly 50,000 acres of grapes in Washington, of which half were considered wine grapes; the other half was overwhelmingly Concord (National Agricultural Statistics Service Web site).

8. See, e.g., Irvine, *The Wine Project*, p. 80: "To Dr. Amerine, Washington state must have seemed like the end of the viticultural universe." Another Davis expert, Professor Singleton, is reported as saying that "Washington will never grow wine grapes" (ibid., p. 219).

9. Ray to Julian Street, 29 September 1940, Julian Street papers, Princeton University, Firestone Library. The full remark is as follows:

   Amerine knows about conditions in Oregon and Washington for grape growing—or has contacts who do. I only know it is done and can be improved upon in eastern Washington. . . . Yes, Washington has every possibility for successful grape growing in its eastern valleys. How successful only further experience would tell. I think the soil would determine the extent of success, for the climate is okay at places, I know.

10. Frank Schoonmaker and Tom Marvel, *American Wines* (New York: Duell, Sloan & Pearce, 1941), p. 119.

11. Maynard A. Amerine, "Some Comments on Wine in America," *Wine and Food* 36 (Winter 1942): 197. E. H. Twight, who had been Amerine's mentor in wine, had done horticultural work in Idaho before World War I and had published a report on the vineyards of the Columbia River basin in 1915.

12. See the discussion in Irvine, *The Wine Project*, p. 135. The method is presented in Bernard Henry, *Studies of Yeasts and the Fermentation of Fruits and Berries of Washington* (Seattle: University of Washington Press, 1936). It would appear to be a kind of syruped fermentation, in which grape concentrate is added to a fermenting must at intervals in order to reach a high alcohol level.

13. Irvine, *The Wine Project*, p. 149.

14. Ibid., p. 410.

15. Ibid., p. 160; Leon D. Adams, *The Wines of America* (Boston: Houghton Mifflin, 1973), p. 338.

16. Adams, *The Wines of America*, p. 335.

17. The report, written by W. J. Clore, C. W. Nagel, and G. H. Carter, is ponderously titled *Ten Years of Grape Variety Responses and Wine-Making Trials in Central Washington*, Bulletin 823 (Pullman: College of Agriculture Research Center, Washington State University, 1976).

18. "Coming: A New Era in Washington State," *Wines and Vines* 50 (April 1969): 21.

19. Lloyd S. Woodburne, "Vintner Views Washington State," *Wines and Vines* 62 (March 1981): 26. Woodburne, a professor of psychology, was the founder of the University of Washington group. He later retired from teaching to take over the full-time management of the winery. Woodburne may be counted among the many who were first led to winemaking by reading Philip Wagner's writings.

20. It is now (as of 2003) the property of Constellation Brands (Canandaigua).

21. "Vinifera in Wash. State," *Wines and Vines* 51 (August 1970): 20.

22. Earlier, before its amalgamation into American Wine Growers, the Pommerelle Company had hired Bradford Webb as winemaker for its berry wines. Webb later made history in California for his work at Hanzell Vineyards: see chapter 9, at n. 102.

23. André Tchelistcheff, *Grapes, Wine, and Ecology*, interview by Ruth Teiser and Catherine Harroun, Berkeley: Regional Oral History Office, Bancroft Library, University of California, 1983, pp. 195–96.

24. Ibid., p. 196. Adams takes the credit for suggesting that Tchelistcheff be invited to consult in Washington (*The Wines of America*, p. 335).

25. The legislative act was sarcastically known as the California wine bill (Irvine, *The Wine Project*, p. 175).

26. "The Evergreen State: 'We're Going to Be No. 2,'" *Wines and Vines* 53 (April 1972): 32. One should note that the planting of Concords continued unabated at the same time: one grower near Pasco put in 1,600 acres in 1972 and expected to have more than 3,000 acres by 1974 to create the "world's largest Concord vineyard" (ibid.).

27. The pest had made its appearance by 1988. The threat of phylloxera was particularly devastating in Washington because one of the important offsets to winter damage was the fact that an own-rooted vine can renew itself quickly from its roots. Vines grafted to resistant rootstocks could not be allowed to grow out again from the roots, since those roots were not of the desired fruiting variety. The increased costs and delays entailed by using grafted vines would be a serious burden (Mike Wallace, "Phylloxera Discovered in Washington," *Vineyard and Winery Management* 15 [March–April 1989]: 12).

28. "The Evergreen State," p. 32.

29. In 1971 there were sixty-six acres of French hybrids in Washington (*Wine Institute Bulletin* [1 February 1973]). These included the red Seibel 1078 and 13053 and the white Seibel 9110 ("Seneca Puts Winery in Wash.," *Wines and Vines* 52 [July 1971]: 10).

30. In 1970, Wagner was negotiating for cuttings from the University of California, Davis, of such vinifera as Melon and Lemberger for planting in Washington (memorandum of 10 August 1970, Philip Wagner papers, box 3, file 31, Cornell University, Kroch Li-

brary). The formula for Yakima Valley Red in 1971 was a blend of Cabernet, Pinot noir, Foch, Baco noir, Boordy Red Blend, Boordy Pinard, and bulk red (ibid., box 3, file 32).

31. Irvine, *The Wine Project*, p. 247.

32. Woodburne, "Vintner Views Washington State," p. 27. The New York association was discontinued in the next year. In Wagner's view, the scheme was "ahead of its time" (Philip Wagner papers, box 4, file 12, Cornell University, Kroch Library).

33. See the interesting photographs illustrating the construction of the Chateau Ste. Michelle Winery and the festivities at its opening in J. Elizabeth Purser and Lawrence J. Allen, *The Winemakers of the Pacific Northwest* (Vashon Island, Wash.: Harbor House Publishing, 1977), pp. 106–15.

34. *Vineyard and Winery Management* 17 (July–August 1991): 15.

35. See the useful list in Irvine, *The Wine Project*, pp. 428–32.

36. The Hogue Winery was sold to the Canadian firm Vincor in 2001.

37. Reed's articles appeared in July 1969: see Irvine, *The Wine Project*, pp. 208–09.

38. Ibid., p. 244. The winning Riesling was a 1972 Ste. Michelle, competing against fourteen wines from California, three from Germany, and one from Australia.

39. "Washington's Bright New Wine," *Time* (27 June 1983): 68.

40. Washington Wine Commission, "Washington Wines: Statistical Review" (Seattle: Washington Wine Commission, 1991); information from the commission, 2002.

41. R. J. Folwell, D. J. Kirpes, and C. W. Nagel, *Washington Wine Grape Acreage, 1982*, Research Circular XC 0648 (Pullman: Agricultural Research Center, Washington State University, 1983).

42. "Washington's Bright New Wine," p. 71.

43. Motto Kryla & Fisher LLP, *Economic Impact of the Washington State Wine and Wine Grape Industries* (St. Helena, Calif.: Motto Kryla & Fisher LLP, 2001), p. 40, from information supplied by the Washington Agricultural Statistics Service.

44. Five hundred tons of Lemberger were crushed in 2000 (U.S. Department of Agriculture, National Agricultural Statistics Service, "Washington Grape Report," 23 January 2001).

45. "Washington Winemen Organize State Society," *Wines and Vines* 55 (June 1974): 52.

46. Unfortunately, the library did not survive the recent transition of the Prosser Public Library from independence to participation in a regional library system. It was decided not to continue the collection, and the books were dispersed. Someone would do well to establish another library in Washington (and Oregon, too).

47. Paul Pintarich, *The Boys Up North: Dick Erath and the Early Oregon Winemakers* (Portland, Oreg.: Wyatt Group, 1997), pp. 2–3.

48. H. B. Howell, "Grape Growing in Oregon," *California Grape Grower* 4 (August 1923): 4. The article reported that three hundred acres were planted in 1923, doubling the existing acreage.

49. John F. Potticary, "Potential for the Development of a Wine and Supporting Wine Grape Industry in Oregon" (Portland: Oregon State Department of Commerce, Economic Development Division, August 1968), p. 5.

50. *Ashland Daily Tidings*, 19 October 1967.

51. One writer has called it "the most marginal of the West Coast wine-producing regions"

(Lisa Shara Hall, *Wines of the Pacific Northwest: A Contemporary Guide to the Wines of Washington and Oregon* [London: Mitchell Beazley, 2001], p. 17).

52. Coury returned to California in 1977. His winery, renamed Laurel Ridge by a new owner in 1986, passed to another owner in 2000 and now operates as David Hill Vineyard.

53. Pintarich, *The Boys Up North*, p. 22.

54. California-trained winemakers continue to figure importantly in Oregon: Ken Wright (Ken Wright Cellars); John Paul (Cameron Winery); Barney Watson (Tyee Wine Cellars); Steve Doerner (Cristom Vineyards); Don Lange (Lange Winery); and Lynn Penner-Ash (Penner-Ash Cellars). The list might be extended.

55. In 2002 applications for approval were pending for the Chehalem Mountains, Ribbon Ridge, Red Hills, Eola Hills, Yamhill-Carlton District, and McMinnville Foothills AVAs; none of them had yet been approved at the end of 2004.

56. Of the 621 acres of vines in the Umpqua Valley in 2003, 72 were of Cabernet Sauvignon, 49 of Merlot, 346 of Pinot noir (Oregon Agricultural Statistics Service, "2003 Oregon Vineyard and Winery Report" [Portland: Oregon Agricultural Statistics Service, February 2004]).

57. According to F. T. Bioletti, "The Rogue River Valley can produce as fine Tokay grapes as any in the country" (Howell, "Grape Growing in Oregon," p. 4).

58. The first Oregon grower to plant vines on resistant rootstocks is said to have been Robert Drouhin; the long and bitter experience of the French with phylloxera made him prudently skeptical about the immunity of a new region (Hall, *Wines of the Pacific Northwest*, p. 18).

59. Philip M. Wagner, "Oregon's Mystery Grape," *Wine East* 16 (January–February 1989): 14–15.

60. Ted Jordan Meredith, *Northwest Wine: Winegrowing Alchemy along the Pacific Rim of Fire*, 4th ed. (Kirkland, Wash.: Nexus Press, 1990), pp. 90–91.

61. This event was so far ahead of the development of the industry that wines from California had to be offered (*Wines and Vines* 51 [July 1970]: 14).

62. According to Hall, the board is a focus of conflict between winemakers in the different regions of the state (*Wines of the Pacific Northwest*, p. 17).

63. *Wines and Vine* 64 (October 1983): 78; *Vinifera Wine Growers Journal* 13 (Summer 1986): 99.

64. *New York Times*, 23 April 1980, III, 18.

65. The number of wineries is, as always, only approximate: the count is varied by new openings, closings, name changes, consolidations, and temporary inactivity, among other causes. The *Oregon Winery Guide* for 2002 issued by the Oregon Wine Advisory Board lists 172 wineries in the state. The contrast to Washington is clear: Oregon, with only about a third of the wine-grape acreage of Washington, nonetheless has more wineries.

66. Matt Kramer, *Los Angeles Times*, 31 October 1996, H, 6.

67. *Wall Street Journal*, 21 September 1981.

68. It is said that the California clone of Chardonnay first grown in Oregon did not ripen properly; other clones since introduced do better.

69. Larry Walker, "Pinot Blanc in Oregon: It's the Real Thing," *Wines and Vines* 81 (January 2000): 132.

70. *Wall Street Journal,* 21 September 1981.

71. Figures from Oregon Agricultural Statistics Service, "2003 Oregon Vineyard and Winery Report."

72. Roy Brady, "History of California Wine," unpublished MS, 5 May 1988, Roy Brady papers, University of California, Davis, Shields Library.

73. The record freeze of December 1990 reduced the state's yield of wine to about a thousand gallons from seven hundred acres of vines (Lawrence Dawson, "Are Idaho Wines Influenced by Altitude?" *Wines and Vines* 73 [April 1992]: 19).

74. Figures from the annual statistical issue of *Wines and Vines.*

75. Summarized from the Idaho Grape Growers and Wine Producers Commission Web site, idahowine.org, August 2004.

76. In the excitement of renewal, some quite extraordinary historical claims are inevitably heard in the new winegrowing states. One Colorado winery affirms in its publicity that before Prohibition Colorado was the second-largest producer of grapes (after Missouri) in the United States (Cottonwood Cellars, "Grape History in Colorado" [2001], copy in the author's collection). An official of the Kansas Department of Commerce has stated that before Prohibition, Kansas and Missouri produced 86 percent of the wine in the United States (*Ottawa* [Kansas] *Herald,* 1 August 2004). The will to believe must be very strong to publish such fantasies.

77. "Varietal Wines from Colorado," *Wines and Vines* 50 (March 1969): 7.

78. Eugene A. Mielke et al., *Grape and Wine Production in the Four Corners Region,* Technical Bulletin 239 (Tucson: University of Arizona, Agricultural Experiment Station, 1980), p. [1]. The commission, funded by federal money, paid for test plots of vines, climate studies, and winemaking experiments, as well as a small winery at the University of Arizona (*Vinifera Wine Growers Journal* 4 [Fall 1977]: 418).

79. Linda Jones McKee, "Colorado: Eastern Wines in a Western Setting," *Wine East* 13 (September–October 1985): 26.

80. See chapter 8, after n. 79.

81. Adams, *The Wines of America,* p. 347.

82. *Vinifera Wine Growers Journal* 4 (Fall 1977): 418.

83. Ibid., p. 419.

84. J. William Moffett, "New Mexico: Land of Enchanting Investment," *Eastern Grape Grower and Winery News* 9 (August–September 1983): 22.

85. The original plan had been for a 300,000-gallon winery, but that was evidently a good deal more than the traffic would bear: see ibid., p. 24.

86. Pamela Ray, "Wineries of New Mexico," *Eastern Grape Grower and Winery News* 11 (December 1985–January 1986): 14.

87. John J. Baxevanis, *The Wine Regions of America: Geographical Reflections and Appraisals* (Stroudsburg, Penn.: Vinifera Winegrowers Journal, 1992), p. 213.

88. Moffett, "New Mexico," p. 26.

89. Roger Larsen, "The Desert Sprouts Winegrapes," *Wines and Vines* 64 (November 1983): 112.

90. Ibid., p. 113.

91. Ibid., p. 114.

92. Ibid.

93. Ibid.

94. Ray, "Wineries of New Mexico," p. 39.

95. *Wines and Vines* 68 (November 1987): 12.

96. "New Mexico Enacts a New Law Granting a Winegrower's License," *Wines and Vines* 69 (June 1988): 14.

97. Figures from the annual directories of *Wines and Vines*.

98. Gordon R. Dutt, "Border Wine Belt Is Emerging," *Wines and Vines* 66 (April 1985): 45.

99. "Arizona Experiments Show Hope for Vinifera," *Wines and Vines* 56 (February 1975): 12.

100. Webb began to use some Arizona grapes from 1982 (Ed Van Dyne, "Arizona's Embryonic Wine Industry: A Dark Horse?" *American Wine Society Journal* 15 [Summer 1983]: 47).

101. Thomas A. Brady Jr., "Arizona's Vintage of 1991," *Vinifera Wine Growers Journal* 16 (Summer 1989): 109, reprinted from *Arizona Wine Growers Association Newsletter*, 1988.

102. When Maple River Winery was bonded in North Dakota in 2002, all fifty states had at least one licensed winery of one sort or another.

CHAPTER 14. CALIFORNIA TO THE PRESENT DAY

1. The figures that follow are from the annual statistical numbers of *Wines and Vines*, supplemented by the reports of the California Agricultural Statistics Service.

2. This figure tells us that nearly a third of California's wineries are crammed into a region containing about 9 percent of the state's wine-grape acreage.

3. White Zinfandel was introduced by the Sutter Home Winery: see Charles L. Sullivan, *A Companion to California Wine: An Encyclopedia of Wine and Winemaking from the Mission Period to the Present* (Berkeley: University of California Press, 1998). White (i.e., pink) Zinfandel had been made before, and was known in the nineteenth century, but its modern popularity begins with the Sutter Home wine.

4. See Jancis Robinson, ed., *The Oxford Companion to Wine*, 2nd ed. (Oxford: Oxford University Press, 1999), *s.v.* "Dealcoholized Wine," for a brief account of how such wines are made.

5. Dave Chupp, "New Wine Regulations," *Vinifera Wine Growers Journal* 4 (Spring 1977): 275.

6. An early discussion of the subject from this point of view is Harry A. Caddow, "Labels and Labels," *Wine Review* 8 (March 1940): 26–28, 48.

7. *Meritage* (to rhyme with *heritage*) is a trademark reserved to members of the Meritage Association for wines made using the traditional Bordeaux blends for red and white wines.

8. Syrah (or Shiraz: not to be confused with Petite Sirah) had 344 acres in 1990; in 2003 the acreage was 17,140. Viognier had 50 acres in 1990, 2,089 acres in 2003.

9. Figures from the Wine Institute Web site.

10. What one concludes from these examples is that the word *premium* has been exhausted and can no longer indicate anything special. As with movies and canned olives, we can expect *super-colossal* and other such terms to appear soon.

11. E.g., Richard D. Hall in "California's Central Valley Face Shrinking Markets, Phylloxera," *Wines and Vines* 72 (July 1991): 50: "A basic problem is that consumers are drink-

ing less but drinking better." Sales of jug wine went down by 8 percent between 1984 and 1986; sales of premium wine rose by 20 percent in 1986 (Jon Frederikson in California Legislature, Senate, Select Committee on California's Wine Industry, *California Wine Production and Marketing Trends: An Overview* [Sacramento: Select Committee on California's Wine Industry, 1987], p. 9).

12. Among the names of the wineries producing cult wines are Bryant Family, Cain, Colgin, Dalla Valle, Grace Family, Harlan Estate, Marcassin, and Screaming Eagle. The list grows as new entrants jostle for position. They have a French equivalent in the *garagistes* of Bordeaux. A few Australian wines such as Grange and Hill of Grace might be classified as cult wines.

13. *Wine Spectator* 27 (31 January–28 February 2002): 55–57. Twelve of the wines listed had no price given, so my average is of seventy-nine wines whose total cost was $17,865.

14. As Richard Smart has observed, the "interesting question" is "the extent to which retail wine prices, which can vary more than a thousandfold, indicate wine quality. The answer is, of course, not very closely" (Robinson, ed., *The Oxford Companion to Wine, s.v.* "Prices").

15. In 1972 the Federal Trade Commission charged Heublein with restraint of trade. The FTC was reacting to the sweeping transformation of the wine industry in California through mergers and acquisitions; it also filed complaints against Gallo and Coca-Cola of New York (which had acquired the Franzia Winery) at the same time. After long proceedings, the charges were withdrawn.

16. The Italian Swiss Colony name belonged to Canandaigua, but Colony to the Wine Group, which also held the Lejon name. The Christian Brothers name now belongs to Heaven Hill Distilleries.

17. The California Association of Wine Grape Growers was formed in 1974 to help meet this crisis.

18. See chapter 10, at n. 3.

19. See chapter 9, after n. 22.

20. *Wall Street Journal*, 4 October 1999, A, 8.

21. Pressure groups such as Free the Grapes, an organization based in Napa County, are opposed by the likes of Americans for Responsible Alcohol Access, whose motto is "Ship the wine, do some time."

22. See a summary of these rulings in Russ Bridenbaugh, "The Direct Shipping Controversy," *Wines and Vines* 82 (January 2001): 152–58.

23. Sara Schorske, "ATF Approves Alternating Proprietors License," *Vineyard and Winery Management* 18 (January–February 1992): 50.

24. The difficulty in distinguishing between a custom-crush client and an alternating proprietor has created some concern among the regulators: see Sara Schorske and Alex Heckathorn, "Precious Privilege in Jeopardy: ATF Re-examines Alternating Proprietorships," *Vineyard and Winery Management* 29 (May–June 2003): 13–16.

25. *Los Angeles Times,* 27 June 2001, H, 4.

26. The UFW was founded in 1962 as the Farm Workers Association; in 1966 it was renamed the United Farm Workers Organizing Committee; from 1973 it was the United Farm Workers, and that name is used in this discussion.

27. *New York Times*, 2 May 1975, 14; 18 May 1975, IV, 5. The "blood" on the grapes alludes particularly to the killing of two farmworkers in the strikes of 1973 but more generally to the unhealthy conditions of a migrant farmworker's life.

28. Enrollment at Davis per the *New York Times*, 16 July 1985, III, 1.

29. The FDA was in charge of food labeling, the BATF in charge of liquor labeling; wine might lie under either authority. The overlap of jurisdictions had long been recognized, and the FDA had historically deferred to the BATF on questions affecting alcoholic beverages. A conflict of authorities was still possible, however, and flared up in this instance. See Iver P. Cooper, "The FDA, the BATF, and Liquor Labeling: A Case Study of Interagency Jurisdictional Conflict," *Food Drug and Cosmetic Law Journal* 34 (July 1979): 373.

30. *New York Times*, 14 January 1978, 8.

31. "Sulfite Labeling," *Wines and Vines* 67 (November 1986): 19. The ruling went into effect in 1987 for all wines containing ten or more parts per million of sulfites. Before this time, the FDA had allowed up to 350 million ppm as safe: most wines contained much less than that amount (*New York Times*, 13 April 1988, III, 14). The measure could be regarded as a form of ingredient labeling.

32. John A. Hinman, "It's a Critical Time in the Wine Industry," *Wines and Vines* 69 (November 1988): 72.

33. Ibid. The federal excise tax on wine was raised in 1991 to $1.07 a gallon for table wine, with a special credit for small producers, who paid only the old rate of 17 cents on the first 100,000 gallons if their total production was under 150,000 gallons.

34. Alcohol itself is not carcinogenic, but "when alcohol is metabolized by mammals, the alcohol is converted into acetaldehyde, which is a known carcinogen" ("Coming to Grips with Proposition 65," *Wine East* 15 [July–August 1988]: 3). Ethyl carbamate, present in minute quantities in wine as a result of fermentation, is a "suspected" carcinogen ("Commonsense Winemaking," *Wines and Vines* 71 [March 1990]: 13).

35. "A Barrel Full of Trouble," *Newsweek* (3 June 1991): 54.

36. "A New Temperance Movement?" *Wines and Vines* 66 (September 1985): 19; *New York Times*, 6 May 1987, III, 16.

37. See the council's advertisement in *Wines and Vines* 72 (September 1991): 24a. This group hoped to include brewers and winemakers as well but had no success in that line (*Vineyard and Winery Management* 17 [July–August 1991]: 14).

38. *Wines and Vines* 72 (December 1991): 35.

39. John Volpe, director of the National Wine Coalition, in *Wines and Vines* 72 (June 1991): 62.

40. The television program was based on an article by Edward Dolnick called "Le Paradoxe Français," in *Health* (May–June 1991).

41. Dan Berger in the *Santa Rosa Democrat*, 26 February 1992.

42. Jon A. Fredrikson, "1992 'Hot' Year for Table Wine," *Wines and Vines* 74 (April 1993): 22. The impact of the program was such that it became known as "the 20 minutes that changed the industry" (*Wall Street Journal*, 19 October 1992, B, 1).

43. "Free ticket to longevity" is Frank Prial's phrase: "Wine Talk," *New York Times*, 25 December 1991, 29. The TTB, after long wrangling over the issue, ruled in 2003 that winemakers could put "directional" statements about health on wine labels—e.g., suggest-

ing that the customer consult the family doctor about the health effects of wine—but only if they added a disclaimer stating that they did not mean to encourage drinking for health ("Health Label Ruling Modified," *Wines and Vines* 84 [June 2003]: 35).

44. Notice 304, *Federal Register*, 12 November 1976. The process began even earlier, in July 1975, when the BATF first signaled its intention to consider the question.

45. This facility was opened in 1994 as the National Grape Importation and Clean Stock Facility, a part of the Foundation Plant Materials Service.

46. "Wine as a 'Food Beverage,'" *Wine East* 16 (November–December 1989): 3, 29.

47. Richard Feeney, "The USDA Role in the Wine Industry," *Wines and Vines* 71 (July 1990): 15.

48. U.S. Congress, House of Representatives, Committee on Agriculture, *Review of the U.S. Department of Agriculture Activities to Assist and Support the U.S. Winegrape and Wine Industry* (Washington, D.C.: GPO, 1992): hearings held 23 October 1991.

49. *Wine Institute News Briefs*, 31 July 1996.

50. A reported 50,000 acres of vines were removed in the Central Valley between 1999 and 2003 owing to overproduction and depressed prices (*California Agriculture* 57 [July–September 2003]: 70).

51. Of the eighteen wineries concerned, five were part of the Kendall-Jackson combination ("A Mass Resignation from Wine Institute," *Wines and Vines* 71 [August 1990]: 14). Jess Jackson of Kendall-Jackson became the first president of the Family Winemakers of California, the rival organization.

52. "Robert Mondavi Winery Exited Wine Institute," *Wines and Vines* 73 (July 1992): 14. Robert Mondavi himself had long been one of the stalwarts of the Wine Institute. His complaint was that the institute was not sufficiently active against the neoprohibitionists.

53. Vines in the Central Valley, where the sandy soil and high temperatures are unfavorable to phylloxera, are often grown on their own roots. Phylloxera is, however, widespread there.

54. Lloyd A. Lider, "Phylloxera-Resistant Grape Rootstocks for the Coastal Valleys of California," *Hilgardia* 27 (February 1958): 287–318.

55. Ibid., p. 303.

56. Lucie T. Morton, "The Myth of the Universal Rootstock," *Wines and Vines* 60 (April 1979): 24–26.

57. Small infestations were also found in Mendocino, Lake, Sacramento, San Joaquin, Alameda, and Santa Clara Counties.

58. A conservative estimate of the cost was $15,000 to $25,000 an acre; some 50,000 acres in Napa and Sonoma Counties were involved, producing a figure between $750 million and $1.25 billion (*California Agriculture* 50 [July–August 1996]: 7).

59. Arthur Lubow, "What's Killing the Grapevines of Napa?" *New York Times Magazine*, 17 October 1993, 60. By 1995 some 12,000 acres of vines had been pulled "as a direct result of biotype B phylloxera" in Napa and Sonoma Counties (*California Agriculture* 50 [July–August 1996]: 10). There were some alternatives to immediate replanting: for instance, one could plant resistant rootstocks between existing vines and so establish a new vineyard before pulling out the old one.

60. See the summary of work in progress by Cliff Ohmart, "Vineyard Views," *Wines and Vines* 84 (March 2003): 18–20.

61. The value of studying clonal variations and of making them available was not much appreciated in California until fairly recent years. That has now changed. The Foundation Plant Materials Service at Davis currently offers 130 selections of Pinot noir alone (Lynn Alley, Deborah Golino, and Andrew Walker, "Retrospective on California Grape Vine Materials Part III," *Wines and Vines* 82 [April 2001]: 67).

62. "Beckstoffer Cautious on the Costs," *Wines and Vines* 76 (June 1995): 26.

63. A leading authority on the subject is Dr. Richard Smart; his *Sunlight into Wine: A Handbook for Winegrape Canopy Management* (Adelaide: Winetitles, 1991), written with Mike Robinson, is widely influential.

64. Although the United States was fourth in wine production in 2003, it was thirty-second in per capita consumption among wine-drinking countries.

65. Bruce Cass, ed., *The Oxford Companion to the Wines of North America* (New York: Oxford University Press, 2000), p. 91.

66. Leon D. Adams, *The Wines of America,* 2nd ed. (New York: McGraw-Hill, 1978), p. x.

67. Paul Lukacs, *American Vintage: The Rise of American Wine* (Boston: Houghton Mifflin, 2000), p. 316.

68. Quoted in "The Long Memories of Prohibition," *Wines and Vines* 64 (September 1983): 36.

SOURCES AND WORKS CITED

ARCHIVAL AND MANUSCRIPT SOURCES

Alcohol and Tobacco Tax and Trade Bureau Library (TTB), Washington, D.C.
   [formerly Bureau of Alcohol, Tobacco and Firearms]:
   Transcripts of hearings, 1933 et seq.
Bowling Green State University Library, Ohio:
   George Lonz papers
California State University, Fresno, Library:
   Roy Brady Collection
Cornell University, Kroch Library:
   Hammondsport Wine Company papers
   Philip Wagner papers
   Widmer papers
National Agricultural Library, Beltsville, Maryland:
   United States Department of Agriculture Wine File
National Archives, Washington, D.C.:
   Federal Emergency Relief Administration Records
   United States Department of Agriculture Records
Princeton University, Princeton, New Jersey, Firestone Library:
   Julian Street papers
Roosevelt Library, Hyde Park, New York:
   Roosevelt papers
   Tugwell papers

Shiloh Museum, Springdale, Arkansas:
    Nelson Wine and Distilling Co. papers
University of California, Davis, Shields Library:
    Leon Adams papers
    Roy Brady papers
    Bureau of Alcohol, Tobacco and Firearms (BATF) Records
    Martin Ray papers
University of Texas, Harry Ransom Humanities Research Center, Austin:
    Alfred A. Knopf papers
Wine Institute Library, San Francisco:
    Committee Reports
    Stabilization Files
    Transcripts of Hearings
    Wine Institute Historical Records

NEWSPAPERS AND SPECIALIZED JOURNALS

American Journal of Enology and Viticulture
American Wine Society Journal
California Agriculture
California Grape Grower (afterward *Wines and Vines*)
California Grower (afterward *Wines and Vines*)
California Journal of Development
California Wine Review (afterward *Wine Review*)
Eastern Grape Grower and Winery News (afterward *Vineyard
    and Winery Management*)
Fruit Products Journal
New York Times
Pennsylvania Grape Letter and Wine News (afterward *Wine East*)
Practical Winery and Vineyard
Proceedings of the American Society of Enologists (afterward
    American Journal of Enology and Viticulture)
San Francisco Chronicle
Vineyard and Winery Management
Vinifera Wine Growers Journal
Wall Street Journal
Wine and Food
Wine East
Wine Review
Wines and Vines
Wine Spectator

ORAL HISTORIES

Adams, Leon D. *California Wine Industry Affairs: Recollections and Opinions.* Interview by Ruth Teiser. Berkeley: Regional Oral History Office, Bancroft Library, University of California, 1990.

———. *Revitalizing the California Wine Industry.* Interview by Ruth Teiser. Berkeley: Regional Oral History Office, Bancroft Library, University of California, 1974.

Amerine, Maynard A. *The University of California and the State's Wine Industry.* Interview by Ruth Teiser. Berkeley: Regional Oral History Office, Bancroft Library, University of California, 1972.

———. *Wine Bibliographies and Taste Perception Studies.* Interview by Ruth Teiser. Berkeley: Regional Oral History Office, Bancroft Library, University of California, 1988.

Baccigaluppi, Harry. *California Grape Products and Other Wine Enterprises: Part II.* Interview by Ruth Teiser. Berkeley: Regional Oral History Office, Bancroft Library, University of California, 1971.

Beckstoffer, William Andrew. *Premium California Vineyardist, Entrepreneur, 1960s to 2000s.* Interview by Carole Hicke. Berkeley: Regional Oral History Office, Bancroft Library, University of California, 2000.

Biane, Philo. *Wine Making in Southern California and Recollections of Fruit Industries, Ltd.* Interview by Ruth Teiser. Berkeley: Regional Oral History Office, Bancroft Library, University of California, 1972.

Bonetti, William. *A Life of Winemaking at Wineries of Gallo, Schenley, Charles Krug, Chateau Souverain, and Sonoma-Cutrer.* Interview by Carole Hicke. Berkeley: Regional Oral History Office, Bancroft Library, University of California, 1998.

Cella, John B., II. *The Cella Family in the California Wine Industry.* Interview by Ruth Teiser. Berkeley: Regional Oral History Office, Bancroft Library, University of California, 1986.

Crawford, Charles M. *Recollections of a Career with the Gallo Winery and the Development of the California Wine Industry, 1942–1989.* Interview by Ruth Teiser. Berkeley: Regional Oral History Office, Bancroft Library, University of California, 1990.

Critchfield, Burke H. *The California Wine Industry during the Depression.* Interview by Ruth Teiser. Berkeley: Regional Oral History Office, Bancroft Library, University of California, 1972.

Deuer, George. Interview by Bernard Skoda, 1974. In *History of Napa Valley: Interviews and Reminiscences of Long-Time Residents,* vol. 2. St. Helena, Calif.: Napa Valley Wine Library Association, 1979.

Dieppe, William. *Almadén Is My Life.* Interview by Ruth Teiser. Berkeley: Regional Oral History Office, Bancroft Library, University of California, 1985.

Di Giorgio, Robert, and Joseph A. Di Giorgio. *The Di Giorgios: From Fruit Merchants to Corporate Innovators.* Interview by Ruth Teiser. Berkeley: Regional Oral History Office, Bancroft Library, University of California, 1986.

Foppiano, Louis J. *A Century of Winegrowing in Sonoma County, 1896–1996.* Interview by Carole Hicke. Berkeley: Regional Oral History Office, Bancroft Library, University of California, 1996.

Fredson, Leonard, and Chris Fredson. Interview by Joseph Vercelli and William Heintz. Healdsburg, Calif.: Sonoma County Wine Library Associates, 1995–1996.

Fromm, Alfred. *Marketing California Wine.* Interview by Ruth Teiser. Berkeley: Regional Oral History Office, Bancroft Library, University of California, 1984.

Gomberg, Louis. *Analytical Perspectives on the California Wine Industry, 1935–1990.* Interview by Ruth Teiser. Berkeley: Regional Oral History Office, Bancroft Library, University of California, 1990.

Joslyn, Maynard A. *A Technologist Views the California Wine Industry.* Interview by Ruth Teiser. Berkeley: Regional Oral History Office, Bancroft Library, University of California, 1974.

Katz, Morris. *Paul Masson Winery Operations and Management, 1944–1988.* Interview by Ruth Teiser. Berkeley: Regional Oral History Office, Bancroft Library, University of California, 1990.

Knowles, Legh F. *Beaulieu Vineyards from Family to Corporate Ownership.* Interview by Lisa Jacobson. Berkeley: Regional Oral History Office, Bancroft Library, University of California, 1990.

Lanza, Horace O. *California Grape Products and Other Wine Enterprises.* Interview by Ruth Teiser. Berkeley: Regional Oral History Office, Bancroft Library, University of California, 1971.

McCrea, Eleanor. *Stony Hill Vineyards: The Creation of a Napa Valley Estate Winery.* Interview by Lisa Jacobson. Berkeley: Regional Oral History Office, Bancroft Library, University of California, 1990.

Martini, Louis M., and Louis P. Martini. *Wine Making in the Napa Valley.* Interviews by Ruth Teiser and Lois Stone. Berkeley: Regional Oral History Office, Bancroft Library, University of California, 1973.

Meyer, Otto E. *California Premium Wines and Brandies.* Interview by Ruth Teiser. Berkeley: Regional Oral History Office, Bancroft Library, University of California, 1973.

Mirassou, Norbert C., and Edmund A. Mirassou. *The Evolution of a Santa Clara Valley Winery.* Interview by Ruth Teiser. Berkeley: Regional Oral History Office, Bancroft Library, University of California, 1986.

Nightingale, Myron S. *Making Wine in California, 1944–1987.* Interview by Ruth Teiser and Lisa Jacobson. Berkeley: Regional Oral History Office, Bancroft Library, University of California, 1988.

Olmo, H. P. *Plant Genetics and New Grape Varieties.* Interview by Ruth Teiser. Berkeley: Regional Oral History Office, Bancroft Library, University of California, 1976.

Ough, Cornelius. *Researches of an Enologist, University of California, Davis.* Interview by Ruth Teiser. Berkeley: Regional Oral History Office, Bancroft Library, University of California, 1990.

Parducci, John A. *Six Decades of Making Wine in Mendocino County, California.* Interview by Carole Hicke. Berkeley: Regional Oral History Office, Bancroft Library, University of California, 1992.

Perelli-Minetti, Antonio. *A Life in Wine Making.* Interview by Ruth Teiser. Berkeley: Regional Oral History Office, Bancroft Library, University of California, 1975.

Peterson, Dr. Richard G. "Self-Interview, 1976." In *History of Napa Valley: Interviews and*

Reminiscences of Long-Time Residents, vol. 2. St. Helena, Calif.: Napa Valley Wine Library Association, 1977.

Petri, Louis A. *The Petri Family in the Wine Industry.* Interview by Ruth Teiser. Berkeley: Regional Oral History Office, Bancroft Library, University of California, 1971.

Peyser, Jefferson E. *The Law and California Wine.* Interview by Ruth Teiser. Berkeley: Regional Oral History Office, Bancroft Library, University of California, 1974.

Powers, Lucius. *The Fresno Area and the California Wine Industry.* Interview by Ruth Teiser. Berkeley: Regional Oral History Office, Bancroft Library, University of California, 1974.

Rossi, Edmund A. *Italian Swiss Colony and the Wine Industry.* Interview by Ruth Teiser. Berkeley: Regional Oral History Office, Bancroft Library, University of California, 1971.

Rossi, Edmund A., Jr. *Italian Swiss Colony 1949–1989: Recollections of a Third-Generation California Winemaker.* Interview by Ruth Teiser and Lisa Jacobson. Berkeley: Regional Oral History Office, Bancroft Library, University of California, 1990.

Setrakian, A. *A Leader of the San Joaquin Valley Grape Industry.* Interview by Ruth Teiser. Berkeley: Regional Oral History Office, Bancroft Library. University of California, 1977.

Skofis, Elie C. *California Wine and Brandy Maker: Elie C. Skofis.* Interview by Ruth Teiser. Berkeley: Regional Oral History Office, Bancroft Library, University of California, 1988.

Stralla, Lou. Interview by James Beard, 1972. In *History of Napa Valley: Interviews and Reminiscences of Long-Time Residents,* vol. 2. St. Helena, Calif.: Napa Valley Wine Library Association, 1979.

Sullivan, Charles L. *Wines and Winemakers of the Santa Cruz Mountains: An Oral History.* Cupertino, Calif.: D. R. Bennion Trust, 1995.

Tchelistcheff, André. *Grapes, Wine, and Ecology.* Interview by Ruth Teiser and Catherine Harroun. Berkeley: Regional Oral History Office, Bancroft Library, University of California, 1983.

Webb, R. Bradford. *Brad Webb: Innovator.* Interview by William Heintz, 1988. Healdsburg, Calif.: Sonoma County Wine Library Oral History, 1991.

Winkler, A. J. *Viticultural Research at University of California, Davis, 1921–1971.* Interview by Ruth Teiser. Berkeley: Regional Oral History Office, Bancroft Library, University of California, 1973.

OTHER PRINTED WORKS

Adams, Leon D. *The Commonsense Book of Wine.* New York: David McKay, 1958.
———. "The Future of Winegrowing in the Southeastern States." *Vinifera Wine Growers Journal* 6 (Summer 1979): 60–64.
———. "Historical Note." In California State Vinicultural Association, *Grapes and Grape Vines of California.* New York: Harcourt Brace, 1981 [orig. 1877], n.p.
———. "Who Caused the Wine Revolution." *Wines and Vines* 60 (February 1979): 39.
———. "The Wine Revolution in America Cannot Be Over-Emphasized." *Wines and Vines* 55 (September 1974): 68–72.
———. *The Wines of America.* Boston: Houghton Mifflin, 1973; 2nd ed. New York: McGraw-Hill, 1978; 3rd ed., 1985; 4th ed., 1990.
Alley, Curtis J. "Certified Grape Stocks Available." *Wines and Vines* 40 (February 1959): 30.

Alley, Curtis J., C. S. Ough, and Maynard A. Amerine. "Grapes for Table Wines in California's Regions IV and V." *Wines and Vines* 52 (March 1971): 20–22.

Alley, Lynn, Deborah Golino, and Andrew Walker. "Retrospective on California Grapevine Materials Part I." *Wines and Vines* 81 (November 2000): 148–52.

———. "Retrospective on California Grapevine Materials Part III." *Wines and Vines* 82 (April 2001): 63–68.

American Winery Directory. Los Angeles: *Wine Review,* annual [1934–49].

Amerine, Maynard A. "The Composition of California Wines at Exhibitions, Part One: White Table Wines." *Wines and Vines* 28 (January 1947): 21–23, 42–45.

———. "The Composition of California Wines at Exhibitions, Part Three: Dessert Wine." *Wines and Vines* 28 (March 1947): 23–25, 42–46.

———. "Dessert Wine Production Problems of California Grapes, I: Introduction." *Wines and Vines* 33 (January 1952): 15–16.

———. "Dessert Wine Production Problems of California Grapes, IV: Muscat of Alexandria." *Wines and Vines* 33 (April 1952): 59–61.

———. "Edmund Henri Twight 1874–1957." *Wines and Vines* 38 (May 1957): 29–30.

———. "An Historical Note on Grape Prices." *Wines and Vines* 27 (October 1946): 28.

———. "The Professional Status of Enologists." *Wines and Vines* 40 (August 1959): 31–32.

———. "The Response of Wine to Aging, Part IV: The Influence of Variety." *Wines and Vines* 31 (May 1950): 28–31.

———. "Some Comments on Wine in America." *Wine and Food* 36 (Winter 1942): 192–99.

———. "Some Facts and Fancies about Winemaking and Wines." Report to the Wine Institute Technical Advisory Committee Meeting, 13 May 1955. Copy in the Roy Brady papers, University of California, Davis, Shields Library.

———. "Wine Production Problems of California Grapes, Part I." *Wine Review* 17 (January 1949): 18–22.

———. "Wine Production Problems of California Grapes, Part II." *Wine Review* 17 (February 1949): 10–11, 21.

———. "Wine Production Problems of California Grapes, Part III." *Wine Review* 17 (March 1949): 10–12.

———. "Wine Production Problems of California Grapes, Part VI." *Wine Review* 17 (July 1949): 6–7, 19–20.

———, ed. *Wine Production Technology in the United States.* Washington, D.C.: American Chemical Society, 1981.

Amerine, Maynard A., and W. V. Cruess. *The Technology of Wine Making.* Westport, Conn.: Avi Publishing, 1960.

Amerine, Maynard A., and Douglas Fong. "Further Studies on Making Wine of Varieties Grown in Region IV." *American Journal of Enology and Viticulture* 25 (1974): 44–47.

Amerine, Maynard A., and Maynard Joslyn. *Commercial Production of Table Wines.* Bulletin 639. Berkeley: University of California, College of Agriculture, Agricultural Experiment Station, 1940.

———. *Table Wines: The Technology of Their Production in California.* Berkeley: University of California Press, 1951; 2nd ed., 1970.

Amerine, Maynard A., and Paul Scholten. "Varietal Labeling in California." *Wines and Vines* 58 (November 1977): 40–41.

Amerine, Maynard A., and Vernon Singleton. *Wine: An Introduction for Americans.* Berkeley: University of California Press, 1965.

Amerine, Maynard A., and E. H. Twight. "Claret." *Wines and Vines* 19 (January 1938): 5, 24.

———. "Sherry." *Wines and Vines* 19 (May 1938): 3–4.

Amerine, Maynard A., and A. J. Winkler. "Angelica." *Wines and Vines* 19 (September 1938): 5, 24.

———. "Burgundy." *Wines and Vines* 19 (November 1938): 5–6.

———. *California Wine Grapes: Composition and Quality of Their Musts and Wines.* Bulletin 794. Berkeley: University of California, Division of Agricultural Sciences, Agricultural Experiment Station, 1963.

———. "Composition and Quality of Musts and Wines of California Grapes." *Hilgardia* 15 (February 1944): 493–673.

Anthony, R. D. "Vinifera Grapes in New York." Bulletin 432. Geneva: New York Agricultural Experiment Station, 1915.

Ash, Charles. "Reminiscences of Pre-Prohibition Days." *Proceedings of the American Society of Enologists* 3 (1952): 39–44.

Asher, Gerald. "The Judgment of Paris Revisited." *Gourmet* 57 (January 1997): 24, 97–99.

Baccigaluppi, Harry. "The Outlook for Wine." *Wines and Vines* 28 (April 1947): 33, 97–98.

Bagshaw, A. E. "How to Secure a Winery Permit." *California Grape Grower* 14 (September 1933): 14.

Ballert, Albert G. "A Report on the Michigan Wine Industry." Prepared for Governor Williams. Lansing: Michigan Department of Economic Development, 1949. Copy in the Wine Institute Library.

Balzer, Robert Lawrence. *California's Best Wines.* Los Angeles: Ward Ritchie Press, 1948.

Barr, Andrew. *Drink: A Social History of America.* New York: Carroll and Graf, 1999.

Bartholomew, Frank H. *Bart: Memoirs of Frank H. Bartholomew.* Sonoma, Calif.: Vine Brook Press, 1983.

———. "'These Are Amiable Wines, Made by Amiable Men.'" *Wines and Vines* 60 (January 1979): 44–45.

Bates, R. P. "The Emerging Florida Wine Industry." *American Wine Society Journal* 17 (Summer 1985): 41–44.

Baxevanis, John J. *The Wine Regions of America: Geographical Reflections and Appraisals.* Stroudsburg, Penn.: Vinifera Winegrowers Journal, 1992.

Benson, Robert W. *Great Winemakers of California.* Santa Barbara, Calif.: Capra Press, 1977.

———. "Regulation of American Wine Labeling: In Vino Veritas?" *UCD Law Review* 11 (1978): 115–99.

Berryhill, Ron. "A Grower Looks at Contract Agreements between Wineries and Growers." *Wines and Vines* 49 (February 1968): 28–29.

Berti, Leo. "Canned Wine: Past Experience and Future Possibilities." *Wines and Vines* 31 (December 1950): 22.

Besone, John J. "Wine Making Traditions Survive at Paul Masson." *Wine Review* 9 (April 1941): 8–11.

Biane, Marius. "How Quality Can Be Controlled." *Wines and Vines* 19 (April 1938): 20–21.

Bigarit, Homer. "Welfare Clients Tend Oklahoma Vineyard." *New York Times,* 26 June 1972, 35.

Bioletti, F. T. "Grape Culture in California: Its Difficulties; Phylloxera and Resistant Vines." Bulletin 197. Berkeley: University of California, College of Agriculture, Agricultural Experiment Station, 1908.

———. "A New Wine Cooling Machine." Bulletin 174. Berkeley: University of California, College of Agriculture, Agricultural Experiment Station, 1906.

———. "The Principles of Wine-Making." Bulletin 213. Berkeley: University of California, College of Agriculture, Agricultural Experiment Station, 1911.

Bioletti, F. T., and W. V. Cruess. "Possible Uses for Wine-Grape Vineyards." Bulletin 14, State Board of Viticultural Commissioners. Sacramento: State Printing Office, 20 May 1919.

Blout, Jessie Schilling. "A Brief Economic History of the California Wine-Growing Industry." San Francisco: Wine Institute, 1943.

Bobo, Carolyn. "University of Texas Is Fostering Wine Production." *Wines and Vines* 64 (November 1983): 46–47.

Boni, Barton. "New Wineries Designed for Efficiency." *Wines and Vines* 28 (February 1947): 34.

Bonner, Charles. *A Rocky Road: The Pilgrimage of the Grape,* ed. John G. Taylor. Fresno: Pioneer Publishing, 1983.

Boswell, Peyton. *Wine Makers Manual: A Guide for the Home Wine Maker and the Small Winery.* New York: Orange Judd Publishing, 1935.

Brady, Roy. *The Brady Book: Selections from Roy Brady's Unpublished Writings on Wine,* ed. Thomas Pinney. Santa Rosa, Calif.: Nomis Press, 2003.

———. "Letter from California: Whither Californian Wine?" *Wine and Food* 127 (Autumn 1965): 59–62.

Brady, Thomas A., Jr. "Arizona's Vintage of 1991." *Vinifera Wine Growers Journal* 16 (Summer 1989): 109.

Brailow, Alexander. "New York—Finger Lakes Region Champagne." *Wines and Vines* 33 (October 1952): 13.

Bridenbaugh, Russ. "The Direct Shipping Controversy." *Wines and Vines* 82 (January 2001): 152–58.

Brook, Stephen. *The Wines of California.* London: Faber and Faber, 1999.

Brown, Dorothy M. *Mabel Walker Willebrandt: A Study of Power, Loyalty, and Law.* Knoxville: University of Tennessee Press, 1984.

Brown, Elbert M. "The Clarification and Stability of Wines in the Pre-Prohibition Era." *Proceedings of the American Society of Enologists* 4 (1953): 1–7.

———. "The TAC—Its History and Its Aims." *Wines and Vines* 32 (May 1951): 21.

Bundschu, Carl. "Distribution Rules Protested." *Wine Review* 5 (April 1937): 10.

Burchard, Hank. "Lorelei Vineyards of Luray: A Cautionary Tale." *Vinifera Wine Growers Journal* 4 (Summer 1977): 336–43.

Burnham, J. C. "New Perspectives on the Prohibition 'Experiment' of the 1920's." *Journal of Social History* 2 (1968): 51–68.

Butler, James L., and John J. Butler. *Indiana Wine: A History.* Bloomington: Indiana University Press, 2001.

Butte, Felix, Jr. "The 1945 Grape Season." *Wines and Vines* 26 (December 1945): 23.

Bynum, Lindley. *California Wines: How to Enjoy Them.* Los Angeles: Homer H. Boelter Lithography, 1955.

Caddow, Harry. "Advertising California Wines." *Wines and Vines* 19 (November 1938): 3, 24.

———. "Annual Meeting of the Wine Institute." *Wines and Vines* 16 (September 1935): 12.

———. "Code of Fair Competition and What It Means to the Wine Industry." *California: Journal of Development* 24 (December 1934): 18, 51.

———. "FAA Regulations and Amendments." *Wines and Vines* 19 (September 1938): 3–4.

———. "Labels and Labels." *Wine Review* 8 (March 1940): 26–28, 48.

———. "Learning the New Label Rules." *Wine Review* 4 (December 1936): 8–9.

———. "The New Wine Labeling." *Wines and Vines* 17 (December 1936): 18.

———. "Permanent Wine Labeling Regulations." *Wines and Vines* 17 (February 1936): 10, 23.

———. "Possibilities of Stabilization." *Wine Review* 4 (May 1936): 10–11.

———. "The Present Wine Market." *Wine Review* 15 (October 1947): 11, 24.

———. "Quality Enforcement Extended into the Winery." *Wines and Vines* 16 (August 1935): 12, 24.

———. "War and the Wine Industry." *Wines and Vines* 23 (May 1942): 15–16.

———. "Wine Industry in Strong Position." *Wine Review* 14 (July 1946): 14–15.

———. "Wine Institute Activities." *Wines and Vines* 16 (May 1935): 12.

Caldwell-Ewart, Carol. "Creating a Winery to Match a Vineyard." *Practical Winery and Vineyard* 22 (January–February 2001): 21–26.

California:

Agricultural Statistics Service. *California Grape Acreage.* Sacramento: annual.

Crop and Livestock Reporting Service. *Acreage Estimates, California Fruit and Nut Crops, as of 1950.* Sacramento: U.S. Department of Agriculture and California Department of Agriculture, annual.

———. *Acreage Estimates, California Fruit and Nut Crops 1919–1953, by Counties.* Special Publication 257: Supplement. Sacramento: U.S. Department of Agriculture and California Department of Agriculture, 1956.

———. *California Fruit and Nut Crops: Acreage, Production, Utilization and Value, 1908–1955.* Special Publication 261. Sacramento: U.S. Department of Agriculture and California Department of Agriculture, 1956.

———. *California Grape Acreage.* Sacramento: annual.

———. *California Grapes, Raisins, and Wine: Production and Marketing.* Sacramento: annual [superseded by *Grape Crush Report*].

Department of Health, Bureau of Food and Drug Inspection. *Wine Standards Hearing, 12 January 1942.* Sacramento: 1942.

Legislature, Senate, Select Committee on California's Wine Industry. *California Wine Production and Marketing Trends: An Overview.* Sacramento: Select Committee on California's Wine Industry, 1987.

———. *Informational Seminar: Wine and the Consumer.* Sacramento: Select Committee on California's Wine Industry, 1989.

California Vineyardists Association. "Form of Organization, Purposes and Functions of the

California Vineyardists Association." Brochure. [San Francisco?]: California Vineyardists Association, ca. 1926.

Campbell, Edward D. C., Jr. "Of Vines and Wines: The Culture of the Grape in Virginia." *Virginia Cavalcade* (Winter 1990): 106–17.

Caputi, Arthur, Jr. "Fifty Years of Research at the World's Largest Winery." *Practical Winery and Vineyard* 22 (November–December 2000): 5–15, 78.

Carosso, Vincent. *The California Wine Industry, 1830–1895: A Study of the Formative Years.* Berkeley: University of California Press, 1951.

Carpy, Charles A. "Freemark Abbey: A Napa Valley Winery Is Reborn." *Wines and Vines* 50 (September 1969): 19–20.

Cashman, Sean. *Prohibition: The Lie of the Land.* New York: Free Press, 1981.

Casler, George L. "New York's Vineyard Industry." *Wines and Vines* 68 (March 1987): 26–28.

Cass, Bruce, ed. *The Oxford Companion to the Wines of North America.* New York: Oxford University Press, 2000.

Cattell, Hudson. "Celebrating Riesling with History and a Tasting." *Wine East* 29 (July–August 2001): 24–27.

———. "Gallo: The Little Winery That Got Bigger." *Pennsylvania Grape Letter and Wine News* 7 (March 1980): 1, 6–7.

———. "Major Investments Spur Long Island Wine Growth." *Wine East* 29 (September–October 2001): 24–29.

———. "Philip Marshall Wagner, 1904–1996." *Wine East* 24 (January–February 1997): 4–6.

———. "Ruth Ellen Church—In Memoriam." *Wine East* 19 (March–April 1992): 5, 29.

———. "Wine as Commitment at Canandaigua." *Wine East* 9 (March–April 1982): 8–10, 17.

Celler, Emanuel. *You Never Leave Brooklyn.* New York: John Day, 1953.

Chambas, Jean-Pierre. "The Growth of the Southeastern Vineyard." *The Sandlapper* [Clemson University] (July 1981): 29–34.

Chamberlain, Bernard Peyton. *A Treatise on the Making of Palatable Table Wines Recommended to Gentlemen, Especially in Virginia, for Their Own Use.* Charlottesville, Va.: Printed for the Author, 1931.

Chapman, P. J., and E. H. Glass. *The First Hundred Years of the New York State Agricultural Experiment Station at Geneva, N.Y.* Geneva: New York State Agricultural Experiment Station, 1999.

Chazanof, William. *Welch's Grape Juice: From Corporation to Co-operative.* Syracuse, N.Y.: Syracuse University Press, 1977.

Cherrington, Ernest Hurst, ed. *Standard Encyclopedia of the Alcohol Problem.* 6 vols. Westerville, Ohio: American Issue Publishing, 1924–30.

Chupp, Dave. "New Wine Regulations." *Vinifera Wine Growers Journal* 4 (Spring 1977): 274–77.

Clark, Norman H. *Deliver Us from Evil: An Interpretation of American Prohibition.* New York: W. W. Norton, 1976.

Clark, Selden. *California's Wine Industry and Its Financing.* New Brunswick, N.J.: Graduate School of Banking, American Bankers' Association, Rutgers University, 1941.

Clemens, Scott. "Making Premium Kosher Wine." *Practical Winery and Vineyard* 16 (March–April 1996): 5–9.

Clore, W. J., C. W. Nagel, and G. H. Carter. *Ten Years of Grape Variety Responses and Wine-Making Trials in Central Washington.* Bulletin 823. Pullman: College of Agriculture Research Center, Washington State University, 1976.

Conaway, James. *Napa.* Boston: Houghton, Mifflin, 1990.

Conn, Donald D. "The California Vineyard Industry: Five Year Report." San Francisco: California Vineyardists Association, 25 April 1932.

Cooke, Giles B. "Cork Culture in Arizona." *Wines and Vines* 24 (June 1943): 18–19.

Cooke, G. M., and H. W. Berg. "Varietal Table Wine Processing Practices in California, I: Varieties, Grape and Juice Handling and Fermentation." *American Journal of Enology and Viticulture* 20 (1969): 1–6.

Cooper, Iver P. "The FDA, the BATF, and Liquor Labeling: A Case Study of Interagency Jurisdictional Conflict." *Food Drug Cosmetic Law Journal* 34 (July 1979): 370–90.

Cox, James J. "A Bit of France in South Carolina." *Wines and Vines* 62 (March 1981): 50–51.

Critchfield, Burke H. "The Status of California Wine in Eastern States." *Fruit Products Journal* 14 (July 1935): 326.

Crosby, Everett. *The Vintage Years: The Story of High Tor Vineyards.* New York: Harper & Row, 1973.

Cruess, W. V. "California Wine Industry Conference." *Fruit Products Journal* 14 (June 1934): 293–94, 308.

———. "Effects of Overcropping." *American Journal of Enology and Viticulture* 5 (1954): 4–12.

———. "Experiments in Sherry." *Wines and Vines* 24 (October 1943): 21–22.

———. "A Few Reminiscences." *Wines and Vines* 33 (December 1952): 17–18.

———. "Grading, Scoring and Classifying Wines." *Wine Review* 3 (May 1935): 13, 18.

———. "Notes on the Use of Concrete in Wineries." *Wines and Vines* 18 (January 1937): 14–16, 23.

———. "Pasteurization and Closures." *Wine Review* 2 (September 1934): 8–9.

———. "Preparation of Yeast Starters for Wine Making." *Fruit Products Journal* 13 (February 1934): 167–68.

———. *The Principles and Practice of Wine Making.* New York: Avi Publishing, 1934; 2nd ed., 1947.

———. "Research in Enology." *California Journal of Development* 24 (December 1934): 10, 51.

———. "Rules for Sound Fermentations." *Wine Review* 5 (September 1937): 17–18.

———. "Suggestions for Increasing Consumer Interest." *Wines and Vines* 18 (November 1937): 6.

———. "Tests on Unfortified Sweet Wines." *Wine Review* 4 (February 1936): 20–21.

———. "Wine and the Fruit Products Laboratory." *Wines and Vines* 25 (December 1944): 39, 42.

Cruess, W. V., and Maynard A. Joslyn. "Crushing and Fermenting White Wine." *Wine Review* 2 (December 1934): 12–13, 15.

———. "Elements of Wine Making." Circular 88. Berkeley: University of California, College of Agriculture, 1934.

Darrow, Terri L. "Winegrowing in Oklahoma." *Wines and Vines* 69 (October 1988): 42–43.

Dawson, Lawrence. "Are Idaho Wines Influenced by Altitude?" *Wines and Vines* 73 (April 1992): 19–21.

Deane, General John R. "The Distillery-Owned Winery: Its Place in the Industry." *Wines and Vines* 30 (November 1949): 13–15.

———. "A Newcomer's Impression of the Wine Industry." Speech at National Wine Week Banquet, Fresno, 11 October 1949. Copy in the Wine Institute Library.

Dobyns, Fletcher. *The Amazing Story of Repeal: An Exposé of the Power of Propaganda.* Chicago: Willett, Clark, 1940.

Duffy, Milton P. "Enforcement of California Wine Quality Standards." *Fruit Products Journal* 15 (August 1936): 355–56, 376.

———. "Wine Standardization Progress." *Wines and Vines* 19 (March 1938): 12–13.

Dutt, Gordon R. "Border Wine Belt Is Emerging." *Wines and Vines* 66 (April 1985): 45–47.

Engelmann, Larry. *Intemperance: The Lost War against Liquor.* New York: Free Press, 1979.

English, Sarah Jane. *The Wines of Texas: A Guide and a History,* rev. ed. Austin: Eakin Press, 1986; 3rd ed., 1995.

Enright, Stratford. "Conditions in the Wine Barrel Store." *Wine Review* 3 (July 1935): 16–18.

Everett, Ed. "The Christian Brothers New Focus." *Wines and Vines* 62 (February 1981): 53–55, 58.

Fabian, F. W. "Michigan." *Wine Review* 11 (August 1943): 54–56.

Feeney, Richard. "The USDA Role in the Wine Industry." *Wines and Vines* 71 (July 1990): 15, 52.

Fessler, Julius. "Stability in Wine." *Wine Review* 14 (October 1946): 28–30.

Firstenfeld, Jane. "Meet a Cheerful Vintner: Redwood's Chuck Daniels." *Wines and Vines* 73 (August 1992): 25–27.

Fisher, M. F. K. "Through a Glass Darkly." *Atlantic Monthly* 174 (November 1944): 107–09.

Fisher, M. F. K., and Max Yavno. *The Story of Wine in California.* Berkeley: University of California Press, 1962.

Folwell, R. J., D. J. Kirpes, and C. W. Nagel. *Washington Wine Grape Acreage, 1982.* Research Circular XC 0648. Pullman: Agricultural Research Center, Washington State University, 1983.

Forker, Olan D., and Bennett A. Dominick Jr. *Toward the Year 1985: Fruit Production and Utilization.* Special Cornell Series 7. Ithaca: New York State College of Agriculture, 1969.

Fosdick, Raymond B., and Albert L. Scott. *Toward Liquor Control.* New York: Harper and Brothers, 1933.

Fournier, Charles. "Birth of N.Y. State Pinot Chardonnay." *Wines and Vines* 42 (January 1961): 32.

———. "A Scientific Look at Vinifera in the East." *Wines and Vines* 42 (August 1961): 27–29.

Fredrikson, Jon A. "The 80s Didn't Deliver on Forecast." *Wines and Vines* 71 (June 1990): 32–36.

———. "1992 'Hot' Year for Table Wine." *Wines and Vines* 74 (April 1993): 21–24, 6.

Freeze, Ken. "Formula Wines Threaten Integrity of Varietal Names." *Practical Winery and Vineyard* 20 (September–October 1999): 5–7.

Freitag, J. H., N. W. Frazier, and W. B. Hewitt. "Pierce's Disease of Grapevines: Vectors, Hosts and Control." *Wine Review* 13 (February 1945): 18–22, 28.

Gallo, Ernest. "Outlook for a Mature Industry." *Wines and Vines* 39 (June 1958): 27–30.

Gallo, Ernest, and Julio Gallo, with Bruce B. Henderson. *Ernest and Julio: Our Story*. New York: Times Books, 1994.

Gardner, M. W., and W. B. Hewitt. *Pierce's Disease of the Grapevine: The Anaheim Disease and the California Vine Disease*. Berkeley and Davis: University of California, Department of Plant Pathology, 1974.

Garr, John D. "A Survey of American Wine Laws." *Food Drug Cosmetic Law Journal* 16 (June 1961): 335–61.

Garrett, Paul. "The Right to Make Fruit Juices." *California Grape Grower* 4 (July 1923): 2–3.

Geagley, W. C. "Michigan Wine Industry." *Wine and Liquor Retailer* (September 1940): 3–5, 8.

George, H. C. "Behind the Scenes . . . How Alabama's Farm Winery Law Came to Be." *Wines and Vines* 60 (December 1979): 37–39.

Gifford, Jim. "Vitis Vinifera in the East: Its Booming Future." *American Wine Society Journal* 15 (Fall 1983): 67–69.

Gohdes, Clarence. *Scuppernong: North Carolina's Grape and Its Wines*. Durham, N.C.: Duke University Press, 1982.

Goldman, Max. "The New York State Industry as It Appears to a Former Californian." *Wines and Vines* 40 (May 1959): 18–19.

Gomberg, Louis. "Analyst Sees 5–6% Annual Growth Rate." *Wines and Vines* 55 (October 1974): 26–27.

———. "California—Land of Great Wines Only?" *Wines and Vines* 43 (January 1962): 24.

———. "The Five-Faced Winery Picture." *Wines and Vines* 61 (September 1980): 40–43.

———. "Gomberg Sees Long Range Wine Grape Surplus Program." *California Grape Grower* (December 1973): 34–35.

———. "Is Consumer Scarcity the Industry's Main Woe?" *Wines and Vines* 57 (September 1976): 30–35.

———. "Lest We Forget." *Wines and Vines* 52 (November 1971): 24.

———. "The Pink Wine Revolution." *Wines and Vines* 51 (September 1970): 56.

———. "Supplying a Demand of 1-Billion Gallons." *Wines and Vines* 53 (February 1972): 22.

———. "To Interpret Statistics Know Which Wines You're Talking About." *Wines and Vines* 60 (August 1979): 22–25.

Goresline, Harry E., and Richard Wellington. "New York Champagnes." *Wines and Vines* 17 (December 1936): 5, 19.

Greenan, George. "Cork: California Trees Produce a Million Acorns." *Wine Review* 13 (July 1945): 14–16.

Hall, Lisa Shara. *Wines of the Pacific Northwest: A Contemporary Guide to the Wines of Washington and Oregon*. London: Mitchell Beazley, 2001.

Hall, Richard D. "California's Central Valley Face Shrinking Markets, Phylloxera." *Wines and Vines* 72 (July 1991): 50–51.

Halliday, James. *Wine Atlas of California*. New York: Viking, 1993.

Harrison, Leonard V., and Elizabeth Lane. *After Repeal: A Study of Liquor Control Administration*. New York: Harper and Brothers, 1936.

Hawkes, Ellen. *Blood and Wine: The Unauthorized Story of the Gallo Wine Empire*. New York: Simon and Schuster, 1993.

Hayes, Irene W. *Ghost Wineries of Napa Valley: A Photographic Tour of the 19th Century.* San Francisco: Sally Taylor and Friends, 1980.

Haynes, Edwin. "45 Years in Wine." *Wine East* 11 (September–October 1983): 10–11, 25–26.

Heald, Eleanor, and Ray Heald. "Firelands Winery—Showcase for Ohio Vinifera Wines." *Practical Winery and Vineyard* 14 (November–December 1993): 44–46.

Hedrick, Ulysses Prentiss. *The Grapes of New York.* Albany, N.Y.: J. B. Lyon, 1908.

Heffernan, William D., and Paul Lasley. "Missouri Grape Industry Past, Present and Future." Columbia: University of Missouri, Extension Division, 1977.

Heinze, Kirk. "The Michigan Grape Industry: Transition, Progress, and Challenge." Special Report 8. East Lansing: Michigan State University, Agricultural Experiment Station, 1983.

Henry, Bernard. *Studies of Yeasts and the Fermentation of Fruits and Berries of Washington.* Seattle: University of Washington Press, 1936.

Hensley, H. K. "The Practice of Refrigeration." *Wine Review* 2 (July 1934): 11–13.

Hiaring, Philip. "Harold P. Olmo: A Vineyardist Is Wine Man of the Year." *Wines and Vines* 69 (March 1988): 16–19.

———. "Sebastiani Vineyards: The Name of the Game Is Growth." *Wines and Vines* 58 (September 1977): 16–21.

———. "World's Largest Bank Sees 650 Million Gallon Market for Wine in U.S. in 1980." *Wines and Vines* 54 (September 1973): 21–24.

Hiaring, Philip E. "A Vinous Tour of Indiana, the Hoosier State." *Wines and Vines* 57 (June 1976): 33–37.

Hicks, Jim. "Space Age Technology to Develop Yellow Rosé of Texas." *American Wine Society Journal* 7 (Fall 1975): 37–39.

Hilgard, E. W. *Report of the Viticultural Work during the Seasons of 1883–4 and 1884–5.* Sacramento: James J. Ayers, Superintendent of State Printing, 1886.

Hinkle, Richard Paul. "Foppiano at the Century Mark." *Wines and Vines* 77 (September 1996): 19–22.

Hinman, John A. "It's a Critical Time in the Wine Industry." *Wines and Vines* 69 (November 1988): 71–74.

Holden, Charles. "Welcoming Remarks." *Proceedings of the American Society of Enologists* 1 (1950): 1–4.

Holliday, Mark. "California's Premium Wines." *Wine Review* 17 (September 1949): 6–7.

Howell, H. B. "Grape Growing in Oregon." *California Grape Grower* 4 (August 1923): 4.

Howie, Millie. "Cuthills Vineyard: A Winery in Pierce, Nebraska." *Wines and Vines* 81 (January 2000): 112–17.

Hughes, Robert. "Metallurgy, Metals, and the Winery." *Wine Review* 3 (April 1935): 12–14.

Hutchinson, John. "Sacramental and Kosher Wines: An Industry Godsend in More Ways Than One." *Wines and Vines* 57 (September 1976): 20–24.

Hutchinson, Ralph B. "The California Wine Industry." Ph.D. diss., University of California, Los Angeles, 1969.

Hutchinson, Ralph B., and William Dunn. "The Constitution, Interstate Commerce and Wine." *Wines and Vines* 48 (April 1967): 20–26.

Hutchison, C. B. "Viticultural and Enological Research Projects at the University." *Wines and Vines* 28 (December 1947): 9–10, 31.

Hutton, Robert W. "Wine at the Library of Congress." *American Wine Society Journal* 10 (Fall 1978): 38–40.

"Importer Now Sells California Wines." *Wines and Vines* 20 (December 1939): 8, 21.

Irvine, Ronald, with Walter J. Clore. *The Wine Project: Washington State's Winemaking History.* Vashon, Wash.: Sketch Publications, 1997.

Jacobs, Julius. "Jeff Peyser: The Man of the Year." *Wines and Vines* 64 (March 1983): 22–27.

Jakisch, Philip F. "Travels with Galet." *American Wine Society Journal* 13 (Spring 1981): 18–19.

James, Marquis, and Bessie Rowland James. *Biography of a Bank: The Story of Bank of America.* New York: Harper and Brothers, 1954.

Johnson, Hugh. "The Wines of California." *Gourmet* 30 (October 1970): 16, 36–45.

Jordan, Rudolf, Jr. *Quality in Dry Wines through Adequate Fermentations . . . A Manual for Progressive Winemakers in California.* San Francisco: Pernau Publishing, 1911.

Joslyn, Maynard A., and Maynard A. Amerine. *Commercial Production of Brandies.* Bulletin 652. Berkeley: University of California, Agricultural Experiment Station, 1941.

———. *Commercial Production of Dessert Wines.* Bulletin 651. Berkeley: University of California, Agricultural Experiment Station, 1941.

———. *Dessert, Appetizer and Related Flavored Wines: The Technology of Their Production.* Berkeley: University of California, Division of Agricultural Sciences, 1964.

Joslyn, Maynard A., and W. V. Cruess. *Elements of Wine Production.* Circular 88. Berkeley: University of California, College of Agriculture, Agricultural Extension Service, 1934.

Kamas, Jim. *Growing Grapes in the Texas Hill Country.* Fredericksburg: Texas Agricultural Extension Service, ca. 2000.

Kelly, Margaret. "The Wine Industry in Ohio." *Wine Review* 7 (January 1939): 15–16.

Kimball, Keith H. "Another Look at Vinifera in the East." *Wines and Vines* 42 (April 1961): 63–67.

Knechel, John A. "Bank of America Lays It On the Line; It's a Rosy 10 Years ahead for Wine." *Wines and Vines* 51 (September 1970): 34–36.

Kramer, Matt. "Oregon's New Pinot Noir Reality." *Los Angeles Times,* 31 October 1996, H, 6.

Kraus, George. *The Story of an Amana Winemaker,* as told to E. Mae Fritz. Iowa City: Penfield Press, 1984.

Krosch, Penelope. "Grape Research in Minnesota." *Agricultural History* 62 (Spring 1988): 258–69.

Kyvig, David E. *Repealing National Prohibition.* Chicago: University of Chicago Press, 1979.

LaFollette, Robert M., Jr. "Never Prohibition Again." *Atlantic Monthly* 171 (January 1943): 37–40.

Lanza, Horace O. "The Grape Products Consolidation." *California Grower* 10 (July 1929): 8.

Lapsley, James T. *Bottled Poetry: Napa Winemaking from Prohibition to the Modern Era.* Berkeley: University of California Press, 1996.

Larsen, Roger. "The Desert Sprouts Winegrapes." *Wines and Vines* 64 (November 1983): 112–15.

Laube, James. *California's Great Cabernets.* San Francisco: Wine Spectator Press, 1989.

Lawrence, R. de Treville, III, ed. *Jefferson and Wine.* 2nd ed. The Plains, Va.: Vinifera Wine Growers Association, 1989.

Leete, Stuart F. "California Wine Moves to Market." *Wine Review* 4 (December 1936): 10–11.

Lefcourt, Martin. "Should Prices Be Lower?" *Wine Review* 13 (September 1945): 14.

Leizear, Richard L. "S. C. Muscadine Winery Denounces Technology." *Vinifera Wine Growers Journal* 2 (Spring 1975): 46–48.

Lender, Mark Edward. *Dictionary of American Temperance Biography.* Westport, Conn.: Greenwood Press, 1984.

"Let's Extol Michigan Wines." *Michigan Beverage Man* (April 1961): 6–7, 13, 16.

Lider, Lloyd A. "Phylloxera-Resistant Grape Rootstocks for the Coastal Valleys of California." *Hilgardia* 27 (February 1958): 287–318.

Lincoln, Elizabeth. "Grapes and Wine in the Nutmeg State." *American Wine Society Journal* 20 (Fall 1988): 84–87.

Lorenzo, Jake [pseud.]. "Tribute." *Practical Winery and Vineyard* 21 (May–June 2000): 74.

Lubow, Arthur. "What's Killing the Grapevines of Napa?" *New York Times Magazine,* 17 October 1993.

Lukacs, Paul. *American Vintage: The Rise of American Wine.* Boston: Houghton Mifflin, 2000.

Mabon, Mary Frost. *ABC of America's Wines.* New York: Knopf, 1942.

McCrea, Eleanor. "Insider's Story of Stony Hill." *Wines and Vines* 63 (November 1982): 52–53.

McDonald, W. N. "The Sales Story of 'Eastern.'" *Wine Review* 8 (September 1940): 8–10.

McEachern, George. "History of the New Texas Wine Grape Industry." In *The Wines of Texas,* ed. Sarah Jane English, rev. ed., pp. 183–93. Austin: Eakin Press, 1986.

McGinty, Brian. *Strong Wine: The Life and Legend of Agoston Haraszthy.* Stanford, Calif.: Stanford University Press, 1998.

McGrew, John. "Why Try to Improve on Perfection?" *Wines and Vines* 54 (May 1973): 22–24.

McKee, Linda Jones. "Colorado: Eastern Wines in a Western Setting." *Wine East* 13 (September–October 1985): 8–9, 26–27.

McKinney, Charles O., and John E. Crosby. "Vineyards in Texas—Past and Present." *Wines and Vines* 71 (June 1990): 55–57.

Magness, J. R., and I. W. Dix. "Vinifera Grapes in the East." Mimeographed report. Washington, D.C.: U.S. Department of Agriculture, March 1934.

Manfreda, John, and Richard Mendelson. *U.S. Wine Law.* Mimeograph. N.p.: John Manfreda and Richard Mendelson, 1988.

Marcus, Irving A. "Blame." *Wines and Vines* 52 (November 1971): 4.

———. "Bulk Dessert Wine." *Wines and Vines* 27 (September 1946): 19, 40.

———. "California's Cooperative Wineries." *Wines and Vines* 34 (March 1953): 8–12.

———. "Give the Devil His Due." *Wines and Vines* 27 (December 1946): 17.

———. "Independent Bottler Faces Tough Times." *Wines and Vines* 27 (April 1946): 23, 71.

———. "Millenium." *Wines and Vines* 48 (October 1967): 4.

———. "New Coops Under Way." *Wines and Vines* 27 (February 1946): 16–17.

———. "Record Crush Still Looms as Good Possibility." *Wines and Vines* 27 (July 1946): 11, 13.

———. "The Seven Fat Years of Table Wine Sales in California." *Wines and Vines* 35 (October 1954): 21–22.

———. "What the New Wine Types Have Accomplished." *Wines and Vines* 44 (January 1963): 14–18.

———. "Wine Price Bugaboo." *Wines and Vines* 26 (November 1945): 11.

Margolis, John A. "Grapes Need a Holiday for Stability of California Grape and Wine Industry." *Wine Review* 16 (September 1948): 6–7, 29.

Marquis, H. H. "California Sherry Production." *Wine Review* 4 (June 1936): 6–7, 22.

———. "The Menace of Second-Hand Barrels." *Wine Review* 3 (May 1935): 19–20.

———. "Selling Wine Out of a Barrel." *California Wine Review* 2 (October 1934): 8–9.

———. "The Vagaries of the Wine Market." *Wine Review* 4 (January 1936).

———. "The Valley of the Crushed Grape." *California Wine Review* 2 (August 1934): 9–10.

———. "Wine in the Hotels of America." *Wine Review* 3 (October 1935): 8–10.

Marshall, L. K. "Better Wine Grapes and the Only Way to Assure Their Availability." *Wines and Vines* 24 (August 1943): 31, 47.

———. "The Position of the Co-ops." *Wines and Vines* 25 (December 1944): 14–15.

———. "Wine Growing in the Lodi District." *American Journal of Enology and Viticulture* 6 (January–March 1955): 33–34.

———. "The Wine Problem." *California Department of Agriculture Bulletin* 26 (January–March 1937): 59–62.

Martin, Harvey W. "Control of Guasti in New Hands." *Wines and Vines* 24 (September 1943): 12.

———. "Schenley Buys Roma and CWI." *Wines and Vines* 23 (November 1942): 9.

Marvel, Tom. Letter to the editor. *California Grape Grower* 15 (September 1934): 18.

Matthews, Patrick. *The Wild Bunch: Great Wines from Small Producers.* London: Faber and Faber, 1997.

Meers, John R. "The California Wine and Grape Industry and Prohibition." *California Historical Society Quarterly* 46 (1967): 19–32.

Melville, John. *Guide to California Wines.* Garden City, N.Y.: Doubleday, 1955.

Mendall, Seaton C. "The Man Who Made It Happen: 1.5–4.5 T/A." *Eastern Grape Grower and Winery News* 5 (February 1979): 12–15.

Meredith, Ted Jordan. *Northwest Wine: Winegrowing Alchemy along the Pacific Rim of Fire.* 4th ed. Kirkland, Wash.: Nexus Press, 1990.

Merz, Charles. *The Dry Decade.* Garden City, N.Y.: Doubleday, Doran, 1931.

Meyer, Justin. "Values of Diversified Cooperage in the Wine Industry." *Wines and Vines* 51 (April 1970): 57–58.

Mielke, Eugene A., et al. *Grape and Wine Production in the Four Corners Region.* Technical Bulletin 239. Tucson: University of Arizona, Agricultural Experiment Station, 1980.

Milhauser, Edgar. "Quality Wine—Why Not Specific Categories?" *Wines and Vines* 33 (May 1952): 6.

Miller, Mark. *Wine—a Gentleman's Game: The Adventures of an Amateur Winemaker Turned Professional.* New York: Harper & Row, 1984.

Mirassou, Edmund. "Are North Coast Grapes Expendable?" *Wines and Vines* 42 (February 1961): 17–18.

Mitchell, Broadus. *Depression Decade: From New Era through New Deal.* New York: Rinehart, 1947.

Mitchell, Roy E. "Texas Wine History." N.p.: Texas Wine and Grape Growers Association, 10 November 1993.

Moffett, J. William. "Changing Regulations for Wine." *American Wine Society Journal* 12 (Summer 1980): 37–39.

———. "New Mexico: Land of Enchanting Investment." *Eastern Grape Grower and Winery News* 9 (August–September 1983): 22–27.

Mondavi, Robert. "Plan for Grape and Winegrowing in the Future." Report to the Wine Institute Technical Advisory Committee, 3 December 1954. Copy in the Wine Institute Library.

———. "A Plea for Generic Promotion." *Wines and Vines* 63 (January 1982): 36–41.

Morrah, Patrick. *André Simon: Gourmet and Wine Lover.* London: Constable, 1987.

Morrison, Paul Cross. "Viticulture in Ohio." *Economic Geography* 12 (1936): 71–85.

Mortensen, E., and U. A. Randolph. "Grape Production in Texas." Circular 89. College Station: Texas Agricultural Experiment Station, 1940.

Mortensen, John A. "Developing Florida's Grape Industry from the Breeder's Viewpoint." *Vinifera Wine Growers Journal* 15 (Fall 1988): 183–86.

Morton, Lucie T. "Elizabeth Furness: Virginia's Wine Pioneer." *Eastern Grape Grower and Winery News* 5 (October 1979): 55.

———. "The Myth of the Universal Rootstock." *Wines and Vines* 60 (April 1979): 24–26.

———. "The Prospects for Texas Wine." *Wines and Vines* 61 (October 1980): 26–33.

———. "An Update on Virginia Viticulture." *Wines and Vines* 62 (October 1981): 47–50.

———. *Winegrowing in Eastern America: An Illustrated Guide to Viticulture East of the Rockies.* Ithaca, N.Y.: Cornell University Press, 1985.

Motto Kryla & Fisher LLP. *Economic Impact of the Washington State Wine and Wine Grape Industries.* St. Helena, Calif.: Motto Kryla & Fisher LLP, 2001.

Moulton, Kirby S. "Will Red Wine, Not White Wine, Be the Wine of Tomorrow?" *Wines and Vines* 58 (September 1977): 36–38.

Mullins, Michael G. "The Future at U.C. Davis." *Wines and Vines* 69 (June 1988): 23–28.

Munson, T. V. *Foundations of American Grape Culture.* Denison, Tex.: T. V. Munson and Son, 1909.

Muscatine, Doris, Maynard A. Amerine, and Bob Thompson, eds. *The University of California/Sotheby Book of California Wine.* Berkeley: University of California Press, and London: Sotheby Publications, 1984.

New York Agricultural Statistics Service. *Survey of Orchards and Vineyards 1996.* Albany: New York State Department of Agriculture and Markets, 1996.

Nightingale, Myron S. "California Methods of Baking Sherry." *Wine Review* 14 (May 1946): 8–9.

Oberst, G. Michael. "The California Wine Industry." Industry Report. San Francisco: Wells Fargo Bank, September 1972.

Ockey, William C. "The Cost of Producing Wine Grapes." *Wine Review* 3 (March 1935): 21–25.

Ohmart, Cliff. "Vineyard Views." *Wines and Vines* 84 (March 2003): 18–20.

Olmo, H. P. "Breeding New Grape Varieties." *Wine Review* 7 (April 1939): 8–10, 32.

———. "Breeding New Wine Grape Varieties." *Wine Review* 18 (February 1950): 7–10, 14.

———. "California's Principal Wine Grape Varieties, Present and Future." *Wines and Vines* 36 (May 1955): 28–29.

———. "Introduction, Improvement and Certification of Healthy Grape Varieties." *Wines and Vines* 32 (July 1951): 7–9.

———. "Our Principal Wine Grape Varieties Present and Future." *American Journal of Enology and Viticulture* 5 (1954): 18–20.

———. "Selecting and Breeding New Grape Varieties." *California Agriculture* 34 (July 1980): 23–24.

———. "Wine Grape Varieties of the Future." *Proceedings of the American Society of Enologists* 3 (1952): 45–52.

O'Neill, John E. "Federal Activity in Alcoholic Beverage Control." *Law and Contemporary Problems* 7 (Autumn 1940): 570–99.

Oregon Agricultural Statistics Service. "2003 Oregon Vineyard and Winery Report." Portland: Oregon Agricultural Statistics Service, February 2004.

Osteraas, Paul. "The Gallo Vacuum Grape Harvester." *Wines and Vines* 47 (April 1966): 49–50.

Peninou, Ernest, assisted by Gail G. Unzelman and Michael M. Anderson. *History of the Sonoma Viticultural Districts: The Grape Growers, the Wine Makers and the Vineyards.* History of the Viticultural Districts of California 1. Santa Rosa, Calif.: Nomis Press, 1998.

Peters, Leon. "Protect Your Stainless Steel." *Wines and Vines* 29 (October 1948): 34–35.

Peterson-Nedry, Judy. *Washington Wine Country.* Portland, Oreg.: Graphic Arts Publishing Center, 1999.

Petri, Louis A. "Wine Quality and the Advertising Program." *Wine Review* 7 (June 1939): 7–8, 10.

Pincetl, Stephanie S. *Transforming California: A Political History of Land Use and Development.* Baltimore: Johns Hopkins University Press, 1999.

Pinney, Thomas. *A History of Wine in America: From the Beginnings to Prohibition.* Berkeley: University of California Press, 1989.

Pintarich, Paul. *The Boys Up North: Dick Erath and the Early Oregon Winemakers.* Portland: Wyatt Group, 1997.

Porchet, Berthe. *La Vigne et le vin en Californie.* Lausanne: Imprimerie Vaudoise, 1937.

Potticary, John F. "Potential for the Development of a Wine and Supporting Wine Grape Industry in Oregon." Portland: Oregon State Department of Commerce, Economic Development Division, August 1968.

Prial, Frank. "Wine Talk." *New York Times,* 7 July 1973, 16; 6 March 1985, III, 13; 18 April 1990, II, 9; 25 December 1991, 29.

Purser, J. Elizabeth, and Lawrence J. Allen. *The Winemakers of the Pacific Northwest.* Vashon Island, Wash.: Harbor House Publishing, 1977.

Pyke, John S. "Wine and National Defense." *Wine Review* 9 (October 1941): 9–10.

Ragan, Allen. *Chief Justice Taft.* Columbus: Ohio State Archaeological and Historical Society, 1938.

Ray, Eleanor, and Barbara Marinacci. *Vineyards in the Sky: The Life of Legendary Vintner Martin Ray.* Stockton, Calif.: Heritage West Books, 1993.

Ray, Pamela. "Wineries of New Mexico." *Eastern Grape Grower and Winery News* 11 (December 1985–January 1986): 12–14.

Reisch, Bruce I., Robert N. Goodman, Mary-Howell Martens, and Norman F. Weeden. "The Relationship between Norton and Cynthiana, Red Wine Cultivars Derived from *Vitis aestivalis*." *American Journal of Enology and Viticulture* 44 (1993): 441–44.

Remington, George. "The Sherries and Ports of Solera Cellars." *Wines and Vines* 29 (November 1948): 53–54.

Richert, Walter S. "Recent Grape Plantings: The Trend Is Backwards." *Wine Review* 7 (December 1939): 6–7, 20.

———. "A Research Program for the Wine Industry." *Wines and Vines* 27 (September 1946): 13, 38–40.

———. "$3,000,000: How Should It Be Spent?" *Wines and Vines* 30 (November 1949): 11–12.

———. "Wanted: More Wine Grapes." *Wine Review* 7 (April 1939): 11–12, 21, 31.

Richert, Walter, and Ben H. Cummings. "Improved Winery Construction." *Wine Review* 5 (May 1937): 8–11.

Riddell, James. "Brandy Production: Past, Present, Future." *Wines and Vines* 49 (January 1968): 19–20.

Rink, James. "Field of Dreams in Jackson County." *American Wine Society Journal* 33 (Spring 2001): 15.

Robinson, Jancis. *Vines, Grapes and Wines: The Wine Drinker's Guide to Grape Varieties.* London: Mitchell Beazley, 1986.

———, ed. *The Oxford Companion to Wine.* 2nd ed. Oxford: Oxford University Press, 1999.

Roby, Norman S., and Charles E. Olken. *The New Connoisseurs' Handbook of California Wines.* 3rd ed. New York: Knopf, 1995.

Rodgers, Marion Elizabeth, ed. *The Impossible H. L. Mencken: A Selection of His Best Newspaper Stories.* New York: Doubleday, 1991.

Roosevelt, Franklin D. *Public Papers and Addresses of Franklin D. Roosevelt,* vol. 2: *The Year of Crisis, 1933,* ed. Samuel I. Rosenman. New York: Random House, 1938.

Rose, Kenneth. *American Women and the Repeal of Prohibition.* New York: New York University Press, 1996.

Rossi, Edmund A. "The Coming Expansion of the Table Wine Market." *Wines and Vines* 25 (December 1944): 29, 47.

———. "Licenses That Burden the Wine Trade." *California Journal of Development* 24 (December 1934): 11, 38–39.

Rossi, Robert D. "Post-Repeal Wine Consumption." *Wines and Vines* 16 (January 1935): 3–4.

Rossi, Robert, Jr. "United Vintners Expands Its Madera Premises." *Wines and Vines* 43 (September 1962): 25, 27.

Roueché, Berton. "Breathing through the Wood." *New Yorker* 23 (29 November 1947): 72–87.

Russell, Meigs B. "Shewan-Jones Plant a Model of Efficiency." *Fruit Products Journal* 13 (December 1934): 104.

———. "Why Masquerade American Wines under Foreign Names?" *Fruit Products Journal* 13 (October 1933): 35–36, 57.

———. "Wise and Far Seeing Policies the Need of American Wineries." *Fruit Products Journal* 13 (March 1934): 197–98.

Ryan, Richard L. "How the ATTD Laboratories Keep Their Eye on You." *Wines and Vines* 42 (July 1961): 18–22.

"Safeguarding the Profit Margin." *Wine Review* 10 (August 1942): 9–12.

Schick, Robert. "The Arkansas Wine Industry." *Wine Review* 14 (June 1946): 8–12, 18.

Schoonmaker, Frank. "Almaden's Great New Vineyard." *Wines and Vines* 41 (August 1960): 21–22.

———. "The Case Is Presented for Varietal Names." *Wines and Vines* 21 (November 1940): 8–9.

———. "The Future of Quality Wine." *Wines and Vines* 26 (December 1945): 21, 37.

———. "The Merits of California Wines." *Wines and Vines* 16 (March 1935): 5, 26.

———. "New Decalogues of Drinking." *Saturday Review of Literature* 11 (3 November 1934): 253, 260–61.

Schoonmaker, Frank, and Tom Marvel. *American Wines.* New York: Duell, Sloan and Pearce, 1941.

———. *The Complete Wine Book.* New York: Simon and Schuster, 1934.

Schorske, Sara. "ATF Approves Alternating Proprietors License." *Vineyard and Winery Management* 18 (January–February 1992): 50.

Schorske, Sara, and Alex Heckathorn. "Precious Privilege in Jeopardy: ATF Re-examines Alternating Proprietorships." *Vineyard and Winery Management* 29 (May–June 2003): 13–16.

Schueneman, Dr. Thomas J. "The Grape in Kansas: Poised for a Winegrowing Comeback?" *Vinifera Wine Growers Journal* 9 (Winter 1982): 225–32.

Sealey, Peter. "Inside Taylor California Cellars." *Wines and Vines* 62 (December 1981): 42–46.

Seff, James. "An Analysis of the Gesell Decisions." *Wines and Vines* 61 (January 1980): 32–34.

Seghesio, Eugene. "Grape Growing in Sonoma County." *American Journal of Enology and Viticulture* 7 (April–June 1956): 77–78.

Shaulis, Nelson, John Einset, and A. Boyd Pack. "Growing Cold-Tender Grape Varieties in New York." Bulletin 821. Geneva: New York State Agricultural Experiment Station, 1968.

Shaw, Robert D., Jr. "The Grapes of Hope." *Vinifera Wine Growers Journal* 1 (Spring 1974): 13–14.

Shear, S. W., and R. E. Blair. *California Fruit Statistics and Related Data.* Bulletin 763. Berkeley: University of California, Division of Agricultural Sciences, Agricultural Experiment Station, 1958.

Sheehan, E. M. "California Sherry Wine." *California Grape Grower* 15 (May 1934): 3.

———. "The Marketing of California Wines." *California Grape Grower* 15 (June 1934): 3.

Shelton, O. M. "Cameo Vineyard Company's Model Plant." *Wine Review* 3 (May 1935): 14–15.

Sifritt, Susan. "The Ohio Wine and Grape Industries." Ph.D. diss., Kent State University, 1976.

Simon, André. "Californian Wines." *Wine and Food* 6 (Summer 1935): 7–12.

———. "First American Impressions." *Wine and Food* 5 (Spring 1935): 3–8.

Sinclair, Andrew. *Prohibition: The Era of Excess.* London: Faber and Faber, 1962.

Smart, Richard, and Mike Robinson. *Sunlight into Wine: A Handbook for Winegrape Canopy Management.* Adelaide: Winetitles, 1991.

Solari, B.C. "And Deliver Us from Glamour." Speech to Los Angeles Advertising Club, 23 October 1962. Copy in the Wine Institute Library.

Sonneman, Henry. "Ohio State Wines." *Proceedings of the American Society of Enologists* 3 (1952): 17–22.

Steenborg, Erich. "Wine Grapes in the State of Washington." *Wine Review* 7 (October 1939): 12–13.

Steuart, Justin. *Wayne B. Wheeler: Dry Boss.* New York and Chicago: Fleming H. Revell, 1928.

Stockley, Tom. *Winery Trails of the Pacific Northwest.* Mercer Island, Wash.: Writing Works, 1977.

Stokdyk, E.A. "The Case for Cooperative Wineries." *Wine Review* 4 (February 1936): 15–16.

Stoll, Horatio F. "The Merits of California Wines." *Wines and Vines* 16 (March 1935): 5, 26.

———. "3.2 Per Cent Wines Make Their Appearance." *California Grower* 14 (May 1933): 3–4.

Street, Julian. "Wine: Cinderella of Repeal." *Scribner's Magazine* 98 (September 1935): 150–56.

———. *Wines: Their Selection, Care, and Service.* New York: Knopf, 1933.

Strutt, Eric. "Let's Look at Radio." *Wines and Vines* 23 (February 1942): 10–11.

Stuller, Jay, and Glen Martin. *Through the Grapevine.* New York: Wynwood Press, 1989.

Sullivan, Charles L. *A Companion to California Wine: An Encyclopedia of Wine and Winemaking from the Mission Period to the Present.* Berkeley: University of California Press, 1998.

———. *Like Modern Edens: Winegrowing in Santa Clara Valley and Santa Cruz Mountains 1798–1981.* Local History Studies 28. Cupertino, Calif.: California History Center, 1982.

———. "March 24, 1967." *Wines and Vines* 48 (June 1967): 68.

———. *Napa Wine: A History from Mission Days to Present.* San Francisco: Wine Appreciation Guild, 1994.

———. *The Society of Wine Educators: A History of Its Inception and the First Ten Years.* Princeton, N.J.: Bob Levine, 2000.

———. *Zinfandel: A History of a Grape and Its Wine.* Berkeley: University of California Press, 2003.

Swarthout, Joseph L. "The New York Wine Industry: Continued Prosperity." *Wines and Vines* 56 (September 1975): 62–65.

Swartout, H.G. *Grape Growing in Missouri.* Bulletin 208. Columbia: University of Missouri College of Agriculture, Agricultural Experiment Station, January 1924.

Taylor, Allan. *What Everybody Wants to Know about Wine.* New York: Knopf, 1934.

Taylor, Greyton H. "New York Wines: Their Place in the Market." *Wines and Vines* 35 (November 1954): 29–30.

———. "Trade Barriers Are a Major Obstacle to Wine Distribution." *Wine Review* 8 (April 1940): 6–7.

Teiser, Ruth, and Catherine Harroun. "The Volstead Act, Rebirth, and Boom." In *The University of California/Sotheby Book of California Wine,* ed. Doris Muscatine, Maynard A. Amerine, and Bob Thompson, pp. 50–83. Berkeley: University of California Press, and London: Sotheby Publications, 1984.

———. *Winemaking in California.* New York: McGraw-Hill, 1983.

Tomkins, John P. "Comments on East Coast Viticulture." *Vinifera Wine Growers Journal* 8 (Summer 1981): 74–81.

Tugwell, Rexford G. *The Battle for Democracy.* New York: Columbia University Press, 1935.

———. *Roosevelt's Revolution: The First Year—A Personal Perspective.* New York: Macmillan, 1977.

Turano, Anthony M. "The Comedy of Repeal." *American Mercury* 39 (October 1936): 168–73.

Turner, B. B. "Our Wines' Reputation." *Wine Review* 9 (July 1941): 8–9.

Twight, E. H. "California Sherry Wine Making." *Wines and Vines* 17 (April 1936): 5, 15.

———. "Improving Sweet Wines." *Wine Review* 18 (June 1937): 14.

———. "Port Wine Making in California." *Wines and Vines* 17 (May 1936): 5.

———. "Sweet Wine Making in California." *California Grape Grower* 15 (October 1934): 4–5.

———. "Sweet Wine Making in California, Part II." *California Grape Grower* 15 (November 1934): 4–5, 7.

———. "Winery Methods Are Not New." *Wine Review* 4 (April 1936): 15.

Twight, E. H., and Maynard A. Amerine. "Port Wine." *Wines and Vines* 19 (February 1938): 5–6.

Udell, Gilman G., compiler. *Liquor Laws.* Washington, D.C.: GPO, 1978.

United States:

Congress. *Tax on Intoxicating Liquor: Joint Hearings before the Committee on Ways and Means, House of Representatives and the Committee on Finance, United States Senate, December 11 to 14, 1933.* Washington, D.C.: GPO, 1934.

Congress, House of Representatives, Committee on Agriculture. *Review of U.S. Department of Agriculture Activities to Assist and Support the U.S. Winegrape and Wine Industry.* Washington, D.C.: GPO, 1992.

Congress, House of Representatives, Committee on Agriculture, Subcommittee on Livestock and Horticulture. *The Status and Prospects of American Wine Production, August 10, 1999.* Washington, D.C.: GPO, 1999.

Congress, House of Representatives, Committee on Ways and Means. *Federal Alcohol Control Bill.* Report 1542. Washington, D.C.: GPO, 17 July 1935.

———. *Legalization of Wine. Hearings, 8 June 1933.* Washington, D.C.: GPO, 1933.

———. *Liquor Tax Administration Bill.* Report 1870. Washington, D.C.: GPO, 1935.

———. *Prohibition: Modification of Volstead Act. Hearings, Dec. 7–14 1932.* Washington, D.C.: GPO, 1932.

———. *To Amend the Revenue Act of 1918, as Amended.* Report 1817. Washington, D.C.: GPO, 17 August 1935.

Congress, House of Representatives, Judiciary Committee. *Hearings on Proposed Modification of the Prohibition Law to Permit . . . 2.75 Per Cent Beverages, Part 1, Part 2.* Washington, D.C.: GPO, 1924.

———. *Liquor Law Repeal and Enforcement Bill.* House Report 1258. Washington, D.C.: GPO, 1935.

Congress, Senate, Committee on Finance. *Hearings on the Liquor Tax Administration Act, 13, 15, 16 January 1936.* Washington, D.C.: GPO, 1936.

Congress, Senate, Judiciary Committee. *Liquor Industry; Hearings, 10, 16, 17 December 1943.* Washington, D.C.: GPO, 1944.

Congress, Senate, Judiciary Committee Subcommittee. *Liquor Industry. Hearings December 1943 and January 1944.* Washington, D.C.: GPO, 1944.

Department of Agriculture. *Agricultural Statistics*. Washington, D.C.: GPO, annual.

———. *Fruits (Noncitrus): Production, Farm Disposition, Value, and Utilization of Sales, 1889–1944*. Washington, D.C.: GPO, 1948.

Department of Agriculture, Beltsville Experiment Station. *Bulletin of the Plant Industry Employees' Association* 10 (June 1956).

Department of Agriculture, Bureau of Agricultural Economics, Crop Reporting Board. *Fruits and Nuts Bearing Acreage 1919–1946*. Washington, D.C.: GPO, 1949.

Department of the Treasury. *Report of the Commissioner of Internal Revenue*. Washington, D.C.: GPO, annual.

Department of the Treasury, Alcohol and Tobacco Tax and Trade Bureau. "Wine." *Code of Federal Regulations, Title 27, Part 1, Chapter 1*, 2004 revision. Washington, D.C.: GPO, 2004.

Department of the Treasury, Bureau of Industrial Alcohol. *Statistics Concerning Intoxicating Liquors, December 1931*. Washington, D.C.: GPO, 1931 [annual].

———. *Statistics Concerning Intoxicating Liquors, December 1932*. Washington, D.C.: GPO, 1932.

———. *Statistics Concerning Intoxicating Liquors, December 1933*. Washington, D.C.: GPO, 1933.

Department of the Treasury, Bureau of Prohibition. *Statistics Concerning Intoxicating Liquors, April 1928*. Washington, D.C.: GPO, 1928.

———. *Statistics Concerning Intoxicating Liquors, January 1930*. Washington, D.C.: GPO, 1930.

Federal Alcohol Administration. *Labeling and Advertising of Wine*. Regulations 4. Washington, D.C.: GPO, 1935.

Federal Alcohol Control Administration. *Code of Fair Competition for the Wine Industry*. Washington, D.C.: GPO, 1934.

———. *Legislative History of the Federal Alcohol Administration Act*. Washington, D.C.: GPO, 1935.

National Commission on Law Observance and Enforcement. *Enforcement of the Prohibition Laws: Official Records*. 5 vols. Washington, D.C.: GPO, 1931. *[Wickersham Report]* *Statutes at Large of the United States of America* 41 (1921).

Tariff Commission. *Grapes and Grape Products*. War Changes in Industry Series, Report 24. Washington, D.C.: GPO, 1947.

———. *Grapes, Raisins and Wines*. Report 134. 2nd ser. Washington, D.C.: GPO, 1939.

Valaer, Peter. "California Brandy Production." *Wine Review* 10 (November 1942): 8–9.

Van Dyne, Ed. "Arizona's Embryonic Wine Industry: A Dark Horse?" *American Wine Society Journal* 15 (Summer 1983): 47–48.

Van Ravenswaay, Charles. *The Arts and Architecture of German Settlement in Missouri*. Columbia: University of Missouri Press, 1977.

Viney, Louis. Letter to the editor. *Wines and Vines* 28 (May 1947): 6.

Vornbrock, Walter. "The Lure of California Land." *Wines and Vines* 66 (November 1985): 20.

Wagner, Philip M. "American Wines." *Wine and Food* 8 (Winter 1935): 77–78.

———. *American Wines and How to Make Them*. New York: Knopf, 1933.

———. "California Thirty Years Ago." *Wine East* 9 (November 1981): 12–14, 21.

———. "Eastern Wine-Growing: Problems and Prospects." *Pennsylvania Grape Letter and Wine News* 5 (February 1979): 1, 4, 7.

———. "The East's New Wine Industry." *Wines and Vines* 60 (March 1979): 24–26.

———. "Federal Aid, Private Research, State Experiments, State Laws and the Winery." *Vinifera Wine Growers Journal* 2 (Fall 1975): 17–19.

———. "The French Hybrids." *American Journal of Enology and Viticulture* 6 (1955): 10–17.

———. "Grapes and Wine Production in the East." In *Wine Production Technology in the United States,* ed. Maynard A. Amerine, pp. 192–224. Washington, D.C.: American Chemical Society, 1981.

———. *Grapes into Wine: A Guide to Winemaking in America.* New York: Knopf, 1976.

———. [Anonymously.] "The Great Wine Boom." *Fortune* 23 (May 1941): 88–95.

———. "Keynoter Philip Wagner." *American Wine Society Journal* 18 (Winter 1986): 125–27.

———. "A Misleading Impression." *Wines and Vines* 59 (January 1978): 50.

———. "More Trouble Than It's Worth." *Wines and Vines* 48 (March 1967): 29.

———. "Oregon's Mystery Grape." *Wine East* 16 (January–February 1989): 14–15.

———. "A Sham Controversy." *American Wine Society Journal* 10 (Spring 1978): 12–15.

———. "Vintage in the Finger Lakes." *Wine East* 26 (May–June 1998): 10–19.

———. "Wagner's Question: Better Name for Hybrids?" *Wines and Vines* 59 (May 1978): 54.

———. *Wine Grapes: Their Selection, Cultivation, and Enjoyment.* New York: Harcourt Brace, 1937.

———. *A Wine-Grower's Guide.* New York: Knopf, 1945.

Wagner, Philip M., and Jocelyn Wagner. "Testing Direct Producers in the East." *Wines and Vines* 24 (September 1943): 16–17.

Walker, Larry. "Pinot Blanc in Oregon: It's the Real Thing." *Wines and Vines* 81 (January 2000): 131–33.

———. "Villa Banfi Winery Is Dedicated." *Wines and Vines* 65 (November 1984): 93.

Wallace, Mike. "Phylloxera Discovered in Washington." *Vineyard and Winery Management* 15 (March–April 1989): 12.

Warburton, Clark, *The Economic Results of Prohibition.* New York: Columbia University Press, 1932.

Washington Wine Commission. "Washington Wines: Statistical Review." Seattle: Washington Wine Commission, 1991.

Watson, Pamela. *Carolina Wine Country: The Complete Guide.* Greenville, N.C.: Woodhaven Publishing, 1999.

Webb, A. Dinsmoor. "A Wine Scholar Looks to the '80s." *Wines and Vines* 61 (February 1980): 20.

———. "Wines of the Future." *Vinifera Wine Growers Journal* 7 (Fall 1980): 195–99.

Wente, Carl. "A Look Backward at the 'Dark Days.'" *Wines and Vines* 43 (December 1962): 17–18.

Wente, Herman. "Wine Moves Ahead!" *Wine Review* 14 (February 1946): 8–9, 28.

West, Charles H. "Are Winery Facilities in California Adequate for the Present Requirements of the Wine Industry?" *Wines and Vines* 16 (March 1935): 4, 21.

Wetmore, Louis S. "Will Post-War Wine Shipments Be Made in Tank Steamers?" *Wines and Vines* 24 (March 1943): 17.

Wienand, E. B. "The Big Four and the Facts." *Wines and Vines* 25 (February 1944): 11.

Wiggans, C. C., and E. H. Hoppert. "Grape Growing in Nebraska." Extension Circular 1257. Lincoln: University of Nebraska, Agricultural College Extension Service, June 1925.

Wiley, Harvey W. *Beverages and Their Adulteration*. Philadelphia: P. Blakiston's Son, 1919.

Willebrandt, Mabel Walker. "Memorandum on the Interpretation of Section 29, Title II, of the National Prohibition Act." In U.S. National Commission on Law Observance and Enforcement, *Enforcement of the Prohibition Laws: Official Records,* vol. V, pp. 9–34. Washington, D.C.: GPO, 1931.

Williams, Howard E. "Prestige Promotion and Thunderbird." *Wines and Vines* 38 (November 1957): 41.

Williams, James R. "Diary of a Farm Winery Bill." *American Wine Society Journal* 16 (Spring 1984): 22–24.

Wine Advisory Board. "The Story of Wine and Its Uses." 5th ed. San Francisco: Wine Advisory Board, 1967.

Wine Institute. *Annual Report*. San Francisco: Wine Institute.

———. "Brief Outline of Important Economic Developments in the California Wine Industry, 1942–1943." Processed document. San Francisco: Wine Institute, September 1943.

———. "The First Twenty Years of the Wine Institute: A Report to Members at the Twentieth Annual Meeting." San Francisco: Wine Institute, 8–9 March 1954.

———. "Historical Wine Tax Summary: Wine Laws, Regulations and Interpretations." Rev. ed. San Francisco: Wine Institute for the Wine Advisory Board, 1 May 1949.

Wines and Vines. *Yearbook of the Wine Industry*. Annual. [Titles vary.]

"The Wines of the U.S." *Fortune* 9 (February 1934): 44–51, 118–22.

Winkler, A. J. "Effects of Overcropping." *American Journal of Enology and Viticulture* 5 (1954): 4–12.

———. "Eighty-Five Years of Work in Viticulture and Enology." Undated typescript [1965?]. Copy in the Wine Institute Library.

———. "Factors Determining Wine Quality." *Wine Review* 5 (September 1937): 8–11.

———. *General Viticulture*. Berkeley: University of California Press, 1962.

———. "Grapes for a Single Purpose." *Wines and Vines* 32 (April 1951): 67–68.

———. "Grape Standardization." *Wines and Vines* 33 (June 1952): 11.

———. "Grape Varieties and Vineyard Expansion." *Wine Review* 14 (April 1946): 72–78.

———. "Grape Varieties for Dry Wines, Part 1." *Wine Review* 4 (May 1936): 6–7, 22–23.

———. "Harvesting and Transporting Grapes." *Wine Review* 4 (August 1936): 14–15.

———. "A Proposed Program for the Introduction, Improvement, and Certification of Healthy Grape Varieties." *Wines and Vines* 32 (July 1951): 7–9.

———. "The Work of the Division of Viticulture." *Wines and Vines* 25 (December 1944): 41, 44–45.

Woodburne, Lloyd S. "Vintner Views Washington State." *Wines and Vines* 62 (March 1981): 26–29.

INDEX

Page numbers in italics indicate illustrations and maps.

Amana Colonies (IA), 178, 281

Ambassador label, 216

American Association against the Prohibition Amendment (AAPA), 5, 6, 7, 46–47, 372n16

American Medical Association, 93

Americans for Responsible Alcohol Access, 477n21

Americans for Wine, 354

American Society for Enology and Viticulture, 145, 313

American Society of Enologists. *See* American Society for Enology and Viticulture

American Vintners Association, 354

American Viticultural Areas (AVAs), 269, 276, 355–56

"American" wine, 72, 441n54

American Wine Alliance for Research and Education (AWARE), 354

American Wine Appreciation Week, 357

American Wine Co., 73, 125, 179, 180, 275

American Wine Growers, 311, 312, 313, 314, 315

American Wine Society, 250, 260–61

Amerine, Maynard A., 78, 86, 91, 101, 102, *103*, 109, 112, 145, 147, 149, 150, 207, 235, 309, 408n36, 415n112, 420n31, 447n53, 471n8; "Composition and Quality of Musts and Wines of California Grapes" (with Winkler), 103–4; *Wine: An Introduction for Americans* (with Singleton), 224, 247, 347

Amity Vineyards, 323

Anaheim (CA), 69

Anderson, Dr. John, 304

Anderson Valley (CA), 211

Angelica wine, 10, 85, 86, 87, 93

Angelo Petri (ship), 196

Animale Cellars, 316

Annie Green Springs brand, 446n39

Antill, Edward, 270

Anti-Saloon League, 2, 21, 23, 50

Apalachee Vineyard, 294

Arakelian, Krikor, 61, 65, 125, 140, 193, 257, 444n6

Aramon grape, 124, 358

Arbor Crest Wine Cellars, 317

Archery Summit Winery, 326

Aristocrat label, 90

Arizona, 336–37

Arizona Vineyards, 337

Arizona Wine Growers Association, 337

Arkansas, 47, 70, 161, 162, 166, 299–300; discriminatory tax in, 181; grape production in, 62; number of wineries in, 70 (1937), 180 (1946), 181 (1950), 299 (1997); vineyard acreage in, 20, 469n47; winemaking in, 180–81, *182*; wine production in, 181 (1945–51)

Arkansas Wine Producers and Fruit Growers Association, 181

Arlington (VA), 169

Arvin Wine Co., 136

Ash, Charles, 390nn30,31

Asher, Gerald, 459n70

Associated Vintners, 312, 314, 317

Association of Chateau Wine Growers, 215

Association of Western Wine Producers, 44, 96

Aubert label, 349

Auchter, Dr. Eugene, 382n10

Auerbach, Richard, 126

Augusta Winery, 277

August Moon concerts (Charles Krug Winery), 218

Auler, Ed, 301

Aurora grape, 262, 332

AxR#1 rootstock, 358–60

Bacchus grape, 167, 170

Bacchus Journal, 246

Bacchus vineyard, 317

Baco, François, 190, 443n94

Baco grape, 272, 324, 333

Bag-in-box, 341

Bailey, Liberty Hyde, 169

Bainbridge Island Winery, 316

Balcom and Moe vineyards, 317

Bali Hai brand, 208

Baliles, Gov. Gerald (of Virginia), 289

Balzer, Robert, 317; *California's Best Wines*, 246; *Private Guide*, 246

Banholzer, Carl, 278

Bank of America, 55, 65, 97, 111, 112, 113, 240, 241, 302, 413n93, 414n96, 446n45, 460n85

Barbera grape, 10, 46, 104, 235; acreage of, 226 (1976), 233 (1974), 343 (2000)

Barberone, 91, 403n71

Barboursville Vineyards, 288

Bargetto family, 17

Barolo wine, 125

Barrel, sales from. *See* Bulk wine, retail sales of

Bartels, Herman, 296

Bartels Winery, 296

Bartholomew, Antonia, 153

Bartholomew, Frank, 152–53

Bauer, Adolph, 66, 398n12

Baxevanis, John: *The Wine Regions of America,* 333

Baxter Winery, 280

Bayless, Alec, 317

Bayuk Cigar Co., 9

Beach, Judge William, 297

Beachaven Winery, 298

Bear Creek Vineyard Association, 66, 79

Beatrice Foods, 241

Beaulieu Vineyards, 16, 54, 62, 68, 90, 105, 107, 119, 126, 232, 241, 244, 345, 346, 401n53, 415n112; Georges de Latour Private Reserve Cabernet Sauvignon, 453n139

Beclan grape, 123

Beer, and Volstead Act, 2, 8, 23, 31

Bellows and Co., 93, 416n7, 432n75

Beltsville (MD), model winery at, 37, 38

Benmarl Winery, 258, 261

Bennion, David, 238

Benoist, Louis, 153, 214

Benson, Robert, 207; *Great Winemakers of California,* 247, 248

Bentonite, 82

Benton-Lane Winery, 326

Berg, Harold, 234

Beringer Brothers Vineyards, 58, 65, 66, 68, 105, 107, 119, 217–18, 244

Berkeley Bank for Cooperatives, 65

Berti, Leo, 54, 213

Besone, John J., 432n72

Bieganowski, Dr. Arthur, 304

Bieganowski Cellars, 304

Biltmore Estate Wine Co., 291–92

Bioletti, Frederic T., 19, 100, 105, *106,* 183

Bisceglia Brothers Winery, 30, 140, 241, 256, 257

Bjelland, Paul, 321

Black, Hollis. *See* Hollis Black winery

Black Pearl grape, 273

Black rot, 162, 185

Blackwell Wine Co., 234

Bleasdale, John Ignatius, 429n37

Blosser, William, 323, 327

Bluebonnet Hill winery, 304

Blue Eye grape, 273

Blue Portuguese grape, 308

Blue Teal Winery, 335

Bolognesi, Alessandro, 170

Bonetti, William, 203, 223

Bonner, Charles, 422n58

Boole, Ella, 7

Boone's Farm Apple Wine, 202

Boordy Vineyard: Maryland, 190, 286; New York, 314; Washington State, 314

Boragno, Joe, 204

Bordeaux wine, 108, 124

Borg, Axel, xvi

Boswell, Peyton, 186, *187,* 188

Bottlers, wine, 56, 89, 135, 144, 157, 402n62

Bottles and Bins (newsletter), 218–19

Bottle sizes, 131, 423n63; metric, 341

Bottling of wine, 50, 83, 142–43; established by war conditions, 133–34, 424n78; as luxury, 88–89, 402nn60,61

Brady, Roy, 214, 218, 235, 237, 328

Brandeis, Louis, 51, 348, 387n81

Brandy, 130, 164, 310; and Christian Brothers, 125–26, 413n87; prorate plan for, 111–12; tax on, 412n76; and whiskey distillers, 126–27

Bridgeview Vineyards, 327

Bridgman, William, 308

Bright's Vineyards, 190, 462n17

BRL Hardy Co., 257

Broich, William, 329

Bronte Champagne and Wine Co., 175, 176

Brookside Winery, 209, 241

Brotherhood Winery, 170

Brother John (winemaker), 157

Brown, Elbert M., 59, 390n28

Bruce, David, 238, 459n70

Bruce, Nigel, 128

Brumley, Baron, 333

Brun and Chaix Winery, 8

Bryson, Joseph, 423n71

Buck, Frank H., 41, 42

Buena Vista Winery, 152, 153, 233, 351

Bulk wine, 66, 165; limited by war, 133, 134; post-war diversion of, 144; retail sales of, 50, 88, 89, 386n72, 402nn57–59; retail sales of, outlawed, 51; shipped by tank car, 89, *91,* *132,* 164; surplus, 157, 158

Firelands Winery, 272

Firestone Vineyard, 351

Fisher, M. F. K., 138, 219, 220

Fisher Ridge Wine Co., 299

Flame Tokay grape, 84, 93, 205, 320

Flerchinger Vineyards, 324

Flora grape, 235

Flora Springs Wine Co., 344

Florida, 295–96; tax in, 49

Florida Heritage Winery, 296

Florida State Fair International Wine Competition, 248

Florin Winery, 79

Flor yeast, 155, 401n46

Flossfeder, Frederick, 105, 106

Flowers grape, 188

Foch grape, 281, 282, 324

Food and Drug Act (1906), 45

Food and Drug Administration, 98, 351, 352, 387n82

Foppiano, Louis, 90

Formula wines, 341

Forrest, Thomas and Elsie. See Thomas and Elsie Forrest Winery

Fortified wines: decline of, 205, 206, 225–26, 227, 340, 343, 448n56, 454n13; dominance of, 57, 61, 143, 158, 160, 177, 181, 435n113, 437n123; "sweet" wine, 389n22

Fortune (magazine), 54, 127

Foster's Group, Ltd., 347

Fougner, G. Selmer, 93, 404n80

Foundation Plant Materials Service, 220

Fountaingrove winery, 16, 58, 106, 107, 119, 120, 125

Fountain Winery, 136

Four Corners Regional Commission, 331, 333, 336

Fournier, Charles, 126, 190, 258, 260

Fox Estate Winery, 316

Foxiness in grapes, 71, 163, 190

Foxwood Winery, 293

France, 119, 126, 190, 354, 415n3

Franciscan Vineyards, 257

Frank, Dr. Konstantin, 169, 258–60, 261, 272, 289, 465n52

Franzia Brothers Winery, 232, 241

Frasinetti Winery, 62, 413n92

Fred Cherry's Personal Wine Journal, 246

Fredonia Products Co., 173, 174

Freemark Abbey Winery, 153, 244, 459n70

Free the Grapes (advocacy group), 477n21

Frei Brothers, 62, 197

Freisa grape, 343

Freixenet, 243

French army, 415n3

French Colombard grape, 64, 207, 234, 235, 339, 430n47, 455n26

French hybrid grapes, 73, 189–91. See also Wagner, Philip

"French paradox," 354

French refugees, 126

French Winegrowers Association, 334

Fresno Beauty grape, 174

Fresno County (CA), 87, 123, 149, 216; vineyard acreage in, 62, 233

Fresno mold, 388n14

Fresno State University, 234

Friedrich, Ed, 295

Fromm, Alfred, 125, 134, 213, 251

Fromm, Norman, 218

Fromm and Sichel, 126, 213, 214, 251

Fruit Industries, 27, 28, 29, 30, 60, 89, 90, 96, 134

Fruit Products Journal, 122

Fruit wines, 178, 180, 188, 229, 269, 282, 293, 309, 320

Fuller, William, 322

Furness, Elizabeth, 467n11

Galet, Pierre: A Practical Amepelography, 247

Gallo, Ernest, 61, 65, 100, 193, 200, 217, 315, 434n94, 444n8; and growth of Gallo Winery, 197–203

Gallo, Julio, 61, 100, 193, 198, 202

Gallo Winery, 31, 61, 128, 134, 140, 159, 192, 208, 223, 225, 233, 237, 257, 302, 319, 340, 349, 415n105; boycott of, 349–50, 350; growth of, 193, 197–203

Gamay Beaujolais grape, 146, 430n42

Gamay grape, 214

Gambarelli and Davito label, 194

Garden Vineyards, 136, 174

Garrett, Paul, 21–22, 28, 29, 30, 39, 40, 41, 60, 74, 162, 168, 171, 187–88, 256, 377n84; Paul Garrett and Co. Winery, 69, 143

Garza, Eligio de la, 356, 357

no mention of california!

San Martin Winery, 241

San Mateo County (CA), 68

San Sebastian Winery, 296

Santa Barbara County (CA), 211, 340; new wineries in, 239; vineyard acreage in, 226, 339

Santa Clara County (CA), 68, 209; new wineries in, 239

Santa Cruz County (CA), 86, 154, 155; new wineries in, 239

Santa Maria Valley (CA), 211

Santa Ynez Valley (CA), 211

Satyricon, 246

Sauterne (U.S.), 17, 29, 46, 69, 91, 93, 162

Sauternes (French), 162

Sauvignon blanc grape, 120, 147; acreage of, 64 (1940), 455n26 (1970, 1979)

Sauvignon vert grape, 207

Sawtooth Winery, 330

Saywell, L. G., 399nn29,30

Sbarboro, Andrea, 32

Scatena Brothers Winery, 32, 417n13

Schapiro Winery, 174

Scharffenberger Cellars, 243

Schenley Corp., 126, 127, 128, 133, 156, 192, 230

Schenley Imports, 127

Scheurebe grape, 343

Schlitz Brewery, 241, 346

Schoenberger, Eugene, 125

Schoonmaker, Frank, 54, 108, 119, 120, 122, 138, 210, 247, 309, 387n3, 416nn7,12, 417n13; and Almadén, 153, 154, 213, 214, 417n13, 433n80, 450n91; *American Wines* (with Marvel), 64, 75, 86, 119, 168, 180, 188; *The Complete Wine Book* (with Marvel), 54; and varietal labeling, 119–21, 122, 123, 124

Schoppaul Hill winery, 304

Schramsberg Vineyards, 239

Schuster and Son winery, 270

Schwarz Winery, 470n65

Sciarone Winery, 401

Scottish and Newcastle Breweries, 347

Screaming Eagle Winery, 344

Scuppernong grape, 39, 40, 63, 168, 188, 256, 383n21

Seagram, Inc., 125, 126, 127, 133, 152, 214, 252, 254, 262

Sears Roebuck Co., 249–50

Sebastiani, Samuele, 16

Sebastiani winery, 16, 137, 231, 351

Security Pacific Bank, 65

Seghesio, Eugene, 148, 239

Seghesio Winery, 148

Seibel, Albert, 190, 443n9

Semillon grape, 120, 123, 214, 455n26

Seneca Foods Co., 314

Seneca Lake (NY), 263

Serendipity Cellars Winery, 324

Setrakian, Arpaxat, 61, 205, 404n2, 448n58

Seven Hills Winery, 324

Seyval grape, 190, 262, 265, 287, 289, 292, 333

Seyve-Villard, Bertille, 190, 443n94

Shandon-Estrella region (CA), 211

Sheppard, Morris, 4, 133, 423n70

Sheridan grape, 186

Sher-po wine, 389n23

Sherry (Spanish), 85, 125

Sherry (U.S.), 10, 17, 56, 58, 69, 70; in eastern U.S., 164, 170; in Michigan, 176; production of, in California, 84–85; solera, 154, 155

Sherry Wine and Spirits Co., 119

Shewan-Jones Winery (Lejon), 32, 58, 68, 126, 192, 346

Shoup, Alan, 319

Sichel, Franz, 125, 213, 251

Sierra Nevada region, 69, 211, 233; new wineries in, 239

Sierra Wine Corp., 237, 458n58

Signature wines, 197, 216

Silver Oak Wine Cellars, 238

Simi Winery, 257, 347, 351

Simmons, Jean, 220

Simon, André, 108–9, 247, 411n65

Simons, Bo, 452n126

Simonton, James, 232

Singleton, Vernon L., 471n8

60 Minutes, 354

Skarstad, John, xvi

Skofis, Elie, 429n35, 434n93

Slip-skin grapes, 163

Smart, Richard, 477n14, 480n63

Smith, Alfred, 4, 30

Smith, Bobby, 301, 304

Smith, F. O., 58

Snake River, 329

Snoqualmie Winery, 315

Tokay (U.S.), 17, 29, 46; production of, in
    California, 85–86
Tomasello Winery, 186, 270, 271
Touriga Francesa grape, 343
Touriga grape, 155
Tourism, 217–18, 244–45
Tourne (milk-sourness), 80, 86, 93
Trail Ridge Winery, 331
Traminer grape, 123
The Treasury of American Wines. See Chroman,
    Nathan
Treaty Line Wine Cellars, 278
Trefethen Vineyards, 239
Trellising, 362
Tressler, Donald, 170
Tri-Cities Northwest Wine Festival (WA), 319
Trousseau grape, 87
Truluck, Dr. James, 293
Truluck Vineyards, 293, *294*
Tualatin Vineyards, 322
Tugwell, Rexford Guy, *36*, 41, 122, 381n1; encour-
    ages winegrowing, 34–35; plans for USDA
    research, 37
Tulare County (CA), 149, 216
Tulare Wine Co., 193, 393n57
Tulipomania, 246
Turner, B. B., 418n17
Twenty-first Amendment. *See* Repeal of constitu-
    tional Prohibition
Twight, E. H., 86, *87*, 397n10, 400n39, 401n54,
    471n11

Ugni blanc grape, 458n58
Umpqua Valley (OR), 321, 323
Underhill, E. S., 171, 172
United Farm Workers, 349–50, *350*
United States: grape production in, 20 (1925),
    163 (1940–49); ideas about wine in, 38, 43,
    51, 54, 57, 207, 217, 366–69; imported wine
    sales in, 116, 118, 415n4; maps of, *xii, 55*;
    number of wineries in, 10, 33, 70 (1936–
    38), 168 (1940), 340 (2000); per capita
    wine consumption in, 56, 389n19; vineyard
    acreage in, 62, 381n135; wine consumption
    in, 42, 157, 225, 226, 343, 384n42, 459n73,
    480n64; wine exports from, 118, 415n3;
    wine production in, 9–10, 20, 42 (1934), 70

(1937), 164 (1940–49), 366; wine "revolu-
    tion" in, 224–31
United States Congress, House Committee
    on Ways and Means, 31, 32
United States Congress, Senate Committee
    on the Judiciary, 129
United States Department of Agriculture (USDA),
    39, 41, 45, 145, 205, 357; aborted plans for
    wine research, 37–38; and vinifera, 169
United States Department of the Treasury, and
    wine regulation, 44, 45
United States Tobacco Co., 315
United Vintners, 192, 193–97, 203, 208, 216,
    225, 241, 345
University of Arizona, 336
University of California, Berkeley, Division of
    Fruit Products: postwar, 144; and restoration
    of winemaking, 99–105, *103*, 409n37
University of California, Davis, 10, *103*, 144, 219,
    221, 234, 322, 357, 409n37; Division of Viti-
    culture, 99–105, 407n28, 409n38, 431n68
University of California, Los Angeles, 145
University of California extension, 251
University of California Press: *The Story of Wine
    in California*, 220
University of Michigan, 251
University of Minnesota Horticultural Research
    Station, 282
University of Texas, 300, 301, 302
University of Washington, winemaking group
    at, 311–12
Upland Winery, 308, 310
Urbana Winery. *See* Gold Seal Vineyards
Utah, 337
Uvas Farming Corp., 335

Vai Brothers. *See* Padre Vineyard Co.
Valaer, Peter, 111
Valdepeñas grape. *See* Tempranillo grape
Valley View Winery, 323
Valliant Winery, 69, 119, 127
Val Verde Winery, 172, 183
Van Duzer Vineyards, 326
Van Gundy winery, 180
Van Nuys, Fred, 129
Varietal, as noun, 417n15
Varietal wines. *See* Wine labeling

Vashon Winery, 316

Veedercrest winery, 459n70

Vercelli, Joseph, 452n126

Veredon Vineyards, 313

Vergennes grape, 166

Vermont, 337

Vermouth (U.S.), 46

Vickers Vineyard, 330

Vidal grape, 262, 265, 272, 281, 287, 292, 333

Vie-Del Grape Products, 140

Vignoles grape, 272, 281

Village Winery, 155

Villa Mt. Eden Winery, 315

Viña Madre Winery, 333

Vincor, 347

Vine-Glo grape concentrate, 29–30

Vineland (NJ), 185

Vine spacing, 361–62

Vine training, 362–63

Vineyardists Inc., 171

Vineyard Management Co., 317

Vinifera. See *Vitis vinifera*

Vinifera Wine Cellars, 259, 261

Vinifera Wine Growers Association, 289

Vinifera Wine Growers Journal, 289

Vino da Tavola brand, 201, 208, 446n34

Vintage (magazine), 246

Vintners International, 254

Vintners' Trade Council, 112

Viognier grape, 343; acreage of, 476n8

Violet Burhard winery, 171–72

Virginia, 162, 166, 187, 188, 287–90

Virginia Dare brand, 29, 39, 60, 74, 90, 121, 168, 256

Virginia Polytechnic Institute, 289

Vitis aestivalis, 71

Vitis Berlandieri, 182

Vitis candicans, 181

Vitis Champini, 182

Vitis cinera, 182

Vitis cordifolia, 182

Vitis labrusca, 71, 190, 268

Vitis Lincecumii, 181, 190

Vitis Monticola, 182

Vitis riparia, 71, 190, 259, 282

Vitis rotundifolia, 162, 168, 182, 290, 293

Vitis rupestris, 71, 182, 190

Vitis vinifera, 71, 183; in Arizona, 337; in

Arkansas, 300; in Colorado, 332; in eastern U.S., 169, 258–60; in Georgia, 294, 295; in Illinois, 281; in Maryland, 287; in New York, 263; in North Carolina, 292; in Ohio, 272; in Oregon, 320, 321; in Pennsylvania, 265; in South Carolina, 293; in Texas, 301; in Virginia, 288–89; in Washington State, 308–10, 314

Volpe, John, 478n39

Volstead, Andrew, 1–2, 20, 22

Volstead Act (1919), 1–2, 4, 5, 8, 9, 19, 31, 95; home winemaking provision in, 20–23, 29, 30; and light wines, 31–32

Voluntary Committee of Lawyers, 6, 43

Vorauer Winery, 183

Vuylsteke, Ronald, 322

Wagner, Charles, 180

Wagner, Philip, 8, 42, 147, 150, 151, 166, 170, 188, 253, 258, 286, 314, 332, 333, 367, 411n69, 436n118, 460n85, 472n30; *American Wines,* 54; introduces French hybrids, 189–91

Walker, Hiram. *See* Hiram Walker and Sons distillers

Wallace, Henry A., 41

Walla Walla AVA (WA), 316

Walla Walla Community College, 318

Wall Street Journal, 245

Ward, Wilson, 299

War Food Administration, 129, 131, 136

Warner Vineyards, 176

War Production Board, 127, 132

Wartime Prohibition, 133, 371n1

Washington, D.C., 290

Washington, George, 287

Washington Association of Wine Grape Growers, 318

Washington State, 70, 162, 307–20; number of wineries in, 70, 310 (1937), 311 (1969), 315; protected status of wine industry ends, 311, 313; vineyard acreage in, 315, 471n7; wine production in, 315

Washington State Liquor Control Board, 309

Washington State University, 318, 319; Wine Project of, 311, 312

Washington Wine and Grape Growers Council, 311, 318

TEXT:	Scala, Scala Italic, Scala Small Caps
DISPLAY:	Scala Sans
CARTOGRAPHER	Bill Nelson
COMPOSITOR:	Integrated Composition Systems
PRINTER AND BINDER:	Thomson-Shore, Inc.